The **Rough Gu**

The Yucatán

written and researched by

Zora O'Neill and John Fisher

ROUGH GUIDES

NEW YORK • LONDON • DELHI

www.roughguides.com

Contents

◀◀ Hacienda Yaxcopoil ◀ The beach at Tulum

Introduction to

The Yucatán

Best known for major tourist attractions like the beaches of Cancún and the awesome temples of Chichén Itzá, the Yucatán Peninsula – the eastern tip of the curving horn of Mexico, facing the Caribbean Sea to the east and the Gulf of Mexico to the west and north – is also still very much the frontier, a swathe of untamed greenery that forms a place apart from the rest of the country. Until the 1960s, this was literally the case, as no road connected the Yucatán with central Mexico. As a result, residents were left to develop their own world-view, one that looked to Europe and Cuba for cultural cues while taking pride in the indigenous Maya culture. Today, it's not uncommon for people born in this region to say they're *yucatecos* first, mexicanos second.

More than anywhere else in Mexico, the Yucatán and the northeastern part of Chiapas reflect native American culture at every level of society: **Maya tradition** is palpable in remote, timeless villages of thatch-roof palapa homes, but also in shopping malls, political campaigns and TV advertisements. Although the Maya as a people are by no means free of the poverty borne disproportionately by indigenous cultures throughout the country, many Maya have prospered, and their culture is incredibly influential. All *yucatecos* use Maya vocabulary, eat Maya cuisine and generally take pride in living in "the land of the pheasant and the deer", as the Maya have called their richly forested terrain for centuries.

Travel in the Yucatán and Mayan Chiapas ranges from blazingly easy, along smooth toll highways in ultra-cushy buses, to virtually impossible, on rattletrap minivans packed with machete-carrying farmers that get mired in muddy tracks. In the latter case, you may be the only passenger remotely upset, as there's a general sense that minor annoyances really are minor, and that there's always something else to do in the meantime. This **laid-back attitude** can be intensely frustrating – or wonderfully relaxing, if you give in to it. You may also be put off by the extremes of wealth and poverty, though these are not as visible here as in the rest of Mexico; similarly, the smog, slums and crime that mark Mexico City are not nearly as evident in the metropolises of the Yucatán, which are generally kept meticulously clean and have relatively few poor areas. Violent crime is almost nonexistent, and for the most part this is a friendly and enormously enjoyable place to visit. Women travellers in particular will appreciate the overall lack of the *machismo* culture so common in central Mexico; in fact, modesty and near formal politeness are the norm.

▲ Angelfish, Cozumel

Between the powdery white Caribbean **beaches**, the wild, dense rainforest that covers the inland peninsula and the muggy river valleys of Chiapas and Tabasco, you'll find a huge variety of attractions. Some, such as the ancient **Maya cities** or the mega-clubs of Cancún, are man-made, while others are natural – UNESCO has established five biosphere reserves in this area, the largest being the 1.7-million-acre Calakmul Biosphere Reserve. Travellers who prefer urban life will enjoy both the sprawling energy of Villahermosa and the gracious tranquillity of Mérida.

Where to go

Cancún, the largest tourist destination in the Yucatán, has a reputation as a spring-breaker's bacchanal, but it offers much more: as a built-from-scratch city carved out of the jungle in the 1970s, it's an interesting urban experiment that also happens to have beautiful beaches and world-class hotels and restaurants. Surrounding resorts such as **Playa del Carmen**, too, are highly developed these days, but continuing down the Caribbean coast you'll find less frenetic towns, such as **San Miguel**, on the reef-ringed island of **Cozumel**, **Tulum** and eventually the isolation of the **Costa Maya**, near Mexico's border with Belize.

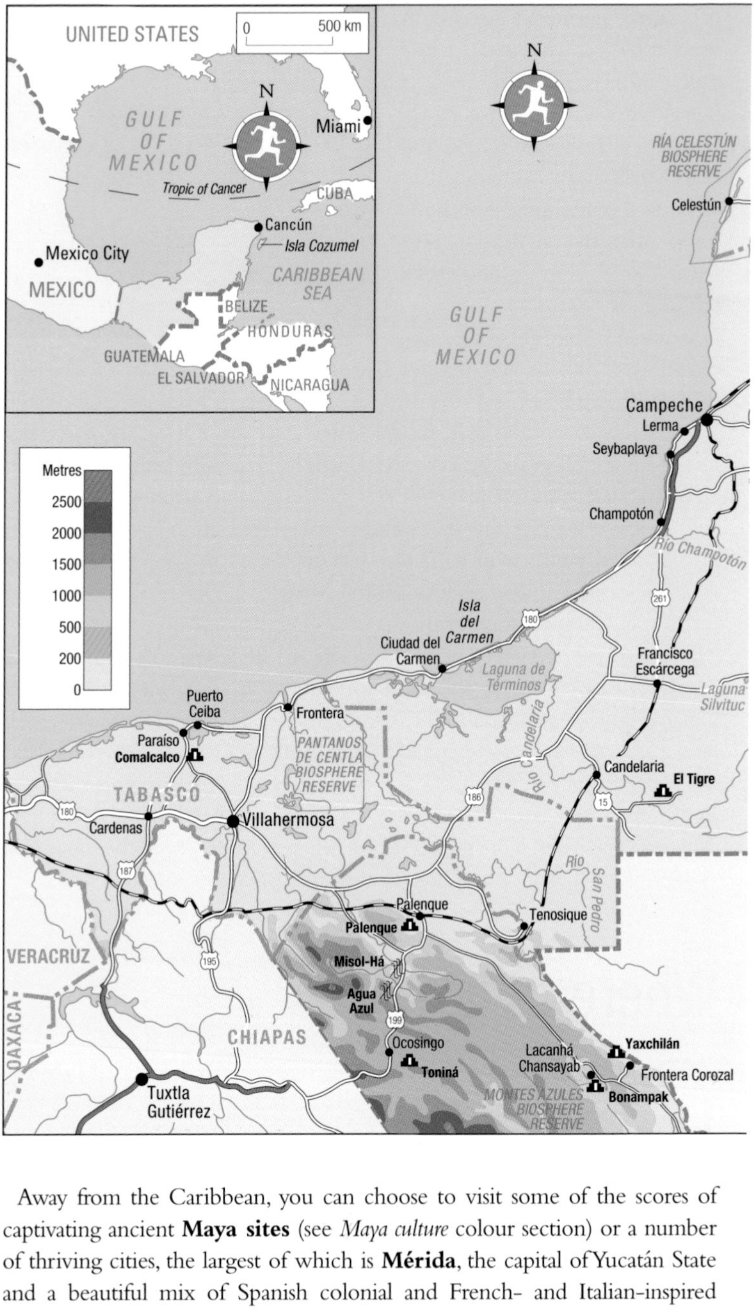

Away from the Caribbean, you can choose to visit some of the scores of captivating ancient **Maya sites** (see *Maya culture* colour section) or a number of thriving cities, the largest of which is **Mérida**, the capital of Yucatán State and a beautiful mix of Spanish colonial and French- and Italian-inspired architecture. On the Gulf coast of the peninsula, the city of **Campeche**, with

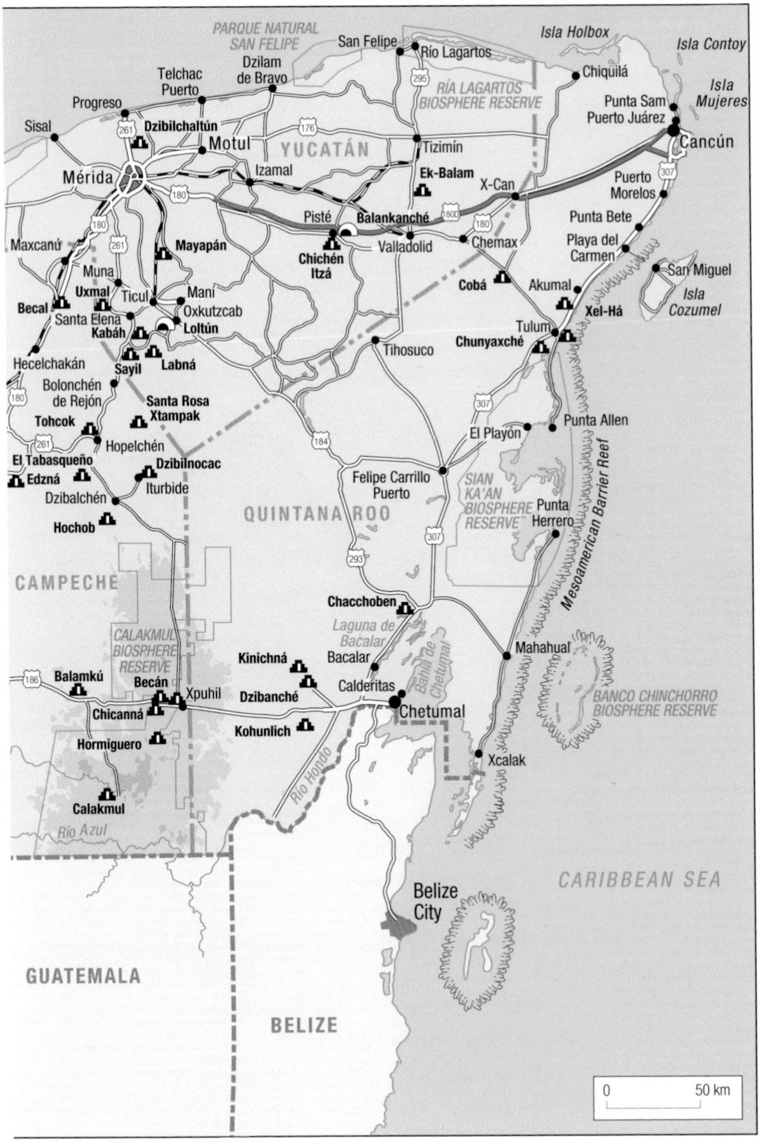

its historic core of pastel-painted buildings, is a tiny gem. South and west of Campeche lies the state of Tabasco, where the Olmecs – considered the originators of all Mesoamerican cultures – flourished more than a millennium before the first Maya cities were built. You can see the enormous stone heads they carved, along with other relics, in the city of **Villahermosa**. Chiapas,

On the beach

The crystalline white sands of the Yucatán's **Caribbean coast** are so transfixingly beautiful that many visitors never go further than their sun chairs for the whole of their vacation. The coast between Cancún and Tulum, known as the **Riviera Maya** (see p.99), complies with the best images of the Caribbean – all glassy water and broad sand; as a result, though, development is intense, and isolated beaches a fast disappearing rarity.

Farther south, the **Costa Maya** (see p.157) around Mahahual and Xcalak offers isolation, but the beaches are generally less attractive, not helped by their mauling at the hands of Hurricane Dean in 2007. Another less crowded alternative is the **Gulf coast** (see p.263 & p.291), along the north and west sides of the peninsula, where the water is not quite so clear but you can enjoy it in perfect solitude. In any case, all of the beaches in Mexico are technically public, so you may lay down your towel anywhere you like. Some hotels will let you use their beach furniture if you order from the bar; elsewhere, beach clubs rent chairs and serve food and drinks, usually for a modest fee.

directly south of Tabasco, was the centre of the Zapatista uprising in the 1990s, though visitors are little affected these days, and the strength of indigenous traditions here, together with the opening-up of a number of lesser-known Maya ruins near the majestic city of **Palenque**, continue to lure travellers.

If it's wildlife you're after, a number of nature reserves are sanctuaries for countless colourful birds and mammals. The **Sian Ka'an Biosphere Reserve**, on the Caribbean coast, comprises a particularly diverse range of eco-systems, while **Ría Celestún** and **Ría Lagartos** (on the west and north Gulf coasts, respectively) enclose bird-filled estuaries. The Calakmul Biosphere Reserve, in the jungle at the heart of the peninsula, encompasses the vast Maya city of Calakmul as well as numerous lesser sites, where monkeys in particular can often be seen among the ruins. Divers shouldn't miss Cozumel, whose coast is lined with lush coral gardens. These are outlying parts of the **Mesoamerican Barrier Reef**, the longest barrier reef in the western hemisphere, running along the Caribbean coast from just south of Cancún all the way to Honduras.

The majority of visitors, of course, base themselves on the Caribbean beaches and venture no further than day-trip distance from their hotels. A

▲ A bar on Isla Mujeres, near Cancún

little more effort, however, is immediately rewarded by leaving the crowds behind to see an entirely different side of local life. A typical travel route through the Yucatán Peninsula begins in Cancún and goes counter-clockwise around the main highways, via Chichén Itzá, Mérida and the surrounding sights, then on to Campeche, with a dip into Tabasco State to see the Olmec ruins, and down to Palenque in Chiapas. A completist will finish the Maya circuit via the **Río Bec** ruins in the southern parts of Campeche and Quintana Roo. Any of these can also be included as a shorter side-trip of a day or so.

When to go

The vast majority of the Yucatán Peninsula is low-lying and tropical, with daytime temperatures in the 30s (around 80°F) year-round. Near the coast the heat and humidity are tempered by the proximity of the water and its sea breezes. Inland, it's noticeably warmer and stickier, while the south – the Costa Maya and inland rainforests – is hotter and wetter than the northern areas around Cancún and Mérida.

◄ Kohunlich ruins, Río Bec area

Summer, from late May to October, can be uncomfortably hot and is in theory the **rainy season**, though just how wet it is varies from place to place. In the heart of the Yucatán you can expect muggy air and a heavy but short-lived downpour virtually every afternoon, which can come as a relief at the hottest time of year. Chiapas is the

Cenotes

Thanks to the porous, limestone ground, there is almost no surface water in the Yucatán. Instead, water collects underground, creating vast caves and caverns. Natural openings to this underground world are known as cenotes (pronounced "seh-NO-tays", from the Maya word "dzonot", sacred well). Cenotes are found all over the Yucatán, and for the ancient Maya were a life-giving source of water as well as a vital part of their religious and ceremonial life. Today, they offer spectacular opportunities for swimming, and for intrepid divers are the gateway to hundreds of kilometres of magnificent cave systems, many of them still barely explored.

wettest state, with many minor roads washed out by autumn. On the Caribbean coast, the rains culminate in **hurricane season** from mid-September to mid-October – you'll get wet weather and choppy seas (as well as plenty of mosquitoes), if not an actual storm.

Winter is the traditional tourist season, with drier air, milder temperatures and clear skies, and in the beach resorts like Cancún and Playa del Carmen, hotels are packed from late December to April. In the early part of the season, through to February, there is still the chance of rainy or stormy days, though these are rarely very long-lasting. Only in the Chiapas highlands, on the very fringes of this area, does it get significantly chilly, even at night.

Average temperatures and rainfall

	Jan	March	May	July	Sept	Nov
Cancún						
Max/Min °F	81/67	84/71	88/77	90/78	89/76	84/72
Max/Min °C	27/19	29/22	31/25	32/26	32/24	29/22
Rainfall (inches/mm)	3.5/88.9	1.6/40.6	4.6/116.8	4.3/109.2	9/228.6	3.8/96.5
Mérida						
Max/Min °F	82/64	90/68	93/70	91/73	90/73	84/66
Max/Min °C	28/18	32/20	34/21	33/23	32/23	29/19
Rainfall (inches/mm)	1.2/30.5	0.6/15.2	2.9/73.7	5.0/127	7.7/195.6	1.4/35.6
Villahermosa						
Max/Min °F	76/66	83/69	89/73	86/74	85/73	79/68
Max/Min °C	24/18	28/20	31/22	30/23	29/22	26/20
Rainfall (inches/mm)	3.6/91.4	1.9/48.3	3.3/83.8	5.2/132.1	13.1/332.7	9.4/238.8

18

things not to miss

It's not possible to see everything the Yucatán has to offer in one trip – and we don't suggest you try. What follows, in no particular order, is a selective and subjective taste of the peninsula's highlights, from stunning ancient ruins and spectacular beaches to folk dancing and traditional crafts. They're arranged in five colour-coded categories, so you can browse through to find the very best things to see, do and experience. All highlights have a page reference to take you straight into the Guide, where you can find out more.

01 **Chichén Itzá** Page **199** • The giant pyramid that towers over the ruined city of Chichén Itzá is an icon of Maya power in the Yucatán Peninsula.

02 Parque La Venta Page **303** • Discover relics of the Olmec civilization, the oldest in Mesoamerica, at this lush park in Villahermosa, which also contains a museum and zoo.

03 Hammocks Page **228** • Yucatecans have perfected the craft of hammock-weaving; the best place to buy one is from a specialist in Mérida.

04 Sian Ka'an Biosphere Reserve Page **152** • The Yucatán's most diverse nature sanctuary contains over one million acres of empty beaches, vibrant reefs, tangled mangroves and lush forest.

05 Palenque ruins Page **309** • The biggest Maya site in Chiapas is remarkable both for its well-preserved architecture and its setting amid stunning waterfalls and pools.

06 **Jarana dancing** Page **230** • Catch this folk dance – a hybrid of Spanish and Maya styles – at a village fiesta if you can; it's also performed weekly in Mérida.

07 **Shrimp tacos** Page **114** • *La Floresta* in Playa del Carmen does them best, but these scrumptious snacks can be found all along the Caribbean coast.

08 **Fortified Churches** Page **256** • Throughout the Yucatán, but especially along the "Ruta de los Conventos", the Spanish built vast fortress churches in the early years of their colonization; today they dwarf the villages around them.

09 The Bonampak murals Page **318** • Still vivid after more than 1200 years, the wall-paintings at this site in eastern Chiapas depict ancient rituals with precise detail.

10 Calakmul Page **183** • The Yucatán's largest ruined city is also the most remote, near the border with Guatemala and deep in a jungle where howler monkeys and jaguars still roam.

11 Haciendas Page **249** • Many of the crumbling grand houses of the Yucatán's wealthy elite have been restored in recent years, as luxury hotels, restaurants or tourist attractions.

12 Scuba diving Page **136** • Below the surface of the Caribbean lies some of the most diverse marine life in the world, best seen in coral atolls around Cozumel; sea turtles also abound along the Caribbean coast, especially at Akumal.

13 Trovador serenades Page **222** • The Yucatán's traditional crooners gather nightly in cafés and on city plazas – hire a trio for a romantic ballad.

14 Caribbean beaches Page **143** • Whether hanging up your hammock or bedding down in a plush resort, the powdery white sand and impossibly turquoise water of the Riviera Maya are irresistible: this one is at Tulum.

15 Smaller sites Page **283** • This is Hochob, but throughout the region are dozens of lesser-known, barely visited, yet spectacular Maya sites; having them to yourself can make the experience more rewarding than the crowded big-names.

16 Whale sharks Page **96** • At the end of every summer, more than two hundred of these enormous, gentle fish gather off the north Gulf coast.

17 Pirámide del Adivino Page **246** • Rising from a unique oval base, the most striking of all Maya pyramids is found at Uxmal, south of Mérida.

18 Cenotes Pages **107**, **139** & **195** • Filled with cool, crystal-clear water, the numerous caverns and sinkholes that riddle the soft limestone bedrock of the peninsula make for a memorable swimming or diving experience.

Basics

Basics

Getting there

The quickest and easiest way to get to the Yucatán is to fly, although you can also reach the peninsula by travelling overland from central Mexico, Guatemala or Belize as part of a longer trip. Unless you've got your own boat, getting there by water is normally possible only on a cruiseship.

The cost of travel to the Yucatán, particularly if you are flying into Cancún, fluctuates greatly according to the season: tickets are at a premium from December to April, when the beach resorts are packed, but they can often be had for a song in the fall. Flights to Mérida and Villahermosa are more stable, but generally more expensive. Note that there are no direct flights to Cancún from Europe – expect to transfer in the US (with all the attendant immigration hassle), or to fly as far as Mexico City, then backtrack on an internal flight.

Barring special offers, the best fares will carry certain restrictions, such as advance booking and fixed dates, with a penalty charge if you change your schedule. They may also limit your stay. Most cheap round-trip fares involve spending at least one Saturday night away. You can occasionally cut costs by going through a **consolidator** or a **discount agent**, who may have a line on charter flights to Cancún; however, departure dates are fixed and withdrawal penalties are high.

Flights from the US and Canada

Flights to Cancún go **from almost every major US city**, but the cheapest and most frequent depart from "gateway" cities in the south and west: Dallas, Houston and Miami, though New York City can occasionally be comparably priced. Round-trip flights from these cities **to Cancún** start at around US$325, rising to US$500 in peak season; figure an additional US$100 or so from other US hubs. **For Cozumel**, flights go on several airlines from Atlanta, Chicago, Dallas, Detroit, Houston, Miami, Minneapolis, Newark and Toronto. Rates from southern cities like Houston and Dallas are typically US$475 year-round. If you're coming from the west coast, it could make sense to go via Mexico City. You can also find attractive deals that include a few nights' lodging in Cancún, Playa del Carmen or Cozumel.

Continental serves **Ciudad del Carmen, Mérida and Villahermosa direct** from Houston, while Aeroméxico offers a few additional flights. The Ciudad del Carmen and Villahermosa flights cater to oilmen and can be prohibitively expensive (US$800–1000), but Mérida is usually about M$500 year-round.

From Toronto, Vancouver, Winnipeg, Halifax, Calgary and Montréal, Air Canada flies direct to Cancún, though not always daily; Cozumel flights go from Toronto and Halifax. Prices start at around Can$600, and cheaper charter flights are plentiful in the winter. Your options expand greatly if you fly via the US.

Flights from the UK and Ireland

Aside from charter flights in high season, there are no direct flights between **Britain** and the Yucatán Peninsula; British Airways goes from London Heathrow to Mexico City, or you can take one of its daily flights to Cancún with a connection in Miami or Dallas.

Good deals can be found if you go **via a European hub**, especially on low-cost carriers like Condor (via Frankfurt) and LTU (via Dusseldorf). Most of the European national airlines fly first to Mexico City, though, so you will have to change planes again to reach Cancún or Mérida. Another option is to fly to the cheapest destination in the US – usually New York City – then take an American budget airline such as Jet Blue to Cancún; plan to stay over, or at least allow a full day's transfer time, to account for immigration processing. The cheapest

Fly less – stay longer! Travel and Climate Change

Climate change is perhaps the single biggest issue facing our planet. It is caused by a build-up in the atmosphere of carbon dioxide and other greenhouse gases, which are emitted by many sources – including planes. Already, **flights** account for three to four percent of human-induced global warming: that figure may sound small, but it is rising year on year and threatens to counteract the progress made by reducing greenhouse emissions in other areas.

Rough Guides regard travel as a **global benefit**, and feel strongly that the advantages to developing economies are important, as are the opportunities for greater contact and awareness among peoples. But we also believe in travelling responsibly, which includes giving thought to how often we fly and what we can do to redress any harm that our trips may create.

We can travel less or simply reduce the amount we travel by air (taking fewer trips and staying longer, or taking the train if there is one); we can avoid night flights (which are more damaging); and we can make the trips we do take "climate neutral" via a carbon offset scheme. **Offset schemes** run by climatecare.org, carbonneutral .com and others allow you to "neutralize" the greenhouse gases that you are responsible for releasing. Their websites have simple calculators that let you work out the impact of any flight – as does our own. Once that's done, you can pay to fund projects that will reduce future emissions by an equivalent amount. Please take the time to visit our website and make your trip climate neutral, or get a copy of the *Rough Guide to Climate Change* for more detail on the subject.

www.roughguides.com/climatechange

high-season fares are usually on Continental or Virgin (connection at Miami with Aeroméxico), but these probably won't beat flights via Europe.

Websites in the UK are not so directly geared to finding Mexican destinations as their US counterparts (for online booking agents, see p.23), so a good flight specialist – such as North South or Journey Latin America (see pp.24–27) – can sometimes work wonders.

Prices for scheduled return flights from London to Cancún range from £600 in the low season to £750 or more in the high season, including taxes; flights to Mexico City are about £625, so it's rarely cheaper to fly there and take an internal flight to the Yucatán. Charter flights, usually flying out of Gatwick or Manchester to Cancún, can be as low as £350 in the low season, though they can go as high as £900 in August, and your stay will probably be limited to two or four weeks. Try My Travel (Ⓣ0870/238 7777, Ⓦwww.mytravel.com), whose charters offer the largest choice of Mexican destinations.

There are no direct flights from Ireland to anywhere in Mexico. Your cheapest way to get there will likely be to take one of the numerous daily flights to London from Dublin, Cork, Shannon or Belfast, then connect with one of the transatlantic flights detailed above. You can also fly from Ireland via the US, from Dublin via Atlanta with Delta, or from Dublin or Shannon via New York (Newark) with Continental. For return tickets from Dublin to Mexico, expect to pay around €850 in the low season to €1000 in the high season, including taxes, and €50–100 more from Cork or Shannon – though ticket prices often depend more on how far in advance you're purchasing, rather than the time of year. From Belfast or Derry, expect to pay around £650 in the low season and £850 in the high season.

Flights from Australia, New Zealand and South Africa

The high season for flights to Mexico **from Australia and New Zealand** is from mid-June to mid-July, and mid-December to mid-January. Tickets can range from A$2600 to A$3200, depending on routing, time of year and how far in advance you make the reservations. You can sometimes find a cheaper itinerary if you book from

Sydney or Auckland to Mexico City, then buy an internal ticket separately – LAN Chile (with a connection in Santiago) and Air New Zealand (connecting in Los Angeles) often have competitive prices.

The Star Alliance airline group (including Air New Zealand, United, Lufthansa, Thai Airways and Singapore Airlines) offers one of the best deals, mile for mile, on round-the-world (RTW) fares from Australia. Prices and deals vary, but the best deal is A$2729/NZ$3125 for 26,000 miles and up to five stops; the only catch is that no Mexican airline is a member of the group, so you can't use the fare to hop around the country. A similar deal is offered by OneWorld (including Qantas, British Airways, Cathay Pacific, American and LAN). Additional specialist tour operators are listed in the "Agents and operators" section, p.24–27.

Coming **from South Africa**, you have to connect in Europe or the US – the latter is almost always less expensive, with flights from SA$1500 to SA$2000, with advance planning. South African Airways flies to Atlanta, connecting with a Delta flight to Cancún, a route that is usually the cheapest, as well as the most direct.

Overland from central Mexico, Belize and Guatemala

If you'll be travelling **by bus** to the peninsula from Mexico City or any point south and east, an invaluable resource is Ⓦwww.ticketbus.com.mx, where you can check schedules and buy tickets for most first-class and deluxe routes, as well as some second-class services. As many bus stations are located outside town, this website will spare you an extra trip to the terminal.

Mérida, the capital of Yucatán state, is also its transport hub, with constant traffic in and out. The main route to the city **by bus from Mexico City** is via Villahermosa, then through Campeche – a twenty-hour ride (7 daily for both Mérida and Campeche), so it's worth splurging on ADO GL, the semi-lux bus line with a bit more room and plusher seats. Villahermosa is just ten hours from the capital (buses run more than hourly), and Campeche

Airpasses in Mexico

If you want to visit several destinations in a fairly short time and venture into central Mexico or neighbouring countries, then an **airpass** is worth considering. The **MexiPass** consists of prebooked and prepaid coupons for internal flights on Mexicana for travellers from outside Mexico. Travel to Mexico can be on any airline (but some fares are lower if you use Mexicana or Aeroméxico), and all flights must be completed within ninety days; you must book routes and dates before you leave your home country. Prices are for one-way flights, based on zones, increasing the further you fly, and do not include domestic departure taxes (currently US$28 per flight): Cancún to Mexico City runs for US$135; Oaxaca to Mérida is US$165. You can also incorporate international flights on the Mexican carriers between the US, Canada and the Caribbean. Because most flights are routed through Mexico City, the pass isn't ideal for hopping around just the Yucatán, but it can offer real savings on longer flights. The best way to find out how (or if) an airpass will benefit you is to call a specialist flight agent – the passes cannot be booked online or through call centres.

If you also want to fly to other parts of the American continent, then Hahn Air's **All America Air Pass** (Ⓦwww.allairpass.com) is worth considering. The pass links Mexico with all the major cities of North, Central and South America and the Caribbean. A routing New York–Mexico City–Cancún–Panama City–San José–New York, for example, starts at US$1016 plus tax, saving almost one-third on flying the same route without the pass. You could also omit a leg and cover that by land. The pass's one drawback for visiting the Yucatán is that it does not include any flights from the US or Canada to Cancún, though you can fly from Houston to Mérida or Villahermosa, or from Mexico City to Cancún.

is seventeen hours. Other buses from Mexico City also go as far as Cancún (11 daily; 24hr). From **Oaxaca**, you'll have to transfer in Villahermosa for points further east.

Mérida's airport also receives frequent internal **flights**, including thirteen daily from Mexico City (1hr 40min). It's also possible to fly from the capital to Cancún (13 daily; 2hr) and Campeche (3 daily; 1hr 40min).

Travellers coming from the Maya sites in northern Guatemala and Belize will find themselves at some very out-of-the-way border crossings. If you want to bypass the potential bureaucratic hassles that come with isolated posts on borders that see a lot of illegal immigration, you can of course fly. Coming **by air from Guatemala,** Taca International (Ⓣ502/2470-8222 in Guatemala, Ⓦwww.grupotaca.com) flies five days a week (Tues & Thurs–Sun) from Guatemala City to Cancún (3hr 15min). Direct flights from Flores also operate to Cancún (1hr 30min). Tickets for both start at about US$290/£145 one-way.

Travellers have several choices when arriving **by car from Guatemala.** The easiest, most frequented checkpoint is at the Talismán Bridge to Tapachula in southern Chiapas, Mexico (which is beyond the scope of this book). An international **bus** runs from Guatemala City through to Tapachula (4 daily; 5–6hr); you have to get off the bus at the border, then reboard on the Mexico side after having your passport inspected. If you arrive at the checkpoint on a second-class Guatemalan bus, you can take one of the many combis waiting on the Mexico side.

If you plan to limit your route in Mexico to northern Chiapas and the Yucatán, then the best crossing is at Bethél, Guatemala, on the Río Usumacinta, opposite Frontera Corozal in Mexico. Buses run from Flores to Bethél (3 daily; 5hr), where you take a thirty-minute *lancha* ride across the river (about US$40 for up to four people). From Frontera Corozal, you can head directly to Palenque or stop off at Bonampak and Yaxchilán. Less desirable (for expense and complex transport connections), yet possible, is the crossing at El Naranjo, which requires an hour-long boat ride to the village of El Ceibo in Mexico; combis run from there to Tenosique. The actual border posts are not regularly supplied with the necessary staff, so it's a good idea to get your passport stamped in Flores before proceeding to the border itself. (Coming the other way, from Mexico to Guatemala, you need to have your passport stamped at the immigration office in Tenosique.)

There are no direct flights **from Belize** to the Yucatán, and given the size of the country, it makes more sense simply to travel **by bus** to the border at Chetumal. Buses run frequently from Corozal in Belize, twenty minutes from the border (and not to be confused with Frontera Corozal, in Chiapas, Mexico) to Chetumal, stopping at the checkpoint and the duty-free shopping zone, then depositing passengers at either the main Chetumal bus station or the main market just northeast of the centre.

Note that no matter where you're coming from, you will need a Mexico-issued tourist card (see p.53) in addition to your passport to enter Mexico. They can be scarce at out-of-the-way border crossings, so if you have the opportunity, visit a consulate in Guatemala City or Belize City to obtain a tourist card ahead of your arrival at the border. Whenever possible, cross the border during daylight, and allow plenty of time in your schedule; **posts typically close after 8pm**. Also note that Mexico observes daylight saving time, while Guatemala does not (although it may begin doing so in 2009). Keep your passport handy once in Mexico, as buses around the border are often stopped in additional immigration sweeps.

By cruise

Several **cruise lines** ply the Caribbean out of Miami, taking in Cozumel (from where you can visit Playa del Carmen) and the more remote port of Mahahual (often called Puerta Maya in cruise literature). A few cruise lines also dock at Progreso. Mahahual was severely damaged by Hurricane Dean in 2007, but as of spring 2008, it was close to reopening. Cruise **prices** start at US$600 per person, plus airfare to the starting point, and go (way) up from there. Agencies specialising in cruises include Cruise World (Ⓣ1-800/228-1153, Ⓦwww.cruiseworldtours.com) and The Cruise Professionals (Ⓣ1-800/265-3838, Ⓦwww.cruiseworldtours.com).

North American cruise lines

Carnival Cruise Lines ⓣ1-888/227-6482, ⓦwww.carnival.com.
Norwegian Cruise Line ⓣ1-800/327-7030, ⓦwww.ncl.com.
Royal Caribbean Cruises ⓣ1-800/398-9819 in the US and Canada, ⓣ0800/018-2020 in the UK, ⓦwww.royalcaribbean.com.

Airlines, agents and operators

Online booking

ⓦ**www.expedia.co.uk** (in UK) ⓦ**www.expedia.com** (in US) ⓦ**www.expedia.ca** (in Canada)
ⓦ**www.lastminute.com** (in UK and US)
ⓦ**www.opodo.co.uk** (in UK)
ⓦ**www.orbitz.com** (in US)
ⓦ**www.travelonline.co.za** (in South Africa)
ⓦ**www.travelocity.com** (in US) ⓦ**www.travelocity.ca** (in Canada) ⓦ**www.travelocity.co.uk** (in UK)
ⓦ**www.zuji.com.au** (in Australia) ⓦ**www.zuji.co.nz** (in New Zealand)

Airlines

Aer Lingus US and Canada ⓣ1-800/IRISH-AIR, UK ⓣ0870/876 5000, Republic of Ireland ⓣ0818/365 000, Australia ⓣ02/9244 2123, New Zealand ⓣ09/308 3355, South Africa ⓣ21/674 3228; ⓦwww.aerlingus.com.
Aerolineas Argentinas US ⓣ1-800/333-0276, Canada ⓣ1-800/688-0008, UK ⓣ0800/096 9747, Australia ⓣ02/9234 9000, New Zealand ⓣ09/379 3675; ⓦwww.aerolineas.com. ⓣ1-800/123-8588 in Mexico.
Aeroméxico US ⓣ1-800/237-6639, ⓦwww.aeromexico.com. ⓣ1-800/021-4010 in Mexico. Codeshare flights with US airlines such as Delta to Cancún.
Air Canada US and Canada ⓣ1-888/247-2262, UK ⓣ0871/220 1111, Republic of Ireland ⓣ01/679 3958, Australia ⓣ1300/655 767, New Zealand ⓣ0508/747 767; ⓦwww.aircanada.com. ⓣ1-800/719-2827 in Mexico.
Air France US ⓣ1-800/237-2747, Canada ⓣ1-800/667-2747, UK ⓣ0870/142 4343, Australia ⓣ1300/390 190, South Africa ⓣ0861/340 340; ⓦwww.airfrance.com. ⓣ1-800/123-4660 in Mexico.
Air New Zealand US ⓣ1-800/262-1234, Canada ⓣ1-800/663-5494, UK ⓣ0800/028 4149, Australia ⓣ13 24 76, New Zealand ⓣ0800/737 000; ⓦwww.airnewzealand.com. ⓣ55/5705-1717 in Mexico.
Alaska Airlines ⓣ1-800/252-7522, ⓦwww.alaskaair.com. ⓣ55/5282-2484 in Mexico. LA, San Francisco and Seattle to Cancún.
American Airlines US & Canada ⓣ1-800/433-7300, UK ⓣ0207/365 0777, Republic of Ireland ⓣ01/602 0550, Australia ⓣ1800/673 486, New Zealand ⓣ0800/445 442; ⓦwww.aa.com. ⓣ1-800/904-6000 in Mexico. Dallas and Miami to Cancún and Cozumel.
British Airways US & Canada ⓣ1-800/AIRWAYS, UK ⓣ0844/493 0787, Republic of Ireland ⓣ1890/626 747, Australia ⓣ1300/767 177, New Zealand ⓣ09/966 9777, South Africa ⓣ11/441 8600; ⓦwww.ba.com. ⓣ55/193-512-3200 in Mexico.
Continental Airlines US & Canada ⓣ1-800/523-3273, UK ⓣ0845/607 6760, Republic of Ireland ⓣ1890/925 252, Australia ⓣ02/9244 2242, New Zealand ⓣ09/308 3350, International ⓣ1800/231 0856; ⓦwww.continental.com. ⓣ1-800/523-3273 in Mexico. Cleveland, Houston and Newark (New York) to Cancún; Houston and Newark (New York) to Cozumel; Houston to Ciudad del Carmen, Mérida and Villahermosa.
Delta Air Lines US & Canada ⓣ1-800/241-4141, UK ⓣ0845/600 0950, Republic of Ireland ⓣ1850/882 031 or 01/407 3165, Australia ⓣ1300/302 849, New Zealand ⓣ09/977 2232, South Africa ⓣ011/482 4582; ⓦwww.delta.com. ⓣ1-800/123-4710 in Mexico. Atlanta, Cincinnati and Salt Lake City to Cancún; Miami to Mérida.
Iberia US ⓣ1-800/772-4642, UK ⓣ0870/609 0500, Republic of Ireland ⓣ0818/462 000, South Africa ⓣ011/884 9255; ⓦwww.iberia.com. ⓣ55/1101-1515 in Mexico.
Japan Airlines (JAL) US & Canada ⓣ1-800/525-3663, UK ⓣ0845/774 7700, Republic of Ireland ⓣ01/408 3757, Australia ⓣ02/9272 1111, New Zealand ⓣ09/379 9906, South Africa ⓣ011/883 2178; ⓦwww.jal.com. ⓣ55/5242-0150 in Mexico.
JetBlue ⓣ1-800/538-2583, ⓦwww.jetblue.com. ⓣ1-800/861-3372 in Mexico. Boston, New York and Orlando to Cancún.
KLM (Royal Dutch Airlines) See Northwest. US & Canada ⓣ1-800/225-2525, UK ⓣ0870/242 9242, Republic of Ireland ⓣ0818/200 018, Australia ⓣ1300/303 747, New Zealand ⓣ09/309 1782, South Africa ⓣ82/234 5747; ⓦwww.klm.com. ⓣ1-800/907-4700 in Mexico (Northwest Airlines).
LAN US & Canada ⓣ1-866/435-9526, UK ⓣ0800/977 6100, Australia ⓣ1800/221 572 or 02/9244 2333, New Zealand ⓣ09/308 3352, South Africa ⓣ11/781 2111; ⓦwww.lan.com. ⓣ1-800/123-1619 in Mexico.

Lufthansa US ⓣ1-800/399-5838, Canada ⓣ1-800/563-5954, UK ⓣ0871/945 9747, Republic of Ireland ⓣ01/844 5544, Australia ⓣ1300/655 727, New Zealand ⓣ0800/945 220, South Africa ⓣ0861/842 538; ⓦwww.lufthansa.com. ⓣ55/5230-0000 in Mexico.

Mexicana US ⓣ1-800/531-7921, Canada ⓣ1-866/281-9343, UK ⓣ0870/890 0400, Australia ⓣ03/9699 9355, New Zealand ⓣ09/977 2213, South Africa ⓣ11/781 2111; ⓦwww.mexicana.com. ⓣ1-800/801-2010 in Mexico. Codeshare flights from the US on American Airlines.

Northwest US ⓣ1-800/225-2525, UK ⓣ0870/507 4074, Australia ⓣ1300/767 310; ⓦwww.nwa.com. ⓣ1-800/907-4700 in Mexico. Detroit, Memphis and Minneapolis to Cancún and Cozumel.

Qantas US & Canada ⓣ1-800/227-4500, UK ⓣ0845/774 7767, Republic of Ireland ⓣ01/407 3278, Australia ⓣ13 13 13, New Zealand ⓣ0800/808 767, South Africa ⓣ11/441 8550; ⓦwww.qantas.com. ⓣ1-800/892-9761 in Mexico.

Ryanair UK ⓣ0871/246 0000, Republic of Ireland ⓣ0818/303 030, International ⓣ3531/249 7791; ⓦwww.ryanair.com.

South African Airways US ⓣ1-800/722-9675, UK ⓣ0870/747 1111, Australia ⓣ1300/435 972, New Zealand ⓣ09/977 2237, South Africa ⓣ0861/359 722; ⓦwww.flysaa.com.

Spirit US ⓣ1-800/772-7117, ⓦwww.spiritair.com. Detroit or Ft. Lauderdale to Cancún.

United US ⓣ1-800/UNITED-1, UK ⓣ0845/844 4777, Australia ⓣ13 17 77; ⓦwww.united.com. ⓣ1-800/003-0777 in Mexico. Chicago, Denver and Washington to Cancún; Chicago to Cozumel.

US Airways US & Canada ⓣ1-800/428-4322, UK ⓣ0845/600 3300, Republic of Ireland ⓣ1890/925 065, Australia ⓣ02/9959 3696, New Zealand ⓣ09/359 8397, South Africa ⓣ11/289 8111; ⓦwww.usair.com. ⓣ1-800/843-3000 in Mexico. Boston, Charlotte, Philadelphia and Phoenix to Cancún; Charlotte to Cozumel.

Virgin Atlantic US ⓣ1-800/821-5438, UK ⓣ0870/574 7747, Australia ⓣ1300/727 340, South Africa ⓣ11/340 3400; ⓦwww.virgin-atlantic.com.

Vivaaerobus.com US ⓣ1-888/935-9848, ⓦwww.vivaaerobus.com. ⓣ1-818/215-0150 in Mexico. Austin, TX, to Cancún.

Agents and operators

Adventure Center US ⓣ1-800/228-8747, ⓦwww.adventure-center.com. Specializes in ecologically sound adventure travel. Ten-day "Yucatán Panorama" starts at US$595 for the trip from Cancún to Palenque and back. The 22-day "Mayan Adventure" (from US$995) includes sites in Belize and Guatemala as well. Prices include transport and hotel, but only a few meals.

The Adventure Company UK ⓣ0845/450 5316, ⓦwww.adventurecompany.co.uk. A good outfit that will tailor itineraries to your needs. Small-group hotel-based excursions include a sixteen-day "Realm of the Maya" tour in the Yucatán, Chiapas, Guatemala and Belize from £1939.

Adventures Abroad US & Canada ⓣ1-800/665-3998, UK ⓣ0114/247 3400; ⓦwww.adventures-abroad.com. Canada-based travel planners providing small-group tours. A seven-day family tour of the Yucatán's ancient sites and fun parks costs US$1657.

Aerosaab Mexico ⓣ984/873-0804, ⓦwww.aerosaab.com. Charter flights on small planes to Chichén Itzá and Holbox, with departures from Playa del Carmen, Cancún and Cozumel. Tour guides optional.

Amerika Venture US & Canada ⓣ1-866/679-7070, ⓦwww.amerikaventure.com. French-run eco-tourism operator with a fifteen-day "Ruta Maya" tour including Guatemala and Belize that costs US$2895; self-drive and other options available, too.

Backroads US ⓣ1-800/462-2848, ⓦwww.backroads.com. Hiking, biking and snorkelling tours to the Yucatán and other destinations, starting at US$3898 per person for a six-day trip. Sporty family packages are available as well.

Bamba Experience UK ⓣ020/8144 2949, Mexico ⓣ1-800/GO-BAMBA; ⓦwww.bambaexperience.com. Hop-on, hop-off backpackers' bus service between Mexico City and Cancún, with potential jaunts into Guatemala.

Bike Mexico Canada ⓣ416/848-0265, Mexico ⓣ999/260-0952; ⓦwww.bikemexico.com. Backroads cycling tours led by serious bike fanatics. Trips range from a week-long excursion around the Ruta Puuc (US$725) to a full tour of the peninsula from Cancún to San Cristóbal de las Casas, lasting three and a half weeks (US$1580).

Cathy Matos Mexican Tours UK ⓣ020/8492 0000, ⓦwww.cathymatosmexico.co.uk. A specialist in Mexico for three decades, Cathy can arrange almost any sort of Yucatán trip from a Cancún beach stay to jungle exploration. Trips favour the unusual and the upmarket. Prices start from around £1000 for a week in Cancún, including flights.

ebookers UK ⓣ0800/082 3000, Republic of Ireland ⓣ01/488 3507; ⓦwww.ebookers.com, www.ebookers.ie. Low fares on an extensive selection of scheduled flights and package deals.

eXito US ⓣ1-800/655-4053, Canada ⓣ1-800/670-2605; ⓦwww.exitotravel.com. Independent travel specialists for Latin America. Website features a particularly useful airfare finder and other invaluable information.
Exodus US ⓣ1-800/843-8272, ⓦwww.exodus.co.uk. Sixteen-day Ruta Maya tour in Mexico, Guatemala and Belize from £1000/US$2565.
Flight Centre Australia ⓣ13 31 33, ⓦwww.flightcentre.com.au; New Zealand ⓣ0800/243 544, ⓦwww.flightcentre.co.nz. Discount package deals to Cancún and the coast.
Future Vacations US ⓣ1-800/233-7260, ⓦwww.futurevacations.com. Vacation packages in Cancún and Cozumel.
G.A.P. Adventures US & Canada ⓣ1-800/708-7761, UK ⓣ0870/999 0144, Australia ⓣ1300/796 618, New Zealand ⓣ800/333 307; ⓦwww.gapadventures.com. Guided adventure trips with some camping and trekking; US$1295 for three weeks on the Ruta Maya through the Yucatán, Chiapas, Guatemala and Belize, or US$795 for a two-week "Ancient Civilizations" trip from Mexico City to Cancún.
Global Exchange US ⓣ415/255-7296, ⓦwww.globalexchange.org. Offers "Reality Tours" to increase travellers' awareness of the way of life in developing countries. Trips to Chiapas to learn about indigenous rights cost US$1000 on average.
Globus US ⓣ1-866/755-8581, ⓦwww.globusjourneys.com. Eight-day tour of the northern Yucatán Peninsula from US$1729.
Green Tortoise US & Canada ⓣ1-800/867-8647, ⓦwww.greentortoise.com. Budget tour operation with strong backpacker roots – lodging is usually at campsites and hostels. Seven days in Chichén Itzá, Mérida and the beaches starts at US$495.
International Student Tours Canada ⓣ1-888/472-3933, ⓦwww.istours.com. Student group-travel company offering week-long resort packages to Cancún (from Can$1219 including airfare).
Journey Latin America UK ⓣ020/8747 8315 or 0161/832 1441, Republic of Ireland ⓣ1800/818 126; ⓦwww.journeylatinamerica.co.uk. Latin America experts with a wide range of mix-and-match tours and holidays, including the haciendas and luxury Riviera Maya hotels, as well as language courses in Mérida. Seven-day Maya city tour from around £421 excluding flights.
Last Minute Club Canada ⓣ1-877/970-3500, ⓦwww.lastminuteclub.com. Travel club specialising in standby flights and packages; membership is Can$40 per year.
Lee Travel Republic of Ireland ⓣ021/427 7111, ⓦwww.leetravel.ie. Flights and holiday packages.
Maya Nature Mexico ⓣ981/811 9193, ⓦwww.mayanature.com.mx. A nine-day tour of Maya heritage sites and natural areas costs US$2139.
MayaSites Travel Services US ⓣ505/255-2279, ⓦwww.mayasites.com. Excellent small custom-tour operation, run by an American and two Yucatecans, all with archeology backgrounds. Special offerings include Carnaval-season tours as well as day-trips to ruins.
North South Travel UK ⓣ01245/608 291, ⓦwww.northsouthtravel.co.uk. Travel agency offering discounted fares worldwide; profits are used to support projects in the developing world, especially the promotion of sustainable tourism.
Peregrine Adventures US ⓣ1-800/227-8747, ⓦwww.peregrineadventures.com. An eleven-day tour down the Caribbean coast into Guatemala costs US$1585; only breakfasts are included.
Premier Travel Northern Ireland ⓣ028/7126 3333, ⓦwww.premiertravel.uk.com. Discount flight specialists.
South America Destinations Australia ⓣ1800/337 050 or 03/9725 4655, ⓦwww.south-america.com.au. Offers a six-day "Yucatán Explorer" tour that includes Oaxaca.
South America Travel Centre Australia ⓣ 03/9642 5353, ⓦwww.satc.com.au. Tours for twelve days in the Yucatán (beginning in Mexico City) from A$1750, not including airfare.
South American Experience UK ⓣ0845/277 3366, ⓦwww.southamericanexperience.co.uk. Flight and tailor-made-itinerary specialists; very good airfare prices.
STA Travel US ⓣ1-800/781-4040, UK ⓣ0871/2300 040, Australia ⓣ13 4 STA, New Zealand ⓣ0800/474 400, South Africa ⓣ0861/781 781; ⓦwww.statravel.com. Worldwide specialists in independent travel that offer student IDs, travel insurance, car rental, rail passes and more. Good discounts for students and under-26s.
Trailfinders UK ⓣ0845/050 5866, Republic of Ireland ⓣ01/677 7888, Australia ⓣ1300/780 212; ⓦwww.trailfinders.com. One of the best-informed and most efficient agents for independent travellers.
Travel CUTS US ⓣ1-800/592-2887, Canada ⓣ1-866/246-9762; ⓦwww.travelcuts.com. Canada's main student travel firm, specialising in student fares, IDs and other travel services.
Trek America US ⓣ1-800/TREK USA, UK ⓣ0845/330 6095; ⓦwww.trekamerica.co.uk. Small-group adventure trips involving camping or staying at budget hotels across Mexico, including a fourteen-day "Yucatan Adventure" tour for £759/US$1571. Flights and food are extra.

Trips Worldwide UK ⓣ0117/311 4400, ⓦ**www.tripsworldwide.co.uk**. Offers an inspired range of tailor-made itineraries to less-visited places, such as Celestún, from £1695 for fourteen days. Also acts as agent for many other recommended tour operators.
USIT Republic of Ireland ⓣ01/602 1906, Northern Ireland ⓣ028/9032 7111; ⓦwww.usit.ie. Ireland's main student and youth travel experts.
Wilderness Travel ⓣ1-800/368-2794, ⓦwww.wildernesstravel.com. Nine days on the Ruta Maya in Chiapas and Guatemala from US$2995 (depending on how many people take the tour).
Women's Travel Club ⓣ1-800/480-4448, ⓦwww.womenstravelclub.com. Organizes women-only tours to Mexico, these are usually short jaunts, and often at a discount. Membership is US$35 per year.
World Expeditions US & Canada ⓣ1-800/567-2216, UK ⓣ020/8545 9030, Australia ⓣ1300/720 000, New Zealand ⓣ0800/350 354; ⓦwww.worldexpeditions.com. Offers a 22-day tour of Aztec and Maya sites from NZ$5295.

Getting around

Although distances in Mexico can be huge, if you're just travelling within the Yucatán Peninsula and Chiapas, the longest slog you'll probably face is an overnight bus between Mérida and Palenque, which can take between seven and ten hours. Public transport at ground level is frequent and reasonably efficient everywhere, though you might want to take an internal flight if you'll be travelling on to (or from) central Mexico.

By air

All of the Yucatán's major cities – Mérida, Cancún, Campeche, Ciudad del Carmen, Villahermosa and Chetumal – have **airports** served by Aeroméxico, Mexicana and, in some cases, smaller affiliates and no-frills airlines. Generally, only Villahermosa and Mérida, as well as Mérida and Cancún, connect; otherwise, you'll probably have to fly back to Mexico City to transfer. Overall, tickets are not terribly cheap, but the time saved over bus travel can make them worthwhile.

The price of a ticket on a particular flight doesn't normally vary from agent to agent, so there's no point in shopping around; it's usually twice as much for a round-trip as a one-way ticket.

Mexicana and Aeroméxico offer multi-flight airpasses, available only outside Mexico (see the box on p.21 for details).

Domestic airlines

Aeromar Mexico ⓣ1-800/237-6627, ⓦwww.aeromar.com.mx. Poza Rica to Villahermosa.
Aeroméxico US ⓣ1-800/237-6639, Mexico ⓣ1-800/021-4010; ⓦwww.aeromexico.com. All major cities, usually via Mexico City.
Aerosaab Mexico ⓣ984/873-0804, ⓦwww.aerosaab.com. Charter flights from Cancún, Cozumel and Playa del Carmen to Chichén Itzá and Holbox.
Alma de México Mexico ⓣ1-800/237-6627, ⓦwww.alma.com.mx. Cancún to Chetumal, Mérida and Villahermosa, as well as destinations in central Mexico; Mérida to Cancún, Chetumal and Villahermosa, and other destinations in central Mexico.
Aviacsa US ⓣ1-702/261-3214, Mexico ⓣ1-800/AVIACSA; ⓦwww.aviacsa.com. Mexico City to Cancún, Chetumal and Mérida; Monterrey to Cancún; Villahermosa to Mérida.
Click Mexico ⓣ1-800/122-5425, ⓦwww.clickmx.com. Mexicana budget subsidiary; Mexico City to Chetumal, Ciudad del Carmen, Cozumel, Mérida and Villahermosa.
InterJet Mexico ⓣ1-800/011-2345, ⓦwww.interjet.com.mx. Mexico City to Cancún, Ciudad del Carmen and Mérida; Monterrey to Cancún.
Magnicharters Mexico ⓣ1-800/201-1404, ⓦwww.magnicharters.com. Mexico City to Cancún and Mérida.

Mexicana US ⓣ1-800/531-7921, Mexico ⓣ1-800/801-2010; ⓦwww.mexicana.com.mx. All major cities, usually via Mexico City.
Vivaaerobus.com US ⓣ1-888/935-9848, Mexico ⓣ1-818/215-0150; ⓦwww.vivaaerobus.com. Monterrey to Cancún, Cozumel, Mérida and Villahermosa.
Volaris US ⓣ1-866/988-3527, Mexico ⓣ1-800/7-VOLARIS; ⓦwww.volaris.com.mx. Guadalajara to Cancún and Mérida; Mexico City to Cancún, Mérida and Villahermosa; Puebla to Cancún.

By bus

Within Mexico, **buses** (long-distance buses are called *camiones*, rather than *autobuses*, in Mexican Spanish) are by far the most common and efficient form of public transport. A multitude of companies run an unbelievable number of them, connecting even the smallest of villages. Long-distance services between major cities use very comfortable and dependable vehicles; remote villages are commonly connected by more rattletrap conveyances.

There are **two basic classes of bus**: first (*primera*) and second (*segunda*). First-class vehicles have reserved seats, videos and air conditioning, and an increasing number of second-class lines on the most popular inter-city routes have the same comforts. The main differences will be in the fare, which is about ten percent higher on first-class services, and sometimes a lot more. More important, though, is the number of stops – second-class buses call at more places, and consequently take longer to get where they're going; *intermedio* service can be guaranteed to stop at every possible junction, while *directo* service can blow through the tiniest towns. Most people choose first class for any appreciably long distance, and second for short trips or (obviously) for destinations only served by a second-class local bus, but you should certainly not be put off second class if the timing or location of the station seems more convenient – and it may even prove less crowded. **Air conditioning** is not necessarily a boon; there's nothing more uncomfortable than a bus with sealed windows and a broken air-conditioner, or a bus chilled to 16°C/60°F.

Deluxe buses form a separate class, running only on important inter-city routes; ADO GL and UNO are the two services in the Yucatán. Fares are around thirty percent higher than for first-class buses, but they have few if any stops, waitress service with free snacks and drinks and air conditioning that works (be sure to keep a sweater handy, as it can get very cold); they may also be emptier. The UNO buses have more fully reclining seats with leg rests, comparable to business-class seats on airlines, as well as movies audible only through headphones (supplied in a little amenities package), which is an improvement over standard service, where blaring kung-fu flicks are the norm. Both ADO GL and UNO have computerized reservations and accept credit cards in payment; you can buy tickets online at ⓦwww.ticketbus.com.mx.

Most towns of any size have a modern bus station, known as the **Central Camionera**, or just **El ADO** ("el ah-day-oh"), as that's usually the primary company operating there. Don't let the word "central" fool you, though, as they can be located a long way from the town centre. Where there is no unified terminus you may find separate first- and second-class terminals, or individual ones for each company, sometimes little more than bus stops at the side of the road. In almost every bus station, there is some form of **baggage storage** office – usually known as a *guardería* or *equipaje* – which charges about US$0.50/£0.25 per item per hour. Before leaving anything, make sure that the place will be open when you come to collect. If there's no formal facility, staff at the bus companies' baggage dispatching offices can often be persuaded to look after things for a short while.

Always check your **route** and **arrival time**, and – whenever possible – buy **tickets** from the bus station or the in-town TicketBus office (for first-class services only) in advance to get the best seats. You'll rarely have any problem getting a place on a bus from its point of origin or from really big towns. In smaller, mid-route places, however, you may have to wait for the bus to arrive (or at least to leave its last stop) before discovering if there are any seats. The increased prevalence of computerized ticketing, however, is easing the problem. Alternatively, there's almost always a bus described as *local*, which means it originates from where you are (as opposed to a *de paso* bus, which started somewhere else), and tickets for these can be bought well in advance.

Weekends, holiday seasons, school holidays and festivals can overload services to certain destinations; again, the only real answer is to buy tickets in advance. However, you could also try the cheaper second-class lines, where they'll pack you in standing, or take whatever's going to the next town along the way and try for a *local* from there.

A common alternative to scheduled bus services is the shared passenger vans called colectivos. These serve heavily trafficked routes on short hops, such as the highway between Playa del Carmen and Tulum; they depart whenever they're full, usually from a designated spot near the main bus station. They also connect very small towns where there is a less frequent or no bus service — in these cases, they usually operate on a fixed schedule, with departures once or twice a day. And in the very smallest towns, they're not vans but regular taxis. In general, they can be marginally cheaper than buses, and they have all the flexibility of a second-class bus: you can be let off anywhere, and flag them down on the highway. The drawback, though, is that they can be less comfortable, as they usually run packed to capacity.

By rail

Mexico's **railways** were privatized in 1995, and since then, though more freight is carried by rail, all passenger services have been withdrawn except for a few services run especially for tourists. In the Yucatán, the deluxe *Expreso Maya,* a service between Palenque and Chichén Itzá, was temporarily halted as of early 2008. There is a slim chance it may be revived, but only on demand by tour groups (Ⓣ999/944-9393, Ⓦwww.expresomaya.com).

By car

Although most people approach the idea of driving in Mexico with some apprehension, doing so in the Yucatán can be a pleasure. The stereotypical "fine"-levying policeman is not so rampant here as in central Mexico; likewise, Yucatecan drivers are more courteous than most visitors expect, and roads are in good condition. Care and concentration will almost guarantee a safe trip: as long as you learn the basic road rules, obey the speed limit and stay off the roads after dark, you should not encounter any real problems.

Renting a car in Mexico is often a very good way of quickly seeing a small area that would take days to explore using public transport. Local rental operations usually charge less than the international chains when you compare full insurance (local companies quote rates that include all necessary coverage). If you rent from an international operation, however, you may be able to skip the insurance and simply use the collision coverage provided by your credit card – but this requires nerve, because if you are involved in an accident, you will have to pay all costs up front and file a claim upon returning home. Daily **rates** with all insurance and unlimited mileage start at around US$50/£26. If you are travelling to Xcalak or Punta Allen during or right after the rainy season, a four-wheel-drive vehicle is a good idea; anywhere else, though, it's unnecessary – fortunately, because some readers have reported hiring a jeep to be a difficult process. Mopeds and motorbikes are also available on Cozumel and Isla Mujeres, but the international companies don't deal with them because of the high frequency of accidents.

Licences from the US, Canada, Britain, Ireland, Australia and New Zealand are valid in Mexico, though an International Driving Permit (basically a translation of your licence) can be useful if your domestic one has no photo on it (contact AAA in the US, Ⓦwww.aaa.org, or the equivalent auto association in your home country).

Mexican **roads and traffic** can seem alarming at first, but if you know the basic courtesies, the experience is less stressful. Traffic circulates on the right, and the normal speed limit is 40kph (25mph) in built-up areas, 70kph (43mph) in open country and 110kph (68mph) on the freeway. Most important of the **road rules** is that a left-turn signal often means it's clear to overtake – slow-moving trucks simply leave their signal on, or a driver may indicate it's clear to pass by turning on his blinker. If you actually want to make a left turn (assuming there is no separate left-turn bay), put on your left-turn signal but pull into the farthest *right* lane, or the hard shoulder if possible – then turn when all lanes are clear. A driver who wants to pass will flash his headlights; you're expected to pull to the right and slow a bit to hasten the process. Another convention is that the first driver to flash their lights at a junction, or where only one vehicle can pass, has the right of way: they're not inviting you to go first. Mexican drivers also use their hazard lights liberally – to signal that they are going slow, or if they are passing loose gravel. Any good road map should explain the common symbols on Mexican road signs, and Sectur has a pamphlet on driving in Mexico in which they're also featured. Don't count on clear highway signage, however, especially on Hwy-307 along the coast south of Cancún, where signs pointing to specific resorts have yet to be moved to align with new left-turn lanes – if you followed the arrows, you'd crash through the concrete median.

Some of the new highways are excellent, and the toll (*cuota*) **superhighways**, such as the one between Cancún and Mérida, are better still, though expensive. Away from the major population centres, however, roads are often narrow, winding and potholed, and cyclists weave along the nonexistent hard shoulder. Rural roads (including the free highway to Chichén Itzá) are punctuated by large **speed bumps** (*topes*) in every town or village. If not crossed at a crawl, *topes* can do serious damage to your car's undercarriage. At any sign of population, slow down and be alert, as they're not always well marked. If you have to drive at night, proceed with care and look out for wildlife, pedestrians and cyclists.

In towns, streets are usually designated one-way, but **signage** can be poor (look for small arrows affixed to lampposts, or arrows painted on buildings). **Theft** is a small threat, so lock everything that might look enticing out of sight (in the boot or trunk of your car). **Petrol stations** (all operated by the national company Pemex) are fairly widespread, but it's always a good idea to fill up before you leave a major town. Standard unleaded is called "Magna" (leaded petrol is no longer sold), and foreign credit cards are not yet accepted. All stations are full service, and while 99 percent of attendants are scrupulously honest, do stay alert while your tank is being filled and when you're paying. One rare but typical scam is for one attendant to distract the driver with idle chatter while a second diverts some of the fuel into another container – they get fuel they can resell, and you drive off with a third less than you paid for. The once-popular scam of not resetting the pump to zero is far less common now that pumps have gone digital; nonetheless, a good attendant will make a point of showing you the zero setting. You should tip all attendants M$5 or M$10, especially if they wash your windscreen. If you're in a remote area and need petrol, look out for hand-painted signs advertising *se vende gasolina*.

A free highway mechanic service, **Ángeles Verdes** (Green Angels), patrols major routes looking for beleaguered motorists. They can be reached by phone on ⓣ01-800/903-9200 and usually speak some English; they're on call only during daylight hours, though. Service is free, though of course they welcome small tips.

Should you have a minor **accident**, try to come to some arrangement with the other party – involving the police will only lead to everyone being carted off to the station, so Mexican drivers will be just as anxious to avoid this situation. If you witness an accident, you may want to consider the gravity of the situation before getting involved. Witnesses can be locked up along with those directly implicated to prevent them from leaving before the case comes up. In a serious incident, contact your consulate and your Mexican insurance company as soon as possible.

For further sound advice on driving in Mexico, request the Road Travel Report from the Association for Safe International Road Travel (ⓦwww.asirt.org).

Car rental agencies

You can either rent from the agencies noted in the "Listings" sections of the Yucatán's major towns and resorts, or arrange your rental before your departure.

Avis US & Canada ⓣ1-800/331-1084, UK ⓣ0870/010 0287, Republic of Ireland ⓣ0214/281 111, Australia ⓣ13 63 33, New Zealand ⓣ0800/655 111, South Africa ⓣ11/923 3660; ⓦwww.avis.com; ⓣ1-800/288-8888 in Mexico.
Budget US ⓣ1-800/472-3325, Canada ⓣ1-800/268-8900, UK ⓣ0870/156 5656, Australia ⓣ1300/362 848, New Zealand ⓣ0800/283 438; ⓦwww.budget.com.
Dollar US ⓣ1-800/800-6000, Canada ⓣ1-800/848-8268, UK ⓣ0808/234 7524, Republic of Ireland ⓣ1800/515 800; ⓦwww.dollar.com.
Hertz US & Canada ⓣ1-800/654-3001, UK ⓣ0870/844 8844, Ireland ⓣ01/676 7476, Australia ⓣ03/9698 2555, New Zealand ⓣ0800/654 321, South Africa ⓣ21/935 4800; ⓦwww.hertz.com. ⓣ1-800/709-5000 in Mexico.
Holiday Autos UK ⓣ0871/472 5229, Australia ⓣ1300/554 432; ⓦwww.holidayautos.com.
Thrifty US & Canada ⓣ1-800/THRIFTY, Australia ⓣ1300/367 227; ⓦwww.thrifty.com.

Hitching

It's possible **to hitch** your way around the Yucatán, but it's not the ideal strategy. Lifts are relatively scarce, and the roadside is often a harsh, shadeless environment if you get dropped at some obscure turn-off. You may also be harassed by the police. Most drivers expect you to contribute to their expenses, which can rather defeat the purpose.

Apart from all this, the standard risks of hitching still apply: robbery is not unheard of, and women in particular (but also men) are advised **not to hitch alone**. You should wait to know where the driver is going before getting in, rather than stating your own destination first. Sit by a door and keep your baggage to hand in case you need to leave in a hurry (feigned carsickness is one way to get a driver to stop).

That said, to get to villages where there's no bus or simply to while away the time spent waiting for one, you may find yourself hitching and you'll probably come across genuine friendliness and certainly meet people you wouldn't otherwise encounter. It does help if your Spanish will stretch to a conversation.

Similarly, hitchhiking is common on the road around Tulum, where fellow travellers often thumb rides between the beach and town, or up the road to Playa. It's also a major form of transport in the interior of the peninsula, where bus service is less frequent, and if you're driving this way, you may want to pick up people who are usually just trying to get to the next town down the road. Riders will always ask how much they should pay as they get out; it's up to you whether to accept any money.

Local transport

Public transport within Mexican towns and cities, usually in the form of buses, is always plentiful and inexpensive, though crowded and, except in Cancún, not particularly user-friendly. Often there's a flat-fare system, but this varies from place to place. Wherever possible we've indicated which **bus** to take and where to catch it, but often only a local will fully understand the intricacies of the system. The main destinations of the bus are usually written on the windscreen, which helps. In bigger places, combis offer a faster and perhaps less crowded alternative, usually for the same price. These minibuses or vans run along a fixed route to set destinations; they'll pick you up and drop you off wherever you like along the way, and you simply pay the driver for the distance travelled.

Regular taxis can also be good value, but be aware of rip-offs – meters are used only on a few taxis in Mérida, and otherwise drivers apply a zone system. In the latter case, fix a price before you get in. In the big cities, tables of fixed prices are posted at prominent spots, such as hotel lobbies, and at the central taxi depot. At almost every airport you'll find a booth selling vouchers for taxis into town at a fixed price depending on the area you want to go to – sometimes there's a choice of paying more for a private car or less to share. In every case you should know the name of a hotel to head for, or the driver may seize the opportunity to take you to the one that pays the biggest commission. Never accept a ride in any kind of unofficial or unmarked taxi.

Cycling

Getting around by **bicycle** is certainly popular with locals – small roads between villages are often crowded with creaky bikes piled high with firewood or the evening's hunting. For this reason, many drivers are more bike-aware than in other countries,

Addresses

In Mexico addresses are frequently written with just the street name and number (thus: Madero 125). Calle (C) means "street"; Avenida (Av), Bulevar (Blv), Calzada and Paseo are other common terms – most are named after historical figures or dates. An address such as Hidalgo 39 8° 120, means Hidalgo no. 39, 8th floor, room 120 (a ground-floor address would be denoted PB, for *planta baja*). Most colonial towns have all their streets laid out in a numbered grid, with odd-numbered streets running east–west, and even ones, north–south. The main plaza at the centre of town is usually at a point where all the numbers converge: calles 59, 60, 61 and 62 in Mérida, for example. In such places a suffix – Ote (for Oriente, East), Pte (for Poniente, West), Nte (for Norte, North), or Sur (South) – may be added to the street number to tell you which side of the two central dividing streets it is.

but this may not make up for the fact that smaller roads have very narrow shoulders, or none at all, often with a sharp drop-off into a ditch. On the other hand, the terrain is almost completely flat, and some municipalities have added paved paths alongside main roads, to allow for all the pedestrian and bicycle traffic. However, this is not to be counted on throughout the peninsula. ADO buses will also load bicycles on buses for a small fee. There isn't yet very much infrastructure for bicycle tourism, but a couple of tour agencies – Bike Mexico (see p.24) and Ecoturismo Yucatán (Ⓣ999/920-2772, Ⓦwww.ecoyuc.com) organize cycling trips, and it's best to join one of these if it's your first visit or long-distance tour. **Within cities**, you will see some local bicycle riders, but hardly anyone cycles for leisure or as a daily commute, as city streets are usually narrow and bus traffic heavy. But if you do ride, stick to smaller streets, and you should be fine. Mérida has an admirable programme called the Bici-Ruta, which closes many downtown streets to car traffic on Sundays (see p.219).

Ferries

Ferries connect islands off the Caribbean coast to the mainland: from Cancún to Isla Mujeres, from Playa del Carmen to Cozumel and from Chiquilá to Isla Holbox. Though not as cheap as they once were, all these services are still fairly inexpensive. The car ferry to Cozumel is reasonably priced and runs frequently. The services to Holbox and Mujeres, however, are all but useless, and very expensive – unless you're planning to stay for a month, it's just not worth taking your car with you. See the relevant chapters for current fares and schedules.

Accommodation

Hotels in Mexico can describe themselves as anything from posadas, hostales and casas de huéspedes to plain hoteles – terms used more or less interchangeably, though the first three are usually reserved for budget operations. Behind the labels, options can range from rustic sand-floor cabañas lit by candles to luxurious pleasure palaces in which all your meals and drinks are prearranged.

Travellers looking for **smaller hotels** have plenty of choice; note, however, that in Cancún's zona hotelera, "small" generally means fewer than three hundred rooms. One agent representing a number of smaller, well-designed resorts, hotels and apartments is the US-based Turquoise Reef (ⓣ1-800/538-6802 in the US, ⓦwww.mexicoholiday.com); on the upper end, Mexico Boutique Hotels (ⓦwww.mexicoboutiquehotels.com) represents a few choice properties. But enormous **resorts** are a dime a dozen, and if you want a week of unencumbered tanning, with only an occasional sightseeing jaunt, you can usually find very good package deals that may even include airfare.

Finding a room is rarely difficult – in most old and not overly touristy places the cheap hotels are concentrated around the main plaza, with others near the bus station (or where the bus station used to be, before it moved to the outskirts of town). The more modern and expensive places often lie on the outskirts of towns, accessible only by car or taxi. The only times you're likely to have big problems finding somewhere to stay are in coastal resorts over the peak Christmas season, at Easter, on Mexican holidays, and almost anywhere during a local fiesta, when it's well worth trying to reserve ahead.

All rooms should have an **official price** displayed, though price is not always a reliable guide to quality – a filthy fleapit and a well-run converted mansion may charge exactly the same, even if they're right next door to each other. To guarantee value, see

Accommodation price codes

All hotel rooms are subject to a twelve-percent **tax**. Some hotels – generally those under US$40/£22 per night – build this into the quoted rate, while most others add it to the bill. Prices listed in this guide are in Mexican pesos, don't include tax and are typically based on **the cheapest available room for two people sharing in high season** (Jan–April in all of the beach areas, plus July and August in the places that see lots of visitors, like Tulum). Additional price hikes go into effect everywhere for the week between Christmas and New Year, and in Semana Santa, the week before Easter. At smaller hotels, it's worth asking for a discount if you walk in off the street; for larger, chain-owned resorts and hotels, booking ahead is the only way to negotiate something lower than the official, or "rack", rate, and online rates can be up to half as much lower. All the accommodation listed in this book has been categorized into one of nine **price codes**, as set out below. **Options** in the ❶ category are rare, found only in Chiapas; ❷–❹ covers basic beach cabañas or simple rooms in small towns, while ❺–❻ is mid-range, usually ensuring air conditioning, comfortable beds and all other standard comforts; anything above creeps into luxury, except on prime beaches, where it just gets your foot in the door of an average room.

❶ M$150 and under
❷ M$151–200
❸ M$201–250
❹ M$251–350
❺ M$351–500
❻ M$501–750
❼ M$751–1100
❽ M$1101–1500
❾ M$1501 and over

your room first. You should never pay more than the official posted rate, and in the low season you can often pay less. The charging system varies: sometimes it's per person, but usually the price quoted will be for the room regardless of how many people occupy it, so sharing can mean big savings. A room with one double bed (*cama matrimonial*) is almost always cheaper than a room with two singles (*doble* or *con dos camas*), and most hotels have large "family" rooms with several beds, which are a tremendous value for groups. In the Yucatán, virtually all budget hotel rooms also have **hammock hooks**, so you can often sling up an extra person that way. The big resorts have lots of apartments that sleep six or more and include cooking facilities, for yet more savings. A little gentle haggling rarely goes amiss, and many places will have some rooms that cost less, so just ask (*¿Tiene un cuarto más barato?*).

Air conditioning (*aire acondicionado* or *clima*) inflates prices and is frequently optional; unless it's unbearably hot and humid, a room with a simple **ceiling fan** (*ventilador*) is generally better. Except in the most expensive places, the air-conditioning units are almost always noisy and inefficient, whereas a fan can be left running silently all night and the breeze helps keep insects away.

When looking at a room, always check its **insect-proofing**. Cockroaches and ants are common, and there's not much anyone can do about them, but decent netting or window-screens will keep out mosquitoes and worse and allow you to sleep. If the mosquitoes are really bad, you'll probably see where previous occupants have splattered them on the walls – it's the same story for bedbugs around the bed.

All-inclusive resorts

All-inclusives are one of the most popular lodging choices in the Yucatán, and the package deals they offer, which include lodging, all meals and gratuities, can be enticing even to travellers who ordinarily wouldn't consider them. For parents with younger children, a package provides a fuss-free programme of activities to keep kids occupied. If you're considering this option, though, don't skimp – cheaper places may seem like a bargain on paper, but the facilities can be run down and the meals bordering on inedible. Plus, prepaid meals may be a waste if you're enticed into the many excellent restaurants in Playa del Carmen, for instance. It also bears mentioning that all-inclusive resorts are perhaps the most useless form of tourism for the Mexican economy; in Cancún, where all-ins rule, less than ten percent of tourism dollars stay in the country. These resorts are also the least likely (at least so far) to be mindful of their environmental impact.

Haciendas

These **grand manors** are one of the great treats of the Yucatán. Ranches or henequen plantations built in the late nineteenth century often went to ruin during the twentieth century, but in recent years have been restored (in varying degrees) to their former luxury, complete with long verandahs, intricately tiled floors, lofty ceilings and lush gardens. Most are within an hour's drive of Mérida, though there are a few in Campeche state as well. *Hacienda Temozón* (see p.249), for instance, between Mérida and Uxmal, has incorporated many of the typical henequen-processing outbuildings into its layout, and played host to Vicente Fox and Bill Clinton. Even if you're not able to splurge on a US$300 room, you can still enjoy the colonial ambience of these sprawling places, sometimes for less than US$50 per night – try *Hacienda Yaxcopoil* (see p.249), south of Mérida; the elegant *Hacienda San Juan de Lizárraga* (see p.236), north of Mérida; or the wonderfully rambling and eclectic *Hacienda San Antonio Chalanté* (see p.209), near Izamal. In addition to the hacienda hotels mentioned in this book, visit Ⓦwww.mayayucatan.com and Ⓦwww.yucatantoday.com (search for "Hacienda Hotels").

Eco-resorts

A growing trend on the Yucatán Peninsula is the so-called **eco-resort**. "Eco-" is a freely used prefix, and often hotels will tout their use of solar panels and wind turbines not because they've chosen this option but because they simply don't have access to the electric grid – as is the case with most of the beach places in Tulum. A truly environmentally sound hotel will also have a wastewater treatment system, a composting procedure and a building plan that minimizes impact on plant and animal life – as well as, ideally, an economic and social relationship with the surrounding native culture. *Genesis Retreat* near the ruins of Ek-Balam north of Valladolid (p.197) is an excellent example, as are *Boca Paila Camps* in the Sian Ka'an Reserve (p.154) and *Villas Chimay* on Isla Holbox (p.95). Note that it's not necessarily less expensive to run a hotel using wind and solar power; you'll be choosing "eco" because you support the premise, not because you'll be getting a bargain. Visit the International Ecotourism Society at Ⓦwww.ecotourism.org for the full list of guidelines, as well as recommended tour operators and lodges.

Campsites, hammocks and cabañas

Camping is easy enough if you are happy simply to crash on a beach, but robberies are common in places with a lot of tourists. There are few organized campsites, and many are first and foremost trailer parks, not particularly pleasant to pitch tents in; however, you can still find a few beach hideaways. Of course, if you have a van or RV, you can use these or park just about anywhere else – there are a few good facilities on the Caribbean coast, including *Acamaya Reef Park* (see p.103) and *Paamul* (see p.136).

In a lot of campsites, you will be able to rent a **hammock** and a place to sling it for the same price as pitching a tent (around US$5/£2.50), maybe less, and certainly less if you're packing your own hammock (Mérida is the best place to buy these, though you can find good ones in more touristy towns if you're picky). The number of dedicated campsites like this is dwindling, though you'll still find a few near the ruins at Palenque and to the south along the Frontier Highway, as well as a very few spots in Tulum. Beyond that, you'll need to tote your own tent or hammock, and rely on personal charm to convince property owners or restaurants to let you bed down for the night.

Beach huts, or **cabañas,** are found at the more rustic, backpacker-oriented beach resorts (mainly Tulum, though a couple of other outposts remain) and sometimes inland. Usually just wood-pole walls with a **palapa** (palm-frond) roof, the shacks will have a cot or hammock, or a place to hang your own. They are frequently without electricity, though as a resort gets more popular, as in Tulum, they tend to transform into sturdier beach bungalows with modern conveniences and higher prices.

Youth hostels

There are only two official Hostelling International hostels in the Yucatán, as well as a number of unaffiliated hostels that maintain excellent standards. In less frequently visited towns, such as Chetumal, you can find a cheap place to bunk at the community sports centre (*villa deportiva*), where travelling student teams often stay. In the official hostels and those geared towards backpackers, you typically pay around US$10/£5 per person for single-sex or shared dorm facilities. A membership card for the HI places isn't necessary, but you may pay more without one. Rules at the *villas deportivas* can be strict (no booze, 11pm curfew, up and out by 9am) but most of the backpackers' favourites are open 24 hours and provide kitchen facilities, laundry, travel advice, Internet and other services. The Hostelling International affiliates are listed at Ⓦwww.hostellingmexico.com. You can make online reservations for these and many other popular facilities.

Eating and drinking

Whatever your preconceptions about Mexican food, they will almost certainly be proved wrong. The cuisine bears very little resemblance to the concoctions served in "Mexican" restaurants in other parts of the world. Nor, as a rule, is it especially spicy; indeed, a more common complaint from visitors is that after a while it all seems rather bland. For a glossary of what you'll find on local menus, see pp.358–362.

Where to eat

Basic meals are served at **restaurantes**, but you can get breakfast, snacks and often full meals at cafés, too, and plenty of **take-out** and **fast-food** places serve sandwiches, *tortas* (sandwiches on fluffy rolls) and tacos. **Jugerías** are devoted to juices and fruit salads, and every city **market** (mercado) has hot-food vendors, too.

Anywhere you dine, even in the fanciest places, don't feel obliged to order a full main course per person, or any more than you're hungry for; wasting food is frowned upon. If you do get too much, it's acceptable to have your leftovers wrapped up to go (*para llevar*).

What to eat

The basic Yucatecan diet is essentially one of corn and its products, supplemented by beans and chiles. Some dishes are spicy (*picante*), but on the whole you add your own seasoning from bowls of chile sauce on the table.

There are at least a hundred different types of **chile**, fresh or dried, in colours ranging from pale green to almost black, and all different sizes (large, mild *poblanos*, for instance, are often stuffed with meat or cheese to make *chiles rellenos*). Each has a distinct flavour, and by no means are all hot (which is why we don't use the British term "chilli"), although the most common, *chiles habañeros*, small and either green or red, are absolutely deadly when eaten straight. Chile is also the basic ingredient in more complex sauces, notably *mole*, a blend of spices that could be called Mexico's version of curry, traditionally served with turkey or chicken. Of the several types of *mole*, the most common is rich *mole poblano*, which involves bitter chocolate. Another novel use of chiles is *chiles en nogada*, in which *poblano* peppers are stuffed with a fruit-laced meat ragout, then covered in creamy walnut sauce and garnished with pomegranate seeds. The colours reflect the national flag, and it's served especially in August and September during the build-up to Independence Day.

Pinto or black **beans** (*frijoles*) usually accompany every dish and are frequently served *refritos*, which means not "refried", but "really fried". **Corn** (*maíz*), in some form or another, also features in virtually everything. In its natural state it is known as *elote,* boiled or roasted on the cob at street stalls, slathered with mayonnaise, crumbly *cotija* cheese, chile-salt and lime. Hulled kernels (*pozole*) are put in meaty soups and stews and have a pleasant yielding texture. Most commonly, though, corn is treated with lye and ground into *masa*, then formed into tortillas: flat maize pancakes served in stacks to accompany your meal. In more expensive or touristy places you might get wheat flour ones (*tortillas de harina*), but these are considered a pretension.

Masa forms the basis of a whole category of Mexican dishes called **antojitos**. Simplest of these are tacos – typically soft (not crispy) tortillas filled with anything from grilled beef to the red pork-and-pineapple combo called *al pastor*. **Enchiladas** are rolled, filled tortillas covered in chile sauce and baked; enchiladas *suizas* are the mildest variety, stuffed with chicken and cheese and topped with a green chile sauce. Tortillas torn up and topped with meat and mild salsa are called *chilaquiles*, a common breakfast dish. *Huaraches*, so named because they resemble sandals, thick ovals of *masa* lightly fried on a griddle and topped with vegetables or meats and cheese.

Masa is also the basis of **tamales**, cornmeal pudding stuffed, flavoured and cooked in corn or banana leaves. They can be either savoury, with shredded pork, or sweet when made with something like coconut and raisins. Steamed tamales (*colados*) are soft, whereas oven-baked ones (*horneados* or *rostados*) have a chewy, crunchy shell.

Northern Yucatán is cattle country, and the **meat** is delicious as long as you're not looking for a melt-in-your-mouth tender slab of steak. Typical cuts like skirt steak (*arrachera*) are sliced thin, grilled to medium and garnished with grilled onions and chiles. (For thick steaks, head to an Argentine restaurant.) Pork is ubiquitous, though usually shredded and used in small portions as flavouring; turkey is also very common. **Eggs** feature on every menu, in the classic Mexican combinations of *huevos rancheros* (fried eggs on a tortilla with red salsa) or *huevos a la mexicana* (scrambled with onion, tomato and chile), as well as the Yucatán-specific *huevos motuleños,* fried eggs on a tortilla with beans, mild tomato salsa, ham, cheese, peas and fried banana slices.

In coastal towns, you'll enjoy a great deal of wonderfully fresh **fish**, shrimp, rock lobster and conch (*caracol*), simply grilled, fried with garlic (*en mojo de ajo*) or made into **ceviche** – doused in lime and left to "cook" in the acidic juice with tomato, onion and plenty of coriander. A *cocktél* is seafood served in a cocktail glass with lime juice, ketchup and chopped onion and chile, usually with a side dish of Saltines. And shrimp tacos – lightly battered fried shrimp seasoned with mayo and chunky *pico de gallo* salsa – are an inexpensive treat. The season for rock lobster (*langosta*) on the Caribbean coast is only September to the end of February – outside that time, it's a frozen and imported product. Shrimp are available year-round – spring is the best time for the fat, succulent pink variety.

Yucatecan specialities

Head inland for more typical **Yucatecan dishes** – see the "Yucatecan food" insert for descriptions of some of the most famous. Look out especially for *pollo* or *cochinita pibil*, chicken or suckling pig wrapped in banana leaves and cooked in a *pib* (a pit in the ground), and anything *en relleno negro*, a black, burnt-chile sauce. Valladolid has its own specialities, including *longaniza*, a bright-red sausage flavoured with cinnamon. In Campeche, *pan de cazón*, a casserole of tortillas and shredded shark meat, and shrimp fried in a coconut batter, are common.

The archetypal Yucatecan treat is the **salbute**, an *antojito* made of a crispy corn tortilla topped with shredded turkey, bright-pink pickled onions, avocado and radish slices and occasionally a salty tomato sauce. *Panuchos* are nearly identical but for an added dab of refried beans slipped inside the fried tortilla.

For anyone interested in learning how to cook Yucatecan food, the Los Dos **cooking school** (Ⓣ999/928-1116, Ⓦwww.los-dos.com) in Mérida offers classes starting from US$75 for a day-long class.

Vegetarian food

Vegetarians can eat well in the Yucatán, although it takes caution to avoid meat altogether. Most restaurants serve vegetable soups and rice, and items like quesadillas, *chiles rellenos* and even tacos and enchiladas often come with non-meat fillings, such as cactus leaves (*nopal*), squash blossoms (*flor de calabaza*) and *huitlacoche*, a fungus that grows on corn and is often called the "Mexican truffle" – it even tastes a bit like bacon. *Queso fundido*, simply melted cheese, is served with tortillas and salsa, and a side of *rajas* (grilled strips of *poblano* peppers). Another boon is the leafy green *chaya* worked into many traditional dishes.

Vegetarianism, though growing, is not particularly common, and a simple cheese and chile dish may have some meat added to "improve" it. Additionally, the fat used for frying is usually lard, so that even something as unadorned as refried beans may not be strictly vegetarian.

Meals

Traditionally, Mexicans eat a light breakfast very early, a snack of tacos or eggs in mid-morning, lunch (the main meal of the day) around two o'clock or later and a late, light supper.

Breakfast (*desayuno*) in Mexico can consist simply of coffee (see "Drinking", below) and *pan dulce* – pastries that usually come in a basket; you pay for as many as you eat. More substantial breakfasts consist of eggs, and at fruit juice places you can have a simple *licuado* (see "Drinking", below) fortified with raw egg (*blanquillo*). Freshly squeezed orange juice (*jugo de naranja*) is available from street stalls in the early morning. You can eat a full meal in a restaurant at any time of day, but you'll eat better by adopting the local habit of taking your main meal at **lunchtime**, when a **comida corrida** or **comida corriente** (set meal, varied daily) is served, from around 1pm to 5pm. In more expensive places the same thing may be known as the *menu del día* or *menu turístico*. You'll usually get a soup, a main dish with a side of beans and a drink or dessert for US$5/£3 or less. More important, the *comida* includes food that doesn't normally appear on menus, such as home-made soups, stews, local specialities, puddings and elusive vegetables. You'll find these set lunches at regular restaurants with broader menus, but also at *cocinas económicas*, open only for the midday meal and catering to neighbourhood workers. Usually managed by local women, they're the best places to sample home-cooked food.

Drinking

The basic drinks to accompany meals are water, the ubiquitous Coca-Cola or beer. If you're drinking water, stick to bottled stuff – it comes either plain (*sin gas*) or carbonated (*con gas* or *mineral*).

Refrescos, jugos and licuados

Soft drinks (*refrescos*) – including Coke, Pepsi and Mexican brands such as apple-flavoured Sidral and the bubblegum-flavoured Pino Negro, made in Mérida, are on sale everywhere. Far more tempting are the **fruit juices** sold at shops and stalls known as *jugerías* or *licuaderías*. Juices (**jugos**) can be squeezed from anything that will go through the extractor. Orange (*naranja*) and carrot (*zanahoria*) are staples, but you should experiment with seasonal tropical fruits – spiky pink *pitahayas*, for instance, yield a drink studded with black seeds, with a flavour like kiwi fruit.

Licuados are fruit mixed with water (*licuado de agua* or simply *agua de...*) or milk (*licuado de leche*) in a blender, usually with sugar added. A banana-milk *licuado* with generous dashes of vanilla and cinnamon is a popular breakfast drink. Combinations get complex and the names colourful: *el vampiro* involves beetroot juice, and *el viagra* combines everything in the shop. *Limonada* (fresh lemonade) is also sold, as are *aguas frescas* – flavoured cold drinks, of which the most common are *horchata* (rice milk flavoured with cinnamon), home-made birch beer and *agua de jamaica* (hibiscus, or sorrel) or *de tamarindo* (tamarind). These are also often sold in the streets from glass jars. Street vendors sell whole green coconuts, into which you can stab a straw, then suck out the clear, faintly sweet juice. Juices and *licuados* are also sold at many ice-cream parlours (*neverías* or *paleterías*); La Flor de Michoacan is a chain operation with an impressive selection of refreshing cold drinks and ice pops.

Coffee and tea

A great deal of **coffee** is produced in Mexico, but in most of the Yucatán it is served as weak *café americano* and *café de olla* (brewed in a clay pot, usually with cinnamon), and instant Nescafé is the default. Good espresso or cappuccino is available in the resort areas and cities. As for **tea** (*té*), typically it's some kind of herb like *manzanillo* (camomile) or *yerbabuena* (mint), but basic *té negro* is usually also available.

Alcohol

Though you can get all of the national brands, the standard **beers** in the Yucatán are the light pilsner Sol, the amber León and Montejo, available in light (*clara*) and dark (*oscura*) brews. Look also for fuller-bodied (and more expensive) brews like Bohemia and Negra Modelo. A popular beer treatment is the *michelada*, in which beer is poured into a salt-rimmed glass with ice, lime juice, hot sauce and Worcestershire sauce; a *chelada* is just the lime, ice and salt. When ordering, say what type of beer you'd like it made with: a *michelada de Sol*, for example.

You'll normally be drinking in bars, but if you don't feel comfortable – this applies to women, in particular (for more on which, see p.60) – you can also get takeaways from most shops, supermarkets and, cheapest of all, *agencias*, single-brand distributors. You pay a **deposit of about 30–40 percent** of the purchase price: keep your receipt and return your bottles to the same store.

Mexican **wine** (*vino* – *tinto* is red, *blanco* is white) is improving. LA Cetto, from Baja California, is the largest producer, and its chardonnay is reasonably good; also look for smaller producers like Monte Xanic, Adobe Guadalupe and Liceaga (especially its merlot). In general, though, wine is expensive, poorly chosen and not very well cared-for.

Tequila, distilled from the cactus-like agave plant and produced in the state of Jalisco, is the most famous of Mexican spirits, served straight with lime and salt on the side. Lick the salt and bite into the lime, then take a swig of tequila (or the other way round – there's no correct etiquette). The better stuff is meant for sipping: *reposados* are somewhat aged tequilas that have taken on a faint woody taste from their casks. *Añejos* are aged longer; some approach Scotch in their smoky complexity. In Cancún and other beach towns, shops are packed with ritzy varieties, though you can find inexpensive good bottles in the grocery store – Cazadores *reposado*, for instance, is smooth and a little sweet, with a slightly lower alcohol content than others.

Mescal (often spelled *mezcal*) is also made from agave; it's usually younger and less refined and has a smoky flavour. The spurious belief that the worm in the mescal bottle is hallucinogenic is based on confusion between the drink and the peyote cactus, also called mescal; by the time you've got down as far as the worm, you wouldn't notice hallucinations anyway. For other spirits, ask for **nacional** (locally produced) varieties if you want a bargain (and perhaps a bigger headache). **Rum** (*ron*), **gin** (*ginebra*) and **vodka** are made in Mexico, as are some very palatable **brandies** (*brandy* or *coñac* – try San Marcos or Presidente).

Whatever you order, if you do it in a more traditional bar or restaurant, you'll be served **botanas** as well. These are complimentary small dishes of snacks, which can be anything from a spicy ground-pumpkin-seed dip (*sikilp'aak*) to morsels of fried fish, or Lebanese ground-meat fritters (*quibi*) or hummus. You can often make a lunch on the snacks alone.

Traditional **cantinas** are for serious and excessive drinking; more often than not, there's a sign above the door prohibiting entry to "women, members of the armed forces and anyone in uniform". Big-city cantinas are to some extent more liberal, but in small and traditional places they remain exclusively male preserves. You can enjoy a lighter, mixed atmosphere at numerous modern bars.

The media

Few of Mexico's domestic newspapers carry much foreign news, and the majority of international coverage does not extend beyond Latin America. Papers can be lurid scandal sheets, brimming with violent crimes depicted in full colour. Each state has its own press, however, and they do vary: while most are little more than government mouthpieces, others can be surprisingly independent.

Probably the best **national paper**, if you read Spanish, is the *Reforma*, which, although in its infancy, has already established an excellent reputation for its independence and political objectivity. Also worth a read is *La Jornada*. With its unabashedly left-wing agenda, it's quite critical of government policy, especially in Chiapas, and its journalists regularly face death threats as a result. As the press has gradually been asserting its independence since 1995, subjects such as human rights, corruption and drug trafficking are increasingly tackled, but journalists face great danger if they speak out, not only from shady government groups but also from the drug traffickers. The worst incidents have been confined to northern Mexico and the border cities. Yucatán and its press, by contrast, remains relatively untouched by the *narcotraficante* intrigue, and it supports several wide-ranging newspapers, from the conservative, long-established *El Diario* to the more liberal tabloids, like *Por Esto*. In Cancún and along the coast, you can also pick up the English-language *Miami Herald Cancún Edition*, but it's mostly a collection of tourism statistics and ribbon-cutting ceremonies at new hotels.

On Mexican **TV** you can watch any number of US shows dubbed into Spanish, but far and away the most popular programmes are the *telenovelas*. These soap operas, produced in Mexico and elsewhere in Latin America, dominate the screens from 6pm to 10pm and pull in audiences of millions. Cable and satellite are now widespread, and even quite downmarket hotels offer numerous channels, many of them American.

No **radio stations** in the Yucatán and Chiapas have regular English-language programmes. In Chiapas, though, you can tune in to the EZLN's broadcast, Radio Insurgente (Ⓦwww.radioinsurgente.org), on different FM frequencies depending on the area. The Universidad Autonoma de Yucatán broadcasts at 92.9 FM from Mérida, with a heavy rotation of classic *trova* and other romantic tunes. If you have a short-wave radio, you can pick up the BBC World Service (Ⓦwww.bbc.co.uk/worldservice), which is broadcast on various frequencies depending on the time of day. The main ones around Mérida are 15,190KHz, 9525KHz and 5175KHz. The Voice of America (Ⓦwww.voanews.com) broadcasts 24 hours on a number of frequencies including 5995KHz, 6130KHz, 7405KHz, 9455KHz, 9775KHz, 11,695KHz and 13,790KHz.

Festivals

Stumbling, perhaps accidentally, onto some Yucatecan village fiesta may prove the highlight of your travels. Usually, these are devoted to the local saint's day, but many fiestas have pre-Christian origins and any excuse – from harvest celebrations to the coming of the rains – will do. The most famous, spectacular or curious fiestas are mentioned here, and the main public holidays are listed in the box on p.57.

Traditional **dances** form an essential part of almost every fiesta. The Maya of the Yucatán and Chiapas are not known for ceremonial dancing or the use of masks, so common and colourful in central Mexico (one exception is the village of Tenosique, in Tabasco, where the dance of *el pochó* re-enacts a jaguar hunt). Instead, festive occasions are marked by dances that merge traditional Maya dress with Spanish or other folkloric forms and rhythms. A variation on the maypole dance, for instance, is common at rural fiestas. Other dances have more recent inspiration: the *degollete* was a protest dance that came about during the brutal Caste Wars of the 1800s; it broadly parodies each of the sharply delimited social classes of the time. The most common festive dance is the *jarana*, featuring a complex and boisterous rhythm produced by a band of clarinets, a contra-bass and several brass instruments. In Mérida, students perform these dances, but it doesn't compare to seeing the same dances performed by enthusiastic amateurs at a village celebration, who go all-out in their most festive *huipiles* and guayaberas and their best gold jewellery.

Carnaval, the week before Lent, is celebrated throughout the Roman Catholic world, and is at its most exuberant in Latin America. Like Easter, its date is not fixed, but it generally falls in February or early March. Carnaval is celebrated with costumes, parades, eating and dancing, most spectacularly in Cozumel and Mérida, and works its way up to a climax on the last day, a Tuesday. Cancún's festivities attract big-name bands, some of which don't even hit the stage until 5am. Smaller towns, however, often have to wait well into Lent to celebrate because the obligatory travelling carnival rides have to make their way from bigger markets.

The country's biggest holiday, however, is **Semana Santa** – Holy Week – beginning on Palm Sunday and continuing until the following Sunday, Easter Day. Still a deeply religious festival in Mexico, it celebrates the resurrection of Christ, and has also become a veneration of the Virgin, with processions bearing her image a hallmark of the celebrations. In Mérida and the towns of Acanceh and Maní to the south, you can see rather vigorous and elaborate Passion plays (see box, pp.42–43) that involve hundreds of people. Many places close for the whole of Semana Santa, and certainly from Thursday to Sunday.

Secular **Independence Day** (Sept 16), in some ways more solemn than the religious festivals, marks the historic day in 1810 when Manuel Hidalgo y Costilla issued *El Grito* (The Cry of Independence) from his parish church in Dolores Hidalgo. It's now marked at midnight on September 15 with a Mass and an impassioned recitation of the *grito* ("Mexicanos, viva México!") in the town plaza, followed by fireworks, music, dancing and parades. In Cancún, the greater part of the month is given over to festivities.

The Day of the Dead (**Día de los Muertos**) begins on November 1, when offerings are made to ancestors' souls, frequently with picnics and all-night vigils at their graves. People build shrines in their homes to honour their departed relatives, but it's the cemeteries to head for if you want to see the really spectacular stuff. Sweetmeats and papier-mâché statues of dressed-up skeletons give the whole proceedings a

Fiestas

January

New Year's Day (Jan 1). Beginning of the Fiesta de los Tres Reyes in the cow town Tizimín (Yucatán), a religious and secular gathering where lots of steak is consumed.

Fiesta de Polk Keken (Jan 6). In Lerma (Campeche), with traditional dances.

Día de La Virgen de Santa Inés (Jan 16–21). An ancient festival with roots in Maya tradition, celebrated in Dzitas, north of Chichén Itzá.

Día de San Sebastián (Jan 20). In Temax, between Mérida and Tizimín, marking the end of a week-long celebration.

El Pochó (variable dates Jan–Feb). On the five Sundays preceding Shrove Tuesday in Tenosique (Tabasco), masked dancers dressed as jaguars and men represent the struggle of good and evil. The celebration concludes with the burning of an effigy of El Pochó, god of evil.

February

Día de La Candelaria (Feb 2). Candlemas: colourful celebrations and candlelight processions at Tecoh and Kantunil (Yucatán) and in Ocosingo (Chiapas). The whole week before (beginning Jan 25) is a fiesta in Valladolid.

Día de San Felipe de Jesús (Feb 5). The village of San Felipe (Yucatán) celebrates its patron saint.

Carnaval (the week before Lent; variable Feb–March). Most riotous in Villahermosa and Mérida, but also big in Campeche, Tixkokob, Ciudad del Carmen and Chetumal, as well as on Isla Mujeres and Cozumel. In Hocaba (Yucatán), re-enactments of the sixteenth-century Maya Inquisition take place. Also the culmination of El Pochó in Tenosique (see Jan).

March

Fiesta del Santo Cristo de la Mora (March 18). Village celebrations in Mayapán.

Feria de Las Hamacas (March 20). Hammock-producing Tecoh celebrates its craft.

Equinox (March 21). Huge gathering for the serpent shadow at Chichén Itzá.

April

Semana Santa (Holy Week, beginning Palm Sunday, variable March–Apr). Passion plays in Mérida, Acanceh and Maní. Ticul has its Tobacco Festival.

Fiesta de Miel y Maíz (April 13–17). In Hopelchén.

Fiesta de San Telmo (April 14–22). Progreso celebrates the patron saint of seafarers.

Feria (second half of April). State fair in Villahermosa, with agricultural exhibits and the crowning of La Flor Tabasco, the state beauty queen.

Fiestas de Santa Cruz (end of April). El Cedral on Cozumel hosts a two-week fair, ending on or near the Día de La Santa Cruz (see May).

May

Día de La Santa Cruz (May 3). Another fiesta in Hopelchén; also celebrated in Celestún, Felipe Carrillo Puerto and Teapa (Tabasco), south of Villahermosa.

Fiesta de la Cruz Parlante (May 12–18). Chancah Veracruz (Quintana Roo), near Felipe Carrillo Puerto, celebrates the Holy Cross that gave inspiration for the Caste Wars.

Feria del Jipi (May 20). In Becal (Campeche), celebration of the Panama hat.

Torneo de Pesca (last weekend in May). Sport-fishing tournament and town-wide party in Puerto Morelos.

June

Día de San Antonio (June 13). Celebrated in Cárdenas (Tabasco), west of Villahermosa.

Fiesta de San Pedro y San Pablo (June 26–30). On Cozumel and in Panaba (Yucatán), north of Tizimín.

July

Fiesta de Nuestra Señora del Carmen (July 15–30). Party in Ciudad del Carmen and Motul (Yucatán), with lots of dancing.

Feria de Santo Domingo (July 28–Aug 5). Town fest in Palenque.

Feria (July 31). In Holbox.

Maya ceremony (dates variable). Held in Edzná to the god Chac, to encourage, or celebrate, the arrival of the rains.

August

Feria (Aug 10–16). Town celebration in Oxcutzcab (Yucatán).

September

Día de San Roman (Sept 14). In Dzan (Yucatán), near Ticul, the end of a four-day festival with fireworks, bullfights and dances. In Campeche, the **Feria de San Roman** lasts until the end of the month.

Día de la Independencia (Sept 14–16). Throughout Chiapas, celebration of the state's annexation to Mexico, in addition to Independence Day.

Equinox (Sept 21). Another serpent spectacle at Chichén Itzá (see "March", opposite).

Día de San Miguel (Sept 29). A major festival in Maxcanú, between Mérida and Campeche, as well as on Cozumel.

October

Los Gremios (end of Sept–Oct 17). Workers' processions around Yucatán, and especially in Mérida, to honour the cathedral's miraculous statue of Cristo de las Ampollas. Ends with a procession around the plaza and the statue's return to its altar on Oct 17.

Pilgrimage (Oct 18). Centred on Izamal (Yucatán), in honour of the miraculous Black Christ of Sitilpech, this starts off ten days of celebration, culminating in dances on the night of October 28.

November

Feria del Estado de Yucatán (first three weeks of Nov). Thrill rides, agricultural exhibits and fried foods at fairgrounds south of Mérida.

Feria de Motul (Nov 4–11). Festival in Motul (Yucatán) with bullfights starting around this time each year.

Feria (Nov 8–13). Held in Tekax, on the road from Mérida to Felipe Carrillo Puerto, with especially lively dances and bullfights.

December

Día de La Inmaculada Concepcíon (Dec 8). Widely celebrated, but especially in Kantunilkin (Quintana Roo), Izamal and Champotón, each of which has a fiesta starting several days earlier. Bullfights in Izamal and Kantunilkin.

Día de La Virgen de Guadalupe (Dec 12). Celebrated everywhere, but the roads around Mérida are filled in the days prior with church groups running relays. On Isla Mujeres, the week prior celebrates the church's statue of the Virgin.

Christmas Fiesta (Dec 25–Jan 6). In Temax (Yucatán), featuring the procession of Las Pastorelas, in which images of the Holy Family are carried from house to house.

Día de Nuestra Señora de La Estrella (Dec 27–Jan 2). Peto (Yucatán) celebrates with a trade fair, bullfights and dancing.

rather gothic air. In the Maya areas, the Day of the Dead is called Hanal Pixan. Simple house altars, with white flowers, candles, water and salt, are built on October 30, in preparation for a sunset dinner on October 31 in honour of children who have died; at noon the next day (November 1), bells chime to herald the departure of the children's souls and the arrival of adult spirits, for whom the same meals are prepared until November 2.

Christmas is a major holiday, and again a time when people are on the move and transport is booked solid for weeks ahead. Gringo influence is heavy nowadays, and after November 20 (the anniversary of the Mexican Revolution, always commemorated with parades of children dressed as Pancho Villa) shop windows and storefronts are crammed with Santa Claus, fake Christmas trees and other Yankee trappings. But the Mexican festival remains distinct in many ways, with a much stronger religious element. It begins around December 16, when people set up Nativity scenes in their homes and perform Las Posadas, re-enactments of the Holy Family's search for lodgings, in town plazas. **New Year's Eve** is still largely an occasion to spend with family, with the actual hour celebrated by eating grapes, one for each strike of the clock.

Sport and outdoor activities

The Yucatán is an active traveller's paradise, from scuba diving and snorkelling in reefs and caves to more leisurely exploits like sailing and horseback riding. Golf, tennis, jet skiing and parasailing are staples at all the big resorts. If you're just up for an afternoon's amble to appreciate the wildlife, you can do that, too.

Sport **fishing** is exceptionally good around Cancún and Cozumel and in Punta Allen, on the flat bays of the Sian Ka'an Biosphere Reserve; there's also good fishing on the Gulf coast. Year-round, you can pick up bonito, barracuda, king fish, grouper, tarpon and the lively bonefish; April to June is the season for mahi-mahi, wahoo and marlin. You can rent catamarans to **sail** on your own in any of the beach resorts, or take one of a number of yachting day-trips from Cancún. Isla Mujeres is a popular yachting port, as well as the finish line for the biennial Regatta del Sol (mid-May, even-number years) that begins in Pensacola, Florida (when the boats arrive, the island throws a big parade and party). The peninsula is also becoming something of a centre for **kiteboarding**, with dedicated enthusiasts in Playa del Carmen and Tulum, and an annual meet in February.

With the vibrant and complex Mesoamerican Barrier Reef running directly off the Caribbean coast, the Yucatán Peninsula, particularly around Cozumel, is one of the top **scuba-diving** destinations in the world. PADI (Professional Association of Diving Instructors) certification courses are offered in such places as Cancún, Playa del Carmen and Xcalak. **Snorkellers** can also enjoy some of the area's under sea wonders – in spots, it's possible to wade to the reef from shore, while a boat trip (with an experienced guide) can make a visit to a more remote coral garden or wall an easy and rewarding experience.

With so many dive spots and countless dive shops willing to take you there, it's important to choose an outfit wisely and be clear and honest about your diving skills and experience; a respectable dive master should not push you to a more advanced dive. It helps if you can find a group of divers of roughly the same level and approach a shop together. Some old hands dive only with guides who have families, a good

Reef behaviour

Coral reefs are among the richest and most complex eco-systems on earth, but they are also very fragile. The colonies grow at a rate of only around 5cm per year, so they must be treated with care and respect if they are not to be damaged beyond repair. Remember to follow these **simple rules** while you are snorkelling, diving or in a boat.

Never touch or stand on corals, as the living polyps on their surface are easily damaged.

Avoid disturbing the sand around corals. Apart from spoiling visibility, the cloud of sand will settle over the corals and smother them.

Don't remove shells, sponges or other creatures from the reef, and avoid buying reef products from souvenir shops.

Don't use suntan lotion in reef areas, as the oils are pollutants and will stifle coral growth; look for special biodegradable sunscreen for use while snorkelling.

Don't anchor boats on the reef. Use the permanently secured buoys instead.

Don't throw litter overboard.

Check ahead of time where you are allowed to go fishing.

Review your diving skills away from the reef first if you are an out-of-practice diver.

indicator that your leaders won't be taking unnecessary risks at your – or their – expense. On Cozumel, would-be snorkellers will want an operator who's willing to travel the distance to the best spots on Colombia and Palancar reefs.

The best coral growth and fish life is around Cozumel, and the reef off Puerto Morelos, though somewhat less lush, is relatively untouched. Cancún is not known for diving, though some spots are excellent for novices, with sandy floors, little current, easy access and plenty to see. Isla Mujeres has easily accessible snorkelling off the Sac Bajo Peninsula as well as a couple of interesting wreck dives. Along the Gulf coast, as on Isla Holbox, for instance, the water is not nearly as clear, and the reef life not as extravagant.

The Yucatán also offers the unique experience of diving in freshwater sinkholes called **cenotes**, part of the vast network of underground rivers, caves and caverns that riddle the limestone bedrock that forms the peninsula. The pristine spring water is gin-clear, and the elaborate rock formations otherworldly. Although many dive shops offer cenote diving packages, not all have the experience to back it up, and most cave-diving accidents have been the fault of guides who took the sport too lightly. Nonetheless, cavern diving (in which you explore a partially open space, with the entrance in clear view) requires only open-water certification; to go deeper into passageways and closed caves, you'll need excellent buoyancy control. **Snorkelling** can be enjoyed by anyone at a number of cenotes, where the proprietors often rent gear as well. An underwater torch can be a big help. Spelunkers can also explore quite a few **dry caves**.

Hiking and trekking

The utterly flat Yucatán Peninsula doesn't yield interesting **hiking** or trekking; you'll have to leave that largely for the highlands of Chiapas. But the various types of scrub forest and jungle are filled with dazzling birds and other wildlife. The few trails where you can hike without a guide are mentioned in the relevant sections of the book, and will occupy only an hour or so of your day. In general, you're better off with a guide who can identify local flora and fauna. **Birdwatchers** will benefit from a tour with Mérida-based Ecoturismo Yucatán (ⓣ999/920-2772, ⓦwww.ecoyuc.com), which also organizes the annual Yucatán Bird Festival. Ecocolors (ⓣ998/884-3667, ⓦwww.ecotravelmexico.com), based in Cancún but operating primarily in the Sian Ka'an Reserve, also offers multi-day camping tours with naturalist guides.

Another great experience is **trekking** to remote Maya ruins. You'll need a bit of Spanish, as the tours are usually geared to Mexican students, but if you can manage that, the thrill of chancing upon unexcavated ruins in the midst of the jungle, or getting a behind-the-scenes look at closed sites, is unparalleled. During Mexican holiday seasons, Servidores Turísticos de Calakmul (Ⓣ983/871-6064, Ⓦwww.ecoturismocalakmul.com.mx) organizes a four-day hike in the Calakmul Biosphere Reserve taking in the ruins of La Muñeca, which you can reach only on foot. They also offer three-day photo safaris and a truly deluxe five-day outing once a year.

Spectator sports

Mexico's chief spectator sport is **soccer** (*fútbol*), and going to a game can still be a thrilling experience, though there are no massive stadiums in the Yucatán (yet). Cancún got its first major team, the Atlante, in 2007 – it will eventually play in a 40,000-seat stadium. The Mérida team is known by the positively non-violent moniker of Los Venados (the Deer). **Baseball** (*béisbol*) is also popular, with the minor-league Tigres playing in Cancún and the major-league Piratas in Campeche. The Leones de Yucatán, another major-league team, are based in Mérida. Almost every town has one or two baseball fields where you can while away a summer night. The atmosphere at these is casual, and entrance fees are nominal or nonexistent.

Bullfights (*corridas*) still take place regularly in Cancún and Mérida, but occur only once a year or so in smaller towns during fiestas, when a bullring complete with stadium seats is erected entirely out of sapling poles. Even if you're leery of the "fight" itself, these small-town events are boisterous fun, with every man who can muster a matador's costume, however camp and bizarre, allowed to compete, and much drink consumed to bolster courage.

Masked **wrestling** (*lucha libre*) is popular in the Yucatán, though not quite a major commercial enterprise here in the same way it is in central Mexico. Nonetheless, local matches can incite great passion – keep an eye out for flyers.

Culture and etiquette

Mexicans are generally very courteous, and in some ways rather formal. It is common, for example, to address people as señor or señora, and being too brusque can give quite a bad impression. Yucatecans use the formal usted address frequently, pepper their speech with such niceties as para servirle (at your service), and ask ¿Mande? (rather than the more abrupt ¿Qué?). They dress as sharply as their income allows – men almost never wear shorts, and women prefer skirts or dresses. Formality, however, does not by any means equal coldness. Strangers may stand a bit closer than you're used to, and touch your arm while chatting.

Religion and family

Two major elements of Mexican culture are family and religion (usually Catholicism, though there's a significant evangelical group as well), though this is obviously a broad generalization. Extended families often go everywhere together – on vacation, to restaurants – and celebrations involve every generation. Don't be surprised if a social invitation from a local turns into a trip back to the house to meet the entire family. Solo travellers in particular are seen as a little sad and lonely, so you might be offered some sympathy hospitality as a result. If you are invited to someone's house, try to bring a small gift such as sweets or flowers (though never marigolds – these are associated with the Day of the Dead), but more important, expect a lot of food that simply should not be refused. (Leaving a bit of food on your plate can help stop the flow – nature abhors a vacuum, as do Mexican hosts.) But when in doubt, the polite answer is "Yes, thank you".

Religion is as much a matter of faith as a social norm that dictates everything from conservative behaviour between the sexes (you'll see young couples canoodling in parks at twilight, but that's usually as far as things go until marriage) to habits such as making the sign of the cross when passing a church. For your part, it is simply polite to avoid open criticism of religion unless you are sure of your company; you should also keep shoulders and knees covered when touring churches (though you'll note this isn't always followed by locals).

Catholicism in Mexico is not nearly as rigid as it can appear on the surface, and major issues are under constant debate. Divorce laws vary from state to state, but it's fully legal and though certainly not a cause for celebration, it's more accepted than it used to be. In 2007, Mexico City legalized early-term abortion within its bounds; elsewhere in the country, the procedure is still available only to rape victims and women whose health is endangered by the pregnancy. Contraception is available in pharmacies, and condoms are openly encouraged for the sake of public health.

Time and appointments

Jaded expats often comment on (nay, complain bitterly about) the phenomenon of "Mexican time", and there is some truth to the fact that things move more slowly in the tropical heat. Punctuality is just not a priority, or even a virtue. Mexicans will say they are doing something *ahorita* – right now – but may not get to it for another hour. This can seem infuriating if you are processing paperwork or building a house, but fortunately you as a traveller are unlikely to be doing these things. In fact, the relaxed attitude towards time can be a bit of a relief if you let yourself live into it. You're rarely expected to show up anywhere on time, either, and might even severely surprise someone if you show up at their home at the precise time invited. Just try not to make plans that rely on, say, dropping off the rental car as soon as the office opens.

Due to both the attitude toward punctuality and general courtesy rules, making appointments can lead to all kinds of misunderstandings. Mexicans find it very impolite to say no, so that if you extend an invitation, you will almost certainly get a positive response – but that is no guarantee the person will turn up. If this seems *not* polite – in fact, a little rude – to you, remember that it can work in your favour, too (especially handy for women). You can always smile sweetly and accept a date with that guy for drinks the next night, then make a graceful exit; it won't be held against you if you simply never appear.

Tipping

The *propina* (tip) is a standard part of Mexican culture, though the amounts are a bit less than in other tipping-heavy countries. Ten percent or so is standard at restaurants – Mexicans usually leave any loose change – though fifteen percent is more common in American-centric areas like Cancún. Always take a look at your bill first – service (*servicio*, usually ten percent) is sometimes included, especially at more formal places. In this case you're not expected to leave anything additional, though of course extra is appreciated. In luxury hotels, tip as you would anywhere – M$10 or M$20 to bellhops and valet parking attendants, plus M$20 or M$30 per day in the room. Staff at smaller, Mexican-run hotels don't generally expect tips, unless the clientele is largely foreign. Tips are also the norm at petrol stations – M$5 or M$10 to the attendant who pumps the fuel, as well as to the one who washes your windshield. Restrooms are usually staffed, and an M$5 tip is standard here – sometimes a sign is posted, sometimes not, and the attendant may or may not have a cup or towel laid out to collect change. (Because tipping is standard in restrooms, it's perfectly acceptable to use one at a restaurant or bar without buying anything.) One exception to the tipping rule is taxi drivers, where only the flat fare is expected. If the driver helps with your bags, though, you might want to add another M$10 or M$20 depending on how much luggage you have.

Smoking

A nationwide smoking ban in restaurants and public spaces is set to go into effect in 2008. How this will be accepted has yet to be seen – the shift will be massive, considering Mexicans have one of the oldest cultures of tobacco consumption in the world.

Shopping

The craft tradition of Mexico, much of it descended directly from arts practised long before the Spanish arrived, is strong in the Yucatán. Regional and highly localized specialities survive, with villages boasting of their reputations for particular skills. You can also pick up a considerable amount of Guatemalan weaving and embroidery.

To buy **crafts**, there is no need these days to visit the place of origin; shops in all the big resorts gather the best and most popular items from around Mexico. On the other hand, it's a great deal more enjoyable to see where the articles come from, and certainly the only way to get any real bargains. The good stuff is rarely cheap wherever you buy it, however, and there is an enormous amount of dross produced specifically for tourists.

FONART shops, which you'll come across in major centres throughout Mexico, are run by a government agency devoted to the promotion and preservation of crafts. Their wares are always excellent, if more expensive than most, and the shops should be visited to get an idea of what is available and at what price. Among the most popular items are: **silver**, the best of which is wrought in Taxco, although rarely mined there; **embroidery**; **leather**, especially tyre-tread-soled *huaraches* (sandals), sold cheaply wherever you go; **glass** from Jalisco; and **lacquerware**, particularly from Uruapán.

Good buys specific to the Yucatán include men's dapper, Cuban-style **guayabera shirts** and Panama hats (known here as *jipis*). Throughout the peninsula and Chiapas, Maya women wear flower-bedecked embroidered **huipiles**, which vary wildly in quality, from factory-made junk to hand-embroidered, homespun cloth. Even the best, though, rarely compare with the **antique dresses** that can occasionally be found, identical in style (as they have been for hundreds of years) but far better made and very expensive. Silver **jewellery** (genuine sterling should be stamped ".925"), either made into fine filigree or set with colourful semiprecious stones, rich amber or milky Mexican opals, can be elegant and inexpensive.

The most popular souvenir of the Yucatán is a **hammock**, and Mérida is probably the best place to buy one, for both price and selection. If you want something you can realistically sleep in, never buy from street vendors or even a market stall – they're invariably of very poor craftsmanship, with thicker strings woven loosely, so they don't hold their shape. Comfort is measured by the tightness of the weave and the breadth: because you're supposed to lie in a hammock diagonally, to be relatively flat, the distance it stretches sideways is far more crucial than the length (although obviously the woven portion of the hammock, excluding the strings at each end, should be at least as long as you are tall). A good way to judge quality is by weight: a decent-size hammock (*doble* at least, preferably *matrimonial*) with cotton threads (*hilos de algodon*, more comfortable and less likely to go out of shape than artificial fibres) will weigh more than a kilo and set you back about US$25/£13. ("*Sisal*" hammocks are generally fraudulent; this rough rope material is seldom used today.)

It is illegal to buy or sell antiquities, and even more criminal to try taking them out of the country (moreover, many items sold as valuable antiquities are little more than worthless fakes).

Markets

For bargain hunters, the **mercado** (market) is the place to head. There's one in every Yucatecan town, which on the traditional market day, one day a week, will be at its busiest with villagers from the surrounding area bringing their produce for sale or barter. By and large, of course, mercados are mainly dedicated to food and everyday necessities, but most have a section devoted to crafts, and in larger towns you may find a separate crafts bazaar. You can also find a lot of fun smaller gift items, such as Spanish classroom vocabulary **posters**, found in stationers, or local foodstuffs, such as **coffee** in Chiapas, inexpensive but fragrant **vanilla** and Yucatecan **honey.**

Unless you're completely hopeless at bargaining, prices will always be lower in the market than in shops, but shops do have a couple of advantages. First, they exercise a degree of quality control, whereas any old junk can be sold in the market; and second, many established shops will be able to ship purchases home for you, which saves the bureaucracy you'll encounter if you attempt to do it yourself.

Bargaining is welcomed only in certain circumstances. In shops there's little chance of significantly altering the official price unless you're buying in bulk, and even in markets most food and simple household goods have a set price. **Bargaining and haggling** are very much a matter of personal style, highly dependent on your command of Spanish, aggressiveness and to some extent on experience. The standard tricks (never show the least sign of interest, let alone enthusiasm; walking away will always cut the price dramatically) hold true; but most important is to know what you want, its approximate value and how much you are prepared to pay. Never start negotiating for something you don't intend to buy. But overall don't let a quibble over a few dollars stop you from buying, and resist the urge to compare prices with fellow shoppers – ten pesos almost certainly means more to the seller than to you, and the "best" price is the one both you and the seller are happy with.

Travelling with children

Travelling with younger kids in this part of Mexico is not uncommon – most Mexicans dote on children, and youngsters can often help break the ice with strangers. Although most of the ritziest resort properties on the Caribbean have a no-kids policy, there are a few very fine exceptions, and you shouldn't have a problem staying at mid-range and budget places.

The biggest concern, especially with small children, is their **vulnerability**. Even more than their parents, children need protection from the sun, unsafe drinking water, heat and unfamiliar food. Remember that diarrhoea can be dangerous for younger children; rehydration salts (see p.55) are vital if your child goes down with it. Also make sure, if possible, that your child is aware of the dangers of rabies and other animal-borne illnesses; keep kids away from all animals, and consider a rabies shot.

For touring, hiking or walking, **child-carrier backpacks** are ideal. They can weigh less than 2kg and start at around US$75/£50. If the child is small enough, a **fold-up buggy** is also well worth packing – especially if they will sleep in it while you have a meal or a drink.

Public breast-feeding is only borderline acceptable – you won't see a lot of mothers doing it, but it's certainly possible in an emergency. Nappies, milk and standard medications are readily available in all but the tiniest towns, and while there may not be a lot of dedicated changing facilities, the inconvenience is largely made up for by the general tolerance and helpfulness toward parents and their little ones. One thing to be aware of, if you try to keep your children away from such things, is the level of on-screen violence typical of the movies shown on buses. You may wish to find seats away from the screen when travelling on long-distance bus journeys to avoid the gore that is likely to be shown.

On the other hand, some things you might want to make a special effort to show children include the monkeys at the reserve in Punta Laguna (see p.151) and any of the scores of cenotes. The cenote near Ek-Balam (see p.197) has a zipline and other activities to keep older kids occupied. As for the haciendas, a livelier place like Hacienda Sotuta de Peon (see p.259) can engage younger kids who may not yet appreciate the ambience of a spooky abandoned place like Yaxcopoil (see p.249). The theme parks of Xcaret (see p.117) and Xel-Há (see p.134) are both a bit expensive, but also relatively safe environments in which younger kids can explore some of the natural elements of the Yucatán, such as cenotes and coral reefs. Older children will likely be fascinated with the caves at Loltún (see p.255) and Xpukil (see p.268). The latter, which lacks lights and defined paths, are probably best reserved for teenagers, though.

For customized and scheduled travel itineraries geared toward adventurous families, contact the US tour agency Rascals in Paradise (ⓣ415/921-7000, ⓦwww.rascalsinparadise.com).

Travel essentials

Costs

Compared with the rest of Mexico, Cancún and the Caribbean coast have a reputation for being expensive. Although in general costs are lower than you'll find at home, prices on the peninsula, compared with the rest of Central or South America, can come as something of a shock. Prices in the text of the guide section are quoted in **Mexican pesos** (M$), but in the tourism-centric coastal areas, these prices can change almost daily, according to the exchange rate with the US dollar.

Prices can also be affected by **season**, and many hotels raise their prices during busy times of the year. Mexicans travel in July and August, the week between Christmas and New Year and the week before Easter (Semana Santa), and these periods overlap with the popular seasons for visitors. Nonetheless, wherever you go, you can probably get by on US$400/£200 a week (you could reduce that if you hardly travel around, stay only in campsites or hostels, live on basic food and don't buy any souvenirs, but that requires a lot of discipline), while on US$800/£400 you'd be living very comfortably.

Food prices can vary wildly, but you should always be able to get a substantial meal in a basic Mexican restaurant for around M$50/US$5/£2.50 – though such value is often available only at lunch. If you're keen to save money, make lunch your major meal, then have lighter snacks for dinner, as locals do. Most restaurant bills come with fifteen percent IVA (*impuesto de valor añadido*, or value-added sales tax) added, and it should be included in prices quoted on the menu. If you intend to travel around a lot, **transport** could be another major expense because distances are so large. On a per-kilometre basis, however, prices are still quite reasonable: the four-hour run between Cancún and Mérida starts at just M$256/US$25/£12.50 on a first-class bus. For more information on **accommodation** prices, see the box on p.33.

Travelling with a group can save a lot. On the beaches, you can get apartments for up to six people for even greater savings. On the other hand, an **International Student or Youth Card**, such as those issued by STA Travel, will not get you much – you might find the occasional reduction on a museum admission price, but usually discounts are extended only to Mexican students.

Service is rarely added to bills, except in more expensive restaurants in the resort towns. The expected tip is about ten percent, while expensive venues tend to call for a full fifteen percent. For more advice on tipping, see p.47.

Crime and personal safety

Despite occasional reports of sordid drug-cartel crimes (Cancún has unfortunately become a trafficking point), you are unlikely to run into trouble in the Yucatán as long as you don't go looking for it. Indeed, the region cherishes its very low rate of violent crime and overall graciousness, and it dismays locals to see travellers clutching their bags tightly and looking around suspiciously in such non-threatening areas as Cancún's zona hotelera or central Mérida.

The precautions to be taken against petty crime are mostly common sense and would be second nature at home: don't wave money around and deposit valuables in the hotel safe. Drivers are likely to encounter problems only if they leave anything enticing visible in their **car**. The vehicle itself is less likely to be stolen than broken into for the valuables inside.

If you're travelling in the Zapatista-controlled areas of the state of Chiapas you will undoubtedly come across guerrillas and the army, but tourists are a target of neither, and you shouldn't encounter any trouble.

Police

In general, police in the Yucatán seem to conform less to the stereotypes of Mexican *federales* (namely, in that they are not quick to make up offences or ask for bribes). Nonetheless, graft does seem to be an accepted part of the job, due to the low wages. This is often difficult for foreign visitors to accept, but it is a system, and in its own way it works well enough. If a policeman accuses you of some violation, explain that you're a tourist, not used to the ways of the country – you may get off scot-free, but more likely the subject of a "fine" will come up. Such on-the-spot fines are open to negotiation, but only if you're confident you've done nothing seriously wrong and have a reasonable command of Spanish. Otherwise pay up and get out. These small bribes, known as **mordidas** (bites), may also be extracted by border officials or bureaucrats (in which case, you could get out of paying by asking for a receipt, but it won't make life easier). In general, it is always wise to back off from any sort of confrontation with the police and to be extremely polite to them at all times.

Should a crime be committed against you – in particular, if you're robbed – your relationship with the police will be different, although it's worth considering whether the lengthy hassles make it worth reporting. **Tourist police** in the resort towns can at least appear more sympathetic, but this doesn't necessarily speed up the process. Some insurance companies will insist on a **police report**, but others will be more understanding. The department you need in order to *presentar una denuncia* (report the theft officially) is the **Procuradoría General de Justicia**.

The Mexican **legal system** is based on the Napoleonic code, which assumes your guilt until you can prove otherwise. Should you be jailed, your one phone call should be to your **consulate** – if nothing else, it will arrange an English-speaking lawyer. You can be held for up to 72 hours on suspicion before charges have to be brought.

Drugs

Drug offences are the most common cause of serious trouble between tourists and the authorities. Under heavy pressure from the US to stamp out the trade, local authorities are particularly happy to throw the book at foreign offenders.

Marijuana (known as *mota*) continues to be cultivated in Mexico. It's widely used, particularly along the Caribbean beaches, but it remains strictly illegal. For possession of even small quantities, you can expect a hefty fine, no sympathy and little help from your consulate. Hallucinogenic mushrooms are also not uncommon. The authorities turn a blind eye to traditional use, but use by non-indigenous Mexicans and tourists is as strongly prohibited as that of any other illegal drug, and heavily penalized.

Cocaine trafficking is a national problem, as Mexico is a major staging post on the smuggling route from Colombian supply to American demand. The cartels do not (yet) exert the social influence in the Yucatán that they do in the northern part of Mexico, but stories abound about suspicious packets washed up on the Caribbean beaches, and equally suspicious sorts reclaiming them. A very thorough drug checkpoint is set up on the highway out from Mahahual. Cocaine use is also widespread and growing, especially in the beach party towns, but you're advised to steer well clear, considering the legal consequences.

Electricity

Theoretically, the voltage in Mexico is 110 volts AC, with simple two-flat-pin rectangular plugs, so most North American appliances can be used as they are. Travellers from the UK, Ireland, Australasia and Europe should bring along a converter and a plug adapter. However, cuts in service and fluctuations in the current do occur, and in cheap hotels any sort of appliance that draws a lot of current may blow all the fuses as soon as it's turned on.

Emergency

General emergency number ☎080; Police ☎060; Fire ☎068; Ambulance ☎065; Green Angels (emergency highway breakdown) ☎01-800/903-9200; Tourism ☎078 (also contact for Green Angels) or ☎01-800/903-9200.

Entry requirements

Citizens of the US, Canada, the UK, Ireland, Australia, New Zealand and much of Western

Europe do not need a visa to visit Mexico as tourists for less than 180 days. Non-US citizens travelling via the US, however, may need a US visa. Visitors entering by land are subject to a M$230/US$23 entry fee, which will be included in your ticket if arriving by air (an additional M$260/US$26, also usually included in the ticket price, is required as an exit tax on all flights).

What every visitor does need is a valid **passport.** On your arriving flight, you'll be given a **tourist card** or FMT (*folleto de migración turística*), which you must keep on hand for the rest of your trip and turn over when you leave. There is a fee for the card (M$230/US$23), and it is usually simply bundled in the price of your plane ticket. (There is also an M$260/US$26 exit tax on all flights – again, usually included in the fare.) If you are **entering by land from Belize or Guatemala**, you will have to pay cash at the border crossing – be sure to get a receipt and hang on to it, as officials further down the line may try to demand the fee again. Note also that it's not uncommon for border posts to run out of tourist cards.

A tourist card is valid for a single entry for **up to 180 days**, though officials will often write in thirty days or less. Be sure to specify you want the full time limit if you know you'll be visiting for a long stretch, as getting an extension can be a time-consuming business. You may also be asked to show bank statements or other proof of sufficient funds for your stay, about US$300 for every week you'll be in Mexico.

Should you lose your tourist card, or need to have it renewed, head for the nearest **Departamento de Migración**, or immigration department office; there are branches in the largest cities. In the case of renewal, if you are near a border, it's far simpler to cross for a day and get a new one upon re-entry than apply for an extension; if you do apply to the immigration department, it's wise to do so a couple of weeks in advance, though you may be told to come back nearer the actual expiry date. Whatever else you may be told, branches of Sectur (the tourist office) cannot renew expired tourist cards or replace lost ones – they will only make sympathetic noises and direct you to the nearest immigration office.

Visas, obtainable only through a consulate (in person or by mail), are required for nationals of South Africa, many Eastern European countries newly admitted to the EU and most non-industrialized countries. Anyone entering the country to work or study, or who will be staying for more than six months, needs a visa. Business visitors need a Business Authorization Card available from consulates, and usually a visa, too. Anyone under 18 needs written consent from their parents if not accompanied by both of them (if accompanied by one, they need written consent from the other).

Mexican consulates and embassies abroad

The following Mexican **embassies and consulates** all issue visas and tourist cards. To find the address of one not listed here, see "Representaciones" at Ⓦwww.sre.gob.mx.

Australia

Embassy 14 Perth Ave, Yarralumla, Canberra, ACT 2600 Ⓣ02/6273 3963, Ⓦwww.sre.gob.mx/australia.

Belize

Embassy 3 North Ring Rd, Belmopan Ⓣ501/822-0406, Ⓦwww.sre.gob.mx/belice.
Consulate Newtown Barracks at Wilson St, Belize City Ⓣ501/223-0193, Ⓔconsular@embamex.bz.

Canada

Embassy 45 O'Connor St, Suite 1000, Ottawa, ON K1P 1A4 Ⓣ613/233-8988, Ⓦwww.sre.gob.mx/canadaingles.
Consulates 2055 rue Peel, Suite 1000, Montréal, QC H3A 1V4 Ⓣ514/288-2502, Ⓦwww.sre.gob.mx/montreal; 199 Bay St, Suite 4440, Commerce Court W, Toronto, ON M5L 1E9 Ⓣ416/368-2875, Ⓦwww.consulmex.com; 710–1117 W Hastings St, Vancouver, BC V6E 2K3 Ⓣ604/684-3547, Ⓦwww.consulmexvan.com.

Cuba

Embassy C 12 no. 518, Miramar, Playa, Havana 11300 Ⓣ7/204-7722, Ⓦwww.sre.gob.mx/cuba.

Guatemala

Embassy Av 2 no. 7–57, Zona 10, Guatemala City 1455 Ⓣ02/420-3433, Ⓦwww.sre.gob.mx/guatemala.

Embassies and consulates in Mexico

Contact information for embassies and consulates can be found at ⓦwww.sre.gob.mx/delviajero – look up your country (US is "Estados Unidos" in "América del Norte"; UK is "Reino Unido") and click on the link labelled "Embajada extranjera en México". For further details of consulate locations, see the "Listings" sections for the relevant cities in this book.

Republic of Ireland

Embassy 19 Raglan Rd, Ballsbridge, 4 Dublin ⓣ01/667 3105, ⓦwww.sre.gob.mx/irlanda.

New Zealand

Embassy 185–187 Featherstone St, level 2 (AMP Chambers), Wellington ⓣ04/472 0555, ⓦwww.sre.gob.mx/nuevazelandia.

South Africa

Embassy 3rd Fl, 1 Hatfield Square, 11101, Hatfield St, Hatfield 0083 ⓣ012/362-2822, ⓔembamxza@mweb.co.za.

UK

Embassy 16 St George St, London W1S 1FD ⓣ020/7499 8586, ⓦwww.sre.gob.mx/reinounido.

US

Embassy 1911 Pennsylvania Ave NW, Washington, DC 20006 ⓣ202/728-1600, ⓦportal.sre.gob.mx/eua.
Consulates are in nearly fifty other US towns and cities, including those in these border states: **Arizona** 1201 F Ave, Douglas, AZ 85607 ⓣ520/364-3107, ⓦportal.sre.gob.mx/douglas. **California** 1549 India St, San Diego, CA 92101 ⓣ619/231-8414, ⓦwww.consulmexsd.org. **Texas** 301 Mexico Blvd, Suite F-2, Brownsville, TX 78520 ⓣ956/542-4431, ⓦwww.sre.gob.mx/brownsville; 910 E San Antonio Ave, El Paso, TX 79901 ⓣ915/533-3644, ⓦwww.sre.gob.mx/elpaso.

Gay and lesbian travellers

Social acceptance of homosexuality is slowly spreading. Mexico's first "out" congresswoman, the left-wing PRD's Patria Jiménez, was elected in 1997, and 2003 saw the passage of a federal law forbidding discrimination based on "appearance, mannerism and expression of one's sexual preference or gender". Beyond this, there's a surprisingly open subculture once you tap into it.

There are **gay bars and clubs** in Cancún, Playa del Carmen and Mérida (visit ⓦwww.sergay.com.mx for "Guia de Lugares", a basic directory, though it's not entirely up to date; also see nightlife listings in this book). Elsewhere, private parties are where it all happens, and you'll need a contact to find them.

As for contacts within Mexico, lesbians can get in touch with Grupo Lésbico Patlatonalli, López Cotilla 996, Guadalajara, Jalisco 44100 (ⓣ333/3825-0598, ⓔpatlas@mail.udg.mx); while for gay men, CIDHOM (Centro de Información y Documentación de las Homosexualidades en México), Cerrada Cuaunochtli 11, Colonia Pueblo Quieto, Tlalpan, México DF 14040 (ⓣ55/5666-5436, ⓔcidhom_colso@yahoo.com.mx), can offer information.

Health

For minor medical problems, head for a pharmacy – look for a green cross and the "**Farmacia**" sign. Pharmacists are trained to diagnose and prescribe, and many speak English. They can also sell many more drugs over the counter than are available at home.

The quality of medical care in Mexico can be quite good (though you will be expected to pay out of pocket); Mérida in particular is a regional centre for medical treatment. Otherwise, most towns have a state-run **health centre** (*centro de salud* or *centro médico*), where treatment is free. Ask a large hotel or your consulate for a recommendation, or get a copy of *MedToGo Yucatan*, published by MedToGo (ⓦwww.medtogo.com).

Travellers in Mexico face few grave health risks. "Montezuma's revenge" (traveller's diarrhoea, aka *turista*) will strike most people at some point. The bounty of fresh fruit is often enough to upset some people's systems, as is a steady diet of cheap margaritas. Watch this intake and wash your hands frequently (there is a sink for this in every restaurant), and you've cut the risk significantly. Water, too, is an issue, though only the most miserable places use tap water (it makes the locals sick, too). In Cancún and Cozumel, the tap water is purified, if not so tasty. If you do get a bout of *turista*, oral **rehydration salts** – *suero oral* (brand names include Dioralyte, Electrosol and Rehidrat) – are a great help. If you can't get these, dissolve half a teaspoon of salt and three of sugar in a litre of water. Yogurt and prickly-pear fruit (*tuna*) are also recommended.

Protect against Mexico's sunny climate with strong **sunscreen** (look for biodegradable brands for use in national parks) and wear a hat. Drink a litre or so of water or fruit juice (not beer or coffee) a day, and don't exert yourself in the hot afternoon.

Malaria is endemic in some small parts of Mexico, though beach resorts like Cancún, Cozumel and Isla Mujeres are malaria-free. You're at virtually no risk unless you'll be spending an extended period in swampy areas. For general comfort, wear long sleeves and repellent (look for an effective natural formulation of essential oils in health stores in Mexico) around sunset. Special mosquito nets for hammocks are also available in Mexico. Mosquitoes carrying **dengue fever** (a disease common in the tropics) have made an appearance in southern Chiapas. They are prevalent during the rainy season and fly during the day, so wear insect repellent all the time in this region. The only treatment is rest, with drugs to assuage the fever.

Other insects include **scorpions**, which can turn up in your shoes or bottoms of sleeping bags. Their sting is not dangerous, only painful; cold-pack the sting to reduce swelling, and seek medical treatment if pain does not lessen within six hours. Few **snakes** in the Yucatán are poisonous, and are unlikely to bite unless actively disturbed.

For comprehensive coverage of the health problems worldwide, consult *The Rough Guide to Travel Health,* by Dr Nick Jones.

Medical resources for travellers

US and Canada

CDC ⓣ1-877/394-8747, ⓦwww.cdc.gov/travel. Official US government travel health site.

Canadian Society for International Health ⓦwww.csih.org. Extensive list of travel health centres.

International Society for Travel Medicine ⓣ1-770/736-7060, ⓦwww.istm.org. US organization with a full list of clinics.

UK and Ireland

Hospital for Tropical Diseases Travel Clinic ⓣ0845/155 5000 or 020/7387 4411, ⓦwww.thehtd.org.

MASTA (Medical Advisory Service for Travellers Abroad) ⓦwww.masta.org.

Tropical Medical Bureau ⓦwww.tmb.ie.

Australia, New Zealand and South Africa

Travellers' Medical and Vaccination Centre ⓦwww.tmvc.com.au, ⓣ1300/658 844. Lists travel clinics in Australia, New Zealand and South Africa.

Insurance

As there are no reciprocal health arrangements between Mexico and any other country, travel insurance is essential. A typical **travel insurance policy** also provides safeguards for the loss of baggage, tickets and a certain amount of cash or traveller's cheques, as well as the cancellation or curtailment of your trip. Most policies exclude so-called dangerous sports unless an extra premium is paid. In Mexico this can mean scuba diving, windsurfing, kiteboarding or trekking, though kayaking or jeep safaris are usually covered. If you have anything stolen during your trip, you must make an official statement to the police and obtain a copy of the declaration (*copia de la declaración*) for your insurance company.

Internet

Internet cafés are thick on the ground in all the larger cities and resort destinations, and the level of service is usually excellent. Depending on where you are, access can cost anything from M$5 to M$25 an hour, with major tourist resorts being the priciest places. Cancún's zona hotelera is the one serious Web wasteland – you're all but locked into using your hotel's outrageously expensive service, unless you head into downtown Cancún and use one of the locals' operations around the bus station. Wireless (Wi-Fi) hot spots are increasingly prevalent (especially in Mérida, where they're installed in many public parks), but don't count on them.

Laundry

Lavanderías are ubiquitous in Mexico. Most charge by the kilo, and for a few dollars you'll get your clothes back clean, pressed and perfectly folded in less than 24 hours. Many hotels also offer laundry services that, although convenient, tend to charge by the item, adding up to a considerably greater cost.

Mail

Mexican postal services (*correos*) are reasonably efficient. Anything sent abroad by air should have an **airmail** (*por avión*) stamp on it. Airmail postcards and letters under 20g cost M$10.50 to the US and Canada, M$13 to Europe and South America and M$14.50 to the rest of the world. Letters should take around a week to North America and two to Europe or Australasia, but can take much longer (postcards in particular are likely to be slow). Dedicated airmail boxes in resorts and big cities tend to be more reliable than ordinary ones.

Sending **packages** out of the country requires examination by customs and much paperwork. Take your package (unsealed) to any post office and they'll set you on your way. Many stores will send your purchases home for you, which is a great deal easier.

Maps

Rough Guides, in conjunction with the World Mapping Project, have produced our own rip-proof, waterproof maps of Mexico and of the Yucatán, with roads, contours and physical features all clearly shown. Obviously we recommend them, and if you compare them for price and clarity with the competition, we are confident that you will prefer them, too.

An excellent alternative is the sturdy laminated Yucatán map published by German mapmaker Borch. At 1:1,000,000, it's a good scale, and covers much of Villahermosa and Chiapas as well; highway details are the most accurate and current available. Rough Guides readers are entitled to a ten percent discount on their Borch purchase at MapsGoneTomorrow.com (Ⓦwww.mapsgonetomorrow.com); enter the coupon code "roughguide".

If you'll be travelling to the Caribbean beach towns and around Chichén Itzá, also see the excellent maps produced by Can-Do Maps, available at Ⓦwww.cancunmap.com. The maps of Cancún, Isla Mujeres, Cozumel, Playa del Carmen, Chichén Itzá and the full Riviera Maya clearly label all hotels, restaurants and rental homes, as well as the usual sights.

In Mexico itself, maps published by Patria and Guía Roji are detailed, but not updated frequently, and newer or smaller roads in the Yucatán are often missing. Both are widely available, though – try large Pemex stations.

For more detailed, large-scale maps (for hiking or trekking), see *Mexico South* (1:1,350,000), which includes Villahermosa and parts of Chiapas, and the *Yucatán Peninsula* (1:500,000), both produced by International Travel Maps (Ⓦwww.itmb.com). INEGI, the Mexican government mapmakers, do produce very good topographic maps on various scales. The company has an office in every state capital and an outlet at Mexico City's airport. Unfortunately, stocks can run low, so don't count on being able to buy the ones that you want.

Money

The new Mexican peso, or **nuevo peso**, usually written $, was introduced in 1993 and is made up of 100 centavos (¢). Bills come in denominations of M$20, M$50, M$100, M$200 and M$500, with coins of 10¢, 20¢, 50¢, M$1, M$2, M$5, M$10 and M$20. The initials MN (*moneda nacional*, or national coin) are occasionally used to indicate that it's Mexican money (not American) that is being referred to; it's clearer when you remember the exchange rate is usually around M$10 to US$1, or M$20 to £1. In Cancún and to a lesser extent Cozumel and Playa del Carmen, many businesses accept US dollars as payment, but rates are usually not favourable.

The easiest kind of foreign currency to change in Mexico is **cash US dollars**. US dollar travellers' cheques come second, although even these are becoming harder to deal with, as currency regulations passed in early 2008 have made it prohibitively difficult for independent cambios (exchanges) to handle them; banks alone are the only guaranteed place to change them. Canadian dollars and other major international currencies such as pounds sterling, yen and euros are a poor third. Dump Guatemalan quetzales and Belize dollars before entering Mexico if possible.

ATMs (*cajero automático*) can be found in all but the smallest towns. The local ATM charge is usually M$7.50 per transaction. All but a very few ATMs are now connected to all the international networks such as Plus and Cirrus; nonetheless, you'll want to carry a small amount of backup cash just in case you encounter problems.

Credit cards are accepted at many better hotels and restaurants. Be sure that you are always charged in pesos, as any US dollar total will likely be at a poorer exchange rate.

Opening hours and public holidays

Only the smallest towns still take any kind of siesta, and businesses are generally open from 9am to 5 or 6pm, and are closed one day a week – usually Monday, but this can vary by town. **Post offices** set their own hours, but you can count on at least Monday to Thursday, 9am to 3pm. **Banks** are generally open Monday to Friday, 9.30am to 4pm, though HSBC branches are open until 7pm.

Public holidays

The main **public holidays**, when virtually everything will be closed, are listed below. Many places also closed on January 6 (Twelfth Night/Reyes).

Jan 1	New Year's Day
Feb 5	Anniversary of the Constitution
March 21	Día de Benito Juárez
Variable	Good Friday and Easter Saturday
May 1	Labour Day
May 5	Battle of Puebla
Sept 1	Presidential address to the nation
Sept 16	Independence Day
Oct 12	Día de la Raza/ Columbus Day
Nov 1–2	Día de los Muertos/ All Saints' Day
Nov 20	Anniversary of the Revolution
Dec 12	Día de la Virgen de Guadalupe
Dec 24–26	Christmas

Phones

Public phones charge very little for local calls, but require a phone card, matched to the brand of phone. It's easier to visit a **caseta de teléfono** (phone office; look for "Larga Distancia" signs), for only slightly more per minute.

Another alternative is to arm yourself with a charge card or calling card that can be used in Mexico; you'll be connected to an English-speaking operator and will be billed at home at a rate that is predictable (for AT&T, dial ⓣ01-800/288-2872; for BT, ⓣ01-800/123-0244; for Canada Direct, ⓣ01-800/123-0200). To contact an operator for collect calls, dial ⓣ92 for numbers within Mexico, ⓣ96 for the US and Canada and ⓣ99 for the rest of the world.

The code for calling *to* Mexico is 52. When dialling to land lines in Mexico, dial "01" followed by the two- or three-digit area code and the seven-digit phone number. When dialling to mobile phones from a land line, dial

Calling home from abroad

Note that the initial zero is omitted from the area code when dialling the UK, Ireland, Australia and New Zealand from abroad.

US and Canada 00 + 1 + area code.

UK 00 + 44 + city code.

Republic of Ireland 00 + 353 + city code.

Australia 00 + 61 + city code.

New Zealand 00 + 64 + city code.

South Africa 00 + 27 + city code.

"044" (for a number in the same area code) or "045" (for a number in a different area code), then the area code and number; when dialling mobile numbers from another mobile, you can dial the area code and number directly.

If you're planning on using your own mobile phone, note that Mexican GSM systems operate on 1900MHz, so European travellers will need a multi-band model. Additionally, the GSM network is relatively new in Mexico, and coverage can be spotty outside the big cities and beach areas. Renting a mobile costs US$4.50–6 per day for a pay-as-you-go phone (usually GSM only). You can buy a SIM card with a local number at Telcel and other mobile-phone stores. They typically cost M$150 and include a M$50 credit.

Photography

Film is manufactured in Mexico and, if you buy it from a chain store like Woolworth's or Sanborn's, costs no more than at home (if you buy it elsewhere, be sure to check the date on the box). Up to twelve rolls of film can be brought into Mexico; spare batteries are a wise precaution. Camera hardware will be prohibitively expensive.

Senior travellers

Mexico is not a country that offers any special difficulties to older travellers. The same considerations as regards scheduling, etc, apply here as to anywhere else in the world. Senior citizens are often entitled to discounts, especially when visiting tourist sights, but also on occasion for accommodation and transport, something which it's always worth asking about.

Study and volunteering

Work permits are almost impossible to get hold of, but you can extend your time in Mexico with classes or volunteer work. Many language schools arrange homestays for around US$20 per night, including meals; particularly recommended is the Institute of Modern Spanish in Mérida (ⓣ1-877/463-7432 in the US, ⓣ999/927-1505 in Mexico, ⓦwww.modernspanish.com), where classes start every Monday and cost about US$300 per week with a homestay. El Bosque del Caribe (ⓣ998/884-1065, ⓦwww.cancun-language.com.mx) is based in downtown Cancún, and International House Riviera Maya (ⓣ984/803-3388, ⓦwww.ihrivieramaya.com) and Playa-Lingua (ⓣ984/873-3876, ⓦwww.playalingua.com) are in Playa del Carmen.

Respected volunteer programmes in the Yucatán include Global Vision International (ⓣ1-888/653-6028, ⓦwww.gviusa.com), which runs volunteer diving programmes to gather data about reefs, as well as a Maya cultural education programme in Tulum. Earthwatch (ⓣ1-800/776-0188 or ⓣ978/461-0081 in the US, ⓣ01865/318 838 in the UK, ⓣ03/9682 6828 in Australia, ⓦwww.earthwatch.org) matches volunteers with scientific monitoring projects; and Willing Workers on Organic Farms (UK ⓣ020/8780 7200, ⓦwww.wwoof.org) links volunteers with agricultural work.

Time

Mexico has four time zones, but most of the country, including the area from the Yucatán to Chiapas, is on GMT–6 in winter and GMT–5 in summer (the first Sunday in April until the last Sunday in October), the same as US Central Time.

Toilets

Public toilets in Mexico aren't always the cleanest, and sometimes there's no paper, although there will often be someone dispensing it outside for a couple of pesos (better just to always carry some with you). Toilets are usually known as *baños* (literally "bathrooms") or as *sanitarios*. The most common signs are Damas (Ladies) and Caballeros (Gentlemen), though you may find Señoras (Women) and Señores (Men) or, more confusing, the symbols of Moon (Women) and Sun (Men).

Because almost every building in the Yucatán has its own septic tank (the limestone bedrock can't support sewage systems), people are scrupulous about not flushing toilet paper. A basket is invariably placed nearby for disposing of paper, and in hotels it's emptied at least daily. You know you're in a very swanky hotel when the basket has gone missing.

Tourist information

The national Secretaría de Turismo (Sectur) maintains a website, Ⓦwww.visitmexico.com, which addresses most basic queries. Once you're in the Yucatán, you'll find **tourist offices** (sometimes called *turismos*) run by state and municipal authorities. Some are extremely friendly and helpful, with free information and leaflets by the cartload; others are barely capable of answering the simplest question. These offices are listed in the relevant city and regional sections throughout the guide. You can also call Sectur toll-free, round the clock in Mexico at Ⓣ1-800/903-9200, or from the US or Canada on Ⓣ1-800/446-3942 and from Europe on Ⓣ0800/6666 2211.

Mexican tourist offices overseas

US

225 N Michigan Ave, Suite 1850, Chicago, IL 60601 (Ⓣ312/228-0517, Ⓔchicago@visitmexico.com); 4507 San Jacinto St, Suite 308, Houston, TX 77004 (Ⓣ713/772-2581, Ⓔhouston@visitmexico.com); 1880 Century Park E, Suite 511, Los Angeles, CA 90067 (Ⓣ310/282-9112, Ⓔlosangeles@visitmexico.com); 5975 Sunset Dr, Suite 305, South Miami, FL 33143 (Ⓣ786/621-2909, Ⓔmiami@visitmexico.com).

Canada

1 Place Ville Marie, Suite 1931, Montréal, QC H3B 2C3 (Ⓣ514/871-1052, Ⓔmontreal@visitmexico.com); 2 Bloor St W, Suite 1502, Toronto, ON M4W 3E2 (Ⓣ416/925-0704, Ⓔtoronto@visitmexico.com); 999 W Hastings St, Suite 1110, Vancouver, BC V6C 2W2 (Ⓣ604/669-2845, Ⓔvancouver@visitmexico.com).

UK

Wakefield House, 41 Trinity Square, London EC3N 4DT (Ⓣ020/7488 9392, Ⓦwww.mexicotravel.co.uk).

Government advisories

Western governments put out the latest information and advice on travel in Mexico. The tone can be extremely over-cautious and generalized – alarmist crime warnings, for instance, are hardly applicable to the Yucatán – but overall, their websites are worth reading before making travel plans, and again before departure.

US State Department Ⓦwww.travel.state.gov.
Canadian Department of Foreign Affairs Ⓦwww.international.gc.ca.
British Foreign & Commonwealth Office Ⓦwww.fco.gov.uk.
Australian Department of Foreign Affairs Ⓦwww.dfat.gov.au.
New Zealand Ministry of Foreign Affairs Ⓦwww.safetravel.govt.nz.

Other websites

You may find the following **websites** useful for travel planning in the Yucatán, Chiapas and Tabasco.

Backyard Nature Ⓦwww.backyardnature.net. Naturalist Jim Conrad spends half the year in the Yucatán and Chiapas. His weekly newsletters are filled with sharp observations about local animals and plants – great reading for anyone planning a birding trip.
Diario de Yucatán Ⓦwww.yucatan.com.mx. The oldest and largest newspaper on the peninsula, published daily in Mérida. In Spanish only.
Exploring Colonial Mexico Ⓦwww.colonial-mexico.com. Run by Espadaña Press, this site concentrates on art and architecture from the colonial era, with an excellent archive of photos and information on Franciscan missions and haciendas in the Yucatán.
INEGI Ⓦwww.inegi.gob.mx. Website of the Mexican government's National Institute for Statistics, Geography and IT, with tables of statistical and geographical information, and maps of things like climate and vegetation. Some of it, but not all, is in English.
Latin American Information Center (LANIC) Ⓦwww.lanic.utexas.edu. The premier Latin American academic website, with extensive links covering topics such as history, politics, culture, religion and food.
Mesoweb Ⓦwww.mesoweb.com. A huge collection of articles and resources on pre-Columbian Mexico and Central America, including the latest archeological news, maps, timelines and articles about life in the Maya world.

Mexico Desconocido ⓦ www.mexicodesconocido.com. The online version of the popular magazine that explores Mexico's backcountry and heritage. A good portion of the articles are available in English.

Mundo Maya ⓦ www.mayadiscovery.com. The online outlet of a now-defunct magazine devoted to Maya culture, with very readable, non-academic articles.

Ruins of Mexico ⓦ www.geocities.com/atlantis01mx/index. An online guide to Mexico's archeological sites, with photos, plans and explanations, which aims to eventually cover all sites, both major and minor. What's on it so far is excellent.

Sac-Be ⓦ www.sac-be.com. Great resource for info on the Riviera Maya. It used to be a monthly print publication, but now operates solely online, posting new articles regularly.

Yucatan Living ⓦ www.yucatanliving.com. Site run by working expats in Mérida, full of news and informative articles on Yucatecan culture.

Yucatan Today ⓦ www.yucatantoday.com. Long-running tourist-info site, extending to all the major destinations in Yucatán state. Info is not always kept up to date, and "reviews" definitely favour advertisers, but for many details it's invaluable.

Travellers with disabilities

Mexico is not well equipped for people with disabilities, but things are improving all the time and, especially at the top end of the market, it shouldn't be too difficult to find accommodation and tour operators that can cater to your needs. The important thing is to check beforehand that tour companies, hotels and airlines can accommodate you specifically.

If you stick to beach resorts – Cancún in particular – and upmarket tourist hotels, you should certainly be able to find places that are wheelchair-friendly and accustomed to having guests who are disabled. US chains are very good for this, with Leading Hotels of the World, Marriott, Radisson, Sheraton and Westin claiming to have the necessary facilities for at least some disabilities in a number of their hotels.

You'll find that, unless you have your own transport, the best way to travel inside the Yucatán may prove to be by air, since buses rarely cater for disabilities, and certainly not for wheelchairs. Ramps are rare, and streets and pavements are not in a very good state. Depending on your disability, you may want to find an able-bodied helper to accompany you.

Women travellers

Machismo may be one of the stereotypical factors in Mexican culture, but in the Yucatán, it's softened considerably by the gentler mores of Maya culture. For women, most hassles will be limited to **comments** in the street. These are generally meant as compliments, but you may soon tire of such astute observations as "Guera!" ("Blondie!"), in which case you'll have to simply tune them out; chances are slim that any retorts on your part, in Spanish or otherwise, will reform a sidewalk lecher. *Yucatecos* are on the whole exceptionally gentlemanly and gracious, and women needn't be too on guard. In the evenings, however, especially anywhere near bars, you're better off walking with a friend.

Any problems are aggravated in the big resort areas, where legendarily "easy" tourists attract droves of would-be gigolos, and the gap between wealthy visitors and the scraping-by population who actually built the place is often quite distinct. There are occasional rapes reported in Cancún and Playa del Carmen, but it's hardly the epidemic that some guidebooks make it out to be. Simply be as sensible as you would ordinarily be: drink in moderation and have a plan with friends for extricating yourself from unwanted male attention.

Away from the cities, though, and especially in indigenous areas, there is rarely any problem. You may, as an outsider, be treated as an object of curiosity (or occasionally resentment), but not necessarily with any implied or intended sexual threat. And wherever you come across it, such curiosity can also extend to great friendliness and hospitality.

The restrictions imposed on **drinking** can be irksome: women are simply barred from the vast majority of **cantinas**, and at worst in so-called Ladies' Bars, "unescorted" women may be looked at with suspicion or at worst refused service. Dining alone in restaurants, on the other hand, is perfectly fine (and you can enjoy a drink with your meal), though if you're alone, other diners and the staff may try to take you under their wing.

Guide

Guide

1

Cancún, Isla Mujeres and Isla Holbox

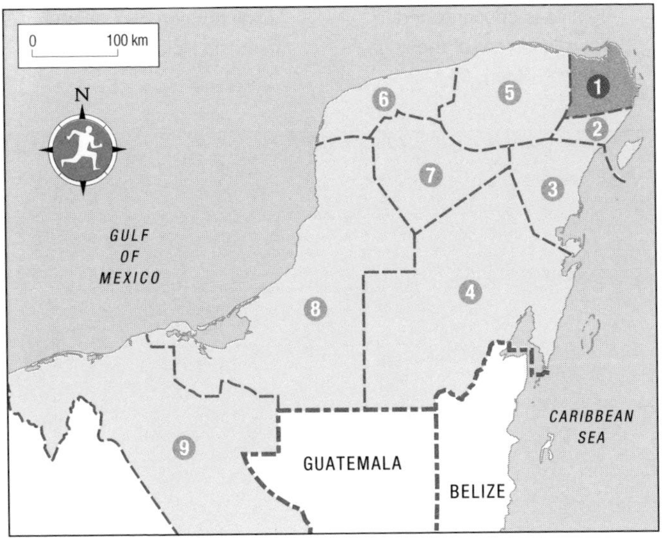

CHAPTER 1

Highlights

* **Parque de las Palapas** Downtown Cancún's social centre comes to life after dark with dancing, craft fairs and vendors selling tasty snacks. See p.73
* **Playa Delfines** An amazingly beautiful stretch of sand in Cancún's zona hotelera. See p.77
* **Punta Cancún** Love it or hate it, Cancún's (in)famous nightlife is concentrated in this wild corner of the zona hotelera. See p.81
* **Isla Contoy** A large island wildlife sanctuary that makes the perfect place for birdwatching, or just playing at castaway. See p.93
* **Whale sharks** Swim with these giant, peaceful fish off the coast of Isla Holbox, some up to 15m long. See p.96
* **Isla Pájaros** This flamingo colony is the highlight of a small but rich bird sanctuary near Isla Holbox. See p.97

▲ Playa Delfines, Cancún

1

Cancún, Isla Mujeres and Isla Holbox

Easily the largest tourist draw in the Yucatán, the resort city of **Cancún** dominates the northern half of Quintana Roo State and, with its large international airport, is the place where most visitors' tours of the peninsula begin or end. Travellers on package tours and cruiseships pack this place by the thousands, in search of sun and margarita-fuelled fun in an environment that's as welcoming of the American dollar as it is of the Mexican peso.

All concrete and glass hotel towers and shopping plazas, this modern city can seem less than charming at first sight. In reality, however, it's really a dynamic, prosperous place that's lined with 20km of astoundingly beautiful **white beaches** and water so clear you can see your plane's shadow on the seafloor as you arrive. Also, contrary to expectation, Cancún can be a culturally rewarding (and not painfully expensive) place to visit if you know where to look.

Isla Mujeres, a tiny island just across the bay from Cancún, affords a slightly more rustic experience, with small, candy-coloured wooden houses lining the narrow streets of the main town. Mujeres is definitely on the tourist route, but there's not a strip mall in sight, and the only entertainment is watching the water lap at the beach around the island's northern edge.

Heading inland, you'll see that Cancún and Isla Mujeres are anomalies – the rest of Quintana Roo's northern half is rural and barely touched by tourism. **Isla Holbox**, a dot of land off the northern Gulf coast, is a typical out-of-the-way spot. It has seen increasing boatloads of visitors in the last few years, but remains a friendly, modest beach getaway where birds can outnumber humans.

A note about prices

Because Cancún, Cozumel and the other big towns along Quintana Roo's northern coast cater largely to tourists, local businesses often quote prices in US dollars, and accept payment in that currency. Moreover, prices for major attractions, tours and the like are often pegged to the exchange rate, so a US$70 hotel room could be M$700 one week and M$770 the next. Prices in this guide are quoted primarily in pesos, but US dollars are used when an attraction or hotel provides that price first and foremost.

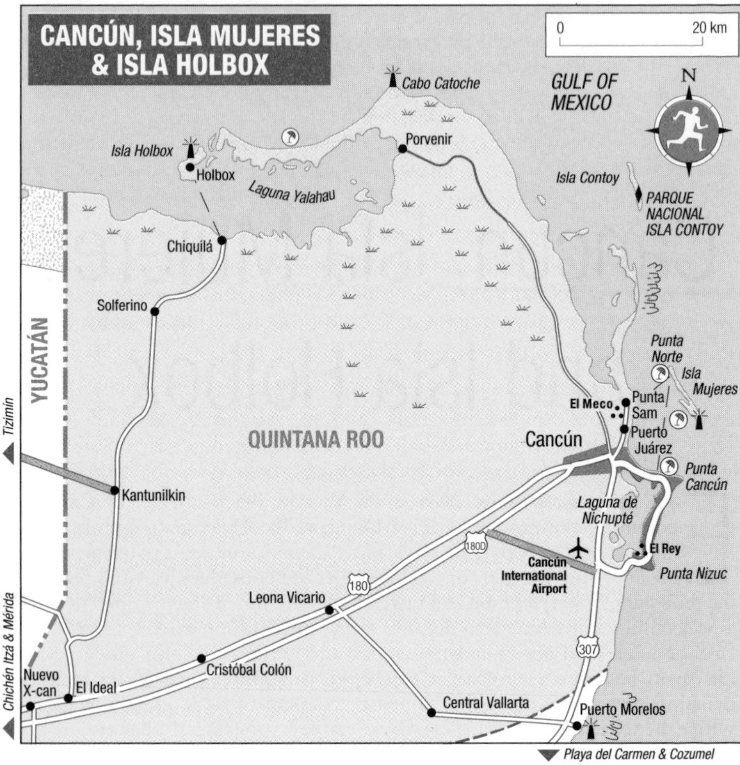

From Cancún, Isla Mujeres is just a half-hour ferry hop, but Isla Holbox is a three-hour bus trip from the airport, followed by a boat ride – precisely what keeps the place quiet.

Cancún

If nothing else, **CANCÚN** is proof of Mexico's remarkable ability to get things done in a hurry, so long as the political will exists. In the late 1960s, the Mexican government decided to develop a new resort area to diversify the economy. Computers crunched weather data, and surveyors scouted the country's natural attractions to identify a 25-kilometre-long barrier island just off the northern Caribbean coast as the ideal combination of beautiful beaches, sparse population and accessible position. The largest settlement in the area was the village of Puerto Juárez, with about a hundred residents, and a small wooden house was the sole structure on the island that was to become Cancún's hotel zone. Construction on the envisioned resort paradise began in 1970, with the initial task being simply to clear enough jungle on the mainland to build a road and bridge to the barrier island. (Jules Siegel, an American who worked for the Mexican tourism ministry during this period, recounts the early challenges, from impossible deadlines to jaguar attacks, in excellent detail in his *Cancun*

User's Guide; see Contexts, p.351.) When the first hotel opened in 1974, it relied on a generator for electricity and trucked in water.

Today the city has a resident population of half a million and hosts some two million visitors a year, the majority from the US and Canada. The place has never been understated or intimate; it's a high-energy resort destination, relentlessly dedicated to entertainment, with jet skis, top-volume mariachis and wet T-shirt contests at rowdy mega-clubs. Restaurants are elaborate theatre (think toga-clad waiters at trattorias), hotels are fantastical pleasure palaces in a constant state of reinvention and the crowds range from college kids to families to senior citizens.

In part because of all this, Cancún has a poor reputation among independent travellers in search of "authentic" Mexico. Prices along the beaches can be steep, and for anyone who has been out in the rest of the Yucatán or is eager to get there, the abundance of concrete and apparent lack of local culture can be off-putting. However, a night spent here on the way in or out doesn't have to be wasted time if you appreciate the city as an energetic, wildly successful frontier experiment, rather than lament the lack of historical sights. A closer look reveals lively salsa clubs, bare-bones beach bars and inexpensive taco stands, all frequented by *cancunenses* who are friendly and proud of the prosperity that the hotels represent.

The city has two quite separate parts: the **zona comercial**, also called the *centro* or downtown, which is the shopping and residential area that has become genuinely earthy as it has aged; and the **zona hotelera**, or hotel zone, the strip of hotels, malls, restaurants and other tourist facilities along a narrow island shaped like a "7". The island is connected to the mainland at each end by causeways enclosing a huge lagoon.

In the zona hotelera, **Paseo Kukulcán** runs the length of the barrier island, from the airport up to **Punta Cancún** (where the road splits around the convention centre and a warren of bars) and back onto the mainland.

From Punta Cancún it's a half-hour bus ride to **Avenida Tulum**, the main avenue in the downtown area that runs north–south and eventually turns into Hwy-307, the highway that follows the length of the Caribbean coast. Avenida Tulum's central blocks are lined with shops, banks, restaurants and travel agencies, as well as the city's most inexpensive hotels – up side streets, but in view. On either side of Avenida Tulum, divided by intersecting avenues, are the giant city blocks known as *super-manzanas*. The oldest ones, part of the city plan laid out in the 1970s (and soon abandoned as growth outpaced the developers' time and budget), are distinguished by winding and looping streets leading to a central park or market. Each *super-manzana* (abbreviated SM) is known by a number; SM 22 contains Parque de las Palapas, the city's main park, along with many of the downtown area's restaurants and bars.

Arrival and information

Charter flights from Europe and South America, along with direct scheduled flights from dozens of cities in Mexico and North and Central America, land at **Cancún International Airport** (Ⓦwww.cancun-airport.com), 20km south of the centre. Most international flights arrive at terminal 3, while domestic flights and some charter flights come into terminal 2. In both of the main terminals, you'll find **ATMs** and **currency exchange** desks just past customs; terminal 2 also has luggage **lockers** (M$70/day).

The best way to the beaches, if your hotel does not provide a pick-up service, is one of the **colectivos** (shared passenger vans) that take you to any part of

Addresses in the zona hotelera

Generally addresses here are given as the nearest kilometre marker on Paseo Kukulcán; the count starts on the north end, near the bridge over from downtown. It's not an exact science: two sets of markers exist, and are out of sync by about half a kilometre, so addresses are guidelines at best.

the zona hotelera for a fixed price (M$75 or US$9); they depart when they're full, but it's seldom a long wait. For downtown, take the ADO/Riviera **bus** (M$35; 6.30am–12.20am) that runs every half-hour from terminal 2 (if you're starting at terminal 3, you can take a shuttle van to the other terminal, or, if the timing's right, you might be put on a Playa del Carmen bus for the short ride down the road). Buy tickets for both services from the desks located after customs – don't get distracted by roving transport touts. **Taxis** are available but cost considerably more, starting at M$200 for the part of the zona hotelera closest to the airport and getting up to M$500 for downtown Cancún and the furthest beach hotels.

All buses, whether first or second class, pull in at Cancún's well-organized main **bus station**, conveniently located on a roundabout at the central junction of avenidas Tulum and Uxmal. **Luggage storage** (daily 6am–9.45pm) is upstairs; rates are M$5–12 per hour, depending on size. You can walk to most downtown hotels, and a city bus stops nearby on Avenida Tulum, running either to the zona hotelera (southbound side of the avenue) or to the Isla Mujeres ferry docks (northbound side).

The **city tourist office** is half a block south of the bus station, inside the city hall at Avenida Tulum 26 (daily 9am–8pm; ⓣ998/884-8073), and the friendly bilingual staff will help with even the smallest enquiries. They also dish out free maps, leaflets and copies of the numerous promotional listings **magazines**, all of which you can also pick up at just about every travel agency and hotel reception. There are other **"tourist information" kiosks** on Avenida Tulum and in the zona hotelera, but most are devoted to selling tours and timeshares. The English-language daily newspaper *Miami Herald Cancún Edition* isn't particularly hard-hitting, but it provides some insight into local politics, along with international news. You can get BBC news in *The International*, an insert in the *Quintanarroense* tabloid.

City transport

All the attractions in downtown Cancún are within walking distance, but you need some sort of transport to get to and around the zona hotelera. **Buses** marked "Tulum–Hoteles, Ruta 1" run along Avenida Tulum every few minutes; the fare is M$4.50 for stops within downtown or M$6.50 to or within the zona hotelera. The ride from downtown to Punta Cancún takes about half an hour. (Several other bus routes go to the zona hotelera as well – all say "Hoteles" on the front window.) Alternatively, shared VW buses (**combis**) run fixed routes throughout downtown – the handiest is north on Avenida Tulum to the Isla Mujeres ferry dock at Gran Puerto and Puerto Juárez (also M$4.50), but otherwise, visitors will have little need for these services, given the frequency of city buses.

Taxis are plentiful and can be hailed almost anywhere. Fares are based on a zone system, rather than a meter, and you should agree on the fare before getting in. Big hotels in the zona hotelera will have sample rates posted, which reflect a small surcharge; rates are slightly cheaper if you flag a cab in the street. Anywhere in downtown is about M$20, and the trip between downtown and Punta Cancún costs around M$110. **Bicycle** rental isn't really advisable (or even available), as distances are too great, and traffic isn't bike-friendly.

Accommodation

Cancún has plenty of lodging options, though much of it very expensive. **Downtown** holds the only hope of a real budget room, and you're only a short bus ride from the public beaches. Many of the **zona hotelera**'s beachfront palaces offer exclusive luxury, with extravagant interiors, glitzy restaurants and numerous pools. Prices here can run well above M$5000 per night in the high winter season, with the least costly options being the lagoon-facing properties, which have no beach but can be booked for just under M$1000 – though note that prices are almost always quoted in US dollars. If you can wait to book until the last minute, though, you might find stunning deals online: as low as US$100 for beachfront hotels in high season. All-inclusive packages used to be the norm, but hotels are increasingly offering room-only pricing (aka "European plan") as well as rooms with kitchenettes (see "All-inclusive resorts" in Basics, p.34).

For those on a tight budget, several places downtown offer **dorm** accommodation; there's nowhere in the city where you can officially **camp**.

Downtown Cancún

Alux Av Uxmal 21 ⓣ998/884-6613, ⓦwww.hotelalux.com.mx. Popular, good-value hotel, if a little dated with its mirror-clad decor; all rooms, though a bit dim, have a/c, TV and telephone. Its real appeal is its easy walk to the bus station. Travel agency on site. 4

Cancún Inn El Patio Av Bonampak 51 ⓣ998/884-3500, ⓦwww.cancuninn.com. A hands-off staff and a location in a residential neighbourhood make this small hotel feel more like a private apartment complex. The thirteen simple rooms encircle a quiet garden courtyard. Easy walk to downtown. 6

Chac Mool C Gladiolas 18 ⓣ998/887-5873, ⓦwww.chacmool.com.mx. This tidy hostel has small four-bed dorms (M$120) as well as a few private rooms, all with a/c. The cool rooftop lounge, with a grand view over Parque de las Palapas, serves M$10 drinks.

Colonial C Tulipanes 22 ⓣ998/884-1535. A decent bargain, in a prime location not far from the bus station and in the middle of downtown's liveliest block. The fifty well-lit rooms are simple and modern, with TV and a choice of a/c or fan, but the place has character, thanks to a small central courtyard. 5

Hostel Laurel C Laurel at Av Uxmal ⓣ998/898-4210, ⓔlaurel41hostel@hotmail.com. Not a hostel at all, but a series of small, well-kept rooms stacked up in a skinny apartment building. Beds are a little lumpy, but this price for a private room (fan or a/c) is hard to beat. 3

Kin Mayab Av Tulum 75 at Av Uxmal ⓣ998/884-2999, ⓦwww.hotelkinmayab.com. This centrally located hotel is clean and secure, with the most comfortable rooms and best pool in its price range (book ahead). Request the back section, by the pool and away from the street noise. 7

Mayan Hostel C Margaritas 17 ⓣ998/892-0103, ⓦwww.mayanhostel.com. If you can't give up the beachfront vibe, opt for a bed in one of the palapa-roof rooms or dorms here, with prices starting at M$100 per person.

The Nest C Alcatraces 49 at C Margaritas ⓣ998/884-8967, ⓔmjkglobal@yahoo.com. This hostel occupies a private home and sports an especially large and lovely communal kitchen. Dorm beds in the colourful a/c room go for M$130, or choose fan-only for M$110. Skip the dismal private rooms, though.

Las Palmas C Palmera 43 ⓣ998/884-2513, ⓔhotelpalmascancun@hotmail.com. Catering as much to Mexican workers and travellers as to foreign backpackers, this place doesn't have the usual hostel party atmosphere – thanks to the kindly owners, it feels almost like staying in a home. And at just M$100, the price for a bed in the big, single-sex a/c dorms is the best in town. There are also a few huge private rooms (starting at M$250), a basic communal kitchen and Internet access. Continental breakfast included.

El Rey del Caribe Av Uxmal 24 at Av Nader ⓣ998/884-2028, ⓦwww.reycaribe.com. Sunny yellow rooms with kitchenettes, plus

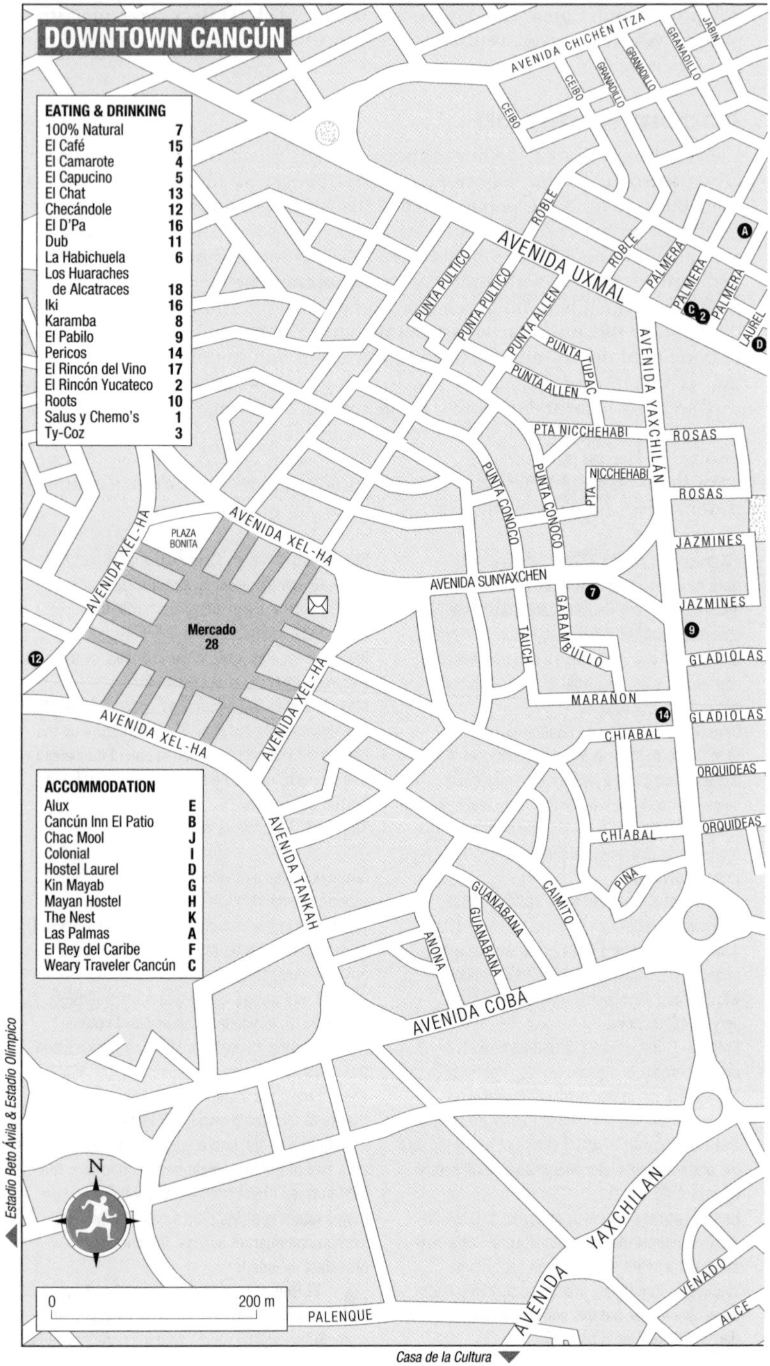
DOWNTOWN CANCÚN
EATING & DRINKING
100% Natural 7
El Café 15
El Camarote 4
El Capucino 5
El Chat 13
Checándole 12
El D'Pa 16
Dub 11
La Habichuela 6
Los Huaraches de Alcatraces 18
Iki 16
Karamba 8
El Pabilo 9
Pericos 14
El Rincón del Vino 17
El Rincón Yucateco 2
Roots 10
Salus y Chemo's 1
Ty-Coz 3
ACCOMMODATION
Alux E
Cancún Inn El Patio B
Chac Mool J
Colonial I
Hostel Laurel D
Kin Mayab G
Mayan Hostel H
The Nest K
Las Palmas A
El Rey del Caribe F
Weary Traveler Cancún C
AVENIDA CHICHÉN ITZA
JABIN
GRANADILLO
CEIBO
AVENIDA UXMAL
ROBLE
PALMERA
LAUREL
PUNTA PULTICO
PUNTA ALLEN
PUNTA TUPAC
AVENIDA YAXCHILÁN
PTA NICCHEHABI
NICCHEHABI
ROSAS
PUNTA CONOCO
JAZMINES
AVENIDA XEL-HA
PLAZA BONITA
Mercado 28
AVENIDA SUNYAXCHEN
GARAMBULLO
TAUCH
GLADIOLAS
MARAÑON
CHIABAL
ORQUIDEAS
AVENIDA TANKAH
PIÑA
CAIMITO
GUANABANA
ANONA
AVENIDA COBÁ
AVENIDA YAXCHILAN
VENADO
ALCE
PALENQUE
N
0 200 m
Estadio Beto Ávila & Estadio Olímpico
Casa de la Cultura

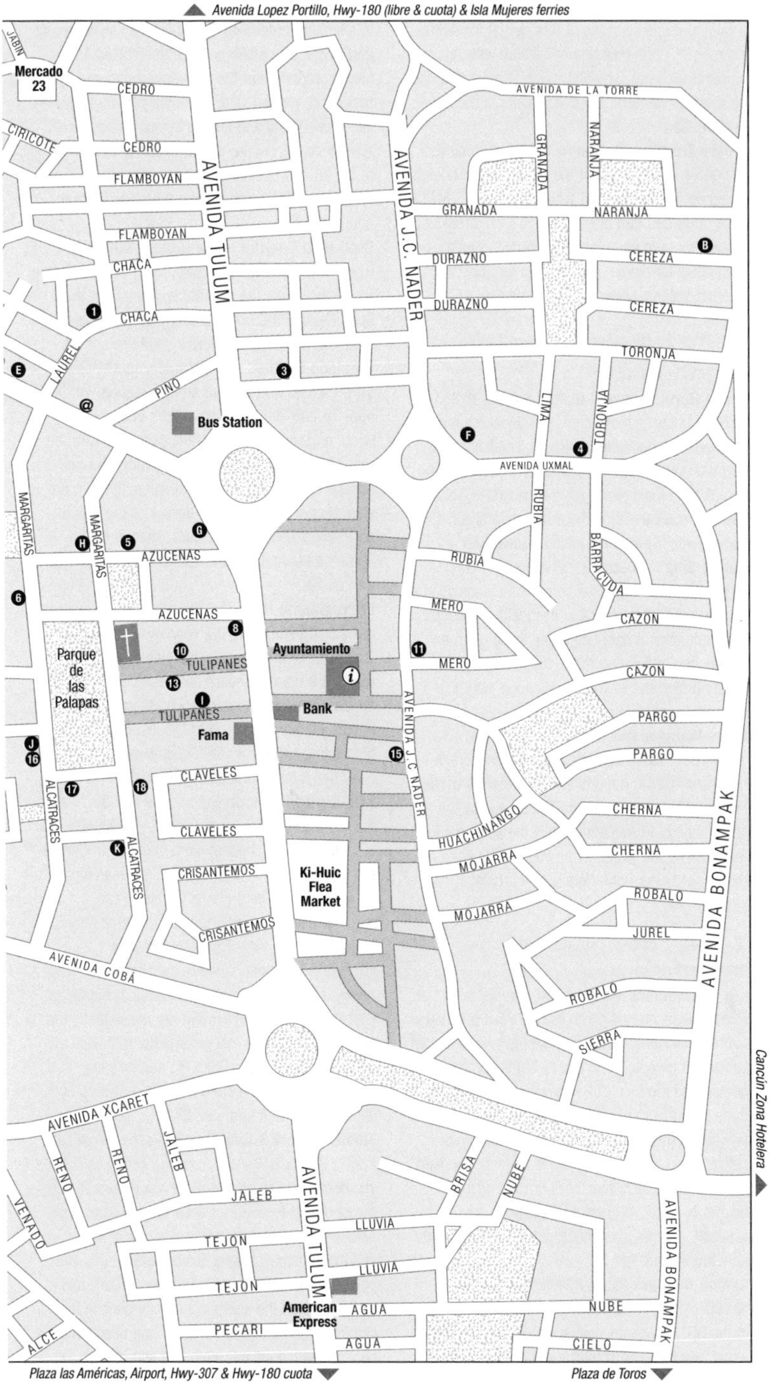
Avenida Lopez Portillo, Hwy-180 (libre & cuota) & Isla Mujeres ferries
Mercado 23
JABIN
CEDRO
CIRICOTE
FLAMBOYAN
CHACA
LAUREL
PINO
AVENIDA TULUM
AVENIDA J.C. NADER
AVENIDA DE LA TORRE
GRANADA
NARANJA
DURAZNO
CEREZA
TORONJA
LIMA
AVENIDA UXMAL
RUBIA
BARRACUDA
MERO
CAZON
PARGO
CHERNA
HUACHINANGO
MOJARRA
ROBALO
JUREL
SIERRA
AVENIDA BONAMPAK
Bus Station
MARGARITAS
AZUCENAS
TULIPANES
Parque de las Palapas
Ayuntamiento
Bank
Fama
CLAVELES
ALCATRACES
CRISANTEMOS
Ki-Huic Flea Market
AVENIDA COBÁ
AVENIDA XCARET
Cancún Zona Hotelera
RENO
JALEB
VENADO
TEJON
LLUVIA
BRISA
NUBE
AGUA
PECARI
CIELO
ALCE
American Express
Plaza las Américas, Airport, Hwy-307 & Hwy-180 cuota
Plaza de Toros

a pool and spa services at this casual hacienda-style hotel – the only one in Cancún with an active ecological sensibility, with composting and solar water heaters. Good discounts in the low season. ❼

Weary Traveler Cancún Av Uxmal at C Palmera ⓣ998/887-0191. One of the older Cancún hostels, cramped but still popular with backpackers. M$110 for a dorm bed (fan only) gets you a full breakfast (cook your own eggs) and a carb-fest of pasta, rice and lentils for dinner. Nice rooftop terrace, plus Internet access, bike rental and laundry.

Zona hotelera: on the lagoon side

Grand Royal Lagoon C Quetzal 8-A ⓣ998/883-1270, ⓦwww.grlagoon.com. Just 36 rooms make up this family-owned hotel, which are small but reasonably well maintained, set around an equally small pool. A few studio rooms have kitchenettes. This is the least you can pay in the zona hotelera, and it's conveniently close to the main boulevard. ❻

Suites Sina C Quetzal 33 ⓣ998/883-1017, ⓦwww.cancunsinasuites.com.mx. Personable staff preside over 33 vast suites, each with either one or two bedrooms, a sofa bed in the living room and a full kitchen and dining room, though some sport a dreary brown decor. The pool is huge, and a sundeck overlooks the lagoon. ❽

Villas Manglar Paseo Kukulcán Km 20 ⓣ998/885-1808, ⓦwww.villasmanglar.com. A blink-and-miss-it hotel hidden in the wilds of the lagoon-side mangroves. You can lounge by the small pool, but the main draw is the sport-fishing tours run by the experienced owners. Upstairs rooms get better light. Continental breakfast included. ❽

Zona hotelera: on the beach side

Ambiance Villas at Kin-Ha Paseo Kukulcán Km 7.5 ⓣ998/891-5400, ⓦwww.ambiancevillas.com. A hotel that feels more like an apartment complex. The big, tastefully furnished double-bed rooms or full suites with one, two or three bedrooms are especially good deals for families or groups. Every room has a terrace or balcony, and the scenic beach is fantastically deep – only the one next door, at *El Presidente* (see below), is better. All-inclusive packages are available, but not good value, since the restaurants here are limited. ❾

Avalon Baccará Paseo Kukulcán Km 11.5 ⓣ800/713-8170 in Mexico, or ⓣ1-800/261-5014 in the US, ⓦwww.avalonvacations.com. Carved-wood furniture and colourful mosaics distinguish this smaller hotel with 27 individually styled rooms and suites. The place is sometimes billed as a luxury property, but the atmosphere is more like a friend's converted villa, with nice personal touches like free snacks and tequila before dinner. As at *Ambiance*, don't take the all-inclusive option due to the limited facilities. Brace yourself for timeshare sales pitches from the larger Avalon operation. ❾

Club Med Cancun Punta Nizúc ⓣ998/881-8200, ⓦwww.clubmed.com. If you're considering an all-inclusive, the original is still one of the best: Cancún's *Club Med* occupies prime real estate at the zona hotelera's southern corner, with long beaches up both sides, snorkelling right off the coast and a large interior lagoon with a pool for late-day sunning. Suites in the Jade wing, on the other side of the property from the rest of the rooms, offer more privacy, and an escape from the gung-ho activities, if that's not your scene. All rooms are done in a hip mix of dark wood and bright colours. Thanks to the French influence, food is vastly superior to other all-ins. ❾

El Presidente Inter-Continental Paseo Kukulcán Km 7.5 ⓣ998/848-8700, ⓦwww.ichotelsgroup.com. One of the zona's oldest hotels, its 306 rooms are more standard business-class look than the chic, minimalist lobby would suggest. More important, however, is what lies just beyond the hotel's back doors: a great, deep beach dotted with palm trees, facing the placid bay waters. ❾

Ritz-Carlton Cancún Retorno del Rey 36, near Paseo Kukulcán Km 14 ⓣ998/881-0808, ⓦwww.ritzcarlton.com. The last word in luxury in Cancún, though with little reference to its Mexican location: its posh chandeliers, tapestries and plush carpeting seem transported intact from some fictional French villa. The hotel boasts a 1.2-kilometre-long beach (where cabañas are converted into private dining spaces at night), as well as food and service that are consistently the best in the city. You can get a taste of Mexico at cooking classes in the slick on-site culinary centre. Rates start around US$500, but drop by almost half in the summer. ❾

Westin Resort & Spa Cancún Paseo Kukulcán Km 20 ⓣ998/848-7400, ⓦwww.westin.com. If you don't want to go the all-inclusive route, this is the next best location for sheer beauty after *Club Med*, with which *Westin* shares a beach. The striking, minimalist hotel has decadent beds and powerful showers. Standard rooms actually feel a bit cosier than the austere, all-white ones in the club tower. An additional west-facing beach and pool on the lagoon get afternoon sun. ❾

Downtown Cancún

With the oldest buildings dating back only thirty years or so, there's no real sightseeing to do in **downtown Cancún**. Whether you're staying here or in the zona hotelera, the real attraction is simply strolling around and soaking up the street life, which is best after the sun goes down. The official centre of town is the **ayuntamiento** (town hall), set back from Avenida Tulum with a large plaza in front. Across the avenue is *super-manzana* 22, a block of small streets lined with restaurants and bars, leading to **Parque de las Palapas**, the cultural and recreational hub where crowds gather on weekend evenings, when there's usually some sort of live music or dance performance on the bandstand. Also look for four smaller parks to the north and south, which often host arts and crafts shows.

Heading west from the park, you reach **Avenida Yaxchilán**, the main nightlife strip. A few touts push menus at tourists, but the clientele at the bar-restaurant is mostly Mexican. Entertainment is limited to karaoke inside and serenades by roving *trovadores* on the open terraces (you can hire these musicians for a private performance – they hang out on the corner of Calle Nacchehabi).

The evening's other main gathering place is the intersection of avenidas López Portillo and Tulum, known as **El Crucero**. There's no formal entertainment here; the southwest corner of this busy crossroads is just a place for families and teenagers to gather, munching *elote* (boiled corn on the cob slathered in mayo, crumbly cheese, lime and chile) or pizza. Head a little bit west on Avenida Portillo and you'll reach a cluster of **market stalls** that cater solely to locals. Although not much of the merchandise may tempt you (meat smokers, underwear and fly-swatters are on offer), it's nice to stroll through a busy shopping area without getting the "Hey, amigo!" sales push.

Two daytime markets also give a sense of the city's hum away from the tourist trade. **Mercado 23**, north of the bus station off Avenida Tulum at Calle Cedro, is a small maze of stalls with the flavour of a village market, complete with butchers and vegetable sellers, as well as herbalists offering cures for whatever ails you. Don't miss the store packed with piñatas, party favours and Mexican candies. The bigger **Mercado 28**, west from the park on Avenida Sunyaxchén, was formerly the city's main general market, but now stocks primarily tourist tat. A few traditional vendors hang on, peddling fresh *masa* and wildly coloured sweets. It's best to visit on a Saturday or Sunday afternoon, when families come for big lunches at the food stalls, which cater to Cancún's population of workers from everywhere else in Mexico, dishing up regional specialities.

The only true historical attraction in the area, **El Meco** (8am–3pm; M$34) is a small archeological site, recommended only for Maya fanatics or anyone who won't get to any inland ruins; head east on Avenida López Portillo, then 3km north on the coast road. The ruins cover less ground than El Rey in the zona hotelera (see p.75), but the buildings, including a tall pyramid, are more substantial. Although it was first inhabited in the Early Classic period, El Meco conforms to the late Post-Classic style of other coastal cities like San Gervasio on Cozumel and Tulum (see Contexts, p.328). A part of a trade network that flourished on the coast after 1100, the city seems to have been an important religious centre as well. Many pieces of jewellery and ceramics were found on the site, as well as a full human skeleton with its skull drilled with numerous holes.

Zona hotelera

Most visitors to Cancún head straight for vacationland: the **zona hotelera** and its clubs, resorts and, of course, **beaches** (see box, p.77). The centre of the action is **Punta Cancún**, the cluster of malls, restaurants and bars around the convention centre at the bend in the "7" formed by the barrier island. East of the main road, on the grounds of the **Dreams Cancun** resort, is Punta Cancún proper, the easternmost point in Mexico. Built by noted Mexican architect Ricardo Legorreta and opened in 1975 as *El Camino Real*, *Dreams Cancun* is the closest thing Cancún has to a historic landmark. It's worth a jaunt inside (just look confident) to admire the hallways filled with greenery, and doors and windows framed with vibrant, typically Mexican colours. As an architectural counterpoint, consider the vast **atrium lobby** of the **Gran Meliá Cancún** resort (Paseo Kukulcán Km 16.5), a neo-Maya pyramid built

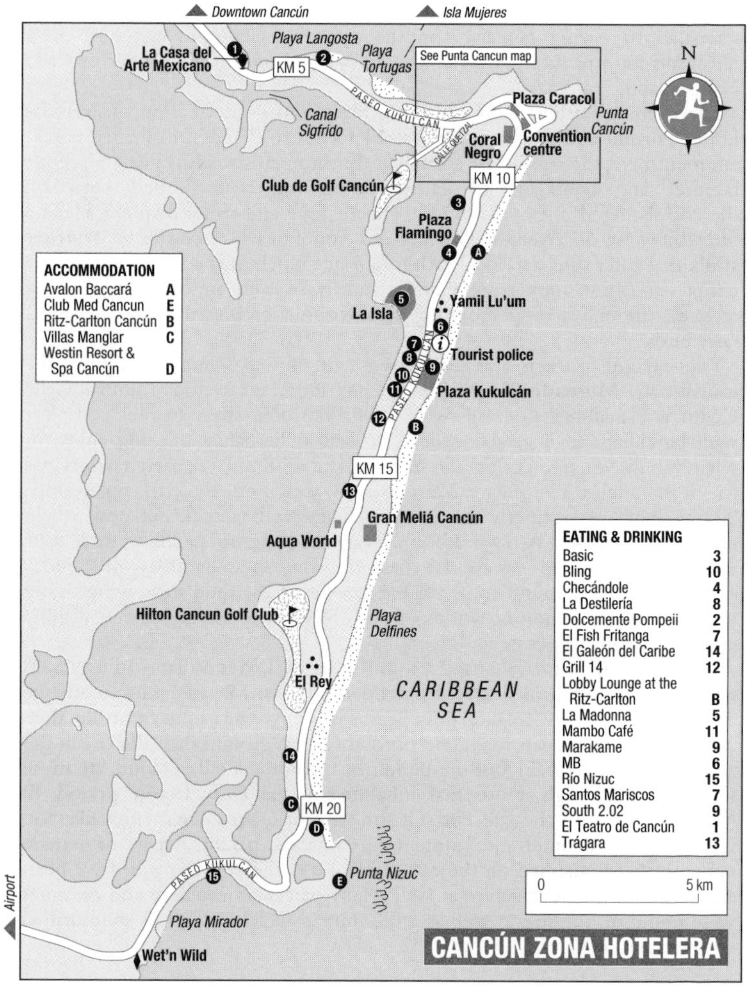

during Cancún's first real boom in the mid-Eighties. From the giant Maya friezes outside to the interior overflowing with cascading plants, koi ponds and waterfalls (as well as dazzled sightseers), it's the pinnacle of Cancún's particular brand of excess.

To catch a bit of culture while you're out here, visit **La Casa del Arte Mexicano** in the Embarcadero complex (daily 9am–9pm; M$55), a lively folk-art museum crammed with musical instruments, children's toys and colourful traditional costumes. Although the collection, grouped by craft and filling two large rooms, isn't particularly academic or rigorously presented, it does contain some beautiful pieces, such as intricate tree-of-life sculptures and painted gourds. If you admire an item, chances are you'll find something similar in the **gift shop**, which is stocked with high-quality pieces (priced accordingly).

The ruins

As if to round out the theme park that is Cancún, there are even a few requisite Maya **ruins**. The largest (which is not saying a lot) are **El Rey** (daily 8am–5pm; M$34), at Km 18, alongside Laguna Nichupté. Here you will likely find yourself alone, save for the enormous iguana population. The late Post-Classic buildings – contemporary with San Gervasio on Cozumel and Tulum – are strung out on a north–south axis. Objects found during excavation suggest this was a stop on the highly developed sea-trade route around the peninsula, disrupted when the Spanish arrived in the early sixteenth century. Not much of this once-thriving city remains; the ruined structures are mostly small-scale residential buildings, with no impressive pyramids to speak of. With the glass-topped pyramid of the *Hilton* looming in the background, today this is a quiet spot for contemplating the rise and fall of civilizations.

Back north a bit around Km 12.5, sandwiched between a couple of hotels (walk down the beach or enter through the lobby of *Park Royal Pirámides*), is the tiny site called **Yamil Lu'um** (free), consisting of two very modest late Post-Classic structures. The name ("hilly land") refers to the ruins' location on the highest point in Cancún, which provides a good view up and down the beach.

Watersports

Although Cancún isn't known for its stunning under-sea life, the reef off **Punta Nizuc** is a passable **snorkelling** spot. Its coral has been damaged by unchecked crowds, but the array of fish is impressive. This area is now a national marine park; if you visit by boat, as most people do, a M$20 entrance fee is charged (though tour operators often don't include this in the quoted price). The typical outing is the so-called "**jungle tour**", which entails riding two-passenger speedboats through the **lagoon mangroves**, then out to the reef (either at Punta Nizuc or to Angel Reef, a little further away but healthier). Aquaworld is the main purveyor (US$66), though you can book something similar through hotels, or directly at any of the numerous docks on the lagoon side. Less ethically, you can dodge the park fee and reach the reef by land: walk through the *Westin* to the beach, then turn right and walk about fifteen minutes down to Punta Nizuc (on *Club Med* property). From there you can cross the rocks and snorkel to your heart's content.

Other reefs off Cancún's coast make good **diving** for beginners, with easy access and little current; contact Manta Divers, at Paseo Kukulcán Km 6.5 (Ⓣ998/849-4050, Ⓦwww.mantadivers.com). A two-tank dive costs about US$62 and a full PADI open-water certification course is around US$389.

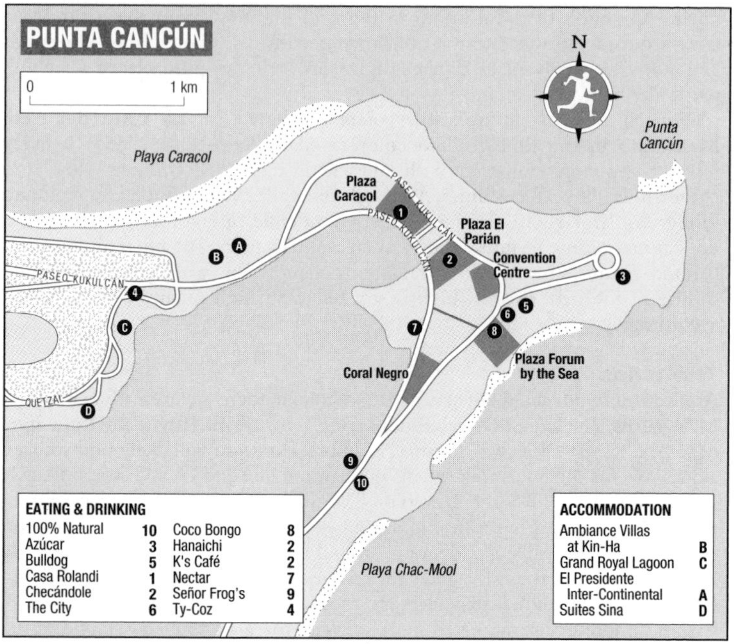

Windsurfing and **kiteboarding** are other options – La Escuela de Tabla Vela, at Paseo Kukulcán Km 3 (Ⓣ998/842-9072), is on the flat bay water, away from the hotels, and therefore the crowds. A two-hour introductory course is US$55. The main kiteboarding school is Ikarus (Ⓣ984/803-2068, Ⓦwww.ikaruskiteboarding.com); its headquarters are in Playa del Carmen, but it holds classes (from US$55 per hour) north of Cancún. Far less strenuously, **parasailing** (US$50 for 10min) is popular, with operators dotting the beach at frequent intervals.

For pure waterfront leisure, head for the winding walkway along **Canal Sigfrido**, opposite El Embarcadero at Paseo Kukulcán Km 4. Especially nice at sunset, you can get an up-close view of the mangroves. Though you might occasionally see kids swimming here, don't be tempted – crocodiles are still plentiful in the lagoon. Signs to "Jardín del Arte" on Avenida Kukulcán point to the parking area.

Eating

Cancún's **restaurants** outnumber hotels many times over, and competition for customers is fierce. Downtown, the most popular eating places line Avenida Tulum and its side streets. Though seafood and steak are the mainstay of many menus, you can also eat Middle Eastern, Yucatecan, Italian, Chinese, French, Cajun and Polynesian fare, not to mention international fast food and items from local chains.

For **budget food**, follow the locals and make for the downtown markets. The biggest is **Mercado 28** (see p.73), where two rows of food stalls and several outlying cafés form a sort of pan-Mexican food court, with specialities from Monterrey, Mexico City, Guadalajara and elsewhere. **Mercado 23** (see p.73), a few blocks north of the bus station, is much smaller but makes a peaceful venue for a decent Mexican lunch. For dinner, food stalls at **Parque de las Palapas** serve *huaraches* (thick tortillas shaped like a shoe sole) and quesadillas, with an array of toppings; they're open until about 11pm.

Almost all of the restaurants in the **zona hotelera** are geared towards one thing only: parting tourists from large amounts of cash. The few recommended here are worth a splurge, or are rare bargains. If you're staying on the beach, you're often better off taking a cab or bus downtown, where you'll find better food at reasonable prices, plus a congenial mix of people.

Cancún beaches

The legendary **beaches** of Cancún are spread out along the barrier island's northern and eastern shores. The north side of the island (the top portion of the "7") faces the tranquil Bahía de Mujeres, where the shallow, pale-green water makes an ideal spot for relaxed swimming, particularly for younger children. Sea grass grows in some places, and though not the best scenery, it's no impediment to swimming and is often home to bright tropical fish. Rocks and cliffs break up the sand at Km 6 and Km 8.5 of Paseo Kukulcán, and continue around the point to Km 9.5 (hotels in these spots have very limited or man-made beaches). The island's scenic east side, where white sand stretches for more than ten kilometres, faces the open Caribbean. While the turquoise waters here appear much more inviting, the waves are sometimes high and currents unpredictable; pay attention to the warning flags and don't swim beyond your comfort zone. On the east side, plan to hit the beach in the morning, as most of the sand is in shadow from the hotel towers by late afternoon; the *Westin* (see p.72) has a small west-facing beach for sunning later in the day.

All of Cancún's beaches are technically open to the public, but hotels carefully guard their furniture against interlopers. At beachfront bars and clubs, however, such as *The City* (see p.82), you may use lounge chairs and umbrellas for the price of a drink or an entrance fee – which also gets you a rowdy party atmosphere.

The ten designated **public beaches**, at intervals along the full length of the zona hotelera, are quieter but have been encroached on by high-rise neighbours, so that many of the turquoise-and-white signs placed by Fonatur (Mexico's national tourism board) now point to not much more than a public walkway and access point between condo developments. The following worthwhile spots are listed in order of their distance from downtown Cancún:

Playa Langosta Paseo Kukulcán Km 5. The best of the bay-facing public beaches, Playa Langosta is a sizeable stretch of sand, with calm, clean water for swimming and a few trees for shade – though it can be hard to find a place to lay your towel at weekends. For refreshments, the adjacent shopping complex is well stocked with bars and convenience stores.

Playa Delfines Paseo Kukulcán Km 17.5. The first public beach that you see on the way from the airport is also the largest. Occupying a sizeable break between hotel developments, Playa Delfines is a wide, sloping stretch of powder-fine sand fronted by incredible turquoise waters and offering an impressive view up the coast. Like the other beaches that face the open sea, the waves can be particularly high here, so sunbathing is the main activity, though it's sometimes possible to surf. Occasional strolling fruit vendors provide the only services.

Playa Mirador Paseo Kukulcán Km 22.5. For the true isolationist, this long, narrow beach on the mainland, dotted with a few palm trees, is usually deserted. Sea grass grows in patches in the shallow water, but the sand is kept very tidy and clean. Bring everything you need for the day, as there are no shops nearby, nor any services at the beach itself.

Downtown Cancún

Cafés

El Café Av Nader 5. This terrace restaurant is busy in the morning, as Cancún's journalists and writers come to enjoy the good coffee and *pan dulce*, along with simple, reasonably priced staples like *chilaquiles*.

El D'Pa C Alcatraces at the southwest corner of Parque de las Palapas. Typical French crepes, both sweet and savoury (M$50 and up), and decent wine by the glass are served late afternoons and evenings. Choose a sidewalk table or inside among plush furniture. Either way, it's very comfortable, and lively at night. Closed Mon.

Dub Av Nader at C Mero. Chilled-out hip café, often with a live DJ. It opens at 8am for breakfast and a morning cappuccino fix, then segues into ice cream and sandwiches for lunch (M$55 and up). Wine and light snacks (*jamón serrano*, olives, salads) are on the menu at night.

El Pabilo Av Yaxchilán 31, in the *Xbalamqué* hotel. Literary coffee shop (dubbed a *"café-brería"*) with good espresso and snacks. The atmosphere is mellow and beatnik-cool, and at night there's usually live guitar or readings. A bulletin board has notices of art openings, concerts and the like.

Ty-Coz Av Tulum, behind Comercial Mexicana. The deluxe main location of this French sandwich shop has more seating, longer hours (open till 10pm) and a slightly bigger menu than its zona hotelera branch. As there, the huge and delicious M$15 *baguette económico*, stacked with ham, cheese and pickled jalapeños, is one of the most enticing options, but croissant sandwiches (from M$30) are tasty as well. Also good for breakfast, with buttery pastries and strong coffee. Closed Sun.

Restaurants

100% Natural Av Sunyaxchén 26 at Av Yaxchilán. As the name implies, the menu at this largely vegetarian restaurant is decidedly wholesome, with fruit salads, veggie burgers and granola, as well as fresh-tasting Mexican dishes. Breakfasts are especially nice, with inventive combos like poached eggs on a bed of nopal leaves and spinach, topped with an almond cream sauce (M$54).

Checándole Av Xpuhil 6. A buzzing, popular restaurant that has been around since the earliest days, with a breezy terrace and a selection of satisfying and fresh-tasting Mexican classics. Entrees like enchiladas start at M$70; set lunch is M$45. Closed Sun.

La Habichuela C Margaritas 25 ⓣ998/884-3158, ⓦwww.lahabichuela.com. Long-established, elegant French-Caribbean restaurant set in a walled garden in front of the park. The featured *cocobichuela* (half a coconut filled with lobster and shrimp in a curry sauce, M$325) draws raves, but simpler, less expensive concoctions are equally good. The sommelier is attentive and enthusiastic. Neighbouring *Labná* applies the same elegant flair to Yucatecan specialities, with somewhat lower prices.

Los Huaraches de Alcatraces C Alcatraces 31 (or enter on C Claveles). This sparkling-clean cafeteria-style restaurant serves breakfasts and filling hot lunches for M$65 and up. But it's just as easy to fill up on the exceptionally delicious *huaraches* and quesadillas (from M$25), all based on chewy, hand-made tortillas tasting of perfectly fresh ground corn. Fillings range from squash blossoms to cinnamon-laced chorizo sausage. Closes at 6pm.

Iki C Alcatraces at the southwest corner of Parque de las Palapas. Potstickers, noodle bowls and savoury coconut-mango soup are some of the highlights at this Asian-fusion restaurant on the park. Set in a futurized palapa where blue neon glows from behind the bar, it has more flair than the showiest restaurants in the zona hotelera, for half the price (everything is less than M$150). Service is excellent. Closed Sun.

Pericos Av Yaxchilán 61 ⓣ998/884-3152, ⓦwww.pericos.com.mx. What opened in 1974 as a four-table *lonchería* is now a phantasmagoria of strolling magicians, crooning mariachis, stilt-walkers and juggling barmen – a little bit of the zona hotelera downtown. The atmosphere is so over-the-top that even sceptical diners might end up dancing around with a sombrero on their head. The food (steaks and enchiladas plus a few intriguing house specials, M$150–250) is tastier than at other dinner-show places.

El Rincón Yucateco Av Uxmal 24. In business since 1981, this stalwart specializes in simple peninsula cuisine such as *panuchos* (M$40 for four) and *brazo de reina* (M$50), a hearty tamale-like dish, all washed down with cold beers. The busy street out front makes the terrace less than ideal, but the nice staff do much to make up for it. Closed Sun.

Salus y Chemo's C Chacá 46. A quiet, pretty neighbourhood restaurant behind the bus station which offers hearty pozole (spicy hominy stew). The set lunch specials (M$45) are consistently satisfying. Closed Sun.

Zona hotelera

Cafés

Checándole Plaza El Parián, Paseo Kukulcán Km 8.7 and Plaza Flamingo, Paseo Kukulcán Km 11. A local fast-food mini-chain with fresh-made Mexican staples, *Checándole*'s two outlets in the zona hotelera are among the few spots in this part of town that offer satisfying, inexpensive local grub. The settings – a strip mall and a food court – aren't ideal, but taco plates start at M$45, while full lunches are M$70 and up. Daily 2–8pm.

K's Café Plaza El Parián, Paseo Kukulcán Km 8.7. Japanese-Mexican fusion is the byword at this tiny place. Try tamales filled with Japanese-style curry, or "taco rice", a stir-fry concoction invented by American Marines in Okinawa in the Sixties – both available for breakfast, if you're up for it. Or try rich miso soup with super-fresh seafood. It's in the inner ring of this little strip mall.

Marakame North end of Plaza Kukulcán, Paseo Kukulcán Km 13.5. Breakfast is served till 2pm at this terrace café with a soundtrack of mellow flute music. Try a poblano-pepper-and-Swiss-cheese omelette for M$60, or just coffee and a basket of tasty *pan dulce*. Lunch offerings include big salads, crepes and pastas, and the service is especially good.

Ty-Coz Paseo Kukulcán Km 6.8. The zona hotelera branch of the French sandwich shop has a shorter menu, but the *baguette económico* is still the highlight. Closes around 6pm.

Restaurants

100% Natural Paseo Kukulcán Km 9.5. Like the downtown original (see opposite), the place to go for health food, though this one is a smaller operation and not so garden-like.

Casa Rolandi Plaza Caracol, Paseo Kukulcán Km 8.5 ⓣ998/831-1817, ⓦwww.rolandi.com. At this Italian-Swiss fixture, the best dishes are done in the wood-burning oven – a fish filet comes out moist and garlicky. Other dishes include house-made spinach ravioli and the occasional venison special. It's expensive (M$170–260), but the cave-like atmosphere, with oil lamps on the tables, is quite nice (provided you get a table out of view of the incongruous flat-screen TV).

La Destilería Paseo Kukulcán Km 13 ⓣ998/885-1086. Waiters give tours of the tequila-making stills which stand in the dining room. Rare for such a theme restaurant, the food is reasonably tasty, varied and relatively inexpensive (M$150 for mains). The real draw, however, is the hundred-plus kinds of tequila, available in tasting flights.

Dolcemente Pompeii Pez Volador 7, near Paseo Kukulcán Km 5 ⓣ998/849-4006. A rare casual restaurant catering to Mexican families and residents in the zona hotelera, serving mammoth portions of hearty Italian food, from hand-made pastas (M$95 and up) to gelato. Hard to find because it's not affiliated with a mall or hotel: turn north in front of the giant Mexican flag. Closed Mon.

El Fish Fritanga Paseo Kukulcán Km 12.5. Hidden down some stairs behind a *Domino's*, this lagoon-side seafood joint is inexpensive, laid-back and frequented by residents. There's a makeshift beach, so you can stick your feet in the sand while you eat, as well as a playground for kids. Fish tacos *a la mayonesa* (M$16) are excellent; if you're feeling adventurous, try the super-tender and tangy octopus tacos (M$18). Full platters – and a full bar – are available, too. Closes at 7pm.

El Galeón del Caribe Paseo Kukulcán Km 19.2. A very rustic restaurant (more like a campsite) off the lagoon side of the road, where fresh fish is grilled over a wood fire for M$100 or so. You're almost guaranteed to be the only non-Mexican there. Get your order in before dusk, as there's not enough electricity to keep the place open after sunset. Opposite the *Club Solaris Premium Class*, the place can't be seen from the road – look for the only cutaway section of curb, a small makeshift parking area and stairs leading down into the trees; if you get to the *Bel Air Collection*, you've gone too far south.

Grill 14 Paseo Kukulcán Km 14 ⓣ998/840-6146, ⓦwww.grill14.com. Chef John Gray is well known for his intimate restaurants in Puerto Morelos and Playa del Carmen, and his newest place is equally reliable, with a broader menu that includes a full sushi bar. Beautiful lagoon setting, with dangerous cocktails – try one at sunset, with the view.

Hanaichi Plaza El Parián, Paseo Kukulcán Km 8.7. At this sparkling little sushi joint, Mexican waiters make small talk in Japanese with the visiting business clientele, serving quite decent sashimi (M$20 per piece) and other standards like beef teppanyaki (M$160).

MB In *Aqua Cancun*, Paseo Kukulcán Km 12.5. Miami chef Michelle Bernstein mixes Latin, Spanish and even Asian flavours in this stylish but not-too-formal restaurant, one of Cancún's best. Small but good wine list, too.

Río Nizuc Off Paseo Kukulcán, near Km 22. Hidden among the mangroves near the opening to the lagoon is this cheap seafood specialist, where ceviche (M$60) and *tikin-xic* fish (M$60) are popular with locals, who gather on weekends to watch the boats whiz by. Daily 11am–5pm.

Santos Mariscos Paseo Kukulcán Km 12.5. A cool seafood joint just south of *El Fish Fritanga* which serves inexpensive treats – wedges of crispy *jicama* topped with shrimp, for instance – to local schoolkids and a few tourists. Unlike most seafood-snack joints, it's usually open till midnight.

Entertainment and nightlife

As Cancún's goal is to encourage some two million visitors a year to have fun, the entertainment scene (huge dance clubs, vast theme bars, top-volume everything) in the **zona hotelera** is lavish – or remorseless, depending on how you look at it. **Downtown** offers a less frenetic scene, with several bars with live bands in SM 22 and along Avenida Yaxchilán. Locals dance on weekends to traditional Mexican tunes at Parque de las Palapas; for a quieter scene, there are a few small, cool bars clustered on Avenida Nader behind the city hall. Apart from the bars and clubs listed below, you may find interesting touring bands, as well as the city's chamber orchestra, playing at El Teatro de Cancún (Ⓣ998/849-5580, Ⓦwww.elteatrodecancun.com) at El Embarcadero.

Cinemas show new American releases subtitled in Spanish; the largest one downtown is the multi-screen Cinepolis (Ⓦwww.cinepolis.com.mx) in Plaza Las Américas on Avenida Tulum, south of Avenida Cobá; tickets are half-price on Wednesday. In the zona hotelera, La Isla mall, at Paseo Kukulcán Km 12.5, also has a theatre (Ⓦwww.cinemark.com.mx).

Bars

Typically embedded in malls or hotels, **bars** can provide a relatively affordable night out, supplementing the usual drinking fare with everything from big-screen sports coverage to romantic piano music in the background. Downtown watering holes often have very good **live musicians** performing at some point in the evening.

▲ Salsa dancing at a Cancún nightclub

Downtown Cancún

El Camarote In the *Plaza Kokai* hotel, Av Uxmal 26 ☎998/884-3218. At this nautical-theme bar, older local gentlemen play backgammon and cards on the front terrace. Inside is a small theatre furnished with captains' chairs and a stage, where crooners perform and couples dance. Thurs–Sat (M$50 cover).

El Capucino C Margaritas near C Azucenas. Local reggae and jam bands play for a mixed clientele of students and assorted bohemian types, though even when there's music, half of the crowd still seems to prefer hanging out and talking on the sidewalk out front.

El Chat C Tulipanes, opposite *Roots*. An Internet café by day, *El Chat* draws a crowd of rock-loving youth in the evenings. When a band isn't playing, it's all Nirvana on the stereo. Also equipped with pool tables.

El Rincón del Vino C Alcatraces 29, south end of Parque de las Palapas ☎998/898-3187. A casual, warmly lit wine bar with a big terrace, this is a great place to sample the best from Mexican vineyards, along with savoury snacks. The scene really gets buzzing around 9pm, when the live music starts – usually mellow *trova* or bossanova singers. Go a little earlier to secure a seat, or make a reservation. Closed Sun.

Zona hotelera

Bling Paseo Kukulcán Km 13.5, opposite Plaza Kukulcán ☎998/840-6014. Take the spiral staircase down to this chic lagoon-side lounge, set on a vast wood deck. The place is popular with well-heeled locals, who come to lounge on overstuffed white sofas while the DJ spins mellow house music.

Lobby Lounge at the Ritz-Carlton Retorno del Rey 36, near Paseo Kukulcán Km 14. Soak up the faux-chateau feel while you sit in the big, comfortable chairs and listen to the tinkling piano. The giveaway you're in Cancún: the sea view and the tequila menu.

La Madonna La Isla mall, Paseo Kukulcán Km 12.5 ☎998/883-4837. A giant reproduction of the *Mona Lisa* presides over this chic, candlelit bar slinging 150 types of martinis (very loosely defined, obviously).

Señor Frog's Paseo Kukulcán Km 10.5 Ⓦwww.senorfrogs.com. Practically synonymous with the name Cancún, *Frog's* is the first stop off the plane for the spring-break hordes. Go for live reggae or karaoke, a wild ride down the water slide into the lagoon or just an anthropological experience. On weekends there's often a US$5 cover.

Trágara Paseo Kukulcán Km 15.6 ☎998/885-0267, Ⓦwww.lagunagrill.com.mx. A breezy lagoon-front lounge whose velvet couches, numerous aquariums and mosaic trim on every surface set a super-cool mood. It's the perfect spot for a sunset drink and a snack from the Asian-fusion finger-food menu. (Look for the sign for *Laguna Grill*, the more prominent adjacent restaurant.)

Clubs

In Punta Cancún in the zona hotelera, giant **nightclubs** face off across the street, and by about 11pm the road is clogged with meandering, scantily dressed thrill seekers and hawkers flogging open-bar deals. The party generally lasts, inside the clubs and out, till 4 or 5am. Most of the clubs charge pricey covers (M$150 and up, cocktails M$70, with open-bar options) and maintain a "no shorts or sandals" dress code. The music can be generic, though during the big spring break season or other festivals, you can catch some international pop and hip-hop stars performing for less than you'd pay at home. The few downtown clubs – including a very popular gay venue – are a bit cheaper but no less dedicated to serious partying.

Downtown Cancún

Karamba Av Tulum at C Azucenas Ⓦwww.karambabar.com. The biggest and busiest gay disco in town, with room for four hundred to dance to pounding house and salsa beats, plus the requisite gay anthems. Most nights see drag acts, strippers and go-go boys galore. M$50 cover; closed Mon.

Roots C Tulipanes 26 ☎998/884-2437. This funky, intimate jazz and blues club has been downtown Cancún's preeminent venue for live music for decades, and often hosts big-name touring musicians. Also serves dinner. Cover is M$50 on Fri & Sat.

Zona hotelera

Azúcar At *Dreams Cancun*, Punta Cancún ☎998/848-7000 ext 7980. Very popular Caribbean club with a ten-piece band that gets the well-dressed crowd grooving to salsa and merengue. Cover is usually M$80; call to reserve a table, as it can get packed. Music starts around 10pm. Closed Sun.

Basic Paseo Kukulcán Km 10.5 ⓣ998/883-2180. The scene is young and the soundtrack heavy on techno and hip-hop at this funky club that's on a floating island just offshore. It's a little smaller (and sometimes cheaper) than the places in Punta Cancún. When the crowd gets overheated, water jets drench the dancers – keep that in mind when you're deciding what to wear.

Bulldog South side of the *Krystal* hotel, Paseo Kukulcán Km 9.5 ⓣ998/848-9851, ⓦwww.bulldogcafe.com. If you hit this place outside the high season (when spring-breakers frolic in the hot tub), you'll probably find more local kids – and more good hip-hop and *rock en español* – than anywhere else. It's the place to catch touring Mexican bands such as Café Tacuba and Molotov.

The City Paseo Kukulcán Km 9.5 ⓣ998/848-8380, ⓦwww.thecitycancun.com. Giant club that has hosted MTV's live spring-break party marathon in years past. Lots of energy is put into a floor show of hip-hop dancers, gymnasts and more to get the crowds worked up. In this respect, *Coco Bongo* is better, but *The City* will occasionally host major international DJs, which means more variety in the music.

Coco Bongo Plaza Forum by the Sea, Paseo Kukulcán Km 9.5 ⓣ998/883-0592, ⓦwww.cocobongo.com.mx. The epitome of the Cancún nightclub experience. The night warms up with a floor show involving trapeze acts, Beyoncé impersonators and roving candid cameras zooming in on the most shapely customers – all while women work the floor doling out tequila shots. It's such a scene that it's not uncommon to see tables of customers in their sixties here, just taking it all in as a tourist attraction. Music, once it really gets started, is of the broadest, most crowd-pleasing variety – but you didn't come here *just* to dance, did you?

Mambo Café Paseo Kukulcán Km 13.5 ⓣ998/840-6498. Cancún's biggest salsa club has a large wooden dancefloor overlooking the lagoon, and it's partially open air so the place doesn't get too steamy hot. The crowd is young, but serious about salsa. There are free salsa classes at 9.30pm and 10.30pm, then live bands – often touring acts from Cuba, the Dominican Republic and Puerto Rico – at around 11pm. Cover is usually M$50. Closed Mon.

Nectar Paseo Kukulcán Km 10.5 ⓣ998/883-3716, ⓦwww.nectarcancun.com. Tucked a little out of view on the opposite side of the strip from the big clubs, this very hip indoor-outdoor lounge has a live DJ spinning ambient beats or hard techno, depending on the night – or day, as it also throws the occasional huge afternoon dance party, or lets its night parties run into the morning hours. Along with the adjacent *Mix Sky Lounge*, *Nectar* hosts touring DJs, too.

Shopping

When it comes to souvenirs, Cancún's mass-market roots are still strong – meaning you'll find infinite quantities of giant sombreros and vaguely obscene T-shirts but precious little quality craftwork (save for in the folk-art museum in the zona hotelera; see p.75). Vast, air-conditioned **malls** dominate the hotel zone, selling everything from bikinis to Rolexes. La Isla mall, at Paseo Kukulcán Km 12.5, is the best, offering a great range of international brands plus plenty to occupy non-shoppers as well. **Prices** are usually fixed, but you can negotiate if you're buying several items at the big clusters of souvenir stalls (confusingly called "**flea markets**"): Coral Negro, at Punta Cancún, has the widest stock of inexpensive Mexicana in the zona hotelera, and the similar Ki-Huic (some signs say "Artesanías Cancún") dominates Avenida Tulum downtown. For a **hammock**, El Aguacate in Plaza Bonita, next to Mercado 28 downtown (see p.73), is the only place that stocks quality ones that will hold up to serious travelling.

You may do better at the **craft shows** that take place every few weeks at Parque de las Palapas. Vendors, whether local artists or visiting craftspeople from other towns, have a more diverse and personal stock and are happy to bargain. For more original **artwork**, check Galería Xaman-Ek in Plaza Caracol, and the Casa de la Cultura in downtown Cancún, west of the centre on Avenida Yaxchilán (ⓣ998/884-8364). The latter mounts new art exhibitions every couple of months – it's the best place to meet local artists and check out the scene.

Moving on from Cancún

If you're heading west **by car** to Valladolid, Chichén Itzá and Mérida, you have a choice between the scenic but speed-bump-filled **free road** (*libre*) or the fast new **toll highway** (*cuota*), running a few kilometres north of the old road for most of its length. From the bus station, drive north on Avenida Tulum about 1km, then turn left onto Avenida López Portillo; after a few kilometres you will have the choice of which road to join. There's another entrance to the *cuota* (but not the free road) off Avenida Tulum (Hwy-307), 1.5km south of the airport. You pay in advance, at the booths on the highway, for the sections you intend to travel along. The toll to Chichén Itzá is M$246; all the way to Mérida is M$311.

First- and second-class **buses** go from the terminal on the corner of Avenida Tulum and Avenida Uxmal. Destinations include Mérida, on the ultra-lux UNO service (7 daily, 6 of which arrive at the *Fiesta Americana*; 4hr), not-quite-as-lux ADO GL (14 daily; 4hr) and standard first and second class (hourly, round-the-clock; 4hr and 6hr); Campeche, on ADO GL (3 daily at 2.30pm, 3pm & 11.30pm; 7hr) and first class (8 daily, 7.45am–11.35pm; 7hr); Chetumal on ADO GL (2 daily at 5.45pm & midnight; 5hr 30min), first class (hourly, 5am–12.30am; 6hr) and second class (roughly hourly, 5am–12.45pm; 7hr); Izamal on second class only (10 daily, 4am–midnight; 5hr); Mexico City on ADO GL (4 daily; 24hr) and first class (9 daily, 8.30am–10pm; 26hr); Palenque on ADO GL (1 daily at 5.45pm; 13hr), first class (1 daily at 7.30pm; 13hr) and second class (8 daily, 2pm–8.30pm; 13–15hr); Playa del Carmen on first class (every 10min; 1hr); Tizimín, all on second class (7 daily; 4hr); Tulum on first and second class (at least hourly, 4am–12.15am; 2hr 30min); Valladolid on ADO GL (6 daily at 4.30am, 8am, 9am, 11.30am, 2pm & 5:30pm; 3hr) and second class (10 daily, 4am–midnight; 4hr); Villahermosa on UNO (1 daily at 6:45pm; 12hr 30min), ADO GL (9 daily, 10am–9.30pm; 12hr 30min), first class (nearly hourly, 7.45am–11.30pm; 13hr 30min) and second class (12 daily, 3pm–8pm; 15hr). There's an ADO ticket office in the zona hotelera, just west of the *Fiesta Americana Grand Coral Beach*.

International **flights** and domestic connections to Mexico City leave regularly from Cancún; from downtown a taxi to the airport costs about M$200; from the zona hotelera, M$200 and up.

Boats to Isla Mujeres

Two companies, Magaña and Ultramar, run passenger **ferries** (M$35; 20min) to Isla Mujeres. Ultramar boats leave from Gran Puerto, at the end of Avenida López Portillo, and Magaña boats depart from Puerto Juárez, 500m north. Nothing distinguishes the services, which depart every thirty minutes (5am–11.30pm), so it's likely you'll just take the boat from Gran Puerto, which is the first one you reach when coming from the centre. Catch a bus ("R-13" or "R-1 – Pto Juárez"; M$4.50) or a combi heading north on Avenida Tulum, or take a taxi from Avenida Tulum (around M$20). Boats also run from Playa Tortugas in the zona hotelera, for substantially more (US$10 one way). Alternatively, you can hire a **private launch** at Puerto Juárez to go directly or stop to snorkel along the way. Rates are negotiable, but a typical trip costs about M$600 for the boat, with stops at three reefs and snorkelling equipment provided.

The **car ferry** (M$185 per car and driver, plus M$14 per additional passenger; 45min) leaves from Punta Sam, 6km north of Gran Puerto, with five departures daily. However, it isn't worth taking a car over to the island, which is quite small and has plenty of bicycles and mopeds for hire.

Film, maps and other basic travel needs are easily purchased at Sanborn's, at the convention centre in the zona hotelera and opposite the bus station downtown. Despite the strong American presence, Cancún is short on English-language

books. Fama, on Avenida Tulum, between calles Tulipanes and Claveles, looks like a basic souvenir shop from the street, but has guidebooks, good maps and mass-market paperbacks tucked away in the back.

Sport

In addition to all the water activities, Cancún offers plenty of other energetic ways to pass the day. **Golf** is popular, with two courses offering especially challenging play and fine scenery. The oldest, recently remodelled by Robert Trent Jones Jr, is Club de Golf Cancún (Ⓣ998/883-1230, Ⓦwww.cancungolfclub.com), which straddles both sides of the boulevard at Km 7.5. The Hilton Cancun Golf Club (Paseo Kukulcán Km 17; Ⓣ998/881-8000, Ⓦwww.hiltoncancun.com) shows particularly creative use of the lagoon setting, with a mangrove trap, a tee on an island and a view of El Rey from the eighteenth hole. Green fees at both start at US$165.

Baseball is a well-attended spectator sport. Root for the local AAA pro team, the Tigres de Quintana Roo, at Estadio Beto Ávila, a bit southwest of the centre on Avenida Xcaret. There are usually eight or nine evening home games per month during the season, from March to September; check the schedule online at Ⓦwww.tigresqr.com (click on "Calendario"). Cheap seats are M$30, and the best ones in the house are only M$95. Cancún's **football** (soccer) team, the Atlante, may have arrived in the city just in 2007, but it has a long history – including victory over the famous Guadalajara Chivas and a triumphant national win in their new stadium. Well-attended games are at the Estadio Olímpico, just west of Beto Ávila.

More geared towards tourists, but still entertaining (if you can stomach the final kill), is the weekly **bullfight** at the Plaza de Toros (Dec–May Wed at 3.30pm; Ⓣ998/884-8248; US$35), at the intersection of avenidas Bonampak and Sayil. To justify the steep entrance price, the *corrida* is preceded by a rather cheesy folk dance show, as well as a bit of audience participation. But the small covered arena has a certain dusty ambience, and this is the only place in the area with a regular bullfight; otherwise, you'll have to wait for a town fiesta to see one.

Bowling is another possibility, at the slick bar-restaurant South 2.02 in Plaza Kukulcán at Km 13 (Ⓣ998/885-0441; M$60 per game), which has eight lanes, as well as some billiards tables.

Listings

Airlines Aeroméxico, Ⓣ800/021-4010, or at Av Cobá 80 Ⓣ998/287-1866, or at the airport Ⓣ998/287-1822; American, Ⓣ800/904-6000, or at Plaza Hollywood Local 1, between Av Xcaret and Av Cobá Ⓣ998/887-3187; Aviacsa, Ⓣ800/AVIACSA, or at Av Cobá 39 Ⓣ998/887-4211, or at the airport Ⓣ998/886-0093; Magnicharters, Av Nader 94 Ⓣ998/884-0212; Mexicana, Ⓣ800/502-2000, or at Av Tulum 269 Ⓣ998/881-9090.

American Express Av Tulum 208 at C Agua (Mon–Fri 9am–5pm; Ⓣ998/881-4025).

Banks Most banks (usually Mon–Fri 9.30am–3pm, Sat 9.30am–1pm) are along Av Tulum, between Av Uxmal and Av Cobá, and in the biggest shopping malls – La Isla, Kukulcán – in the zona hotelera. The HSBC bank, downtown at Av Tulum 192, stays open until 7pm on weekdays.

Car rental Available at most hotels and at the airport, or try Speed Car Rental, Uxmal 22 (Ⓣ998/892-0224, Ⓦwww.thespeedcar.com) downtown, or Buster Rent a Car, Paseo Kukulcán Km 7 (Ⓣ998/883-0510, Ⓦwww.busterrentacar.com).

Consulates Canada: Plaza Caracol, Paseo Kukulcán 8.5 Ⓣ998/883-3060; Germany: Punta Conoco 36 Ⓣ998/884-1898; Netherlands: Martinair office at the airport Ⓣ998/886-0134; UK: at the *Royal Sands*, Paseo Kukulcán Km 13.5 Ⓣ998/881-0100; US: Plaza Caracol, Paseo Kukulcán Km 8.5 Ⓣ998/883-0272.

Internet Immediately across from the bus station and northwest on Av Uxmal are several Internet

cafés; some are *casetas* as well. In the zona hotelera, Web access is significantly more expensive. There's a small café next to the *Bulldog* club that charges M$20 for 20 minutes, and another café in La Isla mall with similar rates.
Laundry Lavandería Las Palapas, on C Gladiolas, at the far side of the park (Mon–Sat 7am–8pm, Sun 8am–2pm), or Lavandería Martinez, across the street from *Las Palmas* hotel. In the zona hotelera there are *lavanderías* in the strip mall opposite El Embarcadero at Paseo Kukulcán Km 4, and next to *Ty-Coz* at Paseo Kukulcán Km 7.7.
Medical emergencies The largest hospital close to the zona hotelera is AmeriMed, Av Tulum Sur 260, behind Plaza las Américas (Ⓣ998/881-3400 or 881-3434 for emergencies, Ⓦwww.amerimedcun.com).
Post office Av Sunyaxchén at Av Xel-Há (Mon–Fri 8am–6pm, Sat 9am–1pm).
Sport fishing *Villas Manglar* hotel (see p.72) specializes in fishing charters.
Travel agencies and tours Most hotels in the zona hotelera have in-house agencies that can arrange day-trips to the chief Maya sites or other attractions along the coast. Otherwise, the student-friendly agency Nómadas has a branch at Av Cobá 5 (Ⓣ998/892-2320, Ⓦwww.nomadastravel.com) and leads affordable tours with guides to Chichén Itzá and other nearby attractions. Ecocolors, C Camarón 32, SM 27 (Ⓣ998/884-3667, Ⓦwww.ecotravelmexico.com), runs single- and multi-day kayaking, birdwatching or cycling tours.

Isla Mujeres

Just a few kilometres off the easternmost tip of Mexico in the startlingly clear Caribbean, **ISLA MUJERES** is substantially mellower than Cancún, drawing people for long stays despite the lack of tourist attractions and wild nightlife. A hippie hangout in the 1970s after wealthy Mexican adventurers paved the way for tourism a decade earlier, the eight-kilometre-long island still retains an air of bohemian languor, with wild-haired baby-boomers passing on travel wisdom to a new generation of young backpackers.

Unfortunately, however, Mujeres is no longer the desert island you may have heard about, and its natural attractions have been developed considerably. Several large hotels have sprung up, thousands of day-trippers visit from Cancún, and the once beautiful **Garrafón coral reef** off the southern tip is now almost completely dead and incorporated into a small-scale family-fun park. Inevitably, too, prices have risen. All that said, the island can still seem a respite to those who've been slogging their way from Maya pyramid to Maya pyramid, or to anyone who is overwhelmed by plastic Cancún – the wooden buildings and narrow streets here have a genuine Caribbean feel.

Isla Mujeres's attractions are simple: first there's the beach, then there's the sea. And when you've tired of those, you can rent a bike, moped or golf cart to carry you around the island to more sea, more beaches and the tiny Maya temple that the conquistadors chanced upon, full of female figures, which gave the place its name. But you'll eventually want to be back under the palms on **Playa Norte**, the big west-facing beach, by late afternoon: Isla Mujeres is one of the few places along Mexico's eastern shoreline where you can enjoy a glowing sunset over the water, margarita in hand. For a truly secluded beach, you can also take a day-trip to the nearby bird sanctuary of **Isla Contoy**.

Arrival, information and island transport

The passenger **ferries** arrive at Isla Mujeres town at two adjacent piers; the car ferry comes in further south on Avenida Medina, at the end of Calle Bravo. The boats leave from Gran Puerto and Puerto Juárez (10min in a taxi from central Cancún, or 15min on a bus) nearly every half-hour from 5.30am; the last is at midnight. From the pier, it's about a twenty-minute walk to the opposite side of the island and the most distant hotels.

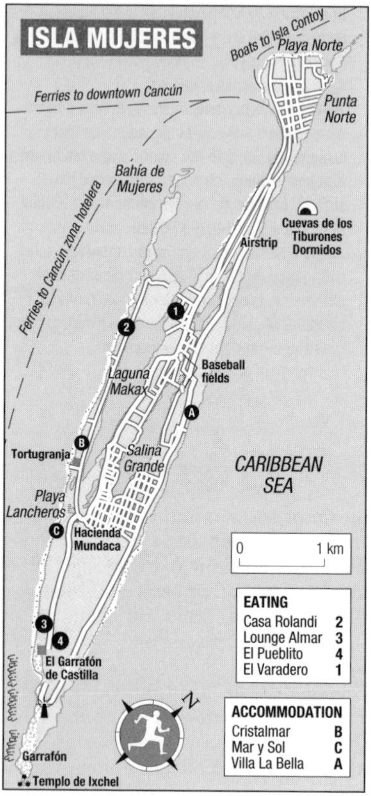

The **tourist office** (Mon–Fri 8am–8pm, Sat & Sun 9am–2pm; ⓦ www.isla-mujeres-mexico.com) is on Avenida Rueda Medina just west of the passenger ferry piers. Here you can pick up leaflets, maps and copies of the free *Islander* magazine (in Spanish and English).

A **bus** runs every half-hour from Avenida Rueda Medina in the main town down to the southern end of the island (M$4), but you may prefer the flexibility of a **moped** (M$100/hr, M$350/24hr) or **bicycle** (M$100/day), as the island is a very manageable size with few hills; alternatively, hire a **golf cart** (M$150/hr, M$600/24hr). Virtually every other storefront rents out all three forms of transport, and prices vary little. You can also take a **taxi** – rates are posted at the stand between the ferry piers, starting at M$23 for hotels in the main town and running up to M$54 to the south end of the island; a tour costs M$160 per hour.

Accommodation

Isla Mujeres has a few solid **budget places** to stay, though they fill up in high season – advance reservations are recommended. Most of the reasonably priced options are on the northern edge of the island; note that on the east-facing coast, the sea is generally too rough to swim in, and the bigger hotels in the centre of Playa Norte have seriously eroded beachfront. For **camping**, you can pitch your tent or sling up a hammock (M$60) in the grounds of the **Poc-Na youth hostel**, Calle Matamoros at Calle Carlos Lazo (ⓣ 998/877-0090, ⓦ www.pocna.com), which opens directly onto a beach. The party-friendly hostel has other sleeping options, from dorm beds (M$90–140) to private rooms with air conditioning (3), though it can be a little less than spotless and has no public kitchen.

Isla Mujeres town

Belmar Av Hidalgo 110, between C Madero and C Abasolo ⓣ 998/877-0430, ⓦ www.rolandi.com. The sunny rooms with big French doors and plenty of extras are a good deal, despite the potentially noisy location above *Rolandi's* pizzeria on the main nightlife drag. (6)

Casa Sirena Av Hidalgo, between C Bravo and C Allende ⓦ www.sirena.com.mx. No need to give up colonial style at the beach: this very tastefully redone old home with six rooms retains some historic details, like tile floors, and added modern bathrooms, minimalist furniture and a breezy roof terrace with a panoramic view (ideal for the daily happy hour). Breakfasts are lavish, and there's even a small pool. Three-night minimum; advance reservations required. (8)

Chi Chi's & Charlie's Northwest corner of the island, end of Av Rueda Medina ⓣ 998/877-0491, ⓦ www.chichisandcharlies.com. The bar on the prime beach spot for sunset-watching also rents eleven rooms – simple, but new construction, so they're in good shape, and certainly the best beachfront deal. 6

Francis Arlene C Guerrero 7 at C Abasolo ⓣ998/877-0310, ⓦwww.hotelfrancisarlene.com. Small family-owned hotel with well-tended courtyards and clean, rather brightly painted rooms with frilly bedspreads, plenty of comforts and choice of a/c or fan. 6

El Marcianito C Abasolo 10 ⓣ998/877-0111. Though lacking the view that *Vistalmar* has, this is otherwise a comparable budget option, with clean rooms with a/c and fairly new bathrooms. All have one double bed; an extra bed can be arranged for M$50. 4

María Leticia C Juárez 28, between C Mateos and C Matamoros ⓣ998/877-0832. Big, airy rooms with or without kitchens and sitting rooms. It's great for long stays, but you absolutely must book ahead. 5

Na Balam C Zazil-Há 118, near Playa Norte ⓣ998/877-0279, ⓦwww.nabalam.com. One of the island's most comfortable hotels, with a pool, lush landscaping and rooms that are elegant but not pretentious. Free yoga classes Mon–Fri. Of all the Playa Norte hotels, this is the only one that still has much of a beachfront. 9

Playa la Media Luna On the northeastern shore ⓣ998/877-1124, ⓦwww.playamedialuna.com. The pastel rooms each have a/c, a fridge and a balcony overlooking the beach, which is a bit rocky, but still swimmable; there's also a pool. Nicely isolated, despite its proximity to town. Continental breakfast is included with all except a couple of "rustic" rooms (US$60) that are smaller and don't face the sea. 8

Plaza Almendros Av Hidalgo, between C Matamoros and C Abasolo ⓣ998/877-1217, ⓦwww.hotelplazaalmendros.com. New rooms with sliding-glass doors open onto a large swimming pool; all have kitchenettes, a/c and sitting areas under a shady portal. 5

Roca Mar C Bravo at C Guerrero, behind the church next to the plaza ⓣ998/877-0101. One of the island's oldest hotels, though well maintained. The big rooms all have balconies, and the small restaurant (see p.91) overlooks the Caribbean. The beach is rocky and the water rough, but there is a pool. 6

Secreto On the northeastern shore ⓣ998/877-1039, ⓦwww.hotelsecreto.com. This whitewashed modern hotel looks more Mediterranean than Mexican; details include enormous fluffy beds, a welcoming outdoor lounge by the pool and a partially sheltered cove. For this level of style and service, the ground-floor double rooms are a bargain; continental breakfast included. 9

Vistalmar Av Rueda Medina at C Matamoros ⓣ998/877-0209, ⓔhotel_vistalmar1@yahoo.com. Brightly painted hotel (the colours seem to change every year or two) just northwest of the ferry pier. Good value, with choice of a/c or fan and big shared terraces with sea views. 4

Elsewhere on the island

Cristalmar On the Sac Bajo Peninsula, 500m north of Hacienda Mundaca ⓣ998/877-0390, ⓦwww.cristalmarhotel.com. The big one- and two-bedroom suites with full kitchens and dining areas are popular with vacationing Mexican families. In addition to the beach, a pool, dive shop and game room keep everyone entertained. Not ritzy, but great staff and a solid bargain. 8

Mar y Sol 5km south from the ferry, on the bay side ⓦwww.morningsinmexico.com. An apartment rental, available by the night or the week. The four studios (each with two beds, a/c, a range and a fridge) are basic, but right on the beach. It's a taxi ride from the action on the north end of the island, but walking distance to the nearby village for supplies, or to Playa Lancheros for lunch. 6

Villa La Bella 2.5km south from the ferry, on the Caribbean side ⓣ998/888-0342, ⓦwww.villalabella.com. This beautifully designed guesthouse is perched above dramatic crashing surf. Swim in the pretty pool instead, or use the hot tub that's fired up on weekends. The five rooms all have king-size beds and fantastic feather pillows; delicious full breakfast is included. 8

The Island

The majority of the tourist amenities on Isla Mujeres are on the northern end in the main **town**, which occupies about a third of the island's area. Nonetheless, it's so compact you can take a quick turn around the sixteen or so square blocks of brightly painted houses in just half an hour. The centre third of the island is also built up, a sort of locals-only "suburb" to the main town. Beyond, a single road runs along the west coast towards the southern tip, passing the ruined pirate abode of **Hacienda Mundaca**, tucked amid low, humid forest, and several quiet beaches, the best of which is **Playa Lancheros**. **Garrafón** park occupies the south end, a watery playland for snorkellers that encompasses the island's single, very small Maya ruin, the **Templo de Ixchel**. The road loops around and continues back up the windy, exposed east coast, where the surf crashes incessantly against the rocks. You can complete the circuit in a golf cart or by bicycle in just a few hours, or make a full day of it, taking time out for beach lounging and a leisurely lunch.

Isla Mujeres town and Punta Norte

Narrow, pedestrianized **Avenida Hidalgo**, lined with tequila bars, crochet-bikini vendors and family-friendly restaurants, cuts through the centre of **Isla Mujeres town**. The street's southern end opens onto the central **plaza**, where tamale and churro vendors set up shop in the evenings. On one side sits a church that's the site of week-long festivities every December celebrating a legendary statue of the Virgin Mary that's on display inside (discovered in 1890 along with two others on the far north coast, the statue is said to walk on the beach occasionally).

Stretched around **Punta Norte**, the northern lip of the town, the island's major beach, **Playa Norte**, represents the archetypal Caribbean beach, with soft, deep sand, plenty of palm trees and bathtub-warm water stretching out at knee height for nearly a kilometre in some spots. The western side, north of the ferry docks, is cluttered with fishing boats and ceviche stands; this is where *isleños* often swim and set up camp with the family on Sundays. At the north-western tip, the beach party goes all week long, with a cluster of bars in perpetual happy hour. Across the northern side, the scene gets quieter. Close to the Avalon Reef Club, the all-inclusive resort on the promontory (and chief timeshare hawker, you can't help but learn), you can **snorkel** a bit. The small bay in front of Casa Maya is particularly calm and a good spot for children to test the waters.

▲ Town cemetery, Isla Mujeres

The only other sight to speak of is the town **cemetery**, on Calle Mateos at Calle Juárez, where you'll find the closing chapter of the saga of Fermín Antonio Mundaca (see below). Nestled between shiny new crypts is the pirate's weather-worn grave, half-buried in sand. It's empty, though: the lovelorn man died alone in Mérida. The grim engraving, allegedly carved by the gloomy Mundaca himself, reads, "Lo que tu eres, yo fui. Lo que yo soy, tu serás" ("As you are, I was. As I am, you will be").

There's little worth **shopping** for on Isla Mujeres, and the densely packed souvenir stands can get old fast. An exception is Artesanías Glenssy, a small shed on Calle Mateos across from the post office packed with a collection of exceptionally beautiful **papier-mâché masks** and headdresses painted in elaborate colours and patterns. Opening hours are erratic, and the artist isn't really geared to selling to tourists, but it's worth taking a peek if you can.

South from town

If you've had enough of lounging on the beach and wandering round town, rent a bike or moped to explore the south of the island. A lone road runs its length, past the dead calm waters of the landward coast and up the other, windswept side.

Heading **south from town**, about halfway down the length of the island and a bit inland lurk the decaying remains of the **Hacienda Mundaca** (daily 9am–5pm; M$10), an old house and garden to which scores of romantic (and quite untrue) legends are attached. The most popular tale reports that in the mid-nineteenth century, the Spaniard Fermín Antonio Mundaca, a reputed swashbuckling pirate (though more likely a run-of-the-mill trader of sugar and slaves), fell madly in love with a young lovely nicknamed La Trigueña ("the brunette"). Attempting to woo her, he built an enormous hacienda in her honour; nonetheless, the lady spurned her suitor and ran off with someone her own age. Mundaca died alone and insane, and his glorious estate went to the dogs. Only one small house has been pieced together, but the entry gate is suitably gothic-looking, as the inscription "La Entrada de la Trigueña" can still barely be made out. A circular garden at the back of the property makes a pleasant and vaguely eerie picnic spot. Near the front and to the right of the main path is a **zoo** of the kind that makes you wonder whether the animals – sprawled sullenly on logs or sunken in pools – are actually alive. The stars are the spider monkeys, quick to pluck food and any other stray items from visitors' hands.

About 100m south of the hacienda (just past the *Isla Mujeres Palace* resort) is **Playa Lancheros**, the best beach outside of Playa Norte. The white sand is pleasantly shaded by palm trees, and it's virtually deserted except at lunchtime. The **restaurant** here produces some great rustic seafood – its speciality is a fantastic *tikin-xic* fish.

Across the traffic circle, another road leads to a government-run **turtle farm** and research centre (daily 9am–5pm; M$20), which breeds endangered sea turtles for release in the wild. Entrance helps fund the preservation project.

Continuing on to the southern tip, you reach the borders of a family-fun nature park, **Garrafón** (daily 9am–6.30pm; Ⓦwww.garrafon.com; US$50, kids US$35), established in 1999 as a way of managing what was left of the small coral reef just offshore, which had suffered serious damage from decades of unsupervized day-trippers. Though much of the coral is dead, you can still see quite a lot of fish, as visitors keep them well fed with park-provided nibbles. In addition, you'll find kayaking, restaurants and "snuba" set-ups (walk under water while breathing through a long flexible tube). The entry price includes meals, towels and snorkel gear.

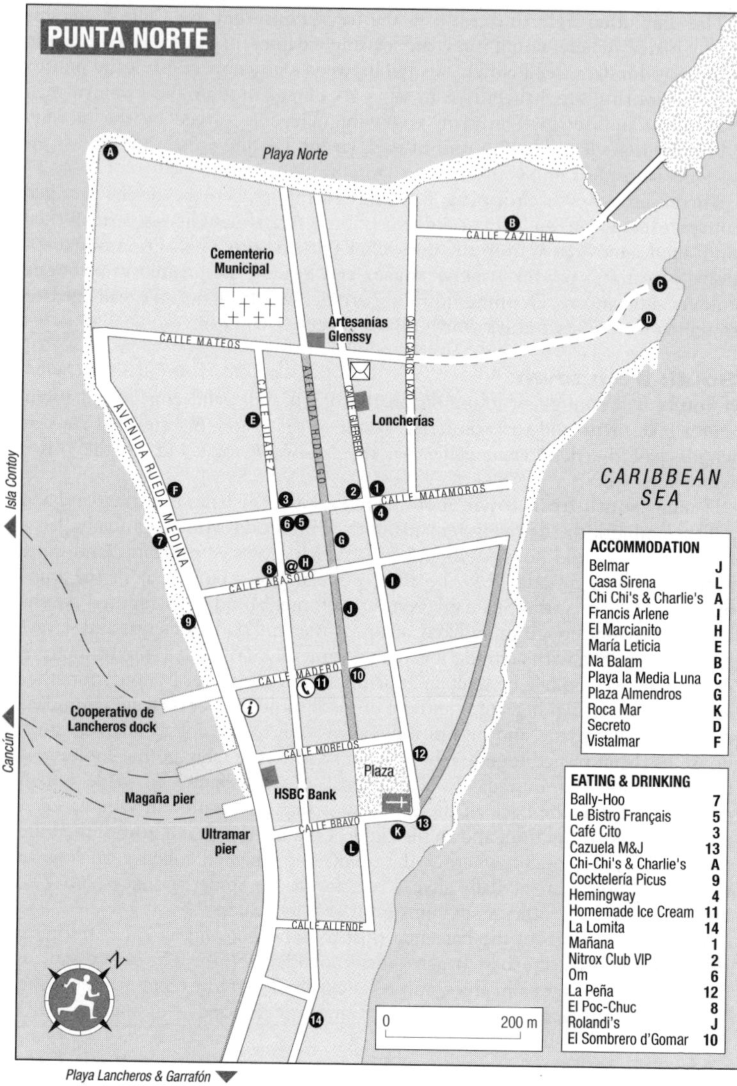

It's much cheaper to snorkel at the adjacent Garrafón de Castilla beach club (M$40). Vigilant workers at the nature park keep interlopers from paddling around on its turf (er, surf), but the beach club has its own protected bay and quite a few fish hanging out.

The entrance to the park is almost at the southern end of the island. Beyond, the road continues to the old **lighthouse**, which affords a decent view back up the coast. A **sculpture park** south of the lighthouse is worth a visit, though it may be closed for renovations. From the park, visitors should also be able to see the **Templo de Ixchel** at the southernmost point of Isla Mujeres (daily 9am–6.30pm; US$5 or free with Garrafón ticket), where Francisco Hernández de Córdoba first arrived in Mexico in the spring of 1517. The temple was filled with female fertility figures, dedications to the goddess Ixchel, which allegedly inspired the Spaniards to dub the place "the island of women". Today the temple isn't very impressive – it's too much of a ruin, in fact – but it is very dramatically situated on low rocky cliffs, and you can often spot large fish basking below. The striking views continue as you head back north to the main town via the narrow, stark east-coast road, dotted with new holiday villas but still quite wild-feeling compared to the rest of the island.

Offshore, there's plenty of sea life to visit. **Las Cuevas de los Tiburones Dormidos** ("caves of the sleeping sharks"), a few kilometres from the northeast coast, is a popular dive spot where tiger, Caribbean reef, lemon, blue and even bull sharks rest in an oxygen-rich fresh-water current that lulls them into stasis. Trips are easily booked through **dive shops** in town, such as Coral at Calle Matamoros 13-A (Ⓣ998/877-0763, Ⓦwww.coralscubadivecenter.com). You can also arrange **snorkelling** trips at the *lancheros* cooperative, north of the passenger ferry landing (M$200; 2hr) at the end of Calle Madero. A popular destination is **El Farolito**, a shallow spot off the tip of the Sac Bajo Peninsula where you're mostly protected from the current. Isla Mujeres is the only other official departure point for tours to the **whale sharks** near Isla Holbox (see p.96); trips from here take longer – at least an hour and a half on a boat – and cost more (about US$125).

Eating

The area along and around Avenida Hidalgo, between calles Morelos and Abasolo, is lined with **restaurants**. For inexpensive, basic Mexican food and great low-priced fruit salads, head for the **loncherías** opposite *Las Palmas* hotel. At night, food **vendors** set up on the main plaza.

Cafés

Café Cito C Juárez at C Matamoros. Visit this colourful, cheery restaurant for healthy yoghurt-granola breakfasts or more decadent crepes and waffles, along with very good coffee.

Cazuela M&J C Bravo at the ocean, past the *Roca Mar* hotel. Enjoy a fine ocean view at this casual café serving inexpensive (mostly Mexican) breakfasts. The signature egg dish is a sort of omelette baked in a *cazuela*, or earthenware casserole. Big glasses of green *chaya* juice are another healthy option. Daily 7am–2pm.

Homemade Ice Cream C Madero, between C Juárez and Av Hidalgo. Just what the sign says – this is one of a handful of excellent gelato vendors in town. Try the lemon cream or one of the intense tropical fruit flavours.

Mañana C Matamoros at C Guerrero. Brightly painted breakfast and lunch café serving everything from falafel to *churrascos* (Argentine-style steak sandwiches, M$68) to Wiener schnitzel (M$65). A secondhand bookshop occupies one corner.

Restaurants

Le Bistro Français C Matamoros 29 at Av Hidalgo. Casual restaurant with an inventive, delicious and reasonably priced menu that's vaguely French-inspired (fish with fennel and capers, for instance). Good breakfasts, too. Daily 8am–noon, 6–10pm.

Casa Rolandi At the *Villa Rolandi* hotel, at the end of the Sac Bajo Peninsula Ⓣ998/877-0500, Ⓦwww.rolandi.com. The menu at this northern Italian restaurant is the same as at its Cancún counterpart (see p.79), but the setting here is superior, on a covered terrace overlooking the turquoise bay.

Cocktelería Picus Av Rueda Medina. Small beachfront hut just north of the ferry landings serving fresh and inexpensive ceviches and shrimp cocktails. In low season it serves lunch only.

La Lomita C Juárez 25-B. Locals line up for a helping of the chef-owner's daily special, anything from bean soup and *chiles rellenos* to pan-fried fish with salsa verde. Fantastic home cooking that's worth the hike up the small hill two blocks south of the plaza. Lunch only.

Lounge Almar Southern end of the island, at *Casa de los Sueños* hotel. The excellent waterfront restaurant at this tiny hotel is open to non-guests. Its Asian-Mexican menu is delicious and different from anything else on the island: definitely try the duck tacos, as well as the poblano-pepper dumplings. Mains are M$120 and up; margaritas, M$60.

El Poc-Chuc C Abasolo at C Juárez. This bargain *lonchería* with red vinyl tablecloths and a giant mural of Chichén Itzá is handily also open for dinner (although not all of the big meals are available at night). Fish soup (M$35) and crispy *panuchos* (M$25) are two reliable offerings.

El Pueblito South end of the island, across from El Garrafón de Castilla beach club. A rustic but tasty place to stop along the way to Garrafón, *El Pueblito* is on the inland side of the road, surrounded by shady trees. A lunch of tacos, guacamole and a couple of beers runs about M$80.

Rolandi's C Hidalgo, between C Madero and C Abasolo. Part of a small family-run chain serving great, reasonably priced wood-oven pizza, lobster, fresh fish and other northern Italian dishes with salads.

El Sombrero d'Gomar Av Hidalgo at C Madero. Hearty portions at reasonable prices are the draw at this two-storey palapa-roof restaurant on the main avenue. Stick with Mexican staples – the *chilaquiles* are good for breakfast.

El Varadero West coast, adjacent to Puerto Isla Mujeres. This super-casual Cuban restaurant is nestled among palm trees on what looks like an unpromising vacant lot – you have to walk back from the road a little to see the small blue-and-white shack. Garlicky pork and refreshing mojitos are the specialities. Tell the cab driver "El Varadero del Burgos", as there's another place with a similar name nearby.

Drinking and nightlife

Isla Mujeres isn't a big **nightlife** destination – in the off-season, only one or two bars can muster any sort of crowd. Occasionally **bars** on Playa Norte will sponsor big parties, but typically the scene consists of beers and perhaps some Jimmy Buffett renditions by a local guitar player.

Bally-Hoo Av Medina near C Abasolo. Swap tales with yachties at this palapa bar on the marina pier; it's the designated hangout for anyone looking to crew a boat.

Chi-Chi's & Charlie's Playa Norte at the end of Av Rueda Medina. Perched on the northwestern tip of the island, this is the perfect bar for a sunset drink (aided by near round-the-clock happy-hour deals).

Hemingway C Guerrero at C Matamoros. A locals' cantina in a Caribbean-style wood house with a porch. The clientele is almost entirely men, and can get rowdy on weekends.

Nitrox Club VIP C Matamoros, between C Guerrero and C Hidalgo ☎998/887-0568. The only disco in town, drawing both locals and tourists. Wed is ladies night, and Fri has Latin music, with free dance classes from 10pm till midnight. Cover is rarely more than M$30. Closed Mon & Tues.

Om C Matamoros, between C Juárez and C Hidalgo. A groovy international-flavoured lounge with pillows on the floor, twenty types of herbal tea and personal beer taps at each table. A good place to meet other travellers.

La Peña C Guerrero on the main plaza. An upstairs bar-lounge popular with younger hostel guests, with a view of the Caribbean, cocktails, DJs and a big movie screen.

Listings

Banks HSBC, on Av Rueda Medina opposite the ferry docks, has an ATM; another ATM is between the two docks.

Books *Mañana* café stocks second-hand English books, and a few new ones.

Bus tickets You can check schedules and purchase tickets for ADO and affiliate buses at a kiosk at the Ultramar ferry pier.

Internet There are several cafés. The one next to *El Marcianito*, on C Abasolo, between Av Rueda Medina and C Juárez, can download photos from cameras; one on the northwest side of the plaza has cheap international calling, too.

Laundry Two laundry services, Tim Phó's and Wash Express, are on C Abasolo. Lava Lounge, on C Guerrero, between C Matamoros and C Abasolo, has Internet access as well.

Post office C Guerrero at C Mateos (Mon–Thurs 9am–4pm); mail is held at the Lista de Correos for up to ten days (postcode 77400).

Telephone A reasonably priced *caseta* is on C Madero, between C Hidalgo and C Juárez; the Internet café on the plaza also has cheap rates.

Isla Contoy

Scores of touts on Isla Mujeres devote their efforts to luring you on a boat trip to the island **bird sanctuary** of **CONTOY**, 30km north of Mujeres. Only 8.5km long, it was designated a national park in 1961, and is now home to some 150 bird species, including large colonies of pelicans, cormorants and frigates. The calm western beaches serve as a nesting haven for sea turtles, while the windy eastern coast is a mix of dunes and limestone cliffs. The boat trip out is leisurely, often with stops to snorkel at reefs along the way; by lunchtime you're deposited on a small beach in a lagoon. Here you may find several other groups, which can dampen the isolated spirit a little, but the total number of visitors is limited to two hundred each day. You have the afternoon to either relax in the sun or explore the wild setting, starting at a small welcome centre and observation tower and going along a path into the mangroves that cover the interior of the island.

You can arrange a jaunt through the fishermen's cooperative, at the dock at the end of Calle Madero. Captain Tony García, with offices at Calle Matamoros 7 (Ⓣ998/877-0229), also takes out his boat, *Guadalupana* – he comes highly recommended by Isla Mujeres regulars. In either case, tours last the whole day and include a basic breakfast, grilled fish for lunch, soft drinks and snorkel gear for about US$55 per person. Tours increasingly depart **from Cancún** as well. Kolumbus Tours (Ⓣ998/884-5333, Ⓦwww.kolumbustours.com) is one good operator – groups are larger, but the boats, replicas of early exploratory sailing vessels, are nifty. Tours cost US$75 and include all the same activities as the Isla Mujeres ones. For an additional M$100 donation, payable on the island, you can take a birdwatching tour with one of the resident biologists. For more information on the reserve, contact Amigos de Isla Contoy (Ⓣ998/884-7483, Ⓦwww.islacontoy.org), which has an office in the Plaza Bonita mall in downtown Cancún (see p.82).

Isla Holbox

A small island off the northeastern point of the peninsula, **Isla Holbox** (pronounced "ol-BOSH") is sometimes touted as a new rustic beach hideaway to fill the place that Isla Mujeres once had in travellers' affections. The one small village, a hospitable, quiet place with a genuinely warm feel, will seem a relief to anyone who has come from the touristy resorts. The gulf waters here do not have the same glittering clarity as the Caribbean (nor any of the vibrant reefs), but they're warm and clean, and the beaches are all but empty. Development is on the rise, of course, but a good part of the island is still very wild, as is the long spit from the mainland that runs east of the island, and all manner of **birds**, including flamingos, thrive here. From mid-June to mid-September, visitors come to see the huge and rare **whale sharks** (see box, p.96) that congregate just off the cape. Sea turtles also nest here during the summer months. The one hitch in paradise: absolutely fearsome mosquitoes during the wet season – no surprise that a popular souvenir T-shirt from here says "Blood Donor". Come prepared with repellent and long pants and shirts.

Getting there: Solferino and Chiquilá

The easiest way to reach Holbox is from Cancún, on the daily direct **bus** (3hr) for Chiquilá, the closest mainland town by ferry. The bus leaves Cancún at 7.50am and 12.40pm. Coming from the west is more difficult: buses leave

Mérida (6hr) and Valladolid (3hr) in the middle of the night and arrive in time for the 6am ferry. Transferring in Tizimín (3hr) is a little easier, with a choice of three daytime buses. You can also take any second-class bus along Hwy-180 *libre* and get off at the tiny town of El Ideal; from there, you can take a taxi north to Chiquilá for about M$300, or, if you time it right, transfer to the bus coming from Cancún, which passes through around 10.30am and 3.30pm.

If you are **driving** from Cancún or Mérida, don't take the toll highway, as there's no convenient exit. You may want to stop in the village of **SOLFERINO**, 42km north of Hwy-180 and 15km south of Chiquilá, which is part of a regional eco-tourism network that offers great opportunities to visit really rural cultures and seldom-seen wild spots. Solferino's main contribution is a **buggy-and-kayak tour** to a nearby cork forest and lake (Ⓣ986/861-3674, Ⓦwww.puertaverde.com.mx). You can go for the afternoon (M$400; 4–5hr) or stay overnight at cabañas for an additional M$100 per person. The minimum group size is three people. As this is still a fairly new tour, the chance of your meeting up with other travellers is slim. If you just want to stretch your legs, at least stop at the **butterfly farm** ("La Casa de las Mariposas", south of the lake tour kiosk, on the west side of the road) or the **orchid garden** and giant ceiba tree (east from the highway – turn at the "Orquideario" sign). Next to the orchid garden is a small **café** and ad hoc gallery run by a friendly and talented Croatian woman.

In **CHIQUILÁ**, the **ferry** for Holbox leaves nine times a day, the first runs at 6am and the last at 7pm (M$40; 30min); you may spot a few dolphins as you cross the lagoon. Holbox is also served by an unreliable **car ferry**, but there's no sense in taking a car to the tiny island. Secure parking is available near the pier (be certain you've set the price before you leave – about M$30 for any portion of a day). You can also hire a private launch (M$250–300), which will

▲ Taxi driver on Isla Holbox

take you directly to your hotel if you like. But don't miss the last ferry: Chiquilá is not a place you want to get stranded. There's a restaurant, a basic hotel, a store and a petrol station, but little else. Note also that there's **no bank or ATM** on Holbox or in Chiquilá – plan accordingly, particularly if you intend to take a trip to the whale sharks, which is a sizeable investment (usually about M$800).

Arrival and information

The ferry moors at a dock on the south side of the island, where there's little but the town generator and baseball field. Golf-cart and *triciclo* (pedicab) **taxis** can take you directly to your hotel if you have already made reservations; a ride to *Villas Chimay*, the hotel furthest from town, is about M$50. Otherwise, it's usually M$10 to the plaza, or about a ten-minute walk north on the wide sand street of Avenida Benito Juárez, which also leads on to the beach, two blocks further. Otherwise, street names are largely irrelevant – all orientation is done from the plaza, as the town stretches for only a few blocks around it.

On the modest main square, called the *parque*, you'll find a **post office** and **money-exchange** desk; there's an **Internet** café one block west, off the southwest corner. There's no official tourist office, though you might receive a **free brochure** on the ferry. Very few people have cars; locals also use the *triciclos* and electric **golf carts**. The latter are available to rent (about M$600/24hr) from several outlets near the *parque*, such as Rentadora Monkeys (ⓣ984/875-2029). You can also get around by **bike** (M$20/hr), though the rentals aren't always maintained very well.

Accommodation

Small-scale hotel development stretches east of town for a couple of kilometres; only one property lies to the west. Out of season (early summer and before Christmas), rates for some of the upmarket rooms can fall by almost half; August, however, can be priced as high as Christmas and Easter weeks. All of the hotels on the **beachfront** are mid-range to luxury, but there are a few decent cheaper options in **town** (and more are on the way – several more *posadas* were under construction as of late 2007), as well as the *Ida y Vuelta* **campground** and **hostel**, with screened shelters for tents or hammocks (M$100) as well as a few beds (M$120), clean bathrooms and a shared kitchen (ⓣ984/875-2344, ⓦwww.camping-mexico.com); there's also a private house for rent (❺). It's located east of the centre, just 200m from the beach, in the block behind *Xaloc*.

Casa las Tortugas On the beach two blocks east of the plaza ⓣ984/875-2129, ⓦwww.holboxcasalastortugas.com. A great little collection of round, two-storey cabañas, beautifully decorated and tucked among dense greenery. Rooms have a mod feel, with polka-dot fabric. A/c is optional; breakfast is included. ❼

Faro Viejo Av Benito Juárez at the beach ⓣ984/875-2217, ⓦwww.faroviejoholbox.com.mx. Tidy, comfortable rooms directly on the beach (the only stretch in town that's free of fishing boats), all with porches. A few suites are ideal for groups, with kitchenettes and porches. Continental breakfast included. ❼

Posada Amapola East side of the plaza ⓣ984/875-2196. This guesthouse with five a/c rooms doubles as a beer wholesaler – convenient. Look for the pink two-storey building. ❺

Posada Los Arcos West side of the plaza ⓣ984/875-2043 ⓦwww.holboxlosarcos.com. Clean, basic rooms, some with kitchenettes, around a small courtyard, or down the street in a separate building. Choice of a/c or fan. ❹

Posada Mawimbi On the beach, next to *Casa las Tortugas* ⓣ984/875-2003, ⓦwww.mawimbi.net. Very similar to *Casa las Tortugas* architecturally, but has a few rooms that are smaller and less expensive. Rooms have a/c, but opt for an upstairs room if you prefer a fresh breeze. ❻

Villas Chimay On the beach, 1km west of town ⓣ984/875-2220, ⓦwww.holbox.info. A wonderful hideaway, and the only lodging on the western beach. Self-sufficient with wind and solar power, and plenty of space between the well-designed bungalows. Also runs tours around the island and to Solferino. 7

Villas Los Mapaches On the beach, two blocks west of Av Benito Juárez ⓣ984/875-2090, ⓦwww.losmapaches.com. Comfortable bungalows with kitchenettes, ideal for longer stays; a larger rental house can accommodate groups or families. 6

Xaloc On the beach, east of town ⓣ984/875-2160, ⓦwww.holbox-xalocresort.com. A compact but well-designed property of eighteen cabañas with rough-hewn wooden canopy beds and particularly well-appointed bathrooms. Smartly divided into areas for families and adults only, with a pool in each section. Free kayaks and snorkel gear, too. 8

The island

Uninhabited until the late nineteenth century (locals claim pirates as their forebears), Holbox today is home to only about two thousand people, most engaged in lobster and shrimp fishing, or selling lobster and shrimp to hungry visitors. All of the population is concentrated in a **small town** on the north coast. With sand streets, wooden houses and almost no cars, it's tranquil in the extreme. Aside from hanging out on the plaza, most activities for visitors involve the wildlife on or around the island.

The biggest such natural attraction, literally and figuratively, is the group of **whale sharks** that cluster off the coast in late summer. A boat tour to see the giant fish takes the better part of the day (M$800 per person including lunch and snorkel gear). You may see dolphins, rays and flying fish on the hour-long boat ride out to where the sharks gather, and tours often stop on the way back at Cabo Catoche, the northern cape, where there's a clutch of fishermen's shacks and a tall lighthouse. Mosquitours (ⓣ984/875-2126, ⓔholbox@turismoalternativo.com) has new boats and informed guides who are respectful of the fish and the regulations concerning them.

Visiting the whale sharks

The whale shark (*Rhincodon typus*, or *tiburón ballena* in Spanish) is a true shark, but earns its name by its enormous size: the largest known fish, it can reach up to 14m in length, and typical adults are between 7m and 10m long. Another common name, the domino shark, comes from its distinctive black skin covered in rows of white dots. The fish's lifespan is also remarkably long, as it can typically live well into its 70s.

Although whale sharks populate the tropical zone around the globe, the shallow waters off Isla Holbox are the only place in the world where such a large population gathers. The fish typically congregate in pods of ten or twenty, but researchers estimate the Holbox group at more than two hundred – perhaps because the swirling water here, where the Gulf of Mexico meets the Atlantic Ocean, teems with plankton, the whale sharks' primary food. Unlike vicious great whites of the popular imagination, whale sharks are gentle filter-feeders; as they glide slowly in circles, they are simply sucking up whatever small sea life is in front of them. Swimming alongside the passive animals poses no risk, except perhaps of getting tossed about by the current from a turning or diving fish.

Whale shark tourism on Holbox has developed very recently, and regulations for visiting the creatures were applied for the first time in 2003. By law, Isla Holbox is the only departure point for tours. Most of the area in which the fish swim is now a marine park, which requires visitors to be accompanied by trained guides, who should make sure swimmers get no closer than 2m to the sharks. Good captains should never attempt to "steer" the sharks with their boats. Take a hat and biodegradable sunscreen if you have it; regular sunblock is prohibited by marine-park regulations.

Other popular tours include **Isla Pájaros**, a very small island wildlife sanctuary inside Laguna Yalahau. A flamingo colony nests here between April and October, along with about 150 other species. Two observation towers give birdwatchers great views at sunset. Also in the lagoon, a fresh-water **spring** wells up among the mangroves on the mainland side – a popular swimming hole that's a side destination for many trips. **Isla de Pasión** is a tiny dot of sand off the west end of the island; a big part of the trip is wading through the shallow water to reach it. Visits to all of these places, as well as to a cork-tree swamp near Solferino on the mainland, can be arranged through most hotels, along with Mosquitours. Any of them can also arrange tours for **fishing**, and a dive shop at *Posada Mawimbi* does **snorkelling** excursions, though the nearby reefs don't compare with those on the Caribbean shore.

One outfit runs **horse-riding** tours (M$350; 2.5hr) to Punta Ciricote, where there is another cluster of flamingos. Enquire where the horses are tethered on the beach, 100m west of *Los Mapaches*, or call ⓣ984/129-9995. **Kiteboarding** is increasingly popular on this breezy island with plenty of empty beach. Classes can be arranged at *Casa Tortugas* (next to *Posada Mawimbi*). Marvin Tours (ⓣ984/875-2103), one block off the northwest corner of the plaza, offers aerial tours in a small plane, especially interesting during the whale-shark season, when you can see just how large the population is. **Fly-fishing** is big here, and Holbox Tarpon Club (ⓣ984/875-2103, ⓦwww.holboxtarponclub.com) is a long-established guide service.

Eating and drinking

The village has very little choice in terms of **restaurants**, but a few are quite good. On the east side of the plaza, *La Cueva del Pirata* is a tasty Italian restaurant, complete with hand-made fresh pasta. Just west of the plaza, off the beach-facing side, *Viva Zapata* serves great fresh fish in banana leaves, as well as chipotle shrimp, pasta and more; the first-floor palapa is a good place to watch the sun go down. On the beach, family-owned *Leo's* serves inexpensive fish and Mexican dishes, and there are also a couple of small *loncherías*. Don't expect any **nightlife** – the closest thing to a full bar is *Carioca's*, on the beach just north of the plaza. Locals generally lounge around on the plaza, where there might be a traditional Mexican *lotería* runner, or some vendors or musicians.

Travel details

Buses

The most useful bus services are those between Cancún and Mérida, and those provided by Mayab, which run at least every thirty minutes between Cancún and Playa del Carmen. Second-class service to smaller towns is provided by Centro, Noreste and Cristobal Colón. The following frequencies and times are for both first- and second-class services. During the summer whale-shark season, there's usually an additional bus from Cancún to Chiquilá, in the early afternoon.

Cancún to: Campeche (7 daily; 7hr); Chetumal (hourly, 5am–midnight; 6hr); Chiquilá (2 daily at 7.50am & 12.40pm; 3–4hr); Izamal (10 daily; 4hr); Mérida (hourly; 4–6hr); Playa del Carmen (every 10min; 1hr); Puerto Morelos (every 10min; 30min); Tizimín (6 daily; 4hr); Tulum (12 daily; 2hr); Valladolid (hourly; 3hr); Villahermosa (14 daily; 12hr).

Chiquilá to: Cancún (2 daily at 7.30am & 1.30pm; 3–4hr); Mérida (1 daily at 5.30am; 6hr); Tizimín (3 daily at 5.30am, 7.30am & 4.30pm; 2hr).

Ferries

Ferry service runs frequently to **Isla Mujeres** and **Isla Holbox**. Although there are car ferries to both, it's not worth taking a vehicle, as the islands are very small.

Chiquilá to: Isla Holbox (9 daily at 6am, 8am, 10am, 11am, noon, 2pm, 4pm, 5pm & 7pm; 30min).

Isla Holbox to: Chiquilá (9 daily at 5am, 7am, 9am, 10am, 11am, 1pm, 3pm, 4pm & 6pm; 30min).

Isla Mujeres to: Puerto Juárez and Gran Puerto, Cancún (every 30min, 5.30am–10pm; 15min).

Puerto Juárez and Gran Puerto, Cancún to: Isla Mujeres (every 30min, 6am–11.30pm; 15min).

Flights

Cancún has a busy international airport with daily flights to Mexico City and other domestic destinations, as well as Tikal in Guatemala and Havana, Cuba. Aerosaab (Ⓣ984/873-0804, Ⓦwww.aerosaab.com) runs charter flights from Cancún to Isla Holbox, Cozumel and Playa del Carmen.

2

Playa del Carmen, Cozumel and the Caribbean coast

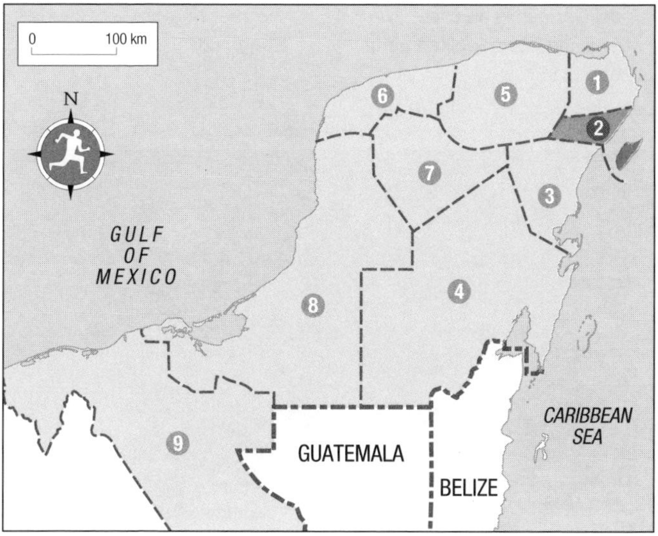

CHAPTER 2

Highlights

✱ **Puerto Morelos Reef** The coral outcroppings off the coast of Puerto Morelos are a great place to learn to dive. See p.103

✱ **La Ruta de los Cenotes** Outside Puerto Morelos, this small road cuts inland through the jungle, passing several beautiful swimming holes. See p.107

✱ **La Quinta** With easily the best nightlife on the Caribbean coast, the central tourist artery through Playa del Carmen is an ever-evolving cosmopolitan party. See p.112

✱ **Mamita's Beach Club** Playa del Carmen's best beach is also its most stylish social scene. See p.115

✱ **Parque Punta Sur** The nature reserve at the southern tip of Cozumel is a must for birdwatchers (look for the Cozumel vireo), and its beaches are beautiful, too. See p.125

✱ **Columbia Shallows** This sandy-floor coral garden off Cozumel's southwest coast teems with colour and life – a mesmerizing place to snorkel. See p.128

▲ Mamita's Beach Club on Playa Norte, Playa del Carmen

2

Playa del Carmen, Cozumel and the Caribbean coast

Development along the spectacular white-sand beaches south of Cancún has proceeded furiously over the last few decades, as landowners have raced to cash in on the resort city's popularity. The tourist authorities granted the area south of Cancún the rather grandiose title **Riviera Maya**, and holidaymakers come in droves to the mammoth gated retreats that dot the coast. That said, finding a relatively deserted stretch of beach is by no means impossible. Immediately south of Cancún, in fact, lies one of the quieter spots: **Puerto Morelos**, a tiny town with clean beaches that has so far avoided unattractive development. (Its other big draw: offshore is the start of the vibrant **Mesoamerican Barrier Reef**, which stretches down to Honduras; the section here is a great, less-visited place to dive and snorkel.) A bit further south, **Punta Bete** is a little sandy point dotted with a couple of basic hotels. By contrast, the phenomenal growth of **Playa del Carmen**, formerly known only as the place where diving fanatics hopped on the ferry to **Isla Cozumel**, has transformed a fishing camp into a major holiday destination in its own right, renowned for its nightlife and gorgeous beachfront.

A half-hour boat ride away, the island of Cozumel is ringed by some of the most beautiful **reefs** in Mexico. From the early Sixties, the barely populated island was a destination primarily for divers, but in the past two decades, the place has boomed like everywhere else, welcoming direct flights from the US as well as massive **cruiseships** at three separate piers. But despite the crush of visitors, you can still find isolated spots to appreciate the island's rainbow-hued underwater gardens. And there's plenty to see on land as well, from the pretty town of **San Miguel** to the deserted eastern coast, known for its empty beaches and rustic bars, where you can while away the time with a margarita or enjoy some fresh grilled fish.

You can explore the mainland coast easily by car, or take cheap and efficient public transport along Hwy-307: both colectivos and second-class buses will stop anywhere you request. On Cozumel, though, there are no such options, so you'll have to rent a car to see the whole island, or join an organized tour.

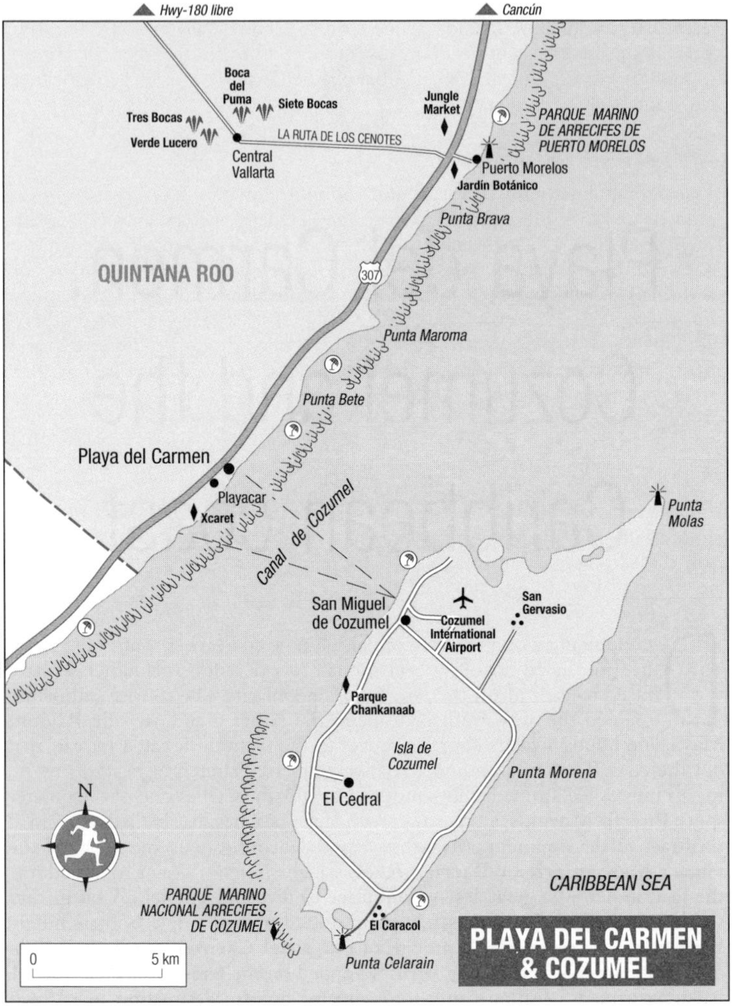

Puerto Morelos

Leaving Cancún behind, **PUERTO MORELOS**, 20km south, is the first town on the coast. Even though it's practically in the shadow of Cancún's hotels, it feels wonderfully remote and barely developed. As the only working fishing village between Cancún and Tulum that hasn't been entirely consumed by tourism, it's so mellow that the afternoon siesta is still observed by most businesses (and many expat-owned places shut entirely in the low summer season). Puerto Morelos's **beach** is pretty and broad, but the main draw here is the **reef**, which lies about half a kilometre offshore and is in healthy condition. For a population of roughly three thousand, the town offers a remarkable number of excellent **restaurants**, ranging from modern-fusion panache to hearty bargain lunches. Inland, on the road to Central Vallarta, some beautiful **cenotes** are also excellent for diving. With a direct bus service from the airport, it's easy for visitors to bypass Cancún altogether, making Puerto Morelos their first stop along the Riviera Maya.

Arrival and information

Buses going down the coast leave the station in downtown Cancún every ten minutes, or leave directly from the airport (11 daily, 9.30am–8.30pm; 20min M$40) and drop you at the highway junction. Taxis wait here to take you the 2km into town for about M$20 (M$25 for some more distant hotels), or you might be lucky enough to meet up with the colectivos or buses that also make the trip, on no discernible schedule. Marand Travel (Ⓦwww.puertomorelos.com.mx), on the southwest corner of the plaza in town, is the unofficial tourist **info** spot, dispensing maps and advising on hotels.

Accommodation

Hotels in Puerto Morelos are split between those right on the beach, and better bargains a few blocks back. If you want to **camp**, your only option is the pleasantly ramshackle *Acamaya Reef Park* (Ⓣ987/871-0132, Ⓦwww.acamayareef.com; M$90), on the beach 5km north of town – look for a signposted turn near the entrance to the Crococun zoo. Cabañas, with shared or private bath, are also available (❻), and the French owner cooks good food.

The Mesoamerican Barrier Reef

Mexico's Caribbean coast faces the second-longest reef in the world (Australia's Great Barrier Reef comes in first). Stretching from Puerto Morelos, just south of Cancún, to the Bay Islands of Honduras, the **Mesoamerican Barrier Reef** hugs the shoreline for more than 700km. The complex eco-system encompasses not just the main coral outcroppings, but also outlying atolls, such as those around Cozumel, the sea-grass beds close to shore and the mangrove swamps that help feed the coral and filter out pollutants from land. The reef is host to more than five hundred species, including the endangered West Indian manatee and extremely rare and slow-growing **black coral**.

Like most coral systems around the world, the Mesoamerican Barrier Reef has suffered a great deal of damage. Some eighty percent of the oldest hard coral has died within just the past thirty years, and slick algae growth in many spots threatens to smother essential reef organisms. Unsurprisingly, the devastation coincides with the tourism boom onshore. Relatively few building projects have directly attacked the reef (though in 2004 a giant new pier in Playa del Carmen was carved straight through the coral), but careless development has taken its toll, particularly on the mangrove swamps, which have been either torn out or used as dumping grounds. At the same time, hurricanes and other natural disasters have put intense stress on the eco-system.

Compared with other stretches of reef around the Caribbean, however, the Mesoamerican system is relatively healthy, and in 1997 the governments of Mexico, Belize, Honduras and Guatemala forged an agreement ensuring their joint conservation efforts. As part of a larger trend along the coast, Puerto Morelos residents successfully campaigned to have their reef frontage designated a national park in 2000, in order to prevent overfishing and other harmful practices. On land, though, building codes are only slowly being adjusted to be less environmentally harmful, and development is continuing unabated – the hope is that the tourism industry won't kill off one of its most profitable attractions.

Amar Inn On the seafront, 500m north of the main plaza ⓣ998/871-0026, ⓔamar_inn@hotmail.com. Very bohemian, family-run hotel on the beach with eight large rooms and cabañas; some with high ceilings, loft beds and kitchenettes. Delicious Mexican breakfast included in rates. ❻

Cabañas Ixchel Av Rojo Gómez, four blocks north of the plaza ⓣ998/871-0180, ⓦwww.cabanasixchel.com. A nice bargain option: "cabañas" (really, tents) are set up in a large beachfront garden and surrounded by greenery. They're outfitted with queen-size beds and other comforts. Rates include breakfast. ❼

Casa Cacahuate C 2 in the zona urbana. ⓣ998/208-9148, ⓦwww.mayaecho.com. With two spacious guestrooms, the "peanut house" is a great chance to be in the forest in relative comfort, as well as to interact with the non-touristy side of Puerto Morelos. It's also a handy place for solo travellers to get acclimated, under the wing of hostess Sandra, a longtime Mexico resident. ❻

Ceiba del Mar 2km north of Puerto Morelos on the coast road ⓣ998/872-8060, ⓦwww.ceibadelmar.com. Distinctive architecture and large pools make this spa resort, five minutes north of town, a standout. As luxury hotels go, it's not as well appointed as *Maroma* (see p.108) near Punta Bete, but neither is it so isolated. The earth-tone rooms have big bathtubs with sea views, and there's a full sauna (open to non-guests by appointment). Rates include continental breakfast and airport transfers. ❾

Hacienda Morelos On the waterfront, just south of the plaza ⓣ987/871-0448, ⓦwww.haciendamorelos.com. Huge, bright rooms strung out in a row, motel-style, all with kitchenettes and bathtubs (a rare treat at this price), plus terraces opening right onto the beach. ❼

Marviya Av Rojo Gómez, 500m north of the plaza ⓣ998/871-0136, ⓦwww.marviya.com. Choose either a room in a big villa (weekly rates only) or one of the expansive studios, rented by a friendly French couple. ❽

Ojo de Agua On the seafront, 400m north of the plaza ⓣ987/871-0027, ⓦwww.ojo-de-agua.com. Bright, sunny rooms (some have a/c) with colourful decor, most overlooking a giant pool; beyond lies a clean beach. The bar-restaurant occasionally hosts a live band. One added perk: sea-view rooms don't cost more. ❻

Posada Amor Av Rojo Gómez, just south of the plaza ⓣ998/871-0033, ⓔpos_amor@hotmail.com. Not on the beach, but friendly, and one of the longest-running hotels in town. Some of the quirky, individually decorated rooms (with shared baths) are the least expensive around, while some other, larger ones with private baths are worth the extra money; ask to see a few. ❺

Posada El Moro Av Rojo Gómez 17, just north of the plaza ⓣ987/871-0159, ⓦwww.posadaelmoro.com. Ten clean, relatively new rooms, some with kitchens, in a pretty little garden; rooms off the street are preferable, though, as the neighbouring bar can be noisy at night. Amenities are excellent for the price: there's a small pool, and continental breakfast is included. ❻

▲ Lighthouse and pier in Puerto Morelos

The Town

A small, modern plaza sits in the centre of Puerto Morelos. The turn-off from Hwy-307 ends here, and **the town**'s only proper streets lead north and south from it, parallel to the beach. The plaza has a small church, a baseball court and a taxi rank and hosts a produce market on Wednesdays. It's also home to the wonderful Alma Libre (Oct–May Tues–Sat 10am–3pm & 6–9pm, Sun 4–9pm; ⓣ998/871-0713, ⓦwww.almalibrebooks.com), probably Mexico's most extensive second-hand English-language **bookshop**, with some twenty thousand volumes to choose from, including a solid selection of books about the area's natural and archeological attractions. If you'll be visiting Puerto Morelos for a while, sign up for the owners' exhaustive email newsletter on everything local, from restaurant openings to speed-bump news. They can also transfer the digital photos from your camera to a CD.

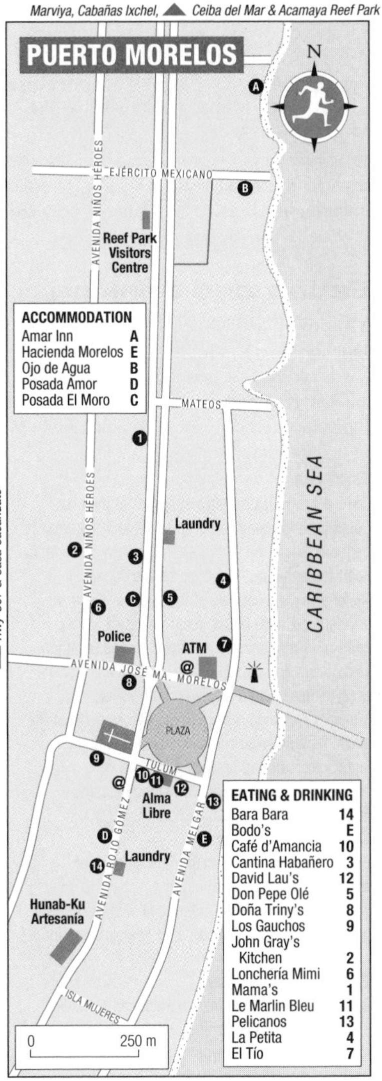

Off the east side of the plaza lies the **beach**, a long wooden **dock** and the old **lighthouse**, a squat little concrete structure knocked Tower of Pisa-style by a hurricane. A newer model has been built behind it, but the old one remains as a town icon. Very attractive and reasonably priced **craftwork**, like hammocks and embroidered clothing, can be found at Hunab-Ku Artesanía, two blocks south of the plaza on Avenida Rojo Gómez. Here you can often see the artisans at work making their goods. If you're in town on a Sunday in high season (Dec–April), also visit the **Jungle Market**, a craft sale and party run by a group of local women – embroidery work is well priced, and there's also good food and music. It starts at 10.30am – most cab drivers know it by the English name, or say "Calle Dos, zona urbana" (M$40).

With a thriving stretch of the Mesoamerican Barrier Reef only 600m offshore, Puerto Morelos is a great place to **dive** or **snorkel**. And, because the area sees nowhere near the traffic of Cozumel or Playa del Carmen, it's also a good spot for novices to start. A national marine park since 2000, the reef can be visited only with a guide, who will take you to shallow coral gardens or, for more advanced divers, a couple of wreck sites. Long-established Almost Heaven Adventures, on the plaza, offers certification courses and one- and two-tank dives (M$400–550), as well as **sport-fishing** charters (around M$2250 for up to four people; 5–6hr) and snorkelling trips (M$220 per person; 2hr). Dive Puerto Morelos, on Avenida Rojo Gómez just north of the plaza (Ⓣ998/206-9084, Ⓦwww.divepuertomorelos.com), is another reliable, informed outfit, offering trips to the local reef, as well as to inland cenotes and Cozumel. And if you're introducing kids to snorkelling, a longtime resident named Valorie Gallagher is especially recommended – ask for her at *David Lau's* restaurant on the plaza.

Eating and drinking

Most of Puerto Morelos's restaurants and nightlife are on the town plaza, a cheerful spot for dinner, followed by a cold beer or an evening stroll. There's also a lot of food sold out of people's houses and yards – keep an eye open for signs. If you're self-catering but want something special, seek out Las Morenas, a small grocery on Rojo Gómez just north of *Amar Inn* – it stocks some gourmet goods.

Cafés

Café d'Amancia Southwest corner of the plaza. Come here for deadly strong coffee and a breakfast bagel or lunchtime sandwich, all in a great vantage point for watching the action on the square.

Doña Triny's West side of the plaza at the main access road. This Mexican café is tiny, but you can't miss it, thanks to its bright-orange paint job. Tasty tacos are just M$7, and lunches are M$40 – everything's cooked up fresh on the spot.

Mama's Av Niños Héroes, three blocks north of the plaza. Homely American-owned breakfast and lunch joint, offering breakfast burritos with veggie chorizo (M$50), oatmeal, fruit smoothies and a wide range of baked goods. Tues–Sat 7.30am–4pm, Sun 8.30am–1pm.

El Tío Av Melgar, just north of the plaza. Get shrimp tacos in the morning and *tortas* and *sopa de lima* at lunch at this hole in the wall. No energy has been wasted on decor; it all goes into the food.

Restaurants

Bodo's South of the plaza in Hacienda Morelos. Flawless Wiener schnitzel and delicious apple strudel: don't ask why you're eating them on the beach in Mexico – just dig in and enjoy. Salads are also delicious, and the view from the terrace is lovely. Closed Wed.

David Lau's South side of the plaza. A longtime Chinese-Mexican restaurateur dishes up General Tso's chicken (M$75) and other standards, along with a full pizza menu (there was an oven in the place when he took over – he's not letting it go to waste). The food is good, but the friendly service is even better. Closed Wed.

Los Gauchos Av Tulum, west of the plaza. From the outside signage, this place looks like any other Mexican restaurant, but it's actually a South American spot, with tasty empanadas (M$15), decent pizza (M$45) and pasta (from M$70), served in a hippie-ish setting. Closed Tues.

John Gray's Kitchen Av Niños Héroes, north of the plaza Ⓣ998/871-0665. Visitors from Cancún often make the short drive down for dinner at this small, casually elegant restaurant. The owner is an ex-*Ritz-Carlton* chef, and his gourmet background shows: the daily menu features simple, smart combos like pan-roasted duck breast with chipotle, tequila and honey, or macaroni and cheese with shrimp and truffle oil. With most entrees under M$200, it's quite a bargain, too. Closed Sun.

Lonchería Mimi Av Niños Héroes, north of the plaza. Look for the pale-green facade on this tidy *cocina económica*, where a team of women cook up daily specials in a spotless open kitchen. Go early, as food tends to run out, and the four tables fill up fast.

Le Marlin Bleu South side of the plaza. This French-owned restaurant is actually best known for its shrimp tacos, which are delectably light and served with the house salsa. Or you can choose from the Gallic side of the menu: a croque monsieur, shrimp in garlic butter and the like.

Pelicanos East side of the plaza, on the beach. A classic seafront restaurant under a giant palapa – you can get better seafood in town, but not with this beautiful view. Traditional *trovadores* often play here in the late afternoon.

La Petita Av Melgar, half a block north of the plaza. This small wooden house surrounded by a sandy yard is where the town fishermen kick back and enjoy the fresh catch of the day, sold by the kilo and served fried, grilled or in a ceviche. A whole *pescado frito* and a few beers will set you back about M$120.

Bars

Bara Bara Av Rojo Gómez, south of the plaza, next to *Posada Amor*. PM's hippest venue, with DJs spinning reggae and house music, and bartenders mixing actual cocktails (beer, in giant *caguama* – aka "tortoise" – bottles, is also available). Closed Mon.
Cantina Habañero Av Rojo Gómez, north of the plaza. Don't be fooled by the spotlights and the fog machine – this is a standard-issue expat bar, where American football is often debated.
Don Pepe Olé Av Rojo Gómez, north of the plaza. A sometimes rowdy local bar scene, which starts in the afternoon. Karaoke is the entertainment of choice once the sun goes down. There's a full food menu, but the place is not renowned for its cuisine.

Listings

ATM Located on the plaza, though there is no actual bank.
Cambios A couple of cambios can be found on the plaza, 7am–10pm.
Internet and telephone There are several long-distance telephones on the plaza, by the police station on the corner, as well as two Internet cafés, one on the south side by Marand Travel and another on the north, by the grocery store.
Laundry Just south of the plaza, across from the *Posada Amor*.

Around Puerto Morelos

The surrounding area contains a few natural attractions that you can visit on half- or full-day trips – having your own car is most convenient, but you can also arrange a taxi for about the same price as renting a vehicle.

Mangrove walk

Just 2km north of town, across the street from the *Ceiba del Mar* resort, a boardwalk runs for about 1km through the **mangroves**. Built and maintained by the hotel, it's a free access point to the swamplands that are home to more than three hundred bird species, such as roseate spoonbills, herons and many migratory songbirds. The boardwalk provides a unique opportunity to explore this eco-system on your own, as the swamps, also home to crocodiles, aren't safe to wade through without a guide. Go early in the morning or late in the afternoon to catch the most bird activity.

La Ruta de los Cenotes and the Jardín Botánico

On the main highway 1km south of the turn-off to town, a concrete Maya-style arch marks the start of **La Ruta de los Cenotes**, a road that cuts through dense forest punctuated by a number of cenotes. These are visited only occasionally by groups from Cancún; you're more likely to have the places to yourself. Sixteen kilometres along the route you pass the very small village of Central Vallarta, a former camp for *chicleros* harvesting sap for the chewing-gum industry. The first cenote you see signs for is **Siete Bocas** (aka Deep Blue) – it's actually a network of caves, accessible only to divers. Just after Central Vallarta, at Km 17 off the right side of the road, **Boca del Puma** (Ⓣ998/886-9869, Ⓦwww.bocadelpuma.com; M$70) has a long zip-line ride and a climbing wall. The least developed site, **Verde Lucero**, is another 1km along on the left; the pretty swimming hole is named for its emerald-green water; there's a smaller zip-line here for swinging into the pool. **Tres Bocas** is another kilometre along – it's more rewarding for divers, as there isn't much surface water. The last operation is **Selvática**, which is open only to prearranged tour groups. Taxis from Puerto Morelos to any of the cenotes cost M$150; a round-trip will depend on how much waiting time you want. Many dive shops in Puerto Morelos (see p.105) also run snorkelling and diving trips out here.

On the east side of the highway, opposite the turn for the cenote route, is the **Jardín Botánico Dr Alfredo Barrera Marín,** also signposted as Yaax Ché (Nov–April daily 8am–4pm; May–Oct Mon–Sat 9am–5pm; M$70). The 148-acre botanical gardens provide a good introduction to the peninsula's native flora. A three-kilometre path leads through medicinal plants, ferns, palms, some tumbledown Maya ruins and a mock-up *chiclero* camp, where you can see how the sap of the *zapote* (sapodilla) tree is tapped before being used in the production of gum. A longer trail leads through an untended chunk of forest (home to spider monkeys, though they usually keep out of sight) to a viewing platform above the canopy. Anyone particularly interested in botany should hire a guide, either at the site or through one of the several tour operators in Puerto Morelos that run day-trips.

Punta Bete

Resorts large and small almost solidly occupy the coast between Puerto Morelos and Playa del Carmen. But there's still public beach access at **PUNTA BETE**, some 25km south of Puerto Morelos, with its turn-off signposted just south of the Cristal/Coca-Cola bottling plant. There's a clutch of good-value hotels, and one good place for a day on the beach. The coast is about 4km from the highway. About 3km along, the road forks at *The Tides Riviera Maya* (Ⓣ984/877-3000, Ⓦwww.tidesrivieramaya.com; ➒), an extremely ritzy hideaway. Taking the left fork, you first reach the turn for *Petit Lafitte* (Ⓣ984/877-4000, Ⓦwww.petitlafitte.com; ➒), a hassle-free resort known for its excellent staff and scores of repeat guests; rates include breakfast and dinner. Close to the beach, but not on it, the charming Swiss-owned *Coco's Cabañas* (Ⓣ998/874-7056, Ⓔmarsilhel@hotmail.com; ➏) has five individual cabañas, a small pool and a restaurant serving very good European cuisine. It's a short walk to *Los Piños* (Ⓣ984/873-1506; ➐), a somewhat dull hotel, but its beach is shaded with palms and is the only spot where **day visitors** can lounge out. For M$200, non-guests can use chairs and a palapa. Second-class buses will drop you at the turn-off to Punta Bete, as will colectivos from Playa del Carmen or Cancún, but it's a hike down to the beach. A cab from Playa del Carmen costs about M$100.

Should you be looking to splurge, head 10km north of Punta Bete to one of the finest luxury hotels on the coast, *Maroma* (Ⓣ998/872-8200, Ⓦwww.maromahotel.com; ➒). Elegant yet informal, with a strong Mexican style, the hotel has grown almost organically over three decades, developing from the original owners' personal home into a group of white-stucco guestrooms tucked amid palm trees.

Playa del Carmen and around

Once a soporific fishing village where travellers camped out en route to Cozumel, **PLAYA DEL CARMEN** has mushroomed in recent years, leaving repeat visitors dumbfounded by the town's transformation into a high-style party town for Europeans, South Americans and Mexico City jet-setters. Like Cancún, Playa – as it's commonly called – has few historic underpinnings. And like other beach towns, it can be a bit pricey, not to mention crowded. With scores of vacationers in countless new condo developments, and curious

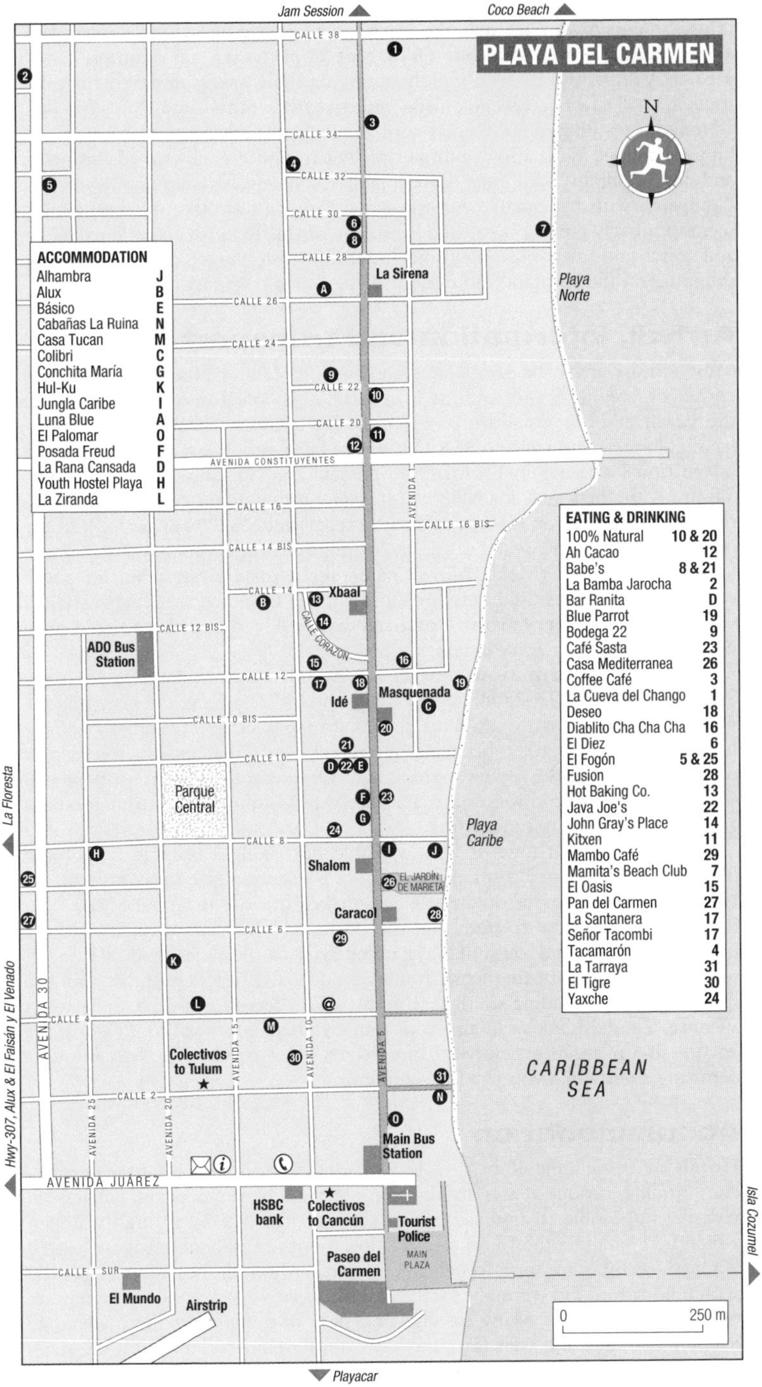
PLAYA DEL CARMEN
Jam Session
Coco Beach
La Floresta
Hwy-307, Alux & El Faisán y El Venado
Isla Cozumel
Playacar
CALLE 38
CALLE 34
CALLE 32
CALLE 30
CALLE 28
CALLE 26
CALLE 24
CALLE 22
CALLE 20
AVENIDA CONSTITUYENTES
CALLE 16
CALLE 16 BIS
CALLE 14 BIS
CALLE 14
CALLE 12 BIS
CALLE CORAZÓN
CALLE 12
CALLE 10 BIS
CALLE 10
CALLE 8
CALLE 6
CALLE 4
CALLE 2
AVENIDA JUÁREZ
CALLE 1 SUR
AVENIDA 1
AVENIDA 5
AVENIDA 10
AVENIDA 15
AVENIDA 20
AVENIDA 25
AVENIDA 30
La Sirena
Playa Norte
Xbaal
ADO Bus Station
Idé
Masquenada
Parque Central
Playa Caribe
Shalom
EL JARDÍN DE MARIETA
Caracol
Colectivos to Tulum
CARIBBEAN SEA
Main Bus Station
HSBC bank
Colectivos to Cancún
Tourist Police
Paseo del Carmen
MAIN PLAZA
El Mundo
Airstrip
0
250 m
ACCOMMODATION
Alhambra J
Alux B
Básico E
Cabañas La Ruina N
Casa Tucan M
Colibri C
Conchita María G
Hul-Ku K
Jungla Caribe I
Luna Blue A
El Palomar O
Posada Freud F
La Rana Cansada D
Youth Hostel Playa H
La Ziranda L
EATING & DRINKING
100% Natural 10 & 20
Ah Cacao 12
Babe's 8 & 21
La Bamba Jarocha 2
Bar Ranita D
Blue Parrot 19
Bodega 22 9
Café Sasta 23
Casa Mediterranea 26
Coffee Café 3
La Cueva del Chango 1
Deseo 18
Diablito Cha Cha Cha 16
El Diez 6
El Fogón 5 & 25
Fusion 28
Hot Baking Co. 13
Java Joe's 22
John Gray's Place 14
Kitxen 11
Mambo Café 29
Mamita's Beach Club 7
El Oasis 15
Pan del Carmen 27
La Santanera 17
Señor Tacombi 17
Tacamarón 4
La Tarraya 31
El Tigre 30
Yaxche 24

cruiseshippers from Cozumel, the town's main centre of activity – Avenida 5, a long, pedestrianized strip one block back from the sea – is often packed to capacity. Visitors can be seen rapidly emptying their wallets in pavement cafés, souvenir and silver-jewellery outlets and designer clothes shops.

Nonetheless, Playa does retain a cool atmosphere, with traces of its roots as a hippie hangout. With a high number of Italian- and French-owned businesses and no buildings over four storeys tall, it's relatively tastefully developed. Compared with hyperactive, Americanized Cancún just 60km to the north, it seems positively cosmopolitan and calm. The **nightlife** in particular is excellent, and you'll find sophisticated cuisine, hotels for most budgets and the best chic shopping on the Yucatán. And of course, the beach is splendid.

Arrival, information and transport

Most visitors arrive on short-haul buses at the central **bus station**, on the corner of Avenida 5 and Avenida Juárez, the main street from the highway to the beach. (Another station, on Avenida 20, between calles 12 and 12 bis, handles longer-haul trips on ADO.) If you're heading to Playa directly from the international **airport** in Cancún, the Riviera bus (11 daily, 9.30am–8.30pm; 55min) is the best deal, for M$80. Otherwise, any number of private minibus operators will take you directly to your hotel (about M$200 per person). At the main bus station, there is short-term **luggage storage** (from M$10/hr) and longer-term lockers (M$50/24hr). There's also a small **airstrip** on the south edge of town, but it's used only for short hops to Cozumel or Chichén Itzá. If you're coming by **ferry from Cozumel**, you will be dropped at the old plaza near Calle 1 Sur (for ferry details, see box, p.117).

The **tourist information centre**, on Avenida Juárez at Avenida 15 (daily 9am–9pm; ⓣ984/873-2804, ⓔturismo@solidaridad.gob.mx), is very helpful, with a multilingual staff who'll do their best to answer any questions you may have. Look in upmarket bars and restaurants for *La Quinta*, a free glossy magazine detailing the town's trendier side. Online, you can plan for your trip or get news on upcoming events at ⓦwww.playa.info, ⓦwww.intheroo.com and ⓦwww.playamayanews.com.

The central area of town is very walkable, but riding a **bicycle** is easy and pleasant, and a bike path runs along Avenida 10. You can hire **taxis** from stands on Avenida 5, or flag one down on the trafficked streets – it's about M$20 from the central bus station to hotels on the north side. To reach smaller towns or beaches just north and south of Playa, **colectivos** are the easiest option: Cancún service (M$30) departs frequently from Avenida Juárez just west of the main bus station, and vans heading south to Tulum (M$25) leave from Calle 2, between avenidas 5 and 10. Taxis can also take you anywhere you need to go along the coast – they're more expensive than colectivos, but far cheaper than any tour company, even when you pay for waiting time.

Accommodation

Hotels are being built all the time in Playa del Carmen, so you'll have no difficulty finding a room. Prices are dropping because of competition, but it's still virtually impossible to find something for less than M$350 in high season – which here includes the European vacation months of July and August, as well as mid-December to April. In general, the further from the sea, the cheaper the accommodation. The central beach is a little narrow, so waterfront hotels are often not good value. Many are also in a state of disrepair, as the owners are happy to sit back and wait for a buyout from developers. Hotels on the main drag, Avenida 5, can be a rough place to sleep due to the bars, but noise from construction is also an issue, especially on the growing north side – if you're sensitive to noise, ask the hotel about nearby projects and request an interior room or pack earplugs. The town has several decent budget hotels, and two places with space for **camping**: the beachfront *Cabañas La Ruina* (M$100) and *Youth Hostel Playa* (M$65).

Hotels

Alhambra On the beach at C 8 ⓣ984/873-0735, ⓦwww.alhambra-hotel.net. This gleaming-white, Moorish-style structure isn't what you'd expect in Playa, but it's one of the best-value hotels on the beach. Some of the equally white rooms are a bit small, but you'll be out on the beach, at the daily yoga classes or getting a massage at the spa. Rates include full breakfast. 8

Alux C 14, between Av 10 and Av 15 ⓣ984/803-2482, ⓦwww.hotelalux.com. *Alux* is a little frumpy, like its downtown Cancún counterpart, but it's also a good deal. A/c is optional, and some rooms have kitchenettes. 5

Básico Av 5 at C 10 ⓣ984/879-4448, ⓦwww.hotelbasico.com. Cool industrial design meets an equally cool clientele – the rooftop pools (converted water tanks) and bar are a hot spot. Rooms have fun details (Polaroid cameras, neon lighting) and floor-to-ceiling windows. Look for the same owners' *Deseo* hotel, at C 12: it has an equally sharp style and is marginally quieter. 9

Casa Tucan C 4, between Av 10 and Av 15 ⓣ984/873-0283, ⓦwww.casatucan.de. A Playa institution, this is still one of its best bargains. Offers basic rooms (some with palapa roofs and shared bath) and excellent-value studios, a big swimming pool, a friendly restaurant and a generally mellow vibe. Book in advance. 6

Colibri Av 1, between C 10 and C 12 ⓣ984/803-1090, ⓦwww.hotel-colibri.com. A beachfront hotel popular with divers that is relatively affordable and well maintained. The cheapest cabaña rooms have palapa roofs, so noise from Calle 12 is an issue; standard rooms have high (solid) ceilings and private terraces. The hotel's own bar shuts down at 8pm, keeping the property fairly calm. 7

Conchita María Av 5, between C 8 and C 10 ⓣ984/873-2336, ⓔhotelconchitamaria@hotmail.com. Surprising budget operation on a prime block – fifteen fan-only rooms, a couple with a small kitchenette and terrace. Top-floor rooms are best, though they're reached by an alarming railing-free staircase. 5

Hul-Ku Av 20 no. 150, between C 4 and C 6 ⓣ984/873-0021, ⓦwww.hotelhulku.com. The slightly remote location is made up for by a very nice pool and shady grounds with hammocks slung around. Rooms all have balconies and plenty of space, though furniture can be a little bit saggy and corners dusty. Nonetheless, excellent amenities for the price. 6

Jungla Caribe Av 5 at C 8 ⓣ984/873-0650, ⓦwww.jungla-caribe.com. On a prime corner on La Quinta, this hotel is nonetheless serene inside, thanks to a shady courtyard (so overgrown, in fact, you can hardly see the pool). Stairs trimmed in black-and-white tiles ascend like an Escher etching to large, cool rooms that are done in a similarly crisp style. It's clean, a little quirky and a bargain in the off season, when rates drop by half. 7

Luna Blue C 26, between Av 5 and Av 10 ⓣ984/873-0990, ⓦwww.lunabluehotel.com. Relatively far from the noisy fray, yet still handy for the beach, *Luna Blue* is built around a central garden with tall palms and other shady trees. Each room has a curvy, palapa-covered terrace, white-washed walls and lots of windows. The American owners are exceptionally helpful. 6

Posada Freud Av 5, between C 8 and C 10 ⓣ984/873-0601, ⓦwww.posadafreud.com. A bit of a hippie holdover: pretty rooms with colourful details smack in the middle of the action at reasonable (and often negotiable) rates. Ground-floor rooms can be loud – it may be worth opting for a back, upstairs room, or if you have a big group, the three-bedroom penthouse. 6

La Rana Cansada C 10 no. 132, between Av 5 and Av 10 ⓣ984/873-0389, ⓦwww.ranacansada.com. One of the oldest hotels in Playa, *La Rana* is friendly, sparkling clean and laid-back. It has communal kitchen facilities and various room options, including a smart two-level suite with beer delivery by bucket from the bar downstairs. Optional a/c. 6

La Ziranda C 4, between C 15 and C 20 ⓣ984/873-3929, ⓦwww.hotellaziranda.com. Spacious, simple rooms are done up in soothing monochromes, each with a private balcony. Thanks to the surrounding greenery, some are so shady that you won't need the optional a/c. A solid bargain and seldom full. 6

Hostels

Cabañas La Ruina C 2 at the beach ⓣ984/873-0405. Playa's most sociable and economical place to stay, still giving backpackers a slice of the good life on the beach despite large hotels looming all around. That said, the really desirable cabañas are comparable in price to regular hotels. ❹

El Palomar Av 5, between Av Juárez and C 2 ⓣ984/873-0144, ⓦwww.elpalomarhostel.com. A bit tidier than *La Ruina*, and still close to the beach, this hostel has the advantage of sand-free floors and big, well-ventilated single-sex dorm rooms (M$120). A few private rooms (❺) have shared baths. There's a communal kitchen on the roof deck.

Youth Hostel Playa Av 25 at C 8 ⓣ984/803-3277, ⓦwww.hostelplaya.com. Cheap, comfortable beds (M$135) and space for camping – though a trek from the beach. Head here if there's no room at *La Ruina* or *El Palomar*, or if you just want a quieter atmosphere. At M$215 per person, private rooms aren't a great deal.

The Town

Avenida 5, called La Quinta, is Playa del Carmen's main tourist thoroughfare. Once a dirt track dotted with a few cabañas, it's now a pedestrian zone stretching 2km north from Avenida Juárez and inching northward every year. It's lined with cocktail lounges, souvenir shops and stylish restaurants, and there's even a tiny Maya **ruin** hidden between the storefronts – look off the south side of La Quinta near Calle 14.

The big local hangouts are the terraced **main plaza** at the end of Avenida Juárez – one corner of which is dedicated to the **Capilla de Nuestra Señora del Carmen**, an attractive modern structure with rustic wood ceiling beams – and the **Parque Central** in front of the town hall on Avenida 20, between calles 8 and 10. This concrete slab has a small amphitheatre that occasionally hosts theatre and musical performances (check with the tourist office if anything's going on). To one side of the park, six stelae are inscribed with the verses of the "Himno de Quintana Roo", an ode to the fledgling state's pioneer spirit and its role as a refuge for the indigenous Maya – very inspiring, but really, all the attention is on the skateboarders who cruise the curving ramps here.

The beaches

One block east of La Quinta, the main **town beach** is a bit narrow and dotted with boats. As a result, there's not a lot of room for lounge chairs – each hotel has a few – or even your towel if you choose to lay out on your own. There are quite a few bars and restaurants, though, and operators offering parasailing, snorkelling or catamaran trips (2hr; M$300 per person). Serious tanners usually head to the better beach at **Playa Norte**, a broad expanse of deep, silky sand that drops into waist-high green water with mid-size swells, which lies to the north, past Avenida Constituyentes. Two beach clubs – *Mamita's* and *Kool by Tukan Beach* – rent acres of chairs, umbrellas and even lounge beds, and serve food and drinks. You can also wander further up the shore and stake out your own spot in the untended areas, or press even further north to the point, called Coco Beach, where there's a casual bar and usually kayaks for rent.

For anyone interested in **scuba diving**, Tank-Ha, on Avenida 5, between calles 8 and 10 (ⓣ984/873-0302, ⓦwww.tankha.com), is a good place to start. The shop offers PADI certification courses, one- and two-tank dives (US$40–70) and twice-daily snorkelling tours (9am & 1.30pm; 3hr; US$40). **Kiteboarding** specialists Ikarus give basic instruction on the beach in Playa, then take you up or down the coast for in-water lessons; visit the shop on Avenida 5 at Calle 20 (ⓣ984/803-3490, ⓦwww.kiteboardmexico.com) for details.

Playacar

The south side of Playa del Carmen abuts a giant, 880-acre condo development called **Playacar**. Its main road is Avenida Xaman-Ha, which winds its

Yucatán food

"The Land of the Pheasant and the Deer" – as the Maya call the Yucatán peninsula – is a bounteous place to eat. For millennia, the forest has augmented the basic diet of corn and beans with turkey, game meats, wild greens and luscious fruits. Locals have also embraced European products: pork, of course, but also Dutch cheese and novel spices. And the sea provides fresh ingredients, too, from succulent shrimp to enormous fish. It's all served up in a distinctive regional cuisine that's both earthy and delicate, not to mention delicious, from breakfast till late-night.

Habañero peppers ▲

Freshly made salsas ▼

Vegetables at a market, Chetumal ▼

The Yucatán table

Yucatecan tables are often full before you even order: a bottle of commercial hot sauce such as Yucateco is standard, plus bowls of gloriously pink pickled onions, grilled and pickled habañero peppers (the peninsula's most potent chile) and a raw chopped salsa of tomato, onion, cilantro (coriander leaves) and more habañero. That's what gives the salsa the name *xnipek*, Maya for "dog's nose", because it will make you sweat.

When the food arrives, though, you'll find none of it is innately spicy. It is, however, colourful: annatto lends a lurid orange stain to dishes like *tikin-xic* (pronounced "TIK-in sheek"), fish wrapped in banana leaves, and *poc-chuc*, pork marinated in juice from the locally grown bitter orange. Food here can also be **staggeringly rich**. The Yucatecans embraced such European exotica as Dutch Edam cheese and concocted some of the world's first fusion food: *queso relleno*, a round of cheese hollowed out and filled with a delectable mix of beef, olives and raisins. On a less exotic note, Yucatecans are strangely

Salsa style

A vital guide to the quality of a restaurant is its salsa – not just the standard condiments like pickled onions and *xnipek*, but also the **cooked salsas**, which can either be red (made with dried chiles) or green (with tomatillos). Grubby bowls refilled with canned supermarket product usually mean the place takes little pride in its food. But a good *casero* (home-cooking) operation will offer a freshly made salsa in a pretty dish. Look for little flecks of black in the mix – these indicate someone took the time to roast the ingredients, which adds a much deeper flavour.

Chaya: the miracle weed

Yucatecan cuisine doesn't involve a lot of vegetables, except for one staple: chaya. Yucatecans use the leaves from the hardy, towering bushes at every meal, starting with an invigorating (and brilliantly coloured) **chaya-pineapple juice** for breakfast. And no wonder – aside from the small catch that it's toxic when eaten raw, it's incredibly healthful. Though its flavour is usually compared with spinach, it trumps that green as a source of iron, calcium, protein and vitamins A and B. Locals swear by it as a cure for everything from diabetes to obesity to bad skin. Rarely has something so healthy also been so tasty.

enamoured with **mayonnaise**, which may or may not be a legacy of French fads in the nineteenth century.

Local ingredients are just as essential. Pumpkin seeds lend a nutty, creamy note to the sauce that douses *papadzules*, tortillas filled with hard-boiled egg. Shredded **turkey** (a bird the ancient Maya domesticated) adds body to the refreshing *sopa de lima*, a citrus-scented broth, and it tops *panuchos*, the small rounds of fried *masa* (the maize paste used for tortillas) that are as popular as tacos for an evening snack. Seafood has been an intrinsic part of the diet, too, and its preparation is usually simpler. Fish is either just fried whole, or diced and mixed with lime juice to make a ceviche.

Wash it all down with a shot of *xtabentun*, a honey-flavoured liqueur allegedly first distilled by the ancient Maya. Or opt for a fresh fruit juice – whatever time of year you visit, something delicious will be in season.

▲ Mayonnaise has a hold in the Yucatán

▼ Fruit juice vendor, Valladolid

▼ Panuchos, a popular Yucatecan snack

Making corn tortillas ▲

Woman at a market, Cancún ▼

Señor Tacombi, a taco-vending VW bus ▼

The Tabasco table

Tabasqueño cuisine is markedly different from Yucatecan food, dictated by the state's proximity to **rivers and the sea**. Locals revere, first and foremost, the alarming-looking *pejelagarto*, a long, skinny gar with nasty teeth; the big ones can be more than a metre long. It's a fresh-water fish, usually plucked straight from the Grijalva river, with a distinctly muddy taste that you'll either love or hate. Served as a cold ceviche-style salad, the flavour is actually nicely offset by bright lime juice and red onions. It's also often packed into deep-fried empanadas, to good effect. Also look out for hearty *chilpachole* – a spicy seafood stew, served with crab claws in season – and anything featuring passionfruit (*maracuya*).

You'll discover that in Tabasco, a good restaurant won't serve you the standard tortilla chips to start. Instead, you'll get a basket of thin fried patties made of plantain mash, starchy and a tiny bit sweet. It's all accented with a distinctive salsa made with **chiltepin chile peppers**. Tiny and green, they look deceptively like capers, but pack a serious punch.

The Chiapas table

Chiapanecos eat a huge range of things. Their diet varies depending on what valley or mountain town they live in, and what ethnic group they belong to. On menus, you can pick out regional goodies because they often start with *t-* or *tl-*. One great example is a cold drink called *tascalate*, a frothy blend of **chocolate** (a regional product), pine nuts, vanilla and sugar. Coffee from the Chiapas highlands is also worth trying. Cafés are getting better at preparing it to European tastes, though locals prefer it brewed weaker and spiced with cinnamon.

▲ Fruit vendors on the main plaza in Playa del Carmen

way southward from the entrance off Calle 1 Sur, with cul-de-sacs leading to beach properties, tennis courts and more than fifteen remnants of small Maya structures; some are marked with signs off the main artery. Playacar's beaches, if they're not fronting a big resort, are often deserted, and the lightly trafficked streets are a good place for a shady bike ride. An **aviary** on Avenida Xaman-Ha (daily 9am–5pm; US$15) is overpriced, but offers an opportunity to check out some sixty species of native birds, including toucans and flamingos. If you won't otherwise have a chance to see them in the southern jungles or on the Gulf coast, it's worth going. From Playacar, you can walk up to town in 45 minutes or half an hour, depending on where you're starting from; taxis cost M$40 or so.

Eating

Playa del Carmen practically bursts with **restaurants** of every kind, and even some of the traditional Mexican places here stay open late. The quality of food is often very good (particularly at the Italian and Argentine places), with correspondingly high prices. **Avenida 5** is lined with dining tables where you can eat all sorts of cuisine – but if you're on a **budget** you'll need to search out where locals go, like the excellent taco carts and fruit vendors on the plaza by the bus station or the inexpensive *comida corrida* and grilled-chicken places starting around Avenida 10 and going further back from the sea. One warning: the turn-over in restaurants in Playa is so high as to make a guidebook writer despair; many of these places may have closed by the time you go looking for them. The good news is that new places will have opened. For interesting developments, try the northern reaches of Avenida 5.

Cafés

Ah Cacao Av 5 at Av Constituyentes. If you prefer your caffeine in the form of chocolate, come to this hip little café for hot and cold cocoa-based drinks, plus truffles, ice cream and Mexican cacao nibs to go (a delicious souvenir). There's also espresso for traditionalists.

Café Sasta Av 5, between C 8 and C 10. Pastries and espresso are the main items at this Italian coffeehouse, and the sidewalk tables are an ideal spot for watching the fashion parade along La Quinta.

La Cueva del Chango C 38, between Av 5 and the beach. Tables are scattered in a big garden filled with birds and a little stream at this outdoor café. It serves till 11pm, but it's a local favourite especially for long, late breakfasts. The menu includes tasty empanadas and crepes with honey, starting at around M$50, and house-roasted coffee. Closes at 2pm Sun.

La Floresta West side of Hwy-307, just north of Av Juárez. This big palapa next to the highway is a road-tripper's delight, serving overstuffed *tacos de camarón*, the perfect marriage of batter-fried shrimp, mayo and chunky tomato salsa. Should you need variety, seafood cocktails and ceviches are available, too.

Hot Baking Co. C 12 bis, between Av 5 and Av 10. Bakery café with muffins, bagels slathered with cream cheese and giant cinnamon rolls. Those with heartier appetites can choose from omelettes and grilled sandwiches (M$50 and up).

Java Joe's C 10, between Av 5 and Av 10. Caffeine junkies stumble to this open-sided coffee bar first thing in the late morning or early afternoon – the regulars are party-happy expats, and the brew is super-strong.

Pan del Carmen Av 30 at C 6. Pick up inexpensive bread, sweet and savoury *hojaldres* (stuffed puff pastry) and *pan dulce* at this fragrant Mexican bakery that's usually well stocked throughout the day.

Señor Tacombi C 12, between Av 5 and Av 10. Clubbers flock to this 24-hour taco vendor built in a groovy VW bus – you'll pay more, but the variety is good, and its breakfast combos are tasty, too.

Restaurants

100% Natural Av 5, between C 10 and C 12. Like the Cancún branch (see p.78), this link in the local mini-chain serves fresh, often vegetarian Mexican food along with big stuffed sandwiches and fresh fruit juices. Not the cheapest, but reliable and set in a big garden. Second branch on Av 5 at C 22.

Babe's C 10, between Av 5 and Av 10. This Swedish-owned Thai noodle house – which also serves a fine Cuban mojito – typifies Playa's international hodgepodge. Dishes like pad thai start at M$90 for a huge portion. An outpost on Av 5 at C 28 has a longer menu.

La Bamba Jarocha Av 30 at C 36. Savour super-fresh ceviche, seafood soup and shrimp *cocktel* in a non-gringo atmosphere. The place is very popular for long business lunches. Look for the beaded curtains on the doors.

Bodega 22 C 22, between Av 5 and Av 10. The bulk of the menu at this cheerful side-street restaurant is vegetarian, with Italian-meets-Mexican flavours. Main dishes start at M$80, and there's a bargain M$65 *comida* for lunch. There's just enough meat to keep carnivores from panicking.

Casa Mediterranea Av 5, between C 6 and C 8. Tucked inside the Jardín del Marieta, this modest little trattoria (there are only about six seats) does toothsome fresh pasta, such as fettuccine with shrimp and squash, for M$100 and up. Unpretentious and delicious.

El Faisán y El Venado C 2, just east of Hwy-307. Very well-priced Yucatecan specialities such as *panuchos* and *carne ahumada* (smoked pork in a citrus marinade) are the draw at this sprawling family-friendly restaurant. Lunch only.

El Fogón Av 30 at C 6 bis. Follow your nose to this basic, brightly lit taco joint that specializes in grilled meat. Big appetites can go for the Taco Loco; throw in an order of *cebollas cambray* (grilled green onions) as well. There's another branch on Av 30 at C 32.

John Gray's Place C Corazón, west of Av 5, between C 12 and C 14 ⓣ984/803-3689. A classy restaurant that, like the original in Puerto Morelos (see p.106), has a simple but consistently satisfying menu, with items like spinach salad and grilled fish with mango salsa. The cosy bar and lounge on the ground floor is great on its own – try the "smoky margarita" made with mescal.

Kitxen Av 5, between Av Constituyentes and C 20. As much a bar as a restaurant, this cool space is owned by a member of legendary Mexican rock group Los Jaguares, so there's often live bands to accompany your meal, which could be anything from a curry-chicken burger to a big vegetarian spread.

El Oasis C 12, between Av 5 and Av 10. *El Oasis* earned its reputation selling shrimp tacos out by the highway, but this new branch has a fuller menu of seafood dishes. The tacos (M$15) aren't quite as good as *La Floresta*'s, but they're the best you can get around La Quinta. Closed Sun.

Tacamarón Av 10 at C 32. The huge shrimp tacos (M$49) at this graffiti-adorned corner café aren't the usual batter-fried snacks, but are sautéed with spices and cheese and rolled in a flour tortilla. If that's too pricey, get one of the many tasty rice dishes (M$39 and up), like the arroz samm.

La Tarraya On the seafront at C 2. A local institution that has been open for more than thirty years, well before Playa was even a gleam in a developer's eye. It still serves standard beach fare like ceviches and *pescado frito* (M$90 per kilo) with plenty of cold beer.

Yaxche C 8, between Av 5 and Av 10 ⓣ984/873-2502. Haute Maya is the agenda at this gracious restaurant: (very) hot peppers stuffed with *cochinita pibil* (shredded roast pork), a Yucatecan shrimp gratin or lobster flambéed in *xtabentun*, a local liqueur. With entrees between M$120 and M$210, it's very reasonably priced, considering the level of service and presentation.

Drinking and nightlife

At night, La Quinta becomes one long street party, and you can find any sort of music in the array of **bars**, though most people will wind up around the intersection with Calle 12, which has the highest concentration of cool **clubs** and **lounges**. If you're looking for a mellower atmosphere, head north of Calle 16, even as far up as Calle 40. Drinks aren't always cheap, but don't let that stop you from going out, as it's easy to meet people, and happy-hour specials can ease you into the night without depleting funds too rapidly.

Bars

Bar Ranita C 10, between Av 5 and Av 10. A crew of regulars – mostly expats – hang out around the horseshoe-shaped bar. Unless there's a live band wedged into the small space, it's a mellow scene and a welcome break from other top-volume places.

Blue Parrot On the beach at C 12. This open-air bar has weathered decades of change in Playa – as the beachfront gets condo-fied, it's the only place lit with torches and sporting rope swings instead of barstools. It has a popular happy hour (5–8pm), then attracts a crowd later in the night with assorted performers and musicians, and usually some dancing. No cover.

Coffee Café Av 5 at C 34. As the name implies, this is primarily a coffee bar, but with wine and beer available along with evening DJs, it can be a very mellow place to hang out at night.

Deseo Av 5 at C 12. The outdoor bar at the stylish hotel draws its inspiration from Miami Beach, with beds to lounge on, easy-on-the-eyes bartenders and classic Mexican films projected on the blank wall over the pool. Drinks are pricey (M$80), but this is the pinnacle of Playa style.

Diablito Cha Cha Cha C 12 at Av 1. Mexico-goes-rockabilly is the loose theme at this retro-cool lounge furnished with Formica tables and vinyl chairs. Fuel up on Asian snacks, or just go straight for the vanilla martinis.

El Diez Av 5 at C 30. A cosy Argentine bar that has all kinds of meaty snacks and pizza sold in big portions, plus beer taps at each table – a potentially dangerous technology. Look for the big numeral 10 on the sign.

Fusion C 6 at the beach. This mellow beach bar, lit by kerosene lamps with tables in the sand, is a great slice of old-fashioned, pre-club-scene Playa. However, it may not survive the adjacent hotel's slated renovations, so visit while you can.

El Tigre Av 10, between C 2 and C 4. Good local spot for beers, ceviches and ridiculously generous *botanas*. Women will probably feel more comfortable accompanied by a man; the billiards area upstairs is men-only. Closes by 5pm.

Clubs

Alux Av Juárez, 400m west of Hwy-307 ⓣ984/803-0713. A trek from the main drag – tell the cab driver "ah-LOOSH" – but worth a visit for its unique setting deep inside a large cave. Dinner of rich, if somewhat overpriced, French-tropical dishes begins at 8pm; a DJ or a floor show of belly dancers and jazz musicians gets started around 10pm. Usually no cover, but drinks are M$70 and up.

Jam Session Av 5 at C 40. At this club hidden away at the north end of the strip, a house band plays blues, jazz and whatever else strikes their fancy, sometimes joined by visiting musicians. If you're feeling overwhelmed by the party scene down by Calle 12, this is a much mellower alternative. Wed–Sat 9am–2pm, Sun 6pm–2am.

Mambo Café C 6, between Av 5 and Av 10 ⓣ984/803-2656. Small salsa club, but with excellent sound and a roster of big-name Cuban and Dominican bands that attracts locals as well as tourists. Cover is usually M$50. Closed Mon.

Mamita's Beach Club On the beach at C 28. The single coolest place to be during the day, with plenty of room to spread out and a hip but not overbearing party atmosphere, complete with a live DJ. Chairs and umbrellas are for rent, but you can spread a towel at the water's edge and still get waiter service for drinks if you like; the food is very good (if a tad pricey). The smaller lounge on the northern edge often stays open into the evening, and occasionally hosts blowout nighttime dance parties.

La Santanera C 14, between Av 5 and Av 10. A super-stylish club with international DJ cred (Rob Garza of global mixmasters Thievery Corporation is a partner) that combines a comfortable, breezy lounge area with diverse music and good strong drinks. The scantily clad party crowd – equal parts visitors and residents – usually staggers out around 5am. No cover.

Shopping

Of all the beach towns, Playa offers the most stylish **shopping**, from folk art to designer flip-flops, though very little of it is cheap. You'll also find the usual pharmacies and giant souvenir marts – generally, shops get more specialized and interesting the further north you go. Prices are fixed at glossier places on La Quinta, but sometimes you can bargain in smaller shops on side streets.

Caracol Av 5, between C 6 and C 8. Richly coloured scarves, meticulous embroidery and other textiles are the main stock at this shop that collects excellent work from Mexico and Guatemala. Don't miss the flat-weave rugs upstairs.

Casita de la Música Av 5, between Av Juárez and C 2. Ignore the standard souvenirs – look instead at the third of the shop devoted to CDs of the latest Mexican pop hits, as well as a decent selection of traditional Yucatecan *trova* ballads and folk music from around Mexico.

Idé Av 5, between C 10 and C 12. Very creative, modern jewellery incorporating semiprecious stones, particularly opals. Pricier than other silver vendors, but the intricate work is unlike anything else in town.

El Jardín de Marieta Av 5, between C 6 and C 8. Look for the small stained-glass sign marking the entrance to this garden courtyard, where you'll find several excellent galleries and craft shops stocking fascinating contemporary paintings and ceramics from local artists, along with wood masks, beautiful weavings and a few gem antiques.

Paseo del Carmen Av 5 at C 1 Sur. Major attractions at this stylish open-air mall include hip Euro chains such as Pull & Bear and Bershka, as well as a few cool bars and lounges like Havana import *La Bodeguita del Medio*, specialising in mojitos.

Shalom Av 5, between C 6 and C 8. This cool boutique will get you dressed for clubbing, Playa-style, with lots of drapey, avant-garde pieces as well as fun, shiny disco duds. Much of the clothing is handmade or one-of-a-kind.

La Sirena Av 5 at C 26. A folk-art shop with all the usual Frida Kahlo-theme items, but one highlight is the selection of small, candy-colour paintings of Chihuahua dogs and Mexican wrestlers – excellent unique gift items.

Listings

Airlines Aeroméxico, ⓣ800/021-4010, or at Av Constituyentes Esq 4 ⓣ984/803-1212; Aviacsa, ⓣ800/AVIACSA, or at Av Constituyentes Manzana 112 ⓣ984/803-4294.

Banks HSBC, Av Juárez, between Av 10 and Av 15 (Mon–Fri 9am–7pm); Bancomer, Av Juárez, between Av 25 and Av 30 (Mon–Fri 9am–4pm); ScotiaBank, Av 5 immediately opposite the bus station. All have ATMs.

Books El Mundo, C 1 Sur, between Av 20 and Av 25, has a friendly and informed staff who are quick to make recommendations on English and Spanish titles alike. Excellent for Maya and Mexican history, or just good beach novels. Closed Sun.

Buses The distinction between Playa's two bus stations is somewhat fluid; typically, long-haul ADO-run trips go from Av 20, between C 12 and C 14, and short-haul services, including Riviera and Mayab buses, leave from the central station, Av Juárez at Av 5. Either way, you can buy tickets for all routes at the central station – just ask which terminal the bus will leave from. For schedules, see "Travel Details", p.131.

Car and bike rental All the large car rental companies have outlets in Playa – most are situated on the main coastal highway at the turn-off into town or in Plaza Marina near the Cozumel ferry pier at C 1 Sur. Try Localiza, Av Juárez, between Av 5 and Av 10 (ⓣ984/873-0580). Isla Bicycleta, C 8 at Av 10 (ⓣ984/879-4992, ⓦwww.playadelcarmenbikes.com), rents mountain and road bikes (US$10/day, US$16/24hr), as well as snorkel gear (US$5/day).

The ferry to Cozumel

Two competing **passenger ferry** services depart from the pier at Calle 1 Sur in Playa del Carmen, for San Miguel in Cozumel, nearly every hour between 6am and 11pm. The prices are the same from both Mexico Waterjets and Ultramar (M$110), and the boats are roughly equivalent as well, so just pick whichever is departing soonest. If you're driving, you can park your car in the secure lot behind the Playa del Carmen bus station for about M$90 per day. Returning to Playa, the ferries depart Cozumel hourly, 5am–10pm.

Transbordadores del Caribe (℡987/872-7688, Ⓦwww.transcaribe.com.mx) operates a **car ferry** to Cozumel from Puerta Calica (also called Punta Venado), 7km south of Playa del Carmen. Immediately past the entrance for Xcaret, follow signs for Calica – there is no indication of the ferry on the highway. It runs seven times Monday to Saturday (4am–6pm) and twice on Sunday (6am & 6pm), with a crossing time of about 1hr 15min; at M$550 per car (with one driver) and an additional M$60 per passenger, it's worthwhile only if you'll be staying on the island more than a few days. Departures from Cozumel back to Calica are between 6am and 8.30pm (8am & 8pm on Sun).

Cinema Cines Hollywood in Plaza Pelicanos, Av 10 at C 10.
Colectivos Vans for Cancún depart from Av Juárez just west of the bus station; for Tulum, from C 2, between Av 5 and Av 10. They run very frequently, from early morning till late-night.
Consulate US: C 1 Sur, between Av 15 and Av 20 ℡984/873-0303.
Internet and telephone The streets off Av 5 hold numerous Internet cafés; one on C 4, between Av 5 and Av 10, has good rates and doubles as a *caseta*. There's also a Telmex *caseta* on Av Juárez, between Av 10 and Av 15.
Laundry *Lavanderías* are scattered every other block on the side streets. Two are Giracaribe Laundry, on Av 10, between C 12 and C 14, and Lavandería Lua, on C 2, between Av 10 and Av 15.
Post office Av Juárez, between Av 15 and Av 20; geared to dealing with tourists. Mon–Fri 8am–2pm.

Xcaret

The huge, surprisingly pleasant and wild theme park of **XCARET** (Mon–Sat 8.30am–9.45pm, Sun 8.30am–6pm; Ⓦwww.xcaretcancun.com; US$69, kids US$34.50) is 6km south of Playa del Carmen. Budget travellers and anyone on a longer trip can pass it up, but if your time is limited or you have children to entertain, the park is an opportunity to experience all of the natural attractions of the Yucatán in one place, such as snorkelling through underground caverns or in a fish-filled bay. There's also a vast butterfly habitat, a cave full of bats, a high-tech aquarium and a sea turtle reserve and education centre. You can also catch a live dance performance or visit a "Maya village", complete with artisans working on traditional crafts. An open-air chapel on the park's highest hill offers respite from the crowds, as well as a fine view. Bus-and-entrance packages are available through every big hotel in Cancún and Playa del Carmen. All Mayab buses stop on request near Xcaret on Hwy-307, a ten-minute ride from Playa.

Isla Cozumel

A forty-kilometre-long island directly off the coast from Playa del Carmen, **ISLA COZUMEL** is far larger than Mujeres (see p.85) and has grown proportionately, particularly to cater to the mainstream tastes of the cruiseship passengers that come ashore here. Nearly every day, up to ten liners, each with

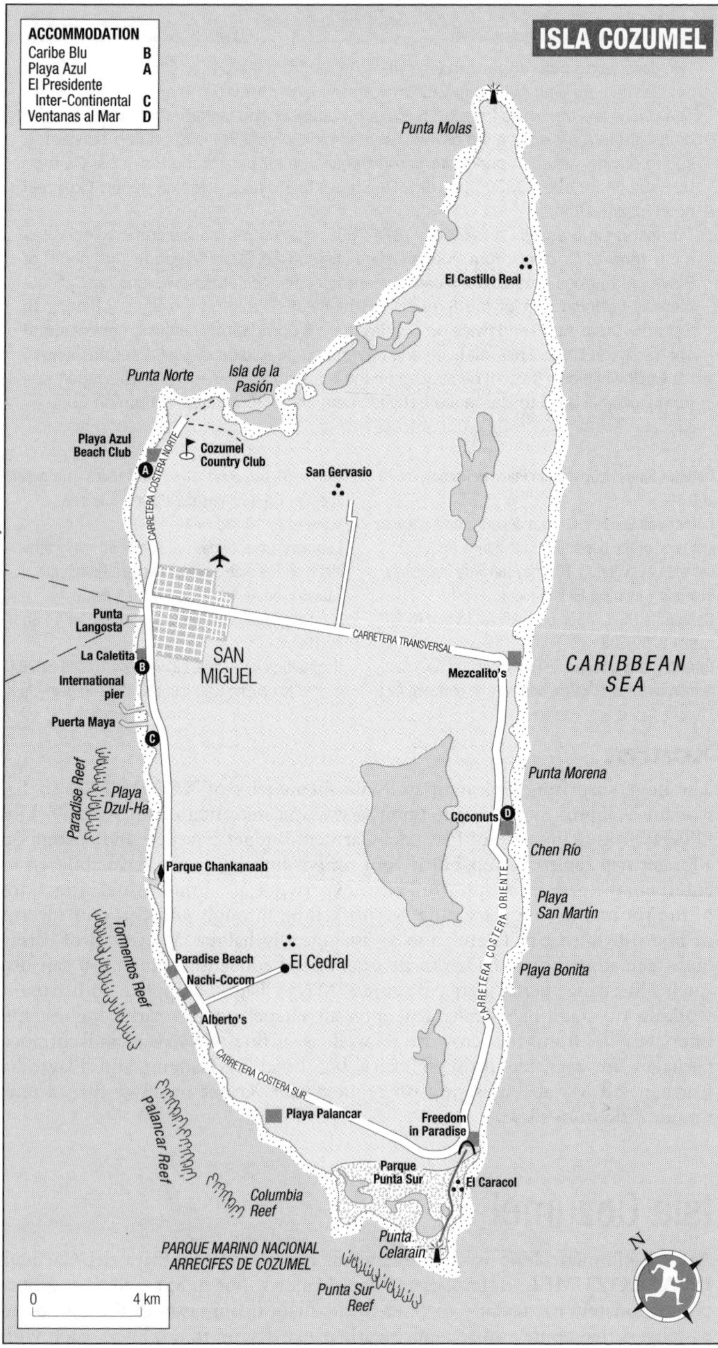
ISLA COZUMEL
ACCOMMODATION
Caribe Blu B
Playa Azul A
El Presidente Inter-Continental C
Ventanas al Mar D
Punta Molas
El Castillo Real
Punta Norte
Isla de la Pasión
Playa Azul Beach Club
Cozumel Country Club
San Gervasio
CARRETERA COSTERA NORTE
Playa del Carmen
Punta Langosta
CARRETERA TRANSVERSAL
La Caletita
SAN MIGUEL
International pier
Mezcalito's
CARIBBEAN SEA
Puerta Maya
Puerta Calica
Paradise Reef
Playa Dzul-Ha
Punta Morena
Coconuts
Chen Río
Parque Chankanaab
Playa San Martín
CARRETERA COSTERA ORIENTE
Tormentos Reef
Paradise Beach
El Cedral
Nachi-Cocom
Playa Bonita
Alberto's
CARRETERA COSTERA SUR
Playa Palancar
Freedom in Paradise
Palancar Reef
Parque Punta Sur
El Caracol
Columbia Reef
PARQUE MARINO NACIONAL ARRECIFES DE COZUMEL
Punta Celarain
Punta Sur Reef
0
4 km
N

several thousand passengers, dock at one of the island's three piers, all just south of the main town of **San Miguel** (often called simply "Cozumel"). As a result, the town's population of 70,000 comes close to doubling on the busiest cruise days in high season (the record is sixteen ships in one day).

But don't be put off by the hordes: even in San Miguel, it's easy to escape into the blocks further back from the sea. Or you can go underwater: the huge, diverse reefs that ring much of the coast offer the best diving in Mexico. These reefs have been dazzling visitors since Jacques Cousteau first brought them to international attention in the early 1960s. The island, which the Maya dubbed *cuzamil* ("land of the swallows"), is also a destination for birdwatchers, as it's a stopover on migration routes and has several endemic species. Parque Punta Sur, a nature park on the southern tip of the island, is a haven for many of the rarest birds. And the windswept eastern coast, with its deserted beaches and pounding waves, provides a beautiful solitary respite.

Some history

In the Terminal Classic period, the few centuries before the Spanish arrived in 1518, the island was a major Maya centre, carrying on sea trade around the coasts of Mexico and as far south as Honduras and perhaps Panama. While this community – one of several along the Yucatán coast that survived the collapse of Classic Maya civilization after 1200 – has long been dismissed by archeologists as the decadent remnant of a dying society, that theory has now been revised. The community's architecture might have declined in the years between 1200 and the Conquest, but large-scale trade, city specialization in particular crafts and even a degree of mass production are all in evidence at the site of **San Gervasio**, the only excavated ruins on the island. Cozumel's later Maya rulers did not wield power in the same grand style as their forebears, but the rest of an increasingly commercialized population was probably better off. The island itself may even have been an early free-trade zone, where merchants from competing cities could trade peaceably.

Whatever the truth, you get little opportunity to judge for yourself – an American air base, built here during World War II, erased all trace of Cozumel's largest ancient city, and the lesser ruins scattered across the roadless interior are mostly unrestored and inaccessible. (The airfield, converted to civilian use, remains the means by which most visitors arrive.)

After about 1600, Cozumel was virtually deserted, the territory of pirates with few settlers. In the mid-nineteenth century, though, as the bitter Caste Wars (see p.332) between the rebel Maya and the Spanish colonists made life on the peninsula highly dangerous and unstable, the island became a place of refuge, and by the 1880s, the town of **San Miguel** was established as a home for the growing population. Over the years, island culture has developed distinct from that of the mainland, with *cozumeleños* relishing their lifestyle, which is somehow even more easy going than on the rest of the coast. San Miguel hosts a particularly colourful celebration of **Carnaval**, the decadent week prior to Lent, with elaborate costumes, parades and exuberant bands and parties.

Arrival, information and transport

Arriving by ferry, you'll be right in the centre of San Miguel, with the plaza just across the street from the pier. From the **airport**, which is at the northeast edge of town (around Av 65), a shared-van service (M$47) makes the short drive into town. If you've come in on a **cruiseship**, you are either on the southern edge of town (at the Punta Langosta pier), or a four-kilometre walk or M$50 taxi ride away (from both the International and Puerta Maya piers). The handiest branch of the **tourist office** (8am–7pm) is in a kiosk on a plaza, straight ahead as you walk off the ferry, where you can get maps and brochures from the helpful staff.

San Miguel has been modernized and is easy enough to get around on foot – though if you're carrying substantial luggage, you'll probably want a **taxi** to get from the ferry dock to any hotel past Avenida 10. **Buses** run around town (M$5), but the only one you might use is the one that runs about once an hour to the beaches and hotels just north and south of town. Look for the northbound bus on Avenida 10, and the southbound on Avenida 15, but note that the majority that go by are for other routes within San Miguel. No buses serve the east side of the island, though, so to get further afield you'll have to go on a tour, take a taxi (fares are posted by the rank at the ferry pier) or rent a vehicle. **Mopeds** give you a bit more freedom, though roads can be dangerously slick in the rain and accidents are frequent. **Jeeps** are available from numerous outlets, but aren't really useful – rental contracts preclude your driving on dirt tracks. A convertible **VW Beetle** is the most popular **car** for tooling around the island, and can handle all the principal tourist routes. You can rent per day from any of the numerous *rentadoras* in the town centre: mopeds cost M$385, jeeps and cars around M$605. Prices vary little, and vendors aren't always into haggling; for cars, you can almost always do better by booking ahead online. **Cycling** is feasible in town, but not recommended down the north–south coast highways, as car traffic is fast and heedless, and hard shoulders are narrow; you could probably get to San Gervasio, if the wind isn't too strong. Rentadora Gallo, Avenida 10 no. 25, between Avenida Juárez and Calle 1 (☎987/869-2444), rents them for M$100 for a day, or M$165 for 24 hours (including a night).

Accommodation

Hotels in Cozumel are divided into two categories: expensive, usually all-inclusive resorts strung out along the coast on either side of San Miguel, and more affordable places in the town centre. Along the beach, the ones to the north require a taxi ride into town, while a few to the south are within walking distance from the action. The spots in town are preferable if you don't want to be isolated from the social scene or are on a budget, though sea views are overrated and overpriced, as they usually come with traffic noise from the **malecón** (San Miguel's seaside promenade) below. In town there is one good hostel option, a recent and welcome addition to the scene (see opposite).

San Miguel

Aguilar C 3 no. 98, between Av Melgar and Av 5 ☎987/872-0307, www.cozumel-hotels.net/aguilar. Quiet, slightly kitschy rooms (no shortage of plastic flowers here), all with a/c, and situated away from the road around a garden with a small pool. The location just two blocks south of the plaza is particularly convenient, and scooter and car hire are available. ❺

Amaranto C 5, between Av 15 and Av 20 ☎987/564-4262, www.tamarindoamaranto.com. Winding staircases and curving walls distinguish these three fanciful stucco palapas and two apartments stacked in a tile-trimmed tower. Rooms – all with fridge and microwave, most with a/c – are clustered around a cosy courtyard and small pool. ❻

Las Anclas Av 5 no. 325, between C 3 and C 5 ☎987/872-5476, www.lasanclas.com. A cluster of well-designed two-storey suites with kitchenettes, all spotless and perfectly maintained; each sleeps up to four with a queen-size bed upstairs and two day-beds downstairs (though the latter are best for kids). The water pressure is probably the best in the whole Yucatán, and a lush central garden makes the place feel extra welcoming. 8

Caribe C 2 no. 332, between Av 15 and Av 20 ⓣ987/872-4283. If you can take the shocking-pink exterior paint job (which doesn't extend to the pastel rooms, luckily), this is a pleasant enough mid-range option – thanks in part to all the flowers around the grounds – and the cheapest place with a pool. 6

Flamingo C 6, between Av Melgar and Av 5 ⓣ987/872-1264, ⓦwww.hotelflamingo.com. Popular with the scuba set, with a rooftop terrace and bar, and a Cuban-fusion restaurant that hosts live salsa bands. Guests can use the beach at Playa Azul. "Courtyard" rooms seem a little stark in comparison with the more stylish (and more expensive) "superior" ones, but they're perfectly functional. 7

Hostelito Av 10 no. 42, between Av Juárez and C 2 ⓣ987/869-8157, ⓔhostelitocozumelmx@gmail.com. Opened in 2007, Cozumel's only hostel is a welcome addition. Dorm beds in clean, fan-only rooms (with slightly cramped bathrooms) go for M$120; private rooms with a/c are also available. A great shared kitchen is an excellent amenity. 3–4

Marruang Av Salas 440, between Av 20 and Av 25 ⓣ987/872-1678. A bargain option if you want to get well away from San Miguel's tourist centre. Rooms are clean, with TVs and firm mattresses, and you can pick up snacks at the market directly across the street. 4

Pepita Av 15 no. 120 at C 1 ⓣ987/872-0098. By far the best of the budget options, with clean, attractive rooms with a/c and TV. Amenities include a pretty courtyard and complimentary coffee in the morning. 5

Posada Letty C 1, between Av 10 and Av 15 ⓣ987/872-0105. The eight rooms at this little hands-off rental operation are well kept – the white-walled rooms contrast with the lively paint jobs in the bathrooms, all done in Easter-basket pastels. 3

Saolima Av Salas 260, between Av 10 and Av 15 ⓣ987/872-0886. Basic and old-fashioned, but clean rooms, with optional a/c. Overall, it's pretty unremarkable, but along with *Posada Letty*, the only decent option in this price range. 3

Tamarindo B&B C 4 no. 421, between Av 20 and Av 25 ⓣ987/872-6190, ⓦwww.tamarindocozumel.com. At this French-owned B & B, rooms have cosy nooks and whimsical touches. Two of the five rooms share a kitchen, while two full suites have kitchenettes at a bargain rate of US$59 (but no breakfast). Full breakfast is otherwise included, and the owner's excellent cooking and island expertise put guests at ease. A/c is an option in some rooms. 5

Elsewhere on the island

Caribe Blu Carretera Costera Sur Km 2.2 ⓣ987/872-0188, ⓦwww.caribeblu.net. Very close to town, with the Blue Angel (an excellent dive shop) and shallow dive training right off the hotel's small beach. All rooms have sea views and private balconies; there's also a pool. 7

Playa Azul Carretera Costera Norte Km 4 ⓣ987/869-5160, ⓦwww.playa-azul.com. Swanky little resort on the best stretch of beach north of town, with fifty elegant sea-view rooms. Guests have access to a spa and gym, and several bars and restaurants; the pool is a bit small, however. Golf and dive packages are available, and rates dip significantly in the low season. 9

El Presidente Inter-Continental Carretera Costera Sur Km 6.5 ⓣ987/872-9500, ⓦwww.ichotelsgroup.com. The sharp-edged modernist design of Cozumel's first luxury hotel, built in 1969, can feel a little severe, but the setting is flawless, with a pretty protected beach and accessible snorkelling from the long pier. All rooms have sea views, and the spa offers lavish treatments. 9

Ventanas al Mar On the east coast, 5km south of *Mezcalito's* beach bar and the intersection with the Carretera Transversal ⓦwww.ventanasalmar.com.mx. This hotel – the only one on the east coast – is powered entirely by wind power. Bring groceries if you plan to stay a while (there's a two-night minimum): the giant rooms and the two-storey suites, which sleep four, have basic kitchenettes, as well as terraces overlooking the crashing surf. Guests get discounts at *Coconuts* restaurant next door, and rates include full breakfast. 7

San Miguel

The only major population centre on the island, **San Miguel** is clean and cheerful and a bit sprawling, with long blocks and low buildings, a few of which are little Caribbean-style clapboard houses that have somehow resisted decades of heavy weather. The primary drawback is that the wide seafront avenue, **Avenida Rafael Melgar**, is all too often a throng of day visitors traipsing from one duty-free diamond shop to the next, and you may be

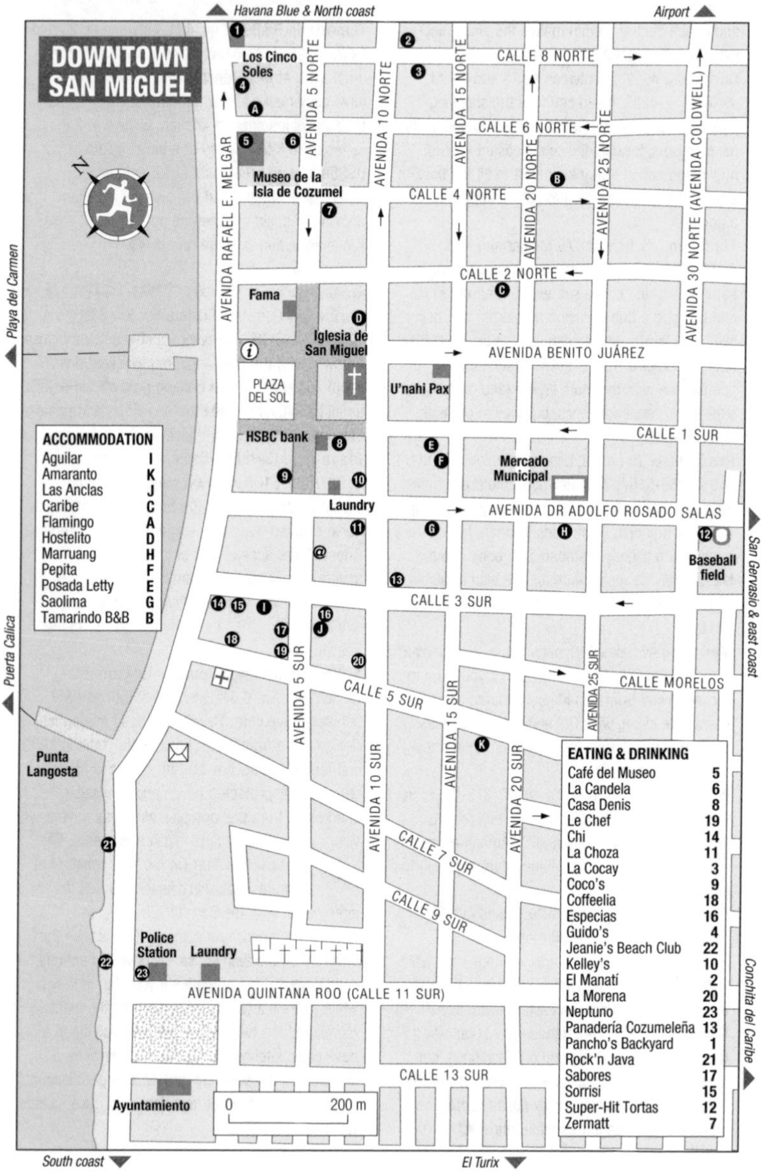

hassled by aggressive salespeople. The weekends, though, are blissfully quiet – no cruiseships generally stop on Cozumel on Sunday, and only a couple arrive on Saturday and Monday.

The town's large main square, the **Plaza del Sol**, stands directly opposite the ferry dock, dominated by a tall clock tower. The plaza is the hub of activity for tourists, though *cozumeleños* also come out on Sunday evenings, when there's live music. It's also popular to **stroll the malecón** (Avenida Melgar), which is graced with grand bronze statues commemorating Cozumel's Maya cultural heritage and long tradition of fishing.

On the malecón between calles 4 and 6, the attractive **Museo de la Isla de Cozumel** (daily 9am–5pm; M$33) has small exhibits on the flora and fauna of the island, its famous reef systems and its history from the Maya era to the present. You'll also see a good collection of Maya artefacts and old photos showing the colourful culture of Cozumel, all labelled in both English and Spanish. In the back on the ground floor, a traditional Maya hut is staffed by a friendly and informative local who will explain (primarily in Spanish) the uses of the various foodstuffs, herbs and accoutrements lying about. Overall, the place is a concise introduction to the primary points of Yucatán history. It occasionally hosts live music and theatre events, and there's a nice café upstairs (see p.128).

San Miguel's name was chosen in the late 1800s, when construction workers unearthed a large, richly adorned statue of St Michael. Research suggests that the statue dates from the early sixteenth century, when Spanish explorer Juan de Grijalva likely brought it to the island as a gift for the native Maya. The discovery inspired townspeople to take San Miguel as their patron saint, and to build the **Iglesia de San Miguel** on the site where the statue was found, one block off the plaza at the corner of avenidas Juárez and 10. The statue of the winged archangel brandishing his sword is still on display on the church altar; Sunday Mass is at 7am, 9am, 6pm and 8pm.

Continuing inland past the church, the town gets more diverse – and affordable. Avenida Coldwell (Avenida 30) is lined with a number of inexpensive restaurants and bars, as well as the main town **baseball field** (at Avenida Salas), which hosts games throughout the summer. The **central market**, on Avenida Salas, between avenidas 20 and 25, is another outlying sight, where the produce and butcher stalls tucked under a high tin roof seem to belong to a completely different town, in contrast to the T-shirt shops around Plaza del Sol. Here you can also find colourful, inexpensive kitchen equipment, bargain lunch counters and juice bars.

The rest of the island

Beyond San Miguel, only a few roads extend across the island. Immediately to the **north** is a small hotel zone. With pleasant sandy **beaches**, it's the best place to go swimming close to town. On the coast road heading **south** from San Miguel, you pass additional hotels; the reef comes very close to shore here, making for easy and scenic **snorkelling** but few natural beaches. About 9km south of town the sand returns, and a number of **beach clubs** offer various activities for every kind of visitor. Just east of the highway, the small village of **El Cedral** is the only other place people live on the island. The south coast road then bends inland, marking the boundary of **Parque Punta Sur**, a nature reserve that encompasses some beautiful beaches and lagoons.

Head east from San Miguel on the dead-straight, cross-island highway – the Carretera Transversal – to reach **San Gervasio**, the island's only excavated Maya ruins, and, after 15km, the **east coast**. Spend time here if you want a very isolated day lounging in a hammock – the further south you go along the water, the fewer people you'll see. You might not be able to swim, however, as the water can get rough on this side. And as appealing as all this is, just offshore is the rich world of the **coral reefs**, more heavily visited than anything the island has to offer above the waterline.

The north coast

Avenida Melgar runs **north out of San Miguel,** first passing a small **public beach**, popular with locals on the weekends, when food vendors set up along the malecón; at the equivalent of Calle 16, north of the turn to the airport, it's the only beach in easy walking distance from the centre of town. The road then leads to a short strip of hotels and one nice **beach club**, Playa Azul (adjacent to the resort of the same name, 4km north of town; daily 10am–5pm), a small patch of clean sand, calm water and a few rocky spots for snorkelling. It's all but empty on weekdays, but on Sunday afternoons it gets a little livelier with local families; there's a M$50 minimum charge. The paved road continues 3km past Playa Azul, then bears slightly inland to end near the Cozumel Country Club (Ⓣ987/872-9570, Ⓦwww.cozumelcountryclub.com.mx), a lush **golf course** set around a large lake.

The south coast

Heading south of San Miguel, Avenida Melgar turns into a small highway that passes several more hotels, all catering to divers. There's accessible **snorkelling** just off the coast, starting at several hotels and beach clubs. Most rent snorkel gear for about M$100; if you think you might visit a few spots, it's worth buying your own. The first spot you reach is **La Caletita**, marked by a bar of the same name. Enter the water here and drift north along a jagged rock-and-coral wall; you'll wind up at *Los Girasoles* restaurant and *Dive Paradise* hotel. The next good place, and probably the best for wade-in snorkelling, is Playa Dzul-Ha, where you'll find the *Money Bar* and a dive shop. The current here usually runs north to south, so you can swim north and drift back, or drift down to the *Fiesta Americana* and walk back along the road. The bar here will probably ask you to pay M$50 for a bracelet – this is a legitimate charge for maintaining the reef as a national park. Dzul-Ha is reached only by the smaller coastal access road; bear right (west) at *El Presidente Inter-Continental* hotel.

Two kilometres further, **Parque Chankanaab** (daily 7am–5pm; US$16) is the island's main tourist destination, though you'll probably want to skip it unless you have children. It's a bit overdeveloped, complete with mini-golf and dolphin pens, and can get very crowded on cruiseship days. It's a good option for kids, however, because its lagoon, which teems with fish, is very calm.

After Chankanaab, the reef runs further from the coast, and swimming and sunning become the main entertainment at the beaches. **Paradise Beach** (daily 9am–6pm; Ⓦwww.paradise-beach-cozumel.net), at Km 14.5, is good for an active day. It can get crowded, but beach chairs and umbrellas are free; kayaks, snorkel gear and floating water-toys moored offshore are US$9. **Nachi-Cocom**, at Km 16.5, offers a more serene beach experience, as it's barely known among cruiseshippers. For a M$200 minimum at the restaurant, you have access to a beautiful beach with shallow water, and an enormous swimming pool and Jacuzzi. Its entrance is not clearly marked: look for a "beach club" sign next to a Maya sculpture. If you get to the *Occidental Allegro* resort, you've gone too far.

A large arch on the inland side of the road at Km 17.5 marks the turn for the village of **El Cedral**, founded in 1847 and now primarily a vacation spot for San Miguel's better-off residents. There's little more here than a small Maya site and a modern Spanish-style church filled with folk art, but in late April and early May the village hosts the ten-day-long **Fiesta de la Santa Cruz**, a huge fair commemorating the meeting of Maya and Spanish cultures, with bullfights, prize-winning livestock and dancing.

Immediately opposite the turn for El Cedral is **Alberto's** beach club, the most rustic, least developed option on the west coast. There's nothing but a small restaurant, which boasts fresh fish caught with its own boats. The place isn't on many tourists' radar, so it stays fairly calm. Just a couple of kilometres south, at Km 19, the last western beach is **Playa Palancar** (daily 9am–6pm). It is a little developed, but attractively so, with winding paths and palm trees amid the lounge chairs. A restaurant serves good *tikin-xic*, and there's a dive shop (closed Sun) where you can arrange a boat ride out to Palancar Shallows (see p.127) just offshore.

Parque Punta Sur

At the southern end of the island, **Parque Punta Sur** (daily 9am–5pm; M$110) covers 2750 acres of lagoons, several lovely beaches and dense mangrove swamps. Visitors drive into the reserve on a very rutted road (treat your rental car kindly). The road passes a pier and viewing tower for admiring the lively crocodile population, as well as the tiny **Templo El Caracol**, which may have been built by the Maya as an ancient lighthouse. When the wind is right, you can hear it whistling through the conch shells embedded in the walls. The road ends at the modern Punta Celarain **lighthouse**, where you can climb to the top for amazing views. Installed in the former lighthouse-keeper's house at the base, the small **Museo de la Navegación** (daily 10am–4pm) has a series of interesting displays covering maritime history on the Yucatán coast and around the world.

From here, a creaking, wood-sided truck transports visitors to the gem of the park: a perfect little crescent of **beach** around a calm bay. Hang out in a hammock, tuck into fried fish at the restaurant (open only in high season) or take a boat tour around the lagoon, which is included in the entrance price. You can also rent snorkel gear (M$100) and paddle out to some small coral heads, dotted with sea fans and often home to hawksbill turtles.

Parque Punta Sur is also a prime spot for **birdwatching**, as the mangroves host a number of migratory species, such as roseate spoonbills, giant frigates and various herons, as well as four endemic ones, including the vibrant Cozumel emerald, the widespread Cozumel vireo and the Cozumel thrasher, thought until recently to be extinct.

San Gervasio

Midway across the island, 6km north of the Carretera Transversal, **San Gervasio** (daily 7am–5pm; M$50) is the largest excavated Maya site on the island. The city was built to honour **Ixchel**, goddess of fertility and weaving, and was one of the many independent city-states that survived the fall of Chichén Itzá; it was also part of a larger trading community on the Yucatán coast, along with Tulum and El Rey in Cancún. Today the ruins are not very impressive to a casual visitor, but, as they are part of a larger nature reserve, they're worth a trip for their scenic setting in the jungle. An early-morning or late-afternoon visit will reveal numerous bird species, butterflies and other wildlife.

Portions of San Gervasio were modelled on Chichén Itzá, with several small plazas connected by *sacbeob*, the limestone-paved white roads built by the Maya. One of the first buildings you reach, the **Manitas** structure, is a small residential room with red handprints all over it. The significance of this somewhat common motif, found at several other Maya sites, is still not understood. Off to the right stands the Chichan Nah, a dwarfish building probably used for ceremonial purposes, as it is similar in scale to the miniature temples at Tulum.

By contrast, Structure 31, closer to the main plaza, is a relatively large residential building with a front portico, a style used primarily by the Chontal Maya of lowland Mexico and Guatemala. In the later centuries, it was likely the seat of the *halach uinic*, the leader of Cozumel. The main cluster of buildings, arranged around a compact plaza, formed the central administrative area; the principal shrine to Ixchel, the **Ka'na Nah**, lies 500m to the northwest along a *sacbé*. The tallest pyramid on the site (though still not particularly towering compared to some mainland structures), it shows a few remnants of painted stucco. Down the

▲ Ruins of San Gervasio, Cozumel

northeast *sacbé*, which is marked by a delicate arch, you'll find the Post-Classic Nohoch Nah temple and the much older Casa de los Murciélagos ("house of bats"), a residential building started in 700 AD.

The east coast

Often impressively wild, Cozumel's **eastern shoreline** remains undeveloped because it faces the open sea, and in most places the water is too rough for swimming. The twenty-kilometre drive along the Carretera Costera Oriente, which runs along the seafront here, is a refreshing contrast to the busier west coast. Along the way, you'll pass tantalizing empty **beaches** (though you should swim only where you see others, and be wary of strong currents) and the occasional no-frills **beach bar**, open only till sundown because there's no electricity.

The first of these as you arrive via the cross-island road (the Carretera Transversal) – and generally the busiest, as it's right at the intersection – is *Mezcalito's*, with *Señor Iguana's* just to the south handling the overflow. The beach here is big and deep, and the party atmosphere strong.

Heading south along the eastern coast highway, you pass a number of variations on the rustic beach-bar theme. Except on Sundays, when locals come out, there's never enough of a crowd to fill all of the bars, and the further you drive, the fewer people you'll see. A short way south along the highway, **Punta Morena** is home to a bit of a surfer scene and a stylish bar-restaurant. The more casual (and usually busier) *Coconuts* bar follows, with a striking view from a tall bluff; the beach below is usually empty. **Chen Río**, a beach a little further on, has two protected coves where you can swim and snorkel (bring your own gear), and the bar serves great margaritas. The restaurant, *El Galeón*, consistently serves some of the best seafood on the strip as well. Just south, the relatively serene **Playa San Martín** is usually the best spot to swim: the currents are not too strong, the sand is kept relatively clean, flags mark the day's swimming conditions and there may even be a lifeguard on duty. Past about 2km of rocky bluffs, **Playa Bonita** has a beach club, also with lifeguards – the water is shallow and umbrellas are for rent. Around a rocky curve is the scenic point called **El Mirador**, where the crashing waves have formed natural rock arches. Finally, the road turns inland at the entrance to Parque Punta Sur and the bar *Freedom in Paradise*, known for its all-reggae soundtrack and savoury shrimp quesadillas.

The reefs

The boundaries of Cozumel's vast marine reserve, the Parque Marino Nacional Arrecifes de Cozumel, encompass the beaches and most of the reefs edging the southern half of the island. The coral has grown into steep drop-offs, massive towers and deep canyons, as well as some beautiful shallow gardens. At the more remote reefs, you can see larger pelagic fish and even dolphins. Regulations require that you be accompanied by a licensed dive guide (see p.130). Expect a M$50 park fee to be tacked on to any organized diving or snorkelling trip you make; beach clubs at snorkelling spots will also ask for the fee, for which you should receive a wristband.

On the western, leeward side, a steady current typically runs south to north, making for easy drift dives and snorkelling. Perhaps the best spot for both **diving** and **snorkelling** is **Palancar Shallows**, about 2km off the southwest coast, an area that ranges from five-metre-deep gardens to a mini-wall dropping 18m. The main strip reef is riddled with fissures and caves, providing nooks for all kinds of sea life as well as shelter from currents. You'll see Cozumel's famous (and rare) **black coral**, as well as giant tube and stove-pipe sponges harbouring brilliantly coloured fish. North of Palancar, the walls at El Cedral and Las Palmas are two excellent spots for **advanced divers**.

A bit to the south, **Columbia Shallows** is the furthest trip most day boats make from San Miguel. Although it's only 10m at its deepest, this sprawling coral garden can still dazzle seasoned divers as well as snorkellers. Sediment-rich run-off from the mangroves that edge the shore help create a thriving eco-system: tall coral towers studded with vibrant sponges and anemones punctuate the floor, and meadows of sea grass are spawning grounds for a remarkable variety of fish. Rays frequent the area, as do nurse sharks and eels. Divers, though, might prefer to stay out of the way of snorkelling crowds nearby in the equally lush **Columbia Deep**, one of the most favoured spots along the reef, meriting repeat visits.

At **Punta Sur**, directly south from the marshes on the southern tip, strong currents (and an hour-long boat ride) deter all but the strongest divers. Those who make the trip are rewarded with a dramatic network of deep caverns and fissures, completely encrusted with vibrant corals and sea fans.

Eating

Many of San Miguel's **restaurants** are overpriced tourist traps catering to a rather bland palate, but beyond the plastic chains and dull steakhouses coasting on their prime plaza frontage, you can find some excellent bargains, as well as a couple of places worthy of throwing down serious pesos. In general, you're better off wandering several blocks back from the seafront for good food and local flavour, and sticking to the large array of casual cafés, rather than the more formal restaurants. The cheapest snacks of all can be had at the city **market**, on Avenida Salas, between avenidas 20 and 25. For a more laid-back atmosphere you can enjoy long, lazy lunches in the palapas dotted every few kilometres along the east coast.

Cafés

Café del Museo Av Melgar, between C 4 and C 6, at the Museo de la Isla de Cozumel. Enjoy a quiet breakfast or early lunch on the upstairs balcony of the city museum. The view of the sea is impressive, the coffee is spiked with cinnamon and the food – from *huevos rancheros* to club sandwiches – is fresh and filling. Closed Sun.

Coco's Av 5 no. 180, between C 1 and Av Salas. At this Cozumel institution, you get American diner-style breakfast from the early hour of 6am till noon – complete with chatty waitresses, free coffee refills and Formica tables – blended with Mexican standards like eggs with *mole* (M$45). The cinnamon rolls are delightfully gooey. Closed Mon.

Coffeelia C 5 no. 85, between Av Melgar and Av 5. A proud local owner presides over breakfast and lunch from her homely kitchen in this sweet café with room to lounge outdoors. The menu mixes fresh Mexican dishes, fruit smoothies and huge Dutch-style pancakes. Breakfast is served all day; in the evening, you might see a singer or storyteller.

Jeanie's Beach Club Av Melgar at C 11. Big American breakfasts – especially waffles – are the attraction here. Plus, you can stick your feet in the sand at the little breakwater beach.

Panadería Cozumeleña C 3 at Av 10. Stop by this sweet-smelling bakery (entrance on C 3) to pick up *pan dulce* to go, or, for a more leisurely light breakfast, settle in at the adjacent coffee shop, a neighbourhood hangout (entrance on the corner).

Sorrisi C 3, between Av Melgar and Av 5. Sure, the upscale Italian food (such as rich shrimp risotto) is quite good, but the real draw is the creamy gelato.

Super-Hit Tortas Av 30 (Coldwell) at Av Salas. Meaty Mexican-style sandwiches with plenty of toppings for just M$20; in the summer, they make an ideal snack before going to a baseball game at the field behind. There's another branch on Av 30 at C 15.

Zermatt C 4 at Av 5. Bakery serving delectably light sugar doughnuts, among other sweet treats.

Restaurants

La Candela Av 5 at C 6. This friendly home-cooked breakfast and lunch spot has a selection of hot dishes – just point at what looks good. Fresh fish specials, too, and breezy terrace seating.

Casa Denis C 1, between Av 5 and Av 10. Open since 1945, *Casa Denis* occupies a little wood-frame house. The Yucatecan mains (*poc-chuc* for M$105) are occasionally a little bland, but the portions are huge, and the fare is leagues better than any other plaza restaurant. The safest bet is a beer and some *panuchos* as you watch the action from your sidewalk table.

Le Chef Av 5 at C 5. Charming, personal place where the chef-owner devises new specials every day, such as various pizzas, grilled fish, creative pastas and, for lunch, fresh sandwiches. Breakfasts are also good. Le Chef himself (aka Eduardo) has also purchased a second restaurant, down the street at Calle 7.

Chi Av Melgar at C 3. This second-floor Asian restaurant caters to cruiseship staff with a full page of Filipino specialities, but locals love it for the standard Chinese dishes; the chefs come straight from Hong Kong and Manila. Entrance is under the Pizza Hut awning. Mains from M$99; Sun buffet for the same price.

La Choza Av Salas at Av 10. Busy and popular palapa-roof restaurant known for its Mexican home cooking, though it has become a little inconsistent. It's best for the daily lunch special, which isn't on the menu; ask the waiter, and you could get a rib-sticking meal for about M$60.

La Cocay C 8, between Av 10 and Av 15 ⓣ987/872-5533, ⓔlacocay@gmail.com. The best place in town for a splurge, with excellent service and inventive dishes such as pork in currant sauce, plus very rich desserts. The menu changes seasonally. Closed Sun.

Conchita del Caribe Av 65, between C 13 and C 15. Well off the tourist track, this locally famous seafood spot – once housed in a renovated garage and now relocated to slightly classier digs – is inexpensive and delicious. Ceviches are particularly good (M$85 for a generous "small" portion). Closes at 6pm.

Especias C 3 at Av 5 ⓣ987/876-1558. Inexpensive Argentine, Mexican and even occasionally Thai dinners (M$12 for snacks like empanadas, about M$50 for salads and M$100 for more substantial main dishes). The dining room is upstairs on a roof terrace. Beware of occasionally erratic opening hours. Closed Sun.

Guido's Av Melgar 23, between C 6 and C 8 ⓣ987/872-0946. *Guido's* is probably best known for its delectable lasagne (M$130), a dense stack of garlicky tomato sauce, meat, cheese and house-made pasta. Also serves pizza from its wood oven (from M$120); seafood mains are about M$200. Check out the lovely garden out back. Lunch and dinner; closed Sun.

El Manatí Av 10 at C 8. Set in an old Caribbean-style wood house, this mellow restaurant has a good prix fixe lunch (M$60) if you want to eat cheap, but not necessarily Mexican. Options may include spaghetti Bolognese or fish with cilantro-cream sauce. The dinner menu is more elaborate (and expensive); there's also live music on the weekends (see p.130).

Pancho's Backyard Av Melgar 27 at C 8 ⓣ987/872-2141. By no means an "authentic" Mexican dining experience – especially at lunch, when it's a favourite with cruiseship passengers – but easily the best service on the island. Very good margaritas, tortilla chips hot out of the fryer and fresh-tasting, slightly dressed-up Mexican entrees (M$100 and up for mains like shrimp with poblano peppers). The vegetarian selection is strong, too.

Rock'n Java Av Melgar 602, between C 7 and Av Quintana Roo (C 11) ⓣ987/872-4405. At this American-owned seafront diner, healthy sandwiches, salads and veggie chilli (between M$40–80) are balanced out by fantastically rich and delicious desserts, such as German chocolate cake. Delivery is available to hotels south of town. Sat 7am–2pm, closed Sun.

Sabores Av 5, between C 3 and C 5. Real home cooking at this lunch-only *cocina económica*, which is run out of the chef-owner's house. Just walk through the living room and kitchen and out to the huge shady garden, where you can choose from several entrees (M$45, or a few dollars more for shrimp dishes). The set price includes soup and an all-you-can-drink jug of *agua de jamaica*. Everything is prepared individually and with care – don't miss it. Mon–Fri noon–4pm.

El Turix C 17, between Av 20 and Av 25, across from Corpus Christi church. Chef Rafael Ponce has cooked as far afield as Montréal, but returned to Mexico to promote the ideals of Slow Food, a traditional cuisine movement. He focuses on Yucatecan dishes like *cochinita pibil* and does a great coconut pie. Dinner only; closed Sun.

Drinking and nightlife

Evening entertainment in Cozumel is generally low-key, as the cruiseship crowd goes back aboard at night. The only real scene centres on the Plaza del Sol, where local families come out to chat and listen to strolling musicians or bands – it's especially lively on Sunday nights. As with everything else on the

Black coral

If you do shop in Cozumel, don't buy **black coral**, an endangered and beautiful type of sea life that is unfortunately sold everywhere. The island used to have one of the largest colonies of this rare, slow-growing species, but it has been severely depleted since the tourist trade started here in the 1960s. Underwater, black coral comes in a variety of colourful tree-like structures (it's name comes from the colour of its skeleton) – don't, under any circumstances, go breaking it off the reefs.

island, drinks can be a little pricey, at least in San Miguel, and happy hours are hard to come by. You could also check out what's happening at the Centro Cultural Ixchel, on Avenida 5, between Avenida Juárez and Calle 2, which hosts concerts and other events.

Havana Blue Upstairs at Forum Shops, Av Melgar at C 10. Done up in shades of – you guessed it – blue, this groovy lounge facing the water has plenty of comfy booths for relaxing over a strong mojito or other Cuban rum concoction. Margaritas are a little cheaper, though, at M$50.

Kelley's Av 10, between Av Salas and C 1. A big open-air bar where you might see your divemaster or tour guide in their off-hours. Very friendly, with a pool table and live music on Fri. Serves big, tasty portions of American food during the day.

El Manatí Av 10 at C 8. Dance up a storm at this casual bar-restaurant, where live reggae or rock bands play to a crowd packed into a tiny area in the back garden (Thurs–Sat 8pm). The place also serves good food (see p.129).

La Morena Av 10, between C 3 and C 5. A restaurant with a back garden serving earthy Yucatecan food, it's also a great place to hang out in the afternoon, when beers cost M$20 and you can fill up on the *botanas* served with each round.

Neptuno Av Melgar at Av Quintana Roo (C 11). Cozumel's only nightclub is heavy on the lasers, fog machines and ladies' drink specials. It's more popular with locals than tourists, and is relatively cheap. Thursday is reggaeton night; Fridays are for salsa.

Dive shops

Of the dozens of **dive shops** in town, Deep Blue, on Avenida Salas at Avenida 10 (Ⓣ987/872-5653, Ⓦwww.deepbluecozumel.com), is one of the best, offering tailor-made small-group tours to some of the most interesting and remote reefs off the island; a two-tank dive is US$68. The shop also runs a full range of certification courses. If you want to **snorkel** you'll need to organize a boat ride out to the reef – all of the dive shops in town should be able to take you (starting around M$300 for 3hr at the closest reefs). To get to the best spots, like Palancar and Columbia, you'll probably have to tag along with a diving expedition, or take a boat directly from Playa Palancar (see p.125). Whether diving or snorkelling, many of the better reefs are a little further south – good tour operators are willing to make the extra effort without complaint. **Sport-fishing** tours are also readily available for the season that runs from March to July; Albatros Charters (Ⓣ987/872-7904, Ⓦwww.gocozumel.com/albatros) can take up to six passengers on full- and half-day trips (from US$420), or contact the experienced guides at fly-fishing operation Pesca Mexicana (Ⓣ1-713/816-0228 in the US, Ⓦwww.pescamexicana.com), who run trips for two starting at US$375.

Shopping

Aside from the town market (see p.123), **shopping** in Cozumel is not immediately rewarding, as the whole seafront has been given over to gem merchants and giant souvenir marts. In this category, however, the handicrafts superstore Los Cinco Soles (Av Melgar at C 8) has a good selection of

jewellery and **housewares** – including elegant, modern pewter serving bowls and lead-free ceramic dishes; various other souvenirs are grossly overpriced, though. Raíces (Av 10, between C 1 and Av Salas) has quirkier **crafts** from around the country, and It (Av 10, between C 1 and Av Juárez), specializes in **textiles**. U'nahi Pax (on Av Juárez at Av 15), sells a variety of Mexican **musical instruments**, from pre-Columbian drums and rattles to elaborate harps and big-bellied guitars, along with a good selection of folk **music** on CD. For more modern music, and all the accessories, stop in at Famous (Av 10, between Av Juárez and C 1), which stocks goth-rocker duds and sells tickets to local concerts. Fama (Av 5, between Av Juárez and C 2) has some **books** and **maps**. In general, if you're interested in buying something of value, do it on a Sunday or Monday (days when there are no ships in port) to avoid any mark-up.

Listings

Airlines Mexicana, Av Coldwell 70-A ☎987/872-3456. For all others, use the national toll-free numbers.
Banks HSBC is on Av 5 at C 1 (Mon–Fri 9am–7pm).
Buses Check schedules and buy tickets for mainland routes at the ADO kiosk at the ferry pier, or at the office on Av 10 at C 2.
Car rental Posted rates are the same everywhere, but you may be able to negotiate when business is slow. Aguilar, in the lobby of the *Hotel Aguilar*, C 3 no. 98 at Av 5 (☎987/872-0307), also rents scooters and bicycles.
Cinema Cinépolis at Av Melgar 1001, between Av Xel-Há (C 15) and C 17.
Consulate US: Plaza Villamar, on the square ☎987/872-4574.
Ferries See box on p.117 for information on passenger and car services.
Internet and telephone The Crew Office, Av 5 no. 201-A, between Av Salas and C 3, has excellent service and can also download images from digital cameras; its international calling rates are usually a little lower than its competitors (closed Sun).
Laundry Lavandería Express, C Salas, between Av 5 and Av 10, is a self-service operation (M$20 per washer). For drop-off service, there are two *lavanderías* on Av Quintana Roo (C 11) just east of Av Melgar; the price is M$10/kilo.
Medical emergencies Hyperbaric chamber and medical clinic on C 5, between Av Melgar and Av 5. You could also visit the 24-hour Centro de Salud, on Av 20 at C 11 (☎987/872-0140). Most doctors are accustomed to dealing with English-speaking patients and those with diving-related issues.
Post office A 10 min walk south from the centre, on Av Melgar at C 7 (Mon–Fri 9am–4pm, Sat 9am–1pm).

Travel details

Buses and colectivos

First-class buses run every ten minutes between Cancún and Playa del Carmen, stopping at the turn to Puerto Morelos on request, and less frequently from the Cancún airport on the same route. Note that buses in Playa del Carmen depart from two stations: one handles largely coastal destinations, while the other has inland and long-distance service. For destinations in between the main towns on the coast, second-class buses will stop anywhere on request, as will colectivos, the white, shared passenger vans that depart Playa very frequently from Avenida Juárez in front of the main bus station (towards Cancún) and on Calle 2, between avenidas 5 and 10 (Tulum-bound). In Cancún, colectivos to Playa depart from the parking lot across Avenida Tulum from the bus station. You can also flag down a colectivo or second-class bus anywhere along the highway – both will stop if they have vacant seats.

Playa del Carmen to: Cancún (every 10min; 1hr); Cancún airport (hourly, 7am–7pm; 1hr); Chetumal (hourly, 6am–midnight; 4hr); Cobá (2 daily; 2hr); Mérida (hourly; 5hr); Palenque and San Cristóbal de las Casas (5 daily; 11–17hr); Tulum (frequently; 1–2hr); Tuxtla Gutiérrez (4 daily; 18–19hr); Valladolid (5 daily; 3hr); Villahermosa (10 daily; 12hr).

Puerto Morelos to: Cancún (every 10min; 30min); Cancún airport (hourly, 8.30am–6.45pm; 20min); Playa del Carmen (every 10min; 30min).

Ferries

The car ferry to Cozumel from Calica, south of Xcaret, takes about 1hr 15min. It's worthwhile only if you'll be spending a long time on the island. See p.117 for prices.

Calica (Punta Venado) to: Cozumel, cars only (7 daily, Mon–Sat 4am–6m, Sun 6am & 6pm).

Cozumel to: Playa del Carmen, passengers only (hourly, 5am–10pm; 30min); cars to Calica (7 daily, Mon–Sat 6am–8.30pm, Sun 8am & 8pm).

Playa del Carmen to: Cozumel (hourly, 6am–11pm; 30min).

Flights

Internal flights connect Cozumel to Mexico City. Playa del Carmen has an airstrip for small planes running on-demand tourist jaunts to Chichén Itzá and Cozumel.

3

Tulum and the Sian Ka'an Biosphere Reserve

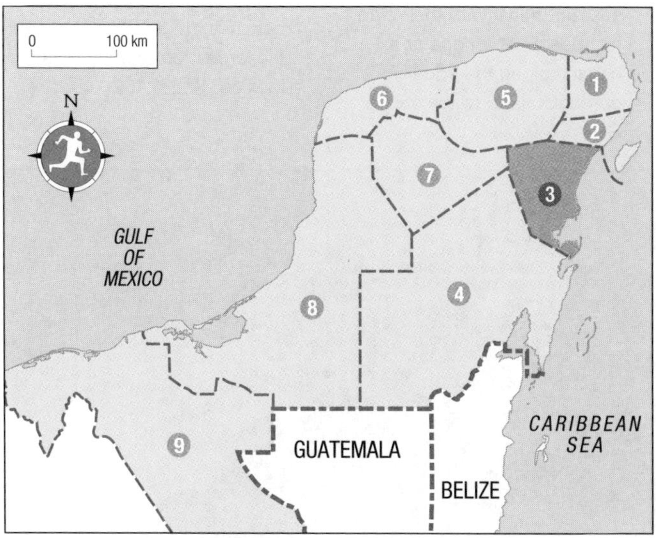

CHAPTER 3

Highlights

* **Playa Xcacel** This beautiful, empty beach is a research station and protected area for nesting sea turtles. See p.138
* **Xel-Há** Despite the theme park appearance (and entry fee!), an area of exceptional natural beauty, teeming with fish and perfect for kids. See p.138
* **Cenotes** The area around Tulum has one of the highest concentrations of scenic cenotes and caverns on the peninsula. See p.139
* **Tulum** See the stirring seafront ruins (with their own tiny beach) or lounge at a cabaña along the equally gorgeous sand to the south. See p.140
* **Cobá** Rent a bicycle to explore these ruins, buried in dense jungle filled with wildlife, then climb the main pyramid for a stupendous view of green in every direction. See p.149
* **Reserva de Monos Arañas de Punta Laguna** This reserve boasts a large population of spider monkeys as well as a tranquil lake great for canoeing. See p.151
* **Sian Ka'an Biosphere Reserve** With tropical forest, mangroves and unspoilt beaches, the reserve is one of the largest protected areas in Mexico. See p.152

▲ The Tulum ruins overlooking the Caribbean

3

Tulum and the Sian Ka'an Biosphere Reserve

The heavily built-up **Riviera Maya**, as the tourism ministry has dubbed this whole stretch of the Caribbean coast, continues south of Playa del Carmen along Hwy-307, with all manner of grand resorts and condo villages lining the flawless sand – interspersed with the occasional, but increasingly rare, empty beach. As you head further south (and put more distance between yourself and Cancún's airport), the beach properties thin out a little. The accommodation here tends to cater to people willing to make the extra drive for a less expensive, more isolated beach experience, culminating in the candle-lit, hippie-inflected cabañas of **Tulum**. On the inland side, the limestone shelf is riddled with some of the peninsula's most impressive **cenotes**, beautiful fresh-water-filled caves that are refreshing and fascinating whether you want to swim, snorkel or scuba dive. Tulum, with its scenic Maya **ruins** and mellow beach-party scene, marks the southern border of Quintana Roo's tourist development. If you're not content just to lie on the beach, you can take a trip northwest to the grand ruins of **Cobá**, a vast Maya city buried in the forest.

After Tulum, the jungle thickens and Hwy-307 narrows and heads inland, skirting more than a million acres of wilderness that have been set aside in the **Sian Ka'an Biosphere Reserve**. The area forms a rich haven for marine and bird life, as well as larger forest mammals. The only village inside the reserve, tiny **Punta Allen**, is a destination for travellers looking for quiet isolation and great fishing. On the edge of the reserve, just off Hwy-307, the rambling ruins of **Chunyaxché** are often empty, while the ancient roads and canals the Maya built here are a great place to spot wildlife. Bus service south of Tulum is not as frequent and flexible as along the Riviera Maya, though certainly still manageable; numerous tour operators will take you into the reserve for a reasonable price.

From Playa del Carmen to Tulum

Almost the entire sixty-kilometre stretch of coast between Playa del Carmen and Tulum has been transformed into resorts or condominium "villages" with gated entrances and little or no access for non-residents to the sea; the most egregious of these is the expensive, sterile **Puerto Aventuras**, 20km south of Playa, which feels like a theme park minus the rides. But amid the slick developments, a few less formal spots survive, such as **Paamul** and **Akumal**, along with some increasingly beleaguered hidden beaches. Everything here is relatively easy to reach from Hwy-307, even if you're travelling by one of the frequent second-class buses or colectivos; the latter run almost constantly between Playa and Tulum and will stop anywhere along the highway. For more structured fun, you can stop off at **Xel-Há**, a semi-natural water park that's nice for kids, or take a cenote tour at **Hidden Worlds**, both just north of Tulum.

Paamul, Xpu-Ha and Akumal

The first community south of Playa, **PAAMUL** is a fancy RV park with an excellent **restaurant** that serves all the standard ceviches and quesadillas, plus succulent main fish and meat dishes, prepared with more care than at typical beach seafood joints. The reef runs very close to shore here, making for some of the best wade-in **snorkelling** within the vicinity of Playa, from a quiet, half-moon beach. The community also operates its own dive centre and two overnight **lodging** options directly on the water – elegant, large rooms with three beds and stunning sea views (❽), or simpler wooden cabañas (❼), both with air conditioning and plenty of hot water (ⓣ984/875-1051, ⓦwww.paamul.com).

Twenty-five kilometres further south, a series of poorly signed tracks lead to **XPU-HA**, whose perfectly white beach curves around in a large, gentle arc. Though the beach is gradually being taken over by development, it's still an especially lovely spot. *Esencia* (ⓣ1-800/561-9162 in Mexico, or ⓣ1-877/528-3490 in the US, ⓦwww.hotelesencia.com; ❾), with 29 beautifully designed rooms, plunge pools and a spa, offers intimate luxury of the most elite kind (from US$600 a night); rare for similar beach properties, kids are welcome. Just next door, the more affordable *Al Cielo* (ⓣ984/840-9012, ⓦwww.alcielohotel.com; ❾) has four beautiful rooms and a pleasantly empty plot of sand out front. Even if the rooms are not in your price range, you can eat in the restaurant, less pricey than it looks, which entitles you to use the beach facilities. Slightly further south, on a track signed *Xpu-Ha Beach Club*, *La Playa* restaurant offers a far less formal beach experience; a friendly place with plenty of locals where for the price of a meal or a few drinks (minimum M$100) you can use the lounge chairs and other beach facilities. The track immediately south of this leads to *Bonanza Xpu-ha* (no tel; ❺) a surviving budget place where you can stay in basic cabañas or **camp** (M$50) on the beach; if you just want to visit the beach, there's a small charge for parking here.

Further on about 10km (turn at "Playa Akumal"), **AKUMAL** is primarily a condo community, but as one of the oldest and best established it has a number of excellent places to eat, interesting shops and several experienced dive and snorkelling establishments. Above all, its main beach offers superb snorkelling, with pretty much guaranteed sightings of turtles just a short way offshore. The Centro Ecológico de Akumal (ⓣ984/875-9095, ⓦwww.ceakumal.org; ❸), just behind the beach, runs a programme monitoring and protecting the local turtle population, and provides a great deal of information on them. As you enter the community through the arch, the *Hotel Club Akumal* (ⓣ984/875-9115,

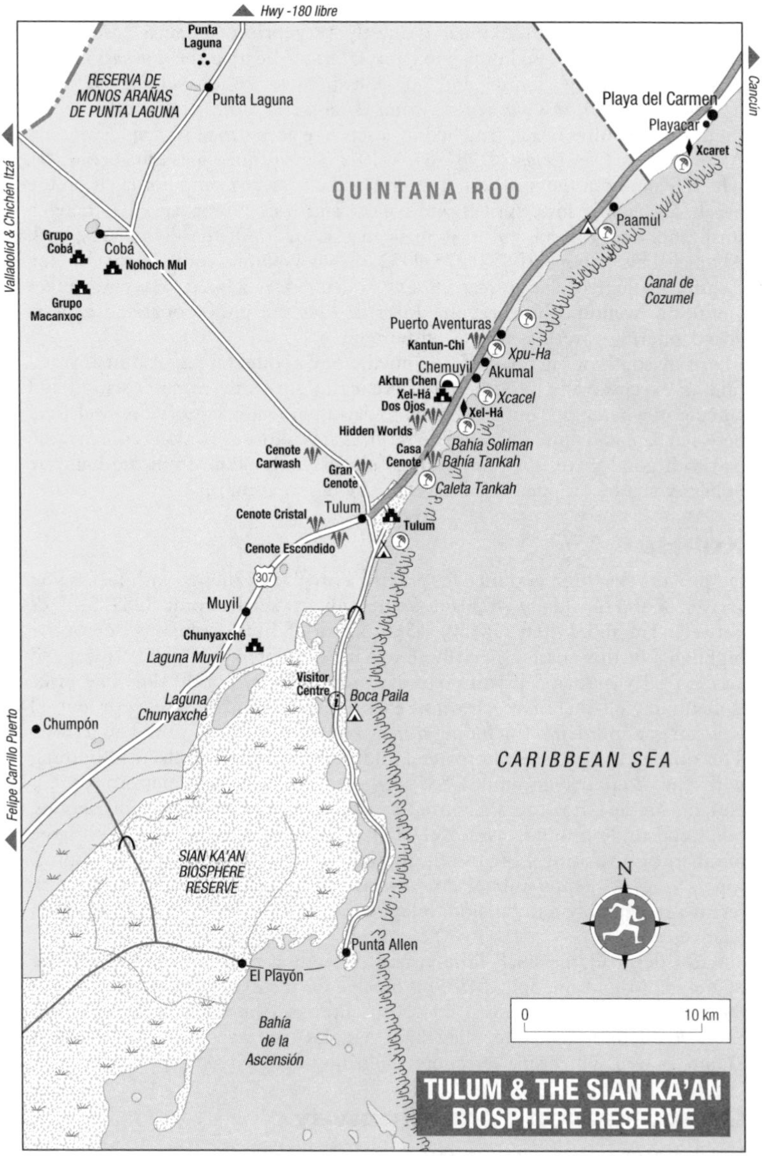

Ⓦwww.akumalguide.com) is one of the best of several operations that rent bikes and offer local tours and services. Of the many places to eat in central Akumal, the chummy *Turtle Bay* **restaurant** is highly recommended, especially for their home-baked goodies at breakfast. For more entertainment, head north up the coast road to *La Buena Vida* beach **bar and restaurant** on Half Moon Bay, a funky place with precarious tree-house seating, bedecked with fish skeletons.

Accommodation in Akumal is mostly very pricey. *Vista del Mar* (Ⓣ1-888/425-8625, Ⓦwww.akumalinfo.com; ⑦), right next to the *Buena Vida*, has reasonable seafront rooms and more expensive condos; *Villas de Rosa* (Ⓣ984/875-9020, Ⓦwww.cenotes.com; ⑦) also has rooms and condos to the south on Aventuras beach (reached by a separate access road signed "Aventuras Akumal"). *Que Onda* (Ⓣ984/875-9101, Ⓦwww.queondaakumal.com; ⑦), which is almost at the northernmost end of the coast road and not right on the beach, has slightly lower prices, and a more laid-back, European vibe; there's a small pool and a good, Italian-influenced restaurant. Of the dive places, both Akumal Dive Shop (Ⓣ984/875-9032, Ⓦwww.akumal.com), right by the Centro Ecológico, and Aquatech Divers (Ⓣ984/875-9020, Ⓦwww.cenotes.com), on Aventuras beach at the *Villas de Rosa*, are professional and experienced, offering cavern as well as offshore diving.

Directly south of the town of Chemuyil, a few kilometres past Akumal, you'll find an exceptionally quiet beach at **Xcacel**, a sea turtle research station and sanctuary where the animals come to lay their eggs; visitors are welcome between 8am and 6pm. There are no services at all – the attraction is the pristine bay with good waves for body-surfing, plus it's only 500m from the highway (where you'd be dropped off if travelling by bus or combi).

Xel-Há

Despite the sky-high entrance fee and the crowds and theme-park feel as you arrive, **Xel-Há** (daily 8.30am–6pm; Ⓦwww.xel-ha.com; US$75, kids between 1m and 1.40m US$50), 13km north of Tulum, remains one of the highlights of this coast, especially if you have children: you can easily spend an entire day here and if you do, it can seem a pretty good value. The price is genuinely all-inclusive – not just lockers, towels and snorkel gear, but all you can eat and drink (including a free bar) for the whole time you're here. The only extras are for photos and additional activities such as swimming with the dolphins (around US$100, but a very slick operation) or less enticing underwater tours. Centred around a natural formation of lagoons, inlets and underground caves, Xel-Há has wonderful snorkelling with large numbers of surprisingly big fish, and activities from kayaking to cliff jumping, rope swings to gently tubing down a river. Through all this it manages to retain a remarkably natural, undeveloped feel, and to absorb the crowds with relative ease.

Across the road, the small, little-visited and only partly excavated **Maya site** of Xel Há (daily 8am–5pm; M$35) is notable for the extant stucco paintings in the Grupo Pájaros, on the east side of the site near the highway. On the west edge, you'll find miniature, chest-high temples that resemble ones found at Tulum, as well as a couple of cenotes, linked by a ruined *sacbé*.

Cenotes along the highway

You'll see signs to cenotes (see box opposite) all along the highway; some are highly developed sites, some mere roadside shacks. Perhaps the most spectacular of the organized cenote parks, certainly for divers, is **Hidden Worlds** (tours daily 9am–3pm; Ⓣ984/877-8535, Ⓦwww.hiddenworlds.com), comprising a cluster of outstanding cenotes and caverns just south of Xel-Há. Guided group snorkelling (M$250–400) and diving (M$500 for one tank) trips run every half hour or so: snorkellers pile into a jeep with a handful of other visitors and trundle through the forest to the enormous Tak Be Ha cavern and constricted Hilario's Well; open-water divers can experience some of the best cenote diving anywhere

Exploring the cenotes

The area north and west of Tulum has one of the largest concentrations of **cenotes** on the peninsula, including Ox Bel Ha, which at almost 170km, is the longest water-filled cave system in the world. Many of them are easily accessible from Hwy-307 or off the road to Cobá (see p.148). Some have been developed as "eco-parks" or adventure centres, and for first-time visitors – especially those who might be leery of tight spaces and dark water – the guides and marked-out trails can be comforting. However, it's also worth visiting one of the less developed alternatives, where for a small entry fee (usually M$50 or so) you are pretty much left to explore by yourself, and fewer visitors means a greater chance of encountering wildlife. If there's worthwhile snorkelling or diving, most will have equipment available to rent, and dive trips (and other visits) can be arranged in every resort. **Divers** must have open-water certification for **cavern diving** (in which you explore within the reach of daylight), while **cave diving** (in which you venture into closed passageways and halls) requires rigorous special training. Though local development threatens the cenotes and the fresh groundwater in the long term, inexperienced and clumsy visitors can do more damage in the short term: wear only **biodegradable sunscreen**; **do not touch** the surprisingly delicate stalactites; never break off anything as a souvenir; **mind your flippers**, as it's easy to kick up silt or knock into the rocks; and be very careful climbing in and out of the water – use the provided paths and ladders.

at the glimmering, sunlit Dos Ojos cenote and the Dreamgate, an awe-inspiring 61-metre-wide cavern. You can also visit these on your own, for a M$50 entry fee paid at Dos Ojos, or with dive companies in any of the resorts.

Other worthwhile organized cenotes include **Ecopark Kantun-Chi** (daily 9am–5pm; Ⓦwww.kantunchi.com; tours M$180–350), between Puerto Aventuras and Xpu-Ha, and Aktun Chen (daily 9am-5pm; Ⓦwww.aktunchen.com tours; M$260), between Akumal and Xel-Há, both of which are lower-key affairs where you walk through rainforest to the caves and cenotes: Kantun-Chi has good snorkelling, Aktun Chen is primarily a dry cave tour. There's a good chance of seeing wildlife along the paths here, especially early or late in the day, as they encourage animals with feeding. Right by Kantun-Chi, **Cenote Azul** (M$50) is a good example of an undeveloped cenote, less spectacular since it's mostly open to the sky, but with some underground swimming.

Soliman and Tankah bays

The final accessible beaches before Tulum are at adjacent **Bahía Soliman** and **Bahía Tankah**, two long, crescent beaches backed mainly by private houses and villas, many of which are available for rental. A number of turn-offs promise *Acceso publico a la playa* – given the development, though, it can be hard to reach the beach or find anywhere to park, a problem that gets worse with every passing year. The best access to Soliman bay is on the track by *Oscar y Lalo's* large roadside restaurant. For Tankah, follow the road signed to the *Blue Sky* restaurant. Behind Tankah beach, the **Casa Cenote** is a great place to snorkel – a network of seven pools that wind through the trees, with plenty of birdlife and supposedly even manatees, though you're unlikely to see the latter. It's right by the *Casa Cenote* restaurant, just before *Blue Sky*; there's no charge, though you may want to use one of the restaurants if you want to park or get to the beach.

Places to stay here include the *Tankah Inn* (Ⓣ984/100-0703, Ⓦwww.tankah.com; ❽), a friendly B&B guesthouse with Wi-Fi, a fridge in each room and many communal facilities, and *Tankah Villas* (Ⓣ984/807-7390,

ⓦwww.sliceofparadise.com; ❼), with two beachfront cabañas and two small *casetas* with kitchen. The latter is near the northern end of the bay, where the reef meets the shore so that you can wade straight out to it. A little further south the **Caleta Tankah Beach Club** (signed "Caleta Tankah") capitalizes on a protected cove with palm trees for shade; between the colourful fish in the sea and a cenote just inland, there's plenty to explore. At the time of writing, however, the place was closed for refurbishment.

Tulum and around

Arguably the most picturesque of all Maya sites, **Tulum**, 130km south of Cancún, is small but exquisitely poised on fifteen-metre-high cliffs above the impossibly blue Caribbean. When the Spanish first set eyes on the place in 1518, they considered it as large and beautiful a city as Seville. They were, perhaps, misled by their dreams of El Dorado, the glorious setting and the brightly painted facades of the buildings – Tulum is no match for the greatest Maya cities in terms of architectural grandeur and finesse. Nevertheless, on account of its location, it sticks in the memory like no other, and draws crowds second only to Chichén Itzá. It is also still an important Maya spiritual and cultural centre.

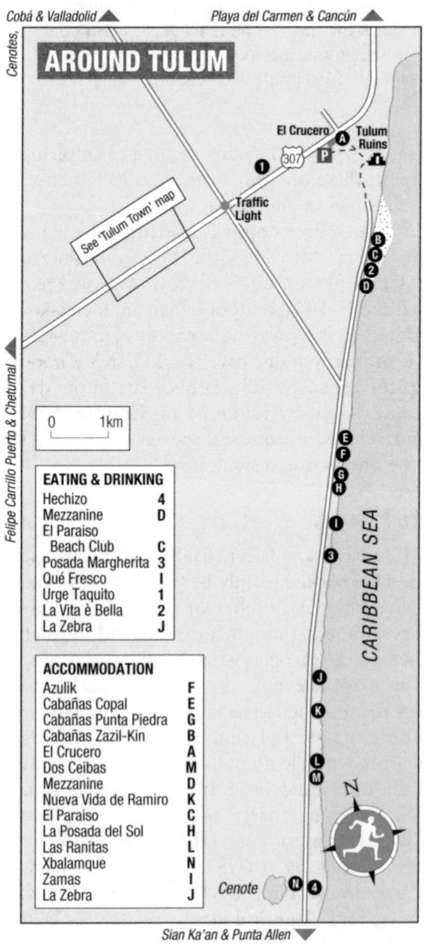

Tulum's beautiful **beach** has been an equally powerful attraction, though its status as a backpacker hangout par excellence is rapidly passing into history as the area develops its infrastructure, both for tourism and new Mexican residents. A few candle-lit, cold-water cabañas still cater to young international travellers, but a larger set of visitors value the more luxurious sensibility of the newer resorts. The actual **town** of Tulum is also growing rapidly, with a population of well over 10,000 swollen by construction and tourist industry workers. You'll find all the basic services here, as well as plenty of restaurants and budget accommodation Tulum is also the easiest place to line up a tour to the Sian Ka'an Biosphere Reserve (see p.152), or a diving or snorkelling excursion to one of the nearby cenotes (see p.139).

Arrival and information

Arriving in Tulum by bus or private transport can be confusing because there are three distinct parts to the community: the ruins, the town and the beaches. Coming in from the north, Hwy-307 first passes a crossroads known as El Crucero, where numerous hotels mark the old entry road to the ruins, and then immediately afterwards the main entrance to the **ruins**, with extensive parking, gift shops and restaurants. The site itself is on the water, 1km east. If you plan to head directly to the ruins, get off the bus here, rather than at the Tulum town station, several kilometres further. Almost two kilometres beyond the ruins there's a traffic light (a giant San Francisco de Asis supermarket is on one corner of the intersection); straight ahead is the beginning of the town proper – Tulum town – strung along either side of the road for a couple of kilometres. Left at the lights, following signs for "Boca Paila–Punta Allen", it's 3km to the junction with the coast road, where the bulk of the local accommodation is strung out along the beach: about one-third of the hotels, including most of the cheaper options, are to the north (towards the ruins), and the remainder run south for some 7km, on a road that eventually enters the Sian Ka'an Biosphere Reserve (heading for the village of Punta Allen). Turn right at the traffic light for the inland road to Cobá.

The **bus** station, open 24 hours, is at the southern end of town, and **colectivos** stop almost next door. To get to the beach hotels, you must hire a taxi from here (starting at M$40), as there's no public transport. Tulum's taxi drivers have a reputation for denying the existence of hotels that don't pay them commission; if you want to get to a particular hotel, insist on being taken there. There's no tourist information office as such, though the *Weary Traveler* hostel (see p.142), just south of the bus station, acts as something of an informal information exchange. You can pick up local maps and brochures here, as well as at many of the popular cafés, travel agencies and dive shops in town.

Accommodation

Although Tulum's beach is an obvious draw, you may want to stay in **town** if you arrive late in the day, have a limited amount of time (and money) or just prefer hot water round-the-clock. Many hotels in the zona hotelera along the **beach road** do not have permanent electricity, relying instead on varying combinations of solar panels, windmills and diesel generators.

Depending on your point of view, the candle-lit ambience of the accommodation on the beach is either rustic charm or expensive primitivism. Either way, the resulting calm – save for the crash of the surf – helps disguise the increasing development. The hotels closest to the ruins (turn left on the beach road) tend to be cheaper: this is where the few surviving sand-floor **cabañas** that attracted the original hippie backpackers can be found – with shared bathrooms and little security. At

▲ A palapa cabaña on the beach at Tulum

the more basic places you should take care both of your possessions and yourself; there have been reports of thefts and even occasional sexual assaults here. To the south (turn right on the beach road), you'll find some ritzier boutique resorts, with jet-set guests and prices to match; many describe themselves as eco-resorts, not always with much justification. Note: the "junction" in addresses given below and throughout refers to the junction of the coast with the road to Tulum town.

In town

Casa del Sol C Polar Pte, about 300m south of the bus station ⓣ984/129-6424, ⓔcasadelsoltulum@yahoo.com. Friendly backpacker hostel with comfortable beds (M$120) in ten-bed dorms – also simple rooftop cabañas and rooms; breakfast and transport to beach included. ❹

El Crucero East side of Hwy-307 at El Crucero, by the pedestrian entrance to the ruins ⓣ984/871-2610, ⓦwww.el-crucero.com. Fun, friendly hotel convenient for visiting the archeological site; one of a group here. Choose very affordable dorm beds (M$100), standard rooms or deluxe rooms with a/c and distinctive murals painted by a local artist, whose gallery is on-site. The bar-restaurant, with its outgoing bartenders (and wireless Internet), is extremely hospitable. ❹–❻

Don Diego de la Selva C Tulum, off the west side of Hwy-307, about 900m south of town ⓣ984/114-9744, ⓦwww.dtulum.com. Quiet, French-owned hideaway just out of town, with a pool and big, white rooms with terraces; two have fans, the other six have a/c. ❻–❼

L'Hotelito West side of Av Tulum, between C Orion and C Beta ⓣ984/136-1240, ⓔl.hotelito@hotmail.com. This tiny, Italian-run hotel, with its palapa roofs and garden courtyard, has a country feel despite its location in the middle of town. The upstairs rooms have high ceilings with fans; downstairs rooms have a/c. ❺

Posada Luna del Sur C Luna Sur 5 ⓣ984/871-2984, ⓦwww.posadalunadelsur.com. Exceptionally comfy, spotless, tranquil rooms set around a small garden. Welcoming and helpful owners and staff create an intimate B&B atmosphere. No children. ❻

The Weary Traveler Av Tulum, just south of the bus station ⓣ984/871-2390, ⓦwww.wearytravelerhostel.com. The best-known and most convenient hostel in town; pretty basic, large dorms (M$120) as well as private rooms. Very party-centric, but a great meeting place. DIY breakfast in the communal kitchen and shuttle to the beach included. ❹

On the beach

Azulik 800m south of the junction ⓣ1-800/514-3066 in Mexico, ⓣ1-888/898-9922 in the US, ⓦwww.azulik.com. One of the most romantic options in the area. Deluxe wood cabins, shielded by trees, are done up with fine linens, and soaking tubs carved from tree trunks perch on cliffs over the crashing surf. A quiet beach lies just to the south. No kids allowed, and no electric light (though there is wireless Internet, and the rooms have fans). ❾

Cabañas Copal 700m south of the junction ⓣ1-800/514-3066 in Mexico, ⓣ1-888/898-9922 in the US, ⓦwww.cabanascopal.com. The round, wood-floor cabañas (plus a couple of older, sand-floored, shared-bath ones) are packed in pretty close here, but they're a decent mid-range option nonetheless. There's no electricity but plenty of hot water, and a clothing-optional beach. Services include bike rental and spa treatments, such as a ritual Maya *temazcal* sauna. ❺–❽

Cabañas Punta Piedra 1.2km south of the junction ⓣ984/116-4296, ⓔcabanaspuntapiedra@hotmail.com. One deluxe cabaña takes up the beach view, but the five fairly basic cabins further back – among the cheapest available on the strip with private bath – are the real draw. Hot water and evening electricity; bike rental and dive shop, too. ❻

Cabañas Zazil-Kin 2km north of the junction ⓣ984/124-0082, ⓦwww.hotelstulum.com/zazilkin. Sturdy, concrete-floor cabañas, a couple with private bath – evening electricity and cold water only – are among the oldest survivors in Tulum (this was formerly the popular *Don Armando*'s), now also with a dozen a/c rooms in a new block. Perennially popular, with a lively bar scene – reserve or arrive early, as rooms go fast. ❹

Dos Ceibas 5.2km south of the junction ⓣ984/877-6024, ⓦwww.dosceibas.com. Small, attractive, Italian-run hotel with a variety of spacious, colourful cabañas in front of a turtle-hatching beach. Solar power and recycling mean their "eco" label is more convincing than most; yoga and meditation classes offered on site. ❻–❾

Mezzanine 1.5km north of the junction ⓣ998/112-2845, ⓦwww.mezzanine.com.mx. The stylish designer rooms at this small boutique hotel are the antithesis of the traditional Tulum experience, though some have great sea views. Mini pool, wireless Internet and beach gear included. ❾

Nueva Vida de Ramiro 4.5km south of the junction T 984/877-8512, W www.tulumnv.com. Peaceful, slightly quirky eco-hotel that relies entirely on wind turbines and solar panels for power. Attractive wood cabins on stilts (all with front decks) are carefully built over and around untamed greenery. The beach is splendid here, and the restaurant serves tasty seafood, fruit shakes and great espresso. 7–9

El Paraiso 1.9km north of the junction T 984/113-7089, W www.elparaisotulum.com. A lively beach club with a party atmosphere at the bar and a dozen comfortable rooms, each with fans, 24-hour electricity and hot water, set back from the water. 8

La Posada del Sol 1.3km south of the junction T 984/876-6206, W www.laposadadelsol.com. The four artfully designed, high-ceiling "jungle" rooms on the wooded side of the road are exceptionally well priced for their size and attractiveness; three beachfront cabañas cost a bit more, but are equally beautiful. There's also an excellent jewellery shop in the lobby. The same owners run the *Posada Lamar*, which has more beachfront bungalows, a kilometre or so further south. 7–9

Las Ranitas 5km south of the junction T 984/877-8554, W www.lasranitas.com. Long-established, understated but comfortable French-owned hotel with fourteen lovely (but expensive) breezy rooms and two family suites, plus tennis courts, a pool and an excellent library. Wireless Internet, 24-hour electricity and hot water. 9

Xbalamque 7km south of the junction, opposite *Hechizo* restaurant, on the inland side of the road just before the entry to Sian Ka'an (no tel). Very simple but clean back-to-nature cabañas with shared bath and sporadic power. At the rear there's access to a cenote, with kayaks for hire to explore. 8

Zamas 1.8km south of the junction T 1-415/387-9806 in the US, W www.zamas.com. Enormous, comfortable rooms, some right on the beach. Hot water and electricity are plentiful, but the style remains bohemian. Good restaurant on site (see p.147). 8

La Zebra 4km south of the junction T 984/115-4726, W www.lazebratulum.com. Luxurious cabañas with 24-hour electricity and hot water, a few on the beach and the rest very close. Wireless Internet in the popular bar-restaurant. 9

The town and the beach

Tulum **town** is in the midst of a growth spurt, with well-groomed central Avenida Tulum giving way to muddy potholes in the back streets. It offers all the basic services and an increasing number of good dinner restaurants and bars, but is utterly devoid of sights or attractions. By day there are generally few visitors because they've all decamped to the **beach**, one of the longest stretches of impeccable white sand along the Caribbean coast. Storms can change the beach rapidly, occasionally washing it away altogether from a particular spot, but it's usually back within a few days. If you're not staying at the beach, the easiest access is at one of the **beach clubs**: there's no charge at these, though you'll pay for lounge chairs and drinks. Elsewhere the beach is open to all, but it can be hard to get to; there's free access if you head far enough south –

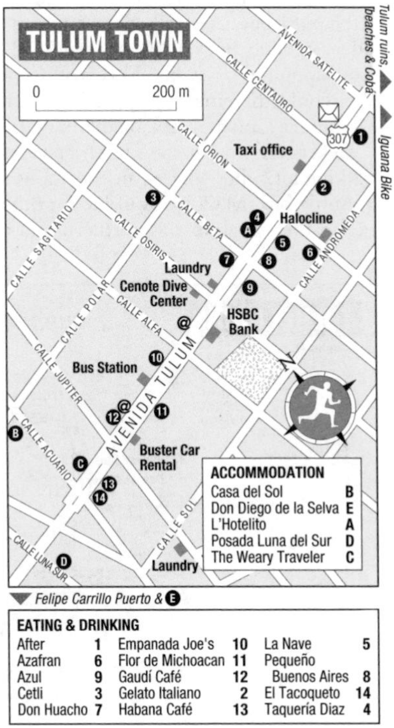

EATING & DRINKING

After	1	Empanada Joe's	10	La Nave	5
Azafran	6	Flor de Michoacan	11	Pequeño Buenos Aires	8
Azul	9	Gaudí Café	12	El Tacoqueto	14
Cetli	3	Gelato Italiano	2	Taquería Diaz	4
Don Huacho	7	Habana Café	13		

especially inside the biosphere reserve – and many hotel bars and restaurants let you use their beach facilities for the price of a meal or drink. The most popular clubs are north towards the ruins: **El Paraiso**, just under 2km from the junction, draws crowds to its fully stocked bar, kiteboarding centre and friendly hippie vibe. If you're looking for more solitude, head immediately north to Playa Maya, a public beach that's generally empty, though you'll have to bring your own towels and refreshments. Next up is **Mar Caribe Beach Club**, which is more of a locals' hangout, with wonderful sand and a great view of the ruins. It can be a rowdy scene at weekends, though, and is also often busy at lunchtime when tour buses call in at the large restaurant.

For something more energetic than hammock-lounging, there are dive shops all along the beach and in town, and plenty of places offering snorkelling and other tours. The dive shop at *Cabañas Punta Piedra* also runs **hiking** trips into the jungle and rents **bicycles**. Other highlights include **cavern snorkelling** tours and **cave diving** in local cenotes, and a variety of **nature tours** into the Sian Ka'an Biosphere Reserve (see p.152). See "Listings", p.147, for details of dive shops and tour operators.

The ruins

On a sunny day, with the turquoise sea glittering behind the weather-beaten grey stones, the first view of the **Tulum ruins** (daily: Nov–April 7am–6pm; May–Oct 8am–7pm; M$48) can be breathtaking, despite the small scale of its buildings, all clustered in a compact mass within fortified walls. The city was built in the late Post-Classic period, after 1200 AD, and was still thriving when the Spanish arrived in the early sixteenth century. The entire site seems a bit haphazard because walls flare outward and doorways taper inward – not the effect of time, but rather an intentional design, and one that is echoed in other sites along the coast, like El Rey in Cancún and San Gervasio on Cozumel. On the whole, the buildings appear less than grand when compared to the majestic Castillo at Chichén Itzá, or the huge pyramids of the Classic Maya sites.

Tickets are sold at the site entrance, about 1km from the main highway and parking lot, where there's an enormous warren of souvenir shops and food stalls; a shuttle bus (M$20) is available for those who don't want to walk. You can also get to the site from the northern end of the beach road; from there it's just a

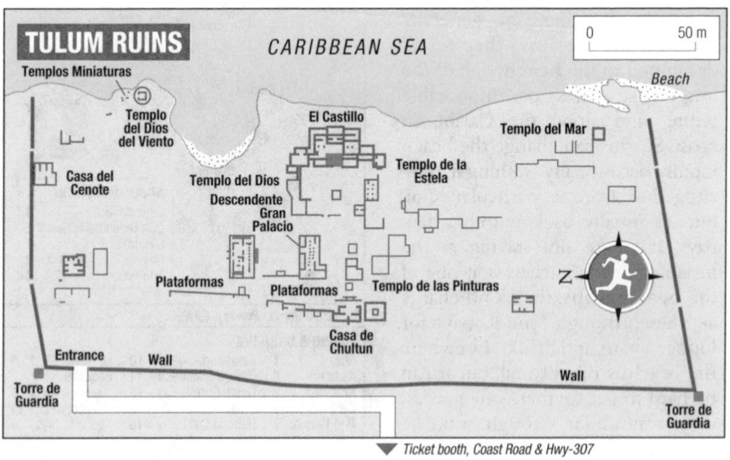

short walk to the ticket office. The area is less than 500m long and takes only an hour or so to see, though you may want to allow time to **swim** at the tiny, perfect beach beneath the cliffs. Arrive in the early morning or late afternoon to avoid the worst crowds, which can be overwhelming here.

You're admitted to the site through a breach in the wall that surrounds the city on three sides (the fourth side faces the sea). This **wall**, some 5m high with a walkway along the top, may have had a defensive purpose, but more likely it delineated the ceremonial and administrative precinct – the site you see today – from nearby residential enclaves. Archeologists believe the towers that mark the corners of the wall were small temples rather than military structures, owing to the altars installed in them. In any case, the walls did take on a defensive role around 1890, in the waning years of the Caste Wars. Maya followers of the Talking Cross liberation movement (see box, p.163) reoccupied the site, where they practised rituals and held out against Mexican armies for more than 25 years.

Virtually all the buildings are now roped off to protect them from the crowds, but they're small enough that you get a pretty good impression from outside. Skirting the northern wall as you walk towards the sea from the entrance, you reach the **Casa del Cenote**, a square structure straddling a water-filled cave; a small tomb occupies its central portion. On the bluff above and to the right are the **Templos Miniaturas**, several scale-model temples, complete with tiny lintels and mouldings, which were probably shrines. Up the hill stands the **Templo del Díos del Viento** (Temple of the Wind God), a small, single-room structure. It's set on a rounded platform; temples to wind gods were traditionally rounded in ancient Mexico so as to present no sharp obstacles to the wind – a design which, though common elsewhere, is seldom seen in this region. This temple finds its twin in a similar chamber, the **Templo del Mar**, which overlooks the water at the southern edge of the site. Alongside it, a wooden stairway leads down to the **beach**.

On the north side of the main promontory, the flared walls of the small temple at the top of the **Templo del Díos Descendente** are emphasized by an additional level of moulding that juts out at an opposite angle. The diving (or descending) god, carved in stone above the narrow entrance of the temple, is one of Tulum's quirks: the small, upside-down winged figure appears all over the city, but in only a handful of places elsewhere in the Maya world. His significance is unclear – he may represent the setting sun, or rain or lightning, or he may be the bee god, since honey was one of the Maya's most important exports. Immediately adjacent to the temple, the imposing **Castillo**, on the highest part of the site, commands fine views in every direction, though visitors, prohibited from climbing it, can only look up at the building from the plaza at its base. The fortress-like pyramid, flanked by steep staircases, probably served not just as a temple, but also as a beacon or lighthouse; even without a light it would have been an important landmark for mariners along an otherwise featureless coastline. Just south of the Castillo, the squat, barely restored **Templo de la Estela** (Temple of the Stele) was named for a commemorative stone tablet found inside, which bears the date 564 AD. As that would have been well before the city's foundation, the tablet was presumably brought here from elsewhere.

Turning away from the sea, you face a cluster of buildings arranged on a city-like grid, with the chief structures set on stone platforms along parallel streets. The most fascinating of these is the colonnaded **Templo de las Pinturas** (Temple of the Paintings). The surrounding gallery you see now, decorated with masks of the rain god Chac, preserved the murals which were painted on the exterior of an older temple. The murals can be seen reasonably well, even from the roped-off path: the predominant images are of Maya gods and symbols of nature's fertility – rain, maize and fish. One remarkable piece, done at a later date than the others, shows Chac seated on a four-legged animal, evidently inspired by the conquistadors with their horses.

Eating

Because the accommodation in Tulum is spread over 10km and the town is so far from the beach, almost every hotel in the area has its own restaurant – ranging from cheap and grungy to very chic. Guests tend to stick to the restaurants in their own hotels, but a few **places to eat** along the coast road merit a special trip. In the village, a number of inexpensive **cafés** serve *comida corriente* (a set meal) and rotisserie chicken, and there's an increasing number of cheerful, mid-range places run by European expats; Italian food is particularly good here. There's also an excellent **bakery**, *Pan del Carmen*, on Avenida Tulum at the corner of Calle Osiris Norte, open daily from 6am to 11pm, which sells good bread and a huge variety of *pan dulce*.

Cafés

Azafran Tulum town, C Orion Sur at C Andromeda. Quiet spot just off the beaten track for excellent breakfasts and home-made bagels; closed evenings.

Empanada Joe's Tulum town, west side of Av Tulum, just north of the bus station. Fast-food style empanadas – savoury and sweet – as well as good coffee, smoothies and icy a/c.

Flor de Michoacan Tulum town, east side of Av Tulum, opposite the bus station. Handy branch of the country-wide chain serving fruit juices and *licuados*, as well as inexpensive Mexican *paletas* (home-made ice pops).

Gaudí Café Tulum town, west side of Av Tulum, just south of the bus station. Good for inexpensive set-price breakfast specials, Spanish sandwiches and decent coffee.

Gelato Italiano Tulum town, east side of Av Tulum, between C Orion and C Centauro. Excellent Italian-style ice cream.

Restaurants

Cetli Tulum town, C Polar Poniente at C Orion. Chef Claudia trained in Mexico City's premier culinary academy, and now offers *Alta Cocina Mexicana* in a lovely setting just a block from the main drag. Very well-priced, refined versions of Mexican classics, such as a delicate peanut-based *mole de cacahuete*. Evenings only, 5–10pm.

Don Huacho Tulum town, west side of Av Tulum, between C Beta and C Osiris. The town's longtime Mexican seafood specialist features the mysteriously spiced *pescado a la Don Huacho*, very fresh ceviche and tasty shark empanadas, which are great with beer.

Hechizo Coast road, 7km south of the junction with the road to Tulum town (turn at Rancho San Eric, on the left shortly before the Sian Ka'an entrance) ☎984/100-0170, ⓔhechizo@bigfoot.com. This gem of a restaurant owned by a former Ritz-Carlton chef is unexpectedly sophisticated. The inspired international menu (watermelon and goat cheese salad, lobster pozole) changes daily; appetizers cost about M$70, mains around M$200. Reservations advised. Closed Mon and parts of the low season.

Mezzanine Coast road, 1.5km north of the junction ☎998/112-2845. Elegant beachside setting for Thai curries and seafood, at prices not much higher than elsewhere.

La Nave Tulum town, east side of Av Tulum, between C Orion and C Beta. A busy town hangout with fresh-fruit breakfasts, inexpensive pizza from a wood-fired oven (M$65 and up) and Italian staples like fresh gnocchi (M$70 and up).

Pequeño Buenos Aires Tulum town, east side of Av Tulum at C Beta Norte. Giant Argentine steaks and *parrilladas* (mixed grills), washed down with some excellent wines from an extensive list (by Tulum standards). The hamburger, using top-quality beef, is great value.

Posada Margherita Coast road, 2km south of the junction at *Posada Margherita* hotel ☎984/801-8493. Fantastic beachfront Italian restaurant with dishes like fresh taglierini with shrimp and zucchini, and fish poached in sea water. The antipasto platter, served on a slice of a tree trunk, is a bounty of piquant cheeses, cured meats and olives. Prices are higher than the informal setting might suggest (around M$160 for entrees), but the food is worth it. Reservations recommended.

Qué Fresco Coast road, 1.8km south of the junction at *Zamas*. A good mid-range Italian restaurant with fresh pastas and a wood-fired pizza oven. Its beachside setting makes it a great way to start the day, too – try the Caribbean French toast.

El Tacoqueto Tulum town, east side of Av Tulum at C Acuario. A dependable *lonchería* with gut-busting daily specials for about M$50, or delicious hot-off-the-grill tacos for even less.

Taquería Diaz Tulum town, west side of Av Tulum, between C Orion and C Beta. Vying for the title of best *taquería* in town, this place specializes in assorted grilled meat fillings. Evenings only; closed Wed.

Urge Taquito West side of Hwy-307, between El Crucero and the traffic lights. Roadside taco place that makes a great lunch stop – good shrimp tacos and ceviche at rock-bottom prices.

La Vita è Bella Coast road, 1.6km north of the junction. Reasonably priced sandwiches and wood-oven pizzas are served throughout the day until 11pm, along with Italian-style steaks and seafood. A cocktail bar opens at 9.30pm, and a European party crowd often gets dancing later under the big palapa.

Nightlife

Although many visitors tell tales of the ultimate beach party in Tulum, tracking down that elusive revel in the sand can be a little difficult. Look for flyers and posters in town, or ask around at cabaña camps and beach clubs like *Zazil-Kin* or *El Paraiso*; there's often some kind of beachfront bongo jam and DJ fest around the full moon. Otherwise, most people stick to their hotel **bars** for an evening's entertainment.

After Tulum town, east side of Av Tulum, between C Centauro and C Satelite. Late-night dance club that's fun when it gets busy, which is not every night. Look out for advertized special events.

Azul Tulum town, east side of Av Tulum, between C Beta and C Osiris. The closest Tulum town comes to a regular nightclub, with fusion food, bar, terrace and a soundtrack of international techno and house. Small dancefloor in the back.

Habana Café Tulum town, east side of Av Tulum, across from *The Weary Traveler*. Cuban bar with a roof terrace and good rum cocktails – usually a lively crowd, especially for Saturday-night parties.

Mezzanine Coast road, 1.5km north of the junction. This super-cool bar-lounge is the only place on the beach where you can regularly find a dance scene. Friday night's *Fiesta en la Playa* channels Ibiza style with European and Mexican DJs; weekend and afternoon parties, too.

El Paraiso Beach Club On the beach, 1.9km north of the junction. This very hospitable beach bar has plenty of room for dancing on the sand. During the occasional massive parties, a big screen shows movies or trippy visuals.

La Zebra Coast road, 4km south of the junction. Tequila bar which hosts a salsa night and pit roast every Sun, plus free salsa lessons Thurs–Sun at 6pm.

Listings

Bank An HSBC with an ATM is in the middle of town, on the east side of Av Tulum, between C Osiris and C Alfa; there's a second ATM on the opposite side of the highway, a block north. Several cambios on the main street will change cash and travellers' cheques.

Bike rental Iguana Bike, C Satelite, between C Andromeda and C Sol (ⓣ984/871-2357), has the best rental bikes in town and also organizes jungle and cenote bike tours.

Car rental Several places on Av Tulum, including Buster (ⓣ1-800/728-8737, ⓦwww.busterrentacar.com), opposite the *Gaudi Café*.

Colectivos gather close to the main bus station, offering service to Playa del Carmen (frequently) and Felipe Carrillo Puerto (every 1–2hr).

Diving There are dozens of dive shops both in town and on the beach: reliable operators include Cenote Dive Center, west side of Av Tulum at C Osiris (ⓣ984/871-2232, ⓦwww.cenotedive.com); Halocline, C Orion Sur at C Andromeda, opposite *Azafran* (ⓣ984/120-6402, ⓦwww.halocline-diving.com); and Acuatic Tulum (ⓦwww.acuatictulum.com.mx), with offices on the beach at *Cabañas Zazil-Kin* (ⓣ984/100-7122) and Hwy-307 by the traffic lights (ⓣ984/871-2508). Extreme Control, at El Paraiso Beach Club, also offers kiteboarding (ⓣ984/745-4555, ⓦwww.extremecontrol.net).

Internet Plenty of places on Av Tulum offer Internet access, and an increasing number of hotels have wireless access. Reliable downtown places include Charlie's, next door to the *Gaudi Café*, and Praetorian, a block north across from the HSBC bank.
Laundry Reliable, inexpensive laundry at Lavandería Los Gemelos, west side of Av Tulum, between C Osiris and C Beta, or Lavandería Burbujas, two blocks east of the main drag on C Jupiter Sur.
Post office On the west side of Av Tulum, between C Satelite and C Osiris, Mon–Sat noon–3pm.
Taxis and transfers The main taxi office is on the west side of Av Tulum, between C Centauro and C Orion; most prices are shown on a board outside (M$40–100 to beach hotels and M$845 to Cancún, for example), but be sure to agree on the price before setting out, anyhow. Airport transfers can also be arranged with the Tucan Kin shuttle (Ⓣ1-800/702-4111, Ⓦwww.tucankin.com), which offers hotel pick-up from M$300 for one passenger (discounts for more than one).
Tours and travel agents Many tours can be arranged by your hotel, with pick-up from the door. Savana Travel Agency, on Av Tulum, next to *La Nave*, is a full travel agency for flights and car rental as well as local tours. The best tours of Sian Ka'an, run by locals, are with the Centro Ecológico Sian Ka'an, whose office is on Hwy-307, in front of *El Crucero* hotel, by the ruins entrance (Ⓣ984/871-2499, Ⓦwww.siankaan.org), or Sian Ka'an Community Tours, west side of Av Tulum, between C Centauro and C Orion (Ⓣ984/114-0750, Ⓦwww.siankaantours.org).

Cenotes near Tulum

As an alternative to the beach, there are a large number of **cenotes** very close to Tulum; a couple of them are the most impressive in the area. In addition to those to the north of town (see p.139), you can also check out **Gran Cenote** (daily 10am–5pm; M$80), just 4km west from Tulum on the road to Cobá. A collapsed cavern that's good for swimming and snorkelling (as well as some spectacular dives), the pool can get very busy in the middle of the day, as it's a popular stop for tours. The dramatic stalagmites and stalactites are well worth braving crowds for, though. You can rent gear here if you don't have your own, and there are toilets and changing rooms, as well as jetties and steps for easy access. So-called because local taxi drivers used to wash their vehicles here, **Cenote Carwash**, aka Aktun-Ha (daily 9am–5pm; M$30), 4km further west, is less impressive on the surface – it's simply a big pond, without any rock structure above – but strap on a snorkel mask or dive tank and you'll be astounded by the underwater rock formations, touted as among the best on the peninsula. Divers have an advantage here, as they can reach the spectacular **Room of Tears cave**, dripping with stalactites, and go below the algae bloom that thrives from March to October, making snorkelling impossible. Both the Gran Cenote and Carwash are easily accessible by second-class bus or a taxi. You may have trouble carrying on from the cenotes to Cobá (see below), however, because the buses are infrequent and often full.

For more solitude, you may want to go instead about 3km south of Tulum on Hwy-307, where **Cenote Escondido** (also called Mayan Blue) lies about 1km east of the main road, and **Cenote Cristal**, a similar distance west. These are secluded spots, open to the sky, good for snorkelling and rarely crowded; pay the joint entrance fee (M$50) at a small kiosk on the west side of Hwy-307.

Cobá and Punta Laguna

Some 50km northwest of Tulum lies the wonderfully isolated Maya site of **Cobá**, worth visiting for its jungle setting and the added fun of getting around the far-flung pyramids by rented bicycle, if you like. Although the ruins aren't as well restored as those at Tulum, their scale is much more impressive, and the dense greenery and wildlife make a good counterpoint to the coast. Moreover, they're not difficult to reach – the narrow but well-paved road out of Tulum leads past the Gran Cenote and Carwash about 48km to a large roundabout, where the village of Cobá and the ruins are just a couple of kilometres to the west. Approximately 20km northeast of the ruins, the **Reserva de Monos Arañas de Punta Laguna** is home to the northernmost community of spider monkeys in Mexico; even if you don't see the critters, the lake here is a beautiful place to canoe. Buses run regularly to Cobá from Tulum, but there's no public transport at all to the monkey reserve. If you don't have a car and would like to visit everything in a day outing, including a stop at Gran Cenote or Cenote Carwash (see opposite), ask at your Tulum hotel about tours, which are typically informal and cost not much more than the taxi fare. If you are doing it yourself, it's well worth getting up very early, or waiting till the end of the day, to get the most from both places.

Cobá

Set in the dense, muggy inland forest amid several lakes, the crumbling ancient city of **Cobá** (daily: Nov–April 7am–6pm; May–Oct 8am–7pm; M$48, parking M$40) is a fascinating site, with clusters of buildings spread out over several kilometres. Sadly, it's far from undiscovered, and in the middle of the day the car park overflows with coaches. Few of these arrive before 10am, however, and most have left by 4pm; outside these hours you can still ramble through the forest in relative peace. There's even the possibility of seeing the local wildlife, including toucans, egrets, coatis and myriad tropical butterflies, such as the giant iridescent blue morpho. A visit here requires at least a couple of hours to see everything and a great deal of walking; renting a **bicycle** (M$30) just inside the site entrance is highly recommended. Otherwise *triciclo* cabs charge M$95 for the tour – many people end up hiring one to bring them back to the entrance when their energy runs out.

Occupied from about 100 AD until the arrival of the Spanish, the site was so long established and legendary that it was even mentioned in the *Chilam Balam* of Chumayel, the Maya book of prophecy and ritual lore written in the eighteenth century, well after the city had been abandoned. The city's zenith was in the Terminal Classic period, around 800 AD, when most of the larger pyramids were built, and its wealth grew from close links with the great cities of Petén, in lowland Mexico and Guatemala. These cities influenced Cobá's architecture and its use of stelae, typically seen only in the southern Maya regions. Cobá also prospered later through its connections with coastal cities like Tulum, and several structures, built around 1200, reflect the style found at those sites.

The first cluster of buildings you reach, right by the entrance, is the compact **Grupo Cobá**, a residential and ceremonial complex where claustrophobic corbel-vault passages lead inside to tiny rooms. The large central pyramid, known as the **Iglesia** (church), was used for Maya ceremonies even after the city ceased to function. There's a small ball-court here, too, with worn carvings; on account of its size, local guides generally claim this was a training court. Up the main path, near the fork, the **Conjunto Pinturas**, named for the paintings inside the temple that sits atop the main building, is a complex assembled with recycled stones in the late Post-Classic era, after 1200.

A kilometre from the fork along the main route is the Nohoch Mul, Cobá's largest and most impressive structure. Along the way is a substantial **ball-court** where you can still see some of the original court markers – an almost 3-D human skull carved at the centre (a feature of many ball-courts, but rarely so well preserved) and a profile of a jaguar warrior with two eroded glyphs at the north end. There are also the rings through which the players would try to get the ball, and a couple of stelae. Just beyond the playing field is the **Xaibé** (Crossroads) pyramid, so named for its position at a major junction of *sacbeob*, the limestone-paved highways the Maya built to connect cities. The pyramid's rounded, stepped design and exceptionally steep, impractical stairway is reminiscent of the Pirámide del Adivino (Pyramid of the Magician) at Uxmal (see p.246), in miniature.

At the end of the path, the looming **Nohoch Mul** reaches a height of 42m, making it far taller than El Castillo at Chichén Itzá, and indeed one of the tallest Maya structures in the Yucatán. Perhaps because it is surrounded by lofty forest trees, it doesn't immediately look that impressive, but once you start to climb the narrow and precipitous stairway, the resemblance to the great pyramids at Tikal in Guatemala becomes more striking. The awesome view takes in nearby lakes as well as the jungle stretching uninterrupted to the horizon. The small temple at the top, similar to structures at Tulum, is a later addition, dating from around 1200 AD. There's a welcome cold-drinks stall at the bottom to reward your efforts.

Retrace your steps to the central fork, where another path leads 1km down a shady *sacbé* to **Grupo Macanxoc**, with a cluster of some twenty stelae, most carved during the seventh century AD. Stele 1 shows part of the Maya creation myth and the oldest date recorded in the Maya Long Count calendar system, which tracks the days since the moment of creation. Other stelae depict an atypically high number of women, suggesting that Cobá may have had female rulers. Clambering between the carvings, you're crossing not natural hills, but unreconstructed pyramids; in a way, these offer a more palpable sense of the civilization that thrived here than some of the more immaculately rebuilt structures.

Practicalities and Cobá village

Five second-class **buses** a day (and one first-class) run to Cobá from Tulum and continue on to Valladolid. The first leaves Tulum at 7am (arriving around 7.40am); the next, which continues to Chichén Itzá after stopping in Valladolid, arrives in Cobá around 10am – you could therefore theoretically cover both sites via public transport from Tulum, though you would be rushed. The last bus back to Tulum leaves at 6.30pm.

The **village** of Cobá, where the bus stops, is little more than a cluster of houses and cabañas beside a small lake, a few hundred metres from the site entrance. There are a number of small **hotels**, however, and several restaurants. For a wonderful bit of tropical luxury, *Villa Coba* (Ⓣ987/872-9300 ext 8101, Ⓦwww.islandercollection.com; ❼) overlooks the lake and comes complete with a swimming pool and an archeological library. The *Hotelito Sac-bé* (Ⓣ984/206-7140; ❹–❺), on the left side of the main street through the village, is a very friendly place with comfortable budget rooms, all en-suite, some with air conditioning. The restaurant here also serves an excellent, generous breakfast. You will also find a couple of **restaurants** overlooking the lake – *La Pirámide*, which serves Yucatecan specialities like *cochinita pibil*, as well as other Mexican dishes, is good. There are additionally numerous no-frills **food stalls** adjacent to the site's entrance.

The lake at Cobá is home to a large population of **crocodiles** (so no swimming!) and turtles. Locals charge tourists M$20 to watch them attract the crocodiles with pieces of chicken at the end of the jetty. But the crocs can often be seen simply basking on the shore right by the road, where they are routinely tormented by tour guides, a practice which you should not encourage. If you do feel like a swim after a sweaty visit to the ruins, a couple of nearby **cenotes** have been opened up to visitors, about 6km beyond the village; you'll see signs pointing the way from the lake, and they're rarely much visited.

Reserva de Monos Arañas de Punta Laguna

From the roundabout outside Cobá, head northeast 18km (following signs for Nuevo X-Can and Cancún) to reach the **Reserva de Monos Arañas de Punta Laguna**, at the small village of Punta Laguna. From the entrance kiosk, you're required to hike with a guide into the forest (M$40 per person, plus M$200 for a guide for a group of up to ten people). As well as the **spider monkeys** here, which congregate in gregarious family groups, there are a few more solitary **howler monkeys** – there's no guarantee you'll see any monkeys

▲ A Central American spider monkey

at all, but the guides generally know where they are. They are at their liveliest in the early morning (preferably before 9am; the guides are locals who live here, so are on site from around 6am) and late afternoon (after 3.30pm), when they feed locally, so you're strongly advised to visit at those times; during the day they often range further afield (beyond the boundaries of the reserve) and are much harder to spot. The trail winds past **unrestored ruins** and a cenote in which many Maya skeletons were found, and where there's a little Maya shrine, lovingly tended. In the middle of the reserve is a big, brackish lake where you can rent canoes (M$60) and paddle around looking for herons and crocodiles. This is very much a community project; some of the local women sell handicrafts at a small shop and there's a simple lakeside restaurant. To reach the area you'll need a car, though some Cobá tours from Tulum, Cancún and Playa del Carmen include a visit to the reserve. Alltournative, for example, have an impressive zip-line here (Ⓣ984/803-9999, Ⓦwww.alltournative.com).

The Sian Ka'an Biosphere Reserve

Sian Ka'an means "the place where the sky is born" in Maya, which seems appropriate when you experience the sunrise in this stunningly beautiful part of the peninsula. The nature reserve is a huge, sparsely populated region sprawling along the coast, south of Tulum. Most of the thousand or so permanent residents here are fishermen and subsistence farmers, gathered in the village of **Punta Allen** and in an experimental agricultural settlement called El Ramonal.

Created by presidential decree in 1986 and made a World Heritage Site in 1987, the Sian Ka'an Biosphere Reserve is one of the largest protected areas in Mexico, covering 1.3 million acres. It contains all of the principal eco-systems found in the Yucatán Peninsula and the Caribbean: approximately one-third of the area is **tropical forest**, one-third fresh- and salt-water marshes and **mangroves** and one-third marine environment, including a section of the Mesoamerican Barrier Reef. The variety of flora and fauna is astonishing. All five species of Mexican **wild cat** – jaguar, puma, ocelot, margay and jaguarundi – live in

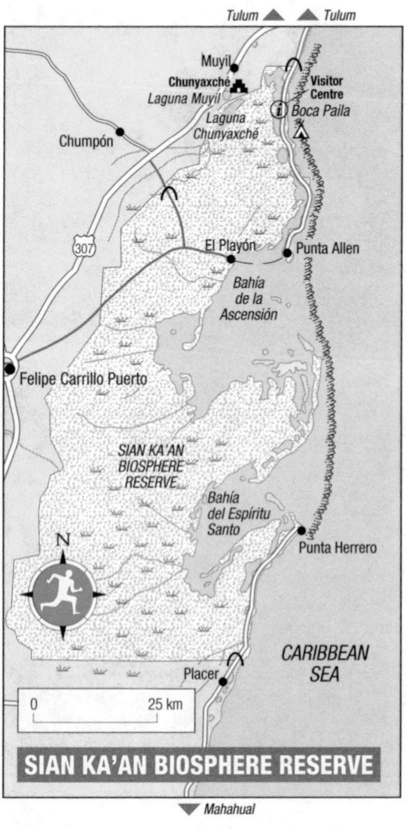

SIAN KA'AN BIOSPHERE RESERVE

the forest, along with spider and howler monkeys, tapir and deer, though all of these are very elusive. More than three hundred species of **birds** have also been recorded (including fifteen types of heron and the endangered wood stork, the largest wading bird that breeds in North America), and the coastal forests and wetlands are important feeding and wintering areas for North American migratory birds. The Caribbean beaches provide nesting grounds for four endangered species of **marine turtle**, while some extremely rare West Indian manatees have been seen offshore. Morelets and mangrove **crocodiles** lurk in the swamps and lagoons.

Although you can enter the park unaccompanied (M$21), most easily on the Punta Allen road south from Tulum's zona hotelera, you will benefit more from an organized tour (from around M$700), which is easily arranged in Tulum (see p.148 for operators). Most include knowledgeable guides who will introduce you to the diverse eco-systems along with a choice of activities – nature walks through the mangroves, swimming in cenotes, boat rides across the lagoons and the ancient Maya canals and maybe fly-fishing or snorkelling around Punta Allen. Whatever you choose, it's a beautiful trip around the fringes of the reserve's vast open spaces, with excellent opportunities for

The UNESCO biosphere concept

Established in 1968 by UNESCO (United Nations Educational, Scientific and Cultural Organization), the biosphere project is an ambitious attempt to combine the protection of natural areas and their genetic diversity with scientific research and sustainable development for local peoples. Biosphere reserves consist of a strictly protected **core area** in which human activity is kept to a bare minimum and the land is typically public property; a designated **buffer zone** used for non-destructive activities such as experimental research; and an outer **transition zone**, merging with unprotected land, where traditional land-use and human settlements are permitted, as is private or community land-ownership.

The success of a biosphere reserve depends to a great extent on the cooperation and involvement of **local people** – the Sian Ka'an management plan, for instance, incorporates several income-generating projects, such as fishing (using low-impact techniques), ornamental plant nurseries and low-impact tourism. But although Sian Ka'an has a relatively large uninhabited core area, the reserve's transition zone is under heavy pressure from the spread of tourism in Tulum – the beach property in this area is particularly valuable, and large plots have been sold off in recent years to wealthy Mexicans and Americans, raising serious concerns that the reserve is being compromised. At the same time, however, nature conservancy groups have been able to purchase plots to maintain untouched areas.

After a lull in the 1990s, Mexico's biosphere programme has regained focus. Including Sian Ka'an, five of the country's fourteen biosphere reserves are in the Yucatán. Calakmul, the largest in the peninsula, was established in 1993 in Campeche State and contains the vast ruined city of the same name. Off the Caribbean coast, the enormous coral atoll named Banco Chinchorro, established in 2003, is a sanctuary for marine life. And the peninsula's sizeable flamingo population is protected in two separate reserves: Ría Celestún, stretching along much of the west Gulf coast, and Ría Lagartos, along the northern coast. Both were natural parks that earned biosphere status in 2004.

For further **information** on the Sian Ka'an biosphere, contact the Amigos de Sian Ka'an, a non-profit organization formed to promote the aims for which the reserve was established. The Amigos support scientific research and produce a series of guide and reference books on the natural history of Sian Ka'an. Their main office is in Cancún (Ⓣ998/880-6024, Ⓦwww.amigosdesiankaan.org).

birdwatching, especially on the sunset tour. There are also less eco-friendly jeep safaris to Punta Allen with mainstream operators, with stops en route and lunch and snorkelling in Punta Allen. If you're doing it yourself, you can stop and swim at deserted beaches almost anywhere along the way, and there's a Visitors' Center about nine kilometres inside the reserve where you can rent kayaks, follow nature trails and arrange boat trips around the lagoons (from around M$1000 per boat).

Accommodation is available at Punta Allen (see below), or at the rigorously eco-friendly *Boca Paila Camps* (ⓣ984/871-2499, ⓦwww.siankaan.org; ❻), located just before the Vistors' Center and run by Centro Ecológico de Sian Ka'an. The camp's sturdy "tent cabins" are hidden among the trees in a prime location beside the beach; guests share bathrooms (with composting toilets), and water is heated with solar and wind power. The staff is very informed about the reserve, and the inexpensive **restaurant** is worth the long drive from Tulum for its sunset view across the jungle. Note that although there are many enticing stretches of sand along the road south from the Tulum hotel zone, biosphere regulations **prohibit camping** on the beach to control erosion – which is not to say it's not done, unfortunately.

Punta Allen

Right at the tip of a narrow spit of land, with a lighthouse guarding the northern entrance to the **Bahía de la Ascensión**, the remote fishing village of **PUNTA ALLEN** is not the kind of place you stumble across by accident. With a population of just five hundred, it's the largest village inside the reserve and a focus of initiatives by both government departments and non-profit organizations promoting sustainable development. Bonefish and tarpon in the bay are a draw for active travellers; layabouts will appreciate the mellow, timeless atmosphere that pervades the sand streets. Telecommunications are almost completely absent, and the most noise you'll hear is the creak of your hammock and the rustle of palm fronds in the breeze. The road south from Tulum's zona hotelera has traditionally helped maintain Punta Allen's special quality: during the rainy season (from late May to October) it was a famously rutted, rollercoaster-like ride. The road is still rough going, but major improvements mean that, in the dry season at least, the 50km drive from Tulum should now take no more than an hour and a half. A colectivo leaves Tulum daily at 2pm (departing from near the taxi office; M$200), and makes the journey in around two hours. Other **roads** into the reserve are far worse, though there's also a bone-rattling, frequently jam-packed colectivo from Felipe Carrillo Puerto (see p.164) to Vigia Chico (also called El Playón), from where a small boat ferries you across the lagoon to Punta Allen – a journey of two to three hours in total. However you get here, bring plenty of cash (there's no bank). **Leaving** Punta Allen with public transport requires an early start, and hence a couple of night's stay if you are actually to spend any time here: the Tulum colectivo will collect you from your accommodation at 5am; the boat followed by the colectivo for Felipe Carrillo Puerto at 7am – sign up beforehand at Tienda Mini-super Caamal to reserve your space.

Entering Punta Allen from the north, past the tiny naval station on the right and beached fishing boats on the left, the first and cheapest of the **accommodation** options is the bohemian *Posada Sirena* (ⓣ984/877-8521, ⓦwww.casasirena.com; ❺–❻), with cabañas for up to eight people. But if you can afford it, ★ *Cuzan Guesthouse* (ⓣ983/834-0358, ⓦwww.flyfishmx.com; ❺–❼), the next hotel south, is far preferable – it specializes in **bonefish tours** and rents wood cabañas and tepees, some with hot water and solar lighting. In the offseason, prices are cut by almost half. The bar and restaurant are great, though you'll need to book meals if you're not staying there. *Serenidad Shardon* (Ⓣ984/876-1827 in Mexico, Ⓣ616/827-0204 in the US, Ⓦwww.shardon.com; ⑥–⑨), just south of the village, offers everything from camping space on the beach (they can provide tents with beds, from M$150–250 per person) and dorm beds (M$150) to all or parts of a big, comfortable beach house.

There are a number of **restaurants** along the beach serving basic, fresh seafood, though none seem to survive long; better bets are *Muelle Viejo*, run by the local nurse, and the restaurant at *Cuzan*. A number of simple tiendas sell basic groceries, supplemented by a **mobile shop** in a truck that travels the length of the peninsula on Wednesdays and Saturdays, selling fresh items not available locally – it usually turns up in the early afternooon. Although there's no dive shop, the hotels generally have some form of **watersports equipment** for their guests and allow non-residents to rent. Fishermen can be persuaded to take you into the reserve for a fee: for instance, a three-hour snorkelling tour, during which you might see some of the local loggerhead turtle population, runs to about M$1200 for a boat; *Cuzan Guesthouse* offers similar tours at similar prices. Victor Barrera is a recommended local guide who takes people **fishing** in the flat waters of Bahía de la Ascensión (Ⓣ998/893-1063, Ⓦwww.macabimarch.com). There are also a number of dedicated fly-fishing lodges in the vicinity, with all-inclusive rates mostly for longer stays – try for example *Pesca Maya* (Ⓣ998/848-2496, Ⓦwww.pescamaya.com) or the *Palometa Club* (Ⓣ1-866/723-7776 in the US, Ⓦwww.palometaclub.com).

On land, for a great view over the bay, you can simply follow the trail south from the village to the **lighthouse**, 2km away, though the route remains somewhat blighted by the destruction wrought by recent hurricanes.

Chunyaxché

Heading south from Tulum, the highway narrows as it runs along the west edge of the Sian Ka'an reserve. After about 20km, you reach the ruins of **Chunyaxché** (daily 8am–5pm; M$29, plus M$40 to follow the boardwalk to the lagoon), at the village of **Muyil**. Take any second-class **bus** leaving from Tulum to Chetumal, or a colectivo, and ask to be dropped at the gate to the ruins. The modest entrance, right beside the highway, has just a ticket booth and restrooms. Despite the size of the site – probably the largest on the Quintana Roo coast – and its proximity to Hwy-307, you're likely to have the place to yourself, as few visitors to the Yucatán travel further south than Tulum.

Archeological evidence indicates that Muyil was continuously occupied from the Pre-Classic period until after the arrival of the Spanish in the sixteenth century. There is no record that the inhabitants came into direct contact with the conquistadors, but they were probably victims of depopulation caused by European-introduced diseases. Most of the buildings you see today date from the Post-Classic period, between 1200 and 1500 AD. The tops of the tallest structures, just visible from the road, rise 17m from the forest floor. There are more than one hundred mounds and temples, and around the central cleared area it's easy to wander and find dozens of buildings buried in the jungle; climbing them is forbidden, however.

The centre of the site was connected by a *sacbé* to the small **Muyil lagoon,** 500m away at the edge of the Sian Ka'an reserve. This is joined to the large

Chunyaxché lagoon, and ultimately to the sea at **Boca Paila,** by an amazing **canalized river** – the route created by ancient Maya traders. Wildlife scatters as you follow the boardwalk that leads through the mangroves to the lagoon. Two wooden watchtowers rising high above the forest canopy will confront you; the rickety climb is not for anyone with the slightest fear of heights. At the end of the path you might find a fisherman offering a boat tour into the reserve, where you'll come across even less-explored Maya sites (there are said to be over twenty small sites within the reserve), some of which appear to be connected to the lagoon or river by **underwater caves**. If you want to be sure of entering the reserve this way, however, it's easiest to do so by arranging it in advance, through one of the Sian Ka'an tour operators in Tulum (see p.148).

Leaving the site, particularly if you're making your way up to Tulum, should be easy enough, provided you don't leave too late. Continuing south, however, could prove a little more difficult, as buses to Chetumal run only every couple of hours, and colectivos are often full when they pass.

Travel details

Buses

Bus service in this area is provided primarily by ADO and Mayab, supplemented by a few second-class Oriente and ATS services. The second-class buses will stop anywhere on the highway on request, but run infrequently – in this case, you're better off in a colectivo.

Cobá to: Cancún (3 daily via Playa del Carmen; 3hr); Chichén Itzá (10am via Valladolid; 1hr 30min); Tulum (5 daily; 40min); Valladolid (4 daily; 1hr).

Tulum to: Cancún (frequently; 2hr); Chetumal (5 daily first class, 11 daily second class, all via Bacalar; 3–4hr); Chichén Itzá (2 daily via Valladolid; 2hr); Cobá (5 daily; 40min); Felipe Carrillo Puerto (4 daily; 1hr); Mérida (3 daily first class, 8 daily second class; 4–7hr); Playa del Carmen (frequently; 1hr); San Cristóbal de las Casas (2 late-afternoon services via Francisco Escarcega and Palenque; 13hr); Valladolid (5 daily; 1hr 30min); Villahermosa (5 daily; 10hr).

Colectivos

White shared vans line up along Av Tulum, close to Tulum's bus station, and depart whenever they are full – every ten or fifteen minutes for Playa del Carmen, and every hour or so for Felipe Carrillo Puerto. They will stop anywhere on request. You can also flag them down from the roadside, and they will stop if they have an empty seat. Pay as you get out.

4

The Costa Maya and the Río Bec

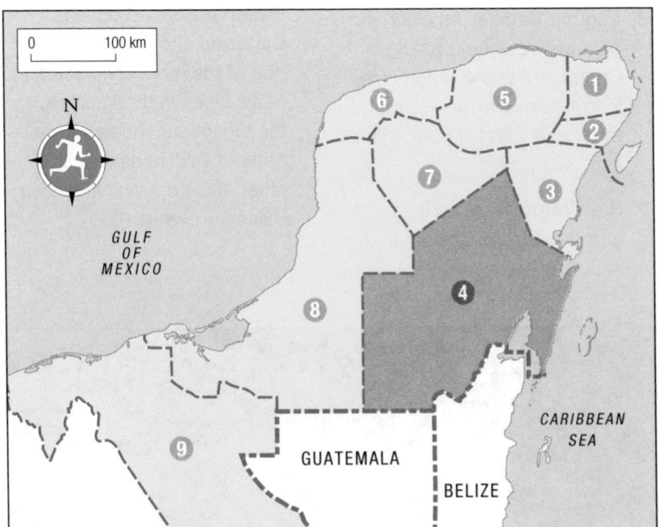

CHAPTER 4

Highlights

- **Mahahual** Rebuilding after the ravages of Hurricane Dean, Mahahual remains a beach bum's fantasy, with a string of cabaña camps and a few friendly restaurants. See p.165
- **Banco Chinchorro** Scores of ships have dashed against this large coral atoll 30km off the coast, creating a vast playground for scuba divers. See p.167
- **Laguna Bacalar** As clear and gloriously coloured as the Caribbean, this 45-kilometre-long fresh-water lake is home to a huge variety of birds and fish. See p.168
- **Río Hondo** Team up with a tour operator in Chetumal to go rafting along this seldom-visited river, which forms Mexico's border with Belize. See p.176
- **Kohunlich** Giant monster masks, a sprawling palace complex with fantastic views and parrots swinging among the enormous fan palms are the main draws at this archeological site. See p.178
- **Calakmul Biosphere Reserve** Centred on Calakmul, the largest (and one of the most spectacular) Maya cities in the Yucatán, the biosphere shelters a vast array of wildlife as well as other ancient cities, including Balamkú. See p.183

▲ On the shore at Laguna Bacalar in southern Quintana Roo

4

The Costa Maya and the Río Bec

South of Tulum, Quintana Roo State noticeably changes character: the jungle creeps up flush against the narrow highway, now just two lanes with the merest whisper of a hard shoulder, and margaritas are in very short supply. With the exception of a growing beach-bum community on the **Costa Maya**, south of the Sian Ka'an Biosphere Reserve, the real personality of this part of the peninsula is found in the inland towns and villages. This region was the centre of the **Zona Maya**, the semi-independent area established by Maya guerrillas during the decades-long Caste Wars that marked the second half of the nineteenth century. Years of grand campaigns and small uprisings finally succeeded in earning the Maya some measure of autonomy, and a lessening of the exploitation they had suffered at the hands of Spanish colonists and Mexican hacienda-owners.

Ancient Maya history, too, is everywhere in evidence along the southern border of Mexico, reached by heading due west out of Chetumal on Hwy-186. The jungle to the south of this narrow road – which was laid down only in the latter half of the twentieth century – is some of the densest and richest in the country, and it contains fantastic Maya ruins, collectively known as the **Río Bec sites**. These tumbledown cities dot either side of the highway well into Campeche State, making for a fascinating archeological tour in an area that's still very unaffected by tourism and barely populated. With mostly older, rickety second-class buses plying the roads, and relatively few places to bunk, the Río Bec is a difficult and sometimes pricey place to explore (taxis provide the only transport to many ruins), but very rewarding if you make the effort.

The first settlement of any size beyond Tulum – a good 100km south – is **Felipe Carrillo Puerto**, a crossroads on the way to Valladolid and Mérida with strong Maya roots. Carrillo makes a good base for excursions into Sian Ka'an (see p.152) and smaller Maya communities inland. The main highway continues through the village of Limones, where a turn-off leads to the Costa Maya towns of **Mahahual** and **Xcalak**, currently in the process of rebuilding after being devastated by Hurricane Dean in 2007. The once isolated beachfronts around these two are rapidly being bought up by wealthy Mexicans and foreigners, so catch them while you can.

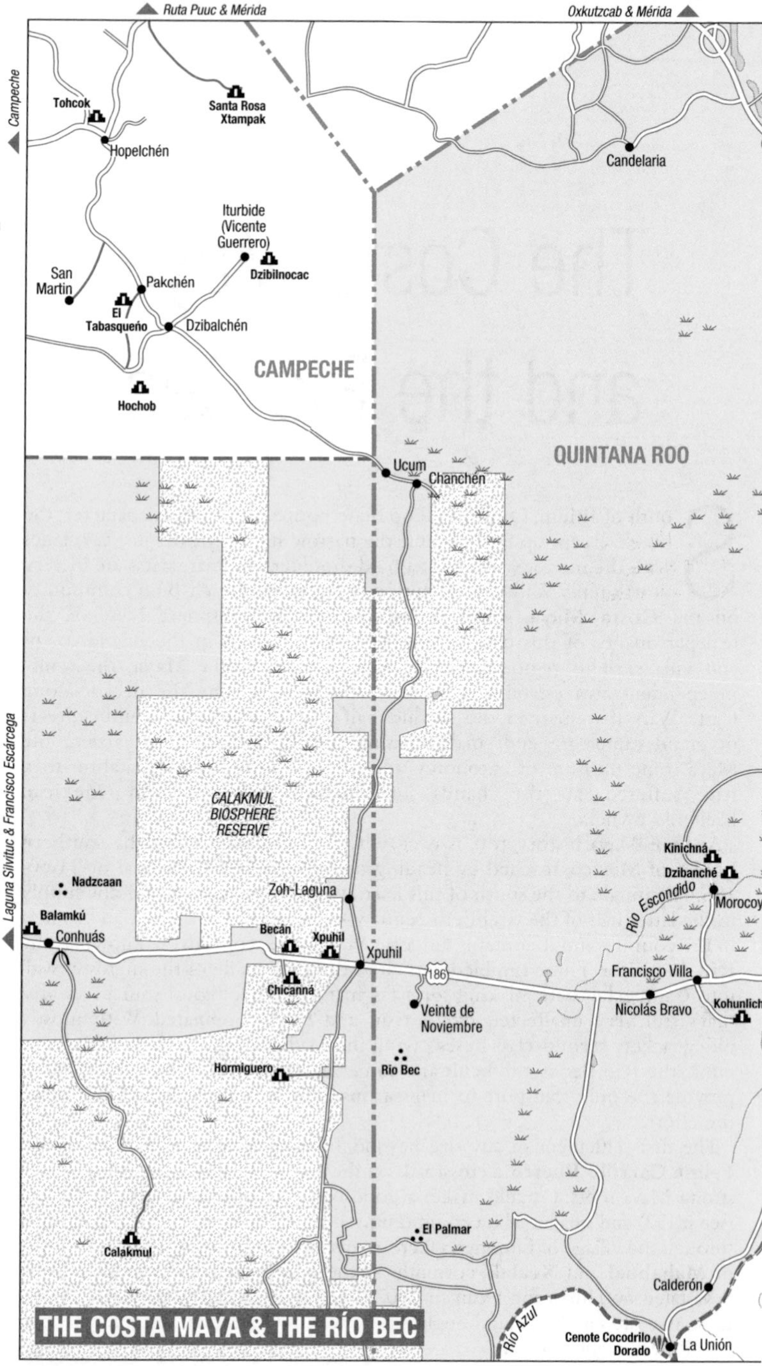

THE COSTA MAYA & THE RÍO BEC

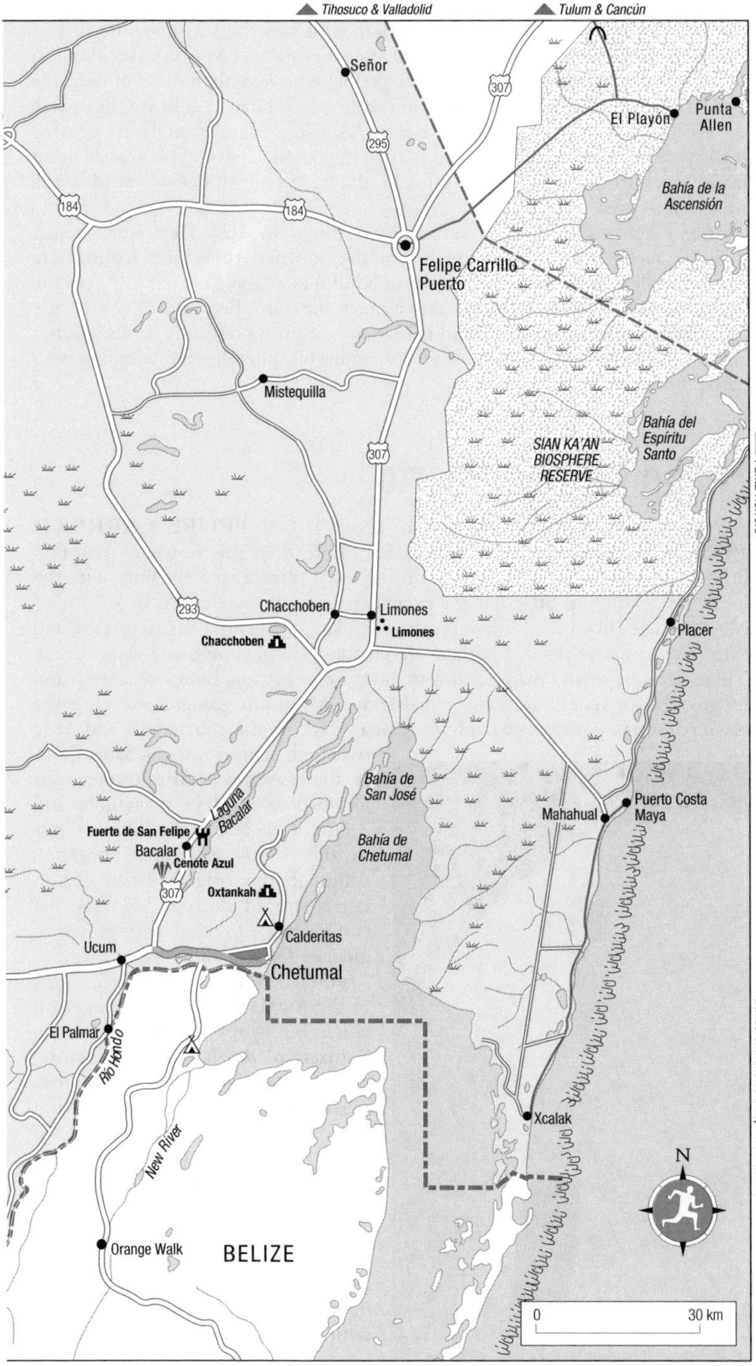
Tihosuco & Valladolid
Tulum & Cancún
Señor
307
295
El Playón
Punta Allen
Bahía de la Ascensión
184
184
Felipe Carrillo Puerto
Mistequilla
307
SIAN KA'AN BIOSPHERE RESERVE
Bahía del Espíritu Santo
Punta Herrero
293
Chacchoben
Limones
Limones
Chacchoben
Placer
Laguna Bacalar
Bahía de San José
Fuerte de San Felipe
Bacalar
Cenote Azul
307
Oxtankah
Bahía de Chetumal
Mahahual
Puerto Costa Maya
Calderitas
Ucum
Chetumal
Banco Chinchorro Biosphere Reserve
El Palmar
Río Hondo
New River
Xcalak
N
Orange Walk
BELIZE
0
30 km

Back on Hwy-307 and continuing south, you pass the seldom-visited Maya ruins of **Chacchoben**, followed by the beautiful **Laguna Bacalar**, an important destination for birds and the people who love them. The impeccably clear lake is also popular with Mexican vacationers. The road ends at **Chetumal**, the state capital and the gateway to Belize. A small, pleasant enough city, situated on a wide bay with a multicultural border-town feel, Chetumal is a good point from which to explore the **Río Hondo**, the wide river that serves as Mexico's southern border.

From Chetumal, Hwy-186 runs west through the **Río Bec** zone, which includes recently excavated and beautifully adorned ruins like **Kohunlich**. Most travellers, though, use the town of Xpuhil as a base. Located just over the border in Campeche State, Xpuhil is near the Río Bec and closer to the Yucatán's largest ruined city, **Calakmul** – awe-inspiring not only for its size, but also for its setting in the centre of an enormous biosphere reserve teeming with native flora and fauna.

Felipe Carrillo Puerto

A modest town with a population of about 15,000, **FELIPE CARRILLO PUERTO** is slow-paced, and visitors (of whom there are very few) will find little to do aside from hanging out on the town plaza in the evenings with the locals. As a jumping-off point for excursions into the wilderness or to smaller Maya villages, however, it's a very pleasant place to spend a night or two, and since it's at a major crossroads, there are plenty of simple hotels and places to eat. These days the town's major claims to fame are its organic honey operation and its greenhouse system, the largest in Mexico. More intriguing, however, is the town's history as the capital of the Zona Maya in the nineteenth and early twentieth centuries. Chan Santa Cruz, as the town was first known, was founded as a Maya stronghold and centre of the cult of the Talking Cross in the 1850s (see box opposite). Although this original town was all but destroyed during the wars, the cultural pride fostered by its period of independence is still evident today.

▲ The Iglesia de Balam Na in Felipe Carrillo Puerto

Along with its original name, most of the town's historical trappings are gone, but you can still visit the **Santuario de la Cruz Parlante**, built on the site of the Talking Cross. Turn west off the main street at the Pemex station, up Calle 69, and the complex is four long blocks down on the right, at the corner of Calle 60. Apparently neglected as it is, and with the remnants of the cross now kept in a smaller village nearby, the sanctuary nonetheless retains an air of mystic power, with the altar topped with several crosses "dressed" in

The Talking Cross movement

In 1850, after the first wave of the Caste Wars ended in the defeat of the Maya at Mérida, a group of rebels led by **José María Barrera** (himself a mestizo) retreated into the forests of Quintana Roo. The story goes that they set up camp near a cenote and discovered a cross, embedded in a tree, that spoke to the group and encouraged them to fight against their oppressors.

The apparition was not unique – such talking crosses and statues, known as *way'ob*, are common in Maya mythology as conduits through which disincarnate spirits speak. While contemporary scholarship is of course a bit sceptical, the Maya were inspired by the phenomenon and galvanized to keep fighting. Following the cross's directions (with the help of a "translator", Manuel Nahuat), and armed with weapons supplied by the British via neighbouring British Honduras, the **Cruzob**, as the fighters soon called themselves, began conducting raids against Franciscan missions and Spanish forts around the central peninsula. The encampment by the cenote grew into a formal town named **Chan Santa Cruz** ("little holy cross"), which functioned as the Cruzob's capital. They established control of territory as far north as Tulum and well inland, and they enforced it ruthlessly: light-skinned non-Maya were typically shot on sight or captured and enslaved.

After the rest of the peninsula was subdued, the Cruzob continued their guerrilla struggle; even after 1901, when the British withdrew support and Mexican armies occupied and gutted Chan Santa Cruz, the rebel Maya held a large patch of the jungle, later negotiating with the Wrigley's chewing-gum company to grant access to *chicle* trees and making a good bit of money in the process. In 1935 they finally signed a treaty, carefully worded to emphasize that they were not conceding, only allowing the Mexican government to rule them. Around the same time, Chan Santa Cruz was resettled and given an innocuous new name, **Felipe Carrillo Puerto**, after a former governor of the Yucatán who was assassinated in 1924. Though they've since stowed the guns, many of the Maya in this area maintain the syncretic religious practices – which meld Catholic elements such as baptism with ancient healing and prayer rituals – that were born out of this violent era.

huipiles, in the distinctive Yucatec Maya way. Photography is forbidden, and you are expected to remove your shoes when you enter.

The other, more imposing relic of the religion is the **Iglesia de Balam Na**, which dominates the main plaza. In a tidy bit of tables-turning, the Cruzob forced white interlopers they'd captured in the jungle to build the first Maya temple of the post-Columbus era, beginning in 1851. Despite its pagan roots, it is almost indistinguishable from a conquistador Franciscan church, with its arched roof and single-nave layout. After the Caste Wars ended in the early twentieth century, the building and the rest of the town were abandoned. Though Chan Santa Cruz was resettled and renamed in the 1930s, the Balam Na was consecrated as a Catholic church only in 1948; its governing order is Irish, as the local population would not accept Spanish priests.

Practicalities

Hwy-307 is known as Avenida Benito Juarez Garcia as it passes through Felipe Carrillo Puerto, which is laid out on a straightforward grid of numbered streets. A **Pemex station**, surrounded by food stalls (some of them excellent), marks the heart of town, though the main **plaza** (bounded by calles 65, 66, 67 and 68) and **bus station** (on the plaza at the corner of calles 65 and 66) are a couple of blocks southwest, just off the highway. A rudimentary **tourist office** (Mon–Fri

8am–2pm & 6–9pm) can be found on the highway, four long blocks south of the petrol station. There's an **ATM** by the Pemex station and a couple more at the bus station; numerous **Internet cafés** are dotted around, including one on the plaza next door to the *Galerias* restaurant. **Colectivos** for Tulum and points north leave from the bus station; for Chetumal, from a tiny separate terminal one block south of here at Calle 63. You can also catch a colectivo (followed by a short boat ride) to Punta Allen: this leaves at 10am and 3pm from the first block east of the highway from the central traffic circle.

For **overnight stays**, a couple of comfortable hotels on the plaza are preferable to those along the highway: the *Hotel Esquivel* (main entry at the rear on Calle 63, between calles 66 and 68; ⓣ983/834-0344; ❺) is only marginally more expensive than, and a definite cut above, *Chan Santa Cruz* (Calle 67 at Calle 68; ⓣ983/834-0021; ⓦwww.hotelchansantacruz.com; ❺); at both, it's worth paying slightly extra for a newly refurbished, air-conditioned room. On the plaza in front of the *Hotel Esquivel*, and under the same management, the *Parilla Galerias* is a reasonably priced restaurant serving tacos and grills, with an unrivalled position for people-watching. Alternatives include *La Placita Maya*, two blocks south of the bus station on Calle 66, for excellent tacos, and a number of simple places on Calle 69, opposite the Pemex station. Also, don't miss the bargain *panuchos* and *salbutes* sold all day at the bus station – even if you're just passing through, it's worth hopping off the bus to savour these quintessential Yucatecan snacks.

Although you can visit nearby nature spots and villages on your own (see below), you'll learn more about the environment and have greater interaction with the local Maya if you travel with the small **tour operator** here. Xiimbal Tours, on the plaza at Calle 65 (ⓣ983/834-1073, ⓦwww.xiimbal.com), seeks to promote sustainable tourism through trips to small Maya communities and visits to local attractions. These include walking tours of Felipe Carrillo Puerto itself, jaunts to the ruins of Chunyaxché, a visit to the **nearby Maya village** of Señor to experience local culture and the lake and a disturbing evening visit to a cave where boa constrictors feed on bats. For a relaxing day out a bit closer to town, call to arrange a visit to Rancho El Angel (weekends only; ⓣ983/834-0358, ⓦwww.flyfishmx.com; M$300), a beautiful and tranquil patch of forested land just twenty minutes south of town, owned by the proprietors of *Cuzan Guest House* in Punta Allen; a typical tour includes **birdwatching**, hiking several botanical trails, swimming and enjoying lunch cooked over a wood-fired grill.

Towards Valladolid and Mérida

Heading northwest from Carrillo, a well-paved, arrow-straight road leads into the densely forested interior and eventually to Valladolid. Along the way you may want to stop off at the scenic **Laguna Azul** lake, 7km from the traditional Maya village of **Señor**, or in **Tihosuco**, where the small but engaging **Museo de la Guerra Castas** (Tues–Sun 10am–6pm; M$5) tells the story of the Maya rebellion (in Spanish). A botanical garden grows at the back, and the gift shop sells locally made herbal treatments. The Franciscan church here is particularly dramatic, its crumbling nave open to the sky and overgrown with vines and weeds. The church was torched during one of the many battles in this town between 1848 and 1865, and until recently stood empty, still blackened by the fires that destroyed it. Now a good part of the interior has been whitewashed and reclaimed for regular church services. At the front on the plaza stands a weathered monument to native son Jacinto Pat, one of the Caste Wars' great leaders.

Colectivos provide the most frequent service to Señor, Tihosuco and Valladolid, departing every hour or so from the Carrillo market, on the northwest corner of the central traffic circle. But you may find it difficult to hop from village to village, as the shared vans are often packed full – hence the particularly high number of locals thumbing a ride along this route. Keep a sharp eye out for people on the roadside if you're driving.

The Costa Maya

The beaches that line the 250km of coast between the southern edge of the Sian Ka'an reserve and the Belize border, while not as scenic as those in Tulum, are quite beautiful in their sheer emptiness. Because of this, the **COSTA MAYA**, as this area is known, has become the object of fascination among those seeking a truly remote getaway, and for people hoping to make some money on this relatively untouched patch of Caribbean-front property (the latter group includes investors in a lavish and bizarrely out-of-place cruiseship pier, the Puerto Costa Maya). Development was temporarily halted by **Hurricane Dean** in August 2007, one of the most powerful hurricanes ever recorded over land, which saw winds of up to 200mph (320kph) ravage Mahahaul, closing the port to cruiseships for a year. It may take several years more to clear up the destruction and beach erosion altogether, though the subsequent reconstruction has also acted as a spur to the government – which has begun improving local services like electricity – as well as developers. For the time being, the two towns in the region, **Mahahual** and **Xcalak**, have a very end-of-the-world feel, and those looking for solitude can certainly find it here. Watersports enthusiasts will also want to make the trek to **Banco Chinchorro**, a divers' playground that was designated a biosphere reserve in 2003.

Infrequent transport has also helped keep the tourist droves at bay. ADO first-class **buses** to Mahahual leave Chetumal at 5am (8.30am on Sun), 1pm and 6.30pm; they return at 7.30am (10.30am on Sun), 1pm and 6.30pm. First-class buses from Cancún leave at 7am (9.30am on Sun) and 11.30pm; they return at 8.30am (12.30pm on Sun) and 5.30pm. Second-class Caribe buses, which continue from Mahahual to Xcalak, depart Chetumal at 6am and 4pm daily; an additional bus runs at 11am on weekends. You can connect with this service at the town of Limones if you're there by 7am and 5pm respectively, and noon for the added weekend service; long-distance services with ADO won't always stop at Limones, however. You can also get a **taxi** from Limones for about M$300–500, depending on your bargaining skills and final destination, and there are **colectivos** from Chetumal which will stop here for you if they have space. Bring plenty of **cash**, as there is no bank or ATM in either Mahahual or Xcalak; for **fuel**, there's a Pemex station on the main road just outside Mahahual.

Mahahual

MAHAHUAL, 60km east of Hwy-307 via a fast, dead-straight highway, is a tiny town of wooden shacks along a narrow beach. Even though the glitzy pier looms a few kilometres north, the pace is still more akin to Playa of twenty years past than to popular Cozumel, and has attracted a small European expat community. Though the damage from Hurricane Dean was severe, the town immediately started to pick itself up, repairing the eroded seafront and constructing a new malecón (seafront promenade). At the time of writing, this process was still ongoing, with the town itself especially hard hit – in particular, few restaurants are fully operational, and hotels outside town are a much more attractive option. Soon, however, much of the work will be completed and cruiseship schedules will return to normal – they call at the pier about four times a week in high season. On those days the community springs to life to accommodate the handful of vacationers who escape the walled compound or go on organized excursions: souvenir stands are set up, and a few jet skis buzz in the shallow, pale-green water off the beach. The town also grows festive during local holidays, especially Semana Santa (the week before Easter) and Christmas, when Mexican families pack the beaches.

The main tourist activity in Mahahual is **snorkelling** or **diving** around the pristine offshore reef. Dreamtime Dive Centre, at Km 2.5 on the coast road south of town (Ⓣ983/834-5823, Ⓦwww.dreamtimediving.com), is a reliable, dedicated shop. You can also hang out on the **beach**, of course, though this can rarely match the immaculate white sands of Tulum; there's lots of sea grass in the water. Further afield, both north and south along the coast road, there are better sands – especially north. Here it's about 22km of decent paved road to **Placer**, where there's some great sand, and a little further to the southern edge of the **Sian Ka'an Biosphere Reserve** (see p.152). An extremely poor road heads on through the reserve, with spectacularly empty beaches alongside almost all the way, as far as **Punta Herrero** (another 25km or so, but likely to be two hours' driving); in the tiny community at the end you may find a fisherman who can take you on a boat tour, or a shack where they'll cook fresh fish for you, but there's no guarantee of either, so bring plenty of water and other supplies. There's **wildlife** outside the reserve, too, with mangroves and small lakes behind the coast road in both directions, but nothing in the way of organized excursions to see them.

Practicalities

Accommodation in Mahahual is basic and generally less expensive than what you'd find in Tulum, especially out of season. Of the places in town, most attractive are *Posada Pachamama* (Ⓣ983/134-3049, Ⓦwww.posadapachamama.net; ❻) and *Los 40 Cañones* (Ⓣ983/123-8591, Ⓦwww.los40canones.com; ❻), both right on the beach with comfortable, modern, air-conditioned en-suite rooms.

The unpaved **coast road** north and especially south of town contains numerous other options, significantly more attractive and peaceful as long as building work continues in town, though hard to reach without transport. *Las Cabañas del Doctor* (Ⓣ983/107-5126, Ⓔprimomm@hotmail.com; ❺), just outside town at Km 2.5 south, has sturdy cabañas (en suite, but no hot water) and rooms (with hot water), across the road from the beach. Continuing south, *Hotel Maya Luna* (Ⓦwww.hotelmayaluna.com; ❼), at Km 4.5, has lovely studios right on the beach, with private roof terraces for stargazing, and a couple of smaller apartments; the restaurant here serves excellent breakfasts (included for guests). At Km 5.5, *Balamku* (Ⓣ983/839-5332, Ⓦwww.balamku.com; ❼) has an eco-friendly outlook, recycling greywater and keeping natural landscaping around its attractive white stucco, thatch-roof cottages. *Travel in'* (no reservations; ❹), at Km 6, is primarily a restaurant, but does have a couple of very simple rooms with shared bath and space to **camp** (M$60) close to the beach. Much further south (at Km 29), wind-powered ★ *Xahuayxol* (Ⓣ983/837-4564, Ⓦwww.xahuayxol.com; ❼) is an excellent spot on a particularly attractive section of beach where the reef is close to shore: you can hire kayaks to head out there, or to explore the mangroves inland. There are comfortable cabañas on the sand, and a good restaurant. The quickest way to get here is to follow the inland Xcalak road until you see the sign. An even more isolated spot is the American-run ★ *Mayan Beach Garden* (Ⓣ983/839-5332, Ⓦwww.mayanbeachgarden.com; ❼) at Placer, 20km north, with just three exceptionally comfortable units right on a beautiful empty beach; an excellent breakfast is included and other meals are available to guests.

Back in Mahahaul, the usual selection of ceviche **restaurants** lines the beach, all very makeshift at present. Hotels on the coast road have more organized alternatives, the best of them being *Travel in'* (see opposite). Open Tuesday to Saturday, evenings only, this is a popular meeting place for the local expat community with an eclectic menu, home-made pita bread and frequent theme nights – tapas on Wednesday, for example, and regular fondue sessions.

Leaving Mahahual, remember that some Caribe buses will go via Xcalak, a very long way round. ADO or the morning colectivo to Chetumal (departs around 10am) are much faster. Note also that on the way out towards the main highway from Mahahual, a military **checkpoint** conducts very thorough searches for drugs and other contraband – but as long as you're not breaking the law, the police are perfectly pleasant.

Xcalak

XCALAK, the only other community in the area, is some 40km south of Mahahual, very near the Belize border. Beyond *Xahuayxol* (see opposite), however, the coast road becomes virtually impassable. Instead, turn back inland after *Xahuayxol* to join the paved route that runs diagonally down from the main road into Mahahual from the highway (or, to bypass Mahahual entirely, turn south off the latter road after 50km). At the tip of the isthmus that stretches like a finger towards Belize, Xcalak was once the largest town in Quintana Roo, but is today a desolate village that never really recovered from being flattened by a hurricane in 1955; steady electricity was restored only in 2004, and Hurricane Dean did further damage. Although there's a fair amount of new building along the beach – mainly private villas – Xcalak is definitely at the back of the queue when it comes to government investment; roads in the village, and along the coast, are severely potholed.

There are no real beaches to speak of here, so the main reasons to visit Xcalak are for superb diving, salt-water fly-fishing and snorkelling. **Banco Chinchorro**, an atoll littered with more than a hundred shipwrecks and encrusted with rainbow-hued coral, is easy to visit via Xcalak, or you can enjoy the clean reef closer to shore. The other local "sport" seems to be trawling for kilos of cocaine washed up on the beach (aka *pez cuadro*, or "square fish"), as smuggling operations occasionally go awry offshore and the cargo is dumped overboard. The same is true in Mahahual, but here it only enhances the generally sketchy feel of the town.

Practicalities

Again, much the best accommodation is along the coast road, though the cheapest rooms are at *La Gaviota* (no tel; ❺) above the general store in the village's main street, one block back from the beach; opposite is an **Internet** and phone *caseta*. Heading north out of town, a small bridge leads to what is sometimes grandly referred to as the zona hotelera. Among the comfortable options here is *Costa de Cocos* (Ⓣ983/839-8537, Ⓦwww.costadecocos.com; ❼), a long-established, laid-back fly-fishing and diving centre with its own fishing boats and dive instructor, plus good snorkelling right off the dock; accommodation is in large, well-constructed wooden cabañas and there's also a popular restaurant, where breakfast is included in the rates. *Tierra Maya* (Ⓣ983/831-0404, Ⓦwww.tierramaya.net; ❼), a little further north, is a bit more beachfront-lux, with comfortable ocean-view rooms and another good restaurant where breakfast is included; nearby, solar-powered *Casa Carolina*

(Ⓣ610/616-3862 in the US, Ⓦwww.casacarolina.net; ⑦) has four plush rooms with simple kitchens. Or if you really want to get away from it all, the charming *Sin Duda Villas* (Ⓣ983/831-0006, Ⓦwww.sindudavillas.com; ⑦–⑨) are 8km further on suspension-breaking roads; rooms and apartments come with kitchen facilities – breakfast (and isolation) also included. There are a couple of simple restaurants in town, as well as *Costa de Cocos* and *Tierra Maya* mentioned above, but by far the best place is *The Leaky Palapa*, on the northern edge of the village, which serves dinner in the winter season (Thurs–Sun) and some weekends in summer. Reservations are recommended here – by email (Ⓔleakypalapa@yahoo.com), in person or through your hotel, which can call them on marine radio. The PADI dive shop XTC (Ⓣ983/831-0461, Ⓦwww.xtcdivecenter.com), just north of the bridge, organizes fishing expeditions, runs **snorkelling and birdwatching trips** (from M$300 per person) and rents snorkel and scuba gear. XTC also offers dive courses and has a licence to dive at Banco Chinchorro.

Laguna Bacalar and around

Glimpsed through the trees to the east as you continue south along Hwy-307, the gorgeous **Laguna Bacalar** resembles the Caribbean Sea, sparkling clear and ranging in colour from palest aqua to deep indigo. The reeds and trees around the water host a variety of **birdlife**, and in the lake you'll find freshwater snails and huge fish that reach nearly 2m in length. At 45km long and, on average, 1km wide, Laguna Bacalar is the second largest lake in Mexico (after Lago de Chapala, south of Guadalajara), linking with a series of other lakes, and eventually, the Río Hondo and the sea.

Chacchoben

Near the northern end of the lake, about 15km south of Limones, a rather grand intersection (built for the benefit of cruiseship passengers) marks the way to the ruins of **Chacchoben** (daily 8am–5pm; M$39), 9km west of the highway. For somewhere so little known, the "place of red corn" is remarkably impressive and, provided you don't coincide with a cruiseship tour, you are likely to have the place to yourself. Unfortunately, a visit does really require your own car (or taxi from Bacalar or Limones), as it is almost impossible to get here by bus. The road beyond Chacchoben continues towards Mérida, via the sites of the Ruta Puuc (see p.251).

Chacchoben, populated from around 250 BC to 1200 AD, flourished above all in the Early Classic period (250–600 AD); it was only rediscovered in the 1970s. Excavated by US archeologist Peter Harrison in the 1990s, the site was officially opened to the public in 2004. Hurricane Dean cleared many of the trees from the site, which has little signage, though local guides are available. The two main excavated areas are separated by a vast Gran Plaza; once paved, this is now totally overgrown, but its extent can be appreciated from above, by climbing the pyramid at the far end. A residential area, barely excavated, lies alongside the plaza, and there are many more unexcavated structures nearby. Of those which have been cleared, the first complex you reach, around Plaza B, had a dual purpose – temple at the front (with stucco decoration of butterflies), administrative area behind. The buildings at the far end are more impressive, including the Gran Basamento, a Petén-style, rounded corner pyramid raised high above its surroundings on a platform. This temple served an astronomical as well as a religious purpose, with portals on top through which the rising sun would shine on significant dates. Palapa thatch protects more stucco decorations.

Bacalar

More Maya remains dot the southern end of the lakeshore, around the town of **Bacalar**, which was a key point on the pre-Columbian trade route. The *Chilam Balam* of Chumayel, one of the Maya's sacred books, mentions it as the first settlement of the Itzá, the tribe that later occupied Chichén Itzá. Now it's a quiet place to stop for a day or two, enjoyed by naturalists as a base for birdwatching and kayaking on the glassy lake. The town is pretty spread out, but its centre clusters on a slope above the water, and most of what you'll need is here, within a couple of blocks of the main plaza and the fortress.

The **Fuerte de San Felipe**, overlooking the lake immediately below the plaza, is Bacalar's only real "sight". Built by the Spanish in the 1730s for protection against British pirates based in Belize (then British Honduras), the fort became a Maya stronghold during the Caste Wars and, in 1901, was the last place to be subdued by the government. Today it is a small, enjoyable **museum** (Tues–Thurs & Sun 9am–7pm, Fri & Sat 9am–8pm; M$50) that displays some of the Maya relics found here, as well as the trappings of pirate days. On the lake a couple of blocks north of here is the **Balneario Magico** (M$5), a pleasant swimming area with a restaurant and palapas for lounging. At the far southern end of the lakeshore road, just where it rejoins the highway, you can have more watery fun at the inky-blue "bottomless" (well, 140m) **Cenote Azul** (7.30am–8pm). Although free, you can only get to the cenote through the restaurant of the same name, so at the very least you'll have to pay for a drink; at weekends the place is busy with local swimmers and dive-bombing teens, entertained by live musicians.

Back in town several **restaurants** along the lakeshore road capitalize on the lake view at weekends, but more reliable for good local food is the basic yet satisfying *Orizaba*, serving inexpensive Mexican classics and a daily *comida corrida*, one block north of the plaza, then one-and-a-half long blocks west. On the plaza itself are *Cosa Nostra,* serving delicious pasta and pizza, as well as salads, sandwiches and snacks; *Sr Cafe*, for good coffee and drinks; and even an ice-cream parlour, *Hawaiian Paradise*.

For **overnight stays**, check out a number of options strung out along the water. Best of the places in town is ★ *Casita Carolina* (Ⓣ983/834-2334, Ⓦwww.casitacarolina.com; ❸–❺), a friendly American-owned guesthouse, a little over a block south of the fort, with seven assorted units, dotted around a garden that slopes down to the water. Accommodation ranges from pretty basic rooms to large apartments that share a kitchen, all with hot water. Another block further south, *Hotelito El Paraiso* (Ⓣ983/834-2334, Ⓦwww.hotelitoelparaiso.com; ❺) has more conventional lakeshore rooms, most with air conditioning, as well as a jetty for swimming and kayaks to hire. Further south along the lakeshore, the wonderfully kitsch and comfortable *Hotel Laguna* (Ⓣ983/834-2205, Ⓦwww.hotellagunabacalar.com; ❺) is a much larger place with a tiny pool, done up with seashell-encrusted lacquer countertops and plaster pillars galore. There's **camping** (M$50) at the Balneario Magico (see above). The **lakeshore outside town** also offers numerous opportunities to stay, often in a somewhat wilder setting, with endless opportunities for birdwatchers: *Villas Ecotucan* (Ⓣ983/834-2516, Ⓦwww.villasecotucan.info; ❺), 5km north of town, is particularly attractive, with comfortable cabañas on agreeably landscaped grounds, sandwiched between the lake and acres of uncleared forest; rates include breakfast and the use of kayaks. Colectivos and second-class buses can drop you off on the highway near the entrance. *Laguna Azul* (983/114-7002, www.laguna-azul.de), at the northern extremity of the lake (look for the sign beside the highway, just south of Pedro Santos, between Limones and the turn to Chacchoben), is still more remote but wonderfully welcoming, with a great little restaurant and bar; choose from en-suite cabañas (5) or camping space (M$45), and rent a kayak to explore the lake. You'll also see signs for various *ranchos* off the highway, offering lake access for a nominal fee and sometimes space to camp.

Other practicalities are easily taken care of: the **bus station** is just off the southwestern corner of the plaza; there's an **ATM** in the centre of the plaza; and various locations offer **Internet** access, including one spot on the way to *Orizaba* restaurant, opposite the huge church. An excellent local web portal, www.bacalarmosaico.com, offers information on all the above and more.

Chetumal and around

If you're heading south to Belize or Guatemala, you can't avoid **CHETUMAL**, 15km from the Belize border and capital of the state of Quintana Roo. Until 1898, when the Mexican navy established the frontier outpost of **Payo Obispo** (Bishop's Point) on this spot, no official border ran through the Bahía de Chetumal, which forms the city's southern edge. Today, elements of the neighbouring country's culture still linger in the little clapboard houses and the residents' often British-sounding names. After being obliterated by Hurricane Janet in 1955, the city has taken decades to reassert itself, but it still has very few notable "sights" to speak of. Indeed, it's largely oblivious to tourists and dedicated almost entirely to unglamorous cross-border commerce – which can be refreshing after the rustic hedonism of the Caribbean beach resorts. Mexicans come to visit the **duty-free zone** between the two countries, a dilapidated mini-mall area accessible by bus, where shops flog an odd assortment of goods: Dutch cheese, Taiwanese hi-fis, American peanuts, reproduction Levis from the Far East, Scotch whisky and more. Likewise, vendors of appliances and cheap lingerie line the main avenue. But despite these modern details, Chetumal retains a certain old-fashioned graciousness, especially palpable in the evenings, when the bay boulevard is filled with lovers and families.

Although it can't really be recommended as a destination for its own sake, Chetumal does make a decent one- or two-day stop for resting and restocking; everything from food to Internet access is easily and inexpensively available here. From the city, you can also make day- or overnight trips to the Río Bec archeological sites or to the little-visited Río Hondo area, both to the west. Be warned, though, that car rental (see p.175) is the one thing in Chetumal that's not a great deal.

Arrival and information

Chetumal's main **bus station** is on the north side of town, a short taxi ride from the centre (about M$15); locker rental costs M$5 per hour. A **bus ticket office** in town, on Avenida Belice, between avenidas Gandhi and Colón, spares you a trip back to the station to buy tickets for ADO and Caribe services. Some **second-class buses**, including Mayab services to Cancún, actually depart from the dusty yard adjacent to this office. The **airport** – currently offering only domestic flights to Mexico City – is 2km west of town. The heart of Chetumal, certainly for tourists, is Avenida Niños Héroes, as it runs down from the Museo de la Cultura Maya and old market to the bay.

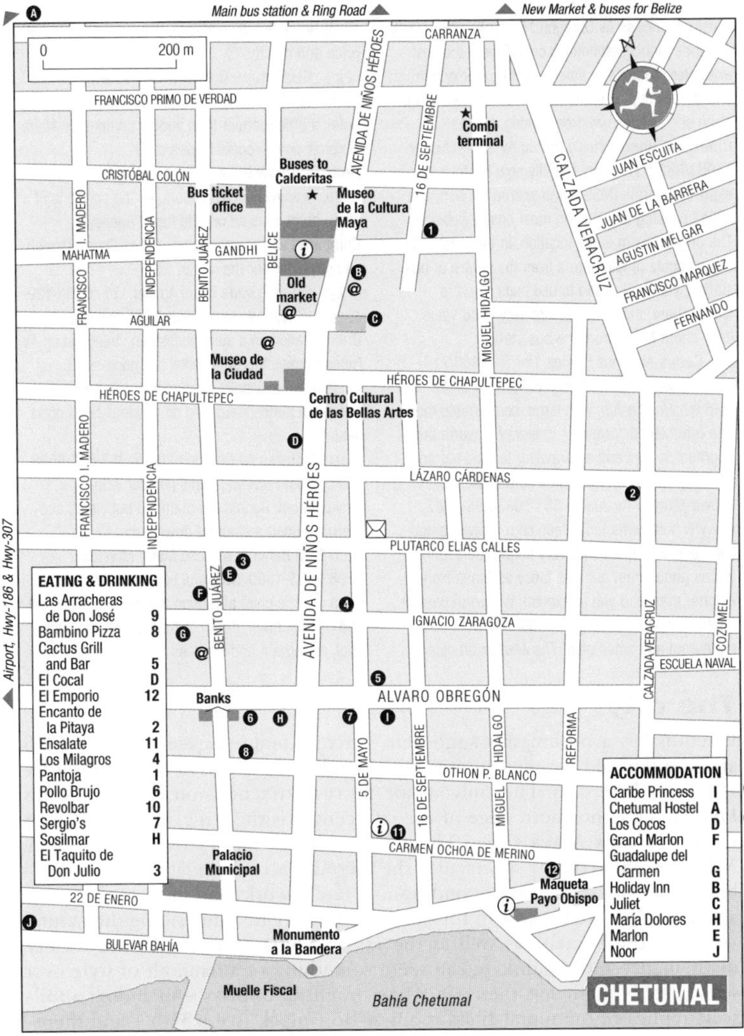

The main **tourist information** office, on Avenida 5 de Mayo at Avenida Carmen Ochoa (Mon–Fri 8.30am–4.30pm; ⓣ983/832-2031), provides helpful bus and hotel information, plus maps; they can also fill you in on nearby attractions in Belize. A smaller kiosk on the malecón at Avenida Hidalgo maintains later hours (Mon–Fri 9am–8.30pm, Sat 9am–3pm). There's also a more convenient, but less knowledgeable, privately run information hut in front of the Museo de la Cultura Maya, just off Avenida Niños Héroes.

Accommodation

Most of Chetumal's **hotels** are on or near Avenida Niños Héroes, in the few blocks back from the malecón; virtually all have off-street parking.

Caribe Princess Av Obregon 168 ⓣ983/832-0900, ⓔcaribe_princess@hotmail.com. One of the best examples of the city's time-warp ritz; smoky mirrors and shades of pink dominate the decor. Rooms are clean and all have a/c; free parking, too. ❻

Chetumal Hostel Sicilia 262 at Av San Salvador ⓣ983/832-8317. Very friendly new hostel with eight-bed dorms (M$90) and shared kitchen, and online booking facilities on most hostel websites. The only problem is the location, in the west of the city a couple of kilometres from the centre or bus station; you really need to use taxis if you're staying here, though these are very good value (only about M$12 from the bus station).

Los Cocos Av Niños Héroes 134 ⓣ1-800/719-5840, ⓦwww.hotelloscocos.com.mx. A better deal than the *Holiday Inn*, with large, comfortable rooms (the refurbished "premier" category is worth the upgrade), a pool and a sprawling terrace bar and restaurant. Also very pleasant suites. ❼

Grand Marlon Av Juárez 88 ⓣ983/285-3287, ⓦwww.hotelesmarlon.galeon.com. Newly remodelled business hotel with very comfortable, quiet rooms (though not quite as fancy as the designer exterior may lead you to expect); it's worth paying a little extra for an executive room. There's also a restaurant and small pool. *The Marlon*, an older sister hotel directly opposite, is a step down in both price and quality. ❻

Guadalupe del Carmen Av Zaragoza 226 ⓣ983/832-8649. Clean and tidy two-storey hotel, a little roomier than budget competitor *María Dolores*; some rooms have a/c. ❹

Holiday Inn Av Niños Héroes 171 ⓣ983/835-0400, ⓦwww.holidayinn.com. All the comforts of a chain hotel, plus an on-site travel agency. Compared to the giant suites at *Los Cocos*, though, you're paying for the name. ❼

Juliet Privada Efraín Aguilar 171 ⓣ983/129-1871, ⓦwww.hoteljulietchetumal.com. Great location on a quiet pedestrian street just off Av Niños Héroes, this small hotel has good-sized, modern, exceptionally clean rooms with a/c and TV. Not much atmosphere (and no parking), but a good deal. ❺

María Dolores Av Obrégon 206 ⓣ983/832-0508. Basic budget offering that's popular with backpackers. Rooms are cramped but clean, and there's a good restaurant downstairs. ❹

Noor Blvd Bahía at Av José María Morelos ⓣ983/835-1300. Beautiful bay views from your room are the chief attraction at Chetumal's newest and priciest hotel; designer furnishings, too, plus pool, restaurant and wireless Internet. ❼

The city

Chetumal is a mishmash of modern concrete buildings erected after 1955 and the few old wooden houses with porches that survive from the settlement's earliest days. The only major tourist attraction, on Avenida Niños Héroes at the northern edge of the city centre, is the large, modern **Museo de la Cultura Maya** (Tues–Thurs & Sun 9am–7pm, Fri & Sat 9am–8pm; M$50). Architecturally spectacular, the museum is in desperate need of refurbishment – it's dark, the air conditioning rarely works and most of the interactive displays are broken. In this state, the flowery text describing the natural world of the Yucatán, as well as the ins and outs of ancient Maya society, mathematics and cosmology, can seem something of a triumph of style over substance. Nonetheless there are a few insightful displays – including a full-scale replica of the mural-filled room at Bonampak (see p.318) – and there's an auditorium with free modern art displays and independent film screenings. On the street in front of the museum, the *Alegoría del Mestizaje* **sculpture** is one of the most striking depictions of the popular theme of the intermingling of Spanish and indigenous cultures, showing modern Mexico born of a conquistador and a Maya woman. Immediately south is a little warren of shops and *loncherías* – what's called the "old" **market** (the newer, larger one, where most of the fresh produce is sold and buses for Belize gather, is 1km northwest along Calzada Veracruz).

A few blocks south of the old market on Avenida Niños Héroes, the **Centro Cultural de las Bellas Artes**, in an impressive 1936 neo-Maya-style school, now houses the **city museum** (Tues–Sun 9am–7pm; M$10), with a collection of romantic memorabilia – from locally made Raleigh bicycles to ladies' hand fans – reminiscent of Chetumal's swashbuckling days, when it was a city of

▲ The Alegoría del Mestizaje sculpture

vaqueros sin caballos ("cowboys without horses"). The state schools for the performing arts are also located here, offering free live performances several evenings a week.

Avenida Niños Héroes continues down to the bay and the spic-and-span **malecón**, popular for fishing and evening strolls. A few blocks east, behind the modern Palacio Legislativo, a small Caribbean-style wooden house contains the fascinating **Maqueta Payo Obispo** (Tues–Sat 9am–3pm, Sun 9am–2pm; free), a scale model of the town as it looked in the 1920s, hand-carved in 1985 by an elderly resident named Luis Reinhardt McLiberty, with the help of local students. The small adjacent museum tells the story of the lighthouse barge *Chetumal*, with which the Mexican army helped establish the town and the country's border with then British Honduras, in order to stop the flow of arms to the rebels defending the Zona Maya. The town was renamed after the barge (itself named after a Maya lord of the sixteenth century) in 1936.

Eating and drinking

The area around the intersection of avenidas Niños Héroes and Obregón has the highest concentration of restaurants in Chetumal, while the **market stalls** south of the Museo de la Cultura Maya have good, inexpensive fare at lunch. **Nightlife** isn't particularly vibrant, but on weekend evenings, when a double-decker shark-shaped party bus cruises up and down the malecón, the plaza is busy with food stalls, and residents flock to the bar-restaurants (and the drive-through liquor store) strung along the seafront east of the plaza.

Las Arracheras de Don José Blvd Bahía, east of the centre. The speciality of this sprawling terrace restaurant, very popular on weekend nights, is meat tacos, from plain old pork to ostrich (*avestruz*), served with a fantastic array of fresh salsas. Want more meat? Steaks are also well priced.

Bambino Pizza Blanco 213. Inexpensive pizza and pasta in a lovely traditional wooden house. Several other bargain options can be found on this block.

Cactus Grill and Bar Av Obregón at Av 5 de Mayo. Attractive Tex-Mex style restaurant, with emphasis on the Mex. Balcony seating lets you watch the world go by.

El Cocal *Los Cocos* hotel. Not the cheapest food in town, but Mexican dishes at this open terrace restaurant are served with great care; breakfast is good, too. The mix of tourists and dressed-up locals makes for a convivial atmosphere, and evenings often see the live keyboard stylings of some crooner or other. Open till 1am Fri and Sat.

El Emporio Av Merino, between Av Hidalgo and Av Reforma. An excellent Uruguayan restaurant in a historic wooden house – great for a splurge. The steaks, served with lashings of garlicky *chimichurri* sauce, are excellent. Good selection of South American wines at decent prices, too.

Encanto de la Pitaya Av Calzada Veracruz at Av Cardenas. A sprawling, casual *restaurante familiar* under a tent, with live bands on weekend afternoons; in the evening, attention turns more seriously to drinking, and the clientele is typically all-male.

Ensalate Av Ochoa, between Av 5 de Mayo and Av 16 Septiembre. This lunch café specializes in baguette sandwiches, with a good range of vegetarian fillings, including avocado, salad and cheese.

Los Milagros Av Zaragoza, between Av Niños Héroes and Av 5 de Mayo. Enjoy tasty, inexpensive food (breakfasts are especially good) at this little sidewalk café, popular with local journalists. Busy day and night.

Pantoja Av Gandhi at Av 16 de Septiembre. Good *comida corrida* (M$45), a favourite with the locals, and hearty dishes like *mondongo* (tripe stew) and *chilaquiles* for breakfast. Closed Sun.

Pollo Brujo Av Obregón, between Av Juárez and Av Niños Héroes. Roasted chicken and nothing else, served fast and hot.

Revolbar Blvd Bahía, east of the centre. Close to *Las Arracheras de Don José* and at the centre of a group of lively places round here, *Revolbar* has themed weekend club nights and visiting DJs with progressive electro sounds, as well as a chilled-out terrace bar.

Sergio's Av Obregón 182. Upmarket but reasonably priced Italian-style restaurant (most entrees are less than M$150) with a few veggie options, such as soups, pizzas and salads, as well as a well-prepared steak.

Sosilmar Av Obregón, in the *María Dolores* hotel. One of the best budget options in town, with good meat and fish and a few splurgy items like *camarones al diablo* (devilled prawns) for M$90. Closed Sun.

El Taquito de Don Julio Av Calles, between Av Niños Héroes and Av Juárez. A good choice for an evening snack if you don't want to walk out to *Las Arracheras Don José*. Make a meal of overstuffed grilled-meat tacos and some *queso fundido* on the fluorescent-lit terrace.

Moving on to Belize and Tikal

Belizean buses run frequently between Chetumal and **Corozal** (1hr), the closest town on the Belize side, though you must get off the bus and walk across the bridge at Subteniente Lopez, the official border crossing, 8km west of Chetumal. Citizens of the UK, US, Canada, Australia and New Zealand do not need a visa. The cheapest, very rattletrap buses leave from the new market – Mercado Lázaro Cárdenas – a long way north on Avenida Calzada Veracruz, at regular intervals throughout the day (more frequently in the morning); you can get over the border for about M$20, and a few of these continue on to **Orange Walk** (2hr 30min) and **Belize City** (5hr). First-class services on better-outfitted vehicles depart from the main bus station (5 daily; around M$100; 3hr to Belize City). There are also two buses a day to Tikal and Flores, via Belize City, leaving at 5am and 6am. Note that cars rented in Mexico cannot typically be driven into Belize. Likewise, there's no air travel straight from Chetumal; you have to cross to Corozal and take an internal flight.

Listings

Airlines Aviacsa, Click Mexicana (Ⓣ983/832-6675) and Mexicana (Ⓣ01-800/801-2010) run daily flights to Mexico City. Aviacsa's office is on Av 5 de Mayo at Av Cardenas (Ⓣ983/832-7676), the others are at the airport.
Buses Most long-haul buses leave from the main bus station on the north edge of town, though some second-class services use the downtown ticket office. For Belize and Tikal, see box, above.
Car rental is expensive in Chetumal; try Continental (Ⓣ983/832-2411, Ⓦwww.continentalcar.com.mx), in the lobby of the *Holiday Inn*, or Bacalar Tours (see "Tour operators", below).
Combis leave from the station on Av Primo de Verdad at Av Hidalgo, making them an easier option than buses for nearby destinations, such as Bacalar (every 30min; 30min), Ucum (hourly from 7am), La Unión (5 daily; 2hr 30min) or Nicolas Bravo (4 daily; 1hr 15min).
Internet Plenty of options, including Arba, with branches in the old market and opposite, on Av Aguilar; C@lix, on Av Juárez near the *Hotel Guadalupe del Carmen*; and Cibernetic, on Av Niños Héroes by the *Holiday Inn*.
Medical services The hospital on Av Juárez, between Av Aguilar and Av Héroes de Chapultepec, is the most centrally located.
Post office on C Plutarco Elias Calles at Av 5 de Mayo (Mon–Fri 8am–6pm, Sat & Sun 9am–12.30pm).
Tour operators are not plentiful in Chetumal, and often need advance notice to arrange something for you. On the plus side, because there are not yet many fixed routes, you can often tailor a trip precisely to your tastes. Villa Manatí, Blvd Bahía 301 (Ⓣ983/129-3204, Ⓦwww.villamanati.com.mx), are the most organized, with tours to the Río Hondo, the Río Bec sites and into Belize. Or try Uchben Kah tours, Av Obregón 306 (Ⓣ983/932-0555, Ⓦwww.uchbenkahtours.com), or Bacalar Tours, Av Obregón 167, opposite the *Caribe Princess* (Ⓣ983/832-3875), a general travel agency where they also rent cars.

Around Chetumal: Calderitas and Oxtankah

On weekends, the town descends en masse on **Calderitas**, a rapidly growing seaside resort just 6km north around the bay. Much the nicest **place to stay** here is the *Yax-Há* RV park (Ⓣ983/834-4127, Ⓦwww.yaxha-resort.com; ❼), which has very comfortable air-conditioned cabañas for up to four people and a large picturesque garden with a swimming pool right on the seafront. *Yax-Há* is one of the last places you reach in Calderitas. You can also hire a **boat here** or at the adjacent *Cahuamo II* bar for various day outings: to the beaches on the nearby empty island of Tamalcab (M$300 for 6–8 people); a tour around the bay to look for manatees (M$1500; 3hr); or to several other nature spots. There are also plenty of waterfront **restaurants** in Calderitas – again, the most pleasant are at the far end of town. **Buses** to Calderitas leave frequently from Avenida Cristóbal Colón, west of Avenida Niños Héroes, behind the museum.

Seven kilometres north of Calderitas, the small Maya site of **Oxtankah** (daily 8am–5pm; M$35) is what remains of a maritime city that was occupied in the Early Classic period (250–600 AD) and exploited ocean resources – specifically salt. It was still occupied when the Spanish arrived. There's a small museum (Spanish labels only) and two main groups of buildings: the Plaza Abejas is the larger, with an altar at the centre overlooked by a temple, a palace and a building known as Estructura IV. Two tombs were found in the temple – you can enter them round the back – and one beneath the altar, while Estructura IV has stucco decorations protected by a huge palapa. The Plaza Columnas consists of a palace, two temples and other unexcavated structures, while a small side path leads to a *chultun*, a bottle-shaped underground cistern. In the middle of it all is a **Franciscan chapel** built by the Spanish. Oxtankah is also allegedly the site of the original **mestizaje**, the intermixing of Spanish and Indian races that literally gave birth to modern Mexico. The legendary first couple were Gonzalo Guerrero, whose ship was wrecked off the coast in 1511, and Za'azil, a high-ranking woman in the Maya tribe that took Guerrero in. Guerrero assimilated, had three children – the first mestizos – and even fought against the Spaniards who arrived a few years later intent on conquering the peninsula. The site is peaceful and wooded, with the flora neatly labelled, including one fantastically huge ficus tree just west of the chapel. You'll need your own transport to get to Oxtankah (follow the shoreline north through Calderitas) or a taxi from Chetumal (around M$150 round-trip with waiting time), as there's no bus.

Shortly before Oxtankah you pass **Ichpaatun**, another Maya city that is not open to the public. There is, however, a pleasant seafront restaurant of the same name, popular with local families at weekends.

The Río Hondo

West and south of Chetumal, the winding, deep-green **Río Hondo**, which forms the border between Mexico and Belize, is an area rich in wildlife, from furry capybaras to massive numbers of bats. A couple of tour operators in Chetumal offer guided day-trips to the area, which are preferable to visiting on your own, as there are only a few villages and no hotels or other services if you get stranded. If you just want to get a glimpse of the area, you can take a long and bumpy trip by car or an early combi bound for La Unión; departures are from the station on Avenida Primo de Verdad at Avenida Hidalgo in Chetumal. You can't linger, though, as the last bus returns from La Unión around 5pm. The forest here is increasingly being cleared for agricultural land, with sugarcane grown in vast quantities.

The closest, most accessible point on the river is the family-friendly *balneario* (bathing area) at El Palmar (M$5 per person, plus M$5 for a car), about 10km south of the town of Ucum and the turn from Hwy-186. There's a well-maintained beach area on the bank, as well as a large spring-fed swimming pool and a small restaurant. You'll see other, similar places signed off the road further south, including a very attractive spot at the village of Alváro Obregón. At the end of the line is the sprawling, sleepy village of **La Unión**. From here the beautiful, emerald-green **Cenote Cocodrilo** is 5km further, on a track only passable on foot (about an hour) or with a truck or four-by-four. The person who owns the land will allow **camping** nearby, but you shouldn't count on this option, as there's often no one around to ask.

The Río Bec and Calakmul

The road that runs across **the south** of the peninsula, Hwy-186 from Chetumal to Francisco Escárcega, passes through some of the emptiest areas of the Yucatán. Many trees have been cleared through subsistence farming practices, or felled for logging or cattle-ranching, but the forest becomes thicker as you travel west toward Campeche State, where a vast tract of land on both sides of the highway is given over to the **Calakmul Biosphere Reserve**, which encompasses the densest jungle on the peninsula.

The area, known as the **RÍO BEC**, is rich in Maya ruins, most of which have been open to the public only since the mid-1990s. Populated during the Classic era, this land forged a link between the Petén cities to the south and the younger settlements just being established in the Chenes area to the north. The enormous site of **CALAKMUL**, located west of the other sites in Campeche State, deep in the wilderness near the border with Guatemala, is the highlight of this area; the view from its main pyramid, the largest in the Maya world, takes in a pure sea of green from horizon to horizon. However, the other sites are also fascinating and substantial, evidence of a land that was vastly more populated a thousand years ago than it is now. Travellers typically arrange tours to the ruins and find accommodation at Xpuhil (see box, below), a village named after the nearby archeological site, on the border between Campeche and Quintana Roo states. Tourist services are rudimentary in this area, but you will often be able to enjoy the ruins and the untamed forest in complete solitude, the antithesis of a visit to Chichén Itzá.

Dzibanché and Kinichná

About 65km out of Chetumal, the first sites you reach are Dzibanché and Kinichná. A well-signed turn-off 5km past the town of Morocoy leads some 15km north to a joint ticket office (8am–5pm; M$39); from here each site is a further kilometre or so. If you're travelling by taxi, specify that you'll be visiting both sets of ruins: it takes little more than an hour to tour everything.

Visiting the Río Bec sites

The typical strategy for visiting this string of ruins is to spend the night in Xpuhil, hire an early-morning taxi to visit Calakmul and Balamkú, and return to Xpuhil to see the ruins in town in the late afternoon. You can then take a late bus to Chetumal or Campeche (see p.270). If you have the time, though, it will be a more rewarding and relaxing visit if you take at least two days and allow yourself to see more. Renting a car in Campeche or Chetumal affords the most flexibility, but taking taxis can cost about the same amount, leaving you the option of continuing on a loop route rather than returning your car.

Using Xpuhil as a base, **taxis** can be arranged through the hotels, though you'll usually get a slightly better rate if you deal directly with the drivers gathered at the crossroads in town. Expect to pay at most M$600 per head to go to Calakmul and Balamkú or to Kohunlich and Dzibanché, half that for Chicanná, Becán and Xpuhil, including waiting time; all prices go down significantly if you have more people in the car (Calakmul is around $1000 for a full load). If you're not in a hurry, it's also possible to start off sightseeing from Chetumal by taking a combi to the town of Nicolas Bravo, hiring a taxi from there to visit Dzibanché and Kohunlich, and then flagging down a second-class bus to Xpuhil.

Alternatively, you could take an organized **tour** to Calakmul from Campeche (see "Listings", p.280, for details).

Dzibanché is the earliest city in the area, thought to be the base for the influential Snake Kingdom (Kaan) clan before it ascended to rule in Calakmul in the early seventh century. Because of its early date, the city is not truly a Río Bec site – the buildings are relatively simple and show none of the later ornate detail. It's a good place to start, though, as the plain buildings, sparse trees and dry soil make a sharp contrast to the sites further down the road and deeper in the jungle. You also get a good idea of the scale of these cities – the inhabitants of Dzibanché were spread over an area of some 40 square kilometres around the ceremonial centre, and you pass a large, semi-excavated plaza on the drive up from the ticket office. Entering the site you come first to Edificio 6, or the **Edificio de los Dinteles**, named for the original wood lintels that were found in the two rooms at the top of the pyramid. The northern one has been replaced, but the southern one remains, dating from the 700s. In the Plaza Gann beyond are several more impressive buildings, among which **Edificio 13** is particularly notable for its stairs carved with the figures of war prisoners. The tallest structures, edificios 1 and 2, lie beyond here on the Plaza Xibalba – each housed tombs of important personages.

At the small site of **Kinichná**, which was most likely a territory of Dzibanché, the centrepiece is a hulking **pyramid**, built layer upon layer by succeeding leaders. Each of its three levels is built in a different style, reflecting three different eras. Sixty-six tall, steep steps lead to the top, but it's well worth the climb for the stunning views in every direction. From here the strategic significance of the site, and of Dzibanché, the tops of whose structures you can just make out, is clear – each occupies an area of higher ground above the endless plain. You can also see the progress of modern land clearance, with most of the surrounding country given over to ranches or the cultivation of corn. The face of the pyramid was originally decorated with giant masks, and though most of the detail has gone (as the result of erosion or theft), you can still make out where these would have been.

Kohunlich

The expansive ruins of **Kohunlich** (daily 8am–5pm; M$46) are beautifully situated a few kilometres past the turn for Dzibanché, then 9km south from the village of Francisco Villa, in a dense jungle of near-prehistoric proportions that's home to green parrots and enormous lurid butterflies. Allow about an hour and a half to visit all of the buildings, spread out among the towering fan palms and linked by a loop trail. The buildings range from the late Pre-Classic to the Classic periods (100–900 AD), and the majority are in the Río Bec architectural style (see box, p.180). But, to quote the early writer and adventurer John L. Stephens, the site is a perfect example of "a strong and vigorous nature..struggling for mastery over art", as even the buildings that have been excavated in the last few decades are once again being consumed by the creeping foliage and moss.

The most famous structure here, the **Templo de los Mascarones**, is named after the five two-metre-high stucco masks that decorate its facade, facing west to the setting sun. Disturbing enough now, these wide-eyed, open-mouthed gods once stared out from a background of smooth, bright-red-painted stucco. Quite whom they represent is a subject of some debate, but most probably they are Kinich Ahau, the sun god, with the features of members of the ruling family. The temple is one of the oldest here, dating from around 500 AD; at some point around 700 AD another pyramid layer was constructed over it (helping preserve the masks), but this has mostly been cleared by excavation.

▲ Stucco mask at Kohunlich

Other structures, following recent reconstruction efforts, include a ball-court, the moss-covered Pixa'an palace and an elite residential area called the **27 Escalones**, worth the detour to see the great views over the jungle canopy from the cliff edge on which it is built (prime real estate was just as valuable 1400 years ago, it seems). Look out throughout the site, too, for evidence of the complex drainage system that collected rainwater in *aguados*, or cisterns. There are also small, square pools to collect water; similar structures were found alongside Maya roads in the forest to provide drinking water for messengers and other travellers.

In a pinch, *Cabañas Kohunlich* (no tel; ❸), right by the junction with the road to the ruins, has very provisional **cabins** with private baths, but stop in first if you want your room made ready, as they don't see a lot of guests. Otherwise, the intimate honeymoon-lux *Explorean* resort (Ⓣ800/366-6666,

Ⓦwww.theexplorean.com; ❾), halfway up the winding road to the site, provides quite a different experience, complete with an infinity pool perched on the hillside. Its **restaurant** and **bar** are open to non-guests, and the view over the jungle canopy can be worth the price of a post-ruins drink.

Río Bec

Despite giving its name to the entire region, the scattered buildings of the city of **Río Bec**, 10km east of Xpuhil and south of an *ejido* (community) named 20 de Noviembre, are frustratingly inaccessible. The area is still under excavation and usually closed to visitors, though some years it opens for a few months in the spring. Ask in the tourist office in Xpuhil about arranging an expedition on horseback, perhaps, as otherwise only four-wheel-drive vehicles can tackle the dirt tracks here. If you do visit, you will see the most extreme example of the Río Bec false-pyramid style: as at Xpuhil, the "steps" on the site's twin towers were never meant to be climbed, with risers that actually angle outwards.

Xpuhil

Thanks solely to its location halfway between Chetumal and Escárcega, the one-street village of **XPUHIL** (also spelled "Xpujil"), straddling Hwy-186 at the border of Campeche and Quintana Roo states, is the de facto base for exploring the Río Bec region. In this it is at least efficient, with food and accommodation all gathered within walking distance, though none is of very high quality. Of the **places to stay** in town, the best choice is the *Hotel Calakmul* (Ⓣ983/871-6029, Ⓔcalakmul04-06@hotmail.com), west of the centre, with pleasant, modern, air-conditioned rooms around a garden (❺) and some very basic cabañas with shared bath (❸). Alternatively, *El Mirador Maya* (Ⓣ983/871-6005, Ⓔmirador_maya@hotmail.com; ❹), at the top of hill on the western edge of town, has decent wooden cabañas with porches, though the noise of trucks struggling up the slope is noticeable at night. Both have adequate **restaurants**, which are significantly more expensive, however, than simpler

The Río Bec style

While Río Bec is the name of a specific archeological site, it also refers to a characteristic **architectural style** common to all of the sites found in this area. Río Bec buildings, most built around 600 AD, were influenced by neighbouring Petén, a region notable for its massive pyramids with rounded corners and the commemorative stelae dotting its plazas.

The Río Bec style's most distinctive feature is a dramatic distortion of the great early pyramids of the Petén. In the Río Bec, the shape of the steep Gran Pirámide at Tikal, for instance, is further elongated to form a tall, slender tower with an unclimbable steep-stepped facade. These are usually built in pairs and topped with temples that are impossible to reach and generally filled in with solid rock; narrow roofcombs add another level of ornamentation to these purely decorative structures. In the lower register, the central doorway is often adorned with the gaping mouth of a god – typically thought to be the ancient deity **Itzamná**, the god of night and day – whose teeth frame the opening. The remaining surfaces of Río Bec buildings are covered with smaller masks of Itzamná and other gods, all hooked noses, curling tongues and rolling eyes, alternating with intersecting crosses and inset stone squares forming checkerboard patterns, another distinctive motif of the region. Tour all the Río Bec sites in a day or two, and you'll come away dizzy from the intertwining grotesquery.

places along the highway. *El Mirador Maya* also offers money **exchange** and arranges taxi tours to the sites. Around the bus station are several phone *casetas* and the Mundo Maya **Internet** café; the local **gas station** is 5km east of town. Xpuhil also boasts an excellent unofficial **tourist information** office (Tues–Sun 9am–1pm & 4–7.30pm; ⓣ983/871-6064, ⓔciitcalakmul@prodigy.net.mx), on the highway at the east end of town. Maintained by a dedicated eco-tourism group that also operates a campsite near Calakmul (see p.185), they can arrange hiking, mountain-biking or horse-riding **tours** (M$1000 to Río Bec, for example) and birdwatching trips, combined with expert archeological knowledge – advance notice is recommended for any of these, and not all the staff (or guides) speak English.

As an alternative to staying in Xpuhil, the tranquil village of **Zoh-Laguna**, 10km north, is an attractive option. Here *Cabañas y Restaurant Mercedes* (ⓣ983/114-9769 or 9933; ③) offers spotless cabins with private baths, and the kindly owners can fix tasty meals on request. You may fall asleep to the sound of your neighbour's satellite TV, but you'll wake to the sound of turkeys, pigs and the other village livestock. The only problem is that the place is increasingly popular, so it's safest to book; should you turn up and there's no space, there are a couple of slightly less comfortable alternatives in the village. If you don't have your own car, you can hire a taxi from Xpuhil (around M$30 one-way), or hop on a colectivo if your timing is right – though this will drop you about 700m from the hotel itself.

Leaving Xpuhil, there are three ADO and three Sur **buses** a day to Chetumal, and fifteen in total to Escárcega, though you may not always be able to secure a seat as these first-class buses can be packed with through travellers. The schedule board in the station does not include several second-class Caribe buses that also operate here – enquire about these if you're in a pinch. **Colectivos** gather in front of the station, but don't run frequently. It's also possible to catch a series of second-class buses heading in the direction of the Chenes sites or to Mérida via Dzibalchén, Hopelchén and the Ruta Puuc, passing through the northern half of the Calakmul Biosphere Reserve on a reasonably well-maintained road.

The ruins

The smallest of all the sites in the area, the Xpuhil **ruins** are less than 1km west along the highway from the bus stop in Xpuhil village (8am–5pm; M$35). Much of the stone carving at this ancient settlement, which was probably a satellite of Becán to the west, is in excellent shape, and you need about half an hour to see it all. The path leads first past a small residential complex, then to the main building, a long, low structure studded with three striking towers (unusual, as other Río Bec buildings have only two); the central one faces west, the other two, east. The stairs up the ersatz pyramids are purely decorative, as they are almost vertical. A narrow, almost equally steep internal staircase leads partway up the the south tower, providing a bit of a view over the neatly cleared grassy plaza that fronts the structure.

Hormiguero

Only the most dedicated Mayaphiles make the effort to reach **Hormiguero** (8am–5pm; M$34), a small site with excellently preserved decoration. It's a bumpy, forty-minute, 22-kilometre drive south from the crossroads in Xpuhil, for a visit that takes only half an hour or so (no buses run this way; taxis charge around M$150 round-trip with waiting time). However, the effort is rewarded by some remarkable, beautifully preserved stone decoration and by it being almost certain that you'll have the place to yourself; even the caretaker is rarely to be seen. Just two structures, tucked in deep forest, have been completely excavated, but plenty of others are visible among the trees. Both the main buildings show a combination of features typical of the Río Bec style: the distinctive monster mouths, later used extensively in the Chenes sites (see p.281), and the impossibly steep towers (although the temples at the tops of these are actually functional, unlike those at Xpuhil). Keep your eyes on the forest floor here as you explore – Hormiguero has its name ("anthill") for good reason.

Becán

Though it covers a relatively small area, **Becán** (daily 8am–5pm; M$39), 6km west of Xpuhil and then 500m north on a signed track, is a very impressive site with several details that set it apart from its neighbours; allow about an hour and a half for a basic tour. The most remarkable feature is the dry **moat**, 16m wide and 5m deep, which surrounds the entire site. This moat and the wall on its outer edge form one of the oldest known defensive systems in Mexico and are unique among Maya sites. The structure has led some to believe that this, rather than present-day Flores in Guatemala, was the site of Tayasal, early capital of the Itzá. Becán was first occupied in 600 BC and reached its peak between 600 and 1000 AD, when it apparently functioned as a regional capital and trade centre.

Unlike many of the excavated sites in the northern Yucatán, most of the buildings here seem to have been residential rather than ceremonial; in fact, the tightly packed buildings – with rooms stacked up and linked with corridors and unusual, winding internal staircases – create a strong sense of dense urbanism, akin to modern apartment blocks.

Enter the ruins through a break in the east wall, and you face an alleyway overhung with a narrow, typically Maya, vaulted arch; passing through, you reach the **Plaza Central**, dominated by the massive 32-metre-high **Structure IX** and the temple-palace complex **Structure X**, topped with the gaping mouth of Itzamná. At its far south end, a glass box protects a beautiful stucco **mask** of the sun god, Kinichná. Though it's nowhere near as large as the Kohunlich masks, the work is marvellously intricate, with much of the original pigment remaining.

Whereas the area around the Plaza Central feels crowded, the raised **Plaza Oriente** exudes a more orderly grandness and was clearly an elite residential area. **Structure I** sports some of the tallest, steepest towers of all the Río Bec sites, topped with small galleries probably used as observatories, and **Structure II** exhibits another typical decorative technique: small limestone cubes inset to form checkerboard patterns and crosses, which represent the cardinal points. Because much of the site was excavated only in the last few decades, the restoration process is meticulously marked throughout: small chips of stone set in the plaster walls mark the edges of the buildings as they were first found; everything above this line is recent restoration. You can climb several of the buildings, and from the tops of the tallest ones, you can just make out the towers of Xpuhil to the east.

Chicanná

Two kilometres west of Becán, **Chicanná** (daily 8am–5pm; M$35) is south of the highway, across from the *Chicanná Ecovillage Resort*. For most of its history, Chicanná was a dependency of Becán, and given the quality of the building and the richness of the decoration, many believe that it was the home of that city's elite. Entering the site, you first reach the large **Structure XX**, topped with a second tier made of stacks of heads traditionally identified as the rain god, Chac, though more recent scholarship suggests they actually depict Itzamná. You can walk inside some of the rooms to see surviving stucco details, such as small human faces. **Structure VI** preserves part of its original roofcomb; all the buildings here, and indeed at most of the surrounding sites, would originally have had similar roofcombs, decorated with depictions of their gods and rulers. Following the path around, you eventually come to the impressive **Structure II**, the design of which gives the site its name ("House of the Serpent Mouth"). Its massive square doorway forms a face and gaping mouth, complete with spiky teeth, thought to be the god Itzamná due to the distinctive crossed eyes and round earrings. The rest of the building is covered in smaller masks of hook-nosed Chac (or Itzamná), made up of intricately carved mosaic pieces of limestone. Many of these are still painted with red stucco, in a style that was developed in this area and the adjacent Chenes cities, then picked up and refined by later builders in the Puuc region to the north.

After visiting the site, you can stop for a drink and a dip in the pool at *Chicanná Ecovillage Resort* (Ⓣ981/811-9191, Ⓦwww.chicannaecovillageresort.com; ❽), which also offers nicely manicured grounds and air-conditioned comfort in large cabañas at a reasonable price. Continuing west on the highway, you reach *Río Bec Dreams* (Ⓣ983/103-7842, Ⓦwww.riobecdreams.com; ❺), a small budget **lodging** option offering cosy wooden "jungalows" with shared bath, or larger private-bath cabañas for families. *Dreams* is also a good travellers' resource, as the Canadian owners are archeology buffs who can advise on the latest site openings and arrange good guided tours; the gift shop is stocked with excellent titles from Mérida's Dante bookshops. Non-guests can stop in at the **restaurant**, with its varied (non-Mexican) menu, for a cold beer and the like.

Calakmul

The vast ruined city of **CALAKMUL** (daily 8am–5pm; M$39) is one of the best Maya ruins for quiet contemplation of the culture's architectural legacy. The site lies sixty kilometres south of Hwy-186, 58km west of Xpuhil, in the heart of the **Calakmul Biosphere Reserve**, which encompasses more than 1.7 million acres of jungle. The reserve's entrance gate on the highway opens at 7am (M$40 per car, plus M$40 per person, to enter the reserve), and it takes an hour, on a paved but narrow road, to reach the ruins. If you arrive early, you'll almost certainly catch plenty of **wildlife** on the ride down – ocellated turkeys, white-tailed deer, peccaries, woodpeckers, hummingbirds and toucans are common, while jaguars roam the forest by night. In total there are said to be 235 species of bird within the reserve and more than 90 mammal species. Even if you don't see anything, you'll certainly hear the jungle life: in the morning, booming **howler monkeys** and raucous **tree-frogs** make the pristine forest as noisy as midtown Manhattan. At about Km 27, a short nature trail leads down to a swampy area; the path is not well maintained, but you don't need to go far to reach the water, in which there are said to be crocodiles; there's also a good chance that spider or howler monkeys will be in the trees overhead.

Although the ruins were uncovered in the 1930s, excavation has been going on only for the past three decades; every year new discoveries yield more revelations about the city's historical significance, and it was designated a UNESCO World Heritage Site in 2002. At the very least, Calakmul is probably the biggest archeological zone in Mesoamerica, extending for some seventy square kilometres; at its peak, it was home to about 200,000 people. The central area alone contains nearly seven thousand buildings and more stelae and pyramids than any other Maya city. The city was founded as early as the sixth century BC, when many large structures were erected, setting out the basic plan of the place. The many stelae – around 120 have been found in all – mostly date from the city's peak of power in the Classic era. Calakmul was finally abandoned by 900 AD, after fourteen centuries of occupation. The **treasures of Calakmul** are on display in the Museo Fuerte de San Miguel in Campeche (see p.278), and include two hauntingly beautiful jade masks. Another was found in a tomb in the main pyramid as recently as January 1998. Also at the museum, you can see the first mummified body ever found in Mesoamerica, from inside Structure XV, which was unearthed in 1995.

Because its architectural style adheres more purely to the plainer Petén tradition, Calakmul is not considered a true part of the Río Bec; unlike the neighbouring cities, which interacted with the Chenes settlements to the north, it looked to the south for trade and culture. Calakmul's primary influence was Tikal, with which it had an often violent rivalry as the two cities' rulers fought for control over lucrative trade routes. The city began as the mighty Snake Kingdom, a powerful clan first based at Dzibanché. Once established at Calakmul, its leaders were referred to with fear and awe, as evidenced in records found at other ruins such as Palenque. Recent hieroglyphic translations reveal how its greatest leader, Yuknoom Ch'een, who reigned between 636 and 686 AD, controlled many smaller cities and outposts through puppet kings. Decades of struggle finally led to a bloody rout of Tikal in 657, but this led in turn to recrimination, and Yuknoom's son, Yich'ak Ka'k' (also known as Jaguar Paw), suffered his own staggering defeat in 695, all but ruining Calakmul. By the middle of the ninth century, the city was basically abandoned.

A choice of three **routes** – *larga, media* or *corta* (long, medium or short) – wind through the excavated areas, with even the shortest loop taking at least a couple of hours (it's a twenty-minute walk just from the car park to the first set of buildings). You could easily spend the better part of a day here, as long as you're stocked with bug repellent, snacks and water. While at times the paths seem to lead away from the buildings, bear with them: all will bring you to the most impressive structures.

There are two main building complexes, the Gran Acropolis and the stunning Gran Plaza, plus many other buildings and smaller groupings scattered through the jungle. Many are individually unremarkable, but the scale of the place is always impressive, as are the many stelae dotted around everywhere, and in particular standing sentinel around the **Gran Acropolis**. Of the lesser areas, seek out especially the **residential section** to the east, where a tight warren of private rooms is built against a section of a large defensive wall that enclosed this elite district of the city.

The real highlights come towards the end of the tour, though. It's at this point that you'll reach **Structure I**, a tremendously tall pyramid. Over one hundred tall steps lead to the top, where no sign of civilization is visible through the jungle canopy in any direction, save for the tops of some of the other neighbouring structures. Nearby is the **Gran Plaza**, where the **Gran Pirámide** (Structure II) is located – it is one of the largest known Maya buildings, with a base covering almost five acres. From the plaza below it's impossible to see the top (1m higher than Structure I), as it recedes in stacked layers of construction, each one added by a new leader. Two giant monster masks flank the central stairway, and one of the temples contained the tomb of Jaguar Paw. Daunting as it may be, the climb yields another awe-inspiring view of nothing but jungle. On a clear day, you can just make out the square top of the Danta pyramid, at El Mirador in Guatemala; it's off the back of the pyramid, slightly to the right.

Just inside the entrance to the reserve you'll see signs to the *Hotel Puerta Calakmul* (ⓣ998/884-3278, ⓦwww.puertacalakmul.com.mx; ⑧), a lovely, upmarket "ecological" retreat with a pool, large cabañas and a beautifully situated restaurant that's open to anyone. Some seven kilometres further, *Yaxche* (also called *Oxte'tun*), could hardly be a greater contrast; a very basic jungle **campsite and restaurant** run by Servidores Turísticos Calakmul (ⓣ983/871-6064, ⓔciitcalakmul@prodigy.net.mx; see p.181). You can sleep in one of their tents here (M$150 per person) or bring your own (M$50), and it's a truly back-to-nature experience, complete with four howler monkeys in residence. The staff can point you to **nature trails** within the reserve, and anyone can stop for a **meal**, though as the kitchen uses all local products, it may not have provisions on hand in slow seasons.

Balamkú and Nadzcaan

Most organized tours to Calakmul stop at **Balamkú** (daily 8am–5pm; M$39), just 5km west of the turn-off to the larger city and 3km north of the highway. The main draw at this small site is a beautifully preserved seventeen-metre-long stucco **frieze**, located in a cluster of buildings furthest from the entrance and protected in a concrete shed embedded inside the central palace; the caretaker should be around to let you in. The embellished wall, crawling with toads, crocodiles and jaguars, seems to undulate in the dim light, and the rolling eyes of the red-painted monster masks, though smaller than those at Kohunlich, are perhaps more alarming here. The elaborate iconography establishes a parallel between the rising and setting sun, as it dips into the underworld, and the dynastic cycle, as kings ascend to the throne, then die and settle in the maw of the earth. Likewise, the frieze's very location inside and under a public space is suggestive of the underworld, although originally it was on the outside of a pyramid, and is preserved so well because another was later built over the top of it. Balamkú is again surrounded by thick forest and full of wildlife; there's often a large troupe of spider monkeys in the trees, especially in the late afternoon.

Less than 1km west of the Calakmul turn, immediately before the town of Conhuas, a dirt road leads 15km north to a sizeable collection of pyramids (some 50m tall), plazas and ball-courts: the city of **Nadzcaan**, which once linked the Petén cities with Edzná further north (see p.281). Stelae found inside the temples are dated around 650 AD. The perimeter of the area contains caves and quarries where limestone was excavated for building. Serious archeological work began here only around 1999, and there are still no services, signage or even entry fee – you're free to thrash around on your own in the untamed undergrowth. The solitude is fantastic, but a visit is advisable only for those with sturdy cars.

If you're continuing on to Escárcega, *La Laguna* **restaurant**, trimmed all over with seashells, makes a good rest stop, just off the highway and overlooking the small but scenic Laguna Silvituc.

Travel details

Buses

Bus service is not as convenient in this corner of the Yucatán as elsewhere; Chetumal is the main hub, especially for long-distance services to other states and into Belize.

Chetumal to: Bacalar (hourly; 30min); Belize City (5 daily via Corozal and Orange Walk; 3hr); Campeche (3 daily via Escárcega and Xpuhil; 7hr); Cancún (at least hourly via Tulum and Playa del Carmen; 4–6hr); Francisco Escárcega (14 daily; 4–5hr); Mahahual (5 Mon–Fri, 6 Sat–Sun; 3hr 30min; see p.165); Mérida (8 daily; 8–9hr); Mexico City (4 daily; 24hr); Palenque and San Cristóbal (3 daily at 7.45pm, 9.15pm & 11pm; 7–10hr); Tikal and Flores, Guatemala (2 daily at 5am & 6am; 12hr); Villahermosa (6 daily; 9–11hr); Xcalak (2 Mon–Fri, 3 Sat–Sun; 4hr 30min; see p.165); Xpuhil (14 daily; 2hr).

Felipe Carrillo Puerto to: Cancún (at least hourly; 3hr); Chetumal (at least hourly; 3hr); Mérida (12 daily; 5hr); Mexico City (3 daily; 24hr).

Mahahual to: Cancún (2 Mon–Fri, 3 Sat–Sun; 4hr; see p.165); Chetumal (5 Mon–Fri, 6 Sat–Sun; 4hr).

Xpuhil to: Chetumal (8 daily; 2hr); Dzibalchén (1 daily at 4am; 1hr 30min); Escárcega (14 daily; 2hr).

Flights

Aerocaribe, Click Mexicana and Mexicana run daily flights between Chetumal and Mexico City.

5

Valladolid and Chichén Itzá

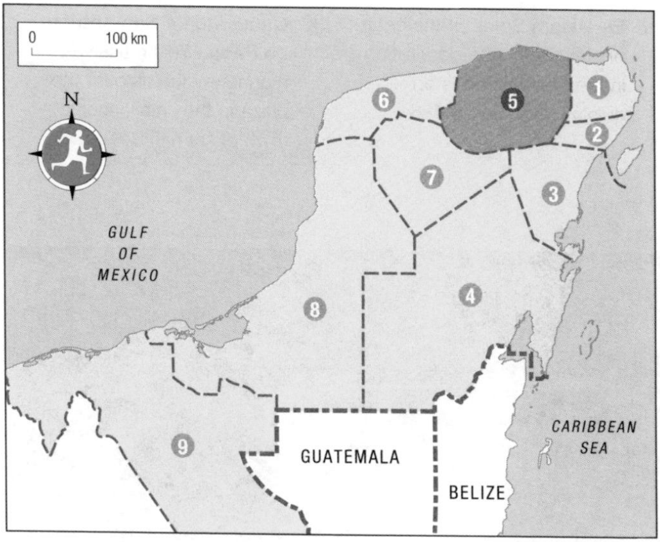

CHAPTER 5

Highlights

* **Iglesia de San Bernardino de Siena** Valladolid's Franciscan mission is the oldest permanent church in the Yucatán. See p.193
* **Cenote Dzitnup** This immense and spectacular cenote is lit by a transfixing beam of sunlight that shines through a hole in its cave ceiling onto glowing blue water. See p.195
* **Ek-Balam** Some of the best-preserved stucco decoration in the Maya world is on display here. See p.196
* **Ría Lagartos Biosphere Reserve** Three small towns inside this strip of marshes along the coast are bases for fishing and birdwatching trips, or simply lazing on the empty beaches. See p.198
* **El Castillo** The giant pyramid that towers over the ruined city of Chichén Itzá is the very symbol of Maya power in the Yucatán Peninsula. See p.203
* **Convento de San Antonio de Padua** This massive monastery looms over the plaza in the small, scenic town of Izamal. See p.208

▲ View across the ruins of Ek-Balam

5

Valladolid and Chichén Itzá

Second only to the beaches around Cancún, the biggest tourist draw in the Yucatán Peninsula are the ancient ruins of **Chichén Itzá**, a beeline west from the coast along Hwy-180 towards Mérida. The vast, well-excavated and fascinating archeological site is dominated by the towering Pyramid of Kukulcán (also known as El Castillo), the most iconic of all the Maya pyramids. While it's not impossible to visit the entire site in a day-trip, the area is huge, and you'll be unnecessarily rushed, not to mention crammed in with the busloads of visitors who pack the place from late morning on. Better to plan instead on staying overnight, either at one of the luxury hotels near the site or in the adjacent village of **Pisté**, which provides budget tourist amenities. An early start will not only help you avoid the worst crowds, but will also give you a chance to see some of the diverse and colourful birds that flourish in the forests surrounding the ruins.

If you're as interested in contemporary Maya culture as in the ancient remains, however, you can't do better than to stay in **Valladolid**, just 40km east of Chichén Itzá and connected by frequent bus and colectivo service. Unfortunately, many visitors in their haste miss this charming, predominantly Maya city that exemplifies the distinct atmosphere and structure of the inland towns built during the Spanish colonial period. Here you'll see the basic blueprint – a central plaza dominated by a cathedral (plus vendors, strolling lovers, taxi drivers and stray dogs) – that's endlessly repeated, on varying scales, in the villages and cities throughout the rest of Yucatán State.

A fascinating counterpoint to Chichén Itzá, the Maya ruins of **Ek-Balam** lie north of Valladolid. The place is distinct from its neighbour in its decorative style, with rare and perfectly preserved stucco adorning the main building. The setting – a swathe of rolling grasslands that covers the northeastern part of the state – is a change, too, as is the complete lack of crowds. From Valladolid, Hwy-295 continues north to the Gulf coast, running through the travel hub of **Tizimín**, a larger city than Valladolid but less scenic. If you're getting around by bus, you'll have to change here to carry on to the **Ría Lagartos Biosphere Reserve**, a sixty-kilometre-long strip of marshland that harbours more than 330 species of birds, including a large flamingo population; the raucous pink creatures are most easily visited from the town of **Río Lagartos**, directly north from Tizimín. Beach lovers can get their fix at the remote towns of **San**

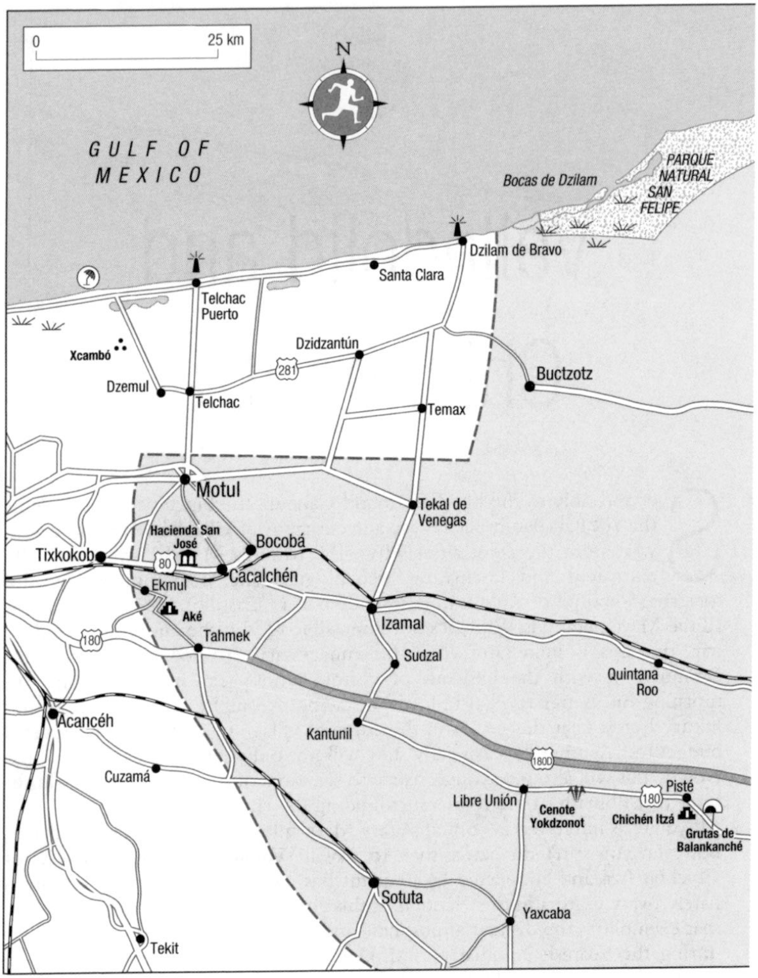

Felipe, west on a narrow road along the coast from Río Lagartos, and **El Cuyo**, twice the distance to the east. From Chichén Itzá or Valladolid, Hwy-180 continues west, with the free and toll roads merging at the town of Kantunil. At this point, you can carry straight on to Mérida, or you can make the very worthwhile detour north to **Izamal**, one of the region's most beautiful small towns, notable for its glowing egg-yolk-yellow buildings and its enormous Franciscan mission church.

If you're driving to Chichén Itzá from the coast, the old highway is more scenic, but slower (about three hours, compared with two and a quarter on the *cuota*). It's also perhaps the most heavily travelled tourist route on the peninsula; brace yourself for the occasionally aggressive souvenir vendor who will besiege your car mid-speed bump.

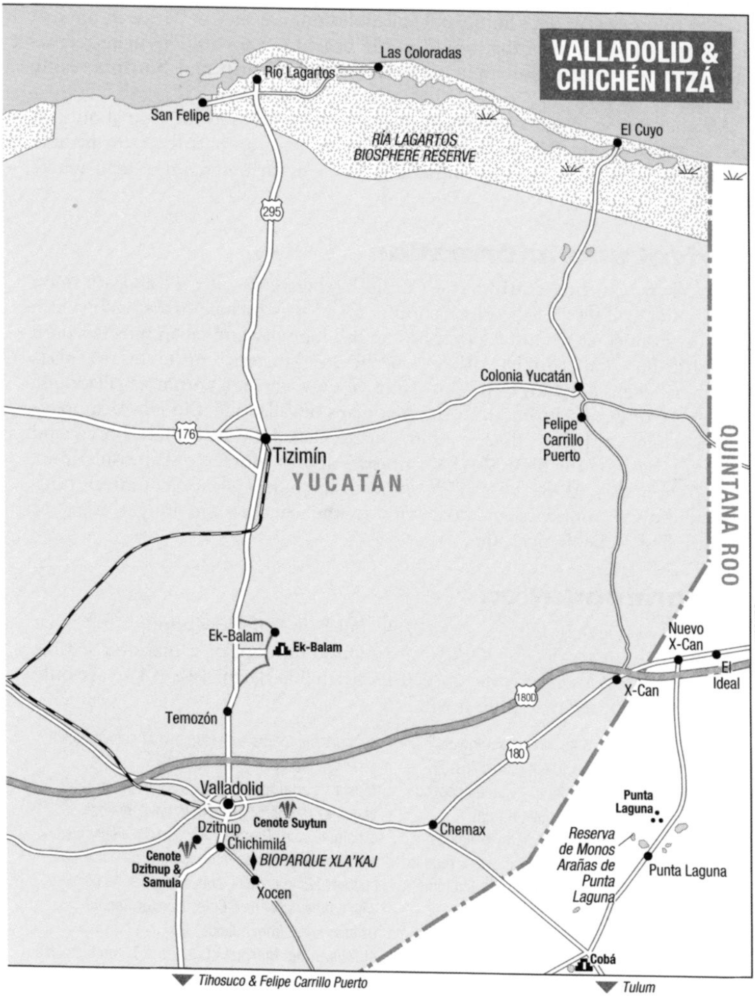

Valladolid and around

About 160km west of Cancún, **VALLADOLID**, the second oldest town in the Yucatán State (after Mérida), took a severe bashing when the Caste Wars began here in 1847. But the city's revolutionary spirit ultimately survived: a bold anti-*hacendado* statement by Maya rebels in Valladolid is credited with being the spark that ignited the Revolution of 1910 (see Contexts, p.335). Despite the damage done by the fighting, the town has retained a strong colonial feel, with towering churches dotting the city grid. Unlike Mérida, with its cosmopolitan bustle, or Campeche's museum-piece, multicoloured centre, Valladolid exudes the quieter, less pretentious attitude of a rural capital, catering to the farmers and ranchers who live in the surrounding counties, while village women gather in the plaza to sell their hand-embroidered huipiles and other craftwork. The slow pace may not be to every traveller's liking, but Valladolid offers a slice of Mexican life that is entirely different from that found in the beachfront towns. The main recreation here is swimming in the nearby cenotes, **Dzitnup** and **Samula**, easily reached by bicycle.

Another reason to work Valladolid into your itinerary is its location about half an hour east of Chichén Itzá, close enough that you can beat the crowds there on an early bus. Also, the accommodation here is far better value than what's available at the ruins.

Arrival and information

Valladolid's main **bus station** is on Calle 39, between calles 44 and 46, just a block and a half west of the plaza; coming on a long-distance first-class bus, you may be dropped at a transfer point on the toll highway and taken into town on a shuttle bus. The **tourist office**, on the southeastern corner of the plaza (Mon–Sat 9am–8.30pm, Sun 9am–1pm; Ⓦwww.chichen.com.mx/valladolid), has plenty of information, including free maps of Valladolid, though it's a pretty casual set-up, and the office is often unattended. However, most hotels and souvenir shops on the plaza also have **maps**. Alberto Morales of Peninsula Tours (C 56 no. 127; Ⓣ985/856-5275, Ⓔpeninsulatours1@yahoo.com.mx) leads walking tours around town, bike trips to the cenotes and longer tours of surrounding archeological sites.

Accommodation

Valladolid's budget hotels are serviceable, but prices are low enough here that you might want to opt for perks like a swimming pool or a mansion setting. Also note that *Genesis Retreat*, an eco-lodge in Ek-Balam (see p.197), is only about twenty minutes outside town.

Casa Hamaca C 49 at C 40, on the southwest corner of Parque San Juan Ⓣ985/856-5287, Ⓦwww.casahamaca.com. Set in a garden packed with fruit trees, this B&B is a quiet retreat. Expansive rooms in the big two-storey building are decorated with elaborate murals and glossy red tile floors. There's also a pool, and massage and other treatments are available. ❽

Casa Quetzal C 51 no. 218 Ⓣ985/856-4796, Ⓦwww.casa-quetzal.com. A pleasant alternative to the plaza hotels, *Casa Quetzal* is a very comfortable guesthouse near the San Bernardino church with a big pool. ❻

Lili C 44 no. 192, between C 37 and C 39 Ⓣ985/856-2163. One block off the plaza, this small, homely hotel rents 21 basic rooms (those upstairs get a little more light) at reasonable rates. ❷

María de la Luz C 42, on the plaza Ⓣ985/856-2071, Ⓦwww.mariadelaluzhotel.com. The best value on the plaza, *María de la Luz* offers clean, comfortable rooms with (somewhat noisy) a/c, all arranged around a small pool. ❺

María Guadalupe C 44 no. 198, between C 39 and C 41 Ⓣ985/856-2068, Ⓔhotel_guadalupe@hotmail.com. The best of Valladolid's cheapies, with well-kept rooms featuring private baths and optional a/c in a small, two-storey 1960s building with a little curvy flair. Colectivos for Cenote Dzitnup leave from outside. ❸

El Mesón del Marqués C 39 no. 203, on the plaza Ⓣ985/856-2073, Ⓦwww.mesondelmarques.com. Lovely hotel in a former colonial mansion, overlooking a courtyard with fountains and lush plants. There's a wonderful palm-fringed pool, and one of the best restaurants in town (see p.194). ❻

Zací C 44 no. 191, between C 37 and C 39 Ⓣ985/856-2167. Pleasant, modern three-storey hotel with a quiet courtyard; the big rooms have either a fan, or, for a few dollars more, a/c and TV. A pool makes it a great bargain. ❺

The city

Valladolid's sedate social scene centres on the **Parque Principal**, bounded by calles 39, 40, 41 and 42. The pretty, peaceful plaza is at its finest at dusk, when the curving love seats are filled with chatting couples and the bubbling

fountain, topped with a statue of a woman in a traditional Yucatecan huipil, is lit from below.

Each of the town's seven central neighbourhoods is named after an elegant church; the two white towers of one, the eighteenth-century **Catedral de San Gervasio**, rise gracefully over the south side of the plaza. The sixteenth-century **Iglesia de San Bernardino de Siena**, 1km southwest of the plaza (Wed–Mon 9am–8pm; Mass daily at 6pm), is the oldest church in town, as well as one of the oldest in the Yucatán. Franciscan missionaries began work on it shortly after the Spanish established Valladolid as an outpost in 1545. The church buildings, which include a large monastery, were once on the very edge of town, so the Franciscans could minister to both the Spanish city residents and the Maya villagers in the surrounding countryside. In 1848, Maya rebels briefly took control of the city and drove the terrified Spaniards out, sacking the church (and much of the rest of the town) in the process; despite this, a fine Baroque altarpiece from the eighteenth century remains, as do some striking seventeenth-century paintings on the side walls. The **monastery** (usually closed to visitors), on the north side, was built over a cenote, so resident monks were self-sufficient, with their own water and food grown on surrounding farmland. For a brief period in the seventeenth century, one of the monk's cells was used as a lock-up for the infamous pirate Lorencillo (legend has it he was lured inland by a beautiful Valladolid resident who had been a passenger on a ship he attacked); Lorencillo's crew rescued him in a raid before he could be executed. To reach the complex, take scenic Calle 41-A, which runs diagonally southwest, starting two blocks west of the plaza. While you're down this way, you can also see the seventeenth-century **San Juan** church on Calle 40 at Calle 49.

East of the plaza on Calle 41, a smaller historic church has been converted to the **Museo de San Roque** (Mon–Sat 9am–8pm; free). Objects from the site of Ek-Balam (see p.196), embroidery and other craftwork from nearby villages and contemporary Maya altars to the rain god Chac comprise the museum's small but diverse collection. For a refreshing break, especially on a hot summer day, head northwest from the plaza to **Cenote Zací**, on the block formed by calles 34, 36, 37 and 39 (daily 8am–6pm; M$15). Right in the middle of the city, it was the water source for the former Maya stronghold of Zací, from where the fierce Cupul clan fought against the first conquistadors. Swimming is not permitted, but it's the easiest cenote to visit, with broad stairs leading down into a huge cavern where light reflects off the green water and glimmers on the walls. The air is cool, and an open-air restaurant affords a fine view. An adjacent "zoo" includes the noble chicken, as well as a white hawk, or *zací*, the old city's namesake.

As the huipil-clad statue in the plaza's fountain suggests, Valladolid is a good place to purchase craftwork; in addition to the women selling their embroidery work, you can also visit the main **craft market**, on Calle 44 at Calle 39, or Yalat, a very nice shop on the northwest corner of the plaza that stocks clothing, Mexican chocolate and locally made soaps. The central city market, the **Mercado Municipal**, is on Calle 32, between calles 35 and 37.

Eating and entertainment

Whatever your budget, to eat well in Valladolid you don't have to stray far from the plaza, where you can get inexpensive **snacks** or treat yourself at a refined **restaurant**. As for **nightlife**, there's nothing much beyond people-watching; a **cinema** on Calle 40, just south of Calle 41, shows first-run American hits.

El Bazar Northeast corner of the plaza. Houses a dizzying selection of inexpensive, always busy *loncherías* and pizzerias. It's also about the only place in town aside from *Hostería El Marqués* where you can eat after 9pm.

La Casa del Café Kaffè C 44, on Parque la Candelaria. Serves organic coffee, juices and little snacks to members of the local arts scene.

Doña Hermelinda C 44, between C 37 and C 39. Succulent stewed pork with white beans is the core ingredient here – you can have it as a taco, a *torta* or (the best) a *pibihua*, a hollowed-out round of chewy fried corn. Cheap and delicious. Open till 8pm.

Hostería El Marqués C 39 no. 203, in *El Mesón del Marqués*. Valladolid's best restaurant is set in a tranquil interior courtyard on the plaza, though it is occasionally packed with tour groups. The menu features Yucatecan classics such as *sopa de lima* and *poc-chuc*, along with city specialities like *escabeche de Valladolid* (chicken in a spicy vinegar broth). Prices are reasonable, starting at just M$60 for mains.

María de la Luz C 42, on the plaza. A popular terrace restaurant that has a basic Mexican and Yucatecan menu, including local dishes like the bright red *longaniza* pork sausage. Good-value lunch and breakfast buffet (both M$50) with American and Mexican dishes.

Plaza Maya C 41, between C 48 and C 50. A delicious little restaurant that accommodates curious visitors by offering a sampler tray of all the Yucatecan staples – not just the usual *panuchos* and *cochinita pibil*, but also *escabeche*, steamed tamales and other treats.

Restaurante San Bernardino de Siena C 49 no. 227. Locally known as *Don Juanito's* and frequented mostly by *vallisoletanos*, this family-run, mid-price restaurant is a great place for a lazy lunch or dinner away from the hustle and bustle of the town centre, two blocks behind Iglesia de San Bernardino. Grilled fish and meat are the specialities.

Yepez II C 41, between C 38 and C 40. Friendly open-air bar and restaurant opposite the Museo de San Roque with live music after 9.30pm, as well as very cheap Mexican snacks (*queso fundido* for M$25). Families come for dinner, but the crowd becomes predominantly male (not too rowdy, though) once the music starts. Open daily till 2am.

Zací C 36, between C 37 and C 39. The restaurant at the cenote is very reasonably priced (mains M$55–75) and features some hearty Yucatecan food, such as *queso relleno* (a wheel of cheese stuffed with spicy-sweet ground meat). The setting is cool and shady. Closes at 6pm.

Listings

Banks Bancomer, which changes travellers' cheques and has an ATM, is next door to the post office on the plaza.
Bicycle rental from the Rey de Béisbol sports shop, C 44 no. 195, between C 39 and C 41, owned by Antonio "Negro" Aguilar, a one-time professional baseball star who is also a great source of local information.
Buses The main station is on C 39, between C 44 and C 46. Some first-class long-distance trips require a change on the *cuota* just north of the city, although this is being phased out. As a result, Valladolid doesn't have as much bus traffic as you might expect, so it's not always the easiest place to get into or out of. You cannot check schedules or buy tickets online at the ADO Website; see p.210 for bus times.
Colectivos depart for Tizimín, Ek-Balam, Cenote Dzitnup and Chichén Itzá from designated meeting points along C 44, one block off the plaza. The Chichén Itzá service is comparable in price to buses (M$15), and may depart more frequently, especially early in the morning.
Laundry in Supermaz, a shopping plaza on C 39, between C 48 and C 50.
Post office on the plaza, C 40 near the corner of C 39 (Mon–Fri 9am–3pm).
Telephone and Internet A Ladatel *caseta* on the plaza also has computers (daily 7am–10pm).

Cenotes around Valladolid

Perhaps the most photogenic swimming hole in the Yucatán, the remarkable **Cenote Dzitnup**, also called X'Keken ("pig") cenote (daily 7am–6pm; M$25), is 7km west of Valladolid on Hwy-180 *libre*. Visitors descend through a cramped tunnel into a huge vaulted cave, where a nearly circular pool of crystal-clear turquoise water glows under a shaft of light from an opening in the ceiling. Bleacher seats and lots of electric lights have been added to accommodate everyone who pops in as part of a bus tour. A dip in the ice-cold water is a fantastic experience, but take a sweater to warm up afterwards, as the temperature in the cave is noticeably cooler than outside. Across the road, at the equally impressive (but smaller and less developed) **Cenote Samula** (daily 8am–5pm; M$25), the roots of a huge tree stretch down into the pool. While Dzitnup is frequently crowded and plagued by small children asking for tips, you may well find yourself alone at Samula.

Colectivos run direct to Dzitnup from outside the *Hotel María Guadalupe* in Valladolid (M$10; see p.192). Alternatively, any westbound second-class **bus** will drop you at the turn-off, 5km from town; then it's a 2km walk down a signed track. You could also take a taxi or, best of all, **cycle** on the paved bike path; the most scenic route is down Calle 41-A to San Bernardino, then along Calle 49, which eventually connects to Avenida de los Frailes, then the old highway and the *ciclopista*.

Or you may want to make the longer trip to **Bioparque Xla'kaj** (M$5), 5km south of town, then 2.2km east on the road to Xocen. Despite the grand name, the destination is simply a huge, open-air cenote with easy access on stone stairs. The surrounding grounds, maintained by the nearby farm community of Chichimilá, are a bit enthusiastically manicured, but there are also refreshments for sale, as well as several nice palapas for **overnight** guests (no tel; ❸). These go for a bargain rate, considering they have individual bathrooms and ceiling fans. Cycling here is possible, if not as nice as the route to Dzitnup – follow the bike path which begins on the south end of town, off Calle 42, then make the well-signed 2.2km ride east.

If you happen to drive by, **Cenote Suytun** (8am–5pm; M$25), 7km east of Valladolid on a cattle ranch, makes a nice break. The admission price covers two pools: Suytun, which is set in a large cave, and a more open sinkhole that's nicer for swimming. They're less splendid than Dzitnup, but also less crowded.

From Ek-Balam to the Gulf coast

The vast majority of traffic from Valladolid heads straight west to Mérida, or back east to Cancún and the Caribbean beaches. A few places north, however, merit exploring – especially if you're looking for wildlife or less-visited Maya ruins. You can easily visit the small but flawless site of **Ek-Balam** 25km north; travel via Tizimín to see the flamingo colony on the coast at **Río Lagartos**; or go to the beach at **San Felipe**, **Las Coloradas** or **El Cuyo**. If you want to go all the way to the coast as a day-trip, you'll need to make an early start – the last bus from Río Lagartos for Tizimín leaves at 5pm. You'll have to return at least to Tizimín to continue on to Mérida, and all the way back to Valladolid for buses to the Caribbean coast.

Ek-Balam

Little-visited but well-excavated, **EK-BALAM** (daily 8am–5pm; M$27) is notable for the high quality and unique details of its sculpture. Enclosed by a series of defensive walls, the compact site is really only the ceremonial centre; the entire city, which was occupied from the Pre-Classic period through the Spanish Conquest, spreads out over a very wide area, punctuated by *sacbeob* (Maya roads) heading out in all directions. The entrance is along one of these ancient roads, leading through a freestanding four-sided arch. Beyond are two identical temples, called **Las Gemelas** (the Twins), and a long **ball-court**. The principal building, on the far side of the plaza, is the massive **Acrópolis**, the stones along its two-hundred-metre-long base adorned with bas-reliefs. Thatched awnings protect the site's finest treasure, an elaborate stucco frieze fully uncovered only around 2000; 85 percent of what you see is original plaster from the ninth century that didn't even require retouching once the dirt was brushed away.

▲ Stucco sculpture on the Acrópolis

A staircase leads up the centre of the building. On the first level, two doorways flanking the steps display near-matching designs of twisted serpents and tongues; in the right-hand carving, the snake's tongue is emblazoned with a glyph thought to represent the city of Ek-Balam. Just below the summit, a **Chenes-style doorway** in the form of a giant gaping mouth is studded with protruding teeth. This is the **entrance**

to the tomb of Ukit-Kan-Lek-Tok, the city's powerful king in the mid-ninth century. The lower jaw forms the floor, while the skulls, lilies, fish and other symbols of the underworld carved below reinforce its function as a tomb gateway. Of the detailed human figures that surround the door, one's disproportionate limbs and deformed hands and feet suggest it is a portrait of a real person – one theory holds that this deformity was a result of inbreeding in the royal class. The figure at the top centre of the mouth is thought to be the king himself. Back on the ground, in the plaza, an exceptionally well-preserved **stele** depicts a king receiving the objects of power from Ukit-Kan-Lek-Tok, the smaller figure at the top of the stele, seated with one leg folded under. Given the rich detail at the site, it's worth hiring a **guide** for about M$350 for a small group. Juan Canul, who has worked on many excavations, is recommended; ask for him at the ticket desk.

In the parking lot at the ruins, you'll find someone selling tickets to the nicely maintained **Cenote Xcanché**, which can be a great afternoon refresher. Entrance starts at M$30, with additional charges for bike rental, rappelling and other activities.

Practicalities

There is no bus service to the site – you'll have to catch a **colectivo** on Calle 44 just west of the plaza (M$40). Look specifically for taxis from the nearby village of Ek-Balam – these are cheaper than a private Valladolid car, which will cost about M$250 round-trip with waiting time. You could also look for colectivos to the village of Santa Rita and walk north from there, which takes about half an hour.

In the village of Ek-Balam itself, *Genesis Retreat* (☎985/852-7980, Ⓦwww.genesisretreat.com; ❺) is a beautiful, bargain-priced **eco-lodge** with a big garden and a bio-filtered pool. The hospitable Canadian owner, who built the place herself, is also dedicated to responsible cultural tourism – her "meet the neighbours" trip around the village to learn about local food and crafts is a highlight. She also organizes periodic nature tours, led by visiting experts, and has a separate piece of property for birdwatching and other outings. *Chaya's*, the **café** at *Genesis*, makes a great stop after the ruins, with treats like avocado ice cream, chocolate-chile cookies and rich crepes of spinach-like *chaya*. To reach the lodge, turn north just outside the gate to the ruins; when you hit the village plaza, turn right, then left, and follow signs off the far corner of the square. If you're taking a taxi to the place, be aware that some drivers may attempt to take you to another, less savoury cabaña lodge around the corner – *Genesis* has a doghouse labelled "Concierge" out front.

Tizimín

If you are travelling by bus from Valladolid to see the flamingos at Río Lagartos, you will have to transfer 51km north in **TIZIMÍN**, the unofficial capital of Yucatán's cattle country. It's a little rowdier than Valladolid (kids from there head north for nightlife), and pleasant enough, but without any specific attractions, it's rarely a stop for travellers. The exception is the **Feria de los Tres Reyes**, which takes place during Epiphany in early January. The fair's festivities, which honour both the Magi of old and the ranchers of today, draw both Catholic pilgrims and cowboys (who relish showing off their barbecue skills). The rest of the year, it's worth arranging your schedule to pass through Tizimín at lunchtime, when you can dine at one of the region's best restaurants, *Tres Reyes*. From the hand-patted, chewy tortillas to the black-as-ink beans to the succulent meats, the fresh food here is full of the very soul of Yucatecan cooking; add charming waiters and an even more charming owner, and it's a memorable dining experience. It's located on the plaza, at calles 50, 51, 52 and 53 – an easy walk from the two bus stations (around the corner from each other at Calle 46 and Calle 47, very near the **market**). If you do find yourself here overnight, the best of the modest **hotels** in the centre is *Hotel San Carlos*, on Calle 54, between calles 51 and 53 (Ⓣ986/863-2094; ❺), while *Posada Maria Antonia*, on Calle 50, just off the plaza between calles 53 and 51 (Ⓣ986/863-2384; ❹), is a good cheap choice. Tizimín also has direct **bus** services to and from Mérida and Cancún.

Río Lagartos

The village of RÍO LAGARTOS, 100km due north of Valladolid, is set on a small spit, surrounded on three sides by water and protected from the open sea by a barrier island. The resulting shallow inlet is inhabited by tens of thousands of **pink flamingos**. Spanish explorers mistook the inlet (*ría*) for a river (*río*), and resident crocodiles for alligators (*lagartos*). The former error, at least, has been corrected, and now the area of marshy flatland along the water in either direction from the town is the **Ría Lagartos Biosphere Reserve** – a popular destination with naturalists, as it's home to almost four hundred bird species. Though there's not much going on in the town itself, the flamingos alone make a visit worthwhile, and the best time of year to see them is the spring nesting season, from April to July; the rest of the year, many migrate to Celestún on the west coast (see p.238). A day-trip from Valladolid is manageable, but if you want to **stay the night**, *Cabañas Escondidas* (Ⓣ986/862-0121; ❸) has a few simple cabins, all with private bath, facing the waterfront on Calle 14, just south of Calle 19; next door, *Posada Isla Contoy* (Ⓣ986/862-0000; ❺) has slightly fancier rooms. The surprisingly flashy *Tabasco Río* (Ⓣ986/862-0116; Ⓦwww.hoteltabascorio.com; ❻) is also an option, where rooms are even a bit stylish. There is **no bank or ATM** in town, so plan accordingly.

You're likely to be swamped by offers to take you out to see the birds as soon as you arrive at the bus station (on Calle 19, just east of the main north–south street through town) or get out of your car. But it's best to either prearrange a trip with Peninsula Tours in Valladolid (see p.192), or head directly west on Calle 19 to *Restaurante Isla Contoy* (daily 7am–10pm), where Río Lagartos Expeditions operate (Ⓦwww.riolagartosexpeditions.com). Here you can arrange a **boat** trip with an experienced English-speaking guide (Ismael Navarro is recommended) to some of the many flamingo feeding sites. The standard tour is two hours and costs M$700 for a maximum of six people; park fees are an additional M$21 per person. A three-hour tour is M$800 and includes a natural "spa treatment" at some remote mud-flats. Arrive early if you're interested in joining up with others to fill a boat. Though it's usually not a problem with these guides, do make sure your boat captain doesn't drive too close to the birds for the sake of photos; also, never pay for the tour before you go out – it's usually a bad sign if your captain demands it.

Río Lagartos Expeditions also runs a night tour (M$800 for a boat) to visit crocodiles, or sea turtles in season (April–July), as well as fly-fishing outings and snorkelling. If you just want to hit the beach, they'll run a boat "taxi" (from M$200) out to the barrier island, where there are a few palapas for shade; you can arrange meals, too.

San Felipe, Las Coloradas and El Cuyo

If it's strictly **beaches** you're after, head west or east along the coast. Twelve kilometres west of Río Lagartos, **San Felipe** sports especially clean streets lined with tidy, colourfully painted, tin-roofed houses. The bay here, which is thick with tarpon, is popular for **fly-fishing**. Most of the buses from Tizimín to Río Lagartos come out here as well; the last one leaves from Río Lagartos at 5.15pm if you want to carry on from there.

There are a couple of good seafood **restaurants** (*Pescadería Danilu*, on the main street, is popular) and one very pleasant waterfront **hotel** in town, *Hotel San Felipe de Jesus*, on Calle 9, between calles 14 and 16 (Ⓣ986/862-2027, Ⓔsanfelip@prodigy.net.mx; ❺), which also has a decent restaurant and offers fishing trips. Otherwise it's about M$50 for a boat from the pier at the east end of the malecón (where you can also get **tourist information**) to the beaches on the spit, where you can set up **camp**. At Mexican holiday times – July, August and Easter week – these spots are crowded; the rest of the year, quite deserted. If you do camp, be sure to bring protection against mosquitoes; if you don't plan to stay over, it's easy enough to arrange for the boat to collect you from the beach in the evening.

With no regular hotels, **LAS COLORADAS** isn't really a practical destination, 20km east of Río Lagartos, unless you're looking for an empty spot on the beach to **camp**. The road out to the village passes through the nature reserve, and past Sendero Peten Tucha, a 2.5km trail through the marshlands that is ideal for birders (Km 8, south side of the road). The road then continues past a long stretch of beach that's the core of the reserve, behind a buffer of yucca and century plants. Note that camping on this beach is prohibited. The reserve abruptly ends at the edge of a vast industrial salt-mining operation, followed shortly thereafter by the village itself – this is the end of the road, and it really feels like it. Just one bus comes out here, at 12.30pm from Río Lagartos.

Another remote beach hideaway, **El Cuyo** lies 50km east of Río Lagartos, but the coast road does not go past Las Coloradas; instead, head east from Tizimín 50km to Colonia Yucatán, then north 38km through rolling farmland to the water. Noreste **buses** make the hour-and-a-half-long trip five times daily from Tizimín. The lagoon you cross on the way is red and foamy from the high salt content (and not pollution), while the town itself is tidy and pleasant, with broad, wild-feeling beaches that are busy only during the Mexican holidays. The *Aida Luz* **hotel** (no tel; ❹), one block back from the beach, is a spick-and-span motel. *Flamingos Cabins* (Ⓣ999/943-7141, Ⓦwww.flamingoscabins.com; ❺) has a more rustic style, but some rooms are equipped with kitchenettes for longer stays. The staff can arrange birdwatching and kayaking tours. Fish is of course the order of the day, and *La Conchita* **restaurant**, one block west of the main plaza, does it best.

Chichén Itzá and around

The most famous, the most extensively restored and by far the most visited of all Maya sites, **CHICHÉN ITZÁ** lies conveniently along the main road from Cancún to Mérida, a little more than 200km from the coast. A fast and frequent bus service runs all along this road, making it feasible to visit as a day's excursion from Cancún, as many tour buses do, or en route between the coast and Mérida. The site, though, deserves better, and to do the ruins justice and see them when they're not entirely thronged with tourists, an overnight stop is highly recommended – either at the site itself or, less extravagantly, in the nearby village of **Pisté** or in Valladolid (see p.191). The relics the ancient Maya

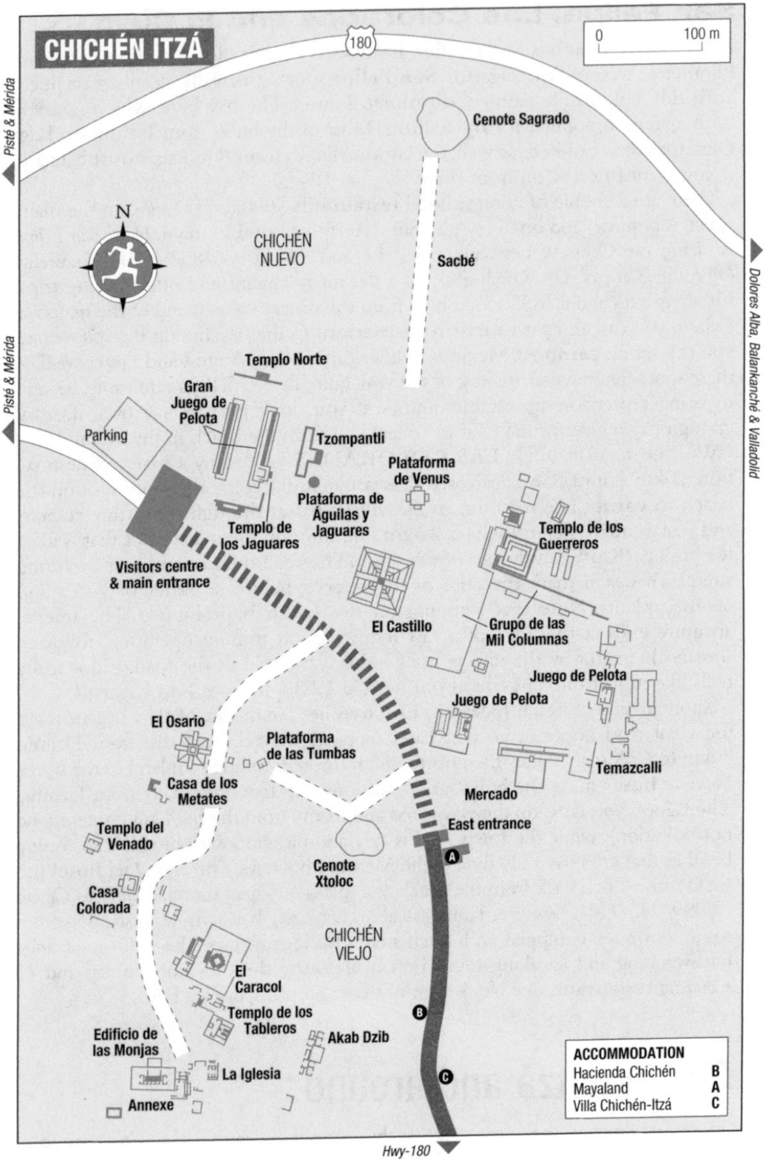

left in the eerie **Grutas de Balankanché** – a cave system a few kilometres east of the ruins – make an intriguing side-trip.

Arrival and information

Arriving at Chichén Itzá, the highway curves around the site to the north, making an arc that merges with the site-access road (once the original highway straight through) on both ends. If you're on a through bus, it may drop you at the junction of the bypass and the access road on the west side, about a ten-minute walk from the entrance. Most **buses**, though, drive right up to the site entrance and also stop in the neighbouring town of Pisté to the west. The rather grandly named Chichén Itzá International Airport, north of the ruins, is in fact a small **airstrip** that receives charter tour flights from the Caribbean coast.

The main **entry to the site** (daily 8am–5pm, though the process of getting everyone out starts at least an hour earlier; M$95, kids free) is on the west side. A parking lot (M$10) and huge **visitor centre** (open until 10pm) houses a museum, restrooms, restaurant, **ATM** and shops selling souvenirs, film, maps and guides. **Guided tours** of the ruins can be arranged here: small-group tours are M$600 for two hours. You can also buy tickets and get in at the **smaller eastern gate** by the *Mayaland* (see below). Book at the hotel reception area for two-hour **horse-riding trips** around the wilder, southern part of the site, Chichén Viejo (US$65 with guide).

The nightly **sound-and-light show** (7pm in winter, 8pm in summer; M$30, or included in the price of a day entrance ticket) is not worth seeing unless you're staying nearby, though it does briefly re-create the shadow-serpent effect (see p.203) on the Castillo (in lurid purple light, no less). Shows are only in Spanish, so if you don't pay for the translation headsets (M$25), shooting stars in the night sky might prove more entertaining. Wear lots of bug spray.

About a half-hour walk west from Chichén Itzá, **Pisté** is a somewhat bleak village straddling the road between Mérida and Valladolid. Its main function is to provide visitors hotel rooms, so they can get up early enough to beat the buses that arrive at the ruins around 10.30am. You'll also find an **Internet** café here, opposite the **bus station**, at the east end of town.

Accommodation

Visitors to Chichén Itzá have a choice of staying in a handful of more expensive **hotels** immediately to the east of the ruins (all but one are on the short access road off Hwy-180, signposted "zona hotelera") or along the main street in the town of Pisté, about 2km west of the main site entrance. In Pisté, most hotels are on the main road, between the village and the ruins, so it's easy to shop around for the best deal. Quality can be low and occupancy high, though, and the few reliable *posadas* have only a handful of rooms apiece. You can **camp** or sling up a hammock at the *Pirámide Inn* (M$50).

Near the ruins

Dolores Alba Hwy-180 *libre* Km 122, 2km east of Chichén Itzá east entrance ⓣ999/928-5650, ⓦwww.doloresalba.com. The best-value hotel on either side of the ruins, with clean, colourful rooms, a good restaurant (see p.202) and two swimming pools, one built out of a natural spring. Transport is provided to the site (but not back). ⑤

Hacienda Chichén Off Hwy-180, near the east entrance to the ruins ⓣ985/920-8407, ⓦwww.haciendachichen.com. Of the two luxury choices at the Chichén Itzá site (*Mayaland* is the other), this place has a more colonial-Mexico feel, with wrought-iron furniture and plenty of greenery, as well as a couple of small ruins within its grounds. Rooms are in individual cottages that housed Carnegie Institution archeologists in the 1920s. ⑨

Mayaland/The Lodge at Chichén Itzá Off Hwy-180, at the east entrance to the ruins ⓣ985/851-0100, ⓦwww.mayaland.com. High-end resort with thatched-hut suites dotted about the gardens. A little more lux than *Hacienda Chichén* – especially in the smaller *Lodge* section, where some bungalows (US$374 and up) have private pools – but lacking any historic ambience beyond the lobby. ⑨

Villa Chichén-Itzá Off Hwy-180, near the east entrance to the ruins ⓣ987/872-9300 ext 8101, ⓦwww.islandercollection.com. Not as lavish as its neighbours, but certainly comfortable. Rooms are set round a patio enclosing a pool and cocktail bar. By night, its library full of archeological tomes doubles as a disco, which is usually empty. ⑦

In Pisté

Felix Inn Just west of *Posada Chac-Mool* ⓣ999/851-0033, ⓔhotelfelixinnchichenitza@hotmail.com. A welcome addition to Pisté's somewhat dreary hotel scene, the *Felix* is a sensible and sunny alternative to the hotels by the ruins. Clean a/c rooms are laid out around a pool, plus a restaurant, an Internet café and Wi-Fi. ⑦

Pirámide Inn Hwy-180 *libre* at the west end of town, next to the bus station ⓣ985/851-0115, ⓦwww.chichen.com. Conveniently situated near the main entrance to the ruins, with a pool, a *temazcal* sauna, extensive gardens and a somewhat New Age clientele. ⑤

Posada Chac-Mool South side of Hwy-180 *libre*, midway through town ⓣ985/851-0270. No frills, and not as cosy (or cheap) as *Kary* or *Maya*, but clean and reliable. Choice of a/c or fan. ④

Posada Kary West end of Pisté; from the bus stop, turn right off Hwy-180 *libre* just before the central intersection and plaza ⓣ985/851-0208. Look for the pink trim on this building with six tidy rooms – good value, and a choice of fan or a/c. ③

Posada Maya West end of Pisté, next to *Posada Kary* ⓣ985/851-0211. Just past *Kary* on a side street, this place, with eight rooms, is an even better deal. Rooms can be a little dark but are livened up with very groovy wood-block prints on the pastel walls. ②

Posada Olalde On C 6, south of the main road; coming from the bus stop, turn left across from *Posada Carrousel* ⓣ985/851-0086. The basic rooms, with fans and hot water, can be a bit dim, but they're very clean. This is one of the quieter spots, since it's off the main road. ③

Eating and drinking

For refreshment near the ruins, or if you're staying overnight, the **restaurant** at the *Dolores Alba* hotel is good and affordable, with basics from hamburgers to tacos, and you can use the pool. Across the road is the package-tour stop *Parque Ikkil* (8am–6pm; M$60), the centrepiece of which is the large Sagrado Azul **cenote**, well appointed with changing facilities and easy-access stairs; skip the unappetizing buffet restaurant, though. If you have your own car, or don't mind hopping on a second-class bus, you could also visit Cenote **Yokdzonot** (see p.207) and its small restaurant, a little to the west of Pisté. In Pisté, the best dining options are *El Carrousel*, for cheap beers and snacks, and *Las Mestizas*, which does some good regional cuisine, such as *poc-chuc* and *brazo de reina*. The pricier hotels all have their own restaurants. At the west end of town, in front of the small plaza, a short row of *loncherías* serve *comida corrida* for about M$45, and are also open in the evenings, dishing up standard snacks. For entertainment at night, the only thing to do is hang out on the plaza and watch the local dogs run around.

The site

Though in most minds the ruins of **Chichén Itzá** represent the very image of the Maya, it's actually the city's sharp divergence from Maya tradition that makes it so archeologically intriguing. Experts are fairly certain that the city was established around 300 AD and began to flourish in the Terminal Classic period (between 800 and 925 AD); the rest of its history, however, as well as the roots of the Itzá clan that consolidated power in the peninsula here after 925, remain hotly disputed. Much of the evidence at the site – an emphasis on human sacrifice, the presence of a huge ball-court and the glorification of military activity – points to a strong influence from central Mexico. For decades researchers guessed this was the result of the city's being invaded and conquered by the Toltecs, a theory reinforced by the resemblance of the Templo de los Guerreros to the colonnade at Tula, near Mexico City. They also found Toltec-style pottery remains and numerous depictions of the Toltec god-king, the feathered serpent Quetzalcoatl (Kukulcán to the Maya).

Work since the 1980s, however, supports a theory that the Itzá people were not Toltec invaders, but fellow Maya who had migrated from the south (which explains why their subjects refer to them as "foreigners" in texts). The Toltec artefacts, this view holds, arrived in central Yucatán via the Itzás' chief trading partners, the **Chontal Maya**, who maintained allegiances with Toltecs in Central Mexico and Oaxaca.

Chichén Nuevo

The old highway that used to pass through the site is now a path dividing the ruins in two: the Itzá-era **Chichén Nuevo** (New or "Toltec" Chichén) to the north and Terminal Classic **Chichén Viejo** (Old Chichén) to the south. If it's still reasonably early in the day, head first to the north. Most buildings here, including the central **Castillo** pyramid, the **Templo de los Guerreros** and an enormous **ball-court**, date from the city's peak, sometime during the Post-Classic period, between 925 and 1200 AD. They have all been very well excavated and restored, though the methods employed in the 1920s by the Carnegie Institution's archeologists relied perhaps a bit more on imagination than academic rigour, according to contemporary critics.

El Castillo

The main path leads directly to **El Castillo** (also called the Pyramid of Kukulcán), the structure that sits alone in the centre of a great grassy plaza. At 25m high, it doesn't compare with larger structures at Cobá and Calakmul, but its simple lines and monumental stairways ascending each face (though only two are restored) rise precipitously to a temple at the top. Visitors are no longer allowed to climb up – probably for the best, considering the difficulty of getting back down.

The design's simplicity is deceptive, however, as a numerological analysis of the building suggests that it is the **Maya calendar** rendered in stone: each staircase has 91 steps, which, added to the single step at the main entrance to the temple, amounts to 365, the total number of days in a solar year. On each face, the central staircase divides 9 terraces into 18, the number of months in the Maya solar year. Additionally, 52, the number of stone panels on each face, is deeply symbolic, representing the number of years required for the two Maya calendar systems (the solar year and the 260-day year) to align and repeat. Most remarkably, the stones are set so that near sunset on the spring and autumn equinoxes, the great heads of the feathered serpent Kukulcán, which are carved into the foot of the main staircase, are joined to the carved tails at the top of the building by an undulating shadow resembling a snake's body. This event lasts just a few hours and draws spectators and awed worshippers by the thousands.

Interestingly, El Castillo is actually a shell. Much of its bulk comes from another pyramid, a miniature version of the exact same proportions inside it, built precisely 52 years earlier. The end of each calendar period called for elaborate rituals and commemorations, often including the construction of larger, grander temples. This kind of nested architecture can be seen at numerous sites, over most of the span of the ancient Maya civilization.

The "Toltec" plaza

El Castillo marks one edge of a **plaza** that formed the focus of Chichén Nuevo, and all its most important buildings are here, many displaying a strong Toltec influence in their structure and decoration. The **Templo de los Guerreros** (Temple of the Warriors), lined on two sides by the **Grupo de las Mil Columnas** (Group of the Thousand Columns), forms the eastern edge of

▲ Grupo de las Mil Columnas

the plaza. These are the structures that most recall the great Toltec site of Tula, both in design and detail – in particular the colonnaded courtyard (which would have been roofed with some form of thatch) and the use of Atlantean columns, representing battle-dressed warriors, their arms raised above their heads. The temple is richly decorated on its north and south sides with carvings and sculptures (originally with paintings, too) of jaguars and eagles devouring human hearts, feathered serpents, warriors and masks with curling snouts (the one undeniably Maya feature). On top (now visible only at a distance, as you can no longer climb the structure) are two superb examples of figurines called **Chac-mools**, thought to have been introduced by the Toltecs: offerings were placed on the stomachs of these reclining figures, which represent the messengers who would take the sacrifice to the gods, or perhaps the divinities themselves.

As with El Castillo, the Templo de los Guerreros was built over an earlier temple, in which some remnants of faded **murals** can be made out (the interior of the temple is very often closed to the public, however). The "thousand" columns alongside originally formed a square, on the far side of which is the building known as the **Mercado**, although there's no evidence that this was actually a marketplace. Near here, to the south, is a small, dilapidated ball-court.

Walking west across the plaza towards the main ball-court, you pass the **Plataforma de Venus**, a raised, square block with a stairway up each side guarded by feathered serpents. Here, rites associated with Quetzalcoatl/Kukulcán when he took the form of Venus, the morning star, would have been carried out. Slightly smaller, but otherwise identical in design, the adjacent **Plataforma de Águilas y Jaguares** features reliefs of eagles and jaguars holding human hearts. Human sacrifices may even have been carried out here, judging by the proximity of a third platform, carved on every side with grotesquely grinning stone skulls. It is likely a **tzompantli,** or "skull rack", a common Toltec (and later Aztec) structure on which victims' heads were displayed.

The Gran Juego de Pelota and the Templo de los Jaguares

Chichén Itzá's **Gran Juego de Pelota**, on the west side of the plaza, is the largest known ball-court in Mesoamerica – with walls some 90m long and an overall field 149m in length. Its design is a capital "I" surrounded by temples, with the goals, or target rings, halfway along each side. Along the bottom of each side runs a sloping **panel** decorated in relief with scenes of the game and its players. Although the full significance of the game remains a mystery, it was clearly not a Saturday afternoon kick-about in the park. On the panel, the players are shown processing from either side towards a central circle, the symbol of death. One player, just right of the centre, has been decapitated (whether it's the winning or losing captain is up for debate). To the left, another player holds his head and a ritual knife. Along the top of the panel runs the stone body of a snake with heads sticking out at either end. In addition, a whispering-gallery effect enables you to hear clearly at the far end of the court.

The **Templo de los Jaguares** overlooks the playing area from the east side. At the bottom – effectively the outer wall of the ball-court – is a little portico supported by two pillars, between which a stone jaguar stands sentinel. The outer wall panels, the left and the right of the interior space, are carved with images of Pawahtuns, the gods who supported the sky and who are thought to be the patrons of the Itzá people. Inside are some worn but elaborate relief carvings of the Itzá ancestors inserted in the Maya creation myth – a forceful proclamation of their entitlement to rule.

Cenote Sagrado

The **sacred cenote** lies at the end of the *sacbé* that leads about 300m from the north side of the plaza. It's an almost perfectly round hole in the limestone surface of the earth, some 60m in diameter and more than 30m deep, the bottom third full of water. It was thanks to this natural well (and another in the southern half of the site) that the city could survive at all, and it gives Chichén Itzá its name (literally "at the edge of the well of the Itzá"). This well was regarded as a portal to Xibalba, the "other world", and it was a repository for small offerings – incense, statues, jade and especially metal disks (a few of them gold) engraved and embossed with figures and glyphs – along with human sacrificial victims, as has been confirmed by dredging operations.

Chichén Viejo

The **southern half of the site** is the most sacred part for contemporary Maya, though the buildings here are not in such good condition. They were built for the most part prior to 925 AD, in the indigenous architectural styles used in the Puuc and Chenes regions. A path leads from the south side of El Castillo to the major structures, passing first the pyramid **El Osario** (the Ossuary, also called the High Priest's Grave), the only building in this section that shows any Toltec-style detail. Externally it is very similar to El Castillo, including the serpent carvings lining the staircase, but inside, most unusually, a series of **tombs** was discovered. A shaft, first explored at the end of the nineteenth century, drops down from the top through five crypts, in each of which was found a skeleton and a trap door leading to the next. The fifth is at ground level, but here too was a trap door, and steps cut through the rock to a sixth chamber that opens onto a huge underground cavern: the burial place of the high priest.

Follow the main path and you arrive at **El Caracol** ("The Snail", named for its curving internal staircase), a circular, domed tower standing on two rectangular platforms and looking remarkably like a modern-day observatory in outline, which is why it's also called "the Observatory". No telescope, however, was mounted in the roof, which instead has slits aligned with various points of astronomical significance. Four doors aligned with the cardinal directions lead into the tower and a circular chamber. A spiral staircase ascends to the upper level, where observations of the stars were made.

Immediately to the south, the so-called **Monjas** (Nunnery) palace complex shows several stages of construction. Part of the facade was blasted away in the nineteenth century, but it is nonetheless a building of grand proportions. Its **annexe**, on the east end, has an elaborate facade in the Chenes style, covered in small heads – these are perhaps of Chac, the rain god, or perhaps of Itzamná, the creator – that combine to make one giant mask, with the door as a mouth. By contrast, **La Iglesia**, a small building standing beside the convent, is a clear demonstration of Puuc design, its low band of unadorned masonry around the bottom surmounted by an elaborate mosaic frieze and roofcomb. Hook-nosed masks again predominate, but above the doorway are also the figures of the four mythological creatures who were believed to hold up the sky: a snail, a turtle, an armadillo and a crab.

About ten minutes' walk south of Las Monjas, a path leads to an additional group of ruins that are among the oldest on the site, but unrestored; this is also a good area for birdwatching, with few people around to disturb the wildlife. Just east of Las Monjas is the **Akab Dzib**, a relatively plain block of palace rooms that takes its name ("Obscure Writings") from undeciphered hieroglyphs inside. Red palm prints – frequently found in Maya buildings – adorn the walls of some of the chambers. Backtrack along the main path to the building opposite El Osorio, the **Plataforma de las Tumbas**, a funerary structure topped with small columns; behind it is a jungle path that heads back to the main east–west road via the site's other water source, Cenote Xtoloc.

Grutas de Balankanché

Just 1.6km east of the *Dolores Alba* hotel (see p.201), the **Grutas de Balankanché** are a somewhat creepy complement to Chichén Itzá's sunlit grandiosity, and a refreshingly cool way to pass an hour. These caverns were reopened in 1959, when a sealed passageway was discovered, revealing a path to an underground altar to the rain god Chac. Tours with taped commentary (in English daily at 11am, 1pm & 3pm; M$54) lead you past an underground pool and stalagmites and stalactites, to a huge rock formation that resembles a ceiba, the Maya tree of life. This is the altar, and around its base lie many of the original Maya offerings, mostly Chac-faced incense burners and other pottery. In places the caves can be cold, damp and thoroughly claustrophobic, despite the rather heavy-handed use of coloured lights. Charles Gallenkamp's book *Maya* has an excellent chapter devoted to the discovery of the caves, and to the ritual exorcism that a local traditional priest insisted on carrying out to placate the ancient gods and disturbed spirits.

Second-class **buses** between Valladolid and Mérida will drop you at *las grutas*, or you can catch a **colectivo** from Calle 44 in Valladolid. A taxi from Pisté should cost about M$50.

West to Mérida

Moving on from Chichén Itzá and Pisté, the most direct route to Mérida is along Hwy-180. If you're travelling leisurely via the *libre* road, you can stop about 14km west of Pisté for a dip at **Cenote Yokdzonot** (9am–6pm; M$20, plus M$10 for a life vest), in the town of the same name – turn south off the highway midway through the village. Any second-class bus will stop on request at the town plaza; the cenote is about 350m south. This large, extremely well-kept swimming hole, with showers and restrooms, opened to visitors in 2007 after a group of local women spent two years cleaning the place up. You can rent snorkel gear (M$25), and with a small **restaurant** serving excellent *poc-chuc* and *panuchos*, it's a great place to wind down after visiting Chichén Itzá. If you have a car, you might also want to detour to the village of **Yaxcabá**. The centrepiece here is a grand Franciscan church topped with three towers, the only one of its kind in Mexico; its eighteenth-century altarpieces are still intact. To reach it, turn south at the village of Libre Unión (8km west of Yokdzonot), then head 18km south.

North of Hwy-180, the small town of **Izamal**, dominated by a beautifully maintained sixteenth-century Franciscan mission, definitely merits a detour. Further along the back road to Mérida, the ancient Maya ruins of **Aké** meld with a working henequen plantation (see box, p.250).

Izamal

A major crafts centre that's also exceptionally scenic, the small town of **IZAMAL** makes a fine day visit or overnight stop, both for its historic monuments and gracious feel. It can also be a good alternative to Mérida as a base for sightseeing, if you prefer the country to the city – in this case, though, it's nice to have a car, as Izamal is served only by relatively slow second-class buses. From Pisté, head west on Hwy-180 *libre* to Kantunil (where the *cuota* and the *libre* merge), then 18km north. To turn north, you actually have to follow signs for the *cuota* to Cancún, then make an awkward U-turn. If you're on the *cuota* heading west, look for a direct right turn off the highway immediately before Km 68. If you miss the turn (easy to do), you can continue to Hoctún, then backtrack from there. By bus from the Chichén Itzá area, you will have to go back to Valladolid, where you can catch one of the two Izamal-bound Oriente buses a day (12.45pm & 3.50pm), or go to Mérida and transfer: buses leave every 45 minutes or so from the Noreste terminal on Calle 50 at Calle 67. Arriving at Izamal's **bus station**, on Calle 32 at Calle 33, you're one block back from (and within view of) one of the two central plazas, set corner-to-corner – walk straight out and you'll be headed in the right direction.

The most immediately striking thing about Izamal is that the convent and all of its buildings are painted a rich ochre colour, which positively glows in the setting sun. The paint job is the by-product of the most exciting event in this quiet town's recent history: Pope John Paul II's visit in 1993. Ancient Izamal was an important religious centre for the Maya, where they worshipped **Itzamná**, mythical founder of the ancient city and one of the gods of creation, at a series of huge pyramid-temples of the same name. Most are now no more than low mounds in the surrounding country, but several survive in the town itself and are fascinating to see rising up right in the middle of the residential grid; a couple of businesses on the main plaza have pyramids literally in their backyards. The largest pile, **Kinich Kakmó** (daily 8am–8pm; free), dedicated to the sun god, has been partly restored. It's just a couple of blocks north of the two central plazas; the helpful brown-clad tourist police roaming the squares have a knack for offering directions the moment you look remotely confused.

Very early in the colonial period, the Franciscans sought to establish Izamal as the centre of their religious leadership. In 1552 Fray Diego de Landa (later responsible for a vicious inquisition and auto-da-fé in Maní) lopped the top off a pyramid and began building the grand **Convento de San Antonio de Padua**, which now anchors the main squares (daily; free). It's impressive not only because it looms above the town, but also because its expansive porticoed yard occupies some 24,000 square metres.

When the complex was completed in 1561, de Landa consecrated it with one of two statues of the Virgin that he had brought back from Guatemala. Several years later, when church leaders from Valladolid attempted to claim the statue, it is said to have become impossibly heavy, and they were forced to leave it in Izamal. In light of this and numerous other presumed miracles, a cult developed that still draws pilgrims from all over the peninsula, even though the original statue burned in 1829 and had to be replaced by its twin. Today Nuestra Señora de Izamal is the official patroness of Yucatán, and during the **fiesta** dedicated to her in August, penitents climb the monastery's broad front staircase on their knees. The statue is usually on view in the *camarín*, a special chapel around the back of the main altar, reached by a long hall that runs adjacent to the nave. The nave is also a good place to admire the flying buttresses supporting the structure. Next to the small chapel is the small **Museo Sanctuario de Nuestra Señora** (Tues–Sat 10am–1pm & 3–6pm, Sun 9am–4pm; M$5 donation), which includes many elaborate gowns that have clothed the statue. This meticulous chronological display is reminiscent of Elvis's Graceland museum – particularly when you get to the silver lamé number from 1974. A few evenings a week, a **sound-and-light show** (Tues, Thurs & Sat at 8.30pm; M$45) is projected on the front facade of the main church. Fray Diego looks on from his post on a pedestal in the plaza on the north side of the monastery.

More recently, the town's artisans – master wood-carvers, papier-mâché artists and embroiderers – have received a great deal of encouragement from Banamex, thanks in part to the bank's ex-president, billionaire tastemaker Roberto Hernandez, who has directed funds to the beautifully done **Centro Cultural y Artesanal** (Mon–Wed & Fri 10am–8pm, Thurs & Sat 10am–10pm, Sun 10am–5pm; M$20). A museum here showcases choice pieces of craftwork from all over Mexico, organized by medium, with a special wing devoted to Yucatecan specialities. There's also a small café (peek behind to see some pyramid remnants), a quiet, perfumed back room where you can get a foot massage, a very nice gift shop and even bicycles for rent (M$40/2hr). These come in handy for visiting the various **artists' workshops** around town, signposted and marked on a **map** dispensed at the museum or the very helpful tourist office (see below). It's all a very casual, non-tacky arrangement, and a great opportunity to just drop in on and chat with some talented locals; be sure to visit the charming Don Esteban, on Calle 26 at Calle 45, who makes striking jewellery from henequen spines.

Practicalities

In the north plaza you'll find a Banorte **bank** with ATM. On the main plaza is a **post office** (Mon–Fri 8am–2.30pm) and the **tourist office** (9am–6pm; ⓣ988/954-0096), should you for some reason not yet have found someone eager to help. An **Internet café** is on Calle 30 just off the plaza, and a **laundry** is one block further. **Horse-drawn buggies** lined up around the plaza will take you for a pleasant *paseo* around the town and the pyramids, as well as out to the old wooden train station (20min; M$40).

Of the very few **hotels** in town, *Posada Flory*, on C 30 at C 27, just off the plaza (Ⓣ988/954-0562; ❸), is a bargain, with ten welcoming rooms (some with air conditioning), operated by a chatty, hospitable woman. For a bit more, *Macan Ché B&B* (Ⓣ988/954-0287, Ⓦwww.macanche.com; ❺), is an assortment of comfortable cottages tucked among rambling gardens a few blocks east of the main plaza, on Calle 22, between calles 33 and 35. Also look for *San Miguel Arcangel*, on the plaza (Ⓣ988/954-0109, Ⓦwww.sanmiguelhotel.com.mx; ❺), a twelve-room hotel furnished with art and antiques; out back, there's a hot tub perched atop a ruined pyramid. A few kilometres south, near the town of Sudzal, and very much worth the drive if you have your own transport, is the rambling, artfully decorated *Hacienda San Antonio Chalanté* (Ⓣ999/132-7411, Ⓦwww.haciendachalante.com; ❺); the owner is a champion horsewoman, and offers riding around the expansive grounds. Rates include breakfast, and dinner is an option.

Back in town, the palapa-roof *Kinich* on Calle 27, between calles 28 and 30, is a good **restaurant** for lunch, with women patting tortillas off to one side and well-priced Yucatecan dishes like *poc-chuc* on the menu. In the evening, *El Toro*, on Calle 30 just east of the convent, also has a hearty Yucatecan menu of dishes like *chaya* tamales and *queso relleno*. You can enjoy coffee or ice cream at *La Estación*, a small courtyard **café** in the arcade leading to *Posada San Miguel*. In the same building, Hecho a Mano, a particularly good craft and **folk-art shop**, is stocked with everything from Mexican wrestling masks to Huichol yarn paintings from Nayarit, as well as photography by the owner; note that the hours (Mon–Sat 10am–2pm & 4–7pm) can be erratic.

Leaving Izamal, buses run to Mérida nearly every thirty minutes; the Oriente buses are preferable because the terminal is closer to the centre. They're nearly as frequent to Valladolid and Cancún, though the faster buses go only five times daily, and all are second-class. Three buses run to Tizimín, and two go to Motul.

Aké

Midway between Izamal and Mérida on the back road via Cacalchén, the **Aké ruins** (9am–5pm; M$27) are partially integrated into an inhabited village – an interesting phenomenon to see if you're in no rush, but not essential to most itineraries. Aké was probably in alliance with the old city of Izamal, as it is linked to it by one of the peninsula's largest *sacbeob*. The most impressive building here is the **Edificio de las Pilastras**, a large platform topped with more than twenty stone pillars, more reminiscent of structures in central Mexico or even Greece than anything in the Yucatán. The Maya rubble intermingles with San Lorenzo de Aké, a working henequen **hacienda**, which, though a bit run-down, is still a fine example of neo-French architecture from the end of the nineteenth century. You're welcome to wander through the machinery to see the fibre-making process. North of the henequen plant, a church has been built on top of one of the old Maya temples. You'll need a car to visit the site, as there's no bus service (though the Auto Centro bus runs the scenic Hwy-80 between Izamal and Mérida every 45 minutes or so). To reach the ruins, turn south off the main road in Euan; in Ekmul, 3.5km south, head east another 5km. The ruins are at the end of the road, beyond an overgrown plaza and the main hacienda building.

Also along this route, 6km west of the village of Cacalchén and 10km east of the turn to Aké, *Hacienda San José* (ⓣ999/910-4617, ⓦwww.luxurycollection.com; ❾), good for a lavish **lunch**, is a nice spot to take in the excellent birdlife in this area. As one of four very tastefully restored haciendas managed by the owners of the *W* and *Westin* hotels, it's also a gorgeous place to **lodge**.

Travel details

Buses

Tizimín is a handy transport hub for northeastern Yucatán – you can go straight from there to Mérida or Cancún, for instance, without returning to Valladolid. Improved bus service at the Chichén Itzá ruins now spares travellers the hike to Pisté for transport. To make your way back to the Caribbean coast from Chichén Itzá, it's best to take any bus you can as far as Valladolid, and if necessary change there for first-class service. You can bypass Cancún by taking a second-class bus to Tulum via Cobá. Note that you can't check schedules or buy tickets for Valladolid on ADO's website.

Chichén Itzá to: Cancún (roughly hourly, 8.35am–5.35pm; 2hr 30min–4hr); Cobá (1 daily at 7.35am; 1hr); Mérida (roughly hourly, 9.10am–5.10pm; 2–4hr); Playa del Carmen (2 daily at 2.35pm & 4.30pm; 3hr 30min); Tulum (4 daily at 7.35am, 8.25am, 2.35pm & 4.30pm; 2hr); Valladolid (roughly every 30min, 8.25am–5.35pm; 45min).

Izamal to: Cancún via Valladolid (roughly hourly, 5am–1.15am; 5hr); Mérida (roughly every 30min, 5.15am–7pm; 1–2hr); Motul (2 daily at 9am & 2.45pm; 1hr); Tizimín (3 daily at 7.30am, 8.30am & 6.25pm; 1hr 30min).

Pisté to: Cancún (roughly hourly, 8.30am–6.30pm; 2hr 30min–4hr); Cobá (1 daily at 7.35am; 1hr); Mérida (roughly hourly, 7am–5.30pm; 2–4hr); Playa del Carmen (3 daily at 7.30am, 2.20pm & 4.15pm; 3hr 30min); Tulum (4 daily at 7.30am, 8.10am, 2.20pm & 4.15pm; 2hr); Valladolid (roughly every 30min, 7.30am–4.30pm; 45min).

Río Lagartos to: Las Coloradas (1 daily at 12.30pm; 45min); San Felipe (5 daily, 8.30am–5.15pm; 30min); Tizimín (13 daily, 5:30am–5.15pm; 1hr 30min).

Tizimín to: Cancún (12 daily, 6.30am–3.30am; 2hr 30min–4hr); Chetumal (2 daily at 4.30am & 1.30pm; 9hr); Chiquilá, for Holbox (4 daily at 4.30am, 11am, 1pm & 2.15pm; 2hr); Las Coloradas (1 daily at 10.30am; 2hr); El Cuyo (5 daily, 7.15am–6pm; 1hr 30min); Izamal (3 daily at 5am, 11am & 4pm; 1hr 30min); Mérida (9 daily, 5.30am–6.30pm; 4hr); Playa del Carmen (1 daily at 8.30am; 4hr); Río Lagartos (8 daily, 5am–7.45pm; 1hr 30min); San Felipe (6 daily, 9.15am–7.45pm; 2hr); Tulum (1 daily at 9.30am; 4hr); Valladolid (hourly, 5.30am–7.30pm; 1hr).

Valladolid to: Campeche (1 daily at 2pm; 6hr); Cancún (roughly every 45min, 6am–3.15am; 2hr–3hr 30min); Chetumal (3 daily at 5.30am, 7.30am & 2.30pm; 8hr); Chichén Itzá (hourly, 7.15am–5.30pm; 45min); Chiquilá, for Holbox (2.45am; 3hr 30min); Cobá (3 daily at 9.30am, 2.45pm & 5.15pm; 2hr); Mérida (roughly every 30min, round-the-clock; 2hr 30 min–4hr); Playa del Carmen (9 daily, 8.30am–5.20pm; 3hr); Tizimín (roughly hourly, 5.30am–8pm; 1hr); Tulum (9 daily, 8.30am–8.30pm; 2hr).

Flights

Charter small-plane tours run from Playa del Carmen, Cancún and Cozumel to a small airstrip near Chichén Itzá (see p.201).

6

Mérida and around

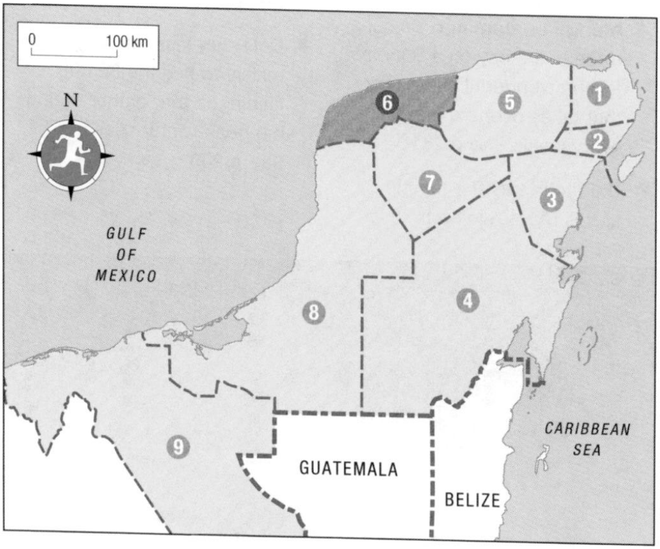

CHAPTER 6

Highlights

* **Catedral de San Ildefonso** The first cathedral built in the Americas is the site of a major pilgrimage in September and October. See p.222
* **Palacio de Gobierno** Inside the Yucatán governor's offices in Mérida, Fernando Castro Pacheco's stirring modernist murals depict local history. See p.224
* **Mérida en domingo** Be sure to be in the city on a Sunday for the wonderful street party that takes over the plaza every week. See p.231
* **Dzibilchaltún** The temple at this Maya ruin north of Mérida aligns perfectly with the sunrise on the equinoxes; the site also has an excellent museum of Maya culture. See p.234
* **Gulf coast beaches** All of Mérida decamps to this shore in the summer, but the rest of the year you'll probably have the sand (and heading further east, the wildlife) to yourself. See p.235
* **Celestún** Visitors flock here mainly to see the 30,000 flamingos that gather during the peak winter season. See p.238

▲ A balloon vendor in front of the Catedral de San Ildefonso in Mérida

6

Mérida and around

If you want to truly appreciate the melding of Spanish and Maya culture that's the cornerstone of local heritage, Mérida, the next most popular stop in the peninsula after Cancún and Chichén Itzá, is the place to come. The capital of Yucatán State is modern and prosperous but also distinctly proud of its past, boasting a rich historical core filled with beautifully decaying mansions, a very good archeology museum, a teeming market and the oldest cathedral in the Americas. It's the region's cultural centre, with a busy schedule of traditional music and dance, as well as the best weekend street party – every weekend – anywhere on the peninsula.

A far more sedate and relaxing city than the Mexican metropolis of popular imagination, Mérida has enough to occupy you for several days and serves as a great base for a handful of easy day- or weekend trips thanks to its location, non-stop flow of buses in and out and ready availability of inexpensive and lovely accommodation (some of those crumbling old homes in the centre have been put to very good use). Outside the city, where the landscape was once a vista of spiky, grey-green henequen plants, many of the former plantation **haciendas** have also been converted into striking hotels.

Though most use Mérida as a base for visiting the great Maya sites of Uxmal and Chichén Itzá (see p.245 & p.199) as well as the scenic Maya ruins along the Ruta Puuc that loops south of the city (see p.251), it's also near the beach. About a half-hour's drive straight north, the resort town of **Progreso** functions as Mérida's collective patio in the summertime and during Semana Santa. Otherwise, it's virtually a ghost town, with green water lapping at the shore and only a few travellers lolling on the sand; some "snowbird" Americans maintain winter retreats here, but mostly this is not a heavily touristed area.

The whole Gulf coast, a bit to the west but largely to the east, is dotted with vacation homes, interspersed with older fishing villages as well as much older Maya ruins like **Xcambó**. The Maya used this low-lying, marshy strip of land to mine salt, one of the great treasures of their time. The *salinas*, or salt flats, harbour diverse birdlife; travelling along the coast highway in the evening, you can often see flamingos and great herons winging home. You'll see even more flamingos if you go west of Mérida to the **Ría Celestún Biosphere Reserve**, a long strip along the Gulf waters where the pink birds roost year-round. There's not much else to do but go swimming or ogle these and hundreds of other types of birds, but doing such could keep you busy for years. Closest to the city, the Maya ruins of **Dzibilchaltún**, best known for their impressive alignment with the rising equinox sun, host a very sophisticated museum, which, with its collection of Maya and Spanish art and artefacts, presents a powerful picture of the interaction between the two peoples from the Conquest to the present.

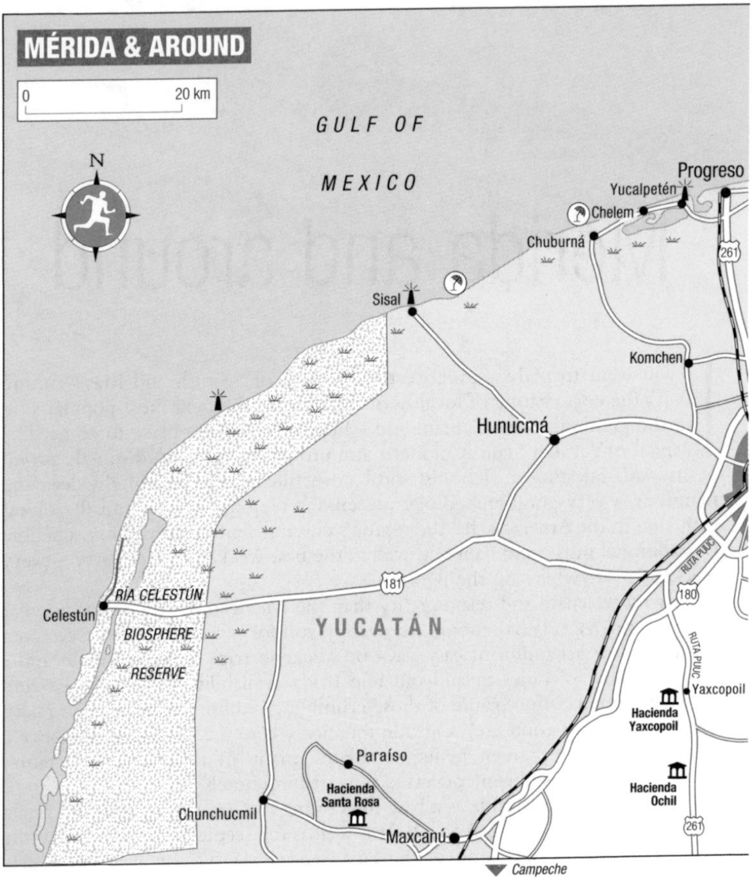

Mérida

In every sense the leading city of the peninsula, **MÉRIDA** bears the nickname "La Ciudad Blanca" (the white city) even though its sprawl of one- and two-storey buildings, once bare white limestone, are now covered in peeling layers of gem-coloured paint. Bus traffic rumbles down its stone streets, but it remains a wonderfully calm and likeable place, with a small-town geniality despite its population of nearly one million. Come dusk, the curving loveseats that dot the numerous parks fill with pairs of lovers, young and old. But don't mistake Mérida for a sleepy backwater: the cultural scene ranges from free traditional entertainment every night of the week (all well attended by older folk in Mérida's version of formalwear – the huipil for ladies and the white guayabera for gents) to avant-garde dance festivals, foreign films, contemporary art exhibitions and lively theatre performances.

This all draws thousands of visitors, both Mexican and foreign. Since 2000, the prosperous city has welcomed a wave of expats and new residents who come from less tranquil places like Mexico City. They mix easily with the Maya, mestizo and

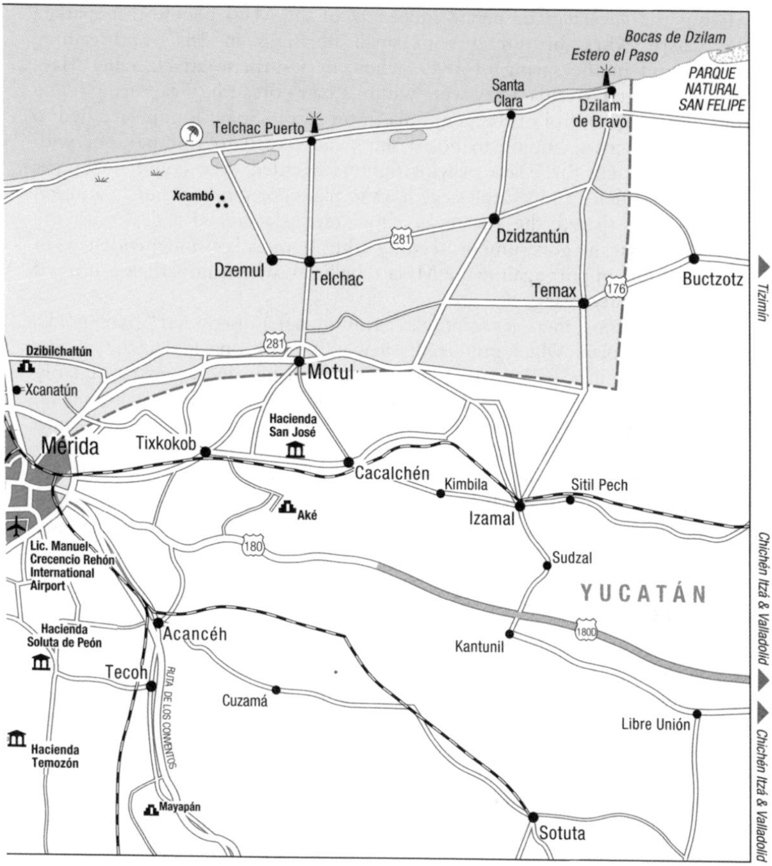

even Lebanese (who came here in the early twentieth century) cultures that define the city's character. Just as important, the newcomers have done a lot to renovate many of the crumbling **historic mansions** that dot the centre. But even as real-estate values skyrocket, the city retains the grace and manners of the past: every street in the centre boasts a well-maintained colonial church or museum, and locals still ride in the little horse-drawn taxis that gather by the plaza in the evenings.

Some history

Founded on January 6, 1542, by conquistador **Francisco de Montejo the Younger** (who also established Campeche), Mérida was the product of a bloody, drawn-out struggle between the Spanish and the local Maya. It was built over, and partly from, the ruins of a Maya city known as **T'hó,** or Ichcansihó, and was intended from the start to be the Spanish capital in the Yucatán. Despite some impressive initial construction around the plaza, however, the city was never a jewel in Spain's crown, largely because the Yucatán contained no gold or other natural wealth. Colonists struggled along with what resources they had: land and forced Maya labour. They established sugarcane and maize plantations outside the city, and looked longingly back to Europe for influence.

It was the *meridanos'* desperate squeezing of the Maya people that sparked the **Caste Wars**, beginning with small uprisings in 1847 and gaining momentum in the spring of 1849, when, in a surprise attack, rebel Maya armies besieged Mérida. They were within a hair's breadth of capturing it and thus regaining control of the peninsula (most of the Spanish populace fled to Sisal on the coast, hoping to board ships and return to Europe), but with victory in reach, the Maya peasant fighters decided they could no longer neglect their fields and left the siege lines to plant corn in hopes of an autumn harvest. Thus spared, the Yucatecan elite quickly arranged a deal with the central Mexican government, ceding the peninsula's independence in exchange for support against the Maya rebellions, which nonetheless ground on for some fifty years.

In the meantime, the *hacendados* (plantation owners) discovered "green gold": the henequen plant, which produced valuable fibre for rope, in demand all over the world (see box, p.250). By 1900, Mérida had become an extraordinarily wealthy city. Much of this wealth was poured into the grandiose mansions on what were then the outskirts of town, along the Paseo de Montejo, and into European educations for the children of the upper classes. The city's wealthy fancied themselves living in "the Paris of Mexico". Today, even with the henequen trade all but dead (it petered out around World War II, when nylon became the material of choice), the city remains elegant, bustling and intellectual.

Arrival

Mérida sees a dizzying amount of **bus** traffic and maintains several small second-class terminals, but visitors are most likely to arrive at one of two main stations, which lie next to each other on the southwest side of town. No city buses provide direct service to the plaza; you'll have to walk (about twenty minutes from any of the stations) or take a **taxi**. Taxis mainly work on a zone system, so a ride to the plaza or a nearby hotel should cost no more than M$30; a ride to hotels on Paseo de Montejo will cost M$40. Drivers will expect a small tip if they handle your luggage. Don't worry about arriving **at night** – only the Noreste bus terminal, near the market, is in an area that feels a little deserted in the evening.

The **Terminal CAME**, reserved for express and first-class services run by ADO, ADO GL, Maya de Oro and (rarely) UNO, is on Calle 70, between calles 69 and 71. You'll arrive here if you're coming directly from Cancún, Campeche or Chichén Itzá. The **Terminal de Segunda Clase**, across the street on Calle 69, between calles 68 and 70, deals with Mayab, ATS, TRT, Sur and some Oriente buses. There's **luggage storage** at the latter station, outside on Calle 70, nearly facing the CAME entrance. Most UNO and many ADO GL services from Cancún arrive at the **Fiesta Americana** hotel, north of the centre off Paseo de Montejo at Avenida Colón. This station is a slightly longer hike to the centre, but a quick cab ride (M$30).

Southeast of the plaza is the **Noreste** terminal, on Calle 67 at Calle 50. Noreste buses arrive here, but so do those operated by Oriente and Lineas Unidas del Sur (LUS). AutoProgreso buses from Progreso and the northern beaches arrive at the dedicated **Terminal de Autobuses a Progreso** on Calle 62, between calles 65 and 67. If you're coming from Izamal on an **Auto Centro** bus, you'll be dropped at a small terminal at calles 65 and 48.

The Lic. Manuel Crecencio Rejón **airport** (Ⓣ999/946-1530, Ⓦwww.asur.com.mx) is 7km southwest of the centre and has a **tourist office** (usually open

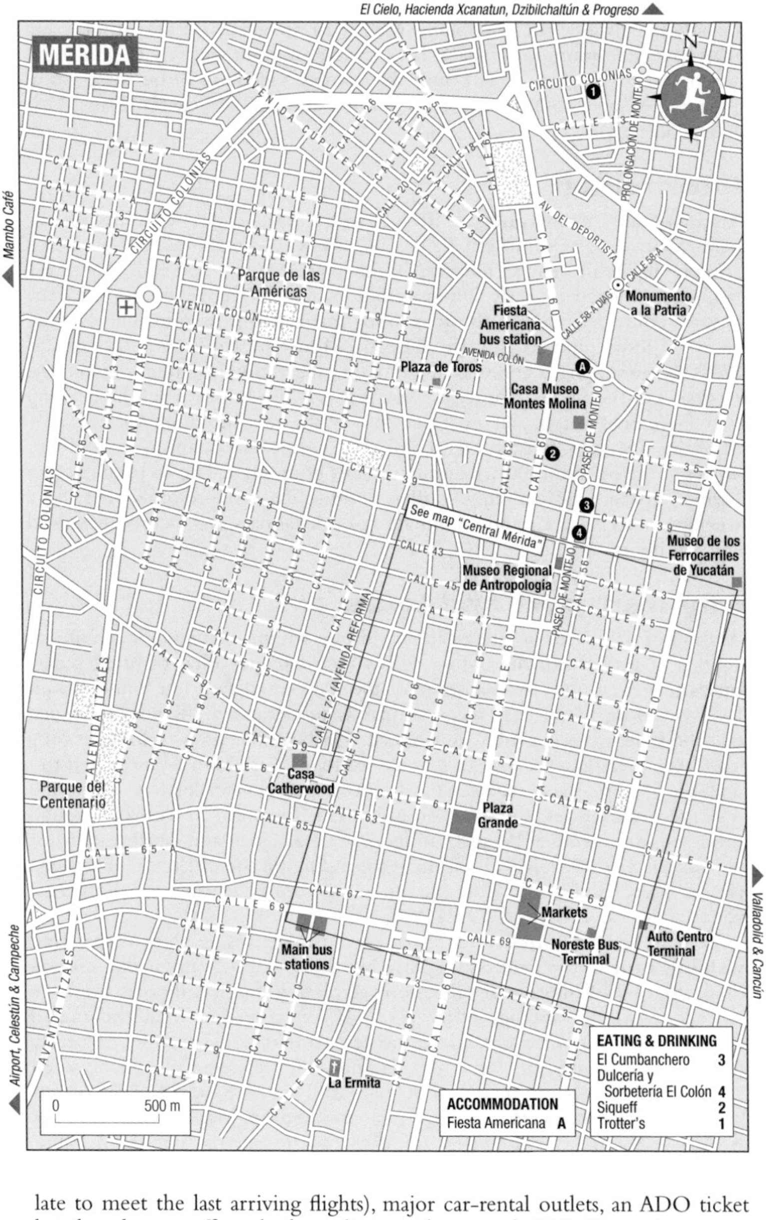

late to meet the last arriving flights), major car-rental outlets, an ADO ticket booth and a post office, plus long-distance phones and ATMs. To get downtown, take a taxi from the stand at the front: buy a ticket (M$135 to the centre) at the desk outside; you may wind up sharing the cab with another passenger. You could also walk straight out and across the parking lot and wait for bus #79 ("Aviación"; M$5); it runs only every 45 minutes or so, though not reliably after 7pm. Combis (marked "Uman") run more frequently along the main road outside the airport, but it's a 500m walk (bear right outside the airport), and they have little room for luggage; look for the stop immediately to your right when you hit Avenida Itzaés. Both the combis and the #79 bus drop off at Parque San Juan, about a ten-minute walk south of the central Plaza de la Independencia.

Information

Yucatán State's main **tourist office** is in the Palacio de Gobierno, on the plaza (daily 8am–8pm; Ⓣ999/924-9290, Ⓦwww.yucatan.travel). This office, and one in Teatro Peón Contreras, on the corner of calles 60 and 57-A, were being remodelled in early 2008; if they've not yet reopened, look in the *palacio*'s courtyard and the theatre's lobby for makeshift booths. The city has its own, less-equipped tourism bureau (Mon–Sat 9am–6pm; Ⓣ999/924-8522, Ⓦwww.merida.gob.mx/turismo), in the municipal building on the west side of the plaza. In any case, you'll usually find some English-speaking staff. Here or at hotels, pick up a free copy of the very thorough *Yucatán Today* magazine (Ⓦwww.yucatantoday.com), in English and Spanish, to find out what's going on around town and in the rest of the state. The website Yucatan Living (Ⓦwww.yucatanliving.com) is another excellent resource, posting a weekly events calendar and commenting on local bars, restaurants, news and cultural items.

City transport and tours

As most of the places of interest in Mérida are within walking distance of one another, it isn't worth the bother of having a **car**, nor even of using public **buses** to get around. To visit some of the less central sites (the museums on Paseo de Montejo, for example), you may want to catch a bus, but be warned that the system is remarkably convoluted. The best strategy is to first get on a main avenue leading the direction you need to go: northbound buses often run up Calle 56, for instance. You can flag buses down at any corner; fares are posted on a green sticker near the door – usually M$5. **Taxis** can be hailed all around town and from stands at Parque Hidalgo, Parque San Juan and the airport. Most use zone fares (M$30, M$40 or M$50 depending on the distance) – but some cars (marked "Radio Taxi") use meters, so they can be cheaper for short trips; you can also call them at Ⓣ999/168-0510.

For basic orientation, Mérida's tourism bureau gives an informative **free walking tour** of the centre every day but Sunday, at 9.30am; make reservations at either of the tourist offices on the plaza (though it departs from the city office, on the west side of the plaza). If you're curious what's behind all the brightly painted facades, take a **garden tour** of some the city's recently renovated mansions, run by the Mérida English Library, on Calle 53, between calles 66 and 68 (Nov–April Wed 9.45am; Ⓣ999/924-8401; M$200). A tour by **horse-drawn carriage** (*calesa*) is slow-paced but relaxing; typical rates are M$200 for an hour-long trip around the centre and up Paseo de Montejo, or M$250 for a longer tour that also visits the out-of-the-way Parque de las Américas and many old houses. Two **bus tours** cover similar routes, going much further afield than you'd ever walk: better to avoid the eyesore red double-deckers and go instead for the festive little open-sided number that departs from Parque Santa Lucía (Mon-Sat 10am, 1pm, 4pm & 7pm, Sun 10am & 1pm; Ⓣ999/927-6119; M$75). Another great way to get to know the culture of the city is through a Yucatecan **cooking class** with Los Dos (Ⓦwww.los-dos.com). The school's day-long "Taste of Yucatán" course

(US$75) starts with a shopping trip to the market and finishes with a meal prepared in a beautiful colonial mansion. A shorter "express" option just takes in the market and lunch at a local restaurant, or you can opt for three-day or week-long intensives.

Riding a **bicycle** can be an excellent way to see the city – catch a little breeze even on the hottest day, and get to the furthest sights with ease. You'll want to be somewhat accustomed to riding in traffic, though, and generally stick to smaller streets, where you won't have to deal with buses. *Hostal del Peregrino* (see p.221) rents bikes by the hour or the day. If you're leery of traffic, wait until Sunday morning to ride – this is the day of the **Bici-Ruta**, when many of the streets downtown, as well as Paseo de Montejo, are closed to cars, and the streets fill with bike riders, performers and more. Bikes are available for rent on the plaza, just for the morning.

Accommodation

Although Mérida can get crowded at peak times, you should always be able to find a room. Unless you have a brutally early bus to catch, there's not much point in staying in the grimier area near the **main bus stations**, nor in the generic upmarket hotels along **Paseo de Montejo**; the far more desirable options are all within a few blocks of the central plaza – which is still just a long walk or a short cab ride from the furthest transport and sights. In addition to the usual hotels, Mérida now has a glut of excellent **B&Bs**, smaller inns and even **hostels**, all housed in converted old homes complete with vintage tile floors and lofty ceilings. The hostels (some of which also have space to **camp** or sling up a hammock) are booming, but some of the newer ones have not proven completely reliable; try to at least call ahead to confirm whether your top choice is open. A glamorous alternative is to stay in a **rental house** from Urbano Rentals (Ⓦwww.urbanorentals.com); they vary in price, but can be quite reasonable if you're travelling with a group or family. A more rural alternative is to stay outside town in a **hacienda**. The closest one is listed here; you may also consider the one guesthouse at Hacienda Yaxcopoil (see p.249). If you're happy to go further afield, check Urbano's options as well as the state tourism website (Ⓦwww.yucatan.travel) for a more-or-less complete list of estates, ranging from ramshackle ruins to ultra-deluxe resorts.

Hotels

Caribe C 59 no. 500, Parque Hidalgo Ⓣ999/924-9022, Ⓦwww.hotelcaribe.com.mx. Mérida's best mid-range hotel is most desirable for its location, just a block from the Plaza de la Independencia, on a pretty, small square of its own. Rooms (fan or a/c) don't have much flair, but the patio restaurant is lovely, as are the views of the cathedral and plaza from the rooftop pool. There's parking, free Internet access and an on-site travel agency as well. ❻

Casa Becil C 67 no. 550-C, between C 66 and C 68 Ⓣ999/924-6764, Ⓦwww.hotelcasabecil.com. This small hotel may need a fresh coat of paint, but the staff is very friendly and helpful, and it's close to the main bus stations. A few rooms have a/c, and there's a kitchen guests can use. Basic continental breakfast included. ❸

Casa del Balam C 60 no. 488 at C 57 Ⓣ999/924-8844 or 999/924-2150 for reservations, Ⓦwww.casadelbalam.com. Good combo of colonial-house style – tiled floors, dark-wood furniture – with all the amenities of a large hotel. Rooms have extra perks like fridges and bathtubs, and there's a shady pool and cosy, wood-panelled bar. Breakfast included. ❼

Casa Lucía C 60 no. 474-A, between C 63 and C 65 Ⓣ999/928-0740, Ⓦwww.casalucia.com.mx. A small, artfully restored hotel across from Parque Santa Lucía that combines European antiques, Persian rugs and typically Méridan details, like heavy wood doors from the original building. The Latin American artwork throughout is excellent. ❽

Dolores Alba C 63 no. 464, between C 52 and C 54 Ⓣ999/928-5650, Ⓦwww.doloresalba.com. Popular mid-range place situated around two courtyards (one colonial-style, and one sporting a dazzling array of mirror glass) and a large swimming pool. Rooms in both sections have TV, phone and a/c. With parking, laundry facilities and more, you get a lot for your money, but the place is a bit out of the way. ❺

El Español C 69 no. 543-C at C 70 ⓣ999/923-2854, ⓦwww.hotelelespanol.com.mx. An upmarket alternative to the adjacent dives, located directly across from the main bus stations. Has a small pool and clean, quiet rooms with powerful a/c. Officially, rates are high, but there's a good chance of a discount promotion. ❻

Fiesta Americana C 56 at Av Colón ⓣ999/942-1111, ⓦwww.fiestaamericana.com. Just off Paseo de Montejo, Mérida's top business-class hotel is often booked with tour groups, but it's a bit of a hike from the centre. It's mentioned here primarily as a landmark: the lobby houses a number of travel and car agencies, as well as a terminal for express buses. ❽

Hacienda Xcanatun 12km north of Mérida on the road to Progreso ⓣ999/941-0273, ⓦwww.xcanatun.com. This eighteenth-century plantation house on lush grounds has been remade as a small, exclusive hotel featuring luxurious suites – some with baths hewn from local rock, some with hot tubs. There's also a full spa and a very good restaurant (see p.230). It's nearly as lavish as the *Hacienda Temozón* (in the Ruta Puuc, see p.249), but about half the price. ❾

Margarita C 66, between C 61 and C 63 ⓣ999/923-7236. A bargain-basement place whose small rooms can be dim and stuffy, but it's certainly the cleanest of the lot in this extremely low price category. You do get a pretty, if slightly dilapidated lobby, a fairly genial atmosphere and optional a/c. ❷

Mucuy C 57 no. 481, between C 56 and C 58 ⓣ999/928-5193, ⓦwww.mucuy.com. Quiet and well run, with clean, good-value rooms (choice of fan or a/c), a small pool and a truly hospitable owner. English-speaking staff and a laundry on the premises. ❸

Posada Toledo C 58 no. 487 at C 57 ⓣT999/923-1690, ⓔhptoledo@finred.com.mx. Grand and well-kept colonial building with beautiful tile floors and heaps of antique furniture. Single rooms can be a little small, but the "honeymoon suite" (M$650) is an amazing confection of French antiques and gold trim. ❺

Trinidad Galería C 60 no. 456 at C 51 ⓣ999/923-2463, ⓦwww.hotelestrinidad.com. Wonderfully eccentric hotel crammed full of bizarre artefacts, sculptures and paintings. Rooms upstairs are lighter and more spacious, but all are individually decorated (some have a/c). Also has a pool, a small breakfast café and two art galleries. The *Trinidad* (C 62 at C 55), under the same ownership, has several cheaper rooms with shared bath (❸), and guests can use the pool at the *Galería*. ❹

B&Bs and inns

Las Arecas C 59 no. 541, between C 66 and C 68 ⓣ999/928-3626, ⓦwww.lasarecas.com. Small, colonial-style guesthouse (one of the few run by a *meridano*) that's a fantastic bargain. Of the five tidy, modestly furnished rooms, two have kitchenettes and three have a/c. All look onto a small central garden and fountain. Breakfast included. ❹

Casa Mexilio C 68 no. 495, between C 57 and C 59 ⓣ999/928-2505, ⓦwww.casamexilio.com. One of Mérida's real treasures, and one of the longest-established B&Bs. In a restored colonial townhouse, this place is a fascinating labyrinth of individually decorated rooms, tranquil gardens, sun terraces and a pool. The full breakfast (included) is delicious. ❻

Casa San Juan C 62 no. 545-A, between C 69 and C 71 ⓣ999/986-2937, ⓦwww.casasanjuan.com. A variety of reasonably priced rooms, some with a/c and all furnished in a very welcoming style, are located in a landmark house midway between the bus station and the plaza. Reserve ahead (two-night minimum), as it's often booked with longer-term residents. Prices include continental breakfast. ❺

Casa Santana C 64 no. 410, between C 47 and C 49 ⓣ999/928-7567, ⓦwww.casasantana.com. Drop-dead gorgeous colonial house with four bedrooms (one of them has two connecting rooms and a shared bath) filled with folk-art treasures and rich textiles. Generous continental breakfast included; there's also a small pool. ❼

Casa Santiago C 63 no. 562, between C 70 and C 72 ⓣ999/928-9375, ⓦwww.mexicanbedandbreakfast.com. Casual house with four rooms and a small pool. Decor is more functional than flashy, beds are comfy and there's a little kitchen. A little further from the plaza than most, but in a pleasant, more old-fashioned neighbourhood where everyone greets you on the street. ❻

Luz En Yucatán C 55 no. 499, between C 58 and C 60 ⓣ999/924-0035, ⓦwww.luzenyucatan.com. Delightful studio rooms and apartments (half have kitchenettes, many have private terraces or patios) in a rambling house, all done in rich colours, plus a pool and plenty of comfortable public space. Wi-Fi is available. Rates are negotiable for longer stays. ❺–❼

Marionetas C 49 no. 516, between C 62 and 64 ⓣ999/928-3377, ⓦwww.hotelmarionetas.com. No antique clutter in this fully renovated colonial home – rooms are sunny, sparely furnished and spacious. The owner designed many of the traditional-style floor tiles herself, and the breakfasts here (included) are memorable. Pool and parking. ⑦

Hostels

Hobo Hostel C 60 no. 432, between C 47 and C 49 ☎999/928-0880, Ⓦwww.hostelhobo.com. This converted home and warehouse is absolutely cavernous, with lots of space for hanging hammocks (M$60). Beds are only M$75, but private rooms (③), with shared bath, are not good value. Unlike other hostels, no breakfast is offered.

Hostal del Peregrino C 51 no. 488, between C 54 and C 56 ☎999/924-5491, Ⓦwww.hostaldelperegrino.com. The more elegant hostelling solution: a beautifully redone house, with an especially nice outdoor kitchen. At M$150 per bed, it's more expensive than others, but a full hot breakfast is included. Private rooms have choice of a/c or fan, and there's free Wi-Fi, as well as bike rental. ⑤

Hostal Santa Lucia C 55 no. 512, between C 62 and 64 ☎999/928-9070, Ⓦwww.hostalstalucia.com. Nice converted house, but arranged a bit awkwardly, with men's dorm beds surrounding the women's section. Dorms (M$85) are fan-only, but private rooms (③) have a/c.

Nómadas C 62 no. 433 at C 51 ☎999/924-5223, Ⓦwww.nomadastravel.com. The longest established of Mérida's hostels, and still the best balance of price and amenities. Dorms (M$92) are spacious and private rooms (③) are clean. There's live music every night, and plenty of helpful advice from the in-house travel agency – guests get discounts on tours to cenotes and the like.

The city

Like the rest of the peninsula, Mérida had little effective contact with central Mexico until the completion of road and rail links in the 1960s, but trade with Europe brought wealth well before then: in the early 1900s, a standard French ship route was Marseilles to New York via Havana and Mérida's port at Sisal. As a consequence the city looks more European than almost any other in Mexico – many of the houses built in the nineteenth century use French bricks and tiles, brought over as tradable ballast in ships that exported henequen.

Mérida's colonial centre (*centro histórico*) is laid out on a simple **grid** of numbered streets: even numbers run north–south, odd from east to west. The city now sprawls much further than most visitors will ever see – particularly up **Paseo de Montejo** (called Prolongación de Montejo in its northern stretch), where chain stores and slick restaurants start to appear – but the centre, which radiates out from the main **Plaza de la Independencia**, is dense with historic attractions and other entertainment. Most sights, from the main market on the south side to the broad boulevard of Paseo de Montejo to the north, are easily reached on foot from the plaza.

Mérida's corners

As you walk around the centre of the city, notice the small red-and-white plaster **plaques** embedded in the walls at many street corners. Originally, the corners were marked not by a written name, but by a statue – most commonly of an animal, but also of things such as a clenched fist or a flower – mounted on top of the building. This cleared up language confusion in the Spanish–Maya city with a universally identifiable "elephant corner" or "cat corner", for example. Corners also came to be known for residents or even abstract ideas, such as "La Libertad" (freedom), the origins of which are now lost to time. Today, the illustrated plaques have replaced the original figures, but often many of the surrounding business names still reflect the old corner designation, and in some cases, the city has devised new designations, like "El Motór Eléctrico" (the electric motor) on a corner near a repair shop. A few of the plaques, such as "La Ermita" (the hermitage), are the last remaining evidence of major buildings that used to serve as landmarks.

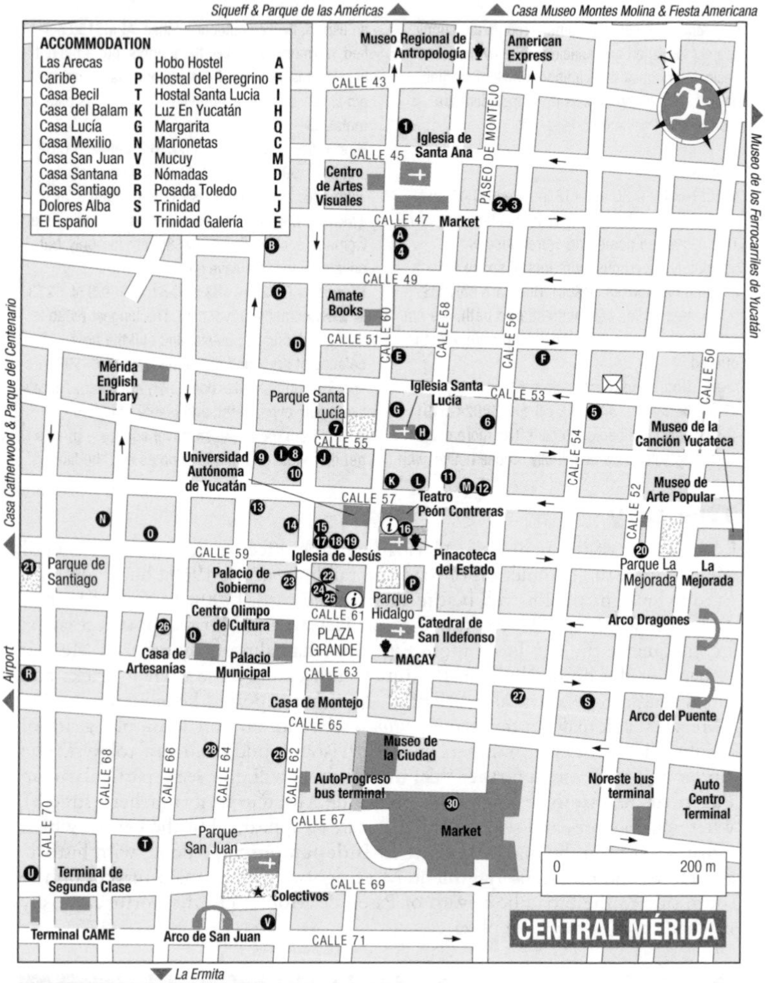

EATING & DRINKING							
Alameda	11	Dulcería y Sorbetería El Colón	25	Ki'xocoatl	7	Pizzería de Vito Corleone	22
Alberto's Continental Patio	13	Fau-San	28	El Lucero del Alba	3	La Quilla	1
Amaro	18	La Habana	17	El Marlin Azul	15	La Reina Itzalana	21
Café Lucía	G	Los Henequenes	12	Mayan Pub	10	Restaurante D'Al	5
Casa de Frida	26	El Hoyo	14	El Mesón de Segoviano	20	El Rodeo	19
La Casa de Todos	9	Impala	2	Pancho's	18	Super Bodega	27
La Cochinita Tuerta	8	Isstey	4	Pane e Vino	24	Taquería La Tia	30
		Jazzin' Mérida	6	La Parroquia	29	El Trapiche	23
				Peón Contreras	16		

The Plaza de la Independencia

The **Plaza de la Independencia,** often called the Plaza Grande or the Plaza Mayor, formed by calles 60, 61, 62 and 63, acts as the hub of the city's life, particularly in the evenings, when couples meet on the park benches and bands of *trovadores* in white guayaberas wait to be hired for serenades. The plaza is ringed by some of Mérida's oldest buildings, including the **Catedral de San Ildefonso** (daily 6am–noon & 5–8pm). Construction on the building began in 1562 and finished before the end of the sixteenth century. Singularly vast and white, it is almost severe in its simplicity, reflecting the trend toward crisper Renaissance design and away from the manically ornate Spanish Plateresque style, inspired by Gothic forms. On its facade, the entwined eagle and snake, symbol of the Mexican republic, is a later addition, replacing the Spanish empire's two-headed Hapsburg eagle, which was removed in 1822. Most of the church's valuables were looted in 1915, as part of the anticlerical movement during the Mexican Revolution. One object that was lost has been recreated: the **Cristo de las Ampollas** (Christ of the Blisters), which is in a chapel to the left of the main altar. According to legend, the original statue of Christ on the cross was carved from a tree in the village of Ichmul that burned for a whole night without showing the least sign of damage; later, in 1645, the parish church at Ichmul burned down, and the crucifix survived, though blackened and blistered. Though the statue was ultimately destroyed during the purge of 1915, the reconstructed image is the focal point of a local **fiesta** from mid-September to mid-October, when each day a different professional group, or *gremio* (taxi drivers, bakers and so on), pays its respects at the church, then parades on the plaza.

Beside the cathedral, separated from it by the Pasaje San Alvarado, the old bishop's palace has been converted into shops, offices and the **MACAY** (Museo de Arte Contemporáneo Ateneo de Yucatán; Wed–Mon 10am–6pm; free), which has the best modern art collection in the region, with permanent displays featuring the work of internationally acclaimed Yucatecan painters Fernando Castro Pacheco, Gabriel Ramírez Aznar and Fernando García Ponce. Ponce's enormous, multilayered collage paintings are particularly striking; one covers the entire wall behind the double staircase at the entrance to the exhibition halls. Temporary exhibitions range from local photographers to European masters on loan from Mexico City museums.

On the south side of the plaza stands the **Casa de Montejo**, a palace built in 1549 by Francisco de Montejo, a captain under Hernán Cortés and the first conquistador to attempt to bring the peninsula under Spain's control. His first effort, in 1527, failed, as did several later forays. His son, Francisco de Montejo the Younger, did what the father could not, securing the northern part of the peninsula in the 1540s. But soon after the father built his triumphant palace, he was stripped of his titles and recalled to Spain; his son moved in, and his family occupied the place until 1828. The building now belongs to Banamex, and most of the interior is used as office space. Visitors are welcome to see the lavishly restored wood-panelled dining room, off the back right corner of the Moorish-feeling courtyard. Above a staid doorway of Classical columns, the facade, in sharp contrast to the cathedral, is richly decorated in the Plateresque style (probably the first instance of it in the New World), with conquistadors depicted trampling savages underfoot. The woolly men with clubs are reminiscent of Spain as well; similar figures can be seen on the Colegio de San Gregorio in Valladolid, Spain, where the Montejos hailed from.

Across the plaza from the cathedral, the **Palacio Municipal** is another impressive piece of sixteenth-century design, with a fine clock tower and a large painting upstairs depicting the *mestizaje*, the birth of the first mixed-blood Mexican. Next door, the gleaming modern **Centro Olimpo de Cultura** contains an auditorium and an art gallery featuring local works and travelling exhibits. In the basement, a **planetarium** has shows about astronomy and science (Tues–Sat 10am, noon, 5pm & 7pm, Sun 5pm & 7pm; M$30); narration is in Spanish, but the imagery is impressive, and the air conditioning can be a treat on a hot day.

Completing the square, the nineteenth-century **Palacio de Gobierno** (daily 8am–10pm) is a must-see; enormous modernist murals by Fernando Castro Pacheco cover the walls on the ground floor and in the large front room on the second floor. They powerfully depict the violent history of the Yucatán and the trials of its indigenous people, though it's interesting to note that the images don't always tell quite the same story as the accompanying texts in Spanish, English and Maya.

North of the Plaza de la Independencia

Most of the remaining monuments in Mérida lie north of the plaza, bordering Calle 60 and the Paseo de Montejo. Calle 60 is one of the city's main commercial streets, lined with its fancier hotels and restaurants. It also boasts a lovely series of colonial buildings, starting one block north of the plaza with the seventeenth-century Jesuit **Iglesia de Jesús**, on the corner with Calle 59, between Parque Hidalgo and Parque de la Madre; if the doors are open, peek inside – the lavish chandeliers and frescoes are an opulent surprize in such a spare church. The building is made of stones from the original Maya city of T'hó, and a few pieces of decorative carving are visible in the wall on Calle 59.

On the same block of Calle 59, the **Pinacoteca del Estado Juan Gamboa Guzmán** (Tues–Sat 8am–8pm, Sun 8am–2pm; M$28) houses a collection of nineteenth-century portraits of prominent Yucatecans and Mexican leaders – Austrian-French Emperor Ferdinand Maximilian, who was executed less than three years into his reign, looks particularly hapless among the crowd of presidents. Back on Calle 60 and continuing north, you reach **Teatro Peón Contreras**, a grandiose Neoclassical edifice built by Italian architects between 1900 and 1908, in the heady days of Porfirio Díaz, the Mexican dictator whose decadence inspired the Revolution. Across the street stands the **state university** (Universidad Autónoma de Yucatán), a highly respected institution that has existed, under various names, since 1624.

One block north of Teatro Peón Contreras, the sixteenth-century **Iglesia Santa Lucía** stands facing the elegant plaza of the same name – a small colonnaded square that used to be the town's stagecoach terminus. Three blocks further on is the **Plaza Santa Ana**, a modern open space, bordered by a small cluster of market stalls. The surrounding neighbourhood is developing something of a contemporary art scene – see what's on at the **Centro de Artes Visuales** (Mon–Fri 9am–10pm, Sat & Sun 9am–7pm; free), the exhibition space for the state university's arts programme. Up and down the block, and further north, are several private galleries displaying a huge range of work, from conceptual sculpture to figurative painting. Head east from here a couple of blocks to reach the south end of Paseo de Montejo.

Paseo de Montejo

Running north from Plaza Santa Ana (Calle 58 at Calle 45), **Paseo de Montejo** is a broad boulevard designed for strolling, its sidewalks dotted with trees and modern sculptures by Yucatecan and foreign artists. It's also lined with the magnificent, pompous mansions of the henequen-rich grandees who strove to outdo each other's high-European style around the end of the nineteenth century. One of the most striking, the Palacio Cantón, at the corner of Calle 43, houses Mérida's **Museo Regional de Antropología** (Tues–Sat 8am–8pm, Sun 8am–2pm; M$39). The Beaux Arts palace, grandly trimmed in wrought-iron and marble, was built at the beginning of the twentieth century for General Francisco Cantón, a railway tycoon and the former state governor, and set off a competitive building boom along the avenue. The walk out **to the museum** from the plaza takes about half an hour, but you can also get there on a "Paseo de Montejo" bus running up Calle 56, or in a horse-drawn **calesa** (about M$150 from the centre to the museum, or pay M$200 for the full hour tour, then get dropped off here).

Given the archeological riches found near Mérida, the collection can seem a bit skimpy, but it's a useful introduction to the surrounding sites nonetheless, with displays (most in both English and Spanish) covering everything from prehistoric stone tools to modern Maya religious practice. You'll find sculptures and other objects from Chichén Itzá and elsewhere, but more interesting are the attempts to give some idea of what it was like to live in a Maya city. Topographic maps of the peninsula, for example, explain how cenotes are formed and their importance to the ancient population, while a collection of

▲ Monumento a la Patria on Paseo de Montejo, Mérida

skulls demonstrates the practices of skull lengthening, teeth filing and dental inlaying (in which precisely cut pieces of turquoise have been set in cavities drilled into the teeth). Other displays cover jewellery, ritual offerings and burial practices, as well as the workings of the Maya calendar. Upstairs, temporary exhibits examine Mérida's history and specific archeological sites. The **bookshop** offers leaflets and guidebooks in English to dozens of ruins in the Yucatán and the rest of Mexico.

A few blocks further north brings you to another grand structure, now the **Casa Museo Montes Molina**, between calles 35 and 33 (Ⓦwww.laquintamm.com; tours in English Mon–Fri 9am, 11am & 3pm; $M50). Built for a Cuban businessman by the same architects who designed Teatro Peón Contreras, it's a shiny white confection of excess, and its interior is similarly grand. A guided tour through its halls, wine cellar and servant quarters is slightly disorienting; amid the delicate antique sideboards and grand oil paintings, you can almost forget you're in Mexico.

Another ten minutes' walk north on Paseo de Montejo, past scores of other old mansions that now contain banks and insurance companies, brings you to the 1956 **Monumento a la Patria**. It is a titan, covered in neo-Maya sculptures relating to Mexican history. Beyond the monument, the street continues under the name Prolongación de Montejo and leads into "new" Mérida, the district of glossy shops and chain restaurants frequented by the younger, wealthier population.

East of the Plaza de la Independencia

If you want to flesh out your impressions of the *centro histórico*, head several blocks east of the plaza to a couple of interesting museums and a generally quieter atmosphere. The first exhibition you reach on Calle 57, just before Calle 50, is the **Museo del Arte Popular de Yucatán** (Tues–Sat 9.30am–7pm, Sun 9am–2pm; M$20), another excellent use of Banamex funding. The Mexican bank has invested in the preservation of artisans' work and skills in a big way, and this very attractive museum shows off some of the best examples of Yucatecan huipiles, jewellery and household items. It also has a small but very nicely stocked gift shop. The museum faces a little park, named for the former monastery of **La Mejorada**, on Calle 59 at Calle 50. The monastery, along with Las Monjas (a convent) on Calle 63 and the now destroyed San Francisco de Mérida monastery (the old market and former post office are built on its ruins), housed the city's devout Franciscan community.

Behind La Mejorada, on Calle 57, before you reach Calle 48, the **Museo de la Canción Yucateca** (daily 9am–5pm; M$15, free on Sun) details the diverse musical influences on the local *trovadores*, from pre-Columbian traditions to Afro-Cuban styles. The presentation, except for one "interactive" room with music clips, is very old-fashioned, with hall upon hall full of vitrines of memorabilia and walls hung with oil portraits of the great composers and singers of the *trova* tradition. The gift shop is an excellent place to pick up some romantic tunes.

A few blocks south of this area and just east of Calle 50, you can also spy two of the old city's entrance **arches** (thirteen of them once studded Mérida's walls from the sixteenth to the early nineteenth century). The Arco del Puente, at Calle 61, sports an adjacent walkway, a 1.2-metre-high tunnel for single-file pedestrians. A third arch, the most elegant, stands on the south side of town, on Calle 64 by the Parque San Juan, marking the former Camino Real ("royal road") that linked the city to Campeche and carried on to Mexico City during colonial times.

South of the Plaza de la Independencia

The blocks south of the plaza are a bit scruffier than the rest of the centre, the streets getting more crowded and the shops more jumbled as you head towards Mérida's main **market**, a huge place between calles 67, 69, 54 and 56. In two linked halls (one old and crumbling, the other new and shiny) plus a clutch of tiny stalls around the periphery, more than two thousand vendors ply their trades. It's a wild scrum of consumer goods, from freshly hacked-up beef to hand-tooled leather belts to more varieties of bananas than you can count on one hand – usually, but not reliably, divided into rough districts. Arrive before noon to see the most bountiful foodstuffs; **craft shops** (many in a separate wing on Calle 60 at Calle 65) are open all day.

Truth be told, the area is not as scrappy as it once was, as the opening of the grand **Museo de la Ciudad** (Tues–Fri 8am–8pm, Sat & Sun 8am–2pm; free) in 2007 inspired a makeover in the surrounding blocks. Set in the old central post office on Calle 65 at Calle 56, it's a beautiful building and an informative exhibit, tracing city history from ancient Maya times through the henequen boom, and you can't beat the price. There's also an art gallery in the building, and texts are in Spanish and English.

Out of the centre

The very dedicated museum-goer can head east of Paseo de Montejo to the **Museo de los Ferrocarriles de Yucatán**, at Calle 43, between calles 44 and 46 (Mon–Sat 8am–1pm; free), to visit the collection of old cars from the Chiapas–Mayab railway line, some of which have been beautifully restored. Sadly, passenger trains are now a thing of the past in the Yucatán, as bus services have proved more efficient. For a taste of modern architecture, you could head to the **Parque de las Américas**, west from Paseo de Montejo on Avenida Colón. The park, inaugurated in 1946, is planted with a tree from every country on the American continent, while the bandstand, library and curving pergolas all display a distinctive neo-Maya style, incorporating motifs from Chichén Itzá and other ancient sites.

Nearby, at the corner of Avenida Reforma (Calle 72) and Calle 25, the **Plaza de Toros** hosts a bullfight once a month or so on Sunday at 3.30pm; ticket prices vary, depending on the event, from M$40 for sunny seats up to M$200 for a shady seat at a major fight. To the west of the plaza, on Calle 59 just past Calle 72, you'll find **Casa Catherwood** (daily 9am–2pm & 5–9pm; M$50), a pretty restored home with an exhibit of English artist Frederick Catherwood's etchings from his excursions to crumbling Maya ruins with John Lloyd Stephens in the mid-1800s. There's a café here, as well. After some refreshment, push on to the sprawling green space of **Parque del Centenario**, on the edge of *centro histórico* at Avenida Itzáes. It contains a **zoo** (Tues–Sun 6am–6pm; free), with a very full aviary. The park is not particularly lush, but it is a nice place to see modern Mérida at leisure. It also has lots of room for children to run around, and other kids for them to run around with. There are boats for paddling about a tiny lake, a mini-chairlift ride and a small-scale train (Tues–Sat 10am–2pm & 3–5pm; M$1) that runs through the zoo area.

Shopping

Mérida's central market has a large section dedicated to **craftwork**, but for real quality you're almost always better off buying in a shop (prices in the market are no great shakes, either, unless you're an unusually skilled and determined haggler). Before buying anything, head down Calle 63, two blocks west of the plaza to the government-run **Casa de Artesanías** (Tues–Sat 9am–8pm, Sun 9am–1.30pm). The fixed prices and general quality will give you an idea what to look for if you bother to go elsewhere, but the shop sells such nice items, such as delicate silver filigree jewellery, that you can safely do a lot of your shopping here. The clothing options are somewhat limited, though. For very high-end crafts from all over the country, head to 100% Mexico, at the south end of Paseo de Montejo, at Calle 47 – the items are not bargain-priced, but all work is signed by the artist. You can pick up cheaper, fun items at Miniaturas, a small store crammed with tiny dioramas (dentist skeletons, priest skeletons, DJ skeletons), as well as movie posters, cut-paper banners and other random treasures.

Arguably the most popular Mexican souvenir is a **hammock** – and Mérida is probably the best place in the country to buy one. Head to Tejidos y Cordeles Nacionales, a top specialist very near the market at Calle 56 no. 516-B, just north of Calle 65. More a warehouse than a shop, it has hundreds of the things stacked against every wall; buy several and you can enter into serious negotiations over the price. Similar stores nearby include the highly respected El Aguacate, on Calle 58, near Calle 73, and La Poblana, at Calle 65 no. 492, near Calle 60. The latter also sells **ahulado**, bright, flower-patterned material (once oilcloth, now almost always vinyl) used as table coverings all over Mexico.

Men will want to look for **guayaberas**, the traditional pleated, embroidered dress shirt that both Cubans and *meridanos* claim to have invented; Filipino traders, who visited both places, probably deserve some credit, too. Since the Revolution put a halt to Cuban guayabera exports, factories in Mérida have flourished, and you can choose from a huge range of colours, with long or short sleeves. Guayaberas Cab, on Calle 60, between calles 65 and 67, does very upmarket versions in pure linen, and will make shirts to measure, in about a week, for M$600 and up. If you won't be in Mérida that long, you can have the shirts shipped to you at a future address in Mexico. Less expensive guayaberas, in polyester-blend fabrics, are found in shops around the market.

Women's **huipiles** are also on sale everywhere, varying wildly in quality, from factory-made, machine-stitched junk to hand-embroidered, homespun cloth. Even the best, though, rarely compare with the antique dresses that can occasionally be found – identical in style (as they have been for hundreds of years) but far better made and very expensive. Vintage Retro Style (Mon–Fri 10am–2pm & 5–9pm, Sat 11am–2pm & 5–8pm), a shop on Calle 60, between calles 47 and 49, occasionally has a few, along with a small assortment of local **antiques** and a fun selection of thrift-store clothing.

Also look for smaller gifts such as Spanish classroom vocabulary **posters** (Papelería El Estudiante, on the south side of the plaza, has a good selection) or local foodstuffs, such as **coffee** and **honey**. Mérida's distinctive *trova* **music** is available in many gift shops on CD; it's especially cheap at the weekly serenade on Parque Santa Lucía, where vendors sell remastered classics or newer songs they've written themselves. You can also try the gift shop at the Museo de la Canción Yucateca (see p.226).

Eating

Good **restaurants** are plentiful in the centre of Mérida, though the best (and some of the least expensive) are open only for lunch. Except for a few high-end places, dinner restaurants are meant for out-of-towners; prices are high and most menus verge on international-bland. Nonetheless, evening is the perfect time to visit the bustling sidewalk cafés on **Plaza Hidalgo**, along Calle 60, between calles 61 and 59, and on **Paseo de Montejo**, where businesses tend to be open later, with some slicker places popular with young locals.

As usual, cheap eats are best at the *loncherías* in the **market**, where you can get good, filling *comidas corridas*; look also in secondary market areas, such as Parque Santa Ana on Calle 47 at Calle 60. You can also easily make a late lunch out of the *botanas* (snacks) served free with beers at the more traditional afternoon bars – see p.231 for these. Around the Plaza de la Independencia several wonderful **juice bars** – notably *Jugos California*, on the southwest corner, and *La Michoacana*, on Calle 61 at Calle 56 – serve all the regular juices and *licuados*, as well as more unusual local concoctions such as home-made root beer. Combine these with something from the **bakery** Pan Montejo, at the corner of calles 62 and 63, to make a great breakfast. For **groceries**, head to the state-run Isstey store on Calle 60, between calles 47 and 49, or to the mega Super Bodega on Calle 63, between calles 54 and 56.

Cafés and Snacks

Alameda C 58, between C 55 and C 57. This old-fashioned lunch café, a popular Lebanese hangout, serves *garbanzos* (hummus) and other Middle Eastern standards.

La Cochinita Tuerta C 62 at C 55. Rich, super-savoury pork gets ladled onto fluffy rolls, then served with cold beer – look for the cheerful one-eyed (*tuerta*) pig painted on the wall.

Dulcería y Sorbetería El Colón C 61, on the north side of the plaza. Popular spot for exotic fruit sorbets, especially coconut; try a *champola*, a big scoop in a tall glass of milk. There's another branch on Paseo de Montejo, between C 39 and C 41, which is a good place to stop after visiting the archeology museum.

La Habana C 62 at C 59. As long as you don't mind cigarette smoke, this is one of the best places to spy on Mérida's older bohemian intellectual crowd, who gather daily to read and argue across the sticky tabletops, while black-and-white-clad waiters dish out Mexican-style diner fare. There's free Wi-Fi and decent coffee.

El Hoyo C 62, between C 57 and C 59. A hip student hangout in the evening, buzzing with both conversation and the hum of blenders and espresso machines, whipping up all kinds of juices and caffeinated drinks. It also serves pressed sandwiches, plus Belgian waffles in the morning.

Impala Paseo de Montejo at C 47. Sidewalk dining until late, with basic sandwiches, burgers and Yucatecan standards, but it's best just for coffee, sweets and people-watching. Daily 6pm–2am.

Ki'xocoatl C 55, between C 60 and C 62. Chocolate junkies head here for frothy, cinnamon-spiked hot chocolate and other local cacao products.

La Parroquia C 62 no. 507, between C 65 and C 67. *Lechería* serving blended milk drinks, yoghurt and fruit plates. Great for a bargain breakfast or a late-night treat (try the cinnamon-laced chocolate milk).

Peón Contreras C 60, adjacent to the Teatro Peón Contreras. Not really recommendable for its food (passable Mexican, plus pizza), but one of the most pleasant outdoor cafés in the city, a good vantage spot for Calle 60's bustle, but away from the actual car traffic.

La Quilla C 60, between C 43 and C 45. The social hub of the burgeoning gallery scene in the immediate vicinity, this funky café is adorned with art and sagging sofas. There's a shady internal courtyard where you can enjoy sandwiches and other light snacks.

Taquería La Tía In the market south of C 65. Catering to night owls with its 3am–2pm opening hours, *La Tía* is guaranteed for a tasty treat any time you stop by. A must-visit when you're at the market – look for it just inside the northwest corner entrance.

Restaurants

Alberto's Continental Patio C 64 no. 482 at C 57 ⓣ999/928-5367. A slice of old-world Mérida, with a beautiful interior courtyard and formal service. The food, which blends Mexican and Middle Eastern flavours, is erratic and wildly expensive, however; better to go just for light snacks and a drink, and a chat with the charming Lebanese owner.

Amaro C 59 no. 507, between C 60 and C 62. Set in a lovely tree-shaded courtyard with a fountain and a romantic guitarist Wed–Sat. A little overpriced, but interesting veggie options, such as *crepas de chaya*, offer a welcome change for non-meat-eaters tired of quesadillas.

Café Lucía In the *Casa Lucía* hotel, C 60 no. 474-A. The good Italian and international menu isn't too outrageously priced, considering the upmarket clientele of local politicos and excellent collection of modern Latin American art on the walls (go at least for a drink to admire this).

Casa de Frida C 61 no. 526 at C 66 ⓣ999/928-2311. Specialising in *chiles en nogada* (chiles stuffed with sweet-savoury beef and topped with a creamy walnut sauce), this eclectic little restaurant is painted in candy colours and romantically lit, sporting a cosy back patio. The food here is definitely prepared with more personal care than most other dinner restaurants in town. Closed Sun.

Casa de Piedra In *Hacienda Xcanatun* ⓣ999/941-0273. Yucatecan-French fusion is the speciality at this elegant place 12km north of town. Dishes like duck glazed with bitter orange and *xtabentun* (a Yucatecan liqueur) are not cheap, but the setting, in the hacienda's old machine-house, is dramatic, and warmed by the glow of candles. Also open for breakfast and lunch, but no dinner Sun.

El Marlin Azul C 62, between C 57 and C 59. Long-time local favourite for excellent but inexpensive seafood (trucked in every morning from Celestún), including tasty fish tacos and perfectly fresh ceviche. Note that it closes at 4.30pm, however, and there's no sign on the blue awning. Also serves breakfast.

El Mesón del Segoviano C 50-A, between C 57 and C 59. A fast-talking Spaniard serves succulent *lechón* (pork leg) – a project for a group – as well as smaller dishes such as incredibly tender octopus salad. In true Spanish style, the only vegetables to be seen are the occasional garnishes.

Pane e Vino C 62, between C 59 and C 61. This wood-panelled restaurant serves workhorse Italian food: simple but satisfying dishes like big cheesy lasagne and large helpings of fresh pasta in creamy sauces. Entrees are all under M$100. Closed Mon.

Pizzería de Vito Corleone C 59 no. 508 at C 62. Inexpensive pizza joint that also does takeaway. Head for tables on the upstairs balcony if you don't want to get roasted by the wood-burning oven.

La Reina Itzalana Parque de Santiago, C 59, between C 70 and C 72. This and a couple of other basic restaurants in the same park are some of the few places near the centre of town to get a casual, super-cheap dinner of *panuchos, salbutes* and *sopa de lima*. Packed with families until 10 or 11pm; also open for lunch.

Restaurante D'Al C 54 at C 53. A typical *cocina económica* serving hearty, stick-to-your-ribs daily specials (about M$30) on flowered tablecloths, but open into the evenings. Also, a rarity at this type of hole-in-the-wall restaurant: beer is served.

Siqueff C 60 at C 35. One of the longest-running Lebanese haunts in town is far from the plaza, but merits a visit to its small Moorish-style garden courtyard for *kafta, kibi* (fried balls of bulgur and meat) and hummus, with guacamole on the side. Venison (*venado*) is an occasional special, and this is also where the signature Yucatecan egg dish *huevos motuleños* was invented in the 1920s. Lunch only.

El Trapiche C 62, between C 59 and C 61 ⓣ999/927-2320. Basic, budget-friendly Yucatecan restaurant, open for every meal, from fresh juices for breakfast to *poc-chuc* for dinner.

Trotter's Circuito Colonias, between C 60 and Prolongación de Montejo. Not at all budget-friendly, but easily Mérida's best and fanciest restaurant. Dining on foie gras and sipping novel cocktails, you won't be submerged in Mexican culture, but you will be rubbing shoulders with the cream of Mérida's social scene. Dress up and make reservations; a taxi from the centre costs M$30.

Drinking, entertainment and nightlife

Mérida is a lively city, and every night of the week you'll find the streets buzzing with revellers enjoying a variety of **free entertainment**. The schedule is fairly fixed: Mondays are dedicated to energetic **jaranas**, vibrant Yucatecan folk dances to a distinctive local rhythm, in front of the Palacio Municipal on the west side of the plaza; Glen Miller-style big band music is at Parque de Santiago on Tuesdays. On Wednesday, there's some kind of free performance at the **Centro Olimpo de Cultura** on the plaza (check the schedule posted outside for other films and lectures during the rest of the week as well). Thursday is the very popular **Serenata Yucateca**, a performance of traditional *trova* songs at the Parque Santa Lucía. Friday is especially busy: even more romantic music at La Ermita, Calle 66 at Calle 77, as well as solo acoustic crooners at the Casa de la Cultura, on Calle 63, between calles 64 and 66, and the **Ballet Folklórico de**

la Universidad de Yucatán, a tourist-oriented but wonderful dance interpretation of traditional Mexican and Maya ceremonies at the Centro Cultural Universitario, Calle 60 at Calle 57. Saturday is the Noche Mexicana, when stalls and musicians set up at the south end of **Paseo de Montejo**. Everything starts at 9pm, except for Tuesday's music, which begins at 8.30pm.

But perhaps the best time to see the Plaza de la Independencia and the surrounding streets is **Sunday**, when vehicles are banned from the area and day-long music, dancing, markets and festivities take over – a real pleasure after the usual traffic rumble. Street markets are set up along Calle 60 as far as the Plaza Santa Ana, and there's a **flea market** in the Parque Santa Lucía.

Other options include the garden behind the Palacio Municipal, Teatro Peón Contreras on Calle 60 (usually some performance every Friday evening and Sunday afternoon; buy tickets in advance). And you can always get a personal **serenade** at the central plaza – trios of *trovadores*, in their white shirts and pants, wait along the edge to be hired by the song or by the hour.

Should you want to see a **film**, first check the schedule at Teatro Mérida on Calle 62, just north of the plaza; its small upstairs cinema often screens art films. Cine Fantasia, on Parque Hidalgo (C 60 at C 59), and Cine Rex, on Parque de Santiago (C 59, between C 70 and C 72), show first-run films, usually American, and ticket prices can be as low as M$25; schedules for both are at Ⓦwww.cineshollywood.com.mx. As a last-ditch effort, head out to the Plaza las Américas mall, which has a multi-screen Cinépolis (Ⓦwww.cinepolis.com.mx).

Bars and clubs tend to be split between traditional places, which are busy in the late afternoon and popular with an older crowd (and even families), and hipper nightspots that get busy later with a younger clientele. Many of the latter are on Prolongación de Montejo, especially around its intersection with Circuito Colónias (just off the north edge of the Mérida map, p.214).

Traditional bars

Apart from the hard-drinking cantinas (and there are plenty of these all over the city, including a couple on Calle 62, just south of the plaza), many of Mérida's more traditional **bars** double as restaurants, with early closing times to match. The emphasis is on cold beer served with *botanas* – small-plate snacks delivered with each round, according to the kitchen's whim – and often accompanied by live music as well.

Fau-San C 64, between C 65 and C 67. A little grittier than the other options here, but still emphasizing food a bit more than drink. Order with restraint, as the *botanas* are very generous.

Los Henequenes C 56 at C 57. A modern reinvention of a traditional bar serving *botanas* and beer, set in an old house and generally busy in the late afternoon. It's perhaps a little too modern, but it does have a local clientele, two-for-one beer specials and live music.

El Lucero del Alba C 47 at C 56. TVs lend an unfortunate sports-bar feel in part of the space, but otherwise this bar is a great place for cold beers or margaritas.

Bars, clubs and live music

La Casa de Todos C 64 at C 55. Very small student bar – more of a clubhouse, really – with a strong leftist bent. Most nights there's a rousing folksinger or two on the tiny stage; other nights, young punk bands. Wed–Sun after 9pm.

El Cielo C 30, between C 15 and C 17 ⓣ999/944-9127. Marvel at Mérida's young wealthies misbehaving at this slick, all-white open-air lounge, the most popular in town. It's in the Prolongación de Montejo area – cabbies will know it. Go before 10.30pm for cheaper entrance; Thurs and Sat are open bar, and the cover can go as high as M$150.

El Cumbanchero Paseo de Montejo at C 39. More convenient than *Mambo Café*, this small salsa bar is owned by the son of the late

Rubén González, of Buena Vista Social Club. Dancing starts around dinner time, with an older crowd at first, who then give way to younger dancers around 10pm. Also open for brunch on Sun.
Jazzin' Mérida C 56 no. 465, between C 53 and C 55. As the name suggests, a good spot for live jazz, usually with a big expat audience. Wed–Sat only.
Mambo Café In the Plaza Las Américas mall. Worth the cab ride (about M$50) if you're looking to mingle with salsa-mad locals in what's considered one of the city's best nightclubs. Touring Dominican and Cuban bands often play here. Free on Wed; otherwise, cover is about M$50. Wed–Sat 10am–3am.
Mayan Pub C 62, between C 55 and C 57. Head through the front colonial house to the garden out back to hear live jazz with Mérida's bohemian crowd.
Pancho's C 59, between C 60 and C 62. A steak restaurant with a pricey haute Mexican menu (and a goofy theme: bandolier-draped waiters, no less), this sprawling space is nonetheless better as a bar – considering it has two of them, plus tasty mojitos and margaritas. Try to hit the happy hour, 6–8pm Mon–Fri.
La Quilla C 60, between C 43 and C 45 Ⓦwww.laquilla.blogspot.com. This artist-friendly café really takes off in the evenings – it often hosts hip-hop shows, DJs, films and other cool events (cover M$20 or M$30), starting at 9pm or so. Even on quiet nights, it's a nice place to drink a beer.
El Rodeo C 59, between C 60 and C 62. A raucous atmosphere, live music and a mixed crowd, as well as a full menu – a good, unpretentious hangout that's not as gritty as a standard men-only cantina.

Listings

Airlines Aeroméxico, Plaza Americana, *Fiesta Americana* Ⓣ999/964-1780; Aviacsa, Plaza Americana, *Fiesta Americana* Ⓣ999/925-6890, or at the airport Ⓣ999/946-1850; Mexicana, Prolongación de Montejo no. 85, between C 15 and C 17 Ⓣ999/944-9105.
American Express Paseo de Montejo 492, between C 41 and C 43 (Mon–Fri 9am–5pm, Sat 9am–noon; Ⓣ999/942-8200, Ⓕ999/942-8210).
Banks Most are around C 65, between C 60 and C 64, have ATMs and are open 9am–4pm. The most centrally located is Banamex, in the Casa de Montejo on the south side of the plaza; it also has an ATM.
Books and maps Amate Books, C 60, between C 49 and C 51 (closed Mon), has an excellent selection of English-language titles on every facet of Mexican culture imaginable, plus Latin American literature and even some magazines, such as *Harper's*, and guidebooks. For maps, though, head to Librería Burrel, C 59, between C 60 and C 62, and if they don't stock what you need, Sanborn's, in the *Fiesta Americana*, may. Librería Dante, on the west side of the plaza and on C 59 opposite Burrel, also sells some guidebooks as well as many useful references, such as field guides, under its own imprint. The Conaculta bookshop adjacent to Teatro Daniel Ayala, C 60 just north of the plaza, carries a good stock of art books, guides and music, though mostly in Spanish. Alternatively, borrow English-language books from the extensive Mérida English Library, C 53, between C 66 and C 68, which also functions as a meeting point for the city's expat community.
Car rental Family-run Mexico Rent a Car, with offices at C 57-A, between C 58 and C 60, and at C 62 no. 483-A, offers not only kind and helpful service, but also has very good rates that include all types of insurance (Ⓣ999/927-4916, Ⓔmexicorentacar@hotmail.com). Otherwise, try the international agencies, most of which have offices in a strip on C 60, between C 55 and C 57, as well as in the *Fiesta Americana*, making it easy to compare quotes.
Consulates Opening hours are likely to be fairly limited, so it's best to phone ahead. Belize: C 53 no. 498, at C 58 Ⓣ999/928-6152, Ⓔconsbelize@dutton.com.mx; Cuba: C 42 no. 200, between C 1-E and C 1-D, Fracc. Campestre Ⓣ999/944-4216, Ⓔconscuba@prodigy.net.mx; Netherlands: C 64 no. 418, between C 47 and C 49 Ⓣ999/924-3122, Ⓔpixan@sureste.com; US: C 60 no. 338-K, between C 29 and C 31, Colonía Alcala Martín Ⓣ999/942-5700.
Hospitals Mérida is the Yucatán's centre for medical care so there is no shortage of doctors. Clinica de Mérida hospital, Av Itzáes 242 at Av Colón (Ⓣ999/920-0411, Ⓦwww.clinicademerida.com.mx), is accustomed to dealing with foreigners.
Internet and telephone *Casetas* are not numerous; you're better off using Skype or a similar service at one of the Internet cafés which dot every street in central Mérida; try Chandler's, in the shopping complex on the north side of the plaza, or the no-name place a little further back, which is marginally cheaper. If you're carrying your own computer, you can use free Wi-Fi in most of the city's parks, including the main plaza.

Moving on from Mérida

As the biggest travel hub in the Yucatán, Mérida has a profusion of **bus stations**, each theoretically dedicated to certain bus companies and regions; in practice, however, the different terminals duplicate routes and services. If you want the fastest long-distance service, go via ADO, semi-deluxe ADO GL or deluxe UNO service at the first-class **Terminal CAME** or the **Fiesta Americana** terminal on Paseo de Montejo (which handles only deluxe service to Cancún – virtually all UNO service goes from here). You might, however, be able to find a comparably fast trip at a lower price at the **Terminal de Segunda Clase** across the street from the CAME; also come here if you're looking for a bus to any town between Mérida and Campeche, or a town on the Ruta Puuc. Slow buses to small towns leave from the **Noreste** terminal, on Calle 67 at Calle 50: visit here for Celestún, and coastal towns east and west of Progreso (such as Chelem, Dzilam de Bravo or San Felipe). It's also the starting point for towns and sights on the Ruta de los Conventos southeast of Mérida, such as Mayapán. Dzibilchaltún and Progreso service runs from the **AutoProgreso** bus station on Calle 62, between calles 65 and 67. Additionally, **colectivos** often provide more frequent service to destinations an hour or two outside of the city, and to smaller villages. These, as well as small buses to Dzibilchaltún, Oxkutzcab and Ticul, congregate at Parque San Juan (Calle 62 at Calle 69). For Progreso, colectivos leave from the east side of Calle 60, between calles 65 and 67. Principal destinations and the corresponding bus stations and services can be found in "Travel details", p.240.

Flights depart from Lic. Manuel Crecencio Rejón airport (Ⓣ999/946-1530, Ⓦwww.asur.com.mx) for Mexico City, Cancún, Ciudad del Carmen and Villahermosa, as well as some international destinations; to get to the airport, catch bus #79 ("Aviación") from Parque San Juan. A taxi from the centre costs about M$80.

The Ruta Puuc bus

Infrequent buses make the more out-of-the-way ruins on the **Ruta Puuc** (see p.251) difficult to visit without your own car, but the Autotransportes del Sur (ATS) company offers a day-trip service for tourists that's budget-friendly, if a bit rushed. The trip costs M$132 and leaves at 8am every day from the Terminal de Segunda Clase, visiting Uxmal, Sayil, Kabáh and Xlapak. You get just long enough at each site to form a general impression, and there's no guide or lunch included in the price. To go to Uxmal only, it's M$75.

Laundry If your hotel doesn't do laundry, try Lavandería La Fe, C 61, between C 62 and C 64, open seven days a week.

Post office C 53, between C 52 and C 54 (Mon–Fri 8am–4.30pm, Sat 9am–1pm).

Tourist police This special squad, dressed in white shirts and brown trousers, roams the plaza, giving directions and otherwise helping visitors (Ⓣ999/930-3200 ext 40062).

Travel agencies and tours For out-of-town trips, student travel agency Nómadas (Ⓣ999/948-1187, Ⓦwww.nomadastravel.com) has good-value excursions to Uxmal and Chichén Itzá, as well as excellent plane fares to Mexico City. For a natural outing, Ecoturísmo Yucatán (Ⓣ999/920-2772, Ⓦwww.ecoyuc.com.mx) runs a day-trip to the cenotes at Cuzamá (see p.258), as well bike trips and other active excursions. Red de Ecoturismo de Yucatán (Ⓣ999/926-7756, Ⓔecoturismo.ac@gmail.com) is a network of very small community eco-adventure projects – stop by the office, C 56-A no. 437, near the Monumento a la Patria (Mon–Fri 10am–2pm, Sat 4–6pm), or email to get all the options, from day biking trips to multi-day camping excursions. Otherwise try Yucatan Trails, C 62 no. 482, between C 57 and C 59 (Ⓣ999/928-2582, Ⓔyucatantrails@hotmail.com), where tours include a handy one-way Mérida–Chichén Itzá–Cancún package; Cuba trips are also available. The knowledgeable Canadian owner offers luggage storage for M$10/day.

The Gulf coast

The distance between Mérida and the port of **Progreso**, the closest point on the coast, is just 36km (thirty minutes to the north by bus). About halfway between the two, a few kilometres east of the main road, lie the ancient ruins of **Dzibilchaltún**, with a **cenote** at the very middle of the site that receives a constant supply of fresh-water from a small spring. The drive out of Mérida follows Paseo de Montejo through miles of wealthy suburbs and shopping malls before reaching the flat countryside.

It's easy enough to visit Dzibilchaltún on the way to Progreso from Mérida: **combis** for Chablecal, which leave from Parque San Juan (Calle 62 at Calle 69) about every half-hour, stop at the ruins; leaving, you can walk or hitch a ride back to the main highway, where you can flag down a Progreso bus. Combis return to Mérida from the corner of calles 80 and 31 near the post office, on the north side of Progreso's Parque Central (note that leaving on Sunday evenings in the summer, with the rest of the weekender crowds, means that you'll have a very long wait). To go straight to the coast from Mérida, **buses** leave from the terminal dedicated to the Progreso service on Calle 62, between calles 65 and 67.

Dzibilchaltún

The archeological importance of the ruins of the ancient city of **Dzibilchaltún** (daily 8am–5pm; M$66) is hardly reflected in what you see. The area was settled from 1000 BC right through to the Conquest – the longest continuous occupation of any known Maya site. More than eight thousand structures have been mapped, but unfortunately, little has survived, in particular because the ready-dressed stones were a handy building material and therefore used in several local towns and in paving the Mérida–Progreso road. In addition, there is virtually no descriptive labelling on the buildings, so it's worth hiring a **guide** (M$200 for up to six people) at the main entrance. Dzibilchaltún features an excellent museum, and the area is part of an **eco-archeological park**, where birders can catch the rough-winged swallow and the Yucatán woodpecker. Allow about two hours to see everything.

Just past the site entrance, the small but smartly done **Museo del Pueblo Maya** (Tues–Sun 8am–4pm) provides an overview of Maya culture and the history of the region up to the present. The exhibits place special emphasis on the continuity of Maya culture and art under Spanish rule, with some beautiful examples of colonial-era wood carvings – including a *retablo* (altarpiece) salvaged from Mérida's cathedral after the Revolution-era fire – as well as samples of huipiles from across the Maya world.

From the museum, a meandering nature trail leads to the **Templo de las Siete Muñecas** (Temple of the Seven Dolls). The temple was originally a simple square pyramid, subsequently built over with a more complex structure. Later still, a passageway was cut through to the original building and seven deformed clay figurines (dolls) were buried, with a tube through which their spirits were meant to commune with the priests. The structure is remarkable for being the only known Maya temple to have windows, and for having a tower in place of the usual roofcomb. A great time to visit is on the **equinoxes**, when the sun shines straight through the tower doors, in a display of ancient astronomical savvy that draws crowds of tourists. In conjunction with the buildings that surround it, the temple is also aligned with other astronomical points and must have served in some form as an observatory.

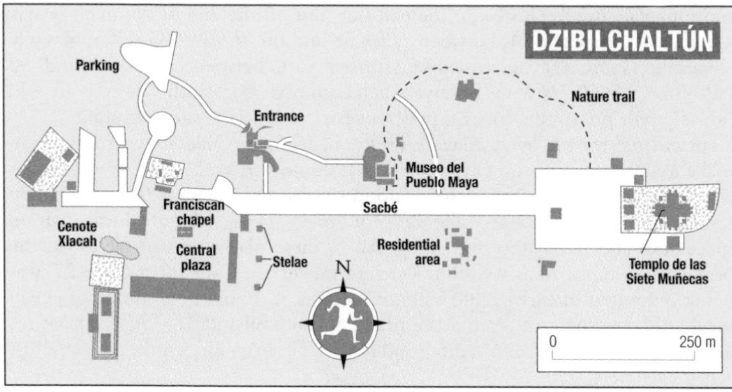

One of the ancient causeways that linked the city's major points runs dead-straight from the temple to another cluster of ruins arrayed around a plaza. The centre of the grassy field is dominated by the shell of a Franciscan chapel built around 1600, and the gates of a cattle ranch from the next century are still standing to the west. A little further west, **Cenote Xlacah**, in addition to providing the ancient city with water, was of ritual importance to the Maya: more than six thousand offerings – including human remains – have been discovered in its deeper end (44m down), which connects to an underground river system. It's also home to a species of spiny fish found only in the Yucatán.

Progreso and around

At first glance, **PROGRESO**, a working port with a six-kilometre-long concrete pier, is unprepossessing, especially at the end of a summer weekend when crowds of day-trippers have just pulled out, leaving beer bottles and food wrappers in their wake. But the beach, really the only reason to visit, is long and broad, with fine white sand, and it makes for a pleasant, non-touristy day out from Mérida. If you're there in the winter, the beach will be empty, except perhaps for a handful of intrepid tourists from one of the cruiseships that docks here occasionally.

If you stray from the beach, you'll discover Progreso is a small place, and it's not difficult to find your way around. The Auto Progreso **bus station** is on Calle 29 (running east–west, four blocks south of the water) at the corner of Calle 82. Calle 80, one block east, is the main street, running north–south and dead-ending at the beach. The **tourist office** (Mon–Fri 8am–2pm, Sat 8am–1pm; Ⓣ969/935-0114) is here, in the Casa de la Cultura at Calle 27; it has only a free map and a couple of flyers, though. On cruiseship days, the courtyard out front hosts a craft market. Also on Calle 80 are a few **banks** with ATMs, and a couple of Internet cafés.

Hotels in town range from very seedy to somewhat overpriced; but because Progreso is a popular family destination, many have large rooms ideal for groups. The high season is July and August and Semana Santa; outside that, prices drop considerably. Best bets include *Hotel Progreso,* Calle 29 no. 142 at Calle 78 (Ⓣ969/935-0039, Ⓕ969/935-2019; ❸), and *San Miguel*, just across the street (Ⓣ969/935-1357; ❸) – they're both several blocks back from the beach but have clean rooms and a choice of air conditioning or fan. A couple of other, more upscale hotels cluster on the east side, just off the end of the main beach: *Casa Isidora*, on Calle 21, between calles 58 and 60 (Ⓣ969/935-4595, Ⓦwww.casaisidora.com; ❻), and *Yakunah*, further east, between calles 48 and 50 (Ⓣ969/935-5600, Ⓦwww.hotelyakunah.com.mx; ❻). Both are set in old houses, with pretty tile floors, a pool out back and an on-site restaurant.

For **eating**, try the lively *Eladio's*, on the malecón at Calle 80, where you can make a good meal of the tasty *botanas* that come free with beers. Also popular is *Sol y Mar*, across the street, for seafood snacks, and *Le Saint Bonnet*, a family restaurant, on Calle 19 at Calle 78, that serves more elaborate local seafood specialities and has a pool for guests. All of these places set out tables on the beach across the road as well. The town's **market**, on Calle 80 at Calle 27, was being renovated in early 2008; when it reopens, it should be a source of cheap meals. Also try the area around the **plaza** at calles 80 and 31 – *El Cordobés*, on Calle 80, is a good place for coffee and snacks. There's a mega-grocery store just across the street.

East of Progreso

Heading **east from Progreso,** the beach is built up for almost 5km. A walk in this direction passes the crumbling mansions of the old henequen exporters, interspersed with modern holiday villas and condominiums. You'll wind up in the fishing village of **Chicxulub Puerto**. You'd never guess that this area is where a massive meteor crashed 65 million years ago, permanently altering the Earth's atmosphere; today the most remarkable thing about Chicxulub Puerto is the excellent *Restaurante Moctezuma* (aka "Los Barriles", for the giant wood barrels that form its front entrance), just east of the small plaza and a favourite local destination for a late seafood **lunch**.

After this, traffic is soon shunted away from the beach and onto the new highway, which runs parallel to the shore about 1km south of the water. The land in between was formerly occupied by coconut plantations, but the tallest tree varieties were highly susceptible to a blight called lethal yellowing disease that spread in the 1980s; now the real estate is given over to holiday homes. At Km 15 on the highway, a smart **viewing platform** (free; follow signs for the *mirador turística*) over the Uaymitún inlet is a great place to see flocks of **flamingos** – not in such great numbers as at Celestún (see p.238), but impressive considering their proximity to the highway. For the best chance of spotting them, go just before the 6pm closing time; the caretakers will rent binoculars for M$10.

If you're driving, you can detour south following signs for Dzemul, passing another flamingo-filled inlet, then to **Xcambó** (9am–sunset), the grass-covered ruins of an Early Classic Maya salt-trading outpost. A thatch-roof chapel, built from the ruins' stones in the 1950s following a reported apparition of the Virgin, sits astride some old foundations, and a huipil-dressed cross stands atop the tallest building. Entrance is free, but you should tip the watchman, who may also show you some human bones allegedly dug up at the site. Continue south on this road to reach *Rancho Komchen*, a private bird sanctuary and casual eco-lodge (Ⓣ999/743-9533, Ⓦwww.komchen.org; ❹) and *Hacienda San Juan de Lizárraga* (Ⓣ999/996-8621, Ⓔsanjuandelizarraga@hotmail.com; ❺, breakfast included), a huge property with a pool, beautiful gardens and very reasonable rates for the big, antiques-filled rooms, including one with its own kitchen and another full-house rental.

Back on the coast road, you reach **Telchac Puerto** after another 10km. This laid-back seaside village is also popular in the summer with escapees from Mérida's city heat. One nice small hotel, *Libros y Sueños* (Ⓣ991/917-4125,

Ⓦwww.l-y-s.net; ④) has tidy rooms, sells English-language books, rents bicycles and runs fishing trips. It's on the west side of town, a bit of a hike if you're coming from the bus stop. The plaza has several good seafood **restaurants** and *Dulcería Chay*, specialising in traditional coconut and lime sweets.

With more time, it's possible to get even further east along an ever-narrowing road, passing a few remaining coconut plantations not killed by the yellowing blight. In **San Crisanto**, 9km east of Telchac Puerto, a village group runs **mangrove tours** for just M$40 per person – you navigate canals on a paddle-boat, winding up at a cenote for a swim. Look for the tour office (Ⓣ999/926-0236) one block south of the main intersection, by the baseball field. After Chabihau, 15km from Telchac Puerto, the holiday homes peter out, and the coast reverts to its wild state. In the village of **Santa Clara** (really just a few buildings stuck between the sea and the salt flats), *La Morena* restaurant serves excellent fresh fish that's worth stopping for; the beach here is tranquil and the view, of virtually nothing, up and down the coast, exceedingly relaxing.

At the end of the road, **Dzilam de Bravo** is a remote fishing village with a sea-defence wall that precludes a beach. *Jean Lafitte* (Ⓣ991/102-1543; ③) is the only **hotel**, but a decent one, with a pool that's sometimes full. The real draw is **Bocas de Dzilam**, 40km away in the Parque Natural San Felipe, a state nature reserve. Set in 620 square kilometres of coastal forests, marshes and dunes, the *bocas* (Spanish for "mouths") are freshwater springs on the seabed; the nutrients they provide encourage the wide biological diversity found here. The wildlife you may see is superb, including turtles, tortoises, crocodiles, spider monkeys and dozens of bird species. To visit, you'll need to track down local guide Javier Nadar, better known as Chacate (ask around for him in the main square). He charges M$850 for a boat and a ceviche lunch (4–5hr; up to five people) and M$350 for shorter trips (3–4hr). If Javier isn't available, ask around at the marina, due east of the plaza a few blocks. A more direct way to get to Dzilam de Bravo is to catch a second-class **bus** in Mérida from the Autobuses del Noreste terminal at the corner of calles 50 and 67. Three buses daily pass through on their way to and from Tizimín and Progreso, and three buses daily leave for Izamal.

West of Progreso

Venturing **west from Progreso** is not as promising as heading east, though in the 19km of coast road, you will find a couple more beach villages, all but deserted during the offseason. To reach them, you must go back inland and around the naval base and commercial port at **Yucalpetén**. Further west, the small resorts of **Chelem** and **Chuburná**, respectively fifteen and thirty minutes from Progreso and easy day-trips from Mérida, have clean, wide beaches and some **accommodation** and restaurants. *Hotel Sian Ka'an* (Ⓣ969/935-4017, Ⓦwww.hotelsiankaan.com; ⑥), in Chelem, is one good option, offering big oceanfront rooms ideal for groups or families, with balconies and kitchenettes, as well as a good fish **restaurant**.

Beyond Chuburná, the coast road, which was damaged by Hurricane Isidore in 2002, is no longer negotiable, and you'll have to turn inland again. It's not worth making a detour back to the coast at **Sisal**, however; unbelievably, this was Mérida's chief port in colonial times (and gave its name to the henequen fibre that was exported from here), but now it's quite shabby and practically deserted.

Celestún

Were it not for its amazing bird-filled lagoon that boasts a large flock of flamingos, **CELESTÚN** – which lies 93km west of Mérida, at the end of a sandbar on the peninsula's northwest coast – would be little more than a one-boat fishing village. The flamingos are most numerous from November to May, when blue-winged teals and shovellers also migrate. To see them in the warm, shallow waters of the 146,000-acre **Ría Celestún Biosphere Reserve**, hire a boat at the official *parador turístico*, just past the bridge on the main road into

▲ Pink flamingos around the Gulf

Celestún. Ask the bus driver to drop you here, as it's a twenty-minute walk back from the main square.

The **ticket system** here is so complex, you might suspect you're being scammed. In fact, it *is* a system, and you should work out the math in advance to know what you're getting into. The pricing is essentially designed to deter people from crowding together in a single boat, as there are plenty of captains and not always a lot of customers. For the standard tour (approximately 1hr), stopping at the flamingo feeding grounds and a fresh-water spring amid the mangroves, groups of four or fewer need to purchase a group ticket (M$500), then individual tickets (M$40) for a total of M$165 per person for four. If, however, you're with a group of five or six (the maximum boat capacity), the rate is simply M$140 per person, so you're not saving much. None of this includes an additional M$40 in taxes per person, or an optional M$200 per boat for a dedicated guide. A two-hour trip, which also visits a "petrified forest" (really, a spooky swathe of salt-choked trees), is M$1000 for the boat plus M$40 per person up to four (M$240 per person for groups of five or six); a guide is M$400. These prices may fluctuate (especially as fuel prices rise), but the basic system should stay the same. If you would like to join a larger group, show up around 10am, as that's when most people arrive, usually on the 8am bus from Mérida.

You may be approached by unlicensed captains outside the *parador*; they will offer a competitive price, but their deep-keel boats are not designed for the inlet, and some passengers have even found themselves pushing their craft out of the mud-flats. These captains may also resort to driving too close to the birds to scare them into giving visitors a spectacular flying display; fortunately, the official captains no longer do this.

For extended **birdwatching** tours, contact Alberto Rodriguez Pisté (Ⓔx2rodriguez@hotmail.com), one of the expert guides at the *parador turístico*; a fluent English-speaker and longtime birder, he can sometimes be found at *Restaurant Celestún*, on the waterfront.

Practicalities

Buses for Celestún depart seventeen times daily from Mérida's Noreste terminal (see p.216), beginning at 5.15am; the trip takes about two hours. The village has half a dozen **places to stay**: beachfront *María del Carmen*, Calle 12 no. 111 at Calle 15 (Ⓣ988/916-2170, Ⓔmcrodriguez@hotmail.com; ④), is the best bet, with balconies overlooking a wide beach (air conditioning is an option), while the *Ría Celestún* **hostel**, on Calle 12 at Calle 13 (Ⓣ988/916-2219, Ⓔhostelriacelestun@hotmail.com), has decent dorm beds (M$65), but is not particularly clean. On the upper end, *Hotel Manglares* (Ⓣ988/916-2156, Ⓦwww.hotelmanglares.com.mx; ⑦) is a comfortable little hotel on the north edge of town. If you really want to escape, the remote and lovely *Eco Paraíso Xixim* (Ⓣ988/916-2100, Ⓦwww.ecoparaiso.com; ⑨) is 10km north of town. Operating primarily on wind and solar power, it offers well-appointed cabañas, excellent showers and a deserted beach; rates include breakfast (though don't go for the "halfboard" options, in which dinner is also included, as dinner is better in town).

Of the several **seafood restaurants** along the beach, *La Palapa* is the biggest and priciest, but unfortunately one of the only really reliable ones. For cheap home cooking, visit the *loncherías* by the small market (just off the inland side of the plaza). There's also a bakery, a bank (but **no ATM**) and a petrol station.

If you are travelling by car, you can avoid retracing your route completely by taking a series of small roads back to Hwy-180 south of Mérida. Leaving

Celestún, turn south 23km east of town, then east in Chunchucmil. This village and those that follow are all former henequen haciendas where the ruins of the old buildings stand on every central plaza, strikingly similar in layout and architecture. One of these, *Hacienda Santa Rosa* (ⓣ999/910-4852, ⓦwww.starwood.com; ⑨), has been beautifully renovated as a hotel (see p.268). You will rejoin the highway at **Maxcanú**, either returning to Mérida (about 50km) or continuing south to Campeche.

Travel details

Buses

Wherever you go in this corner of the Yucatán, you'll have to pass through Mérida, but bus service from there is more frequent than any other city in the Yucatán. Cristóbal Colón (OCC) and ADO (and its deluxe UNO) provide first-class service. A number of other companies provide second-class service, ranging from relatively direct routes on comfortable buses with ATS and Mayab, to very slow local routes on rattletrap buses with Noreste (to the north coast and Celestún), Oriente (points east, such as Izamal and Chichén Itzá, as well as Celestún) and Líneas Unidas del Sur (LUS - towns southeast of Mérida).

Celestún to: Mérida (15 daily, 7.30am–6pm; 2hr).

Mérida (AP=AutoProgreso; C=Terminal CAME; FA=Fiesta Americana; N=Noreste; SC=Terminal Segunda Clase) to: Acanceh (N: 8 daily, 5.30am–8pm; 45min); Bolonchén de Rejón (SC: 5 daily; 2hr); Campeche (C: at least hourly, round-the-clock; FA: 1 daily at midnight; SC: at least hourly, 4.15am–9pm; 2hr 30min–4hr); Cancún (C: 40 daily, including three on UNO, round-the-clock; FA: 14 daily, including six on UNO, 6am–12.45am; N: 17 daily via Valladolid, 6am–8.20pm; SC: 20 daily, 6am–midnight, 2 daily via Carrillo Puerto at 5.45am & 1.30pm; 4–8hr); Celestún (N: 17 daily, 5.15am–8.30pm; 2hr); Chetumal (C: 4 daily at 7.30am, 1pm, 6pm & 11pm; SC: 7 daily, 7am–midnight; 6–8hr); Chichén Itzá (C: 3 daily at 6.30am, 9.15am & 12.30pm; N: 17 daily, 6am–8.20pm; 1hr 30min–2hr); Chicxulub Puerto (N: 19 daily, 4.45am–9.30pm; 1hr); Chiquilá for Holbox (SC: 1 daily at 11.30pm; 6hr); Ciudad del Carmen (C: 26 daily, 4am–1.20am; SC: 10 daily, 6.30am–9pm; 5hr 30min–7hr); Cobá (N: 1 daily at 5.20am; SC: 2 daily at 5am & 9.55pm; 6hr); Cuzamá (N: 7 daily, 5.40am–9pm; 1hr 30min); Dzibilchaltún (AP: hourly; 30min); Dzilam de Bravo (N: 7 daily, 5am–8pm; 4hr); Escárcega (C: 7 daily, 8.30am–11.50pm; SC: 3 daily at 11am, 1.10pm & 3.40pm; 4hr 30min–6hr); Felipe Carrillo Puerto (SC: 10 daily, 4am–10pm; 2hr 30min); Frontera (SC: 2 daily at 7pm & 9pm; 8hr); Hecelchakán (SC: 30 daily, 4.15am–7.15pm; 2hr); Hopelchén (SC: 5 daily; 2hr 30min); Izamal (N: 23 daily, 4.45am–9pm; 1hr); Maní (N: 8 daily, 5.30am–8pm; 2hr); Maxcanú (SC: 30 daily, 4.15am–7.15pm; 1hr 45min); Mayapán (N: 8 daily, 5.30am–8pm; 1hr); Mexico City (C: 14 daily, 10am–11.30pm; 21hr); Motul (N: 9 daily, 5.45am–8pm; 45min); Oxkutzcab (SC: 12 daily, 6am–6.30pm; 2hr); Palenque (C: 6 daily at 8.30am, 7.15pm, 8.15pm, 9pm, 10pm & 11.50pm; 7hr 30min); Playa del Carmen (C: 17 daily, 4.20am–1.45am; N: 1 daily at 5.20am; SC: 6 daily via Cancún, 6am–11.35pm, 2 daily via Cobá at 5am & 9.55pm; 5–7hr); Progreso (AP: every 30min; 45min); Río Lagartos (N: 3 daily at 6am, 4pm & 5.30pm; 6hr); Sancrisanto 3 daily at 7.15am, 10.15am & 6.30pm; 1hr 45min); San Felipe (N: 1 daily at 5.30pm; 6hr 30min); Santa Elena (SC: 5 daily; 1hr); Sisal (N: 3 daily at 12.20pm, 4pm & 7pm; 2hr); Telchac Pueblo (N: 3 daily at 7.45am, 3.15pm & 6.45pm; 1hr); Telchac Puerto (N: 7 daily, 7am–6.30pm; 1hr 30min); Ticul (SC: 12 daily, 6am–6.30pm; 1hr 45min); Tizimín (N: 15 daily, 5.30am–8.20pm; 4hr); Tulum (C: 4 daily at 6.30am, 10.40am, 12.40pm & 5.45pm; N: 1 daily at 5.20am; SC: 6 daily via Cancún, 6am–11.35pm, 2 daily via Cobá at 5am & 9.55pm; 4–6hr); Uxmal (SC: 5 daily; 1hr); Valladolid (N: 17 daily, 6am–8.20pm; SC: 20 daily, 6am–midnight; 2–3hr); Villahermosa (C: 33 daily, including two on UNO, 7.15am–1.20am; FA: 1 daily on UNO at 9.30pm; SC: 3 daily at 11am, 7pm & 9pm; 8hr 30min–10hr 30min); Yaxcaba (N: 1 Sat–Mon at 6.15pm; 3hr).

Progreso to: Tizimín (3 daily via Telchac Puerto and Dzilam de Bravo; 2hr); Mérida (every 30min; 45min).

Flights

Flights depart daily from Mérida's airport for Mexico City, Veracruz and Villahermosa.

Maya culture

More than any other Mesoamerican culture, the Maya have been subject to the fantasies of later explorers, who even imagined they might be extraterrestrials. But perhaps the most damaging idea is that the Maya people disappeared after their pyramid cities crumbled. In fact, they're alive and well in the Yucatán peninsula, where indigenous culture is more integrated into modern life than in any other part of Mexico. The legacy of the Maya – the raw stone of the ruins – comes alive when you see it next to the culture today.

Exploring the ruins of Tulum ▲

Iglesia de Balam Na, a Maya stronghold ▼

A Jaina figurine ▼

The Maya past and present

At its peak a thousand years ago, the ancient Maya empire had a population of some two million, based around at least forty substantial cities, including Chichén Itzá, Calakmul and Uxmal. Eventually the empire splintered, and, after the **Conquest**, collapsed. But despite the best efforts of the Spanish Catholics, the culture persisted, and the ancient religion even helped fuel a rebellion in the nineteenth century. The **Caste Wars**, as the decades-long resistance came to be known, were the only really successful indigenous uprising in Latin America. The Maya fought for more than fifty years, and even succeeded in briefly establishing an **independent state** that was recognised by the British.

The art of the ancient Maya

Outside of the ruined buildings themselves, the most famous Meso-american artworks are probably the **Jaina figurines**, a collection of small clay animals and people found on the Maya burial ground of Isla Jaina (see box, p.269). The thousands of statuettes depict everyone from queens to village governors to weavers, and their timeless, expressive features give a clear impression of the Maya as people, rather than just as pyramid-builders. Other art forms, seldom seen at ruined sites, are **plaster sculpture** and **fresco painting**. Because plaster is so fragile, little of either kind of work has survived, but the elaborate figures at **Ek-Balam** (see p.196) and the murals at **Bonampak** (see p.318) are a reminder that the ancient world was much more ornate and colourful than the grey stone we see today.

Touring the sites

Travellers often aspire to "do" all the major Maya sites in a single trip: Chichén Itzá, Uxmal, Palenque and Calakmul. But it's more realistic to focus on one and explore the surrounding smaller ruins, giving you time to appreciate living Maya culture, too. Not far from Chichén Itzá lie **Ek-Balam** and **Cobá** (an excellent place to spot wildlife), but be sure to also stop in the town of **Valladolid** (see p.191), where Maya women from surrounding villages come to sell their embroidery. South of Mérida, **Uxmal** anchors the **Ruta Puuc**, a circuit that passes several smaller but equally ornate ruins, as well as the **Grutas de Loltún** (see p.255), a network of caves where the ancient (and not-so-ancient) Maya conducted rituals. South from **Palenque**, along the border with Guatemala, sits **Bonampak** and riverside **Yaxchilán**, reachable only by boat. You may see offerings and incense at the altars in these remote yet vibrant spots. Also stop in Palenque town's small **textile museum** (see p.306) to see the variety of weaving produced by the Maya group in Chiapas. The most remote site of all is **Calakmul**. Once you've gone that far, don't miss the odd towers of the **Río Bec** sites (see p.177) to the west.

Now there are some six million Maya, spread throughout the Yucatán, Tabasco, Chiapas and neighbouring Belize and Guatemala. They're barely visible in Tabasco but vibrant in Chiapas, home to the Lacandón, Tzeltal, Tzotzil and Chol Maya. On the peninsula itself, the majority are **Yucatec Maya** – that is, related to or current speakers of the Yucatec variation of the Maya language, which is spoken everywhere and often incorporated into Spanish as slang. In the Yucatán the culture is most visible, a point of regional pride even among those who have little or no Maya roots.

▲ The Grutas de Loltún were used by ancient Maya

▼ Statue, Palenque's museum

▼ Maya woman in a huipil, Chetumal

Jarana dancing, Mérida ▲

Maya boys in Chiapas, near the Lacandón jungle ▼

Maya woman with corn ▼

Beyond the ruins

After you've toured the archeological sites, check out these other ways to experience Maya culture in the Yucatán peninsula.

Party down

Rituals like El Pochó predate the Conquest, and **town fiestas** highlight the local *jarana* dance. For a list of festivals in the Yucatán peninsula, see p.42.

Camp out

After visiting Bonampak, stay the night with the **Lacandón** in their village near the ruins; they are the most remote of the Maya groups, and their knowledge of the surrounding forest is vast. See p.320.

Take to the water

At the ruins of Muyil, hire a small boat to tour the canals dug in the mangroves by early Maya traders. See p.155.

Pay respects

Visit the shrine of the **Talking Cross** in Felipe Carrillo Puerto, the stronghold of the Maya resistance during the Caste Wars. See p.162.

Meet the neighbours

Guests at *Genesis Retreat* in the village of Ek-Balam can **visit local Maya** houses and learn to make tortillas and weave hammocks. See p.197.

Visit the artists

In Izamal, craftspeople open their workshops to visitors, demonstrating embroidery, jewellery-making and other skills the Maya have honed for centuries. See p.207.

Eat up

The **food** on your plate was probably eaten by Maya thousands of years ago as well. See p.36 and p.358 for menu items.

7

Uxmal and the Ruta Puuc

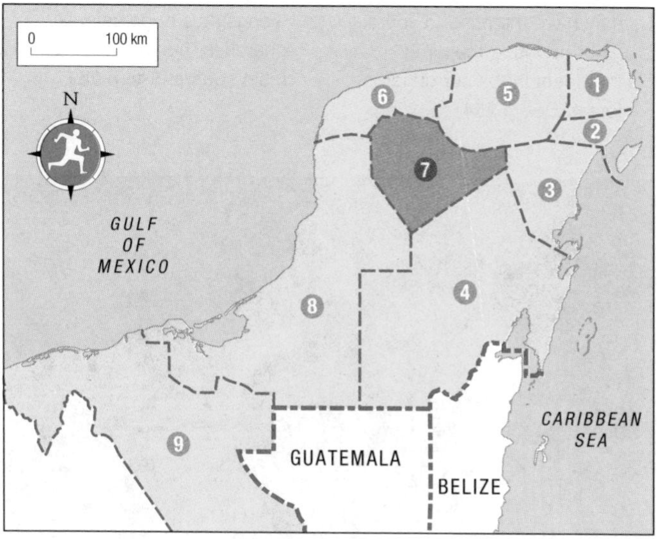

CHAPTER 7

Highlights

* **Uxmal** Along with Chichén Itzá and Palenque, this is one of Mexico's three greatest ancient Maya sites, boasting some of the region's finest architecture. See p.245

* **Haciendas** Stay at a restored nineteenth-century hacienda and get a sense of henequen plantation life. See p.249

* **Sayil** If you can get to the vast site of Sayil early, you may have the ruins to yourself – not counting the birds that teem in the surrounding forest. See p.254

* **Grutas de Loltún** Visit these spectacular caverns, which trace their geologic history to the Stone Age. See p.255

* **Fortress churches** Designed to awe the native population, the fortified churches along the Ruta de los Conventos are still impressively enormous. See p.256

* **Acanceh** Virtually unknown, a hefty ancient pyramid stands alongside a huge colonial church in this rural town's main square. See p.257

▲ A hacienda north of Uxmal

7

Uxmal and the Ruta Puuc

About 80km south of Mérida in the Puuc hills lies a group of the peninsula's most important archeological sites. Chief among them is **Uxmal**, second only to Chichén Itzá in size and historical significance, yet perhaps greater in its initial impact and certainly in the beauty and harmony of its unique architectural style. The **Ruta Puuc** itself heads down from Mérida to Uxmal and then, along Hwy-261, on to **Kabáh**, not far beyond, before turning east along a minor road past **Sayil**, **Xlapak** and **Labná**. Though Uxmal is firmly established on the tourist trail, and perpetually crowded, these lesser Maya sites are surprisingly little-visited. If these places or their equivalents were in Europe or the United States, you wouldn't be able to move for tourists: here, however, if you time your excursion right, you may get a vast site covering several square kilometres entirely to yourself. The Ruta Puuc sites themselves are not only rather accessible – particularly if you are coming from Mérida, the main city in Yucatán State – but they are also very well restored, in comparison with many of the other ancient Maya cities.

Though the Puuc sites are the undoubted highlight, there are plenty of other attractions to blend into the mix when touring this area. The Ruta Puuc takes in contrasting **haciendas** at Yaxcopoil, Ochil and Temozón on the way to

The Ruta Puuc bus

All the Ruta Puuc sites are far enough apart that it's impractical to visit more than a fraction of them by bus, unless you're prepared to spend several days and endure a lot of waiting around. If you are reliant on public transport, the simplest way to visit the main Maya sites is to take the **"Ruta Puuc" day-trip bus** (M$132), run by Autotransportes del Sur from the second-class bus station in Mérida. This departs daily at 8am, returning to Mérida at 3.45pm, and stops for twenty minutes at Xlapak, thirty minutes each at Labná and Sayil, fifty minutes at Kabáh and two hours at Uxmal. Though very rushed at every site, since Uxmal is the last visited it's possible to stay here longer and pay for a later bus back. Alternatively, almost every travel agency in Mérida offers some kind of Ruta Puuc or Ruta de los Conventos trip that includes meals and a guide, with prices starting from around M$400 per person.

Uxmal, while beyond Labná it passes the crumbling Hacienda Tabi as well as the impressive caverns of the **Grutas de Loltún**. These are just outside **Oxkutzcab**, on the old main road from Mérida to Quintana Roo, and from here you can return to Mérida via **Ticul** and Muna, or take the fast new road past the Maya ruins of **Mayapán**.

The latter route, known as the **Ruta de los Conventos**, bypasses a string of villages with gigantic fortified churches, relics of the early years of the Spanish occupation. The most impressive of these is the Franciscan monastery of San Miguel in **Maní**, and while the other villages en route are far less visited, many of them offer other attractions in the form of minor ruins, caves or **cenotes**, the latter especially impressive at Cuzamá, where a horse-drawn rail cart will take you to Los Tres Cenotes.

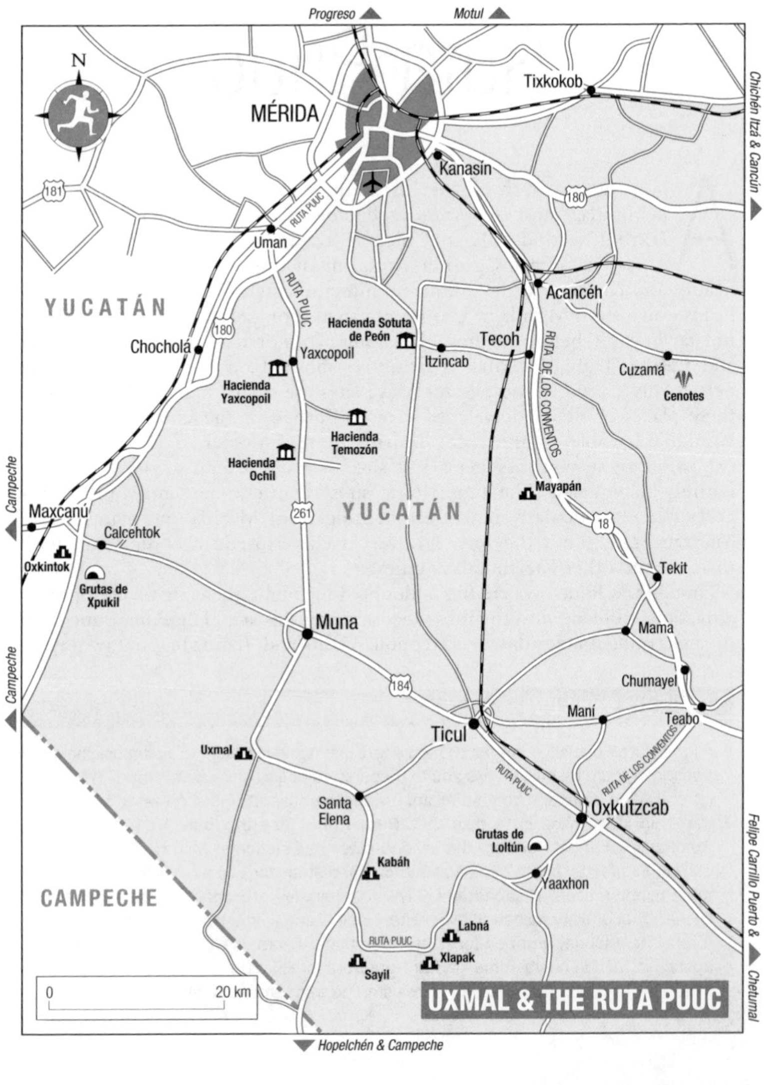

It's possible to cover this area by bus, though with some difficulty (see box, p.233). If you **rent a car,** you can more easily explore all of the key sites in two days (three would be more relaxed), either returning to Mérida by evening or finding a **room** around Uxmal or in Santa Elena, Oxkutzcab or Ticul. For details of car rental agencies in Mérida, see p.232.

Uxmal and around

The UNESCO world heritage site of **UXMAL** (pronounced "OOSH-mal", meaning "thrice-built") represents the finest achievement of the Puuc-region Maya. Rising to power when many southern cities were disintegrating, Uxmal fell into its ultimate decline near 1000 AD. Its spectacular buildings remain, however, encrusted all over with elaborate, and sometimes grisly, decoration. Admittedly, they look the way they do in part because there has been a huge amount of reconstruction, primarily done in the 1930s and some of it quite haphazard. But most visitors will probably feel that the mix of accessibility and preservation has been judged about right, and it's a hard site not to enjoy. In fact, it's potentially more rewarding than a visit to Chichén Itzá, as the crowds are (somewhat) smaller, the decorative detail is fascinating and you can still climb one of the pyramids.

To enjoy the site as its best, try to arrive close to opening time, when you'll share the space with chattering swallows and only a few other visitors. You can see the major buildings easily in a couple of hours; by the time you head out around 11am, the buses will have arrived in convoys. If you can't get such an early start (it helps to stay the night nearby, though the drive from Mérida takes about an hour), know that at least there's plenty of space for people to disperse once you get past the packs of guided tours thronged around the largest pyramid.

Arrival, information and accommodation

Several **buses** a day run direct from Mérida to Uxmal, and any bus heading down the main road towards Hopelchén (or between Mérida and Campeche via Hopelchén) will drop you just a short walk from the entrance. There's a pay **car park** (M$10) at the modern **entrance to the site** (daily 8am–5pm; M$98), where the small but handy **tourist centre** includes a basic museum (Spanish only), a Dante bookshop, a state-run craft store, a snack bar, phones, an ATM and an espresso vendor. You can hire a **guide** for M$550 for a small group. Uxmal's **sound-and-light** show (daily; M$30, or free with day entry ticket) starts at 7pm in winter and 8pm in summer: the commentary is in Spanish (translation equipment is available for M$25) and of dubious historical accuracy, but the lighting effects highlight the relief decorations on the walls beautifully. Once the novelty has worn off, the bats, fireflies and shooting stars will entertain you. No inter-city buses run late enough to get you back to Mérida after the hour-long show, though you might be able to talk your way onto a Turitrans-mérida tour bus, which visits the site every night (or just book directly with the company: ⓣ997/924-1199, ⓦwww.turitransmerida.com.mx). Otherwise, a taxi from Mérida costs around M$500 for a round-trip with waiting time.

Several **hotels** can be found very close to the site, none of them in the budget category. All are subject to sudden arrivals of huge tour groups, sometimes causing a noticeable dip in the quality of service and food, but they are also likely to offer deals when not full. Two are right at the site's entrance: *Villa Uxmal* (ⓣ987/872-9300 ext 8101, ⓦwww.islandercollection.com; ❼) is probably the best value here, with a pool and tennis courts, though the air-conditioned rooms are relatively small; *The Lodge at Uxmal* (ⓣ998/877-2495, ⓦwww.mayaland.com; ⑨) is much more spacious, but grossly overpriced, with published rates above US$300. *La Palapa*, the hotel's breezy **restaurant** and bar, is a convenient spot for a cool drink, however. Across the main road from the site entrance (an easy 500m walk), the colonial-style *Hacienda Uxmal* (ⓣ998/887-2495, ⓦwww.mayaland.com; ⑨) is a sister hotel to *The Lodge*, though it has far more reasonable rates. Other accommodation nearby, but not within walking distance, includes budget options in Santa Elena (see p.252) or the ultra-lux *Hacienda Temozón* (see p.249).

The site

The main restored buildings are set out on a roughly north–south axis in a large cleared site; the alignment of individual buildings often has astrological significance, usually connected with Venus or the Sun. Little is known of the city's history, but what is clear is that the chief monuments, and the city's peaks of power and population, fall into the Terminal Classic period, 800–1000 AD. Though there are indications of settlement long before this, most of the buildings that you see date from this time. After 900 AD the city began to decline, and by 1200 Uxmal and the Puuc sites, together with Chichén Itzá, were all but abandoned. The reasons are unknown, although political infighting, ecological problems and loss of trade with the Toltec site of Tula, near Mexico City, may have played a part. Later, the **Xiu Dynasty** settled at Uxmal, which, along with Chichén Itzá and Mayapán, became part of the League of Mayapán (see p.259). From here, in 1441, the rebellion originated that finally overthrew the power of Mayapán and put an end to any form of centralized Maya authority over the Yucatán.

The Pirámide del Adivino

Entering the site, you first see the great **Pirámide del Adivino** (Pyramid of the Magician) rising before you. The most remarkable looking of all Mexican pyramids, it soars at a startling angle from its unique oval base to a temple some 30m above the ground – though some scholars claim that its shape is unique only because it has been wrongly rebuilt. The legend of the pyramid's creation tells that an old sorceress, who lived in a hut where the pyramid now stands, hatched a dwarf son from an egg and encouraged him to challenge the king to a series of tests – all of which the dwarf won, thanks to a little magic. Finally the king challenged him to build a pyramid overnight: the dwarf succeeded, and became ruler of Uxmal. Despite the legend, however, archeological evidence shows at least five separate stages of construction – six if you count the modern restoration, which may not correspond exactly to any of its earlier incarnations.

Visitors are not permitted to climb this pyramid, but from the base of the rear (east) stairway – facing you as you enter the site – you can see a tunnel that reveals **Templo III**, one of the earlier levels. At the top, surrounded by a platform, the temple at the summit has a facade decorated with interlocking geometric motifs. Walk around to the west face of the pyramid into the **Cuadrángulo de los Pájaros** (named for the macaws that stud the roofline of the building on the west side) to admire the even steeper stairway that runs down either side of a second, older sanctuary in a distinctly different style. Known as the **Edificio Chenes** (or Templo IV), it does indeed reflect the architecture of the Chenes region (see p.281), its entire front forming a giant mask. At the bottom of the west face, divided in half by the stairway, you'll see the very first stage of construction – the long, low facade of a structure apparently similar to the so-called "Nunnery" (see below).

The Cuadrángulo de las Monjas and the Casa de las Tortugas

Directly behind the pyramid, the **Cuadrángulo de las Monjas** (Nunnery Quadrangle), a beautiful complex of four buildings enclosing a plaza, is one of many here named quite erroneously by the Spanish, to whom it resembled a convent. Whatever it may have been, it *wasn't* a convent; theories range from a military academy to a sort of earthly paradise, where intended sacrificial victims would spend their final months in debauchery. The four buildings, probably all constructed between 895 and 906 AD, are each set on a slightly different level, possibly representing the four main levels of the Maya universe. The facade of each is decorated with complex patterns of stone reliefs, full of religious symbolism – the quadrangle itself is a slightly irregular shape, apparently to align with Venus.

All four sides display Maya architectural skills at their finest – the false corbel vaults of the interiors were built about as wide as they could be without collapsing (wooden crossbeams provided further support), and the frontages are slightly bowed in order to maintain a proper horizontal perspective. The **north building**, raised higher than the others and even more richly ornamented, is probably also the oldest. Approached via a broad stairway between two colonnaded porches, it has a strip of plain stone facade (from which doors lead into vaulted chambers) surmounted by a slightly raised panel of mosaics, featuring geometric patterns and human and animal figures, with representations of Maya huts above the doorways. The **west building**, which has been heavily reconstructed, boasts even more varied themes, and the whole of its ornamentation is surrounded by a coiling, feathered rattlesnake with the face of a warrior emerging from its jaws. The **east building** mirrors the west one in its proportions; its snake decorations, however, run in long horizontal bars.

An arched passageway through the middle of the **south building**, the lowest of the four, provided the square with a monumental entrance directly aligned with the **ball-court** (ham-handedly rebuilt with cement) outside. Today a path leads through here, between the ruined side walls of the court and up onto the levelled terrace on which stand the Palacio del Gobernador (see below) and the **Casa de las Tortugas** (House of the Turtles). This very simple, elegant building, named after the stone turtles carved around its cornice, ably demonstrates another constant theme of Puuc architecture: stone facades carved to appear like rows of narrow columns. These probably represent the building style of the Maya huts still in use today, consisting of walls of bamboo or thin branches lashed together. The plain bands of masonry that often surround them mirror the cords that tied the hut walls in place.

The Palacio del Gobernador and the Grupo Sur

It is the **Palacio del Gobernador** (Governor's Palace) that marks the finest achievement of Uxmal's builders. Explorer and writer John L. Stephens, arriving at the then virtually unknown site in June 1840, had no doubts as to its significance: "If it stood this day on its grand artificial terrace in Hyde Park or the Garden of the Tuileries, it would form a new order…not unworthy to stand side by side with the remains of the Egyptian, Grecian and Roman art." The palace faces east, away from the buildings around it,

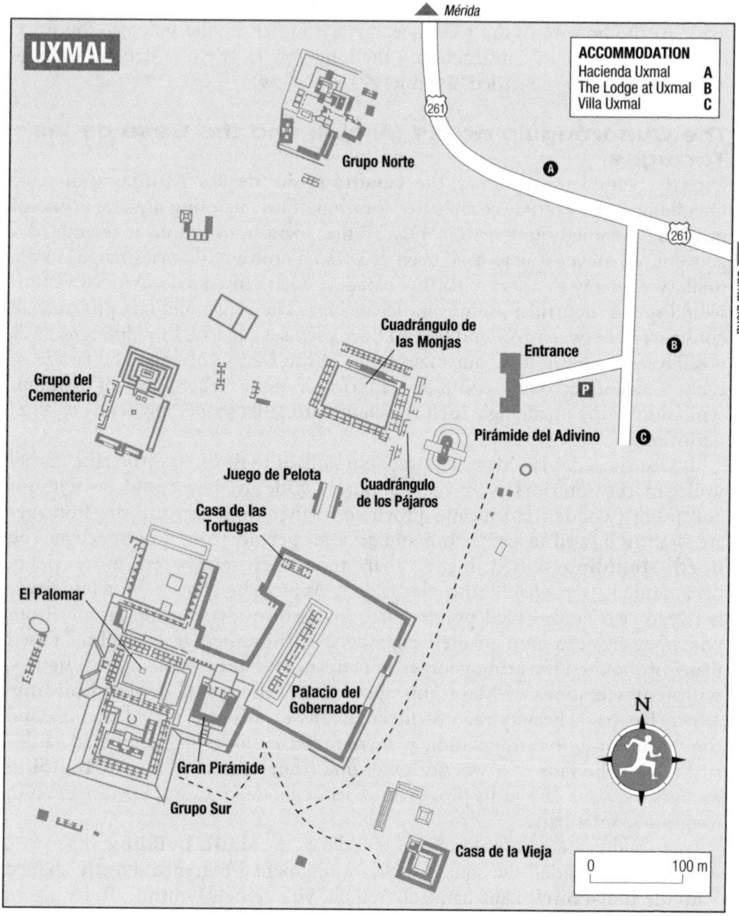

probably for astronomical reasons – its central doorway aligns with the column of the altar outside and the point where Venus rises. Long and low, it is lent a remarkable harmony by the use of light and shade on the facade. Strong diagonals run through its broad band of mosaic decorations, particularly in the steeply vaulted archways that divide the two wings from the central mass, like giant arrowheads aimed at the sky. Close up, the mosaic is equally impressive: curly-nosed masks (perhaps of Chac, the rain god, though also possibly of Itzamná, the creator) alternate with grid-and-key patterns and stylized snakes. In addition, the patterns vary in depth, lending the whole facade a rippling texture. Inside, the chambers are narrow, gloomy and unadorned; but at least the great central room, 20m long and entered by the three closer-set openings in the facade, is bigger than most. At the back, the rooms have no natural light source at all.

Behind the palace stand the crumbling buildings of the **Grupo Sur** (South Group), with the partly restored Gran Pirámide (Great Pyramid) and El Palomar (The Dovecote). You can climb the rebuilt staircase of the **Gran Pirámide** to see the temple on top, decorated with macaws and more curly-nose masks – some of these have even smaller carved faces set inside their mouths. **El Palomar** is what remains of a quadrangle which was originally like that of the Nunnery. It is topped with a great latticed roofcomb which resembles a dovecote, or pigeon loft, giving the structure its name.

After you've taken in the main site, the outlying structures are rather anti-climactic, but the scrub forest is the perfect place to spot some of the Yucatán's more distinctive birds, such as the turquoise-browed motmot, with its pendulum-like tail. Look especially along the path that runs off the south side of the Palacio del Gobernador. The trail leads to an odd display of small **stone phalluses**, protected by a thatch roof – collected from all over the site, they're evidence of a fertility cult centred in Uxmal (they're also worked into the back of the building on the west side of the Nunnery Quadrangle). The largest of the phalluses is on display in the small museum in the visitors' centre. The **Pirámide de la Vieja** (Pyramid of the Old Woman), probably the oldest surviving building at Uxmal, is now little more than a grassy mound with a clearly man-made outline, while the **Grupo del Cementerio** (Cemetery Group) is also not restored. Nevertheless, traces of carved hieroglyphs and human skulls are visible in the low altars in the middle of this square.

Eating

If you're looking for lunch after your visit and you don't fancy the buffets at the hotels at the site entrance, numerous **restaurants** can be found along Hwy-261 towards Mérida, many of them catering mainly to tour groups. One good option is *Restaurante Cana-nah*, next to the otherwise dumpy *Rancho Uxmal* hotel, about 1.5km north of the site. The food is tasty and inexpensive, and diners are welcome to use the swimming pool.

Northeast towards Mérida

Between Uxmal and Mérida, there are few towns of any note, and with new roads being built and the old ones improved, it's possible to bypass virtually all the settlements en route. However, several restored haciendas offer compelling reasons to break your journey or even spend a night.

Just west off Hwy-261, about 30km north of Uxmal, the attractively refurbished **Hacienda Ochil** (11am–7pm; ⓣ999/910-6035, ⓦwww.haciendaochil.com) operates as a very good restaurant (standard meals for M$85), along with a small henequen **museum** displaying old photos and henequen at various stages of processing as well as a group of excellent *artesanía* stores and workshops. Some of the old railway lines along which carts of henequen were transported have been restored to working order, and you can also see the plant being grown; occasionally there are demonstrations of the entire production process. The entry fee of M$20 is waived if you're eating at the restaurant. For pure luxury, **Hacienda Temozón** (ⓣ999/923-8089, ⓦwww.luxurycollection.com; ⑨), about 8km off Hwy-261 to the east, is one of the grandest of the haciendas that have been converted into hotels; on its sprawling grounds you'll find two cenotes, a dramatic swimming pool and a gym in the old machine room. There is also a rather lavish international restaurant on the premises – its breakfasts, however, are not too expensive, and this makes a good early start to a trip to Uxmal, if you time it right.

Some 10km further north, **Hacienda Yaxcopoil** (Mon–Sat 8am–6pm, Sun 9am–1pm; M$50, kids free) lies on the edge of the village of the same name. At its height, the place employed four hundred people, but now the main house

Haciendas and henequen

The country all around Mérida is liberally dotted with the crumbling remains of old **haciendas**, an increasing number of which are being restored as luxury hotels, restaurants or tourist attractions in one form or another. The oldest of them had their origins as early as the seventeenth century, when Spanish colonists were granted vast landholdings on which they raised cattle or practised other forms of agriculture. The heyday of the haciendas, however, was the end of the nineteenth century and the beginning of the twentieth, when the henequen boom brought vast wealth to their owners.

A type of agave cactus from which fibres can be extracted for use, above all, in the manufacture of rope and twine, **henequen** is also known as *sisal*, after the port on the Yucatán coast from which it was originally shipped (though technically, *sisal* and henequen are slightly different plants). The great, spiky leaves are harvested by hand, taking just a few from each plant every year to prolong the plant's life. The collected leaves are transported to the **machine house**, crushed and shredded to extract the individual fibres; the introduction of steam-powered machinery to do this initiated the boom, and at some of the haciendas you can see the original nineteenth-century equipment.

Henequen still grows throughout the area, but is now processed only in small quantities: the market for the "green gold" that paid for so many of Mérida's grandiose mansions collapsed in the 1940s with the invention of artificial fibres, though by then the haciendas were already in decline from their high point between the turn of the century and the end of World War I – foreign competition and redistribution of land following the Revolution having dealt the first blows.

The bigger haciendas were virtually self-sufficient and self-ruling fiefdoms – some even printed their own money. Each had a grand house at the centre, where the owner or his overseer would live, with the machine room for processing nearby. Surrounding these were the workers' one-room homes, the company store (where many workers and their families were kept permanently in debt, from generation to generation) and other outbuildings including a chapel, pump room, stables, jail and, at the more enlightened places, a hospital and school. Some had a dedicated station on the main rail line, connected by narrow gauge lines on which the henequen and the processed fibres would be transported by horse-drawn cart.

stands in a state of picturesque disrepair – peeling walls, sagging ceilings and rooms full of mildewed tablecloths and faded pictures. If you're the only visitors, one of the employees will offer his services as a guide – this can be very illuminating (though only if you can understand Spanish), but it's also nice just to wander around the place, which is full of poignant corners. There's a water tank (used as a swimming pool) with changing rooms, a beautifully preserved old pumping engine by a well and lush orchards that you're free to wander, still watered by the original irrigation system. One room is dedicated to Maya relics unearthed when the plantation was expanding, with ancient carved stones, *metates* (used for grinding corn) and pots. Note the old machine rooms in a separate block – though beware of rocky floors and unprotected drops. If you really want to escape the crowds, there's a wonderful **room to rent** here, a huge, tiled, high-ceilinged space with two double beds, a fridge, coffeemaker, bathroom and terrace. You can cook over a fire or they'll bring meals in for you (Ⓣ999/927-2606, Ⓦwww.yaxcopoil.com; ❻).

If you're travelling by bus, *Yaxcopoil* and *Ochil* lie right beside the road, so it's easy enough to be dropped here and flag down another to continue your journey; buses to Muna, many to Ticul and any that pass Uxmal roll by.

The Ruta Puuc

From Uxmal, the **RUTA PUUC** continues south through the town of Santa Elena, a handy base for exploring this region. The road continues to the site of Kabáh, and shortly afterwards turns left (east) along a minor road to the market town of Oxkutzcab. The Maya sites of Sayil, Xlapak and Labná are all along this road, as are the Grutas ("caves") de Loltún and, with a bit of a detour, Hacienda Tabi.

If you're on a day-trip from Mérida, you can get from the caves onto the fast new highway via Mayapán (see p.256) without even entering the town of **Oxkutzcab**. However, if you're taking things at a more leisurely pace, want somewhere to stop over or are reliant on public transport, then either Oxkutzcab or **Ticul**, the larger, livelier alternative, are the places to head.

Many of the organized **tours** cover this route in the opposite direction, starting with a visit to the Grutas de Loltún and ending up at Uxmal in the late afternoon in time for a tour followed by the sound-and-light show. If you're staying at Uxmal or nearby and start early, there's a good chance of seeing the smaller Puuc sites when very few other people are around.

Two things seem particularly striking when visiting the Puuc sites today. First, though each has its unique features, the overall impression is of a consistent **style** – the geometric patterns of Xlapak are echoed at Labná; the masks with the upward-curling noses that abound at Kabáh are also seen – in slightly less profusion – at Uxmal and all the other sites. The other striking factor is the extraordinary change in **population**. Today, along the entire route from Uxmal

The Puuc style

As with Chichén Itzá, the **Puuc sites** were once thought to be the product of invading Toltecs from central Mexico, but are now accepted as being as authentically Maya as Tikal or Palenque. Though Uxmal is easily the best-known today, the less celebrated sites were originally more important. The earliest significant examples of Puuc style are found at sites like Oxkintok (see p.266) and Edzná (see p.281), but at the height of the Classic era it was the area around Kabáh and Sayil that dominated the region. Sayil at its height had a population of some 17,000 and the whole region, now barely inhabited, may have supported hundreds of thousands. Uxmal rose to dominance only at the end of the Classic period, around 800 to 900 AD, perhaps thanks to the city's relationship with the **Chontal Maya** of the Gulf coast lowlands, who became the Yucatán's most important trading partner by the Terminal Classic period (800–1000 AD). The Chontal Maya themselves traded extensively with Oaxaca and central Mexico and are thought to have passed on their architectural styles and themes to the Yucatán.

Each Puuc site has its unique characteristics, but they also share marked similarities in architectural and artistic technique, religious symbolism, hieroglyphic writing and settlement patterns – scarcely surprising since there were also great causeways (*sacbeob*) linking the main centres. **Puuc architectural style** is characterized by buildings of classical proportions, decorated with broad stone mosaic friezes of geometric patterns, or designs so stylized and endlessly repeated as to become almost abstract. The face of what may be **Chac**, the rain god, is everywhere. He must have been more crucial here than almost anywhere, for Uxmal and the other Puuc sites have no cenote or other natural source of **water**, relying instead on artificially created underground cisterns known as **chultunes**, jug-shaped and coated with lime, to collect and store rainwater. In recent years almost all of these have been filled in, to prevent mosquitoes breeding.

to Labná you'll see just one small town at Santa Elena; 1200 years ago, there were several hundred thousand people living here.

Santa Elena

The village of **SANTA ELENA**, sixteen kilometres south of Uxmal, and just seven from Kabáh, is worth visiting mainly for the magnificent view from its large **church**, which dominates the skyline for miles around from a position atop a small hill. Ask for the sacristan, who will open the door to the spiral staircase that leads to the roof. Beside the church is a morbidly interesting small **museum** (daily 8am–6pm; free) with displays on local funerary practices, including the 200-year-old mummified remains of four children that were discovered under the church floor in 1980.

Two exceptionally pleasant **places to stay** are located on Hwy-261 as it bypasses the village centre, making them particularly accessible – both are popular, so book ahead. The *Flycatcher Inn* (no tel, ⓦwww.geocities.com/flycatcherinn; ❺–❻, breakfast included), a B&B with seven rooms and a separate guest cottage, all decorated with local craftwork and furnished with lovely pillow-top beds; air conditioning is optional. It's about a five-minute walk south from the main square, or through-buses from Mérida will drop you on the highway very nearby. A little further south is *Sacbe Bungalows* (ⓣ985/858-1281, ⓦwww.sacbebungalows.com.mx; ❸–❹), where a hospitable Mexican-French couple offer basic but spotless bungalow rooms with porches, dotted about the spacious, lovingly planted grounds. There is also a very nice **camping** area (M$40 per person). For a small additional charge the owners will cook you a delicious breakfast and supper. In between the two hotels are two small **restaurants**: *El Chac Mool* does decent, inexpensive local food (closes at 8pm), while *The Pickled Onion* (Mon–Sat 1–9pm, Sun 5–9pm), owned by a British expat, has a more international menu, but also does excellent versions of local dishes, like *lomitos de Valladolid*; vegetarians will appreciate the fresh salads and the *chaya* soufflé. *La Central*, slightly further away in the village's main square, also offers good, simple meals. Note as well that, after the sound-and-light show at Uxmal, you may be able to hitch a ride back to Santa Elena with Uxmal's workers – check with your hotel, who may also be able to arrange some kind of shared transport.

Ticul

Located 80km south of Mérida on Hwy-184, **TICUL** is another good base for exploring the Puuc region, though not especially scenic. Historically an important centre of Maya shamanism, it's also a shoe-manufacturing town. Streets here are lined with shoe shops, and there's an annual Feria de Zapatos (Shoe Festival) in the fall – if you're in the market for some totally impractical sparkly sandals, this might be just the place. Thanks to its position on what used to be the main road between Mérida and the Quintana Roo coast (the newly upgraded highway via Mayapán now takes much of the traffic), Ticul is also an important transport centre, well served by **buses** to and from Mérida, and with services to Cancún and the east coast.

The centre of town is around the junction of calles 25 and 26, with a large plaza to either side, plus a massive church and several **hotels** in the immediate vicinity. Simplest of these is the friendly *Sierra Sosa*, Calle 26 no. 199-A, between calles 23 and 21 (ⓣ & ⓕ997/972-0008; ❸), where basic rooms have a shower and fan (upstairs is better), though air conditioning and TV are available. A smarter alternative is the *Plaza*, Calle 23 no. 201, between calles 26 and 26-A

(Ⓣ997/972-0484, Ⓦwww.hotelplazayucatan.com; ④), with TV, telephone and air conditioning in all rooms. But it pays to go slightly further afield, to *Posada Jardín* at Calle 27 no. 216, between calles 28 and 30 (Ⓣ997/972-0401, Ⓦwww.posadajardin.com; ④), which has four excellent-value cabins with separate sleeping and sitting areas, air conditioning, TV, fridge and coffeemaker, set in a lovely, bright garden with a small pool.

Ticul's best-known **restaurant,** *Los Almendros*, is the original location of what is now a small chain and claims to have invented *poc-chuc* and other Yucatecan dishes – unfortunately that's no guarantee you'll get a great meal, but it's worth a try. It's on Calle Principal, heading out of town towards Oxkutzcab, in a big building complete with a pool, and packed with families at weekends. Back in the centre, there's a good pizzeria, *La Gondola*, at the corner of calles 23 and 26-A. For an inexpensive *comida*, try the *Lonchería Carmelita*, at the corner of calles 23 and 26, or, as usual, least expensive of all are the *loncherías* near the bus station. For night-time dining, don't miss the *tortas* at the front of the market on Calle 23, between calles 28 and 30.

Buses from Mérida and elsewhere use a station directly behind the church at the corner of calles 24 and 25-A. **Colectivos and trucks** for Mérida, as well as Santa Elena, Oxkutzcab and surrounding villages, set off when they're full from various points in the immediate vicinity of the bus station – for Mérida, from around the corner of calles 24 and 25; for other destinations, mainly from Calle 25-A, alongside the church. Other practicalities are also central – the **Banamex bank** facing the plaza on Calle 26, just off Calle 25, has an ATM; directly opposite is a good **Internet café**. A small, locally run **tourist information office** (Ⓣ997/972-2350) can be found on the corner of calles 23 and 26, above *Lonchería Carmelita*.

Kabáh

The extensive site of **KABÁH** (daily 9am–5pm; M$35), meaning "Mighty Hand", stretches across the highway some 25km from Uxmal. Much of it remains unexplored, but the one great building, the **Codz Poop**, or Palace of Masks, lies not far off the highway to the east, near the main entrance. The facade of this amazing structure is covered all over, in ludicrous profusion, with goggle-eyed, trunk-nosed masks – to get into the doorways you need to tread over the masks' noses. Even in its present state – with most of the long, curved noses broken off – this remains the strangest and most striking of all Maya buildings, decorated so obsessively, intricately and repetitively that it almost seems the product of an insane mind. A couple of lesser buildings are grouped around the Codz Poop, directly in front of which stands a rare, working *chultun* (an underground cistern) with a concave stone floor gathering water into the underground chamber.

The other main buildings of the site lie across the highway. At first almost invisible through the trees, **La Gran Pirámide** is an unusual circular pyramid – now simply a green conical mound that, once you spot it, is so large you can't believe you missed it. It is thought that this Great Temple, erected on a natural elevation, functioned as a "house of the gods", where priests offered sacrifices or interpreted divine messages. Just beyond, a sort of triumphal arch marks the point where the ancient thirty-kilometre causeway, or *sacbé*, from Uxmal entered the city. Though only traces have been found, it is believed that such causeways once linked all the major sites here.

Leaving Kabáh, you may have to virtually lie down in the road to persuade a bus to stop for you, as they are often full or on a hell-bent schedule. Ask the guards at the site for the bus times, and be ready at the roadside looking desperate. Getting a ride with other visitors, though, is pretty easy, and with luck you may even meet someone touring all the local sites.

Sayil

A sober, restrained contrast to the excesses of Kabáh, the site of **SAYIL** (daily 8am–5pm; M$35) lies some 5km along a smaller road heading east off the highway, from a junction 5km beyond Kabáh. Once one of the most densely populated areas in the Puuc region, it is estimated that up to 17,000 people inhabited Sayil from 700 AD to 1000 AD. In the early part of that period, before the ascendancy of Uxmal, Sayil was probably the foremost centre of the region. Today the site is dominated by one major structure, the extensively restored, eighty-metre-long **Gran Palacio** (Great Palace), built on three storeys, each smaller than the one below. Although several large masks with protruding noses adorn a frieze around the top of the middle level, the decoration mostly takes the form of bamboo-effect stone pillaring – seen here more extensively than at any other Puuc site. The interiors of the middle level, too, are lighter and airier than usual, thanks to the use of broad openings, their lintels supported on fat columns. The upper and lower storeys are almost entirely unadorned, featuring plain stone surfaces with narrow openings. Water for the palace's inhabitants was once provided by eight *chultunes*.

Few other structures have been cleared, and those that have are widely scattered in the forest. The distances between cleared sites not only give a strong impression of how big Sayil once was – it's a brisk, sticky, fifteen-minute walk from the Gran Palacio to the Palacio Sur (see below) – but also mean there's plenty of surviving tropical forest here, and plenty of wildlife. You'll see birds of all sorts, including hummingbirds, and there's a chance of spotting monkeys and other larger animals, such as the racoon-like coati. From the Gran Palacio a path leads through the forest, past the piled stones of unexcavated remains, to **El Mirador**, a small temple with a roofcomb, and a large stele carved with the phallic figure of Yum Keep, god of fertility, now protected by a thatched roof. A signed turn-off leads to a group of buildings dominated by the Palacio Sur as well as the **Templo de las Jambas Jeroglíficas**, named for the uninterpreted glyphs carved all around one half-buried doorway. The **Palacio Sur**, when you finally reach it, is a large, little-restored structure with another characteristic bamboo facade, overlooking a ball-court, along with some unrestored mounds that make up the rest of the Grupo Sur and mark the end of the ceremonial *sacbé* through the site. You've actually been following this *sacbé* for much of your walk through Sayil, though there's little evidence of that fact to the untrained eye.

Xlapak and Labná

It's around 10km from Sayil to Labná, and just over halfway lies **XLAPAK** (daily 8am–5pm; free). Maya for "old walls", Xlapak is the smallest and least-visited of the Puuc sites, dominated by just one restored building, a small, elegant palace with huge masks above its doorways and at the corners. Between the masks, the walls are adorned with geometric patterns. The remains of a *chultun* can be seen on the far side. There's almost no signage at all at Xlapak, and from the palace unmarked trails lead through the forest to other nameless, half-uncovered mounds, again characterized by geometric patterns.

The ancient city of **LABNÁ** (daily 8am–5pm; M$35), historically far smaller and less important than Sayil, is in many ways a more impressive site. There has been more clearance and reconstruction here, so that the main buildings – the Palacio, the Edificio de las Columnas, El Mirador and the Arco de Labná – can all be seen as part of a harmonious whole. The **Palacio**, near the entrance, is similar to, though less impressive than, that of Sayil. Traces of sculpture include a crocodile-snake figure with a human face emerging from its mouth – thought to symbolize a god escaping from the jaws of the underworld.

The main sites are clearly joined by the remnants of a raised *sacbé*, the best-preserved portion of which leads from the Palacio to the **Arco de Labná**. Originally part of a complex linking two great squares, like the Nunnery at Uxmal, it now stands alone as a sort of triumphal arch. Both sides are richly decorated: on the east with geometric patterns; on the west (the back) with more of these and niches in the form of Maya huts or temples. Nearby **El Mirador** is a barely restored temple mound topped by the well-preserved remains of a tall, elaborate roofcomb. An inner passageway at one time led to the site's principal temple. Many of Labná's buildings were originally adorned with human figures; you can still see the lower half of one standing by the roofcomb of El Mirador as well as painted stucco remnants inside the "huts" atop the Arco. The last of the main structures, the **Edificio de las Columnas**, is a long, low building, its facade punctuated by five doors, characterized by the classic Puuc-style bamboo column decoration from which it takes its name.

Grutas de Loltún

The **Grutas de Loltún** (daily 9am–5pm, accessible only with guided tours, at 9.30am, 11am, 12.30pm, 2pm, 3pm & 4pm; M$20, plus M$30 for the tour) are the most impressive easily accessible caves in the Yucatán. The hour-long tours, most in good English, concentrate on strange rock formations and the patterns seen in giant stalactites and stalagmites (including the inevitable Virgin), but there's also plenty of fascinating history and some spectacular caverns. Mammoth bones discovered here attest to prehistoric periods of climate change, and the caves were revered by the Maya as a source of water long before they built their cities. At the entrance, a huge bas-relief warrior guards the opening to the underworld, and throughout are traces of ancient paintings and carvings on the walls. The surrounding jungle is visible through the collapsed floor of the last gallery, on which ten-metre-long tree roots have anchored themselves.

Outside you'll find two decent, if slightly pricey, **restaurants**: *El Guerrero* has its tables set out right by the exit from the caves (reached down the side road beside the caves); *Los Aluxes de Loltún* is on the main road directly opposite the entrance. Both have fairly standard Mexican menus, with tasty *panuchos* and the like. **From Oxkutzcab** (see below) the short taxi ride to the caves will cost you approximately M$50, or **colectivos** and trucks that pass the caves leave from Calle 51 next to the market. If you get there by 8.30am you may be able to catch the truck taking the cave employees to work. Getting back is more difficult, as the trucks are full of workers and produce, but if you wait something will turn up.

Oxkutzcab

OXKUTZCAB has all the facilities you might need, but not a great deal else; its main claim to fame is a huge daily **fruit market**, bustling in the mornings, where local produce, notably citrus, is sold, mostly by the crate or sack. The centre of town is around the junction of calles 51 and 50, where the main plaza and the *mercado* are separated by a hefty Franciscan church.

Buses to Mérida via Ticul (2hr) leave about every hour from the **bus station** on Calle 51 at Calle 56; colectivos come and go from Calle 51, beside the market. One clean, basic **hotel**, *Hospedaje Duran* (☎997/975-1748; ❷), is centrally located on Calle 51, opposite the market, but the *Hotel Puuc*, at calles 55 and 44, on the way out of town towards Labná (☎997/975-0103; ❸), is much preferable and only marginally more expensive. Its bright, clean rooms have air conditioning and TV. The Banamex **bank** on Calle 50, opposite the plaza, has an ATM, and there's an **Internet café** at the corner of calles 51 and 52. Basic **restaurants** and *loncherías* skirt the market area; for something slightly more upmarket try the *Restaurante Peregrina* at the *Hotel Puuc* or, in the evening, *Caffe Centro* on Calle 51, by the market.

The Ruta de los Conventos

The **Ruta de los Conventos** ("Convent Route") can easily be followed from Mérida as a day outing. Get an early start, then end with a leisurely late lunch at one of the destination restaurants along the way. Or if you've already explored the Ruta Puuc, you can head back to Mérida this way, starting in Oxkutzcab. The route itself is something of a recent invention by the tourist authorities, for although it's true that almost all the villages along the way do have impressive, fortified churches or monasteries – above all at **Maní** – the same can be said of towns and villages throughout the Yucatán. Nevertheless it's a worthwhile and enjoyable excursion, with a fascinating and wholly Yucatecan mix of churches, minor Maya ruins, caves and cenotes, set against a backdrop of small towns and villages that see relatively few tourists. If you follow Hwy-18 you can turn off to almost any town en route and find a vast, ancient church, but the highlights of the route are **Acanceh**, with its remarkable blend of ancient and modern; **Los Tres Cenotes** where, as the name suggests, three cenotes lie along the tracks of a hacienda's old rail system (the journey itself is much of the attraction); and the late Maya site of **Mayapán**.

The **churches** themselves date mainly from the seventeenth century or even earlier, when the Spanish were trying to establish their control. They were built so huge partly to impress, partly as symbols of Christianity's domination over traditional gods (often on the site of Maya temples, using the stones from the older buildings) and partly as fortresses and places of refuge in times of trouble – windows are few, high and narrow, and interiors are relatively plain.

Leaving Mérida by car, the easiest route is to take Calle 69 to the Periférico, and then follow signs to Mayapán. The improved highway – **Hwy-18** – that this takes you to bypasses all of the towns and villages mentioned below, but on the whole they're well signposted and only a short way from the new road.

Hacienda Tepich & Acanceh

Just 5km beyond Mérida's ring road on Hwy-18, **Hacienda Tepich** is the old henequen plantation in the town of Tepich Carrillo. The main house has been renovated just enough to be a functioning (and tasty) **restaurant** (noon–4pm) that specializes in rabbit dishes. Squeamish diners should probably go somewhere else, but anyone who appreciates locally grown food will also appreciate the fact that the live, pre-dinner rabbits are hopping around the grounds. There are other traditional Yucatecan dishes, too, whose ingredients are somewhat less conspicuous. Before or after your meal, you can stroll the vast, overgrown grounds. You'll have to ask for directions in town, and don't be deterred if the gates are closed – this is usually just to keep the horses in.

Another 7km beyond Tepich, **ACANCEH** (pronounced "Ah-kan-KAY") is somewhere that could exist only in Mexico. This town, with its extraordinary mix of Maya, modern and colonial architecture, almost entirely ignored by tourism, is in many ways a perfect introduction to the route. Penetrating through the scrappy outskirts of what is a sizeable town, you arrive suddenly at the central plaza where, beside the church – a sixteenth-century Franciscan

▲ Church and pyramid in Acanceh

construction that in any other setting would command your attention – is a large Maya **pyramid** (daily 8am–5pm; M$29). Behind this is a second smaller pyramid, and nearby there's a third – all of them surrounded by people's backyards and the everyday life of the town. At the top of the large pyramid, protected under thatched shades, are four huge stucco masks; though all four have been defaced they can still easily be made out. It's not known exactly whom they represent, but they are old (Early Classic or before) and some of the finest of their kind that survive: some say that the features show Olmec influence. Acanceh was an important Maya centre before many of its better-known neighbours were, reaching its high point in the Early Classic period (300–600 AD) before gradually declining in the face of the rising power of nearby Mayapán.

The ancient Maya **Palacio de los Estucos** is about four blocks away, behind the market (get directions from the booth at the main pyramid). Though fenced, it seems to be open all day and is usually deserted save for some truly huge iguanas. A long, low building, the palace may have been an elite residential complex as its name suggests, or possibly an administrative centre. At the top is a corbel-arched passageway and, under cover, the stuccos from which the palace takes its name. These are far from complete, but there are plenty of easily identifiable figures, animals and glyphs.

Los Tres Cenotes

The trip to **Los Tres Cenotes** ("The Three Cenotes") at **Cuzamá** is a significant diversion from the Ruta de los Conventos, and a time-consuming one likely to take at least three hours. For locals it's usually a Sunday afternoon jaunt; busy at weekends, the area is practically deserted during the week, though transport is always available. The starting point is the **Hacienda Chankanaan**, which you'll find by following signs to Cuzamá, beyond Acanceh. Almost nothing survives of the hacienda buildings, but the cenotes lie among the semi-abandoned henequen fields, reached by the hacienda's old narrow gauge rail lines. Arriving at the hacienda you'll be hailed by locals offering *carritos* (or *truks*), the rickety, wooden, horse-drawn rail carriages in which you take the trip (about M$150 per *carrito*). These can seat four or five in some discomfort, with no brakes, suspension or proper seats. The journey is roughly 45 minutes each way, plus as long as you choose to spend at the cenotes. Uncomfortable or not, you get a real sense of journeying back in time as you leave the road behind and head off along the wobbly tracks through the fields.

The first cenote, **Chelentún**, is the easiest to access, with a concrete stairway down to the water, but also the least appealing. The second, **Chansinic'ché**, and third, **Bolonchoojol**, are much more attractive, but reached by steep, terrifyingly rusty metal ladders, repaired in places with any materials that came to hand. It's well worth it, though, for the cool, clear water at the bottom – plenty of small fish testify to its cleanliness – and the spectacular views as sunlight spears through the narrow openings above. Bolonchoojol, in particular, is famously photogenic. To enjoy the trip to the full, do as the locals do and bring along a picnic, as well as swimming gear and towels.

To get to Cuzamá from Mérida, there is bus service (see "Travel Details", p.261), but you can also take a combi from the Parque San Juan – the ride takes two hours. You'll then need to take a *triciclo* taxi from the combi stop to Hacienda Chankanaan, another M$10 or so. If you're already in the area, look for combis in Acanceh.

Tecoh

Next stop along the Ruta proper, **TECOH** has another vast, fortified church on its plaza, but its main claim to fame is an extensive cave system, the **Grutas de Tzabnah** (Mon–Fri 10am–5pm, Sat & Sun 8am–5pm; M$30), containing no fewer than thirteen cenotes. This is a trip only for the cave enthusiast, however: there's no lighting except for the flashlights you and your guide will carry, and the caves are slippery, dark, low-ceilinged and full of bats. Taking the full tour involves crawling through tight, muddy passageways as well as various steep inclines where you need a rope. There are some impressive caverns along the way, and at the far end a welcome swim in the tenth cenote, but you'll get muddy and sweaty again on the way out – at least until plans to put in a staircase and lighting are realized. Not surprisingly, perhaps, there are few visitors except at weekends, when locals descend. Near Tecoh, you'll also see signs pointing you west to **Hacienda Sotuta de Peón** (Mon–Sat, tours at 10am, noon & 2pm; ⓣ999/960-8551, ⓦwww.haciendatour.com; M$250, M$125 for kids aged 3–12), just outside of Itzincab. In terms of dilapidation, it's the polar opposite of Yaxcopoil (see p.249), although fortunately it's not so well groomed that it's no fun. Set up as a sort of living history museum, the grounds are actually in use as a henequen plantation; a guided tour on a horse-drawn rail cart takes you to each point in the processing. Entrance is a bit pricey, but this also includes access to a cenote and a large swimming pool. As such, it's a good alternative to the cenotes at Cuzamá if you have smaller children.

Mayapán

Roughly halfway from Mérida to Maní, the ruins of **MAYAPÁN** (daily 8am–5pm; M$29) lie right beside the road. The most powerful city in the Yucatán from the thirteenth to the fifteenth century, Mayapán's history is in some dispute. According to Maya chronicles it was one of the three cities (the others being Chichén Itzá and Uxmal) that made up the **League of Mayapán**, which exercised control over the entire peninsula from around 987 to 1185. The league broke up when the **Cocom Dynasty** of Mayapán attacked and overwhelmed the rulers of an already declining Chichén Itzá, establishing itself as sole controller of the peninsula. However, archeological evidence suggests that the Maya chronicles must be wrong, as Mayapán does not appear to have been a significant settlement until the thirteenth century. The rival theory has Mayapán founded around 1263, after the fall of Chichén Itzá.

Whatever its history, Mayapán became a huge city by the standards of the day, with a population of some fifteen thousand (rulers of subject cities were forced to live here, perhaps even as hostages, so they could be kept under control), on a site covering five square kilometres, in which traces of more than four thousand buildings have been found. Its hegemony was maintained until 1441, when Ah Xupan, a Xiu leader from Uxmal, finally led a rebellion that succeeded in overthrowing the Cocom and destroying their city, thus paving the way for the fractured tribalism that the Spanish found on their arrival, making their conquest considerably easier.

What can be seen today is in some ways a disappointment, and certainly no match for the Classic Maya sites. The buildings, by Maya standards, were relatively crude and small – at best poor copies of what had come before – and only a small proportion of them have been restored (a visit doesn't take long). This has led to the widespread dismissal of the Mayapán society as "decadent" and failing, but a powerful case can be made that it was merely a changing one. As the priests no longer dominated here (hence the lack of great ceremonial centres), what developed instead was a more genuinely urban society: highly militaristic, no doubt, but also far more centralized and reliant on trade than any previous Maya culture.

The site has its undeniable attractions, too. If you've already been to Chichén Itzá, you may experience déjà vu: the main structure, the so-called **Castillo de Kukulkán**, looks like a miniature rendition of the Castillo at the larger site. Steep, narrow steps lead to an unshaded platform from where there's a seemingly infinite view across the surrounding plains. Low down at the rear of the building are stucco reliefs of decapitated warriors – there's a niche where their heads would have been, where perhaps the heads or skulls of real enemies were displayed. Elsewhere there are rows of columns, again similar to Chichén Itzá, as well as gaping snake heads protruding from staircases. Scattered throughout are numerous frescoes, carvings and stuccos (look for the thatched shelters), many with their original colours still visible. Keep an eye out also for the cenote – it's not one you can swim in (it's tucked underground, the entrance shaded by banana palms) but it's one of no fewer than 26 similarly small springs scattered across the ancient city.

Maní and around

Continuing south from Mayapán along Hwy-18, there's a string of villages distinguished by their huge fortress-like churches; most see few tourists and have no facilities apart from the odd general store. Many of the women here still dress daily in elaborately embroidered huipiles, and there's a real sense of traditional rural life. The churches are generally open during the day, though there's no guarantee of this.

Before reaching Maní, you'll pass a number of other small villages whose mammoth churches are pretty plain on the inside, though enlivened somewhat by a few naive carvings of saints. **Tekit**, a village otherwise devoted to farming, has some good examples of these, while at **Mamá**, the vast, crumbling fortress of a church is cathedral-like in scale, and probably the oldest on the route. Dedicated to the Virgin (celestial images around the intricately carved entrance represent the Queen of Heaven), it dates originally from the sixteenth century, but has been much altered and added to during the centuries since. If you can get in, be sure to look at the beautiful wall-paintings in the room behind the altar, as well as the cloister-style garden courtyard around a well. In **Chumayel** the rather smaller Templo de la Purisima Concepción has a brightly gilded altar set off by whitewashed walls, and at **Teabo** there's another monster-sized church, albeit not quite on the scale of Mamá. Beyond Teabo, an entirely new section of road extends towards Peto on the way to Felipe Carrillo Puerto and Chetumal, so take care not to miss the turn (by a giant Pemex station) for Oxkutzcab and Maní.

MANÍ, just 12km north of Oxkutzcab, is the most historic of the towns along the Ruta de los Conventos. Founded by the Xiu after they abandoned Uxmal, it was, at the time of the Conquest, the largest city the Spanish encountered in the Yucatán, though almost no trace now survives. Avoiding a major confrontation, Maní's ruler, Ah Kukum Xiu, converted to Christianity and became an ally of the Spanish. In 1548, one of the earliest and largest **Franciscan monasteries** in the Yucatán was founded here; this still stands, surrounded now by Maya huts. About the only evidence of Maní's past glories are the ancient stones used to construct it and the walls around the town. In front of the church, in 1562, Bishop Diego de Landa held an infamous auto-da-fé, in which he burned the city's ancient records (because they "contained nothing in which there was not to be seen the superstitions and lies of the devil"), destroying virtually all surviving original Maya literature. The monastery itself offers an enjoyable wander through courtyards and cloisters full of plants, flowers and old wells, while the church has some fine, elaborately carved altars and saints in niches. Maní has little else to offer beyond an entrancingly slow pace of life, though Méridans often come down here on day-trips to dine at *El Príncipe Tutul-Xiu*, on Calle 26, between calles 25 and 27, a festive palapa-roof **restaurant** that has been serving Yucatecan standards for more than thirty years (Tues–Sun 11am–7pm).

Travel details

Buses and combis

Few major buses originate in this region, as they tend to pass through on their way from Mérida to Chetumal or Campeche, and most of the local buses originate in Mérida. There is no first-class service to the area; ATS, Sur and Mayab operate second-class buses. Lineas Unidas del Sur covers the Ruta de los Conventos. Departures in Mérida are either from the Terminal de Segunda Clase (towns on the Ruta Puuc) or the Noreste Terminal (towns on the Ruta de los Conventos). Because Ticul is on a major highway, there's plenty of second-class service onward to the Caribbean coast.

Mérida to: Acanceh (8 daily, 5.30am–8pm; 45min); Cuzamá (7 daily, 5.40am–9pm; 1hr 30min); Maní (8 daily, 5.30am–8pm; 2hr); Mayapán (8 daily, 5.30am–8pm; 1hr); Oxkutzcab (12 daily, 6am–6.30pm; 2hr); Santa Elena (5 daily; 1hr); Ticul (12 daily, 6am–6.30pm; 1hr 45min); Uxmal (5 daily; 1hr 15min).

Ticul to: Bacalar (3 daily at 4am, 8.40am & 6.40pm; 5hr 30min); Boloncheh de Rejón (1 daily at 7pm; 1hr); Campeche (1 daily at 7pm; 3hr); Cancún (8 daily, 4.30am–1.30am; 8hr); Chetumal (3 daily at 4am, 8.40am & 6.40pm; 6hr); Felipe Carrillo Puerto (10 daily, 4am–1am; 4hr 30min); Hopelchén (1 daily at 7pm; 2hr); Mérida (14 daily, 4.30am–9pm; 1hr 45min); Oxkutzcab (21 daily, 4am–1.30am; 30min); Playa del Carmen (8 daily, 4.30am–1.30am; 6hr 30min); Santa Elena (1 daily at 7pm; 30min); Tulum (8 daily, 4.30am–1.30am; 5hr 30min).

Combis and colectivos

Given the short distances, it's usually much easier to go by combi or colectivo. They run more frequently than buses (especially in Santa Elena, where they're the only originating service), and prices are generally a tiny bit cheaper as well.

Mérida to: Oxkutzcab (2hr); Santa Elena (1hr 15min); Ticul (1hr 45min).

Santa Elena to: Campeche (5 daily; 2hr 45min); Merida (8 daily; 1hr 30min).

8

Campeche

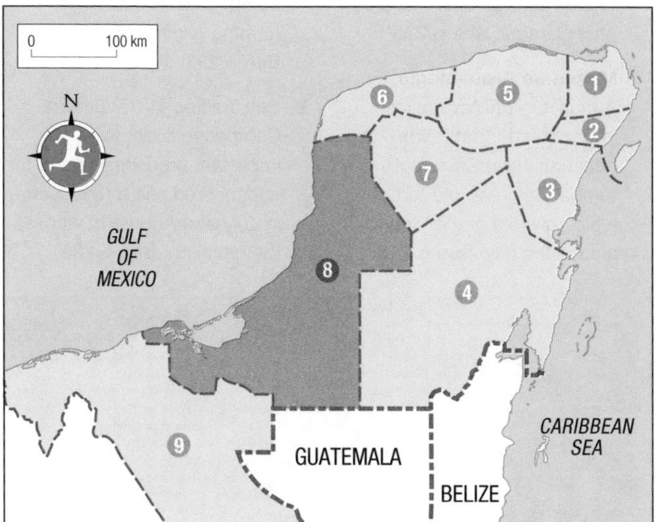
0
100 km
N
GULF OF MEXICO
1
2
3
4
5
6
7
8
9
GUATEMALA
BELIZE
CARIBBEAN SEA

CHAPTER 8

Highlights

* **Caves** Riddled with cave systems, the area includes two of the Yucatán's largest at Calcehtok and X'tacumbilxuna'an. See p.268 & p.285

* **Campeche's centro histórico** Surrounded by brash modern Mexico, this fortified colonial settlement, beautifully preserved as a UNESCO World Heritage Site, conjures past glamour. See p.275

* **Museo de Arqueología** A museum of Maya relics in Campeche that holds treasures from Calakmul's tombs. Set in an old fort, it also gives a grand view across the city. See p.278

* **Edzná** The Maya's mastery of the land is evident at this great site, whose ancient population was dependent on an elaborate system of drainage and irrigation. See p.281

* **Chenes sites** Home to a wildly decorative architectural style, in which buildings look like monsters or gods, complete with doorways forming gaping mouths. See p.283

* **Sea Turtles** The southern Campeche coast is an important breeding ground for endangered sea turtles; come in July and August to witness the hatching. See p.285

▲ A bulwark in Campeche's centro histórico

8

Campeche

The third of the three states that make up the Yucatán Peninsula, Campeche is far less visited than its neighbours, even though its capital city is a UNESCO world heritage site and the area's importance in the ancient Maya world grows ever clearer with time. The ruins of **Edzná**, **Oxkintok** and the **Chenes sites**, notably **Hochob**, are indeed magnificent, but it is the city of **Campeche** that is the region's highlight – a place that evokes an era when pirates were a constant threat, and the wealth of the Americas flowed through on its way to Spain. Today it combines the feel of Old Spain in its superbly preserved colonial centre, the frantic chaos of modern Mexico in its raucous outskirts and the hot, heady atmosphere of a tropical port that's half-asleep in the mid-afternoon.

Campeche State is located on the southwest part of the Yucatán Peninsula, where the coastline with the Gulf of Mexico curves from a north-south direction to east-west. The **main route** through the area is Hwy-180, which heads down from Mérida to Campeche and then around the coast via Ciudad del Carmen to Villahermosa. Hwy-261 takes a more leisurely course from Mérida towards Campeche, heading inland via Uxmal and Hopelchén, with access to the Chenes sites along the way. At Hopelchén, a minor road heads south through barely inhabited forest to Xpuhil. Hwy-261 joins up with Hwy-180 just south of Campeche, but then turns inland again towards the dusty junction town of Escárcega. Here it meets Hwy-186, which runs right across the south of the state – east via Xpuhil and the Río Bec sites to Chetumal, west and south towards Palenque and Villahermosa. There is a good **bus service** on all these major highways, with Campeche as the hub, but away from these routes the country is sparsely inhabited. In this area there's barely any transport at all, and, for that matter, very few roads.

Mérida to Campeche along Hwy-180

The direct road from Mérida to Campeche, taken by first-class buses and all *directo* services, is **Hwy-180**, which follows the line of the old colonial Camino Real, the Spanish trade route connecting Gulf ports with central Mexico. This is a fast, flat drive of 160km or so, especially quick if you take the superhighway for the first half of the journey. This road bypasses the most interesting stops on the way, however, including the Maya site of **Oxkintok** and the hat-producing town of **Becal**. Entering the state of Campeche the superhighway narrows, and there's a further worthwhile detour to **Hecelchakán,** where a small archeology

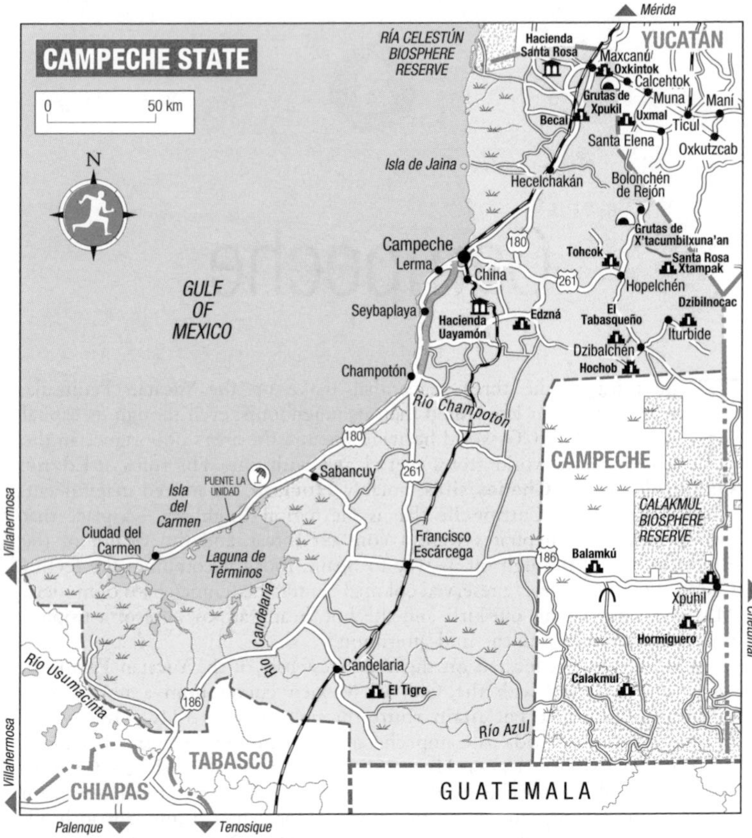

museum displays figures from nearby Isla de Jaina (the island itself is not publicly accessible) and other nearby sites.

The longer route follows **Hwy-261** for almost 250km past Uxmal and Kabáh (see Chapter 7), entering Campeche State near **Bolonchén de Rejón**. Much slower as it winds through the hills inland, this is also a far prettier route with a number of possible stops. Uxmal and Kabáh themselves could take the best part of a day, while several of the smaller Chenes sites are reached from **Hopelchén**. As you approach Campeche, Edzná is also not far off this road. It's easy going if you're driving, of course, and a bit slower – but still feasible – by bus, as many second-class services follow this route. With an early start you should be able to go this way, take in at least one site and continue the same day. Only Uxmal and Kabáh, though, actually lie directly on the road.

Oxkintok

Only recently excavated, **OXKINTOK** (daily 8am–5pm; M$35), in Yucatán State, is a large and beautifully maintained site, relatively little visited. The ruins are signed off Hwy-180, a few kilometres along a minor road that leads to Muna and Uxmal and then a dusty white track to the site itself. They are not easily reached by bus – you'd have to get to Maxcanú and take a *triciclo* taxi for several kilometres from there. Similarly, there are no facilities or shops of any kind nearby, so be sure to bring some water and perhaps pack a lunch; there are picnic tables under palapa shades near the entrance and further into the site.

Oxkintok was probably the dominant city in the region during the Early Classic period (c.250-600 AD), thanks in part to a strategic position among low hills which command the route from the coast at Celestún to Uxmal and Sayil, and also to Dzibilchaltún and the salt lagoons to the north and west. It is among the earliest of the Puuc sites, and although power later passed to the better-known cities further south, Oxkintok continued to be inhabited right through the Classic Maya era.

The site features three main groups of buildings: Ah Dzib, to the right as you enter; Ah Canul, to the left; and Ah May, directly ahead of you. Tzat Tun Tzat, the so-called "**Maya labyrinth**", is behind the Ah Dzib group, to the right of Ah May. All of the structures here are old – older than most you'll see at other Puuc sites – and for that reason are on the whole smaller, less decorated and perhaps a little cruder than those at the great sites. Nonetheless, this proto-Puuc style contains many of the seeds of the architectural forms that would reach their height at Uxmal. The **Ah Dzib** group is the oldest of all, dating mainly from the Pre-Classic era (c.300 BC–250 AD). The small ball-court here was equipped with a *temazcal*, a steam-bath similar to those still used by the Maya today, where players would undergo ritual purification before a game.

Sadly, the labyrinth – El Laberinto or **Tzat Tun Tzat** – the most famous individual structure here, is closed to the public, so you can no longer explore its sixteen rooms on three levels and numerous dimly lit passageways. It is a highly unusual building for this era, with its tiny windows and rooms: locals claim that there are tunnels, as yet undiscovered, linking the labyrinth to other buildings here, or even to nearby caves. This fits neatly with ancient myths that at Oxkintok there was an opening to Xibalba, the Maya underworld.

Between the labyrinth and the Ah May group, a damp depression, alive with plants, cacti and butterflies, marks the site of an ancient cistern, or *aguada*. Scattered around the site are also numerous underground *chultunes*, their openings usually blocked with flat stones or metal discs. The **Ah May group** itself, also known as the Plaza Suroeste, offers great views of the surrounding countryside, studded with unexplored mounds. The Palacio Junquillos (building MA-9) was built later than most at the site: its dressed-stone walls with simple bamboo-column decoration overlook a large plaza, very reminiscent of the style at other Puuc sites.

The **Ah Canul** group is the largest and perhaps most impressive of all. Most of the facade of El Palacio Ch'ich (CA-7) has crumbled, but a couple of columns survive, carved with human figures that still stand sentinel over the plaza in front of them. In the centre of the plaza, you can make out the opening to a large *chultun*, while adjacent to it lies the Palacio del Diablo, of which almost nothing remains save the column from which it takes its name, carved with a figure with two holes in the top of its head. The Spanish thought that horns had sprouted from these – hence the name. There were once many other human figures adorning these buildings, but neglect and easy access mean this site has been very heavily looted. The Palacio Pop (CA-3) is among the oldest structures at the site: on its floor, remnants of a painted palm mat design have been found (a palm mat, or *pop* in Maya, was a symbol of authority).

Around Oxkintok

More than twenty **cave systems** are found in the countryside around Oxkintok – some are single caverns, others huge interconnecting areas. It is suspected that many of them are further connected to each other in ways not yet discovered. There's plenty of evidence that they have been used by the local population since prehistory, as a place to live, a place of refuge (including as recently as the nineteenth century, during the Caste Wars; see p.332) or a place of worship. You may well be accosted at the entrance to Oxkintok by a local guide offering to take you to one of these caves, and if you have the time and are prepared for a bit of walking over rough ground, it's an opportunity worth taking (the guide will almost certainly speak no English, though).

One local cave, **Aktun Usil**, with its entrance in the middle of a field not far from Oxkintok, is a short drive on a rough track followed by a little clambering over rocks. It is named *ak-tun* (tortoise-stone) because the domed cavern roof is shaped like the inside of a tortoise shell. It seems that this cave was used purely for ritual purposes: no sign of habitation has been found, but there were burials, possibly of priests, symbols painted on the ceiling and found items including dozens of stingray spines, used for ritual blood-letting.

The best known of the local caves, though, are the **Grutas de Xpukil**, which some claim to be the largest cave system in the Yucatán; they're near the village of Calcehtok, signed off the road from Hwy-180 to Muna, not far beyond Oxkintok. You'll usually find someone to guide you at the entrance, and you are strongly advised not to go in without a guide, as there are no paths or lighting – just an alarmingly rickety metal ladder leading down into a hole. Nonetheless, the cool breeze emanating from the mouth of the cave can be motivating on a hot day, and the basic tour of less than an hour (M$200 for up to four people) will show you some impressively large vaulted caverns, in whose stalactites and stalagmites you'll find faces and the shapes of deer and other animals. It will also probably leave you pretty dirty (the guides love to claim that the mud you are covered in is actually bat guano, which may be, in part, true). Longer trips are real explorations and for potholing enthusiasts only, involving as they do a great deal of climbing, sliding and squeezing through narrow gaps.

Inside the caves all sorts of pre-Hispanic objects have been found, including obsidian knives, ceramics, sculptures and lots of bones, some from human burials. Anything of any value has long since been removed, but in some of the deepest caverns the guides still offer to show you human skeletons. There are also numerous *haltunes* – water-collecting basins carved out by the Maya.

Maxcanú, Becal and Hecelchakán

The old highway has been routed around all the towns it used to pass through, so you'll need to turn off to visit any of the following. Although there are motels and the odd restaurant along the highway, you'll find far more characterful places away from it. **MAXCANÚ**, the nearest town to Oxkintok, is a sizeable rural centre, but something of a backwater now that the highway bypasses it. There's little going on here – you'd probably only stop in to break up your journey or get something to eat – but you could take a look at the recently renovated church of San Miguel on the main plaza. Directly opposite the church's main doors is an incongruously fancy bar where locals enjoy good home-made **food**; alternatively, try the reliable *Restaurante San Valentín*, not far off the plaza beyond the market. If you want to **stay** in this region, just about the only option is the ultra-luxury on offer at the gorgeous *Hacienda Santa Rosa* (Ⓣ999/910-0088, Ⓦwww.luxurycollection.com; ⑨). Some of the eleven rooms here have their own private gardens and plunge pools, and there are extensive grounds with native plants as well as a beautiful main pool. You could also call in here for a meal, though since it's so small it would be wise to phone in

The Jaina figurines

The **Isla de Jaina** (which means "the place of the house on the water" in Maya) is the source of thousands of beautiful, detailed **clay figurines** that now grace the collections of museums throughout the world as well as at Hecelchakán and Mexico City. Typically just 10–20cm tall, the figures depict ordinary Maya as well as priests, lords, warriors and ball players, and they have provided a huge proportion of what is known today about everyday Maya life – what people wore, what they looked like, how they entertained themselves. The figures were placed in the graves of the people they depicted, often held in their hands or laid on their chests. Many of them also work as rattles or whistles, and clearly they were meant to accompany their owners to the underworld, perhaps as offerings or companions, or to make a noise to attract attention or ward off evil spirits.

Over 20,000 tombs have been counted on the island, and though some archeologists argue that they were the burial sites of local residents, it seems far more likely that Jaina was some kind of necropolis where people from all over the region were buried. Its western location may have been symbolic of the setting sun, or the island may have marked an entrance to **Xibalba**, the Maya underworld. Initially, perhaps, this was an elite burial place: early interments have few figurines, but of very high quality. As the burial location gained in popularity, the quality of the figures declined – increasingly they were made in moulds rather than entirely by hand, and they began to feature ordinary people as well as members of the upper class.

In many ways, however, it is these "lesser" figurines that are of most interest: they depict people going about their daily activities – weavers with their waist-looms, ball players at the doors of temples, dwarfs, musicians, the sick, the blind – and show clothing in great detail, revealing clearly that what people wore was dependent on their social status. They also record ancient Maya physical characteristics – short stature, hooked noses and straight hair – as well as artificial features like intentionally deformed skulls and teeth ornamentation.

The island was occupied throughout the Classic Maya period, from as early as 250 AD to as late as 1000 AD, though whether it was purely a ritual centre or a city in its own right is again a matter of some disagreement. In order to build here, the ancient Maya were forced to transport materials from the mainland: they did so in sufficient quantity to construct two substantial pyramids, as well as many lesser buildings.

advance to let them know. The hacienda, in the village of Santa Rosa, is extremely hard to find; it's off Hwy-180, near Maxcanú, about 10km down unmarked roads, past Granada. (For a more affordable hacienda option, press on south to *Hacienda Blanca Flor*; see p.270).

About 20km further, **BECAL**, just across the border in Campeche State, is famous for the manufacture of baskets and, above all, the ubiquitous Yucatecan **jipis**, or "Panama" hats (genuine Panama hats, confusingly, come from Ecuador). Like Maxcanú, this is a hot, slow-moving place where little seems to happen, but it's interesting to see a village so consumed with a single cottage industry – a fountain made of concrete hats even graces the town square. If you pull over here you're likely to be approached by a friendly local offering to show you round, which basically means being taken to a nearby hat shop – though you may get a short tour in the back of a *triciclo* thrown in, with a stop at one of the town's many *cuevas* (the cellars in which the villagers traditionally make and store their hats, where the damp, cool conditions keep fibres soft and flexible). Ask your guide to point out a *jipi*, too, the fibrous plant from which the hat-making material is extracted. There doesn't seem to be a great deal to choose from between the many hat shops; they all sell similar products at prices ranging from around M$120 to M$1200, depending on quality, which is mainly determined by the fineness of the fibres and tightness of the weave. The best hats can supposedly be crumpled into a ball and will spring back into shape.

A little under halfway from Becal to Campeche, **HECELCHAKÁN** lies just off the highway, where a road to the **Isla de Jaina** turns off. Despite the tempting signs, there's little point following the dusty road to the sea, as there's no access to the archeological site or the island itself, and the surrounding coast is windswept and entirely lacking in facilities. You can, though, view some fine examples of the Jaina figurines (see box, p.269), as well as many other objects from local sites, in Hecelchakán's small and recently refurbished **Museo Arqueológico del Camino Real** (Tues–Sat 8am–7.30pm; about M$29), housed in an elegant old mansion on the main plaza. The other side of the vast colonial square that marks the centre of town is presided over by the impressive church of San Francisco de Asís, a sixteenth-century foundation whose dome and towers are later additions.

On the plaza itself, among wonderful topiary hedges in animal and geometric shapes, a couple of *loncherías* serve tacos, *tortas* and juices for a quick lunch. If you're looking for **accommodation** around here, the *Hacienda Blanca Flor*, a short way north of Hecelchakán near the village of Poc-Buc (at Km 85.5 on the highway; ⓣ999/925-8042 or 996/827-0266, ⓦwww.blancaflor.com.mx; ❽) has sixteen large, comfortable rooms with air conditioning in a converted seventeenth-century hacienda. It was one of the first hacienda hotels (opened in 1988) and occasionally shows its age a little, especially in the bedroom decor, but it's set on a beautiful working ranch, complete with a nice pool and live animals, such as lambs, goats and horses. Simple but excellent meals are available.

If you're driving, you may also want to stop outside the prison about 12km north of Campeche – stalls along the road here sell excellent-value **hammocks**, all woven by inmates.

Campeche

Capital of the state that bears its name, startlingly beautiful **CAMPECHE** is one of Mexico's finest colonial gems. At its heart, relatively intact, lies a historical port town still surrounded by hefty defensive **walls and fortresses**; within them, interspersed with the occasional grand Baroque church, are elegant eighteenth- and nineteenth-century houses painted in pastel shades, hundreds of which have been restored to their former glory. Nonetheless, the place doesn't feel like an outdoor museum, with appliance stores and Internet cafés occupying many of the historic shopfronts. Around the old **centre** are the trappings of a modern city that is once again becoming wealthy, while the **seafront**, built on land reclaimed from the sea, provides a thoroughly modern vista.

In the past, few travellers stopped here, preferring to sweep by en route to Palenque or Villahermosa, though more visitors – almost entirely European – are beginning to spend at least a few days in the immaculately preserved and tranquil streets which compare favourably with Mérida's. For the moment at least, Campeche remains unblighted by tourist overkill, and though the city is growing, it's still the sort of place where businesses shut down for the afternoon. Here, *campechanos* live up to their reputation as some of the most gracious and friendly people in Mexico.

Some history

In 1517 a crew of Spanish explorers under Francisco Hernández landed outside the Maya town of Ah Kin Pech, only to beat a hasty retreat on seeing the forces lined up to greet them. Not until 1540 did the second-generation conquistador **Francisco de Montejo the Younger** found the modern town – which he named Villa de San Francisco de Campeche – and from here set out on his mission to subjugate the Yucatán. From then until the nineteenth century, Campeche was the chief port on the peninsula, exporting goods from throughout the region, but above all **logwood** (*Haematoxylum campechianum*, a tree also known as *palo de campeche* or *palo de tinte*), the source of a red dye called haematein, which attracted huge prices in Europe. Although logwood was planted – and still grows – throughout the Caribbean, the finest is said to be that from Campeche. The rapidly accruing wealth made Campeche an irresistible target for **pirates** (see box, p.272) until locals finally prevailed upon the Spanish authorities to fortify the city. Construction of the **walls**, with their eight massive *baluartes* (bulwarks), began in 1686 after a particularly brutal massacre of the local population, and the original defences were completed in 1704. Much of the wall has been demolished and replaced by a ring road, but two substantial sections survive, along with seven of the eight original *baluartes*.

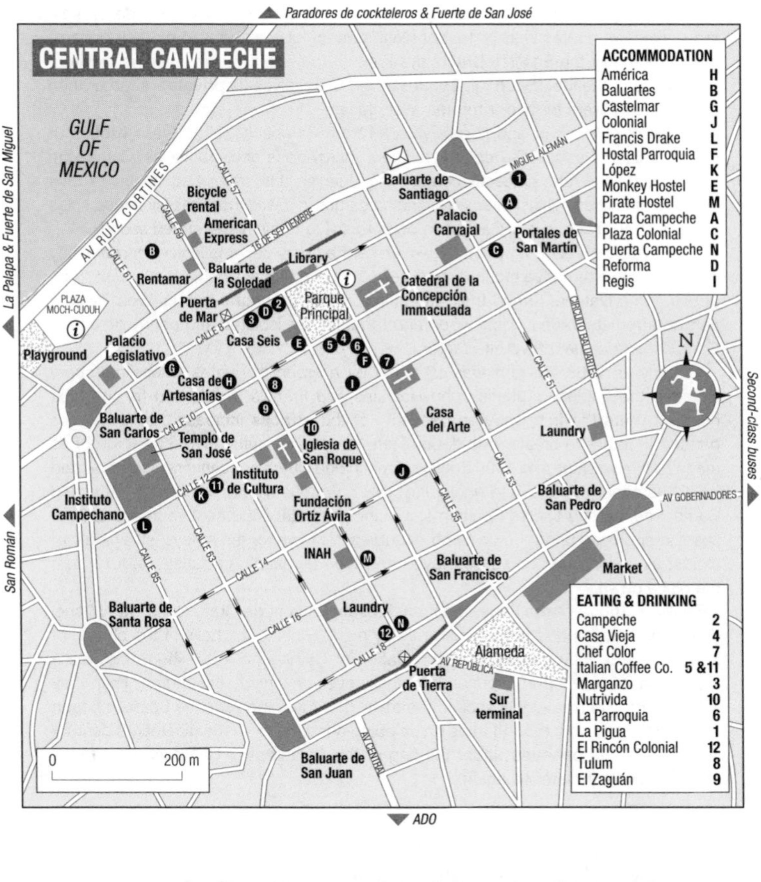

Arrival

Campeche has two **bus stations**, for first- and second-class services, as well as a separate minor terminal for local and rural buses, including those to Edzná. The **first-class** station, or ADO, is a little more than 2km east of the centre on Avenida Central. There are taxis outside (pay about M$35), or buses and colectivos (M$4.50). Of the buses and colectivos, almost any one immediately outside on Avenida Central should take you into town – look for "Mercado" or "Centro", and you'll be dropped at the market, just outside the historic centre on the landward side. The **second-class** terminal is about 600m northeast of the city walls on Avenida Gobernadores; you could walk to the city centre (turn left on Gobernadores) or take a bus: cross Gobernadores and look for anything marked "Centro" or "Mercado". You can get off here, and enter the historic centre through the Puerta de Tierra. Or you can stay on the

The pirates of Campeche

For about three hundred years, beginning in the mid-sixteenth century, the wealth of the Spanish colonies in America proved irresistible to **pirates**. Many were based in the West Indies, from where they could prey on shipping as it passed, but the Campeche coast, above all the sheltered waters and unpopulated islands of the Laguna de Términos around modern-day Ciudad del Carmen, was also a popular hideout. Despite their swashbuckling and violent reputation – far from undeserved – the majority of pirates were in fact at least semi-official, authorized by their governments (primarily the English, Dutch and French) to seize Spanish shipping in return for a share of the loot. Such raiders described themselves as **privateers** rather than pirates; many were former or future naval officers.

Cargos of gold, silver and jewellery sailed from Campeche, as did less exotic but equally valuable goods like cotton, feathers, hardwoods and, above all, Campeche logwood. By the late sixteenth century the Spanish authorities had begun to take effective measures against piracy by sending cargos in fewer, more heavily armed ships and assembling convoys in Caribbean ports to sail to Spain under armed escort.

The privateers were not put off, however: as their prey became less vulnerable they came up with alternative tactics – bad news for Campeche. Unable to ply their trade at sea, the privateers turned their attention to **raiding coastal towns**. Wealthy as a port and from its trade in local wood and tobacco, the isolated and poorly defended Campeche became a favourite target.

As early as 1568 the port was attacked by a group of pirates whose members included the English captains John Hawkins and Francis Drake, and for the next hundred years the frequency and severity of the **attacks** increased, as privateers banded together to create formidable fleets for joint assaults. In 1663 a force of as many as twelve ships and 1500 English, French and Dutch buccaneers – commanded by Christopher Myngs and including the notorious Henry Morgan – attacked Campeche, seizing twelve Spanish ships and over 150,000 pesos in treasure. Four years later a band under Lewis Scott occupied the town for three days, stripping it of almost everything that could be moved and then demanding a ransom not to burn the place down.

Finally, in 1685, a force under the French pirate Laurent de Graff, along with Michel de Grammont, invaded the town silently by night. Ringing the bells of the church of San Francisco, they gathered the population of Campeche – for whom this was a signal to assemble – and imprisoned virtually everyone inside the church. Then they systematically and savagely sacked the town. The following year, the Spanish began to fortify the city and, though raids on shipping continued into the nineteenth century (when privateers operated under the flag of the Texan navy), Campeche itself was never seriously threatened again.

bus – virtually all wait a bit here before continuing round the line of the city walls to the post office, nearer the Parque Principal and the sea. These are also the points of departure to get back to the bus stations: look for "Av Central" or "ADO" (first class) and "Gobernadores", "Universidad", "ISSTE" or "Terminal Sur" (second class). Some buses from **Edzná** and other local destinations such as Champotón use Sur's local terminal on Avenida República, just south of the market, by the Alameda Francisco de Paula Toro (a major promenade), a block from the Puerta de Tierra.

To get to or from the **airport**, about 10km southeast of town, you'll have to take a **taxi** (M$80). **Drivers** coming from Mérida will turn off Hwy-180 (which bypasses the whole city some kilometres inland) north of the city and drive in along the seafront. Unless you backtrack completely, leaving town can be a little tricky: the two main arteries are Avenida Gobernadores, running northeast out to Hwy-180, and Avenida Central, which runs more due east. Where it joins with Hwy-180, jog north a few hundred metres for the direct route to Edzná and Hwy-261 (the back way to Mérida), or turn south to continue to Champotón. The safe bet is to follow the seafront road straight south, to eventually wind up at the old Hwy-180; if you want the fast toll road south to Champotón, turn left at the Pemex and backtrack a few kilometres to the highway entrance.

Information and city tours

Campeche's **state tourist office** (daily 8am–4pm & 6–9pm; ⓣ981/811-9229 or 1-800/900-2267, ⓦwww.campechetravel.com) is in the tent-like building on Plaza Moch-Couoh, on the seaward side of the very mod Palacio Legislativo. It's helpful and there's usually someone there who speaks English. You can pick up brochures on attractions throughout the state, though specifics on activities outside the city are somewhat limited. They also have a list of independent **guides** (speaking various languages) who lead tours of the city and archeological sites, though you might be expected to provide the transport. The **city tourist office** is more accessible, right on the Parque Principal, on Calle 55, alongside the cathedral (see p.276); however, it's rather less organized and has fewer brochures. The staff is helpful for common queries. Smaller **information booths** at the bus stations, in the Baluarte de San Pedro and in the Casa Seis, are not always manned, but do have leaflets, maps and details of activities and tours.

For a concise overview of the city, take the **tranvía tour** on one of two open-sided buses that depart from the Parque Principal. The city route (daily, hourly, on the hour 9am–1pm & 5–9pm) is a 45-minute trundle around all the main sights and *barrios*, including outlying areas you'd be unlikely to walk to – it's especially nice in the evening, when the doors of the historic churches you pass are all flung open. The other bus runs south along the seafront and up to Fuerte de San Miguel (daily, hourly, on the hour 10am–1pm & 6–9pm), or north to the Fuerte de San José (daily 9am & 5pm). All cost M$70, and usually provide excellent live commentary in both Spanish and English (put in a language request when you buy your ticket).

Accommodation

Campeche's **hotels** are only just beginning to match tourist demand – there are relatively few to choose from, and those at the budget end can be shockingly shabby. The few decent ones are within a couple of blocks of the Parque Principal; a couple more upmarket choices are just outside the old city walls. In any case, avoid rooms overlooking the street, as Campeche's narrow lanes magnify traffic noise. There are also two good **hostels** and one super-luxury hotel. If you're looking in this category, you might also want to check out the *Hacienda Uayamón* (see p.283), 21km out of town on the way to Edzná.

América C 10 no. 252, between C 59 and C 61 ⓣ981/816-4588, ⓦwww.hotelamericacampeche.com. Set in an elegant colonial building with a small courtyard, the a/c rooms are actually rather chic and modern. With continental breakfast thrown in, they're a decent value, though you don't get a pool here, as you do at *López*. ❺

Baluartes Av 16 de Septiembre 128, between C 59 and C 61 ⓣ981/816-3911, ⓦwww.baluartes.com.mx. Of the two neighbouring, bland and modern hotels on the seafront (the other is the *Del mar*), this one is the better value, as it doesn't charge extra for water-view rooms. There's a large pool, but it's been overshadowed by construction on a new wing begun in early 2008 – a room on the south side will avoid potential ruckus. ❼

Castelmar C 61 no. 2-A, between C 8 and C 10 ⓣ981/811-1204, ⓦwww.castelmarhotel.com. A welcome renovation of what had been an exceedingly dumpy hotel. Saved: old floor tiles, large courtyard and soaring ceilings. Added: dull but modern bathrooms, a pool, a/c, satellite TV and free Wi-Fi. Continental breakfast included. Its style and value have made the 26 rooms very popular, so book ahead. ❼

Colonial C 14 no. 122, between C 55 and C 57 ⓣ981/816-2222. The only attractive budget place in town, but also one of the best hotels in the Yucatán: an airy courtyard building with conscientious owners who keep the place immaculate and running just as it did fifty years ago, only now with a/c in a few of the rooms, painted Easter-egg hues. It's vintage in the best way; book ahead. ❸

Francis Drake C 12 no. 207, between C 63 and C 65 ⓣ981/811-5626, ⓦwww.hotelfrancisdrake.com. This small hotel in a renovated colonial building has lavish rooms and a few suites (though they lack the high ceilings of *Plaza Campeche* and *Castelmar*). The staff here is particularly helpful. ❻

Hostal Parroquia C 55, between C 10 and C 12 ⓣ981/816-2530, ⓦwww.hostalparroquia.com. Next door to the restaurant of the same name, this converted colonial home has a good mix of attractive dorms (M$90 per bed) and private rooms with high ceilings around a very pleasant courtyard. Somewhat limited kitchen, but laundry services available; rates include continental breakfast at the restaurant. ❸

López C 12 no. 189, between C 61 and C 63 ⓣ981/816-3344, ⓦwww.hotellopezcampeche.com. A nicely renovated hotel catering to Mexican business travellers (complete with free Wi-Fi and a newspaper in the morning); modern a/c rooms are in a pretty Deco-era building with open halls. Continental breakfast in the café included, and there's even a small pool. ❺

Monkey Hostel C 57 at C 10 ⓣ1-800/CAMPECHE, ⓦwww.hostalcampeche.com. In a prime location on the west side of the plaza, this long-established backpacker haven has a helpful staff, clean rooms and a host of services, from laundry to local tours. Breakfast is included. Single-sex dorm beds are M$80; basic double rooms (❷) are also available.

Pirate Hostel C 59 no. 47 between C 14 and C 16 ⓣ981/811-1757, ⓔpiratehostel@hotmail.com. The public areas and general vibe are nice at this hostel, though the dorms (M$90) and private rooms (❸) are in a utilitarian new building in the backyard, behind the colonial place that overlooks the street; all other facilities match the competition, and the location is quieter.

Plaza Campeche C 10 at Circuito Baluartes ⓣ981/811-9900, ⓦwww.hotelplazacampeche.com. Immediately outside the old wall on the north side, the *Plaza Campeche* is a higher-end place with some character and friendly service – attractive, antique-looking furniture fills the large rooms, which have lux marble baths (including tubs). There's also a very small pool, a bar and wireless Internet. The same management's *Plaza Colonial*, on C 10 just inside the walls, has smaller rooms, but the same bathroom fixtures, for a bit less. ❽

Puerta Campeche C 59 no. 61, between C 16 and C 18 ⓣ981/816-7508, ⓦwww.luxurycollection.com. Located just inside the Puerta de Tierra, Campeche's finest hotel (by a wide margin) occupies the shell of a colonial home that sprawls down most of the block, all restored to maximize the romance of the past – the pool winds through crumbling walls, and the restaurant has a formal elegance that local business lunchers like, though anyone will feel comfortable on the breezy terrace. ❾

Reforma C 8 no. 257, between C 57 and C 59 ⓣ981/816-4464. A very basic, very central hotel with rooms around a courtyard, and a couple with balconies overlooking the city walls. Faded splendour would be the polite description of the decor (chipped and broken would be the less so); it's mentioned here simply as the city's cheapest option that's still remotely habitable. ❷

Regis C 12 no. 148, between C 55 and C 57 ⓣ981/816-3175. Seven very large rooms, all with a/c as well as fans, arranged around a small patio – a decent alternative to the *Colonial* or the *López*, and about halfway between the two in price. ❹

The city

Perhaps the greatest pleasure to be had in Campeche is simply wandering around the old streets or seafront – especially in the early evening, as the air cools, the lights come on behind the grilled windows of the old homes and locals come out to stroll, or to jog, bike or blade along the waterfront **malecón**, which runs for several kilometres north and south of the centre. Along the way plenty of museums, churches, mansions and fortresses punctuate each block, though only the **archeological museum** in the Fuerte de San Miguel could really be described as a "must-see" (note that it, and every other museum, is closed on Mondays).

As you explore, it's worth remembering that even-numbered **streets** run parallel to the sea, starting inside the ramparts with Calle 8; odd-numbered streets run inland. The plaza, or **Parque Principal**, is bordered by calles 8, 10, 55 and 57. Outside the ring of the old city wall, the grid system is less strictly adhered to; the **market**, immediately outside the wall on the landward side, is as far as you're likely to need to venture into the modern city except when you arrive or leave. Much of the city wall itself has been demolished and replaced by a ring road – **Avenida Circuito Baluartes** – but two substantial sections survive, along with seven of the eight original *baluartes* (bulwarks). The city defences were completed by two large fortresses, overlooking the city from hills along the coast in either direction: the **Fuerte de San Jose** to the northwest, and the **Fuerte de San Miguel** to the southeast. With the exception of the forts, everything that follows is within easy walking distance of the central plaza.

The Parque Principal

The obvious starting point for exploring Campeche is the **Parque Principal**, the city's main plaza, and the fine colonial buildings that surround it. It's at its

▲ Bicycling on the malecón

best on weekends, when the streets around it are closed to car traffic, and food vendors set up. Musicians play, and crowds flock to the *lotería* tables – Campeche's variation of this game of chance is more complex than most, with a much larger pool of cards. Just off the corner of the square, a musical fountain provides a pretty light show.

Chief among the monuments on the plaza is **La Catedral de Nuestra Señora de la Concepcion**, founded in 1540, the year the town was established, and one of the oldest churches on the peninsula. The bulk of the construction, though, took place much later, and what you see today is a relatively ordinary Baroque structure with bulbous white towers. Directly across the plaza, the **Centro Cultural Casa Seis** (daily 9am–9pm; free) is a mansion that has been restored to something approaching its nineteenth-century glory, with fine furnishings and paintings. Under the central patio is a giant cistern: rain that fell on the house was collected and could be drawn up from the well-like structure in the centre. Today Casa Seis hosts art exhibits and cultural performances, including musical *serenatas* most Thursday evenings, and there's a good café on-site, as well as a tasteful craft shop.

On the seaward side of the plaza, the **Museo de Arquitectura Maya** (Tues–Sun 9.30am–5.30pm; M$29) is housed in the Baluarte de la Soledad. The small but interesting collection of columns, stelae and stone details from Edzná and other local Maya sites are arranged by regional style, such as Chenes, Puuc, etc, which is extremely informative. Likewise, its presentation of a sketch outline of the decoration next to most of the carved stone helps train your eye to see the details. In front of the city wall, a beautiful building contains the well-used public **library** (with a good reference section that's open to anyone). Formerly the city's main barracks, this structure comprised government offices before it was destroyed by Hurricane Isidore and rebuilt as a library. On the fourth, inland side of the square, elegant *portales* (arcades) shelter a row of not very elegant shops.

Around the plaza

Leaving the plaza to wander the old city streets, there are a number of other grand old houses that you can see inside, many converted to schools, hotels or offices. Two notable ones include the **Palacio Carvajal**, on Calle 10, between calles 51 and 53, an elaborate Moorish-style colonial house that was formerly the city home of the fabulously wealthy owners of Hacienda Uayamón (see p.283) and now houses government offices (Mon–Fri). The other is the **Fundación José Ortiz Ávila**, in the former home of an ex-governor of the state at Calle 59, between calles 12 and 14. The Fundación contains Ávila's library and a huge collection of guns. Opening hours are a bit erratic, but entry is free and it remains open till late in the evening. The state offices of **INAH** (the national archeology commission), too, occupy a pretty old home on Calle 59, between calles 14 and 16 – there's a nice gift shop selling reproduction Maya pottery, plus a small exhibit on central Campeche's zoning and preservation issues. On Calle 55, between calles 12 and 14, look out for the **Casa del Arte** – not really a remarkable building, but its rooms are turned over to sometimes fascinating art exhibitions, all with free admission.

There are plenty of colonial churches, too, most of them open sporadically for services. Among the finest is the **Templo de San José**, at the corner of calles 63 and 10. Though it was begun in the mid-seventeenth century, many of the church's most striking features date from the end of the eighteenth, in particular the wonderful tiled facade. One of the mismatching towers also incorporates Campeche's original lighthouse. The church is now part of the

Instituto Campechano, so you can get in during school hours; you'll often find temporary exhibitions here. Another elegant sight is the church and monastery of **San Roque**, also known as San Francisquito, on Calle 12, between calles 59 and 61. The beautifully restored red gilt altars crowd the walls of the narrow chapel. The monastery portion now houses the **Instituto de Cultura**, which has an attractive courtyard where occasional art displays and concerts are staged (Mon–Fri 8am–9pm, Sat & Sun for special events and church services only).

The city wall and museums

Heading southwest along the old city wall from the Baluarte de la Soledad (the one facing the plaza) takes you past the flying-saucer-like Palacio Legislativo to the **Baluarte de San Carlos**, which has cannons on the battlemented roof and, underneath, the beginnings of a network of ancient tunnels that runs under much of the town. Mostly sealed off now, the tunnels provided refuge for the populace from pirate raids, and before that were probably used by the Maya. The *baluarte* houses Campeche's **Museo de la Ciudad** (Tues–Sun 9.30am–5.30pm; M$29), a tiny but rather lovely collection of local memorabilia that includes excellent silver, models of ships, an ancient ship's compass and the like.

From here you could walk right around the old centre following the line of the wall, but in practice it's much more interesting to cut through the old streets. Those on this southwest side, calles 57, 59 and 61, for example, are far less commercial than those around the plaza, with more of a sense of history. Calle 59 will lead you eventually to the **Puerta de Tierra** (daily 9am–4pm), the main gate on the landward side, which now sits in the middle of another well-preserved stretch of wall. It hosts a perfunctory pirate museum (M$30), but you can also pay just to climb up to the ramparts (M$10) and walk along the top of the walls in either direction, to the Baluarte de San Juan or the Baluarte de San Francisco. It's shadeless and exposed up there, but the views are intriguing; from the **Baluarte de San Francisco** to the north, you can look out at some of the busiest parts of the new town, along with the **Alameda Francisco de Paula Toro**, the Havana-inspired promenade next to the market. Head south towards the **Baluarte de San Juan** and turn in the other direction and you can gaze down over the neatly restored colonial facades to see just how much still lies derelict behind them. An optional audio guide (M$40) identifies some of the other landmarks you can spot from here. This section of the wall also hosts an enjoyable **sound-and-light show** (Tues, Fri & Sat 8pm; M$50, or M$80 with translation), starting from the Puerta de Tierra, which includes a walk along the wall in the company of the "soldiers" guarding it.

Beyond the city wall

If you take the city *tranvía* tour (see p.273), you'll see much of what's interesting outside the city wall. Perhaps most striking is the way that, to the northeast especially, the *barrios* of San Martín, San Francisco and Guadalupe look little different from the city centre, their streets lined with low colonial houses, albeit here in a much less glamorous state of repair. Indeed, these are some of the oldest parts of the city – the Iglesia de San Francisco marks the site of the first Mass given in Mexico, in 1517, in what was then the Maya settlement of Ah Kin Pech. There are good places to eat out here, including a number of *loncherías* under the arcades of the **Portales de San Martín**, not far beyond the wall. Nearby, another of the city bulwarks, the Baluarte de Santiago, has been adapted to house the **Jardín Botánico Xmuch'haltún** (Mon–Sat 9am–9pm, Sun 9am–4pm; M$10), with a small collection of native plants. A good destination for an evening stroll is the neighbourhood of **San Román**, especially its massive church, where the altar is dominated by an enormous black crucifix, originally set in place in 1565, when the church was first built. Head south on Calle 10 and look for the blue bell tower.

Substantially further from the centre, the two outlying **forts**, in opposite directions along the coast, require transport to get to. Each is wonderfully preserved, with a dry moat and cannons among the battlements that still look ready to blast approaching ships out of the water. The **Fuerte de San Miguel**, on a height overlooking the coast, some 4km southwest of the centre, is in fact one of the city's chief attractions, or at least the impressive **Museo de Arqueología** (Tues–Sun 9.30am–5.30pm; M$29) that it houses is. Though the information provided is in Spanish only, the beautiful relics, from all over the peninsula, speak for themselves. Maya artefacts from Edzná and Jaina predominate, including delicate Jaina figurines, many of which are cross-eyed (a feature that the Maya considered a mark of beauty). There's also some fine sculpture and pre-Hispanic gold, but the highlight is the treasure from the tombs at Calakmul. The most important of the burials is identified here (though the identification doesn't seem to be widely accepted) as that of the Calakmul ruler Jaguar Paw (see p.184); the jade death masks are mesmerizing and the jewellery and other objects that accompanied the dead fascinating. Look at the views over the ramparts, too, which are wonderful at sunset. To get here you can take a city bus along the coast road (look for "Lerma" or "Playa Bonita"), but that will leave you with a stiff climb up the hill to the fort. An easier alternative is to take the *tranvía* or a taxi on the way here and walk down to the road to get a bus back into town.

The **Fuerte de San José** (Tues–Sun 9.30am–5.30pm; M$29), completed in 1792, occupies a similarly superb defensive position on the opposite side of the city – it's immediately uphill from the *paradores de cockteleros* (see p.opposite), though the roads leading there are not so direct. Its museum contains armaments, scale models of the city and ships and sundry items salvaged from shipwrecks, such as centuries-old Dutch gin bottles, with Spanish-only commentary. While the museum is not as compelling as the other fort's, the view north to the green swathe of protected marshland is striking; also look south for the mammoth modern statue of Benito Juárez, Mexico's great reform president of the mid-1800s, on the next ridge. To get to the fort, look for buses marked "Bellavista", starting from in front of the Alameda, just south of the market – they make the climb all the way up the hill so you don't have to, going within a block of the entrance. A taxi from the centre costs M$25.

Originally, the city defences dropped straight into the sea, but now they face a reclaimed strip of land on which stand the spectacularly modern Palacio de Gobierno and state legislature building, a series of striking **sculptures** representing various aspects of the city – piracy, warfare at sea, fishing – and several big hotels. The area has been made less severe with the installation of a vast **playground** next to the state tourist office. It's a wild sight in the evening, when it's completely crawling with local kids.

If you're desperate for **beaches**, you could take one of the buses along the waterfront marked "Playa Bonita" or "Lerma", two seaside destinations not far beyond San Miguel, south of the city. But while Playa Bonita is the better of the two, with palapas for shade or to hang your hammock under, it's still pretty dreary – either crowded and rowdy on weekends or depressingly empty during the week.

Eating and drinking

Restaurants abound in the centre of Campeche, especially along calles 8 and 10. **Seafood**, served almost everywhere, is a good bet; try the *pan de cazón* (a kind of lasagne made with layers of tortillas and shredded shark meat) or shrimps (*camarónes*) in spicy sauce. For breakfast, the cafés along Calle 8, near the government offices, offer everything from tacos to fresh juices and pastries. Later in the day, the café in the centre of the plaza serves excellent coffee and home-made ice cream, and Campeche's **market**, just east of the walled city, is surrounded by *comedores* offering cheap and tasty lunches. Another local favourite is the stretch of *paradores de cockteleros* on the malecón, on the north side of town – hop in a cab or seafront bus to reach these seafood-vending kiosks that are open until around 4pm (6pm on weekends). At **night**, people head to Portales de San Martín (see p.277) for snacks. Bars aren't open late, but definitely stop by the rooftop terrace bar at *Puerta Campeche* (Fri & Sat only) for the gorgeous view.

Campeche C 57, on the Parque Principal. Large, unfussy restaurant next door to the *Hotel Campeche*, with an extensive menu of Yucatecan specialities and Mexican food in general, all at reasonable prices.

Casa Vieja C 10 no. 319, on the Parque Principal. Cuban-owned restaurant that serves tasty international cuisine with a well-appointed balcony overlooking the main square. Prices match the classy setting, but if your budget doesn't stretch to a full meal, you can just stop in for one of the excellent rum cocktails.

Chef Color C 55 at C 12. Cafeteria-style service and plastic folding chairs give this little lunch spot the feel of a church basement, but the home-made food – hearty dishes like pork with beans – is delicious, fast and cheap. Lunch only.

Italian Coffee Co. C 10, on the plaza. This slick café satisfies cravings for espresso as well as less traditional drinks, such as Oreo frappés; it sets out plaza-front chairs on weekends. Grilled sandwiches and assorted muffins are also available, though they're not cheap. A larger space, all gleaming brass and copper, is on C 12, between C 61 and C 63. Free Wi-Fi draws local teens and laptop drones, who fill the lounge chairs in the evening.

Marganzo C 8 no. 267, between C 57 and C 59. Somewhat touristy but pleasant nonetheless, and not as expensive as it looks. The varied menu includes tasty crab quesadillas and generous *botanas*.

Nutrivida C 12 no.157, between C 57 and C 59. Health-food store serving vegetarian and wholegrain snacks, sandwiches, juices and the like. Mon–Fri 8am–2pm & 5.30–8.30pm, Sat 8am–2pm.

La Palapa Resurgimento, 2.5km south along the malecón from the city centre. A good goal for a malecón stroll, this large bar is right on the water, and delicious *botanas* are served with every drink.

La Parroquia C 55 no. 8, between C 10 and C 12. Traditional, family-run café with high ceilings, echoing with the clink of dishes and buzz of conversation. Open 24 hours, with free Wi-Fi. You could easily eat all three meals here: delicious home-made yogurt for breakfast, daily lunch specials and lighter, toothsome evening snacks like *pan de cazón* and tamales. Check your bill – ten percent for service is sometimes added, sometimes not.

La Pigua Av Miguel Alemán 179-A ⓣ981/811-3365. Follow C 8 north beyond the wall to one of the city's most legendary restaurants, beloved for its elegant presentation of seafood. Not exactly cheap, but a bargain when you consider the quality. For dinner, make reservations if you can.

El Rincón Colonial C 59 at C 18. A charming old-fashioned men's cantina, complete with swinging doors and ceiling fans. Women get relegated to the ladies' lounge next door – not quite as picturesque, but it is air-conditioned.

Tulum C 59, between C 10 and C 12. A mellow, candlelit bar-restaurant in a colonial-style courtyard where you can eat baguette sandwiches and the like. *Tulum* usually hosts romantic crooners playing acoustic guitar or keyboard, and there's never a cover.

El Zaguán C 59 no. 6, between C 10 and C 12. Small, friendly bar-restaurant, with tables in wooden booths, serving inexpensive but good local and Mexican specialities, including *pan de cazón* and *mole poblano*. Closed Sun.

Listings

Airlines Aeroméxico, ⓣ981/816-5678 at the airport, operates a variety of internal flights.
American Express Inside the VI-PS travel agency, C 59, between Av Ruíz Cortines and Av 16 de Septiembre, near the *Hotel Del Mar*. Mon–Fri 9am–8pm, Sat 9am–1pm; ⓣ981/811-1100, ⓦwww.viajesprogramados.com.
Banks HSBC, C 10 at C 55, is just off the main square and has an ATM; Banorte is on the southeast corner of the plaza.
Bicycle rental Aventura (ⓣ981/811-9191 ext 405), on C 59 in the *Hotel Del Mar* parking lot, rents cruisers with baskets (M$25/hr or M$100/day) and can lead tours around town with advance warning. Rentamar (ⓣ981/811-6461, ⓔrentamar@aol.com), across the street, rents mopeds (M$100/hr).
Buses and colectivos Separate terminals for first-class services from ADO, Sur and others, and second-class Autobuses del Sur, ATP and TRP (see p.272). For buses that make stops on Hwy-180, or for Escárcega, Hopelchén, Bolonchén de Rejón and Iturbide (for the Chenes sites), you'll need the second-class terminal. Colectivos for the same destinations depart from Gobernadores as well – you'll pass the marked stops on the walk to the bus station. For Champotón, Seybaplaya or Sabancuy, go to the smaller, secondary Sur terminal by the Alameda (see p.273). For Edzná there are departures from in front of this same terminal (though they're not Sur buses) at 7am, 8am, 9am and 10am. You can buy first-class tickets at the Ticketbus office inside the Edzná Tours travel agency, on Circuito Colonias at C 8.
Car rental Maya Car Rental (ⓣ981/816-0670) in the *Hotel Del Mar*, Localiza in the *Hotel Baluartes* (ⓣ981/811-3187) or through Xtampak Tours (see below).
Internet and phone There are Internet cafés on every street in the centre of Campeche, most charging approx M$15 per hour. You can send a fax from Ah-Kim-Tel *caseta*, C 10, between C 57 and C 59.
Laundromats Good ones include Klar, C 16 no. 305 at C 61, and Lave Klin, Av Circuito Baluartes Norte, between C 14 and C 16.
Post office In the Palacio del Gobierno Federal, Av 16 de Septiembre at C 53 (Mon–Fri 8.30am–3.30pm).
Shopping Casa de Artesanías Tukulná, C 10 no. 333, between C 59 and C 61, is a particularly well-stocked craft shop, with items like tortoiseshell combs, fine Panama hats and Campeche-style *lotería* sets. Casa Seis, on the plaza, has a smaller but also quite fine selection. (With these options right at hand, the mega Bazar Artesanías, near the convention centre on the malecón, is not worth the walk.) The Librería Levante, C 12, between C 59 and C 61, next to the Instituto Cultural, is a wonderful place to browse glossy art books, though almost everything is in Spanish.
Taxis Taxis within the city are inexpensive. They're usually waiting at the bus stations, and there are taxi-stands throughout the centre, though they're a little hard to flag on the street. To call a cab try ⓣ981/816-2363, 816-2359 or 816-2355.
Tours and travel agencies Xtampak Tours, at C 57 no.14, between C 10 and C 12 (Mon–Sat 8am–3pm & 5–9pm; ⓣ981/811-6473, ⓔxtampac_7@yahoo.com.mx), runs trips to Edzná as well as longer outings to all the Chenes sites, Calakmul and more. Prices are reasonable – starting at M$180 for Edzná – and you can take transport only, or opt for a guide (M$700/day). *Monkey Hostel* (see p.274) also arranges budget tours. For regular travel services, airline tickets and the like, try VI-PS (see "American Express", above) or the agencies in the lobbies of the hotels *Del Mar* or *Baluartes*.

Edzná and the Chenes sites

Some 50km from Campeche lie the ruins of **Edzná**, the only local site reasonably accessible by bus (and even then, with a bit of trouble). Though this is an area where the so-called **Chenes** style of architecture (see box opposite) dominated, Edzná is far from a pure example of it, as it also features elements of Río Bec, Classic Maya and Puuc design (especially that of Uxmal; see p.245). Beyond Edzná, Hwy-261 leads towards Hopelchén and the ruins of Hochob, Dzibilnocac, El Tabasqueño and Santa Rosa Xtampak. These other sites are tough to get to unless you have your own transport, and often have just one important structure. However, the buildings are spectacular and there's a real sense of adventure in getting there – especially as you may well be the only visitor.

The Chenes style

Chenes **architecture** is characterized by highly decorative facades, often on relatively small buildings. Above all, it features buildings whose doorways form the mouth of a giant mask, created out of stone reliefs, that often takes up the entire front of the building. No one is quite sure who the mask is meant to be – some contend it represents Itzamná, the Maya creator god, in the form of a giant serpent, while other say it is a *witz*, a deity representing mountains and earth. *Chen* means "well" in local Maya and is a fairly common suffix to place names in this region, where towns have grown up around these sources of water. The Maya cities were no doubt equally dependent on wells, but they're not in evidence at any of the sites.

Edzná

Yet another Maya site that's far more impressive than its relative obscurity might suggest, **EDZNÁ** (daily 8am–5pm; M$39) reached the height of its power very early, in the Pre-Classic period from around 250 BC to about 150 AD. At this time, the flood-prone, marshy valley in which Edzná lies was transformed by a drainage system of canals, aqueducts (one stretching 12km) and reservoirs into highly productive, terraced agricultural land supporting a population of thousands. Handily located on major trade routes between the coast and the Maya highlands, Edzná became the dominant power in the region. After 150 AD, however, possibly as a result of war, the city declined and there was virtually no more building until the height of the Classic era, from 600 AD onwards. Most of what you see now dates from around 700–900 AD; you'll need a minimum of an hour to visit.

The main plaza of Edzná is dominated by the raised **Gran Acrópolis**, atop which stands the site's largest structure, the great **Templo de los Cinco Pisos** (Temple of the Five Storeys). A stepped palace-pyramid more than 30m high, each of its storeys contains chambered "palace" rooms: while solid temple pyramids like this are relatively common, as are multi-storey "apartment" complexes, it's rare to see the two combined in one building. At the front, a steep monumental staircase leads to a three-room temple, topped by a roofcomb. It's a hot climb, but the view from the temple is one of the most impressive in the Yucatán. On the way, notice the hieroglyphic inscriptions (as yet undeciphered) on the first four steps and, halfway up, three giant, crumbling masks. At the top, looking out over two plazas, the further on of which must have been capable of holding tens of thousands of people, it is easy to imagine the power that the high priest or king commanded. Beyond lie the unexcavated remains of other large pyramids, and behind them, the vast flat expanse of the Yucatán plain. Inside the west-facing temple a stele of the god of maize was illuminated by the setting sun twice a year, on the very dates when maize was planted and harvested.

Descend back to the Gran Acrópolis, where the **Templo del Norte** demonstrates two separate stages of construction; an original pyramid with stepped sides, and a later one finished with sloping stone. Behind it, the **Patio Puuc** has the characteristic column-like decoration of the Puuc style. Down in the main plaza itself, the clear lines of two ceremonial *sacbeob* can be seen leading away from the Gran Acrópolis. The **Nohochná** (*Casa Grande* or Big House), across from the Gran Acrópolis, is some 55m long and includes a room used as a *temazcal* (sauna), with stone benches and hearths over which water could be boiled. The steps on its front may have been used as seating for events and rituals in the plaza – the acoustics at the site allow you to hear

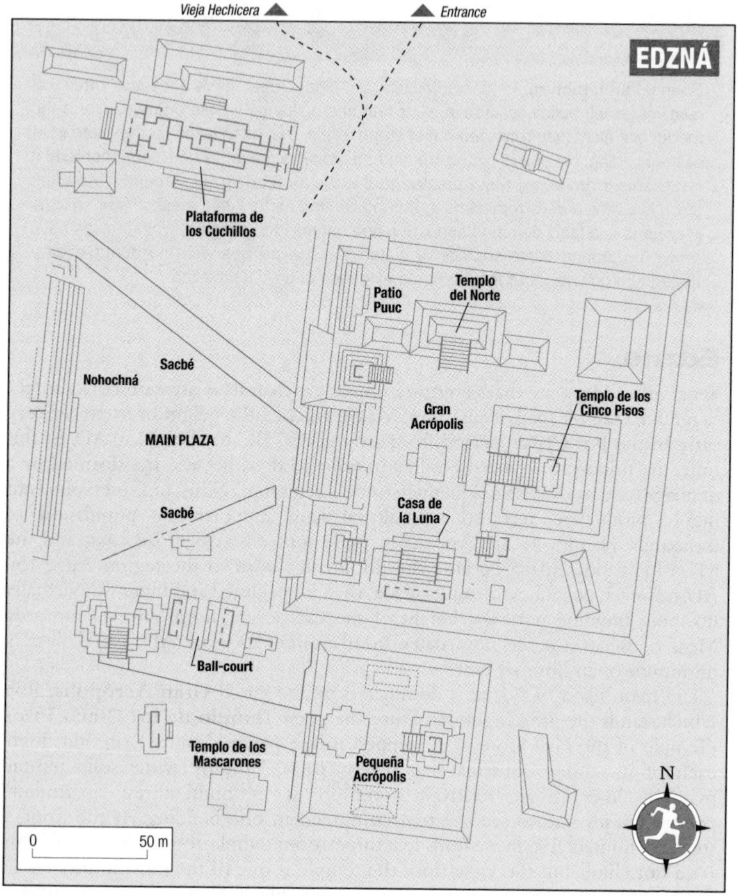

announcements made from the top of the Templo de los Cinco Pisos clearly. The buildings around the **Pequeña Acrópolis** are rather older and smaller, but impressively decorated, above all the **Templo de los Mascarones** (Temple of the Masks), where two haunting stucco masks represent the Sun god – rising on the east (left-hand) side, setting on the west. If you walk beyond this main cleared area, following the signs to the **Vieja Hechicera**, you'll get a better idea of the scale of the original city, and also of the challenges faced by its builders – there's a great deal of water and marshy ground here. At the end of the path, some five minutes' walk, is another large plaza, with a partially restored pyramid rising from it.

Practicalities

Buses leave from Campeche in the mornings in front of the Sur terminal on Avenida República, south of the market (see p.273); the last ride back to Campeche is at 3.30pm, but double-check with the driver on the way there. A **tour** with Xtampak Tours in Campeche (see p.280) doesn't cost a lot more, and gives you a little more flexibility with time. A **sound-and-light show** runs every Friday and Saturday (8pm; M$112) – it involves walking among the illuminated buildings, so wear good shoes. Bug spray and long sleeves help, too. Xtampak offers transport-only tours for this as well.

The only **accommodation** closer than what's in Campeche is at the wonderful and congenial *Hacienda Uayamón* (Ⓣ981/829-7257, Ⓦwww.luxurycollection.com; ⑨), off the fast road to Edzná (follow this route to bypass the village of China). Founded as a cattle ranch as early as the sixteenth century, its vast lands were raided by pirates in the seventeenth, but it reached its height in the nineteenth century, when its production of sugar, logwood and, above all, henequen, made it one of the largest, wealthiest and most famous haciendas in the country. Most of the rooms – each of them unique, and many with a private outdoor terrace and plunge pool – are in the old workers' housing scattered throughout the extensive grounds. There's exuberant birdlife here, and armadillos and other small animals are often seen around the rooms. Amenities from horse-riding to massage are on offer. The hacienda's **restaurant** is a good option for a romantic dinner – you can have a table set up on the terrace overlooking a centuries-old ceiba tree, its split trunks intertwining. Call ahead for a reservation.

The Chenes sites

Examples of true **Chenes** style are accessible only with a car or exceptional determination. The chief sites are reached from the village of **Hopelchén**, about 90km east of Campeche. Here a road heads south, newly paved all the way to Xpuhil; if you take it, be sure to fill your tank at Hopelchén, as it's almost 200km with very few services, especially as you get further south onto the newly paved stretch through tropical forest. Hopelchén itself has basic facilities, including a branch of Bancomer with an ATM on the plaza, and a simple **hotel**, *Los Arcos* (Ⓣ999/958-0260, Ⓔhiram_aranda@hotmail.com; ②), on the corner of the plaza at Calle 23, near where the buses stop. You might also want to check out the interesting wood altar in the eighteenth-century Church of San Antonio de Padua.

The first of the local archeological sites is **Tohcok** (daily 8am–5pm; free), right beside the highway, immediately outside Hopelchén as you approach from the west. This is no more than a single unrestored building, but it's worth five minutes as you drive past; the friendly site guardian will point out the main features in rapid-fire Spanish. The more significant Chenes sites lie off the road to the south. **El Tabasqueño** (daily 8am–5pm; free), reached by a 4km track from the village of Pakchén, and about 30km from Hopelchén, has a temple with a doorway in the form of the mouth of a monster (typical of the Chenes style) surrounded by hook-nosed masks as well as a tower, which is unusual. The most beautiful of the Chenes sites, **Hochob** (daily 8am–5pm; M$29), can be found 15km down a paved side road that turns off just outside Dzibalchén. Even this is very modest – it basically consists of a lovely little hilltop plaza with one very elaborately decorated building; other structures are buried, almost imperceptibly, in the dense forest all around. That decorated building (romantically named "Structure 1") is beautiful, however – a three-room temple (low and fairly small, as are most Chenes buildings) with a facade entirely covered in richly carved, stylized snakes and masks. The central chamber is surmounted by a crumbling roofcomb, and its decoration takes the form of a huge mask, with the doorway in the shape of a gaping mouth: hooked fangs frame the opening, while above are the eyes and to either side elaborate decoration on the ears. Surrounding the plaza are

▲ Detail of mask carving at Hochob

other small structures (including one with part of a roofcomb), their facades softly carpeted with green moss.

Dzibilnocac (daily 8am–5pm; free), the Place of the Painted Vault or of the Great Painted Turtle, is something of a contrast – a very large, flat site that is undergoing substantial restoration. Currently, little of it is open to view, but while there's nothing to match the beauty of Hochob, there are plenty of elaborate facades and masks typical of the Chenes style, and one very pretty little pyramid with a temple on top. Dzibilnocac is also the one Chenes site that's relatively easy to get to by bus. It lies on the edge of the small town of Iturbide (or Vicente Guerrero, as many of the road signs and buses know it), 18km down a badly potholed road from Dzibalchén, which has frequent second-class service from Hopelchén and Campeche. To be on the safe side, arrive early and check return times on arrival.

In the other direction from Hopelchén, Hwy-261 heading north towards Mérida passes one other Chenes site at **Santa Rosa Xtampak** (daily 8am–5pm; M$29), 32km off the highway on a rough paved road. Only recently rediscovered and partly restored, this site mirrors Edzná in size and importance, as well as in its history: it developed very early, around 800 BC – Xtampak means "old walls". Its style, too, is predominantly Chenes, but with Puuc and a variety of other influences. In its heyday there were no fewer than ten ceremonial plazas here, built across a naturally raised but artificially levelled platform. Numerous semi-ruined structures can still be explored, the most important of them being a three-storey palace. As at all of these sites, curly-nosed masks and doorways in the form of mouths are constant motifs.

Back on the main highway, you pass the **Grutas de X'tacumbilxuna'an** (Tues–Sun 10am–5pm; M$50, or M$80 with translation) shortly before Bolonchén de Rejón. This cave system is another that claims to be the largest in the peninsula, and certainly it's an impressively vast hole, some 350m deep, into which you descend. A newly installed sound-and-light show relates a tale of a wronged Maya princess and tantalizing descriptions of other parts of the cavern that you unfortunately never get to see. If you can muddle along with the Spanish commentary, it's an interesting diversion; paying the extra for simultaneous translation definitely places it in the realm of overpriced. **Bolonchén** itself is an attractive little town, with nine decorative wells outside its church (in fact, Bolonchén means "nine wells"), but offers no compelling reason to stop.

South from Campeche

South of Campeche, Hwy-180 splits into free (*libre*) and toll (*cuota*) roads. The old seafront route is winding and scenic, alternating between rolling hills fuzzy with sea grass and reeds, and striking vistas of the green Gulf waters; the only flaw is that it can be very slow, especially given the likelihood of tailing an underpowered delivery truck servicing the small towns along the way. The toll highway (M$53), however unremarkable, is straight, fast and easy. It ends just outside **Champotón**, a sleepy port at the mouth of the Champotón river that's famous for its seafood cocktails. Here, Hwy-261 heads due south towards **Escárcega**, where it meets cross-country Hwy-186: to the east this will take you past the Río Bec sites to Chetumal and the Riviera Maya; west it heads towards Palenque and Villahermosa, with the opportunity to turn off for **Candelaria** and the site of **El Tigre**, both in the wildlife-rich, little-visited valley of the Candelaria river. Hwy-180 meanwhile heads southwest to the Isla del Carmen and the steamy oil port of **Ciudad del Carmen**, en route to Villahermosa via the coast.

Along the coast

Leaving Campeche on the free **coastal road** you head first through **Lerma**, the city's port, with major oil facilities and a sizeable fishing fleet. There are some good fish restaurants here, but it's not an even remotely attractive place. Immediately afterwards you hit the town beaches at Playa Bonita (see p.278), then a long inland stretch of road winds around the hills, with occasional access points to the sea. From here on, southern Campeche State is low, flat, hot and monotonous; the white sand **beaches** frequently look tempting, but they're generally less attractive close up, with coarse sand and shallow water that smells none too clean. That hasn't stopped development here, though, and it's a little worrisome to see beach houses and resorts built right at the waterfront, with no allowance made for the flood plain that stretches inland for nearly a kilometre. There are usually thousands of shells, though, and the beaches along this stretch of coast, from Campeche all the way down to Ciudad del Carmen, are important breeding grounds for endangered green, Kemp's Ridley and hawksbill **turtles**. There are a number of places where the turtles are protected and where, in nesting season (May–Sept, but busiest in July and Aug), you may be able to witness the young turtles making their way to the sea. One such spot is **Xpicob** (Ⓣ981-812-5887, Ⓦwww.xpicob.com), where you can also rent kayaks – look for the turn between Playa Bonita and **Seybaplaya**, where the highway finally rejoins the coast. It's a torpid place that's home to dozens of small fishing boats and thousands of pelicans and other seabirds. There's another sea-turtle reserve here as well; visits, though, are probably best arranged as a tour from Campeche, as there may well be no one around if you just turn up.

The free and toll roads come together again near **Champotón**, a growing fishing village at the mouth of the broad Río Champotón. Here in 1517 a Spanish force under Francisco Hernández de Cordoba landed – having been driven away from Campeche and caught in a storm – to replenish their stocks of fresh-water. They were surprised by a Maya force and heavily defeated; Hernández de Cordoba died of his wounds a few days later, and the place became known as the Bay of the Bad Fight. Today it's more famous for delicious and fabulously cheap shrimp cocktails and *ceviche*, served up at *coctelerías* all along the surrounding beaches. Trips upstream, where there's kayaking, fishing and a chance to visit a couple of crumbling haciendas, can also be organized, most easily at one of the tour agencies in Campeche. If you do want to arrange one locally, enquire at one of the local **hotels**, the *Snook Inn* (Ⓣ982/828-0018, Ⓔsnookinnchamp-oton@hotmail.com; ❺), a modern, motel-style place with a pool, as well as TV and air conditioning in all rooms, or the *Hotel Geminis* (Ⓣ982/828-0008, Ⓔmarcastl@yahoo.com.mx; ❹–❺), somewhat older, simpler and cheaper, but also with a pool and optional air conditioning and TV. Both are on Calle 30 close to the main road, on the south side of the river's mouth, right by the bus station and market.

Most visitors heading in this direction turn inland at Champotón, on their way southeast towards Escárcega for Chetumal or Palenque. If you're heading to Villahermosa, however, opt for the improved highway south of Champotón en route to **Ciudad del Carmen**. Although this isn't really a compelling destination, the drive down the coast is fast and pretty, passing along some lovely stretches of beach. Though not actually a beach town (it's 2km inland from the coast highway), **Sabancuy** is quite pleasant, perched on a glassy green inlet that you can tour by boat with the fishermen moored by the village's little waterfront plaza. Further along the coast, **Isla Aguada** is another beachy spot that sees few visitors outside of Easter vacation; it also has a sea-turtle nesting site. Both towns have very basic hotels. Sabancuy is served by regular buses from Campeche, and you can get off at Isla Aguada on any second-class bus – you'll know you're there when you reach the Puenta de la Unidad (M$49 toll), which crosses the eastern entrance to the Laguna de Terminos, joining the Isla del Carmen to the mainland. If you're driving, be careful not to exceed the 50kph speed limit; traffic cops posted at either end of the bridge are notorious for demanding heavy fines on the spot. Locals fish off the bridge, and in the evening you'll often see kids holding up strings of fish for sale.

Ciudad del Carmen

The only town of any size on the 35-kilometre-long Isla del Carmen, **CIUDAD DEL CARMEN** doesn't merit a special trip except perhaps during Carnaval (the week before Lent), which it celebrates with gusto, and its lively **fiesta** in the second half of July, celebrating the town's namesake, Our Lady of Carmen. If you do wind up here, you'll find a place that offers occasionally bizarre contrasts. The conquistadors landed in the town in 1518, but the first real settlers, in 1633, were pirates (see p.272), for whom the island made an ideal base from which to prey on shipping. Nowadays, the money's in shrimp (a giant bronze prawn presides over one central traffic circle) and oil, pumped out of the Gulf. The industry has forced prices up, so you won't find many bargains.

Penetrate as far as the seafront **Plaza Central** (bounded by calles 24 and 22, parallel to the shore, and by calles 31 and 33), however, and there's a small-town Mexican feel, hot and crowded. A renovated malecón runs along the seafront, and from here the source of the town's growth is immediately apparent – there are oil rigs just offshore. In this seafront area, the few relics of the town's colonial past are also visible. To see what little of the old town survives, head south from the plaza to calles 22 and 25, where the pretty Iglesia de Jesús presides over the **Parque Juárez**, a beautifully preserved colonial square. North on Calle 22, near Calle 41, a small **museum** (Mon–Fri 9am–6pm; M$15) charts the history of the city; fittingly, there's also an exhibit about the wonders of petroleum, plus a small-scale pirate ship where kids can walk the plank. The main beach in town is **Playa Norte**, due north of downtown, about ten minutes in a taxi. The broad swathe of sand is very lively on weekends, though not particularly scenic.

Practicalities

Ciudad del Carmen is a very big place, but once you've found your way downtown there's no need to stray more than a few blocks. ADO (first-class) and Sur (second-class) **buses** use the same station on Avenida Periférica Oriente, a very long way out. To get to the centre, take a taxi or colectivo (5am–11pm; about 20min). There's a downtown ADO ticket office on Calle 24, next to the *Hotel Zacarias*. There's also a surprisingly busy little **airport**, not far off the highway east of town. From here, a taxi will be your only option. The **tourist desk** (Mon–Sat 9am–9pm) in the modern government offices on the malecón, in front of the central plaza, is helpful but not always manned and, though they have plenty of information on Campeche State, there's little about Ciudad del Carmen itself (apart from an incomprehensible map). You'll find several **banks** on Calle 24, just south of the plaza: Banamex and Bancomer, both at the junction with Calle 29-B, have **ATMs**, and there's another in the Ayuntamiento building, on the seaward side of the plaza. The **post office** (Mon–Fri 9am–3pm) is on Calle 22 at Calle 27. There's a handy **Internet café** in the Plaza Delfin, on Calle 20, across from the Plaza de Artesanías y Restaurantes.

Most of the accessible budget **accommodation** in town is around the plaza, near the waterfront. At fiesta time places fill up, so book ahead. The big, basic *Hotel Zacarias* (Ⓣ938/382-3506; ⑤), on the plaza at the corner of calles 24 and 31, has rooms with a choice of air conditioning or fan; *Hotel Victoria* (Ⓣ938/382-9301; ⑤), at calles 24 and 27, is a little more comfortable but not great value. More luxurious is the *Hotel del Parque*, on Calle 33, between the plaza and the waterfront (Ⓣ938/382-3046; ⑥), where all rooms have air conditioning, TV and a phone. **Food** in Ciudad del Carmen is a mixture of specialities from the Yucatán Peninsula and the more spicy flavours of the state of Tabasco, with an emphasis on shellfish. One of the nicer places to enjoy it is *La Fuente*, at calles 20 and 29, on the waterfront, a traditional Mexican café serving simple food round-the-clock (*cochinitas* on weekends are super-succulent). Immediately north of the plaza, a huge new white footbridge crosses to the malecón. At the landward end of this is the Plaza de Artesanías y Restaurantes, with more than a dozen small restaurants, cafés and *neverías* (ice-cream parlours), though not much sign of any *artesanías*. Another option is *Portal Regis*, in the pedestrianized section of Calle 33 by the main church, with tables right on the plaza and a lunchtime *comida*. More upmarket hangouts favoured by expat oilmen include *Los Pelicanos,* Calle 24, between calles 29 and 29-A, with a Tex-Mex menu and a well-stocked bar that's a popular early evening hangout, and *Il Giglio*, a pricey pizzeria nearby on Calle 24, opposite the *Hotel Victoria*.

Escárcega

The town of **ESCÁRCEGA** (officially Francisco Escárcega, though the full name is seldom used) is south of Champotón on the inland route, where Hwy-261 meets the east–west Hwy-186. Known as the ugliest town in the region, it has been given a superficial makeover with topiary in the medians and some new chain stores, but that can't disguise the noise of downshifting trucks and other traffic rumbling through at all hours. Unfortunately, it's likely you will put in some time here: if you're heading to or from Xpuhil and Calakmul along the Río Bec (see p.177), or by direct road to Chetumal or Palenque, this could be the spot where you'll have to make a bus transfer.

The **ADO bus station** (where OCC and some ATS services also arrive) is on the edge of town at the junction with the highway; from there to the centre and the **second-class bus station** (for Sur and other ATS buses) it's 1.5km straight east – a long walk or a short cab ride. In the **centre** there's a branch of Bancomer with an **ATM** on Calle 27, more or less opposite the Sur terminal, and there are numerous basic places to eat and some very grungy hotels nearby. Much better **food** options, however, can be found near the ADO. Of the cluster of restaurants around the junction of the two highways, try *La Teja,* on the west side and blessedly screened from traffic by lots of plants. If you need to **stay**, the gaily painted *Hotel Escárcega* on the town's main drag (Ⓣ982/824-0186, Ⓔhotelescarcega@hotmail.com; ❸–❹) has tidy enough rooms with air conditioning or fan, but if you definitely want your climate controlled, *Gran Hotel Colonial del Sureste*, a bit further east (Ⓣ982/824-1908; ❹), is a much better value. There's also a little **tourist office** on the highway at the western edge of town.

El Tigre and Candelaria

The site of **EL TIGRE** (daily 8am–5pm; M$24), 75km from the highway via a road that is very badly potholed in places, is a diversion that, even with your own vehicle, will take at least three hours plus time spent at the site. Not surprisingly, many people don't make it down here. If you do, yours may be the first name in the visitors' book for days.

El Tigre is often identified as Itzamkanac, which is where Cortés had Cuauhtémoc, the last Aztec emperor, executed in 1524; he also found extensive cocoa plantations here, and supposedly built many bridges. Certainly there's plenty of water: from the high ground the site occupies there are wonderful views over the Río Candelaria and its wetlands, and the ancient city had an important river port that gave it widespread trade connections. The port is being excavated, but is not part of the site you see. What you do see consists primarily of a small plaza with a ball-court below it. The main pyramid here has a huge stucco mask, and there are two more, similar to those at Edzná, on the smaller pyramid nearby. They're easily spotted because of their thatched protective roofs. Major excavation is ongoing here, with dozens of workers frequently on-site and lots of clearance work being carried out.

This new work involves relatively little reconstruction, and what there is uses different coloured materials so that what is original and what's new is immediately apparent.

The drive down here from the highway is an interesting one, through land that has been relatively recently settled and cleared of forest. In an attempt to help preserve what is left, the state government is promoting eco-tourism in the region, and you can get numerous glossy leaflets at tourist offices or in various hotels. Their efforts centre on **CANDELARIA**, a former railway town (the old station now sells women's stretchy clothing), where there's now not much action at all – you, the visitor, will likely be the most exciting thing in town. It sits on the Río Candelaria, lined with a fancy new malecón, though everyone still seems to prefer the plaza for a stroll. The river offers waterfalls and wonderful opportunities for observing bird and animal life. To date, however, there's almost no infrastructure to support the eco-tourism claims, apart from the ability to hire a *lancha* (small boat) through one of the **hotels** for a trip on the river. If you do want **to stay** here, the *Hotel Itzamkanak*, on the main road through town (Ⓣ982/826-0127; ❹) has decent rooms with air conditioning (though no ceiling fans), or the *Hotel del Bosque* (Ⓣ982/826-0395; ❸), signed just off the road as you come into town, is a simpler place with fan-cooled or air-conditioned rooms. If you do happen to come on a bus, you'll be limited to what's near the plaza: *Posada Santa Rosa* (Ⓣ982/826-0077; ❷) has cell-like rooms, but is at least clean and quieter than the bigger hotel directly on the plaza. For food, *Taquería Faby*, on the plaza, is cheerful, and *Restaurante Lupita*, next to the *Hotel Itzamkanak*, is a friendly spot serving excellent plain **meals** and an inexpensive lunchtime *comida*. **Buses** run from the second-class station in Escárcega (12 daily, 8.30am–8.30pm; 1hr 30min). To get from Candelaria to El Tigre via public transport, ask about combis in front of the hotel on the plaza.

Travel details

Buses

ADO, ADO GL and UNO are the major first-class services in the state of Campeche, augmented with service from ATS and Cristóbal Colón (OCC). ATS also runs *económico* service, departing from second-class terminals. Sur and Maya de Oro are the other two second-class bus companies, and for villages in the Chenes region and along Hwy-180 en route to Mérida, they're the only option.

Campeche on **first class** to: Cancún (11 daily; 7hr); Champotón (22 daily, 6am–11.45pm; 45min); Chetumal (1 daily at noon; 6hr); Ciudad del Carmen (at least hourly; 3hr); Escárcega (13 daily, 11am–2.20am; 2hr); Mérida (every 30min, round-the-clock; 2hr 30min); Palenque (7 daily at 11am, then 9.40pm–12.30am; 5hr 30min); Villahermosa (28 daily, 9.30am–3.50pm; 5hr 30min–6hr 30min); Xpuhil (1 daily at noon; 4hr). On **second class** to: Becal (every 30min, 3.45am–9.15pm; 45min); Bolonchén de Rejón (5 daily at 6am, 9.15am, noon, 2.30pm & 5pm; 2hr); Candelaria (6 daily at 6am, 7.40am, 10am, noon, 2pm & 4pm; 4hr); Champotón (at least hourly, 4am–10pm; 1hr 30min); Chetumal (2 daily at 8.15am & 10pm; 8hr); Ciudad del Carmen (7 daily, 5.30am–10pm; 4hr); Dzibalchén (12 daily, 6.45am–6.30pm; 2hr); Escárcega (at least hourly; 3hr); Hecelchakán (every 30min, 3.45am–9.15pm; 1hr); Hopelchén (12 daily, 6am–4.30pm; 2hr); Iturbide (9 daily; 2hr 30min); Maxcanú (every 30min, 3.45am–9.15pm; 1hr 15min); Mérida (6 daily at 6am, 8.15am, 9.15am, noon, 2.30pm & 5pm; 3hr 30min); Sabancuy (12 daily, 6.30am–7pm; 2hr); Santa Elena (5 daily at 6am, 9.15am, noon, 2.30pm & 5pm; 2hr); Seybaplaya (every 30min; 45min); Uxmal (5 daily at 6am, 9.15am, noon, 2.30pm & 5pm; 2hr 30min); Villahermosa (2 daily at 9.05am & 10pm; 8hr); Xpuhil (4 daily at 5.15am, 8.15am, 6.30pm & 10pm; 4hr).

Escárcega on **first class** to: Campeche (15 daily; 2hr); Cancún (21 daily, most after 8pm; 9–11hr); Champotón (5 daily at 5.50am, 10.50am, 1.30pm, 3.45pm & 12.50am; 1hr 30min); Chetumal (23 daily; 4hr); Ciudad del Carmen (1 daily at 9.45pm; 2hr 30min); Mérida (10 daily, most after midnight; 4hr 30min); Palenque (7 daily at 4.05am, 4.10am, 5.50am, 12.50pm, 11.35pm, 12.55am, & 2.20am; 3hr); Villahermosa (21 daily, but no departures between 8.30am–2.40pm; 4–5hr); Xpuhil (6 daily; 2hr). On **second class** to: Campeche (21 daily; 2hr 30min–3hr); Champotón (23 daily, 5am–4.30pm; 2hr); Chetumal (4 daily at 7.45am, 11.30am, 1.30pm & 10.30pm; 5hr); Ciudad del Carmen (8 daily, 4am–4.30pm; 3hr); Mérida (1 daily at 11am; 6hr); Sabancuy (8 daily, 4am–4.30pm; 1hr); Villahermosa (3 daily at 8.45am, 10.30am & 4.30pm; 6hr); Xpuhil (4 daily at 7.45am, 11.30am, 1.30pm & 10.30pm; 2hr 30min).

Flights

Perhaps because **Campeche** is so close to Mérida, its "international airport" currently has no international flights and only two flights daily to Mexico City on Aeroméxico. In fact, the airport at **Ciudad del Carmen** is busier, with one daily flight to Veracruz on Alma and at least twice-daily service to Mexico City with Mexicana.

9

Villahermosa and Palenque

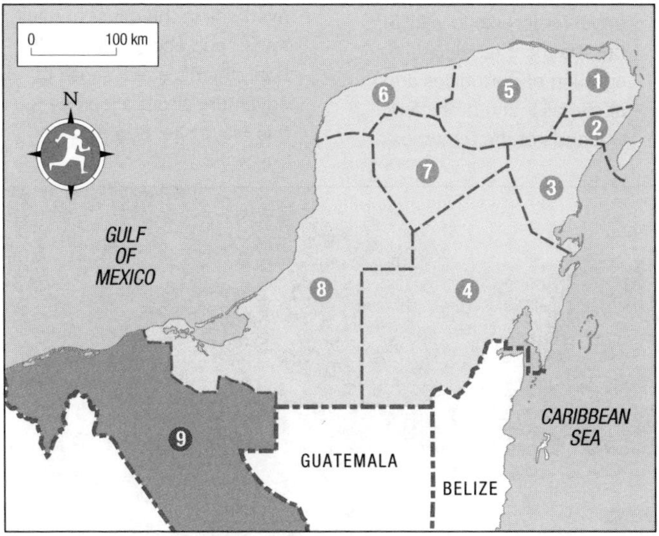

CHAPTER 9

Highlights

* **Parque La Venta** Don't miss the giant stone heads at this reconstructed Olmec site in the heart of Villahermosa. See p.303

* **Palenque** One of the Maya's greatest achievements, Palenque is striking both for its beautiful architecture and its dramatic mountain setting. See p.305

* **Wildlife** You don't have to travel far for exotic wildlife, but the most fabulous spotting opportunities are above all in the protected wetlands of the Pantanos de Centla and the unspoilt tropical forests that crowd the Guatemalan border. See p.295 & pp.317–321

* **Waterfalls** West and east of Palenque, a series of rivers running off the mountains forms a string of spectacular waterfalls, most famously at Agua Azul and Misol-Há. See p.313

* **Yaxchilán** Set on the riverbank in the midst of thick forest, and accessible only by boat, there's a real sense of adventure about a journey to this Maya site. See p.321

▲ Lanchas on the riverbank near the ruins of Yaxchilán

9

Villahermosa and Palenque

Though not technically part of the Yucatán, **Villahermosa** and **Palenque**, across the state borders in Tabasco and Chiapas respectively, are culturally and historically bound to the peninsula. There's no doubt that the great Maya site of Palenque, which sits on the very edge of the vast plain of the Yucatán, is intimately connected to the Yucatán Maya sites. The entire region, in fact, with its slow-moving **tropical rivers** making their way to the Gulf, was a vital trade highway for the ancient Maya, as it was for the Olmec before them. In addition to Palenque, the region boasts important Maya sites at **Bonampak** and **Yaxchilán**, on the banks of the mighty **Río Usumacinta**, as well as at **Toniná**, higher in the mountains near the town of **Ocosingo**. All of these, as well as the magnificent **waterfalls** that tumble down alongside the road from Ocosingo to Palenque, can easily be visited on day-trips if you're based at Palenque.

Villahermosa, capital of Tabasco, is by far the largest city in the region, busy and wealthy from the oil that's extracted all over the state. It's also a virtually unavoidable road junction, especially if you're travelling by bus. At its supreme attraction, the Parque La Venta, you'll find the most important objects from the Olmec site of La Venta (including the giant basalt heads for which the Olmec culture is primarily known) displayed in a steamy jungle setting. This is one of the very few opportunities to see anything created by the Olmecs, the predecessors of the Maya.

Not far from Villahermosa, the Maya site of **Comalcalco** lies en route to the coast. Here, an abundance of clay and shortage of stone meant that the Maya constructed their pyramids from bricks, making for an extraordinary and unexpected site. The **coast** itself, with alternating estuaries and sand bars, salt marshes and lagoons, is well off the beaten track. A road runs very close to the shore, however, enabling you to reach the deserted beaches. These have somewhat limited facilities – even the main coastal town, **Paraíso**, is a tiny place.

This area is also exceptionally rich in **wildlife**, which you'll experience above all if you visit Bonampak or Yaxchilán, off the Frontier Highway at the edge of Mexico's last unspoilt tropical forests. Though development is making inroads at a frightening pace, vast tracts of forest are protected, and a little adventure will guarantee some exotic sightings. Monkeys are common

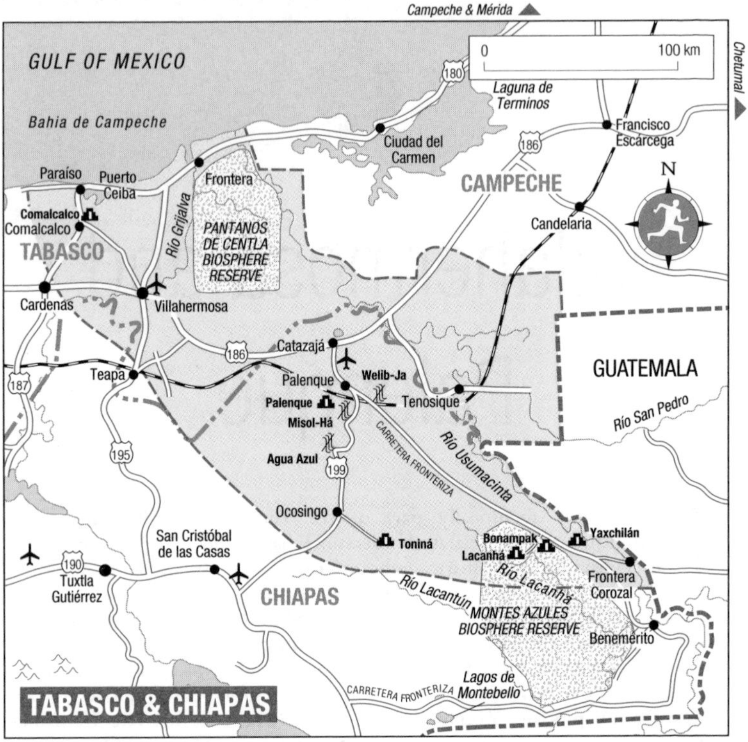

at many of the sites, as are birds of every description and crocodiles basking on the banks of the Río Usumacinta. As they approach the sea, the rivers come together to form vast flood plains where natural reserves have been established, most accessibly at the Pantanos de Centla Biosphere Reserve, to protect the unique flora and fauna.

En route to Villahermosa

Despite the best efforts of the state tourist board, few visitors view the state of Tabasco as more than a transit corridor to Palenque; most people have to change buses in Villahermosa. There are a couple of worthwhile stops, though, especially if you're coming from Campeche via **the coast**. This is a beautiful drive passing through a spectacular wildlife area, the **Pantanos de Centla Biosphere Reserve**, and it's never hard to find deserted beaches and lagoons. If you hug the coast the whole way (instead of turning inland after Frontera), you'll pass the unique ruins of **Comalcalco**, on the road south to Villahermosa. They're a fascinating contrast to the Yucatán's limestone ruins, and even merit a day-trip out from Villahermosa, especially if you combine them with a jaunt to one of the local **cacao haciendas**.

Frontera and the Pantanos de Centla Biosphere Reserve

Baking and half-asleep, the town and working port of **FRONTERA**, about 90km west of Ciudad del Carmen, seems unchanged since Graham Greene visited in 1938 and immortalized it in *The Lawless Roads*: "The carcasses of old stranded steamers held up the banks. And then around a bend in the river Frontera…a white blanched street running off between wooden shacks." In fact, it was at the time the main port for southern Mexico, with river steamers providing the only access to the roadless interior.

Modern advances in highways and trucks now mean the sole reason for staying in Frontera is to visit the 17,200-square-kilometre **PANTANOS DE CENTLA BIOSPHERE RESERVE**, a vast wetland area positively teeming with wildlife. Among the more exotic species here (few of which you are actually likely to encounter) are jaguar and tapir, osprey and tiger heron, and, in the water, manatee and crocodile. But there are also hundreds of bird species, especially in the lush marshy waterways accessible by boat, and the mangrove forests are full of rare orchids. To get there you will almost certainly need your own transport, unless you're lucky enough to catch one of the few combis to Jonuta – head through Frontera and continue west on the highway a few kilometres, then take the Jonuta road, just before the huge bridge over the river. Ten kilometres south, on the riverbank, the Desarrollo Ecoturístico Punta Manglar (open daily, but most activities available only at weekends; ⓣ913/398-1688) offers guided walks, canoe and ferry trips and other educational **activities** in the reserve, plus it has a small **restaurant**. A few kilometres further down, the Centro de Interpretación Uyotot-Já (ⓣ913/131-3274; M$20 admission includes a guided tour) is a

▲ Wild crocodile in the Yucatán

somewhat larger tourist centre with an observation tower, restaurant, boat trips (from about M$500 for up to ten people) and walkways over the marshy riverbanks. There are also a few perfectly functional cabañas here for **spending the night**.

Practicalities

Frontera offers little in the way of excitement – with time on your hands the best thing to do is head to the mouth of the Río Grijalva and the picturesque, palm-filled **Playa del Bosque**, about 12km north and easily accessible by local bus or combi. In town, virtually everything you'll need is around the plaza, including banks and a couple of nondescript **hotels**; the *Marmor Plaza* (Ⓣ913/332-0001; ④) on Juárez, just left of the delicate Gothic-style church, is the best option, with reasonable-value, air-conditioned rooms. For tasty shrimp or an inexpensive *comida*, try *El Conquistador*, in a crumbling colonial building on the opposite side of the church. The **bus stations** are pretty handy: arriving by second-class bus, turn left out of the terminus and walk two blocks along Madero to get to the plaza; from first-class head left along Zaragoza, then right, and walk three blocks down Madero to approach from the other direction. There are frequent services to Villahermosa and Ciudad del Carmen.

The Tabasco coast

About 30km west of Frontera, Hwy-180 turns south and inland – this is the route fast buses take to Villahermosa. If you continue straight west, however, you wind up on a little-travelled **coastal route** that skirts the ocean and passes through wetland areas. Mangrove swamps and lagoons formed by the deltas of the great Usumacinta and Grijalva rivers are covered with flocks of feeding waterbirds, and if you look hard enough you may spot the odd crocodile. However, if it's beaches you've come for, you should adjust your expectations – the sand is grey-brown and, though generally clean, you're rarely out of sight of the refinery or other oil installations. The real appeal of the area is simply being somewhere that virtually no tourists make it to. There are few hotels along this stretch, but plenty of spaces for **camping** – often amid swarms of mosquitoes and sandflies. With your own vehicle you could pretty much pick your spot; on public transport the coast is harder to get to, though many local villages are well served, and from any one of them a *triciclo* (these are abundant, and many of them are motorized) can take you wherever you wish.

Two of the most obvious beaches to head for are **Playa Pico de Oro**, a quiet stretch about 20km along the road, and a few kilometres north of the main road. Further along, **Playa Azul** is a favourite for watersports enthusiasts. The beaches *look* magnificent – seemingly endless fine sand strands backed by palms, with palapa shelters for shade – but you may find them deserted and windswept or, during holiday times, packed with rowdy crowds and litter. West of Laguna Santa and Laguna de Mecoacán, the village of **Puerto Ceiba** has a *parador turístico* that offers ferry trips and outdoor activities. Dozens of palapa seafood restaurants serve fish straight out of the lake, many of them concentrated at El Bellote, just outside Puerto Ceiba by the bridge across the lagoon (though you can't miss the views of oil refineries).

Paraíso

After Puerto Ceiba, the road widens into a divided highway, leading into the larger town of **PARAÍSO**, a weekend escape for Villahermosa denizens on the banks of the Río Seco. It's a pleasant place, with some beaches nearby and a sleepy atmosphere if you need to wind down, and if you're looking for somewhere to spend the night it's preferable to Frontera. There are plenty of buses heading this way, though Paraíso's **bus stations** are not too central. The ADO station is an inconvenient 1km south of the centre along Benito Juárez, the main road: turn right out of the station and keep walking – eventually you'll see the town's most distinctive monument, the plaza's twin-towered colonial church, across the river up ahead. The main second-class station, with departures for points along the coast, is a fifteen-minute walk north of the centre; to get into town head south (left) and aim for the church towers. Combis might drop you on the town side of the main bridge over the river, just off Juárez and a short walk from the centre, but they might also bypass this and head to the second-class terminal. One quality **hotel** in town is *Sabina*, on the east side of the plaza (Ⓣ933/333-0016, Ⓦwww.hotelsabinatabasco.com; ❹), with freshly painted, clean air-conditioned rooms and TV, private bathrooms and drinking water. A slightly more expensive alternative is the comfortable *Solimar* (Ⓣ933/333-2872; ❻), a block north of the plaza at Ocampo 114; this business-style accommodation is where the oilmen stay when they are in town. Both hotels have good **restaurants**, though there are some more moderately priced alternatives, as well as plenty of juice bars, on and around the plaza. *Real de la Costa*, next to the *Sabina* hotel on the plaza's east side, is perhaps the best, with a wide selection of Mexican food, meats, pastas and seafood dishes; *El Parillan*, on Juárez near the bridge, serves excellent charcoal-grilled chicken and other meats. On the west side of the plaza you'll find several Internet cafés, including *Compucentro*. Local **beaches** Playa Limón or Playa Paraíso are an easy twenty-minute combi ride north of Paraíso; busy at weekends, the wide, palm-studded sands are entirely deserted during the week.

Comalcalco and the cacao region

The area between the coast and Villahermosa is the heart of Tabasco's **cacao-growing region**. About 10km south out of Paraíso, you reach **Hacienda Cholula** (Ⓣ933/334-3815), a small business producing organic chocolate in the old-fashioned way. There are guided tours (daily 9am–5pm; M$100 per group, English-speaking guides usually available) and a shop where the end product, traditional Mexican drinking chocolate, is for sale. It comes in solid blocks, with grainy sugar, that are crumbled into hot milk and water, then whisked to produce a drink. The tour is short but fascinating, with a brief overview of the entire process, from the young cacao plants to the final production of chocolate. It's also something of a nature trek – there's a large troupe of howler monkeys here as well as innumerable birds (and thousands of mosquitoes), and alongside the cacao the hacienda grows coffee, cinnamon and bananas.

Just south of Cholula lies the westernmost known Maya site, **COMALCALCO** (daily 8am–5pm; M$39). Built in the Classic period, it was occupied around the same time as Palenque (250–900 AD), with which it shares some features, and it may have been ruled by some of the same kings. The area's lack of stone forced the Chontal Maya to adopt a distinctive, almost unique, form of construction: kiln-fired brick. As if the brick-built pyramids themselves were not enough to distinguish this site, the builders added an element of mystery to the process – each brick was stamped or moulded with a geometric or representational design before it was fired. This design was deliberately placed facing inwards, so that it could not be seen on the finished building.

You can see the astonishing designs on the bricks in Comalcalco's excellent little **museum**, though the labels are in Spanish only. Animals depicted include crocodiles, turtles, frogs, lizards, dogs and mice, while those portraying the sculpted faces of rulers display an advanced level of artistry. One of the most amazing figures is of a skeleton that appears to be leaping out at you from the surface of the brick. The abundant clay that provided such a versatile medium for architects and artists here also formed the basis for many more mundane artefacts. Comalcalco means "place of the *comales*" – fired clay griddles for cooking tortillas – and these and other clay vessels have been excavated in great numbers. Some of the largest jars were used as **funerary urns** and several are on display here, including one with an intact skeleton.

Though there are dozens of buildings at Comalcalco, only around ten or so of the larger ones have been restored. Owing to the fragile nature of the brickwork you're not allowed to enter or climb on many of them, but you can follow a path up to Structure 3 and around the Palacio. Entering the site, you first come to **Templo I**, a tiered pyramid with a massive central stairway and the main structure of the **North Plaza Cluster**. Originally, the whole building (like all of the structures here) would have been covered with stucco made from oyster shells, sculpted into masks and reliefs of rulers and deities, and brightly painted. Only a few of these features remain – the exposed ones protected from further erosion by shelters, while others have been deliberately left buried. Facing Temple I at the opposite end of the site is the **Gran Acrópolis**, a complex of buildings, some of which are still being excavated, raised above the plaza. Here you can climb up to **El Palacio** for some excellent close-up views of the brickwork, including a series of massive brick piers and arches that once formed an enormous double-corbelled vault, 80m long and over 8m wide – one of the largest enclosed spaces the Maya ever built. There's a fine stucco mask of Kinich Ahau, the Maya sun god, on **Templo VI**, and at the side of **Templo V**, a small, corbel-arched room contains stucco reliefs of nine richly dressed, half-life-size figures apparently conversing, or even arguing – they may represent the **Lords of Xibalba**, the Maya underworld.

Carrying on to Villahermosa is quick and easy on the highway straight south to Cardenas. The town of **Comalcalco** itself, surprisingly large but unremarkable, lies west of this highway and a bit south of the ruins. The slower route, winding southeast through countless *tope*-strewn towns, though, is more interesting, especially when you reach **Cupilco**, notable for the exuberantly decorated **Templo de la Virgen de Asunción**. The paint-job – gold and blue with floral patterns – is truly astounding, a beautiful example of the distinctive *tabasqueño* approach to sacred spaces.

Practicalities

It's easy enough to get to Comalcalco by **bus from Villahermosa** in around an hour and a quarter: the most frequent service is from Comalli Bus, with departures from Calle Gil y Sáenz, a couple of blocks northwest of the ADO terminal. Also look for the marginally faster and more frequent red, white and blue **combis** (M$10) that leave from just down the street. Additionally, ADO has one departure in the mid-morning, and Transportes Somellera runs an hourly service from the second-class bus station. Once in the town of Comalcalco, look for green combis (M$5), about a block past the bus terminal, to get you to the ruins. Also, any bus heading north will pass by the turn for the *ruinas*, but you'll have to walk about 1km to the site entrance. A taxi costs about M$25. For **drivers**, the ruins are signed off the main highway on the northern edge of town, immediately opposite an overpass bridge. **Returning**

to Villahermosa, TRT buses pass by on the highway every 45 minutes or so, taking the fast route via Cardenas; Allegro and Comalli buses go the slow route via Cupilco, every half-hour.

There are no official **guides** at Comalcalco, but Eugenio Martínez Torres, an expert on the site, can often be found at the entrance, or you can call in advance to arrange a tour (ⓣ933/327-4629; around M$250 per group). There's a small **café** and toilets at the site, and plenty of buses back to Villahermosa and on to Paraíso, running along the main road. It's hot and humid here, so water and insect repellent are both necessities.

Villahermosa

At first sight, **VILLAHERMOSA** – or "Beautiful Town" – doesn't live up to its name. Sprawling and crowded, traffic-choked and manic, it feels far more like a big city than Mérida or anywhere else in the Yucatán. Stay a while longer, though, and the place can start to grow on you. Ancient streets are interspersed with impressive ultra-modern buildings, art galleries and museums, and swathes of green space and vast lakes wind through the city, inspiring the sobriquet "La Esmeralda del Sureste" (The Emerald of the Southeast). Amid the attractive plazas of its revitalized downtown, you'll spot the broad sweep of the **Río Grijalva**.

In fact, Villahermosa's position on the water became a liability in November 2007, when heavy rains led to intense and sudden flooding here and throughout the state, displacing tens of thousands of people and wrecking most of the state's fall harvest. However, by early 2008, Villahermosa had recovered significantly, with buildings freshly painted and the streets cleared of mud. Visitors probably won't notice the damage, except in a few of the museums, which may still be undergoing repairs.

Most of what's to be seen in Villahermosa is in a relatively small area in the centre, plus the essential **Parque La Venta** some 3km away. This outdoor archeological exhibition and zoo, in a jungle setting on the bank of a lagoon, is the highlight of any visit. It provides one of the few accessible glimpses of the ancient **Olmec** civilization. The other focus of interest lies in the pedestrianized streets of the **Zona Luz** (also known as the Zona Remodelada, or simply La Zona), the downtown district, alongside the Río Grijalva.

Arrival and information

Arriving at one of Villahermosa's **bus stations**, you're in the midst of some hectic traffic. The **first-class** terminal (better known as the ADO) is an efficient modern building just off the main highway through town. There's luggage storage here (daily 7am–8pm; M$5 per item) and a small tourist information booth. To get to the centre there are reasonably priced taxis or a number of combis passing outside the terminal – look for those labelled "Parque Juárez" or "Malecón". Otherwise, it's at least a twenty-minute walk to town: cross the street and walk up Calle Merino or Calle Fuentes for six long blocks, then turn right at Madero, which will eventually get you to the Zona Luz and most hotels.

To get from the ADO to the **second-class terminal**, turn left on Avenida Mina, walk three blocks to the highway, Bulevar Adolfo Ruíz Cortines, turn right and cross it on the overpass. Not all second-class buses use the main terminal, but they all stop within a block or so – it's thoroughly crowded and chaotic. To get from this terminal to the centre, cross Ruíz Cortines on the overpass, then head east (left) alongside the road towards the river, then turn right to follow Avenida Madero towards the centre. Outside the second-class terminal, **combis** are plentiful, though they will not take you directly to the Zona Luz – look for "Madero", for example, or "CICOM". **Taxis** are more direct (for about M$30 to the centre), but not as easy to find as at the ADO. If you **drive** in, be warned that parking can be elusive near the centre.

Villahermosa's busy regional **airport**, the Aeropuerto Carlos A. Rovirosa, lies about 13km east of the centre on the highway towards Escárcega and Palenque. No buses run to the centre from here; a taxi will set you back around M$150.

Despite the growth in visitor numbers, there's no handy **tourist office** in Villahermosa. Small booths at the airport, ADO and Parque La Venta have a jumble of leaflets (more on the state than the city, and also available at many hotels), but nothing very useful. The main state and federal offices (Mon–Fri 8am–6pm, Sat 8am–1pm; ⓣ993/316-2889 ext 217) are in government buildings at the junction of Paseo Tabasco and Avenida de los Ríos, near the Tabasco 2000 shopping centre area, and too far from the centre to be of much use.

Accommodation

Hotels in Villahermosa are not great value on the low end: most **budget** options are on Avenida Madero or Calle Lerdo de Tejada, close to the heart of things, though none is particularly praiseworthy. A few of the more **upmarket** hotels, on the other hand, are actually very well priced when compared with more touristy cities, but a steady stream of Pemex employees and conventioneers can keep the rooms full. With a couple of exceptions, these pricier places are located in the Tabasco 2000 district, about 2.5km west of the centre along Paseo Tabasco, not far from La Venta.

Best Western Madan Av Madero 408 ⓣ993/314-0518, ⓦwww.bestwestern.com. Excellent-value mid-range option, with quiet a/c in the well-kept modern rooms and an exceptionally nice staff. The café downstairs is a busy meeting place. 6

Del Centro Av Madero 411 ⓣ993/312-2565. Functional but unexciting budget spot, and not exactly spotless. Rooms can be rented alone, with shared bath (in which case they're overpriced), or a group can take over a wing and use it as an apartment. 3

Miraflores C Reforma 304 ⓣ993/312-0022, ⓦwww.miraflores.com.mx. A bit cheaper than the *Best Western*, this independent hotel has all the same amenities (parking, a lobby bar and café, lobby Wi-Fi), though they're not quite as slick and new. Rooms all have nice balconies, and the staff is friendly. 6

Olmeca Plaza Av Madero 418 ⓣ993/358-0102, ⓦwww.hotelolmecaplaza.com. A rare higher-end option in the centre, with slick modern rooms and a swimming pool; published rates can seem steep, but there's usually a promotion on. 7

Oriente Av Madero 425 ⓣ993/312-0121. The best of the budget options, though a bit pricier than its neighbours – you're paying for a big tile-floor room that's actually clean, with a very firm bed and a decent bathroom. The mint-green paint job and pink staircase are a bonus. 4

Palomino Palace Av Javier Mina at corner of C Fuentes, across from the ADO terminal ⓣ993/312-8431. Conveniently located for late arrivals and usually has rooms available, but overpriced for what you get. Rooms, some with a/c, all have private shower and TV. Bar and restaurant. 5

Plaza Independencia C Independencia 123 ⓣ993/312-1299, ⓦwww.hotelesplaza.com.mx. Well-furnished, comfortable rooms and suites – with a somewhat retro-Mexican flair – in a blessedly quiet block just off the Plaza de Armas, behind the church. There's a lift, a pool, a good restaurant, a bar with live music and free off-street parking. 6

Quality Inn Cencali Paseo Tabasco at C Juárez ⓣ993/313-6611, ⓦwww.qualityinnvillahermosa.com. The best-value spot in the Tabasco 2000 area. Set in quiet, luxuriant gardens on the shore of a lagoon, the *Cencali* has an inviting pool, comfortable, well-furnished rooms with a/c and suites with beautiful tiled bathrooms; upstairs rooms have balconies. Parque La Venta is a 1km walk. ❽

Quinta Real Paseo de la Choca 1402 ☎993/310-1300. The best of the city's luxury hotels, done up in grand mansion style, with vast rooms and two pools. It's 5km west from the centre, but right by the city's outer ring road, making it easily accessible for drivers, yet not too far from Parque La Venta. ❾

San Miguel C Lerdo de Tejada 315 ☎993/312-1426. Rooms (all with private bath) are very basic and potentially noisy, but at least the sheets are clean. Competes with *Tabasco* for cheapest rates. ❷

Tabasco C Lerdo de Tejada 317 ☎993/312-0077. Spartan but functional place similar to adjacent *San Miguel* – rooms are smaller, but the hallways not quite so scary, and there are some quiet rooms in the back of the building. ❷

The city

Sandwiched between the Río Carrizal and the Río Grijalva, Villahermosa's streets wind up hills and around vast lakes, making it a bit hard to navigate. An outer ring road runs next to the Carrizal on the west side, while Bulevar Ruíz Cortines forms a loose inner ring. The historic centre, the **Zona Luz**, hugs the west bank of the Grijalva, just a bit south of Ruíz Cortines. Everything of interest is confined to a walkable area between two main squares, Parque Juárez to the north and the Plaza de Armas in the south. Ruíz Cortines also leads around to **Parque La Venta**, a forested area that offers an accessible glimpse of the Olmec civilization as well as a fine zoo – it is Villahermosa's must-see attraction. East of the city, you'll find the entertaining **Yumká**, an expertly run safari park that allows you to step out into a recreation of the African wild.

Downtown

The oldest part of Villahermosa can be found **downtown**, in the **Zona Luz**, where vestiges of the nineteenth-century city (the original colonial buildings were built mostly of wood and have perished) survive on streets busy with shoppers and commerce. Many of the main shopping blocks are now pedestrianized, and the buildings are gradually being restored. Parque Juárez, on the northern end of the Zona, at the junction of Avenida Madero and Calle Zaragoza, is bustling in the evenings, as crowds swirl around watching the street entertainers. Facing the plaza on the east side, the futuristic glass **Centro Cultural de Villahermosa** (Tues–Sun 10am–8pm; free) presents changing exhibitions of art, photography and costume, as well as film screenings and concerts, plus a good café. Works in the exhibitions are usually for sale.

West of the park, on the corner of calles Sáenz and Lerdo de Tejada, the distinctive pink and purple paint on **La Casa Siempreviva**, dating from the early twentieth century, immediately catches the eye. Now a free gallery with a small café, it has tiled floors, arched stained-glass windows and some later Art Deco features. In the 1930s, it was home to journalist and women's rights activist Isabel Rullan. Just a couple of doors down at Calle Sáenz 203 is another old mansion turned into a museum – the **Casa Museo Carlos Pellicer** (Tues–Sat 10am–7pm, Sun 10am–4pm; free), filled with bits and bobs related to the life of the Villahermosa-born poet and anthropologist who was the driving force behind the rescue of the stone carvings of La Venta. In the side streets are other small **art galleries** – look around for signs of current shows. The steps at the far end of Calle Lerdo lead to the small, tree-shaded **Parque Los Pájaros**, where budgerigars sing in a large, globe-shaped cage and water flows through blue-tiled fountains and pools.

Heading on south, Villahermosa's **Museo de Historia de Tabasco**, at the corner of Avenida 27 de Febrero and Calle Juárez, was damaged in the 2007 flood and is slated to reopen in 2009. But the main attraction is the building

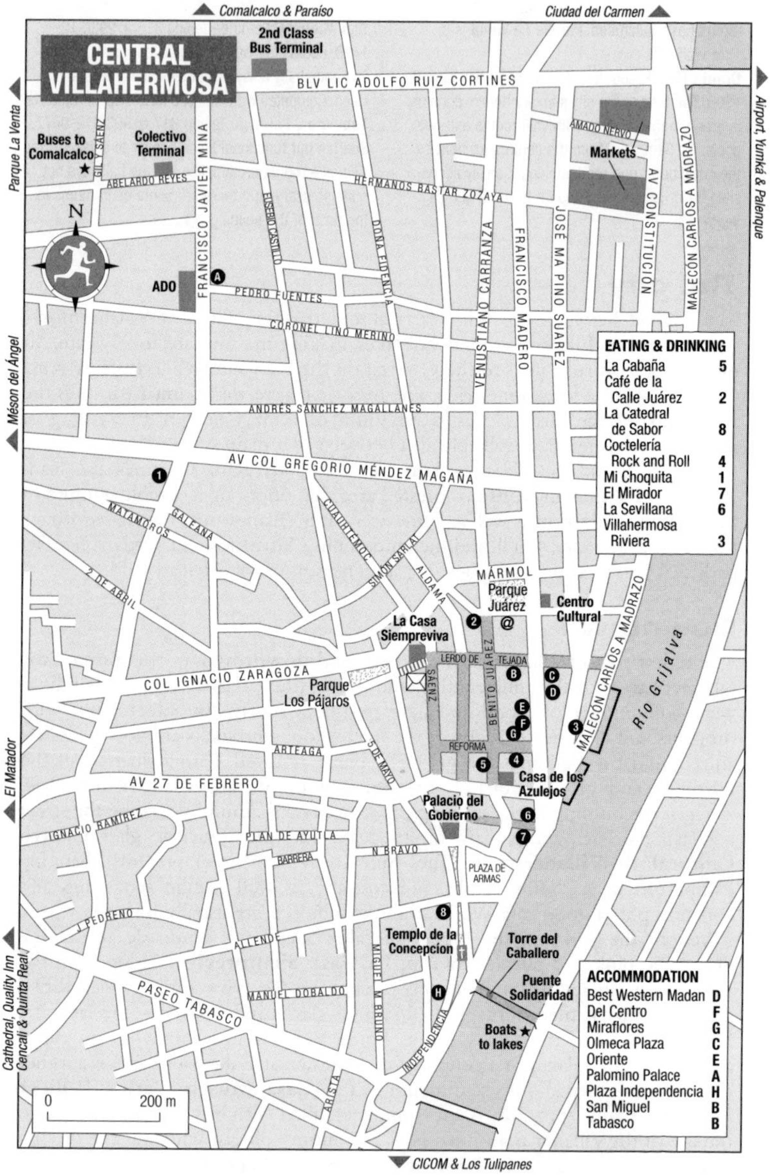

itself (c.1900). Popularly known as the **Casa de los Azulejos**, it is covered top to bottom in blue tiles. Look up to see the statues of nymphs and classical figures perched on the railings around the roof.

A couple of blocks further south, the grand **Palacio del Gobierno** looks onto the **Plaza de Armas**, a patch of green adjacent to a sprawling expanse of concrete. You can poke your head inside the government building to see what temporary exhibition is on, but the building is attractive on its own, with classical columns, turreted corners and a clock tower. Across the park to the south lies the pretty white **Templo de la Concepción**, commonly called "La Conchita". The church was first built in 1799, but this and its successor were each demolished – the present building dates only from 1945. Facing this traditional civic plaza is a more modern public space, usually busy in the cool of the evening, when there's often live music. Steps lead up to the **Puente Solidaridad** footbridge over the Río Grijalva, overshadowed by a rather bleak square tower, its observation deck unreliably open to the public. Cross the water to reach jetties with boats offering tours up and down the river.

If you're tempted, incidentally, by the impressive-looking silhouette of Villahermosa's **Catedral del Señor de Tabasco** – with one of the tallest church spires in Mexico, and easily visible from the Plaza de Armas – know that it's a longer walk than it looks, about twenty minutes up Paseo Tabasco. Once you get there, you'll find that the spires are just about all that exists. The rest of the Gothic building, begun in 1973, is only very slowly being constructed.

The CICOM complex

A fifteen-minute walk south from the Zona Luz, or a short combi ride, brings you to Villahermosa's cultural centre, **CICOM** (Centro de Investigaciones de las Culturas Olmeca y Maya). But you probably won't want to make the trek until 2010, when the complex's centrepiece, the **Museo Regional de Antropología Carlos Pellicer Cámara** reopens after a massive overhaul. Its collection of Olmec and Maya artefacts is vast and beautiful. In the meantime, the only other real attraction here is an excellent restaurant (see p.305).

Parque La Venta and around

A visit to Villahermosa's **Parque La Venta** (daily 8am–4pm; M$40) could easily fill half a day. The most important artefacts from the Olmec site of La Venta, some 120km west of Villahermosa at the border with Veracruz State, were transferred here in the late 1950s, when they were threatened by Pemex oil explorations. Little is known about the **Olmec culture**, referred to by many archeologists as the mother culture of Mesoamerica (see p.325). Its legacy, which included the Long Count calendar, glyphic writing, a rain deity and most likely the concept of zero and the ball-game, influenced all subsequent civilizations in ancient Mexico. That it developed and flourished in the unpromising environment of the Gulf coast swamps 3200 years ago only adds to its mystery.

Although hardly the exact reproduction of the original site it claims to be, the Parque La Venta does give you a chance to see a superb collection of artefacts. The most significant and famous items in the park are the four gigantic **basalt heads**, whose apparent African features present a curious puzzle. There's a whole series of other Olmec stone sculptures; follow the numbers as the path winds through the park. In their zeal to recreate an authentic jungle setting, the designers have included monkeys, agoutis (large rodents) and coatis (members of the raccoon family), which wander around freely, while crocodiles, jaguars and other animals from the region are displayed in the zoo's sizeable enclosures. The mosquitoes add an unplanned touch of reality. You can also visit the park at night for a rather good **sound-and-light show** (Tues–Sun 8, 9 & 10pm; M$100) that involves strolling from monument to monument, dramatically illuminated amidst the shadowy trees. For this event, you must buy tickets and enter at a second gate about 250m southwest along Paseo Tabasco.

Parque La Venta is set inside the much larger **Parque Tomás Garrido Canabal**, which stretches along the shore of an extensive lake, the **Laguna de Ilusiones**. There are walking trails here and boats for hire, or you can climb the Mirador de los Águilas, a tower in the middle of the lake. Also in the park, opposite the La Venta entrance, the small **Museo de Historia Natural** (Tues–Sun 9am–5pm; M$15) features displays on the animals and plants of Tabasco, focusing on the interaction between humans and the environment.

To get to La Venta, take a taxi or hop on one of the combis that pass on Avenida Madero in the city centre ("Tabasco 2000", "Circuito 1", "Parque Linda Vista", "Fracc Carrizal", among others); they also run along the highway from the second-class bus terminal. A taxi from the centre costs M$40.

Beyond La Venta, many of the combis continue down Paseo Tabasco to the **Tabasco 2000** area. This extension of the city is an impressive, if soulless, example of modern Mexican architecture, with concrete shopping malls, government buildings and a planetarium, as well as a number of large hotels.

Yumká

Villahermosa's major ecological attraction, **Yumká** (daily 9am–5pm, last entry 4pm; Ⓦwww.yumka.org; M$50, kids M$25), named for the Chontal Maya dwarf-god who looks after forests, is an enjoyable combination of a safari park and an environmental studies centre. The park covers more than six square kilometres, so after a guided walking tour of the Tabasco jungle, complete with monkeys, you board a train for a trip round enormous paddocks representing the savannahs of Africa and Asia. Elephants, rhinos, giraffes and antelopes are rarely displayed in Mexico and almost never in such spacious surroundings. After a stop at the **restaurant**, you can take a boat ride on the hippo-filled lagoon (M$20).

Yumká is 14km from the centre of Villahermosa, very close to the airport. **Combis** leave regularly from along Calle Amado Nervo behind the market at the top end of Avenida Constitución, and a park-operated **shuttle bus** (M$15) departs from Bulevar Ruíz Cortines, west of Parque La Venta (Sat & Sun 9am, 10.30am, noon & 1.30pm). A taxi will set you back M$170.

Eating and drinking

The Zona Luz boasts only **fast food** or bland hotel fare, with a couple of exceptions noted below. For the former, head for Calle Aldama, north of its junction with Calle Lerdo de Tejada: at this junction there's a *Flor de Michoacan* ice-cream place, and heading up Aldama you'll find half a dozen taco and pizza joints. For a wider choice, better quality and more cosmopolitan flavours you're best off travelling out towards Tabasco 2000, where the hotel **restaurants** are amongst the best in the city. As ever, the **market** – here, a vast, tidy two-storey complex trimmed in white wrought-iron trellises – is good for fruit, bread and cheap tacos. It's several blocks north of the Zona Luz on Avenida Constitución. For **nightlife**, check out the various clubs on the malecón around Avenida 27 de Febrero, some facing the water and others on structures jutting into the river – all far smarter than you might expect.

La Cabaña C Juárez, opposite the Casa de los Azulejos. Traditional café where local gents linger over their coffees and conduct their business. Food is served, though it's rather pricey – you may be better off eating at *Café de la Calle Juárez*, up the street, with a decent breakfast and *comida*.

La Catedral de Sabor C Independencia, adjacent to the church. Cool down with a refreshing *horchata de coco* – a Tabasco speciality – at this little sidewalk stand at the Plaza de Armas. A more formal café (with a/c) is next door.

Coctelería Rock and Roll C Reforma 307. Directly opposite the *Hotel Miraflores*, a bustling place with excellent seafood cocktails, ceviche and prawns, accompanied by live marimba music.
El Matador C César Sandino 101-A at Av 27 de Febrero. Open nearly round-the-clock, this is the most famous taco stand in Villahermosa, renowned for its *gaonera*, a succulent *taco al pastor* topped off with melted cheese. Portions are enormous, but you can work up an appetite on the 1.5km walk. Follow Av 27 de Febrero south off Paseo Tabasco; the restaurant is in a triangle intersection on the left.
Méson del Ángel Av Gregorio Méndez 1604 ⓣ993/315-8616. A popular spot for expense-account meals, as well as local celebrations, this white-tablecloth joint melds Spanish appetizers (good garlic soup) with steaks and fresh seafood. It's in the Tabasco 2000 area; pay M$45 for a taxi.
Mi Choquita Av Javiér Mina 304-A. Good, inexpensive breakfasts and regional dishes prepared in a typical Tabascan style as well as an excellent-value lunchtime *comida*. It's located a few blocks south of the bus station.
El Mirador Av Madero 105 ⓣ993/314-3495. Excellent seafood restaurant with river views, and not unreasonable prices. Try the delicious *róbalo* (bass), but don't go late – it's open only until 8pm.
La Sevillana Av Madero, just north of *El Mirador*. Swanky little gourmet shop with a takeout deli (lots of Spanish ham) and liquor store, plus a sit-down café serving expensive but tasty sandwiches.
Los Tulipanes In the CICOM complex. Lovely riverfront restaurant, a bit formal (and unstinting on the a/c). Sample delicious renditions of Tabasco cuisine: shrimp with coconut and passionfruit salsa, fresh corn tortillas stuffed with seafood, crab soup. Very well priced, considering the massive portions. Open till 6pm.
Villahermosa Riviera Av Constitución 104, 4th floor ⓣ993/312-4468. Luxurious and relatively expensive, with fantastic food that merits the price (rarely more than M$180). Views along the river at sunset are magical, and there's often live music.

Listings

Airlines Aeroméxico, Periférico Carlos Pellicer Cámara 511 ⓣ993/314-9262, or at the airport ⓣ993/356-0005; Mexicana, Via 3 no. 120 in the Plaza D'Atocha mall, Tabasco 2000 ⓣ993/316-3132.
Banks There are branches of all major banks at the airport, throughout the centre and in Tabasco 2000; most have ATMs.
Buses and combis To get to the first-class terminal take a "Central" or "Chedraui" combi (the latter go to a huge department store behind the terminal); most of these also go past the second-class terminal. Between them, ADO and Cristóbal Colón operate dozens of services to all the main destinations. For smaller destinations within Tabasco State, more frequent services go from the main second-class terminal: look here for Allegro buses to Comalcalco via Cupilco, and TRT buses for other destinations. Combi service can be preferable in many cases, as it's more frequent and direct – look for vans parked around the main combi terminal on C Abelardo Reyes near Av Javier Mina, just north of the ADO terminal.
Internet access Internet cafés aren't as common as you'd expect. Look for Ciberware, C Aldama 521, or G&C on C Zaragoza, facing Parque Juárez. Rates rarely top M$10/hr.
Laundry Top Klean on Av Madero, between C Reforma and Av 27 de Febrero (closed Sun).
Post office C Sáenz at C Lerdo de Tejada, opposite La Casa Siempreviva (Mon–Fri 9am–3pm, Sat 9am–1pm).
Travel agents and tour operators There's no shortage of travel agencies in the Zona Luz, and all the big hotels have a tour desk to arrange domestic flights and trips to Palenque. Creatur, Paseo Tabasco 1404 in Tabasco 2000 (ⓣ993/310-9900, ⓦwww.creaturviajes.com), is particularly helpful, with a multilingual staff.

Palenque

Set in thick jungle buzzing with insects in the foothills of the Chiapas mountains, **PALENQUE** is hauntingly beautiful. For many, it is the finest of Mexico's Maya sites: less crowded than Chichén Itzá, larger than Uxmal, with a far more spectacular setting than either. Although more structures are being excavated every year, it is not a huge site – you can see everything in a morning

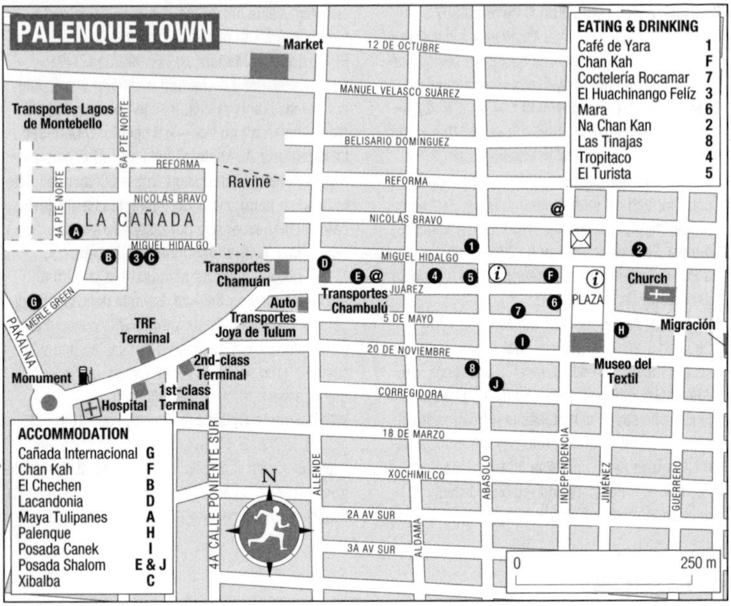

– but it is a fascinating one, strongly linked to the lost cities of Guatemala while keeping its own distinctive style.

Nine kilometres east of the ruins, the **town of Palenque** (officially Santo Domingo de Palenque, though no one ever says this) has more than 65,000 inhabitants and every facility a visitor might need. An excellent base for exploring the ruins and the waterfalls in the nearby hills, it is lively enough, with music in the turquoise-painted plaza most evenings. But, save for a small **museum** on the plaza devoted to the textiles of Chiapas, it has no real intrinsic appeal. As there are a number of excellent camping sites, cabañas and hotels near the ruins, you may prefer not to stay in town at all.

Arrival and information

Arriving on any long-distance bus, you'll be at one of two nearly adjacent **bus terminals** on Avenida Juárez, just off the main highway through town. If you know when you're leaving it's worth buying your onward ticket as soon as you arrive – or at any rate as soon as possible – as buses out of Palenque can be very crowded, particularly the more popular first-class services towards Mérida or San Cristóbal de las Casas. Palenque's three main streets, avenidas Juárez, 5 de Mayo and Hidalgo, all run parallel and lead straight up to the **plaza**, the Parque Central. The **tourist office** (Mon–Sat 9am–9pm, Sun 9am–3pm; ⓣ916/345-0356) is in the Plaza de Artesanías, on Avenida Juárez at the corner of Calle Abasolo, a block below the plaza; the staff more often than not gives wrong information, and a street map if you're lucky. There's another booth on the east side of the plaza, with a sometimes sharper staff. You'll generally get better **information** from local tour operators (see "Listings", p.309) or at your hotel.

Accommodation

In Palenque town, there are plenty of **hotels** on the streets leading from the bus stations to the plaza, especially Avenida Hidalgo (though the traffic noise means these are best avoided) and Avenida 20 de Noviembre. The other option is the area called **La Cañada,** named for the ravine that divides it from the town centre. With brick-paved streets and soft lighting, it feels a little like a chic subdivision, but set in a quiet swathe of trees (birds and monkeys are audible in the morning) and only a short walk from the action, it's a good compromise between the noisier town proper and the isolation of the ruins. Most hotels here are more upmarket, but there's one very good budget option. You'll also find a host of places lining the **road to the ruins**, in every category from luxury hotel to campsite, though the latter options are becoming fewer. Note that some places charge up to fifty percent more during peak times – July and August, Semana Santa and Christmas.

In town

Chan Kah Av Juárez at C Independencia ⓣ916/345-0318, ⓦwww.chan-kah.com.mx. The most upmarket accommodation in town (and the only one with a lift), this comfortable spot has big rooms with a/c, many with balconies overlooking the plaza – the drawback being the noise, of course. ❺

Lacandonia C Allende no. 77 at Av Hidalgo ⓣ916/345-2333, ⓔhotel-lacandonia@hotmail.com. Plant-covered balconies set a pretty tone at this mid-range hotel; the twenty rooms have wrought-iron furniture, a/c and fans. There's a café downstairs, as well as parking. ❻

Palenque Av 5 de Mayo 15 ⓣ916/345-0188, ⓔhotelpalenque@prodigy.net.mx. A grand hotel from another era, the *Palenque* has a groovy Sixties feel, complete with two-tone green rooms – though fortunately, bathrooms are new, and there's a very large pool. ❺

Posada Canek Av 20 de Noviembre 43 ⓣ916/345-0150, ⓔposada_canek@hotmail.com. One of several *posadas* along this street, *Canek* describes itself as a youth hostel, though it doesn't have the usual party vibe. It's great-value, as single beds in shared rooms are M$60, and the staff looks after solo travellers like family. Double rooms, some with private bath and a street-side balcony, are huge. Luggage storage is available, as are tours. ❷

Posada Shalom Av Corregidora at C Abasolo ⓣ916/345-2641. Spotless enough to please even the pickiest travellers, the white rooms all have ceiling fans (a/c is optional). The perks really add value: parking, laundry, even continental breakfast delivered to your room. There's an equally clean branch at Av Juárez 158 (ⓣ916/345-0944), but the location is noisier. ❷

In La Cañada

Cañada Internacional C Merle Green ⓣ916/345-2093, ⓔreservascanada@hotmail.com. Clean new rooms (the hotel opened in late 2007), with bamboo headboards and other jungle-inspired touches, though there's also a/c, if you prefer a less authentic jungle experience. A small pool is a plus. ❻

El Chechen C Merle Green at Av Hidalgo ⓣ916/345-1008. Formerly a backpacker flop, this place has been scrubbed down and is now run by a very conscientious family. Just sixteen rooms, all with private bath (the brown tile looks suspect, but it's actually new and clean). Parking, too. ❹

Maya Tulipanes C Cañada 6 ⓣ916/345-0201, ⓦwww.mayatulipanes.com.mx. Opposite *El Chechen*, this rather bland but very comfortable hotel has a/c rooms, shady grounds, a small pool and a good restaurant. ❼

Xibalba C Merle Green at Av Hidalgo ⓣ916/345-0411, ⓔxibalba02@prodigy.net.mx. Pretty white rooms are accented with green and brown, giving a vaguely natural feel, but the space is not very large. Staff is friendly, though, and there's also a good restaurant and helpful travel agency. ❻

On the road to the ruins

Chan Kah Resort Village 4km from town, on the left ⓣ916/345-1134, ⓦwww.chan-kah.com.mx. Luxury brick and stone cabañas, rather tightly packed in a lovely forest and river setting, humming with birdlife. Amenities include three stone-lined swimming pools and a restaurant. ❽

El Columbre 3.5km from town on the right, then another 2km ⓣ916/345-0165. Thatch-roof concrete cabañas here have private bathrooms and are decorated with the owner's quirky paintings. There's a pool overlooking the valley, and a shared kitchen. The catch: for the extra ride off the main road, you'll need a car or a taxi – or energy and little luggage – to get there. ❷

Elementos Naturales 6km from town, on the left ⓔenpalenque@yahoo.com.mx. Dorm beds

(M$120) are a good option at this sprawling place; hammock or campsites are available, too (M$50), as are cabañas. It's a bit quieter than *Mayabell*, but not so carefully maintained. ❷–❹

Mayabell Camping and Trailer Park 6.2km from town, on the left (inside the park boundary and 300m from the site museum) ⓣ916/341-6977, ⓦwww.mayabell.com.mx. A backpackers' favourite with something for everyone. In addition to palapa shelters for hammocks and tents (from M$40), *Mayabell* has vehicle pads with electricity and water (from M$150), and some very comfortable private cabañas with hot water. The tiled, shared showers have hot water as well, and there's a restaurant, Internet access, swimming pool and *temazcal*. The site is rarely crowded, though it can be rowdy. ❺

El Panchán 5.1km from town, on the left, just before the park entrance ⓦwww.elpanchan.com. A large complex incorporating a number of different cabaña operations, separated by screens of trees and sharing a couple of restaurants. The vibe might be a little too nouveau-hippie for some, but most places are excellent deals. It's easy to take a combi here and then compare rates by walking around to the various options. One drawback is that there's no swimming pool anywhere (despite mention on the website). *Margarita and Ed's* (ⓣ916/341-0063, ⓔedcabanas@yahoo.com; ❷–❹) is the cleanest and best-value of the places here, with thatched cabins or conventional double rooms with a/c. *Jungle Palace* (ⓣ915-348-0520; ❶) has a stream running between its thatch cabañas and a "no drums" policy. *Don Mucho's* should be avoided if you want to go to bed early – the cabañas are right by the restaurant, where there's live music and fire-spinning at night.

Rancho Quiloma 2.5km from town, on the left ⓣ916/345-4066, ⓦwww.quilomaranch.com.mx. Up on a hill overlooking the green valley, the handful of clean and modern rooms here all have a/c (though no ceiling fans, unfortunately, nor screens on the windows) and a swimming pool right out front. Two more rustic wood cabins at the back look onto dense forest – these have fans, but they're the same price as the other rooms. ❹

Eating and drinking

Food in Palenque town is fairly basic, and most restaurants serve up similar pasta and pizza to customers who've really only come for the ruins. There are also several places along the road to the site – some of which cater mainly to tour groups – including a couple in *El Panchán* (see "Accommodation", above). The bigger hotels in La Cañada have attached restaurants, and though standards are generally fine, prices are higher than in town. **Avenida Juárez** also has several budget options between the bus stations and the plaza, while **Avenida Hidalgo** has more Mexican-style food, with several taco places and even a couple of seafood restaurants. There's a good Mexican **bakery**, *Flor de Palenque*, on Calle Allende, next to the Chambalú colectivo office.

Café de Yara Av Hidalgo at C Abasolo. Café culture comes to Palenque – try the cappuccino (from a proper espresso machine) and breakfasts especially. Dinner (about M$60) is also decent, and it's a spot to get a green salad.

Chan Kah Av Juárez at C Independencia, on the plaza. The hotel has a first-floor terrace bar-restaurant with great views over the action on the plaza. Prices reflect the location, but this is a good place for an early evening drink.

Coctelería Rocamar Av 5 de Mayo, between C Abasolo and C Independencia. Seafood is the speciality at this spot, which is hugely popular with locals. Known for generous portions and reasonable prices.

Don Mucho On the road to the ruins, 5.1km from town. The social centre of *El Panchán*, serving Mexican and Italian food in the evening, with music after 8pm. Great for breakfast (around M$40) or a leisurely lunch after visiting the ruins, though sometimes busy with small tour groups.

El Huachinango Felíz C Merle Green at Av Hidalgo. A bi-level restaurant in La Cañada that serves great fish and shrimp baked in banana leaves, among other seafood. Prices are reasonable (less than M$100), and the setting is pretty and quiet – a nice break from restaurants in town.

Mara Av Juárez at C Independencia, on the plaza. A pleasant little café from which to watch the plaza scene. Tacos are good here, but you can get big platters as well, or just a few cold beers.

Na Chan Kan Av Hidalgo at C Jiménez. Good-value breakfasts and set meals; an enjoyable location for coffee and people-watching.

Las Tinajas Av 20 de Noviembre at C Abasolo. Pleasant, family-run open-sided restaurant with a wide menu of meats, fish, chicken and pasta (M$70) in addition to the usual Mexican fare.

Unfortunately, no *comida* special, but portions are big enough to share.

Tropitaco Av Juárez, between C Allende and C Abasolo. The biggest skewer of *pastor* pork in town, served hot and fast to the constant drone of blenders whipping up fruit drinks. For something more substantial, go for the *torta de bisteck*, garnished with griddle-fried cheese.

El Turista Av Juárez at C Abasolo, opposite the tourist office. Excellent *jugos* and *licuados*.

Listings

Banks Several along Av Juárez have ATMs and will change traveller's cheques; the best exchange rates are at Banco Azteca/Western Union, at the back of the giant Elektra electrical and furniture store on Av Juárez, not far from the bus stations.

Buses and combis For first-class service on ADO and Cristóbal Colón to Villahermosa, Campeche and beyond, departures run from the first-class terminal on Av Juárez; for frequencies and travel times, see "Travel Details", p.322. The second-class terminal, just down the street, has some very rickety but frequent services to Ocosingo. For other destinations, combis are your best bet. At least five different companies on or near C Allende operate vans, each to different areas. The most useful are Chambalú, for the Palenque ruins and the major waterfalls, and Chamoán, for Bonampak and Frontera Corozal.

Internet Internet cafés are plentiful. They include Ciber-konqueror, just past the post office on C Independencia at Av Nicolas Bravo; RedMay@, on Av Juárez, near the Elektra store; and Cibernet, on C Independencia, near Av 20 de Noviembre.

Laundry Several in town, including a good one on Av 5 de Mayo at C Allende.

Post office On C Independencia, a block from the plaza (Mon–Fri 9am–6pm, Sat & Sun 9am–1pm).

Tours Walk the streets of Palenque and you'll be accosted by hawkers offering a huge variety of tours to local attractions, above all the waterfalls at Agua Azul and Misol-Há (p.313) and the ruins of Bonampak and Yaxchilán (p.318 & p.321). There are also trips to Tikal in Guatemala or to Toniná, and adventure tours, including kayaking and horse-riding. Prices vary according to season (and even time of day if there's one seat left to fill) but start from around M$100 for the waterfalls, and M$600 for a day-trip to Bonampak and Yaxchilán. Be sure to check what's included – entrance fees, meals and English-speaking guides most importantly. The agents listed below are consistently reliable.

Travel agents/tour operators Two of the best are Na Chan Kan (Ⓣ916/345-0263, Ⓔnachan@tnet.net.mx), with a small office on Av Juárez, just up from the bus station, and a main office on Av Hidalgo at C Jiménez, and Viajes Shivalva, based at the *Hotel Xibalba* in La Cañada (Ⓣ916/345-0411).

The ruins of Palenque

The **ruins of Palenque** occupy the top of an escarpment marking the north-western limit of the Chiapas highlands. Superficially, the site bears a closer resemblance to the Maya sites of Guatemala than to those of the Yucatán, but ultimately it's unique – the **towered palace** and **pyramid tomb** are like nothing else, as is the site's abundance of reliefs and glyphic inscriptions. The setting, too, is remarkable. Surrounded by hills covered in deep green jungle, Palenque is right at the edge of the great Yucatán plain – climb to the top of any of the structures and you look out across an endless stretch of low, pale-green flatland. If you arrive early enough in the day, the mist still clinging to the treetops and the roaring of the howler monkeys lend an exotic, if a bit macabre, ambience.

Founded around 100 BC as a farming village, it was four hundred years before Palenque began to flourish, during the Classic period (300–900 AD). Towards the end of this time the city ruled over a large part of modern-day Chiapas and Tabasco, but its peak came during a relatively short period in the seventh century, under two rulers, **Hanab Pakal** (**Jaguar Shield**) and **Chan Bahlum** (**Jaguar Serpent**). Almost everything you can see (and that's only a tiny, central part of the original city) dates from this era.

Ruin practicalities

Getting to the ruins of Palenque, 9km from town, is no problem. Two **combi** services, Chambalú and Otolúm, run at least every fifteen minutes (6am–6pm; M$10 one-way) from their terminals on Calle Allende, either side of Avenida Juárez, and will stop anywhere along the road to the ruins – useful if you're staying at one of the hotels or campsites nearby. After 6pm, you'll have to either walk or take a **taxi** (M$50). There are also plenty of organized **tours** from town (see p.309).

The **ruins** (daily 8am–5pm, last entry 4.30pm; M$48 including museum) are in the **Parque Nacional de Palenque**, which takes an additional M$20 at the park gate, just after *El Panchán*. (If you're staying inside the park, at *Mayabell*, for example, you only have to pay once – just hold onto your ticket.) The main road first passes a nice *artesanías* shop, a café and the site **museum**. It's possible to buy a site ticket here, after 9am (but not on Mondays, when the museum is shut), then enter at the gate across the road, hiking up to the main part of the site via the waterfalls trail. But most people will press on to the main site entrance, at the top of the hill another 2km up a winding road. In this area, there's a small **café** and numerous souvenir stalls selling drinks, as well as toilets and some expensive lockers. Guides officially cost M$350 for groups of up to seven people, but that's open to negotiation. Signs inside the site are in English, Spanish and Tzeltal – the shared Maya language in this area.

Even if you have your own **car**, you may still prefer to take a combi, as this enables you to exit on the downhill side of the site by the museum, and spare yourself having to hike back up to your vehicle. If you do drive, know that there's very little space for parking at the main entrance on top of the hill.

El Palacio and around

As you enter the site, **El Palacio**, with its extraordinary watchtower, stands ahead of you. The path, however, leads to the right, past a row of smaller structures – one of them, the so-called **Tumba de la Reina Roja** ("Tomb of the Red Queen"), is open inside, and you can climb in to see a sarcophagus still in place. This is nothing, though, compared with the structure's neighbour, the enormous **Templo de las Inscripciones**, an eight-stepped pyramid, 26m high, built up against a thickly overgrown hillside. You are not permitted to climb the pyramid, so you just have to imagine the sanctuary on top, filled with a series of stone panels carved with hieroglyphic inscriptions relating to Palenque's dynastic history. Deep inside the pyramid is the **tomb of Hanab Pakal** (615–683 AD). Discovered in 1952, this was the first such pyramid burial found in the Americas, and is still the most important and impressive. Some of the smaller objects found inside – the skeleton and the jade death mask – are on display at the Museo Nacional de Antropología in Mexico City, but the massive, intricately carved stone **sarcophagus** is still inside. One of the most renowned iconographic monuments in the Maya world, the sarcophagus lid depicts Pakal at the moment of his death, falling into Xibalba, the underworld, symbolized by a monster's jaws. Above the dead king rises the **Wakah Kan** – the World Tree and the centre of the universe – with **Itzam-Ye**, the Celestial Bird, perched on top representing the heavens. In order that the deified king buried here should not be cut off from the world of the living, a psychoduct – a hollow tube in the form of a snake – runs up the side of the staircase, from the tomb to the temple.

In June 1994, another remarkable tomb was discovered in **Templo XIII**, a pyramid next to the Templo de las Inscripciones. This burial, currently the only one open to the public, is considered by archeologists to date from a similar period to that of Pakal, and its sarcophagus contained a number of jade and obsidian grave goods, as well as vessels of food and drink to sustain the deceased on the way to Xibalba.

The centrepiece of the site, **El Palacio**, is in fact a complex of buildings constructed at different times to form a rambling administrative and residential block. Its square **tower** (the top floor of which was reconstructed in 1930) is unique, and no one knows exactly what its purpose was – perhaps a lookout post or an astronomical observatory. Bizarrely, the narrow staircase winding up inside starts only at the second level, though you're not allowed to climb it. Throughout you'll find delicately executed **relief carvings**, the most remarkable of which are the giant human figures on stone panels in the grassy courtyard, depicting rulers of defeated cities in poses of humiliation. An arcade overlooking the courtyard held a portrait gallery of Palenque's rulers, though many of these have been removed.

South of El Palacio and adjacent to the Templo de las Inscripciones, a small path leads to the **Templo del Bello Relieve** (**Templo del Jaguar**). This shaded walk delivers you almost immediately into thick jungle, with only the sound of the rushing water from the adjacent stream to disturb you. More temples are being wrested from the jungle beyond, but the paths are closed, and though the path leads eventually to the *ejido* of Naranjo, you won't be

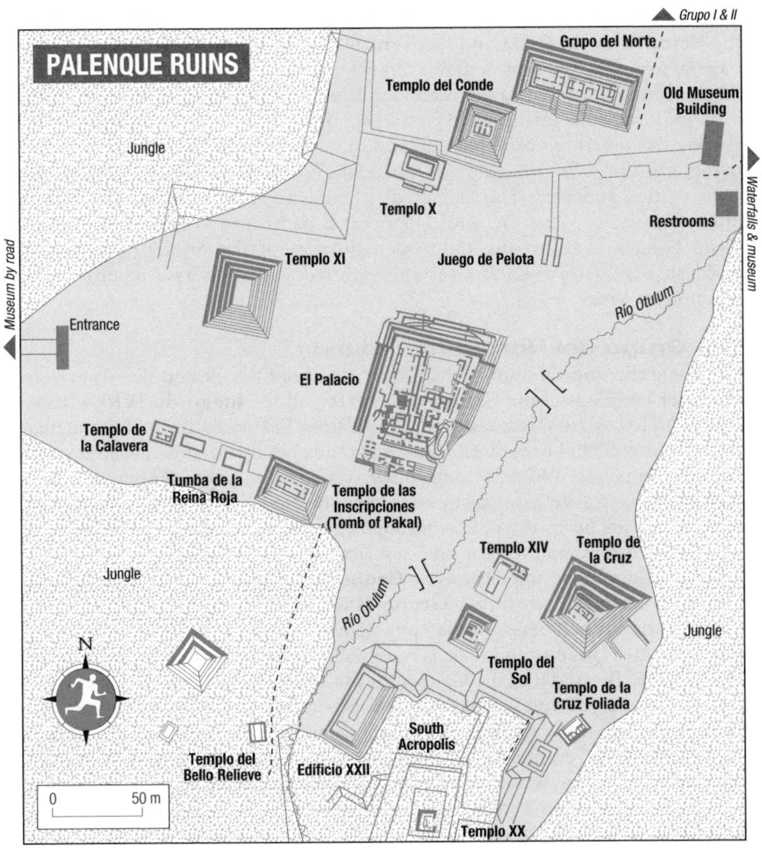

permitted to pass much further into the forest without a guide. Even so, clambering around here, it's easy to believe you're walking over unexcavated buildings, as the ground is very rocky and some of the stones don't look naturally formed.

The Grupo de la Cruz and around

The main path then leads across the Río Otulúm, one of several streams that cascade through the site. As it passed through the city in its heyday, the Otulúm was lined with stone and used as an aqueduct; the reinforcement also kept the stream from overflowing its banks and undermining the foundations of the surrounding buildings. On the way up the hill, structures are tucked back in the greenery – this area, called the South Acropolis, is rarely open to the public, as there is ongoing excavation work here. Explorations in 1999 revealed a painted tomb at **Templo XX** and a stone throne at **Templo XIX**, inscribed with over two hundred glyphs, among other funereal goods, but these have yet to be opened for viewing, as the structures have not yet been stabilized. Some of the items are now in the site museum.

The path ends in the plaza of what's called the **Grupo de la Cruz**, oddly oriented away from Palenque's more central buildings (it seems the South Acropolis was an extension of the Grupo de la Cruz, however, so the whole district was significantly larger than it appears now). The **Templo del Sol**, the **Templo de la Cruz** and the **Templo de la Cruz Foliada** are all tall, narrow pyramids surmounted by a temple with an elaborate stone roofcomb. All, too, contain carved panels representing sacred rites – the cross found here is as important an image in Maya iconography as it is in Christian, representing the meeting of the heavens and the underworld with the land of the living. On the right-hand side of the Templo de la Cruz, God L, one of the gods of the underworld, is depicted smoking tobacco – so far the oldest known image of someone smoking. A small path next to the Templo de la Cruz Foliada leads to the only open portion of the South Acropolis, a building with a replica relief carving, covered with elaborate glyphs and a triumphant king.

The Grupo del Norte and around

Following the Río Otulúm to the northern edge of the cleared site, you reach the lesser buildings of the **Grupo del Norte** and the **Juego de Pelota** (ball-court), on lower ground across a grassy area from El Palacio. Beyond them, two **paths** lead downhill towards the museum. One goes down some perilous stairs behind Grupo del Norte, leading down via the buildings of **Grupo I** and **Grupo II**, intricate complexes of interconnected rooms. The other path follows the stream as it cascades through the forest and flows over beautiful limestone curtains and terraces into a series of gorgeous pools (no swimming allowed, though). It initially skirts **Grupo C**, a small cluster of buildings minimally restored and cleared. **Grupo B** is a small residential complex right on the path, located between the aptly named **Baño de la Reina** (**Bathing Pool of the Queen**) and a small waterfall on a second stream, the Arroyo Murciélagos. Beyond this, the **Grupo de los Murciélagos** is another residential area where you can see remnants of the original drainage systems as well as benches and stairways. The paths join again just after a suspension bridge crossing the river; eventually the route emerges on the main road opposite the museum. If you don't want to exit here, it's best to make a loop by going down via Grupo I and II – the steeper route – then making your way back up by the other, somewhat easier trail.

The museum

Palenque's excellent **museum** (Tues–Sun 9am–4.30pm; included in site entry price), on the road 1.5km from the site entrance, will give you a good idea of the scale of Palenque, and a look at some of its treasures. There are fine displays of many of the glyphs and carved relief panels found at the site, as well as examples of the giant ceramic censers (incense-burners) in the form of gods or mythological creatures, a number of which were found in extraordinarily good condition. An intricate model of El Palacio reveals how it would have appeared in the Classic period – with the tops of the buildings adorned with roofcombs – and there's a map of the entire site showing that only around a quarter of the structures have been excavated (at its height, the population may have reached 100,000). The back wing is devoted to a replica of Pakal's famous sarcophagus lid from the Templo de las Inscripciones – entrance is restricted to small groups, every thirty minutes or so.

Beyond Palenque

Any of the following destinations can easily be visited as a day-trip from Palenque, and each can also be made part of a longer excursion, with plenty of accommodation options along the way. The easiest way to do this is with a **tour**, and there are dozens to choose from (see "Listings", p.309), or if you have your **own transport**. However there are also good bus and combi connections in every direction.

To the south, a series of stunningly beautiful **waterfalls** is the chief attraction on the winding mountain road that heads from Palenque towards **Ocosingo**. The awesome cascades on the Río Shumulhá at **Agua Azul** and the exquisite waterfall at **Misol-Há** are usually visited on a day-trip from Palenque, but it's also possible to visit them independently and stay nearby, or to make this part of a more extended excursion taking in Ocosingo itself and the nearby ruins of **Toniná**. There are several places to stay in Ocosingo, and it's an opportunity to experience something of the atmosphere of the Chiapas highlands, though the ruins are the real reason to visit.

Heading slightly further east will take you to the Usumacinta river and the spectacular Maya sites of **Bonampak** and **Yaxchilán**. Impressive ruins aside, this is an opportunity to experience something of the remaining tropical forest and the teeming wildlife around the banks of the river.

To make an outing with locals, rather than tourists, visit **Catazajá**, at the junction with Hwy-186, where a huge lake is a popular weekend outing, and also home to a small pod of manatees. Autotransportes Joya de Tulum's combis (M$15), drop you near but not at the lake – taxis (M$5) wait to do the final shuttle to the "Playas". Down at the waterfront are numerous restaurants – try *El Pelicano* or *El Manatí* – and *lanchas* available for trips on the lake with its abundant birdlife.

Misol-Há, Agua Azul and Agua Clara

Just 18km from Palenque, **Misol-Há** (M$10 entry), a 25-metre waterfall, provides a stunning backdrop to a pool that's safe for **swimming**. A fern-lined trail leads along a ledge behind the wide cascade, where there is a refreshing spray and the lush rainforest is filled with bird calls. Most tours arrive here early (around 9.30am) or at lunchtime and spend no more than half an hour, so if you can visit mid-morning or mid-afternoon you'll find things much quieter. There's inexpensive **accommodation** in beautifully situated wooden cabañas (☎0155/5329-0995 ext 7006; ❺), where the roar of the waterfall will lull you to sleep. The cabins, the **restaurant** (mainly catering to tour groups) and the **craft shop** on site are owned and run by the San Miguel *ejido*; each cabin has a private bathroom and electricity, and some are family-size, with kitchens. With your own car, this is a potential alternative to staying at Palenque; for those relying on public transport, the falls are an easy 1.5km walk from the road.

Pressing on up the winding mountain road, you reach the turn for **AGUA CLARA** (M$10), 56km from Palenque. This is a more recently developed river attraction that is also on many tour itineraries. Here the water is calmer and you can rent kayaks and small boats to explore the river, or trek a couple of kilometres through the forest to a quiet natural pool where the Tulijá and Shumulhá rivers join. There's also horse-riding.

Another 8km along the highway is the turn for **AGUA AZUL**; the falls themselves are 4km further down a track in the Parque Nacional Agua Azul. Overall it's a more active place, with swallows darting through the cascades' spray, kids thronging the parking lot and a long row of souvenir stands and empanada cafés. Nonetheless, the whole area around the cascades is exceptionally beautiful, with dozens of lesser falls found both up- and downstream. If it's safe to walk upstream (it may not be in the rainy season) you'll come across a perilous-looking bridge over the river and eventually an impressive gorge where the **Río Shumulhá** emerges out of the jungle-covered mountain. At the right time of year, the river is alive with butterflies. Higher up, the swimming is a little safer, too – but don't go in at all if you're not a strong swimmer. People drown here every year, and though a few signs warn of dangerous currents, they don't mark all the perilous spots.

Agua Azul is a major tour destination. If you come **by bus** (not on a tour), you'll be dropped at the crossroads, where there are usually taxis (M$10) waiting to take you to the base of the falls. Otherwise it's a 45-minute walk to the waterfall and at least an hour's sweaty hike back up. Villagers have set up two tariff stations along the road, at each of which (if they're manned) you'll be charged M$10. Simple **cabañas** (❹) are also available for rent – enquire at the Modulo de Información near the car park. And although you may want to get as far from the tourist scrum at the entrance to the falls as possible, keep in mind that **violent attacks** have occurred here in the past. A heavy federal police guard has been a major deterrent in recent years, but you're always safer with other people nearby.

The easiest way to visit two or three of these spots is with a **day tour** through Transportes Chambalú in Palenque. It runs van tours to Misol-Há and Agua Azul at 10am and noon, spending thirty minutes at Misol-Há and three hours at Agua Azul. A departure at 9am also stops at Agua Clara. All tours cost M$100 per person.

Ocosingo & Toniná

Pressing on up into the mountains past the waterfalls, a visit to **Ocosingo** and the nearby Maya site of **Toniná** will give you a sense of the Chiapas mountain heartland – a complete contrast to the relative lowlands of Palenque. The unrelenting winding road makes it a slow trip, but a fascinating one, through scores of tiny villages where women's colourful clothing changes with each ridge you cross.

Ocosingo

By the time you reach **OCOSINGO**, you're at an elevation where pines have replaced tropical trees. A fair-sized town, this is a sort of regional capital, still close to its country roots, with cowboy-hatted men in from the ranches and women selling *maíz* from great bubbling vats. The streets are lined with single-storey, red-tiled houses, and the air is thick with the scent of wood smoke. There's little to see beyond the **plaza**, surrounded by *portales* and a big old country church on the east side, and the **market**, vast and crowded with people from all sorts of different ethnic groups. But if you're coming from the Yucatán, it's striking to see just how culturally different this area is.

The area around Ocosingo is something of a **Zapatista** stronghold, and as recently as 2003 the nearby *Rancho Esmeralda* (see below) was seized by the rebels. You'll see plenty of signs proclaiming Zapatista control in the region ("Pueblo Zapatista…el pueblo manda y el gobierno obedece" – "Zapatista town…the people command, the government obeys"). Also look out for some striking murals on buildings at the north edge of town. There are army check-points, but tensions are generally low, and tourists should not be affected.

Practicalities

Buses stop on Ocosingo's main road or at a makeshift terminal nearby. To get to the plaza turn left out of the terminal and walk down the hill for about four blocks until you reach Calle Central, then turn left for a further two blocks. You'll find pretty much everything you need within a block or two of here.

Accommodation options are plentiful, including the *Hotel Central* (Ⓣ919/673-0024; ❸), on the north side of the plaza, where good-size rooms have fans and TV, and *Hotel San José*, just off the northeast corner of the plaza along Calle 1 Ote Nte (Ⓣ919/673-0039), with clean, comfortable budget rooms (❶) as well as some fancier ones with cable TV and air conditioning. The best of the lot for arranging further adventures, however, is the colourful and friendly *Hospedaje Esmeralda* (Ⓣ919/673-0014, Ⓦwww.ranchoesmeralda.net; ❸), a traveller's meeting place at Calle Central Norte 14, half a block north of the plaza, which has a range of shared-bath and en-suite rooms for one to four people. If you're travelling alone they can sometimes arrange shares, plus the place doubles as a **tourist information** office. The welcoming staff can help book light aircraft flights over Toniná (from the airfield just outside town), horse-riding trips (M$200; 1hr 30min) or travel to attractions further afield, including Tikal in Guatemala. The *hospedaje* started life as the *Rancho Esmeralda*, a hotel and campsite in a rural setting near Toniná, and there's a folder of newspaper reports documenting the seizure of the *Rancho* by the Zapatistas, as well as plenty of other reading material to borrow.

The *Esmeralda* also has a good **restaurant**, and there are several other budget **places to eat** surrounding the square, most serving a standard Mexican menu of tacos and tortilla dishes. *El Campanario* on the north side is very friendly and has a well-priced menu; the bright-yellow *El Desván*, on the opposite side of the plaza, is a slightly fancier place that serves pizza as well as the usuals. In the **food market**, indigenous women sell fruits, vegetables and local cheeses, including the round waxy *queso de bola* and the delicious creamy *queso botanero*. To get there turn right at the church for one block, then left along Calle 2 Sur Oriente for another four.

There are a couple of **ATM**s, one at Banamex on the plaza, and another at Banco Santander, opposite *Hospedaje Esmeralda* on Calle Central Norte. A few **Internet** cafés can be found along this road as well, including Compuchat, near the plaza, and Xanav (9am–2pm & 4–10pm; Ⓣ919/673-1334) at no. 40-C, which doubles as a travel agent for domestic flights.

Leaving Ocosingo by road is easy enough until mid-evening, with frequent buses to Palenque (16 daily; 3hr 30min), and buses and combis onwards to San Cristóbal de las Casas (12 daily; 2hr). The last Autotransportes Tuxtla-Gutiérrez (ATG) buses in either direction officially leave at 7.30pm – though they're *de paso* (stopping) buses and so are likely to run late. Cristóbal Colón services continue well after midnight in both directions.

Toniná

Some 14km east of Ocosingo, the Classic-period Maya site of **TONINÁ** (daily 9am–3.30pm; M$39) is large and impressive, and yet it sees few visitors. At its height, Toniná was a great power in the Usumacinta river basin. The city defeated Palenque and captured its ruler in 699 AD, and ruled from then until after 900 AD, when it became the last of the great Maya centres to fall victim to the disaster that led to their abandonment. It's also the site of the **latest recorded Long Count date**, corresponding to 909 AD.

When approaching Toniná, you'll see its modern **museum** (daily 8am–5pm; included in site entry price), which is well worth a look before heading off to the ruins. There's also a helpful model of the site, as well as drawings of some of the relief carvings still in place in the buildings – seeing these first will help you discern the images more clearly. The museum's collection ranges from exuberant images of the chocolate god to obscure details about skull shapes of the various Toniná inhabitants, who came in two waves and practised very different rituals. You'll also see many of the sculptures and relief carvings that were removed from the exposed parts of the site and preserved indoors here. In ancient times Toniná was a major ritual site, and it displays an almost single-minded obsession with images of bound prisoners and decapitation – panel carvings show the process, and many statues have had their stone heads chopped off. Seeing them all packed together in the gallery space is a bit unnerving. Labelling throughout is in Spanish only, but the objects are striking enough on their own.

The **ruins** of Toniná, a five-minute walk from the entrance, are virtually all one enormous building. A broad grassy plaza was once surrounded by smaller buildings and some ball-courts. **Ball-court 1** exemplifies Toniná's preoccupation with prisoners; built around 699, possibly to celebrate the great victory over Palenque, it has representations of bound captives instead of the usual rings for the balls to pass through.

But the real focus is the **Acrópolis**, a series of seven artificial terraces built into the hillside, incorporating dozens of temples and other buildings on its various levels. This is the "house of stone" that gave the site its Tzeltal name. A flashlight is useful to explore the labyrinthine interiors – there are warrens of small rooms and even internal staircases ascending from one terrace to the next. As you climb the hill there's plenty to explore, but look out above all for the reliefs and stucco masks that survive in situ, easily spotted under their protective thatch or corrugated-iron roofs. The most extraordinary of these is the enormous (16m x 4m) **Mural de las Cuatro Eras**, on the sixth platform. This amazingly well-preserved stucco codex tells the story of Maya cosmology by following the eras of the world as they were created and destroyed. The worlds are depicted as decapitated heads surrounded by flowers. A grinning, skeletal Lord of Death cheerfully holds a defleshed human head.

The final two levels are crowded with temples, and the climb to the summit is by steep, narrow steps. At the top is the **Templo del Espejo Humeante** (Temple of the Smoking Mirror), built around 840 AD, where you will be rewarded with awesome views. In the foreground, the pasture-land that surrounds the cleared site is studded with unexcavated mounds.

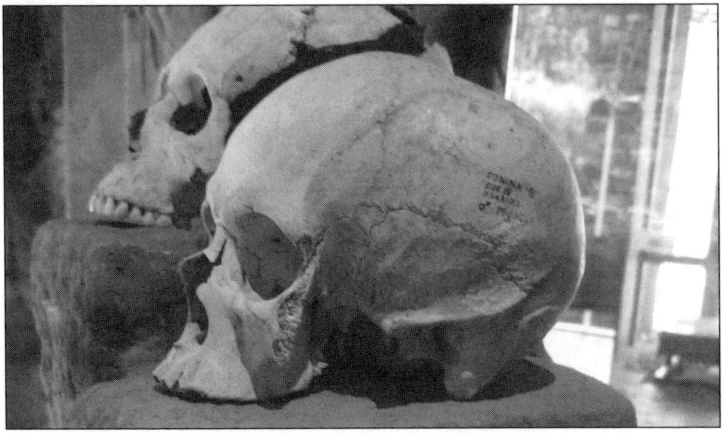

▲ Display of skulls in the archeological museum at Toniná

To reach Toniná **from Ocosingo**, you can take one of the frequent combis (M$10) that leave from the market area – look for those marked "Predio/Ruinas". A taxi will cost around M$70 one-way. At the entrance to the site itself (a walk from the museum), a small **café** sells packaged snacks, as well as locally made macadamia-nut products and espresso, made from local beans.

The Frontier Highway

The Carretera Fronteriza (**Frontier Highway**) provides access to the Usumacinta valley and the Lacandón forest, and the great Maya sites located here: **Bonampak**, famous for its murals, and **Yaxchilán**, a vast city on the riverbank. Following the river (also the Guatemalan border) through small settlements and wild forest, the remote highway has a reputation for being dangerous. A steady military presence has made the area relatively safe, however, and though it's not advisable to drive the road after dark, it is certainly no problem to travel this way in your own car. Army checkpoints are frequent, so be sure to carry your passport.

Another reason the area has become safer is, unfortunately, the increasing human settlement, which has meant, in turn, the destruction of the forest. Whereas you used to find untamed green less than sixty kilometres out from Palenque, the road is now lined for the most part with tidy farm plots and occasional blue-and-red-painted wood houses all the way to the town of Frontera Corozal, the starting point for trips to Yaxchilán. Tourism infrastructure has grown, though this is still one of the most adventurous places to visit in this part of Mexico. In particular, there's an amazing opportunity to stay overnight in deep forest, in the company of the Lacandón Maya, who have lived here for millennia. The good news is that large areas are protected, and wildlife remains abundant, even if you need a keen eye to spot the howler monkeys or the toucans that hide in the treetops.

The easiest way to visit Bonampak and Yaxchilán is through a **tour** from Palenque (see p.309), whether as a day-trip or overnight, with accommodation at the Lacandón Maya community of **Lacanhá Chansayab**. In either case, make sure that meals and site entry fees are included. It's also not difficult to make the trip on your own, so you can arrive at the remote sites relatively alone, and not with a merry band of twenty. **DIY trips** are also substantially cheaper, although the final cost will depend on finding people to share the boat trip from Frontera Corozal to Yaxchilán. The starting point is the Transportes de Chamoán combi office on Avenida Hidalgo, near the corner of Calle Allende in Palenque – for M$60 at the most, these vans will take you anywhere on the Frontier Highway, ending in Frontera Corozal. (Other bus companies offer cheaper service, but you're dropped on the highway and will have to take a taxi to Frontera Corozal for an additional M$20 per person.) The first departures are around 5am, and they run at least every hour until 5pm. If you're **driving**, note that the last petro station is at the turn for Metzabok, about 40km beyond Palenque. For details on local accommodation and transport, see Lacanhá Chansayab or Frontera Corozal (see p.320).

Welib-Ja

About 30km southeast of Palenque, the beautiful waterfalls of **WELIB-JA** (8am–5pm; M$10) are smaller but far less visited than Agua Azul or Misol-Há. And because they're only 500m from the road, they're also a lot easier to reach by public transport (take the Chamoán combi and ask to be let off at the *cascadas*). A little forest path leads alongside the river and down to the base of a towering split cascade, close enough that the mist sprays over you. There's a sensible sign advising "Don't get in the water if you can't swim", but otherwise you're left to your own devices. There are a few palapas for picnicking in the shade, as well as a protected kids' swimming area, upstream from the falls. Getting back to Palenque shouldn't be hard, as long as you start looking for a ride by 4.30pm or so – flag down standard combi vans as well as the pick-up trucks fitted with bench seats.

Bonampak

The outside world first heard of **BONAMPAK** ("Painted Walls") in 1946, when Charles Frey, an American conscientious objector to WWII who had taken refuge deep in the forest, was shown the site (though not its famous **murals**) by the Lacandón. The first non-Maya to see these murals – astonishing examples of Classic Maya art – was the American photographer Giles Healey, who arrived shortly after Frey's visit, sparking a long and bitter dispute over exactly who was responsible for their discovery. Bonampak's actual buildings are small and not the most spectacular, but the murals definitely make it worth the visit – there is very little like them elsewhere in the Maya world, and even in their somewhat decayed state, the colours are vivid and the imagery memorable.

The **entrance to the site** (daily 8am–5pm; M$36) is just a couple of huts selling sodas, as well as some Lacandón woodwork. Guide service is on offer, though English-speakers are rare. You are usually closely supervized, especially near the Temple of the Frescoes. No flash photography of the frescoes is allowed. You'll need just an hour to see the whole site, but allow at least another hour and a half for working out the various transport details (see "Practicalities", p.320).

The site

After crossing the defunct airstrip, you enter the site at the northwest corner of the main plaza, bounded by the foundations of some palace-style buildings. In the centre of the plaza **Stele 1** is of a larger-than-life **Chan Muan**, the last king of Bonampak, dressed for battle. Standing at nearly 7m, it is one of the tallest in the Maya world; you'll encounter other images of him throughout the site.

The Lacandón

You may already have encountered the **Lacandón Maya** selling exquisite bows and arrows at Palenque. Though today many wear their simple white robes and uncut hair for the benefit of tourists, the Lacandón have been the most isolated of all the Mexican groups. Their ancestors are believed to have migrated to Chiapas from the Petén region of Guatemala during the eighteenth century. Prior to that the Spanish had enslaved, killed or relocated the original inhabitants of the forest.

The Lacandón refer to themselves as "Hach Winik" (true people); "Lacandón" was a label used by the Spanish to describe any native group living in the Usumacinta valley and western Petén outside colonial control. Appearances notwithstanding, some Lacandón families are (or have been) quite wealthy, having sold timber rights in the jungle, though most of the money has gone. This change has led to a division in society, and most live in one of two main communities: **Lacanhá Chansayab**, near Bonampak, a village dominated by evangelical Protestants, some of whom are developing low-impact tourist facilities (see p.320); and **Nahá**, where a small group attempt to live a more traditional life.

Ahead, atop several steep flights of steps, lies the **Acrópolis**, built on at least two smaller structures underneath. On the lower steps more well-preserved stelae show Chan Muan preparing himself for blood-letting and apparently about to sacrifice a prisoner.

Splendid though these scenes are, the highlight of the site is the famed **Temple of the Frescoes**. Inside, in three chambers on the temple walls and roof, the renowned **Bonampak murals** depict vivid scenes of haughty Maya lords, splendidly attired in jaguar-skin robes and quetzal-plume headdresses; their equally well-dressed ladies; and bound prisoners, one with his fingernails ripped out, spurting blood. Musicians play drums, pipes and trumpets in what is clearly a celebration of victory.

Dated to around 790 AD, the murals show the Bonampak elite at the height of power: unknown to them, however, the collapse of the Classic Maya civilization was imminent. Some details were never finished and Bonampak was abandoned shortly after the scenes in the temple were painted. Though time and early cleaning attempts have taken their toll, you can still make out some vivid scenes (it helps immensely if you can study colour photos of replica murals beforehand). No more than three people at a time are permitted in each chamber, so you may have to queue to see them.

Room 2, in the centre, is the heart of the scene: it contains a vivid, gruesome depiction of battle and the defeat of Bonampak's enemies. Tortured prisoners lie on temple steps, while above them lords in jaguar robes are indifferent to their agony. A severed head has rolled down the stairs as Chan Muan grasps a prisoner (who appears to be pleading for mercy) by the hair, clearly about to deal him the same fate. The chambers to either side continue the story with celebrations of the victory and the arrival of rulers of vassal states to pay tribute. In **Room 1** an infant wrapped in white cloth (the heir apparent?) is presented to assembled nobility under the supervision of the lord of Yaxchilán, while musicians play trumpets in the background. **Room 3** shows more celebration and the execution of captives, while Chan Muan's wife, **Lady Rabbit**, accompanied by noblewomen, prepares to prick her tongue to let blood fall onto the paper in a clay pot in front of her. The smoke from burning the blood-soaked paper will carry messages to ancestor-gods. Other gorgeously dressed figures, whose senses in real life would have probably been heightened by hallucinogenic drugs, dance on the temple steps.

Practicalities

Bonampak lies in a small national park controlled by the Lacandón, on the fringe of the much larger Montes Azules Biosphere Reserve. However you get here, you are permitted to enter the forest only via Lacandón transport. When you get off a combi at the highway, **taxis** are waiting by a big palapa to take you to the site – about 12km into the forest – for M$70 per person. Arriving in your own car, you can continue into the forest about 3km to a parking area at the turn for the village of Lacanhá Chansayab, then get on a rattling old combi to the ruins there, for the same price – the transport is rougher, but you'll want to do this if you're planning to drive to the village for lodging. You can also **rent a bike**, but the business is set up another 250m *past* the combi parking area, and the combi drivers may tell you the bikes don't exist. If you don't have your own car and want to rent a bike, you'll have to explain this to a taxi driver at the highway – you should be able to negotiate a lower rate for the shorter ride. You could also conceivably **walk** to the ruins: the first 3km are fairly exposed (you might be able to hitch a ride for this stretch), but the remaining 9km are pleasantly shaded, with no major hills.

If you want to spend the night, the easiest option is at the combi parking area, a simple place called *Camping Margarito* (from M$70 per person), which also runs a **restaurant**. But there are more – and nicer – **camping spots and cabañas** in and on the way to the village of **Lacanhá Chansayab**, reached by the other road leading out of the parking area. The same Lacandón drivers can take you, for M$20 per person, and it's easiest if you have a particular spot in mind – the village is too spread out to walk around comparing options. Prices at all places are about M$25 for camping, M$80 for dorm beds where available, M$200 for shared-bath rooms and M$300–400 for private-bath options – the differences come in the upkeep of the facilities. None of the ten or so operations currently has a phone, but there's little chance you'll wind up with nowhere to sleep.

The first place you pass en route to the village is *Campamento Servicios Turísticos Lacandones*, where tent sites are set by a rushing river; a few concrete cabañas have private bathrooms. *Tucan Verde* is next, a rough spot recommendable only for camping, as the cabañas have been neglected. *Ya'aj Ché*, further along on the right and next to a small stream, is much preferable: a few lovely shared-bath wood cabins have good mosquito nets and porches by the water, or you can go for large concrete rooms with en-suite facilities. *Río Lacanjá*, to the left at the main village junction, is very popular with tours – it doesn't get too excited about walk-up business, though it does have a well-groomed set of cabins. Other recommended spots are run by old hands Vicente Kin Bor and Enrique Paniagua – look for signs at the village junction. Every place will be happy to arrange guides to the gorgeous rivers and waterfalls in the forest, and you can reach the **Lacanhá ruins** in under two hours from here. There's also a **hiking trail** to Bonampak (with some interpretive labels). The hike is wonderful in the dry season (Jan to late April) – be prepared for mud at other times.

Frontera Corozal

Another 15km along the Carretera Fronteriza is the turn for the narrow paved road to the settlement of **FRONTERA COROZAL**, on the Mexican bank of the Usumacinta, 19km off the highway. From here you can take a boat downriver to the ruins and jungle of **Yaxchilán**. A village checkpoint charges M$15 per person, and you may also be asked to show your passport, even if you have no intention of crossing the river to Guatemala. The community **museum** (7am–7pm; free) showcases the history of the settlement, founded only in 1976, and the relationships between the Chol, Lacandón and Tzeltal people, along with local archeology, flora and fauna. Its **restaurant** also has one of the only telephones in the village.

Should you want **to stay**, there are a few options. *Escudo Jaguar* (ⓣ00/502-5353-5637, calling Guatemala; ❹) is the longest-established place, and though its rooms are clean, spacious and comfortable, they're also the top choice for tours and can fill up early. *Nueva Alianza* (ⓣ00/502-5353-1395, calling Guatemala, ⓦwww.ecoturlacandon.com), behind the museum, is more natural-feeling, with big group rooms in wood cabañas (M$110 per person), camping space (M$50 per tent) and private cabañas (❸–❻); many of the latter are in a wooded area kept intentionally dark at night. Away from the riverfront (follow signs to the right off the main street), in a little pink-and-green two-storey building, *Posada Lizbeth* (❸) is tidy and clean, and rooms have hot water and fans.

To reach Yaxchilán, you need a *lancha* – a narrow riverboat with benches along the side and a tin roof for shade. A number of companies compete for business, but your best bet is to head straight down to the cooperative office at the riverfront (ⓣ00/502/5362-9599, calling Guatemala, ⓦwww.yaxchilan.com.mx), which has marginally lower prices. As with all the operations, fares vary with group size, with one to three people paying M$600 total, four paying M$700, and so on. If you're looking to share a boat you might also want to walk over to *Escudo Jaguar* – even though it's pricier, at M$650 for three, it's still listed in all the guidebooks as the main boat operator, so it's where most travellers ask to be dropped off. You also pay your site entrance fee wherever you buy your boat ticket (really, a kid runs with your money up to the INAH ticket office by the museum). The **river trip** is fabulous in itself, down a broad, fast-flowing river with Mexico on one bank, Guatemala on the other, and usually a great deal of wildlife including crocodiles to help pass the time. The journey downstream to Yaxchilán takes around half an hour; the return more than twice as long. To allow enough time at the site, the latest you should get on a *lancha* is 2pm. If you're heading **back to Palenque** or Lacanhá Chansayab the same day, you'll have to go much earlier, as the last buses and combis leave from in front of the cooperative office at 4pm (the earliest one leaves at 4am, with departures at least every hour all day).

Yaxchilán

A large and impressive site, accessible only via the river, **Yaxchilán** (daily 8am–4.30pm; M$46) was an important Classic-period centre. From around 680 to 760 AD, the city's most famous kings, Escudo Jaguar (Shield Jaguar) and his son Pájaro Jaguar IV (Bird Jaguar), led a campaign of conquest that extended Yaxchilán's sphere of influence over the other Usumacinta centres and may have established alliances with Tikal and Palenque. The buildings occupy a natural terrace above the river, with others climbing steep hills behind – a superb natural setting. Not so many people make the trip to this evocative site, and you'll often be alone in the forest with nothing but moaning howler monkeys around you. Giant trees keep the site shady, but nonetheless the jungle heat can be palpable. Bring plenty of water, as there are no services at the ruins.

From the entrance, the main path leads straight to the Gran Plaza, but if you have the energy for climbing, it's more rewarding to explore the wilder parts of the site first. Follow the branching path to the right leading up the hillside to the **Pequeña Acrópolis**, a set of thirteen buildings. A lintel on the most prominent ruin, known as **Edificio 42**, depicts Escudo Jaguar with one of his warriors. Walk behind here to find another narrow trail down through the jungle, over several unrestored mounds, until you reach a fork: to the right, the path climbs steeply once again, until it reaches **Edificios 39–41**, also called the Templos del Sur, 90m above the river level. These buildings probably had some kind of astronomical function. High above the river, this is a good place to spot parrots and other canopy-dwellers.

Retrace your steps to the main path, and continue until it emerges at the back of **Edificio 33**, the most famous building at the site, also known as El Palacio. It overlooks the main plaza from a high terrace. The lintels here are superbly preserved, and inside one of the portals is a headless statue of Pájaro Jaguar IV. In ancient times the building was a political court; more recently, it served as a religious site for the Lacandón Maya.

Descending 40m down the stairs in front brings you to the long **Gran Plaza**. Turn back to look up at the Palacio: with the sun shining through the building's roofcomb and tree roots cascading down the stairs, this is what you imagine a pyramid lost in the jungle should look like. To your left, just above ground level, **Edificio 23** has a few patches of coloured stucco around its door frames, just one patch of many well-preserved paintings and relief carvings that appear on the lintels of buildings surrounding the long green lawn. Some of the best works were removed in the nineteenth century and are now in the British Museum in London, but the number and quality of the remaining panels is unequalled at any other Maya site in Mexico. Many of these show rulers performing ritual events. This can also be seen on **Stele 1**, right in the middle of the plaza, near the base of the staircase. It depicts Pájaro Jaguar IV in a particularly eye-watering blood-letting ceremony, ritually perforating his penis. **Stele 3**, originally sited at Edificio 41, has survived several attempts to remove it from the site and now lies at the west side of the plaza, where it shows the transfer of power from Escudo Jaguar to Pájaro Jaguar IV.

Heading back to the entrance, pass through **El Laberinto** (The Labyrinth) at the plaza's northeast corner, where you can walk down through dim passages and out onto the main path.

Travel details

Buses

Villahermosa is the major transport hub, with services to all points in Mexico. Palenque does not have quite enough services – if you can't get a seat on the bus you want, it may be easier to take any bus available to Villahermosa, then transfer for onward service. ADO provides first-class service throughout the region, while Cristóbal Colón (OCC) serves Chiapas and Transportes Regionales de Tabasco (TRT) serves its own state. ATS runs into the Yucatán peninsula, and is usually a bit cheaper, and slower – more like second-class service, though its buses use the ADO terminals. Second-class companies usually cover only small regions, and are useful in Tabasco for destinations like Comalcalco, Paraíso and Frontera. The travel times given are for first-class services only. Allow at least thirty percent longer for second-class services, which run at least as frequently.

Villahermosa to: Campeche (21 daily; 6hr 15min); Cancún (30 daily, including one on the deluxe UNO service; 12hr); Chetumal (11 daily; 8–9hr); Mérida (25 daily, including two on UNO; 8–9hr); Mexico City (26 daily, including four on UNO; 11–13hr); Oaxaca (3 daily; 12hr 30min); Palenque (14 daily; 2hr 30min); Tenosique (14 daily; 3hr 30min); Tuxtla-Gutiérrez (17 daily; 4–5hr); Veracruz (28 daily, including one on UNO; 6–7hr).

Palenque to: Campeche (6 daily, 8am–12.55am; 5hr); Cancún (9 daily, 5.20pm–11.10pm; 13hr); Chetumal (8 daily; 7hr); Mérida (6 daily, 8am–12.55am; 7hr 30min); Mexico City (1 daily at 9pm; 14hr); Oaxaca (1 daily at 5.30pm; 15hr); Ocosingo (15 daily; 3hr); Playa del Carmen (9 daily, 5.20pm–11.10pm; 11hr 30min); San Cristóbal de las Casas (14 daily; 5hr); Tulum (8 daily, 5.20pm–11.10pm; 10hr); Tuxtla-Gutiérrez (13 daily; 6hr 30min); Villahermosa (12 daily; 2hr 30min).

Flights

Villahermosa has a major airport with frequent daily flights to Mexico City and many other domestic destinations, including Veracruz and Mérida.

Contexts

Contexts

History

The history of the Yucatán is inextricably linked with that of the surrounding territories. The indigenous Yucatec Maya, whose extraordinarily advanced culture and sphere of influence extended as far south as present-day Honduras, lived in a constantly changing pattern of local allegiances until the arrival of the Spanish in the early sixteenth century. Subsequently part of a loose political entity controlled from Spain – at times under the power of Mexico, sometimes thrown in with Guatemala and Central America – the Yucatán was, very briefly, an independent state, before being subsumed into the newly formed Mexico in the 1820s.

Prehistory

The exact date when human beings first crossed the Bering Strait into the Americas is debatable, but the earliest widely accepted figure is around 15,000 years ago. Successive waves of nomadic Stone Age hunters continued to arrive until around 6000 BC, pushing their predecessors gradually further south. Some of the earliest signs of human presence in the Yucatán can be found in the peninsula's many caves, such as the Grutas de Loltún, where prehistoric paintings can be seen.

The first signs of settled habitation – the cultivation of corn, followed by the emergence of crude pottery, stone tools and even of trade between the regions – come from the **Archaic** period, around 5000 to 2000 BC. Thereafter, similar patterns of settlement start to appear throughout **Mesoamerica**, an area stretching from the mid-north of modern Mexico south into the heart of Central America. The first established civilization does not appear until the **Pre-Classic** or Formative era (2500 BC to 250 AD), with the rise of the Olmecs.

Still the least known of all the ancient societies, the **Olmecs** are regarded as the "mother culture" of Mesoamerica, inventors of the calendar, glyphic writing, a rain deity and probably also the concept of zero and the ball-game. What you see of them in museums today, or above all at the **Parque La Venta** in Villahermosa, is a magnificent artistic style, exemplified in their sculpture and in the famous colossal heads. These, with their puzzling "baby-faced" features, were carved from monolithic blocks of basalt and somehow transported over ninety kilometres from the quarries to their final settings – proof in itself of a hierarchical society commanding a sizeable workforce.

By the end of the Pre-Classic period, Olmec civilization was already in decline. La Venta, the most important cultural centre, seems to have been abandoned around 400 BC, and the other towns followed over the next few hundred years. As the Olmec weakened, new civilizations grew in strength and numbers, establishing cities throughout central Mexico at sites such as Monte Albán (near Oaxaca), Cuicuilco, in the great Valley of México (where Mexico City now stands) and above all **Teotihuacán (northeast of Mexico City)**, the first truly urban society in Mesoamerica, whose architectural and religious influences reached as far south as the Maya heartlands of Guatemala.

The Pre-Classic Maya

The first identifiably **Maya** settlements appeared in the Guatemalan highlands from around 1500 BC. From here, over the next few hundred years, the Maya spread in all directions, including north to the lowlands of the Yucatán Peninsula. Early villages were little more than temporary encampments, but gradually the cultivation of corn, beans, squash and chile allowed for the development of larger settlements. These were always near a water source, which in central Yucatán usually meant a cenote. The **spread of agriculture** allowed the population to grow, and with population growth came a society that was increasingly hierarchical and specialized. At this time, pottery replaced stone implements, woven cloth supplanted animal fur and writing, art and science began to flourish. Thatched, oval or rectangular Maya huts, recognisable to today's inhabitants of the Yucatán, formed the basis of these early villages, but buildings of increasing size and complexity were soon constructed specifically for religious purposes.

Recent discoveries suggest that by the late Pre-Classic period, some Maya settlements, above all in the Guatemalan highlands, were becoming very sophisticated indeed, and that previous assumptions about the timing of the development of Maya civilization may have to be brought forward. In the Yucatán, development lagged behind, but even here cities of substantial size were growing up. Among the **early sites** are Calakmul, close to the Guatemalan centres, and Edzná, where a system of canals and moats helped drain agricultural land and defend the city. Along with Dzibilchaltún and Oxkintok, these early cities all lie on routes leading from the highlands to the Gulf coast, with its salt pans and trading opportunities.

The Classic era

It was in the **Classic period**, however, from around 250 AD to 900 AD, that the Maya reached their peak of power and achievement. While in Europe the Roman Empire was in decline, in Mesoamerica the Maya were embarking on six-and-a-half centuries of extraordinary technological, architectural, artistic and scientific advance. Without the use of metal tools, draught animals or the wheel, they built **city-states** that controlled hundreds of thousands of people, created intricate **statuary** and sculpture and devised a **mathematical and calendar system** far more advanced than those known in the "civilized" world. For more on Maya achievements, see p.343.

Again, the first great centres of the Classic period were not in the Yucatán but in the highlands further south – cities such as Tikal, Copán and Kaminaljuyú. The most celebrated cities of the Yucatán, on the whole, were latecomers: Palenque, Yaxchilán, Uxmal and Chichén Itzá all flourished towards the end of the Classic era. Which is not to say that Yucatán was not thriving, just that important sites like Calakmul or Sayil lived to some extent in the shadow of still greater powers further south.

Conflict and downfall

There was never a single Maya empire, but rather a series of independent – yet interdependent – city-states in an almost constant state of shifting **alliances,**

rivalry and war. War was necessary not just for control over rivals and access to their resources, but also to increase a ruler's prestige and provide captives, preferably high-born, for ransom and sacrifice. Some, such as Calakmul and Tikal, or Yaxchilán and Palenque, seem to have been traditional rivals; others, like Yaxchilán and Bonampak, or Sayil and its Puuc neighbours, enjoyed long-standing alliances.

Among the major conflicts that we know about – mainly from carvings or even paintings (such as the famous Bonampak murals) created to celebrate the victory – the battles between the great centres of Tikal and Calakmul stand out. In 562 AD **Calakmul** succeeded in putting together an alliance with Yaxchilán and others that inflicted a major and lasting defeat on Tikal. It was only when this alliance fell apart that Tikal was able to take its revenge, humiliating Calakmul and its ruler, Jaguar Paw, in battle in 695.

Further west, **Palenque**, under its rulers Hanab Pakal (Jaguar Shield) and Chan Bahlum (Jaguar Serpent), spent much of the seventh century asserting its authority over the Usumacinta basin region, forcing Yaxchilán into subservience. A hundred years later, the roles were reversed, as **Yaxchilán** became the greater power – again under two kings, Escudo Jaguar (Shield Jaguar) and his son Pájaro Jaguar IV (Bird Jaguar) – and Palenque the subject. Similar swings of power affected central and northern Yucatán, too, where **Uxmal** and later Chichén Itzá rose to dominance at the very end of the Classic era.

Quite what caused the **downfall of Classic Maya civilization** remains the subject of fierce debate, yet what is certain is that societies throughout Mesoamerica suffered a similar fate at similar times. Teotihuacán, the great power of central Mexico, was abandoned as early as 750 AD (at the end of a long decline), and within a hundred years many of the great Maya centres, in particular those in the highlands, followed suit. Maya societies in the Yucatán were among the last to retain their authority, but by around 950 AD they too were in terminal decline, if not abandoned altogether. Only Chichén Itzá continued to thrive.

Numerous theories attempt to explain the Maya collapse, among them the notion that it was caused by invaders from the north, occupying a vacuum left by the fall of Teotihuacán. Certainly Teotihuacán's demise must have severely affected its trading partners throughout Mexico, possibly setting off a **chain of disasters** that had a cumulative effect. More likely than invasion, though, the causes were natural, with the Maya paying the price for their success: overpopulation exacerbated by the failure of harvests, perhaps resulting from overexploitation of the land. Such events can easily be imagined spilling over into the political sphere in a rigorously structured society. A loss of faith in rulers and priests could have led to rebellion, or wars between cities may have broken out over increasingly scarce resources.

Post-Classic society

If the Yucatán saw the final flourish of Classic Maya civilization at sites like Uxmal, it also saw the most powerful surviving **Post-Classic societies** (900 to 1500 AD), above all at **Chichén Itzá**. This was the one city in the entire Maya land – or at least the only one we know of – that not only revived its former glory, but from around 1000 AD on, may have even surpassed it. For many years it was believed that the revival of Chichén Itzá was the result of an invasion by the **Toltecs**, whose capital was at Tula in central Mexico. Certainly there are many apparent links between the two cities, not just in architecture, but in a new obsession with war and sacrifice, and with the legendary feathered-serpent god **Quetzalcoatl** (Kukulcán to the Maya). These days, though, most archeologists believe that Chichén Itzá remained under Maya control, albeit with strong trading and cultural links with the Toltecs. This theory sees not an invasion by a foreign power, but rather the arrival of a new Maya clan, the **Itzá**, driven north by the collapse of their cities in Guatemala.

Whatever their origins, the Itzá consolidated their influence, and Chichén Itzá remained the dominant power in the peninsula until it was abandoned in the first half of the thirteenth century. Shortly afterwards, around 1263 AD, the Itzá ruler Kukulcán II founded a new city, **Mayapán**. A walled city with some 10,000 inhabitants, it led a broad alliance of small city-states that united the Yucatán for some two hundred years. Some of these were based at the great old centres like Uxmal and Chichén Itzá, others were newly prosperous towns, especially on the Caribbean coast, such as Tulum, Xel-Há and Cozumel. What Mayapán lacked, however, was the great architecture and vast ceremonial centres of its predecessors – signs, perhaps, of a less hierarchical, more trade-based society. **Maritime trade** certainly flourished in the late Post-Classic age. Christopher Columbus himself (though he never got to Mexico) encountered a heavily laden boat of Maya traders, plying the sea between the Yucatán and Honduras.

Mayapán's supremacy ended in 1441 after an attack by the Xiu people, based at Uxmal. From then until the arrival of the Spanish, the Yucatán's city-states continued to form alliances and enmities, and apparently to prosper, but they remained disparate, with no central authority or dominant group.

The Spanish Conquest

Having heard tales of gold and empires to be claimed in the new territories ever since Columbus's accidental discovery of the Americas in 1492, the Spanish started to probe the Mexican coast from their bases in Cuba. The first expedition to land in the Yucatán was led by **Francisco Hernández de Cordoba** in 1517. Cordoba discovered Isla Mujeres, but after being driven away from Ah-Kin-Pech (Campeche) by hostile natives and caught in a storm, his team landed at the mouth of the Río Champotón to replenish their stocks of fresh-water. There they were surprised by a Maya force under Moch Cuouh and heavily defeated. Cordoba died of his wounds a few days later, and the place became known as the Bay of the Bad Fight. The following year, **Juan de Grijalva** sailed round the Yucatán and up the coast as far as present-day Tampico, reporting back on the wealth of central Mexico.

The most notable Spanish invasion, of course, began with **Hernán Cortés**'s landing on the coast near modern Veracruz on April 21, 1519 (Good Friday). With him were just 550 men, a few horses, dogs and a cannon, yet in less than three years they had defeated the Aztecs and effectively established control over most of Mexico. Mopping up the rest of the Aztec Empire was a relatively straightforward task for the conquistadors, but it took twenty more years to overcome the Maya.

The defeat of the Maya

Almost immediately after their campaigns in central Mexico, the Spanish turned their eyes south. During the 1520s Pedro de Alvarado and his brother

Gonzalo conquered most of what is now Guatemala and the southern Mexican highlands of Chiapas. In 1526, **Francisco de Montejo**, a veteran of the Grijalva and Cortés expeditions, travelled to Spain to petition the king for the right to conquer the Yucatán. The following year he landed at Cozumel with about two hundred men, and from there crossed to the mainland. At first, his task seemed an easy one: most local chiefs, aware of the conquests elsewhere, swore loyalty to the Spanish Crown. However, as he advanced inland he found towns already deserted, and his troops began to suffer ambushes and attacks. In a pitched battle at **Aké** (near modern Tizimín) 1200 Maya warriors were killed, but Montejo also lost nearly half his force and the Maya refused to surrender. Leaving behind a small garrison, Montejo retreated to Veracruz to gather a larger army.

In 1531, Montejo returned with his son, **Francisco de Montejo the Younger,** and defeated the Maya at Campeche, setting up a base there. Montejo the Younger waged a successful campaign in northern Yucatán, making alliances and declaring Chichén Itzá his capital. Meanwhile, his father had travelled to Maní, where he established friendly relations with the **Xiu**, who a century earlier had brought about the downfall of Mayapán. Again, however, many Maya allies turned on the Spanish, and by 1535 the Montejos were forced to withdraw once more from the Yucatán, their troops demoralized by the fierceness of the resistance and the lack of financial reward for their efforts.

The final chapter in the conquest of the Yucatán began in 1540, when Montejo the Younger returned to Campeche with a yet larger force, founding Mérida two years later. What really tipped the scales this time was the support of the Xiu, whose leader in **Maní** converted to Christianity. The Xiu dominated much of western and northern Yucatán and most of their subject cities either followed their lead or were easily subdued. The east continued to resist, but armies led by Montejo's cousin (another Francisco de Montejo) gradually established power. By 1546, the Yucatán was firmly under Spanish control.

Colonial rule

Cortés was appointed governor of **Nueva España** (New Spain) in 1522, and there followed three hundred years of direct Spanish rule, under a succession of 61 viceroys personally responsible to the Spanish king. The boundaries of the new territory initially stretched from present-day Panama to the western states of the US, although it wasn't long before internal struggles erupted over their control. In 1542, the state of **Guatemala** was formed, whose territory included the Yucatán, though 23 years later Guatemala found itself yet again a part of New Spain. Guatemala was ultimately re-established as a state in 1570, but this time the Yucatán was attached to Mexico. There it would remain throughout the colonial era, albeit never wholly absorbed thanks to the difficulties of communication with the centre.

For the Spanish, the initial colonial concerns were reconstruction, pacification and conversion. To this end they began building grand towns (to a plan, with a plaza surrounded by a grid of streets, laid down in Spain) and constructing **churches**, often in areas that had been sacred to the Maya or on top of their pyramids. The cathedral in Mérida was built in 1561 on the ruins of a Maya temple; in Maní, the stones of the old temples were used in the construction of the monastery. Churches were built like fortresses, to awe the Maya population and to serve as refuges for the white population if necessary. Moreover, they were built in places sacred to the Maya, to encourage them to worship there and prove the superiority of the new god; mass conversions were the order of the day.

The most dramatic and immediate consequence of the Spanish Conquest and colonization, however, was the **decimation of the Maya population**, not through war or famine (though some died that way), but as a result of successive epidemics of infectious **diseases**, including smallpox, measles and influenza, to which the New World had no immunity. It has been estimated that within a century, the native population of Mesoamerica was reduced by as much as ninety percent. Not surprisingly, the effects were catastrophic, and not only for the Indians themselves. The few survivors were treated more and more like slaves.

The Spanish Crown theoretically offered some protection to the native population – outright slavery was outlawed, for example – but in practice Spanish authority was very distant from the ordinary people of the Yucatán. Indeed, many Maya were overseen by Maya chiefs, who collected tax and tribute on behalf of the colonial authorities. Some priests, too, attempted to champion indigenous rights, notably **Bartolomé de las Casas** in Chiapas, but they were few and far between. In the Yucatán, it was a Franciscan friar, **Diego de Landa**, later bishop of Mérida, who was responsible for one of the most notorious acts of all. In 1562 he held an auto-da-fé on behalf of the Inquisition, at which 42 local Indians were tortured and executed for heresy, and over twenty Maya codices (hieroglyphic books recording Maya history and beliefs) were burnt. This constituted virtually every known written Maya record at the time. Ironically, Landa, whose acts were condemned in Spain, is responsible for much of what we do know of the ancient Yucatecan Maya. Perhaps as an act of contrition, he later gathered all the information he could discover about the Maya, and compiled it in his famous book, *Relación de las Cosas de Yucatán*.

Pirates and traders

For much of the Yucatán, the colonial era settled into a pattern of semi-enslavement for the Maya population on vast landholdings granted to Spanish colonists. The region was far from the centre of Mexico and outside the mainstream of its politics; since it had few natural resources, it was largely left to itself. The exception was around the coasts, where persistent piracy led much of the population to flee inland. From bases in the uninhabited areas around the Laguna de Términos (near modern Ciudad del Carmen), pirates and privateers, many of them British, operated with impunity throughout the seventeenth century. They preyed on vessels travelling between Veracruz and Cuba, exploited local resources of logwood and mahogany and frequently raided coastal towns, above all Campeche. Finally driven out at the beginning of the eighteenth century, they moved round the coast and, in 1763, with official British support and following numerous battles with Spanish fleets, founded **British Honduras** (now Belize) with the old pirate population as its basis.

What wealth there was in colonial Yucatán, and indeed throughout Mexico, was concentrated in the hands of a tiny local elite and the imperialists in Spain. The governing philosophy was that "what's good for Spain is good for Mexico", and towards that end all **trade**, industry and profit was exclusively aimed. No local trade or agriculture that would compete with Spain were allowed, so the cultivation of vines or the production of silk was banned. Heavy taxes on other products – coffee, sugar, tobacco, cochineal and silver and other metals – went directly to Spain. This didn't prevent the growth of a small class of extraordinarily wealthy **hacendados** (owners of massive estates or haciendas), whose money funded the architectural development of colonial towns like Mérida and

Campeche. These were transformed from fortress-like huddles at the beginning of the colonial era to supreme examples of Baroque extravagance by its end. However, Spain's policies did stop the development of any kind of realistic economic infrastructure, or even of decent roads linking the towns. Throughout the colonial era there was no practical overland route from the Yucatán to central Mexico, for example.

Even among the wealthy there was growing **resentment**, fuelled by the status of Mexicans: only "**gachupines**", Spaniards born in Spain, could hold high office in the government or Church. Of course, such people constituted a tiny percentage of the population. The rest were **criollos** (creoles, born in Mexico of Spanish blood), who were in general educated, wealthy and aristocratic, and **mestizos** (of mixed race), who dominated the lower ranks of the Church, army and civil service, or lived as anything from shopkeepers and small ranchers to bandits and beggars. At the bottom of the pile were the surviving Maya.

Independence

By the beginning of the nineteenth century, Spain's status as a world power was in severe decline. In 1796, British sea power had forced the Spanish to open their colonial ports to free trade. At the same time, new political ideas, realized with the French and American revolutions, were transforming the world. Although the works of such political philosophers as Rousseau, Voltaire and Paine were banned in Mexico, the opening of the ports made it inevitable that their ideas would spread, especially via traders from the newly established United States. Literary societies set up to discuss these books quickly became centres of **political dissent**.

The spark, though, was provided by the French invasion of Spain, as colonies throughout Latin America refused to recognize the Bonaparte regime, and the campaigns of Bolívar and others in South America began. In Mexico, the "gachupine" rulers proclaimed their loyalty to Ferdinand VII (the deposed king) and hoped to carry on much as before, but creole discontent was not to be so easily assuaged. In Querétaro, the first leaders of the independence movement emerged from a literary society: **Father Miguel Hidalgo y Costilla**, a creole priest, and **Ignacio Allende**, a disaffected junior army officer.

When their plans for a coup were discovered, the conspirators were forced into premature action, with Hidalgo issuing the famous **Grito** (cry) of Independence – "¡Méxicanos, viva México!" – from the steps of his parish church in Dolores on September 16, 1810. The mob of Indians and mestizos who gathered behind the banner swiftly took the major towns of San Miguel, Guanajuato and others to the north of the capital, but their behaviour – seizing land and property, slaughtering the Spanish – horrified the wealthy creoles who had initially supported the movement. In 1811, Hidalgo's army, huge but undisciplined, moved on the capital, but at the crucial moment Hidalgo decided to retreat, and his forces broke up as quickly as they had been assembled. Within months, Hidalgo, Allende and the other ringleaders had been captured and executed.

By this time most creoles, frightened at what had been unleashed, had rejoined the ranks of the royalists. But many mestizos and much of the indigenous population remained in a state of revolt, finding a new leader in the mestizo priest **José María Morelos**. Morelos was not only a far better tactician than Hidalgo, he was also a genuine radical. By 1813, after a series of highly successful guerrilla campaigns, he controlled virtually the whole of central and northern

Mexico, with the exception of the capital and the route from there to Veracruz. At the **Congress of Chilpancingo**, he declared the abolition of slavery and the equality of all races. However, the royalists fought back with a series of crushing victories. Morelos was captured and executed in 1815, and his forces, now led by Vicente Guerrero, were reduced to carrying out the occasional minor raid.

Ironically, it was the introduction of liberal reforms in Spain, of just the type feared by the Mexican ruling classes, which finally brought about **Mexican Independence**. Worried that such reforms might spread across the Atlantic, many creoles pre-empted a true revolution by assuming a "revolutionary" guise themselves. In 1820, **Agustín de Iturbide**, a royalist general but himself a mestizo, threw in his lot with Guerrero; in 1821, he proposed the **Iguala Plan** to the Spanish authorities, who were hardly in a position to fight, and Mexico was granted independence.

The Yucatán declares independence

Always culturally, as well as geographically, distinct from the rest of Mexico, the Yucatán briefly attempted to go it alone as a nation. This was not as radical a notion as perhaps it sounds – Chiapas was in a similar situation, while Guatemala and the territories of Central America, after having been invited to join Mexico, chose to go their separate ways. Yucatán's independence initially lasted a matter of months, however, before both the Yucatán and Chiapas joined the new nation of Mexico.

The post-independence years were chaotic to say the least, with constant changes of government, and in 1835 a new regime in Mexico City under General Santa Ana attempted to impose far more central control on the regions. Local discontent culminated in the **Mérida Congress** approving a declaration of independence for the Yucatán. At first, the Yucatán's governor, Santiago Méndez, blocked it, saying that the Yucatán would recognize the rule of the central government if the old constitution was reinstated. Promises were made but swiftly broken by President Santa Ana, and the Yucatán formally declared independence in 1841. Mexican flags were replaced by the flag of the **Republic of Yucatán** – five stars on a green field and one white horizontal stripe between two red.

Soon the Yucatán was suffering from loss of trade as Mexico blockaded its ports. Still more significantly, the Caste Wars broke out in 1847. Desperate for help, Méndez offered sovereignty over the Yucatán to any nation that helped defeat the rebellion. Although the US considered the offer seriously, it was the newly wealthy Mexican government, following the end of the Mexican-American War, that took him up, and the Yucatán was again reunited with Mexico on August 17, 1848.

The Caste Wars

The **Caste Wars** were one of the most successful indigenous uprisings in history, creating an autonomous Maya state that survived for over fifty years. Yet their origins were at least as much political, over land and labour rights, as they were racial. Initially, at least, the uprising was supported by poor mestizos as well as the Maya.

For all its promises, the effect of independence on most people in Mexico was simply a change of ruler, from the Spanish to locally born creoles. Indeed, for the lowest rungs of the population, this development actually made things worse: the protection of the Spanish Crown disappeared, and the liberalization of **land** laws allowed the privatization of previously communal land. Meanwhile, the power of the Church was barely diminished, but with a reduction of funds from the government the burden of tribute on the poor became even greater. At the same time, the loss of Spanish trade meant major changes to agriculture. **Henequen** was first planted in the 1830s, and by 1845 had become the Yucatán's chief export (see box, p.250); sugarcane was also widely introduced. As a result, forest that had previously been communal was taken over by the great haciendas and cleared. These supposedly unexploited forest areas were often sacred to the Maya, homes to their gods. Water, too, was sold off, with cenotes and springs that had been in communal use for centuries handed over to private owners.

In the battles for independence, and also in the internal struggles which had pitted Campeche against Mérida (a reflection of the wider struggles between liberals and conservatives throughout Mexico), many Maya had been recruited to **armed militia**, often with promises of land or freedom for their service. Such promises were rarely honoured, but the participants were taught the use of arms and military organization – training the white elite of the Yucatán would regret.

The spark that ignited the Caste Wars is generally taken to be the execution, in July 1847, of rebel leader **Manual Antonio Ay** in Valladolid. That same year Valladolid, Tepich and Tabi were sacked by the rebels, and much of their white population slaughtered. By May 1848 a loose alliance of Maya forces, led by **Cecilio Chi** and **Jacinto Pat**, occupied almost the entire peninsula and advanced to within 24km of Mérida and 8km of Campeche, where the white population had taken refuge. Allegedly, the only reason the governor had not

▲ Henequen workers waiting to go home

issued orders for a complete evacuation of the Yucatán was the shortage of paper in the besieged city. At the very point of victory, however, the spring rains came, and the Maya army evaporated as its soldiers went back to their fields to plant corn.

Within months, the Mexican-American War ended, the Yucatán accepted Mexican sovereignty and well-equipped **Mexican troops** poured in to suppress the rebellion. The rebels were pushed back into the southeastern corner of the state, in what today would be southern Quintana Roo, and both Chi and Pat were assassinated in 1849. The fighting had left perhaps 200,000 people dead or displaced in the Yucatán, and over the next ten years as many as two thousand Maya were arrested and sold as slaves in Cuba.

Chan Santa Cruz

In 1850, the **Talking Cross** appeared to a group of Maya (see box, p.163). They believed their gods had spoken to them through it, urging them to fight for independence. The same year, the town of Chan Santa Cruz (later Felipe Carrillo Puerto) was founded and would become the cultural, military and political capital of the ongoing Maya rebellion. From here the Maya administered a growing state, supplied with arms and other necessities from British Honduras, and launched occasional guerrilla attacks into Mexican territory. At its peak the **Maya nation of Chan Santa Cruz** controlled all the land from modern Playa del Carmen to the border of British Honduras, and inland as far as Tepich and Tihosuco; it was recognized by Britain (which benefited from the trade) as a de facto independent nation.

Chan Santa Cruz was never allowed to live at peace, however, and the Mexican government fomented rivalries with other Maya groups, supplying them with weapons and promising land rights. By the 1890s, the people and their leaders grew weary, and with the dictator Porfirio Díaz in power in Mexico City, British relations with Mexico improved. Partly to protect their huge new investments (in rail construction for example), the British government recognized the sovereignty of Mexico and closed the border between Chan Santa Cruz and British Honduras, cutting off the Maya nation's main line of supply. In 1901, Mexican general Ignacio Bravo occupied the town of Chan Santa Cruz, destroying the Talking Cross and officially ending the war. The final battle was anti-climactic, with the Maya short of arms and their army crippled by the diseases the Mexicans brought with them. Quintana Roo was made a territory of Mexico in 1902 (finally achieving statehood in 1975).

Isolated resistance to the Mexican republic continued for many years, with major incidents in 1917 in Vigia Chico and 1933 in Dzula, and outbreaks of rebellion reported even in the 1950s. Many of the original causes of the war, however, disappeared (at least in theory) when the victorious revolutionary armies marched into the Yucatán in 1915, bringing with them promises of land reform and the cancellation of debt labour.

Dictatorship and revolution

Distracted by the Caste Wars and as physically isolated as ever, the Yucatán was largely a spectator during the civil wars that tore central Mexico apart from 1855 to 1876. The liberal reforms that resulted, above all the reduction of the power of the Church, reached the Yucatán late, and trickled down. In 1876 a new radical liberal leader, **Porfirio Díaz**, overthrew the elected government and proclaimed his own candidate president. The following year he assumed the presidency himself, and was to rule as dictator for the next 34 years. At first his platform was a radical one, but it was soon dropped in favour of a brutal policy of **modernisation**.

In many ways the achievements of his dictatorship were remarkable: some 16,000km of railway were built (including the line from Mexico City to Mérida), industry boomed, telephones and telegraphs were installed and major towns, reached at last by reasonable roads, entered the modern era. In the countryside, Díaz established a police force, the notorious *rurales,* who stamped out much of the banditry (though later, their corruption made them almost as bad as the bandits). But the costs were high: rapid development was achieved by handing over huge swathes of the country and its people to foreign investors, who owned the vast majority of the oil, mining rights, railways and natural resources.

This was also the era when the vast **haciendas** of the Yucatán reached their peak of power, wealth and privilege. Able to rely on the forced labour of a landless peasantry, whose serfdom was ensured by wages so low that they were permanently in debt to their employers, they had little interest in efficiency or in production for domestic consumption. By 1900, the entire land was owned by some three to four percent of its population. The rich became very rich indeed; Yucatán's poor had lower incomes and fewer prospects than they had had a century earlier.

With the onset of the **twentieth century**, opposition was growing to Díaz, not just among the poor, but also the young, educated middle classes, concerned above all by the racist policies of their government (which favoured foreign investors above native ones) and by the lack of opportunity for themselves. In 1910, **Francisco Madero** ran against Díaz for president. When he was imprisoned and the election awarded to Díaz, revolutionary forces took up arms. In the northern state of Chihuahua, **Pancho Villa** and **Pascual Orozco** won several minor battles, and in the southwest, **Emiliano Zapata** began to arm indigenous guerrilla forces. After numerous revolutionary successes, Díaz fled into exile, and on October 2, 1911, Madero was elected president.

Like the originators of Independence before him, Madero had no conception of the forces he had unleashed. He freed the press, encouraged the formation of unions and introduced genuine **democracy**, but failed to do anything about the condition of the peasantry or the redistribution of land. The renewed fighting between revolutionary factions continued, on and off, for nearly ten years. Even later, in the 1920s and 1930s, there were sporadic attempts at a Catholic counter-revolution.

Again, the Yucatán was only peripherally involved, with all the major battles taking place in northern and central Mexico. When **Salvador Alvarado** marched into Yucatán at the head of a revolutionary army in 1915, the resistance of the conservative local elite was swiftly overcome.

The Yucatán in modern Mexico

The first president who was in a secure enough position to start to make real progress towards the revolutionary ideals was **Plutarco Elías Calles**, elected in 1924. Work on large public works schemes began – roads, irrigation systems, village schools – and about eight million acres of land throughout Mexico were given back to the villages as communal holdings, *ejidos*. At the same time, Calles

The end of the ejido?

Land reform was one of the great promises of the Mexican Revolution, and its most cherished legacy. Land redistributed after the Revolution was parcelled out in communal holdings, known as **ejidos**, which could not be sold as they belonged to the state. At a local level the land was held communally, divided up by the communities themselves, following the pre-Hispanic and colonial tradition. In the 1990s, however, the constitution was amended to allow the sale of *ejido* lands. Many peasants and indigenous communities feared that their landholdings would now be vulnerable to speculators or corrupt officials. And as most poor communities exist in a state of almost permanent debt, people believed that their land would be seized to cover outstanding loans, worsening their economic plight still further. All too often they have been proved right.

instituted a policy of virulent **anticlericalism**, closing churches and monasteries, and forcing priests to flee the country or go underground. Through the 1930s, Calles continued to control his successors from behind the scenes, steering national politics to the right in the bleak years of the Depression.

Lázaro Cárdenas, elected in 1934, revived the revolutionary momentum. As the spokesman of a younger generation, Cárdenas set up the single broad-based party that was to rule Mexico for the rest of the twentieth century, the **PRI** (Party of the Institutionalized Revolution). He set about an unprecedented programme of reform, redistributing land on a huge scale (170,000 square kilometres during his six-year term), creating peasant and worker organizations to represent their interests at a national level and incorporating them into the governing party. He also relaxed controls on the Church to appease internal and international opposition.

In 1938, he nationalized the **oil companies**, an act that has proved one of the most significant in shaping modern Mexico and bringing about its industrial miracle. For a time it seemed as if yet more foreign intervention might follow, but a boycott of Mexican oil by the major consumers crumbled with the onset of **World War II**, and was followed by a massive influx of money and a huge boost for Mexican industry as a result of the war.

In the Yucatán, the so-called Mexican miracle was slower to take hold, and the fifty years following the Revolution were ones, on the whole, of gradual decline. Though the lot of the peasantry improved hugely thanks to land distribution and the break-up of the haciendas, in economic terms the region went backwards. Many of the haciendas had been damaged during the Revolution, and henequen production was also hampered by the confusion following land redistribution and the loss of much of the workforce to work their own fields. At the same time, new sources of henequen in Asia and South America were becoming available. With the widespread replacement of henequen products by artificial fibres in the 1940s, Yucatecan agriculture lost its final overseas markets. It was not until the 1970s that the modern world started to catch up with the Yucatán. There were two chief drivers: the selection of **Cancún** for massive government investment in tourism, and the exploitation of **oil** reserves off the Gulf coast of Campeche. Suddenly the area was wealthy again, and development since, above all in tourism, has been unrelenting.

The final decades of the twentieth century were traumatic for Mexico. Vast oil revenues and a one-party state proved an ideal breeding ground for **corruption**, which permeated every level of government. Despite the country's wealth, a huge foreign debt had been built up, and in the 1980s, falling oil prices and rising interest rates provoked a major **economic crisis**. Public faith in the governing party was further shaken by the 1985 **earthquake** that devastated Mexico City and again revealed widespread corruption, both in the distribution of aid and in the contracts that had been awarded to erect sub-standard buildings in the first place. The governing party was further damaged by the outbreak, in 1994, of the **Zapatista** rebellion in Chiapas, a revolt that, though currently quiet, is still not entirely resolved. Finally there were **drugs**, with cartels smuggling vast quantities across the border into the US, protected by corrupt police and government officials. Their wealth and ruthless use of violence for many years made the cartels inviolate, and even today the government struggles to contain them.

All these crises, and the loss of their traditional support (even though they could still rely on the party machine to deliver election victories, earned or not) forced the PRI into ever more **radical change**, and in the 1990s much of the old party ideology was torn up in the name of economic reform. Most significantly, the NAFTA free trade treaty was signed with the US, and the *ejido* system (see box, opposite) was reformed. At the same time, the electoral system was cleaned up. For the first time, the PRI started to lose elections.

Into the new millennium

On July 2, 2000, **Vicente Fox Quesada**, the candidate of the right-wing PAN party, was voted in as president. It was a landmark event. Not only was he the first opposition candidate ever to have been democratically placed in power, it was also the first peaceful transition between opposing governments since independence. Furthermore, it was the end of seven decades of PRI rule and of the world's longest-surviving one-party dynasty. At a national level, the decline

Drug-running in the Yucatán

The Yucatán was not exempt from the worst excesses of **corruption and drugs**. Indeed, as a stronghold of the PRI's old guard, it witnessed one of the most extreme cases. **Mario Villanueva**, governor of Quintana Roo from 1993 to 1999, disappeared a few days before his term of office – and his immunity from prosecution – ran out. He spent two years on the run before finally being arrested in Cancún in 2001.

On the one hand he is alleged to have taken millions of dollars in bribes from developers of the Riviera Maya coast, riding roughshod over ecological considerations and the rights of *ejido* landholders. At the same time, it is claimed that, with his direct involvement, Cancún and the surrounding area became one of the major shipment points used by Colombian drug cartels moving their products to the US. In June 2007, Villanueva was found guilty of money laundering by the Mexican courts, but acquitted on the more serious drugs charges. He was released on the basis of time already served, but immediately rearrested on a request for extradition to the US; he remains in jail, fighting desperately against extradition.

Although serious damage was done to the trade by his arrest and that of many associates, the war against drugs continues. In 2004, following the murder of three federal agents, the Cancún attorney general's office was occupied by the Mexican army, and over twenty senior local government and police officials arrested, suspected of involvement in the continuing drug trade. And in 2007, after nearly ten tons of cocaine were seized from two US-registered planes, more arrests were made in Cancún.

of the PRI continues: in the 2006 presidential elections, PAN candidate **Felipe Calderón** defeated the candidate of the left (with the PRI nowhere) by less than half a percentage point. The close and controversial result left Calderón weakened, though he has gradually established more authority. Most strikingly, a feature of his government has been an all-out military campaign against the drug cartels; whether it's effective or not remains to be seen.

The Yucatán, meanwhile, is known by Mexican political commentators as "**The Land of the Dinosaurs**" for the continuing grip that the PRI party machine maintains here. Although PAN and other parties have made some progress, all three current state governors in the Yucatán are members of the PRI (Ivonne Ortega in Yucatán, Jorge Hurtado in Campeche and Félix González in Quintana Roo), and the legislatures are generally dominated by them, too. PAN does provide the mayor of Mérida (César Bojórquez) and others across the state, but, if anything, their influence in the region seems to be in decline as the PRI reasserts itself.

Environment and wildlife

The Yucatán Peninsula, Tabasco and the lowlands of Chiapas contain some of Mexico's richest wildlife areas, with particularly outstanding birdlife. Lush tropical forests in **Chiapas** and **southern Yucatán** contain the remaining populations of monkeys and large cats, as well as parrots and toucans, while the flat uplands and coastal areas of the **Yucatán Peninsula** host a fabulous collection of migrating birds, including large flocks of greater flamingos. Snorkelling or diving along the Mesoamerican Barrier Reef and islands in the Caribbean reveals schools of brilliantly coloured fish.

Unfortunately, as in many countries suffering economic hardship, much of this natural beauty is under threat either from direct hunting or from the indirect effects of **deforestation** and **commercialization**. It is imperative that visitors be respectful of the natural environment and support the vital educational programmes working to preserve it.

It should be stressed that not only is it extremely irresponsible to buy, even as souvenirs, items that involve wild animals in their production, but it is also generally **illegal** to bring them back to the UK or the US. This applies specifically to tortoiseshell, black coral, various species of butterfly, mussels and snails, stuffed baby crocodiles and cat skins. Trade in living animals, including tortoises, iguanas and parrots (often sold as nestlings), is also illegal, as is uprooting cacti.

Geography

The Yucatán Peninsula is a single limestone platform, one of the largest on the planet. An accretion of layers of decayed reefs, it's rarely more than a few feet above sea level. There's no visible sign of it now, but 65 million years ago, an enormous meteor slammed into the north Gulf coast near the town of Chicxulub Puerto; this is the meteor that is thought to have brought about a catastrophic climate change and the extinction of the dinosaurs. The climate here, fortunately, is more stable today. The region is entirely within the **Tropic of Cancer**, and rainfall varies across the landmass, though generally there are only two seasons: a hot, wet one, from mid-May to mid-November, and a temperate, dry one, through most of the winter and spring. Hurricanes are a risk between August and November, and, due to the lack of elevation, they have on occasion swept well inland. Hurricane Isidore did substantial damage to Mérida in 2002, and Hurricane Dean hit land on the Caribbean coast in August 2007, sweeping all the way from the south of the peninsula to the Gulf of Mexico.

Most of the Yucatán's geographic interest lies underground. Despite the total lack of visible rivers, a reserve of fresh-water is trapped just below the limestone surface, occasionally exposed through sinkholes called **cenotes**, and filling vast and beautiful **caves**, some more than 100m deep. In 2001 and 2002, explorers discovered three human skeletons that are more than 10,000 years old in caves here; several prehistoric elephants and other giant Pleistocene animals have also been brought to light. Because limestone is so porous, however, the aquifer is very easily contaminated, and scientists are only now starting to advise the government on safe modes of growth and development.

By contrast, **Tabasco** is almost entirely a coastal plain, shot through with rivers that have their sources in the mountains of **Chiapas** and Guatemala. In the foothills in the south of the state, and all over more mountainous Chiapas, the rivers take the form of dramatic **waterfalls**. The extensive river system comes with its own liabilities, namely flooding. Eighty percent of the state of Tabasco was inundated in November 2007, after a particularly heavy rainy season caused the Usumacinta and Grijalva rivers to rise well beyond their banks. What laid the groundwork for the disaster – which displaced more than 20,000 people – was that Tabasco's ground level has sunk in the last century, due to heavy petroleum extraction and other mining, as well as deforestation.

Vegetation

The Yucatán Peninsula's vegetation is influenced by its low elevation. No mountains provide runoff water, but the extensive coastline brings regular and fairly reliable rain along with year-round warm temperatures. The northern portion is primarily **dry deciduous scrub**, filled with tamarind and bay cedar. Much of the thorny scrub has been cleared to grow maize, citrus fruits and **henequen**, a variety of agave cactus used for the production of rope. A swathe of **seasonal tropical forest**, where many of the low acacias and ceibas lose their leaves in the dry season, covers the centre, mostly in Yucatán State. Bougainvillea, hibiscus and flame trees add dramatic colour in these areas. **Tropical rainforests** extend across the base of the Yucatán Peninsula and through Tabasco, containing mahogany, cedar, rosewood, ebony and logwood, as well as over eight hundred species of wild orchid. Extensive **mangrove forests** line much of the Gulf coast and the Caribbean. Throughout, though, charcoal cutting or slash-and-burn agriculture has substantially denuded the original forest. Similarly, tourism growth along the coast has eaten away at the mangroves – a short-sighted move, as runoff from the trees' root systems nourishes the coral reefs that draw travellers in the first place.

The tropical forests provide both **chocolate** (from the cacao trees of Tabasco and Chiapas) and **vanilla**. Also harvested are chicle, from the latex of the **sapodilla** tree (used to make chewing gum), and wild rubber and sarsaparilla. **Herbs** used in the medicinal or pharmaceutical industries include digitalis from wild foxgloves and various barks for making purges and disinfectants. **Dioscorea mexicana**, a wild yam unique to Mexico that flourishes in Tabasco and Chiapas, was the source of the first lab-created progesterone, enabling the invention of oral contraceptives.

Insects

Insect life is incredibly abundant and diverse, particularly in the southern tropical rainforests, which teem with everything from assorted **gnats** to long columns of fungus-eating **leafcutter ants** to swarms of carnivorous **army ants**, which can devour much larger insects, even giant **grasshoppers** (called *langostas*, or lobsters). Lovelier are the colourful **butterflies** that can, at peak times of year, fill the air like snow. But for the most part, insects make themselves known through the variety of bites and sores they inflict. **Mosquitoes** are particularly troublesome; malaria is still a small risk in jungle areas. The **garrapata**, a tenacious tick found everywhere livestock exists, readily attaches itself to human hosts. And while **scorpions** live throughout the Yucatán, they are generally not lethal (and are in fact eaten dried as a purported wart cure); **tarantulas** are also encountered in the drier areas, and they too are not poisonous.

Fish and reptiles

Because the Yucatán has few rivers above ground and only one substantial lake, fresh-water fish are few. Only in Tabasco is there significant diversity. Of the more than one hundred species in Tabasco's Río Usamacinta, one of the most remarkable is the prehistoric-looking, sharp-toothed **pejelagarto**, a type of gar – its name, derived from the Spanish words for "fish" and "lizard", accurately describes its appearance. The Yucatán cenotes and lagoons contain two **endemic species**, the Mayan cichlid and the banded tetra, while deep in the underwater cave systems, several varieties of eyeless fish flourish.

Offshore, the waters contain over one hundred significant marine species. Among the more prevalent are **swordfish**, **snapper**, **bonefish**, **tarpon** and **mackerel**. **Shrimp** and **spiny lobster** are also important commercial species, and deep ocean beds and coastal irregularities provide rewarding fishing in the waters of the Campeche Bank on the Gulf of Mexico. The Laguna de Términos, near Ciudad del Carmen, hosts the country's largest fishing fleet. A variety of sharks cruise the reefs, but the most remarkable ones are the placid **whale sharks** that congregate off the coast of Isla Holbox at the end of every summer, in what is perhaps the largest community in the world.

As for **reptiles**, iguanas and smaller lizards are at home in the forests and at seemingly every archeological site, while crocodiles populate the mangrove swamps and other brackish lagoon areas. **Marine turtles**, including the loggerhead, green, hawksbill and leatherback, are still found off many stretches of undeveloped waters and shores on the Gulf and Caribbean coasts. Hunting of both adults and eggs is against the law, but numbers have been greatly reduced, as illegal hunting continues. Nonetheless, programmes to protect turtle nests have been established in many of the major tourist areas, which may help boost the population in the future. Outside the Chiapas jungle (where the fer-de-lance viper makes its home) the number of poisonous **snakes** is relatively few – only rattlesnakes are found in the scrub forests, and assorted large green tree snakes are much more common. Amphibian life is similarly abundant; varieties include salamanders, several types of **frog** and the massive **cane toads** that have invaded nearly every continent.

Birds

Between the marshes and scrublands of the northern Yucatán Peninsula and Tabasco, and the dense rainforests in the south and Chiapas, this region is a delight for birdwatchers. During the winter migratory season, some two billion birds pass through. Among the diverse species (more than five hundred in the jungles alone) are resplendent **red macaws** and **parrots**, which make a colourful display as they fly amongst the dense tree canopy. The cereal-feeding habits of the parrot family have not endeared them to local farmers, and for this reason (and their continuing capture for sale as pets), their numbers have also been seriously depleted in recent times. Red macaws are now seldom seen outside of the southern fringes of Chiapas. Larger **game birds**, such as curassow, chachalaca and especially the ocellated turkey (eaten by the Maya for millennia) can be seen on the ground. Keel-billed **toucans** can also be spotted in the southern jungles – Maya legend has it that the tips of their bills are red because they dipped them in the blood that covered the land during the nineteenth-century Caste Wars. Another distinctive species in the Yucatán is the large turquoise-browed **motmot** (*toh'* in Maya), called the clock bird (*pájaro reloj*) because it switches its long tail feathers rhythmically like a pendulum.

The most familiar large birds of Mexico, however, are the carrion-eating **turkey vultures**, which migrate from North America and are often seen soaring in large groups. The Yucatán is also one of the last remaining strongholds of the small **Mexican eagle**, depicted on the Mexican flag.

Large numbers of coastal lagoons serve as feeding and breeding grounds for a wide variety of aquatic birds, some of them winter visitors from the north. Foremost among these are the substantial flocks of graceful **flamingos** that can be seen at selected sites along the western and northern Gulf coasts.

Mammals

The central Yucatán forest has traditionally teemed with **agouti**, **opossums** and **coatimundis**, but these have been seriously depleted by overhunting. Long-legged **pacas** (*tepescuintle*) have suffered greatly, as they have a reputation for being particularly tasty; they, at least, are now being semi-domesticated. **Spider** and **howler monkeys** are still plentiful in the Chiapas jungle and around Calakmul, though their numbers are also decreasing as their territory shrinks.

The largest ground-dwelling mammal in the region is the **tapirs**, a distant relative of the horse, with a prehensile snout, usually never found far from water. Two species of **peccary**, a type of wild pig, wander the forest floors in large groups seeking their preferred food (roots, palm nuts and even snakes), and there's the smaller **brocket deer**. The **jaguar**, so revered by the Maya, is severely endangered.

The drier tropical and subtropical forests of northern Yucatán produce a more varied ground cover of shrubs and grasses, which supply food for the **white-tailed deer** and abundant small rodents such as the spiny tree **rat**, which in turn provides food for a variety of predators such as the **margay** and **jaguarundi**. Other large mammals that can still be found in small numbers are large and small **anteaters** and **armadillos**. The reefs and lagoons that run along the Quintana Roo coast, as well as the brackish Laguna de Catazajá in Chiapas, have small colonies of the large aquatic **manatee** or sea cow, a docile creature that feeds on sea grass.

The Maya belief system

Like so many ancient cultures, the Maya have been subject to the fantastical theories of explorers as well as the imaginings of armchair spiritualists: "The Maya were not aided by extraterrestrial beings," a sign at several archeological sights clarifies, "What they accomplished was due to their ingenuity and hard work." It doesn't help, though, that the archeological record is so spotty, partially due to the fragile limestone in which the Maya predominantly built, but more the fault of the Spanish conquerors who were not content just to destroy the physical symbols of the Maya but were also bent on systematically replacing the pagan culture with Catholicism.

Much of our knowledge of the ancient Maya, then, is derived from the surviving traditions, handed down through generations, often in secret to protect them from Spanish pillaging. The **Chilam Balam**, for instance, are cumulative records of lore and prophecy recorded in various villages in Latin script in the late seventeenth and early eighteenth centuries. Experts also draw on various Spanish contemporary accounts, as well as the sculpture, pottery and jewellery retrieved from tombs. Images carved into the ruins of buildings offer clues, while the breakthrough in decoding the hieroglyphic system, a success of just the past few decades, has contributed greatly to the historical record. Further hints come from other Mesoamerican cultures, as the Maya share a great deal with the Aztecs and Toltecs, as well as the earliest related culture with a strong archeological record, the Olmecs.

The Olmec influence

The cities of the **Olmecs**, the first great Mesoamerican civilization, formed a template that was traced by subsequent cultures, including the Maya. They were the first Mesoamerican civilization who literally set their cosmology in stone, making a permanent record of their rulers and the gods and spirits with whom they communed. The Olmec place of creation was the mighty volcano of **San Martín**, in the south of modern Veracruz State, and they built a replica – a sacred artificial mountain, complete with fluted sides – in their city at **La Venta** in Tabasco. This was the original Mesoamerican **pyramid**, a feature that recurs in virtually every subsequent culture. Into the base of their volcano pyramid the Olmecs embedded huge **stelae**, flat carved stones portraying ruling dignitaries communicating with gods and spirits. These were the first stelae in Mesoamerica, and later versions fill the plazas of ruined cities in the Maya world and all over Central America.

One stele at La Venta depicts a **World Tree**, a symbol of the "axis mundi" at the centre of the Mesoamerican universe. With its roots in the earth and its branches in the heavens, the tree links the underworld of the dead with the earth and sky. Though this was perhaps the first such representation, World Trees have been found in cities all over Mesoamerica. Among the Maya, the World Tree is specifically the spreading boughs of the silk-cotton (ceiba) tree. At Palenque there are several images of the ceiba, including one on the lid of a ruler's sarcophagus, where the ruler is shown falling through a World Tree inscribed in the night sky – the Milky Way.

Opposite Mexico's first pyramid, the Olmecs built a **gateway** to the spirit world, home to a pantheon of gods, spirits and the souls of dead ancestors, in the form of a sunken, court-shaped plaza with an enormous pavement of blocks made of the mineral serpentine. They added two large platforms topped with mosaics and patterns depicting aquatic plants. Such symbols appeared all over Mesoamerica in the ensuing centuries, often decorating ball-courts or ceramics.

The Olmecs also developed the ritual **ball-game** that appears in every subsequent Mesoamerican culture. Usually played in a ball-court shaped like the letter "I", the game featured players, in teams of two or three, who scored points by using their thighs or upper arms to hit a ball through hoops, or at markers embedded in the court walls. The penalty for losing the most important games was death, though it has been suggested that the winners were sacrificed in some cities.

In general, the basic structure of Olmec society – a theocracy ruled over by a priestly and regal elite who communicated with and propitiated the spirit world through sacrifice and ritual blood-letting – would change little throughout Mesoamerica until the arrival of Cortés.

The calendar

For the Maya, the stars were embodiments of gods, and the constellations re-enactments of cosmic events; they regarded the three stars below the belt of Orion as the place of creation itself. Their interest in the constant shifting of the heavens was aided by the invention of the **calendar**, probably by the Zapotecs of Monte Albán in about 600 BC.

By the time of the Classic Maya (250–900 AD), the 260-day calendar, depicted as a wheel, had become the most significant tool in prediction and divination. Every number and day had its own meaning; each of the twenty-day names had a specific god and a particular direction, passing in a continuous anticlockwise path from one day to the next until a cycle of time was completed. This calendar was

▲ A Maya calendar

used alongside a 365-day calendar, roughly matching the solar year, but lacking the leap days necessary to give it real accuracy. This was divided into eighteen groups of twenty days plus an unlucky additional five days. Each twenty-day grouping and each solar year also had a supernatural patron. When the two calendars were set in motion and running concurrently, it took exactly 52 years for the cycle to repeat.

In addition to these two calendars, the Pre-Classic Maya developed what is known as the **Long Count**, recording the total number of days elapsed from a mythological date when the first great cycle presumably began. Under this elaborate record system, all became sacred, and every event, from the planting of crops to the waging of war, had to occur at the correct spiritual time.

The pantheon

The ancient Maya worshipped a staggering number of gods who represented virtually every facet of life, from specific activities (Ek Chuah oversaw trade and commerce, for instance) to places, such as the maize fields, where squat, mischievous *aluxes* were believed to stand guard. The deities' relative importance varied across the Maya world, but typically the Sun God, most often called **K'inich Ahau**, was considered the supreme deity. As the creator, he took several forms: by night, he became the Jaguar God, guarding the way to the underworld. Characterized by crossed eyes and buckteeth, he was one of the oldest gods in the Mesoamerican tradition, and was also worshipped by the Olmecs. After 900 AD, in the Post-Classic era, he was conflated with **Itzamná**, a powerful god credited with inventing writing and the tradition of scribes. Itzamná is often depicted with a toothless mouth (signifying his old age) and a hooknose, holding a pen; his consort is **Ixchel**, goddess of fertility. Also vital to the pantheon is the rain god **Chac**, who is widely identified with the many curly-nosed masks that adorn Maya temples and other buildings, though more recent scholarship suggests that these may actually be Itzamná.

The Maya's relationship with their gods was not one of simple worship, but of struggle and outwitting. Life was not so much borrowed time as time won by trickery from the gods of death. Maya vases, buried with the dead, often depict scenes from the **Popul Vuh**, the creation epic of the Quiché Maya tribe, in which the **Hero Twins**, two proto-humans with godlike powers, defeated the **Lords of the Underworld** through a series of tricks and their expertise in the ball-game.

In the Yucatán, this connection to the spirit world was made all the more tangible by the **caves** and **cenotes** that riddle the peninsula. These, it was believed, were open gateways to the underworld, and as a result many were considered sacred and were the site of numerous rituals. Though the ancient Maya were not as bloodthirsty as the Aztecs of central Mexico (whose cosmology rested on the gods' seemingly insatiable appetite for human hearts), their rituals do seem to have included **human sacrifice**. When the main cenote at Chichén Itzá was dredged, for instance, it was found to contain numerous skeletons, and Fray Diego de Landa recorded details of sacrifices in the mid-sixteenth century.

The Spanish conquistadors and the Franciscan priests who accompanied them toppled a pantheon that had been in place for centuries. Hundreds of thousands of books were burnt, priests executed and temples overturned. Such is the tenacity of the traditional beliefs of the Maya, though, that even five hundred years of effort have not been enough to eradicate them entirely, as anyone who has entered a rural church in the Yucatán or witnessed the rituals of the Day of the Dead – called Hanal Pixan by the Maya – can attest.

Books

Most big US book stores have an enormous array of books about, from or set in Mexico, as well as a few novels. In the rest of the English-speaking world there's far less choice, though the best known of the archeological and travel titles below should be available almost anywhere. Amazon.com and other US booksellers online can also ship worldwide, of course. Books with a ⛹ symbol are highly recommended.

For **specialist sources** in the UK, try the Latin America Bureau (Ⓣ020/7278 2829, Ⓦwww.lab.org.uk), which publishes books on the region's current affairs and politics, mostly from a radical left-wing perspective, and Canning House Library (Ⓣ020/7235 2303, Ⓦwww.canninghouse.com), a superb reference resource.

Travel

⛹ **Graham Greene** *The Lawless Roads*. In the late 1930s, Greene was sent to Chiapas and Tabasco to investigate the effects of the persecution of the Catholic Church. The result was this classic account of his travels in a very bizarre era of modern Mexican history. *The Power and the Glory*, published later, is an absorbing fictionalized version, centred on the exploits of a "whiskey priest" on the run from the authorities.

Michel Peissel *The Lost World of Quintana Roo*. In 1958, Peissel, then 21 years old, bushwhacked on foot through the virtually empty fringe of the peninsula. Definitely worth snapping up if you find a used copy, as it's a great depiction of an area that has changed rapidly in just a few decades.

Nigel Pride *A Butterfly Sings to Pacaya*. The author, accompanied by his wife and 4-year-old son, travels south from the US border in a Jeep, heading through Mexico, Guatemala and Belize. Though the travels took place over 25 years ago, the pleasures and privations they experience rarely appear dated.

John Lloyd Stephens *Incidents of Travel in Central America, Chiapas, and Yucatán*. A classic nineteenth-century traveller, Stephens, acting as American ambassador to Central America, indulged his own enthusiasm for archeology. His journals, full of superb Victorian pomposity, make great reading. The best editions include the fantastic original illustrations by Frederick Catherwood; a Smithsonian edition combines some of these with modern photographs.

John Kenneth Turner *Barbarous Mexico*. Turner was an American journalist who travelled through nineteenth-century Mexico. This exposé of the workers' conditions in the Yucatán's plantations did much to discredit the regime of Porfirio Díaz.

Ronald Wright *Time Among the Maya*. A vivid and sympathetic account of travels from Belize through Guatemala, Chiapas and Yucatán, meeting the Maya of today. The book's twin points of interest are the ancient Maya and the recent violence involving the Zapatistas.

Fiction and poetry

Jorge Ibargüengoitia *The Dead Girls, Two Crimes* and others. One of the first modern Mexican novelists translated into English, Ibargüengoitia was killed in a plane crash in 1983. These two are both blackly comic thrillers, superbly told, the first of them based on real events.

Octavio Paz (ed) *Mexican Poetry*. Edited by Paz (Mexico's leading man of letters in the post-revolutionary era) and translated by Samuel Beckett, this is as good a taste as you could hope for of modern Mexican poetry. Some of Paz's own poetry is also available in translation.

Earl Shorris *In the Yucatán*. This novel, the story of a Mexican-American lawyer and a Maya mystic who bond in jail, has its flaws, but its background detail is excellent, providing a good dose of political commentary and cultural information about the Maya. Shorris is also the author of numerous non-fiction titles including *The Life and Times of Mexico*, a somewhat rambling history that's fascinating to dip into.

B. Traven. Traven wrote a whole series of compelling novels set in Mexico. Among the best known are *Treasure of the Sierra Madre* and *The Death Ship*, but of more direct interest if you're travelling are such works as *The Bridge in the Jungle* and the other six books in the *Jungle* series. These latter all deal with the state of the peasantry and the growth of revolutionary feeling in the last years of Díaz's dictatorship, and if at times they're overly polemical, as a whole they're enthralling.

History

Inga Clendinnen *Ambivalent Conquests: Maya and Spaniard in Yucatán 1517 to 1570*. A product of meticulous research that documents the methods and consequences of the Spanish conquest of the Yucatán, Clendinnen's book examines events from the viewpoints of both the Spanish and Maya. In particular, she probes the extent to which the Maya ever truly converted to Christianity or believed themselves subjugated.

Bernal Díaz *The Conquest of New Spain* (trans J.M. Cohen). This abridged version of Díaz's classic, *Historia Verdadera de la Conquista de la Nueva España*, is the best available in English. Díaz accompanied Francisco de Cordoba and Juan de Grijalva on their initial forays into the Yucatán, then joined Cortés's campaign of conquest. It's a magnificent eyewitness account that makes compulsive reading.

Brian Hamnett *A Concise History of Mexico*. The book kicks off with a brief examination of contemporary issues and then jumps back to the time of the Olmecs. A combined chronological and thematic approach is used to analyse the social and political history of Mexico from then to the present day, making for a good general introduction.

Nelson Reed *The Caste War of the Yucatán*. Reed's book is the authority on this tumultuous and defining era in Yucatán history, with great detail on the Talking Cross movement. A must-read for anyone intrigued by this period.

Hugh Thomas *Conquest: Montezuma, Cortés, and the Fall of Old Mexico* (US); *The Conquest of Mexico* (UK). Same book, different title, but either way a brilliant narrative history of the Conquest by the British historian previously best known for his history of the Spanish Civil War. A massive work of real scholarship and importance but also humorous and readable, with appendices on everything from Aztec beliefs, history and genealogy to Cortés's wives and lovers.

The ancient Maya

Michael D. Coe *The Maya.* The best available general introduction to the Maya, now in its seventh edition: concise, clear and comprehensive. Coe has also written several more weighty, academic volumes. His *Breaking the Maya Code*, a beautifully written history of the decipherment of the Maya glyphs, owes much to Coe's being present at many of the most important meetings that led to the breakthrough.

David Drew *The Lost Chronicles of the Maya Kings.* Ignore the title – this is actually a very thorough yet accessible account of almost all aspects of the Maya in a single volume, by a British archeologist and broadcaster.

M.S. Edmonson (trans) *The Book of Chilam Balam of Chumayel.* The *Chilam Balam* is a recollection of Maya history and myth, compiled by the Maya over centuries; this version was written in Maya in Latin script in the eighteenth century. Although the style is not easy, it's one of the few keys into the Maya view of the world.

Diego de Landa *Yucatán Before and After the Conquest* (ed William Gates). A translation of the Franciscan monk's *Relación de las Cosas de Yucatán.* De Landa's prior destruction of almost all original Maya books as "works of the devil" makes his own account the chief surviving source on Maya life and society in the immediate post-Conquest period. Written in 1566 during his imprisonment in Spain on charges of cruelty to the Indians, the book provides a fascinating wealth of detail.

Mary Ellen Miller *Maya Art and Architecture.* An excellent survey of the artisanship of the Maya, organized by media, from stelae to pottery. Miller's *The Art of Mesoamerica: From Olmec to Aztec* gives a broader view.

Mary Ellen Miller and Karl Taube *The Gods and Symbols of Ancient Mexico and the Maya: An Illustrated Dictionary of Mesoamerican Religion.* A superb modern reference on ancient Mesoamerica, written by two leading scholars. Taube's *Aztec and Maya Myths* is perfect as a short, accessible introduction to Mesoamerican mythology.

Linda Schele, David Freidel et al. At the forefront of the "new archeology" school, the authors have been personally responsible for decoding many Maya glyphs, thereby revolutionizing and popularizing Maya studies. Although their writing style, which frequently includes recreations of scenes inspired by their discoveries, is

The music of the Yucatán

The Yucatán peninsula has historically looked to the Caribbean and Europe, rather than central Mexico, for culture. This is most strongly reflected in its music, particularly *trova yucateca*, which melds Cuban and European rhythms with local sounds, amounting to a music entirely unlike the brassy, boastful mariachi style associated with Mexico.

Instead, **trova yucateca** features dreamily sentimental ballads performed most typically by trios of string musicians. It came about as an outgrowth of Cuban music, which was fashionable in Mérida in the late nineteenth century. The city's upper class, rich from the surrounding henequen plantations, loved nothing better than to dance the elegant, romantic *habanera* and *guaracha,* imports from Cuba. At the same time, to reinforce Mérida's self-made reputation as "París en miniatura", children were groomed for French salon society, with music lessons as part of their acculturation.

Some of these youngsters grew up to be composers, adapting Cuba's vibrant dance music to the Yucatecan setting. This meant incorporating the Spanish-inspired rhythm of the **jarana**, danced in the Maya towns during fiestas, and penning heartfelt paeans to local Maya women. The singers conveyed their gallantry and sensitivity with oiled hair, limpid eyes and starched shirts. By the 1920s, *trova yucateca* was in full flower, and the songs of this era, such as "Caminante del Mayab", "Ojos Tristes" and "Beso Asesino", are often compiled on albums and performed today by succeeding generations.

Though you may see trios made up of instruments other than the usual guitar, *mandolín* and *tololoche* (double bass guitar), or solo lounge crooners with more modern tousled hair and unbuttoned shirts instead of guayaberas, today's *trovadores* still hold closely to tradition. This remains music of romance, nostalgia and seduction. In Mérida, you can experience it every night of the week if you like, as *trova* trios gather on the Plaza de la Constitución and can be hired for a single serenade or an entire evening's entertainment.

Back home, **recordings** are hard to come by, though Amazon and other online sources can usually come up with the odd compilation (such as *La Inolvidable y Anorada Trova Yucateca*, a 2-CD set on RCA International) and assorted one-off imports (the Pentagrama label is usually reliable) from bands like Los Condes or Los Dandy's. You can also listen to a number of great free samples on ⓦwww.yucatan living.com, including some in Maya. Locally there's plenty of choice, thanks to a tradition of home CD production by current *trova* artists; most markets will have a wide selection.

controversial to some fellow professionals, it has also inspired a devoted following. *A Forest of Kings: The Untold Story of the Ancient Maya* and *The Blood of Kings*, by Linda Schele and Mary Ellen Miller, detail how the ancient Maya were ruled by hereditary kings, lived in populous, aggressive city-states and engaged in a continuous entanglement of alliances and war. *Maya Cosmos: Three Thousand Years on the Shaman's Path*, by Schele, Freidel and Joy Parker, is perhaps more difficult to read, but continues to examine Maya ritual and religion in a unique and far-reaching way.

Robert Sharer *The Ancient Maya.* The classic (and weighty) account of Maya civilization, now in a completely revised and much more readable sixth edition, yet as authoritative as ever. Required reading for archeologists, it provides a fascinating reference for the non-expert.

Dennis Tedlock (trans) *Popol Vuh.* Translation of the Quiché Maya bible, a creation myth from the only ancient civilization to flourish in rainforest terrain. The Maya obsession with time can be well appreciated here: dates are recorded with painstaking precision.

Society, politics and culture

Rick Bayless *Rick Bayless's Mexican Kitchen.* Aimed at ambitious chefs, this tome has more than 150 recipes but no photos. The country's gastronomic heritage is explored in detail with a special focus on the myriad types of chile that form the heart of Mexican cuisine. More accessible is Bayless's *Mexico One Plate at a Time* (though it features no Yucatecan dishes, unfortunately), with careful instructions and thorough coaching, including a testimony in favour of lard.

Fernández de Calderon Candida *Great Masters of Mexican Folk Art.* A grand and gorgeously photographed coffee-table book produced by the cultural wing of Banamex, with portraits of the artisans alongside their works.

Macduff Everton *The Modern Maya: A Culture in Transition.* Everton's black-and-white photographs document Maya village life with affection and an eye to socio-economic issues.

Nancy and Jeffrey Gerlach *Foods of the Maya.* A solid introduction to the Yucatecan culinary tradition, very well tested for non-Mexican kitchens.

Diana Kennedy *The Essential Cuisines of Mexico.* Kennedy was a pioneer in bringing the multifaceted cuisine of Mexico to the attention of Americans when she published her first cookbook in 1972. This book is an almost overwhelming reference, but compiled with love. Pair with *From My Mexican Kitchen: Techniques and Ingredients* if you're completely new to Mexican cooking.

Dan La Botz *Democracy in Mexico.* Examines the political landscape of modern Mexico and puts it into historical context by analysing the major defining events of recent decades – the 1968 student massacre, the 1985 earthquake, the 1994 Zapatista uprising, amongst others – in terms of a rising political consciousness.

Elena Poniatowska A pioneer in the field of testimonial literature and one of Mexico's best-known essayists and journalists. To write *Here's to You, Jesusa!* Poniatowska befriended and interviewed her real-life cleaning lady. Narrated in the first person, the text is compelling, lively and at times ribald; Jesusa herself is now a celebrity on the literary circuit. Other works available in English include *Massacre in Mexico*, a collage of testimonies by people present at the 1968 massacre of students in Tlatelolco.

John Ross *Rebellion from the Roots.* An absorbing early account of the build-up to, and first months of, the 1994 Zapatista rebellion, and still the definitive book on the subject. Ross provides a detailed and informative background to the event, showing how the uprising was no surprise to the Mexican army. He's also the author of *Mexico in Focus*, a short but authoritative guide to modern Mexican society, politics and culture – worth reading before a visit.

Guiomar Rovira *Women of Maize.* Rovira, a Mexican journalist, witnessed the Zapatista uprising in Chiapas on New Year's Day, 1994. Interweaving narrative, history and the personal recollections of numerous women involved in the rebellion, this book provides extra ordinary insight into the lives of indigenous people.

Chloë Sayer. Sayer is the author of numerous books on Mexican arts, crafts and associated subjects, all of them worth reading. *The Arts and Crafts of Mexico is* perhaps the best general introduction you can find, while titles like *Textiles from Mexico* illustrate the depth of her knowledge.

Joel Simon *Endangered Mexico*. Eloquent and compelling study documenting the environmental crisis facing Mexico at the end of the twentieth century. Accurate and very moving, it's essential reading for those wanting to know how and why the crisis exists – and why no one can offer solutions.

Mariana Yampolsky and Chloë Sayer *The Traditional Architecture of Mexico*. The enormous range of Mexico's architectural styles, from thatched peasant huts and vast haciendas to exuberant Baroque churches and solid, yet graceful public buildings, is encompassed in this inspired book. While most of Yampolsky's superb photographs are in black and white, a chapter on the use of colour emphasizes its significance. The quality of Sayer's text raises it above the average coffee-table book. (For guides to ecclesiastical architecture in Mexico, see R. and R. Perry, below.)

Other guides

In Mexico, the best and most complete series of guides are published by **Guías Panorama** – they have small books on all the main archeological sites, as well as more general titles.

Carl Franz *The People's Guide to Mexico*. Not a guidebook as such, more a series of anecdotes and words of advice for staying out of trouble and heading off the beaten track. A brilliant read; perennially popular, and deservedly so.

Joyce Kelly *An Archaeological Guide to Mexico's Yucatán Peninsula*. Detailed and practical guide to more than ninety Maya sites and eight museums throughout the peninsula, including many little-known or difficult-to-reach ruins; an essential companion for anyone travelling purposefully through the Maya world. Kelly's "star" ratings – based on a site's archeological importance, degree of restoration and accessibility – may affront purists, but they do provide a valuable rubric when deciding where to go.

Richard and Rosalind Perry *Maya Missions*. One in a series of expertly written guides to the sometimes overlooked treasures of Mexico's colonial religious architecture; *More Maya Missions* covers Chiapas. These specialist offerings, ideal for travellers who want more information than most guidebooks can provide, are not widely available, though you can usually find them in tourist book stores in the areas they cover.

Jules Siegel *Cancun User's Guide*. Siegel, a freelance journalist, moved to Mexico in 1981, then worked for the tourism ministry in the nascent resort city. His self-published tome is as much an ode to this underappreciated city and the people who built it as it is a practical guide, with shopping and eating recommendations. Affectionate, opinionated and guaranteed to change your outlook on Cancún.

Wildlife

Rosita Arvigo *Sastun: My Apprenticeship with a Maya Healer.* The author established an organic herb farm in Belize and then studied with the region's best-known medicine man for five years. Her story is worthwhile for anyone interested in herbal treatments; more detail can be found in her *Rainforest Home Remedies.*

Les Beletsky *Tropical Mexico: The Ecotravellers' Wildlife Guide.* An excellent field guide with colour plates of birds, reptiles and mammals found throughout the Yucatán and Chiapas.

Ernest Preston Edwards *A Field Guide to the Birds of Mexico and Adjacent Areas: Belize, Guatemala, and El Salvador.* Some 850 species are shown in colour plates, with names in English, Latin and Spanish.

Steve Gerrard *The Cenotes of the Riviera Maya.* This self-published full-colour guide is hard to come by outside Mexico, but it's worth tracking down if you'll be doing any cave diving, as it's meticulously thorough.

Steve Howell and Sophie Webb *The Birds of Mexico and Northern Central America.* A tremendous work, the result of years of research, this is the definitive book on the region's birds. Essential for all serious birders.

Paul Humann and Ned DeLoach *Snorkeling Guide to Marine Life: Florida, Caribbean, Bahamas.* A clear field guide to corals, fish, plants and other underwater life off the Caribbean coast, with 280 colour photos.

Thor Janson *Maya Nature: An Introduction to the Ecosystems, Plants and Animals of the Mayan World.* A good complement to an illustrated field guide, as the 196 colour photographs show animals in their natural habitat.

R. T. Peterson and E. L. Chalif *Mexican Birds.* The classic ornithological guide to Mexico. The text is excellent, but drawings are limited to indigenous examples only. Migratory species are included in additional (North American) guides, which can be frustratingly impractical.

Victoria Schlesinger *Animals and Plants of the Ancient Maya: A Guide.* More than a field guide, this book also examines the cultural significance of the over one hundred species that were present in ancient Maya times.

Language

Language

Mexican Spanish

Once you get into it, **Spanish** is actually a straightforward language, and in Mexico, people are eager to understand and help even the most faltering attempt. **English** is widely spoken, especially in the tourist areas, but you'll get a far better reception if you at least try to communicate with people in their own tongue. You'll be further helped by the fact that Mexicans speak relatively slowly (at least compared with Spaniards) and that there's none of the awkward lisping pronunciation.

Rules of pronunciation

Relative to English, the rules of **pronunciation** are clear-cut and strictly observed. Unless there's an accent, words ending in D, L, R and Z are stressed on the last syllable; all others, on the second last. All vowels are pure and short.

A is somewhere between the A sound of "back" and that of "father".

E as in "get".

I as in "police".

O as in "hot".

U as in "rule".

C is soft before E and I, hard otherwise: *cerca* is pronounced "SER-ka".

G is a guttural H sound (like the ch in "loch") before E or I, and a hard G elsewhere: *gigante* pronounced "hi-GAN-te".

H is always silent.

J is the same sound as a guttural G: *jamón* is pronounced "ham-ON".

LL sounds like an English Y: *tortilla* is pronounced "tor-TEE-ya".

N is generally as in English, but in the Yucatán is often pronounced M at the ends of words ("Yuca-TAM").

Ñ with the tilde (accent), spoken like NY: *mañana* is pronounced "ma-NYA-na".

QU is pronounced like an English K.

R is rolled, RR doubly so.

V sounds more like B: *vino* is pronounced "BEE-no".

X has an S sound before consonants; has an H sound between vowels in place names, like México ("MEH-hee-ko"). In Maya words, X sounds like SH: Xel-Há is pronounced "shel-HA".

Z is the same as a soft C: *cerveza* is pronounced "ser-VAY-sa".

Useful words and phrases

Although we've listed a few essential words and phrases here, if you're travelling for any length of time some kind of **dictionary** or **phrasebook** is a worthwhile investment. *The Rough Guide to Mexican Spanish* is an excellent practical guide, correct and colloquial, and will have you speaking the language in no time. One of the best small Latin American Spanish dictionaries is the University of Chicago version (Pocket Books), widely available in Mexico, although the Langenscheidt pocket dictionary is handy because its yellow plastic cover holds up well. If you're using an older dictionary, bear in mind that CH, LL and

Ñ are traditionally counted as separate letters and are listed after the Cs, Ls and Ns respectively; most current dictionaries, however, follow more familiar alphabetizing procedures, though Ñ retains its own section.

Basics

Sí, No	Yes, No
Abierto/a, Cerrado/a	Open, Closed
Por favor, Gracias	Please, Thank you
Empujar, Tirar	Push, Pull
¿Dónde?, ¿Cuándo?	Where?, When?
Con, Sin	With, Without
¿Qué?, ¿Cuánto?	What?, How much?
Buen(o)/a, Mal(o)/a	Good, Bad
Aquí or Acá, Allí or Allá	Here, There
Gran(de), Pequeño/a	Big, Small
Éste, Eso	This, That
Más, Menos	More, Less
Barato/a, Caro/a	Cheap, Expensive
Hoy, Mañana	Today, Tomorrow
Ayer	Yesterday
Ahora, Más tarde	Now, Later

Greetings and responses

¡Hola!, Adiós	Hello, Goodbye
Buenos días	Good morning
Buenas tardes/noches	Good afternoon/night
¿Qué tal?	How do you do?
Hasta luego	See you later
Lo siento/disculpeme	Sorry
Con permiso/perdón	Excuse me
¿Cómo está (usted)?	How are you?
De nada or por nada	Not at all, you're welcome
(No) Entiendo	I (don't) understand
¿Habla (usted) inglés?	Do you speak English?
(No) Hablo español	I (don't) speak Spanish
Mande?	What (did you say)?
Me llamo...	My name is...
¿Cómo se llama usted?	What's your name?
Soy...	I am...
inglés(a)	...English
americano/a	...American*
australiano/a	...Australian
canadiense	...Canadian
irlandés(a)	...Irish
escosés(a)	...Scottish
galés(a)	...Welsh
neozelandés(a)	...New Zealander

*Mexicans are from the Americas, too, so describing yourself as American can occasionally cause offence. Another option is "estadounidense" (or, more simply, "de Los Estados Unidos", from the United States) if you are a US American.

Hotels, transport and directions

Quiero…	I want…
Quisiera...por favor	I'd like...please
¿Sabe...?	Do you know...?
No sé	I don't know
(¿)Hay...(?)	There is... (Is there...?)
Deme... (uno así)	Give me... (one like that)
¿Tiene...?	Do you have...?
...la hora	...the time
...un cuarto	...a room
...con dos camas /cama matrimonial	...with two beds/ double bed
Es para una persona (dos personas)	It's for one person (two people)
...para una noche (una semana)	...for one night (one week)
¿Está bien, cuánto es?	It's fine, how much is it?
Es demasiado caro	It's too expensive
¿No tiene algo más barato?	Don't you have anything cheaper?

¿Se puede...?	Can one...?
¿...acampar (cerca) aquí?	...camp (near) here?
¿Hay un hotel cerca aquí?	Is there a hotel nearby?
¿Por dónde se va a...?	How do I get to...?
Izquierda, derecha, derecho	Left, right, straight on
Por acá, por allá	This way, that way
¿Dónde está...?	Where is...?
...la camionera central or el ADO	...the bus station
...la estación de ferrocarriles	...the railway station
...el banco más cercano	...the nearest bank
...el cajero automático	...the ATM
...el correo	...the post office
...el baño or sanitario	...the toilet
¿De dónde sale el bus para...?	Where does the bus to ...leave from?
Quisiera un boleto (de ida y vuelta) para...	I'd like a (return) ticket to...
¿A qué hora sale (llega en...)?	What time does it leave (arrive in...)?
¿Qué hay para comer?	What is there to eat?
¿Qué es eso?	What's that?
¿Cómo se llama éste en español?	What's this called in Spanish?

Numbers and days

un/uno/una	1
dos	2
tres	3
cuatro	4
cinco	5
seis	6
siete	7
ocho	8
nueve	9
diez	10
once	11
doce	12
trece	13
catorce	14
quince	15
dieciséis	16
diecisiete	17
dieciocho	18
diecinueve	19
veinte	20
veintiuno	21
treinta	30
cuarenta	40
cincuenta	50
sesenta	60
setenta	70
ochenta	80
noventa	90
cien(to)	100
ciento uno	101
doscientos	200
quinientos	500
setecientos	700
mil	1000
dos mil	2000

primero/a	first
segundo/a	second
tercero/a	third
quinto/a	fifth
decimo/a	tenth

lunes	Monday
martes	Tuesday
miércoles	Wednesday
jueves	Thursday
viernes	Friday
sábado	Saturday
domingo	Sunday

Yucatec Maya basics

Yucatec is the variant of Maya spoken throughout the Yucatán Peninsula and northern Belize. (Maya in Chiapas and Guatemala speak other variants: Tzotzil, Tzeltal, Quiché and others.) An estimated one million people speak Yucatec, whether in small villages in central Yucatán State (which has the highest number of native Yucatec speakers) or on the city streets of Mérida. Most Maya are also at least conversant in Spanish, but they will generally appreciate any effort you make to communicate in their language. If you are interested in learning more, look for Gary Bevington's *Maya for Travelers and Students*, which provides a good introduction to the structure of the language, with a basic dictionary, as well as commentary on Maya culture. In Mexico, you may be able to find *Metodo Fácil para Leer, Escribir y Hablar la Lengua Maya*, by Jésus Rivero Azcorra and published in Mérida; it has English translations as well, and supplies more complete phrases than Bevington's book, though many are often obscure – "Clean out that iguana", for instance.

For pronunciation, spelling here reflects the modern academic style, and is fairly phonetic. An X is spoken as "sh", and an apostrophe is a light glottal stop, or pause. Draw out double vowels, and try to keep stress equal on all syllables.

What's up?	Ba'ax ka wa'alik?
Not much	Mixba'al
How are you?	Biix a beel?
I'm fine	Ma'aloob
Where are you going?	Tu'ux ka bin?
I am going to Mérida	Inka' bin a Ho
What's your name?	Ba'ax a k'aaba'?
My name is...	In k'aaba'(e)...
Where are you from?	Tu'ux ka tah?
Let's go	Ko'osh
See you later	Ka'ka't(e)
See you tomorrow	Samaal
Yes	He'le'
No	Ma'
I	Ten
You	Tech
Is there...	Yan he'...
There is...	Yan...
There is no...	Mina'an.../Na'am...
What's that?	Ba'ax lela'?
How much?	Bahuux?
Thank you	Dyos bo'otik
You're welcome	Mixba'al
Bon appétit!	Hach ki' a wi'ih!

Food and drink terms

On the table

Azúcar	Sugar
Cuchara	Spoon
Cuchillo	Knife
La cuenta	The bill
Mantequilla	Butter
Pan	Bread
Pimienta	Pepper
Queso	Cheese
Sal	Salt
Salsa	Sauce
Servilleta	Napkin
Tenedor	Fork

Cooking terms

A la parilla	Grilled over charcoal
A la plancha	Grilled on a hot plate
A la tampiqueña	Thin strips of meat served with guacamole and enchiladas

A la veracruzana	(Usually of fish) stewed with tomatoes, onions and green olives
Al horno/horneado	Baked
Asado/a	Broiled
Barbacoa/pibil	Wrapped in leaves and herbs and steamed/cooked in a pit
Con mole	In *mole* sauce, based on a rich spice paste; *mole poblano* (with bitter chocolate) is the most common
Empanizado/a	Breaded
En mojo de ajo	Fried with slow-cooked garlic
Frito	Fried
Poco hecho/a punto/ bien cocido	Rare/medium/well-done

Breakfast (desayuno)

Chilaquiles	Tortilla strips with shredded chicken and tomato sauce
Huevos...	Eggs...
...a la mexicana	...scrambled with tomato, onion and chile
...con jamón	...with ham
...con tocino	...with bacon
...motuleños	...fried, served on a tortilla with beans, ham, cheese, tomato sauce, peas and fried sweet plantains
...rancheros	...fried, served on a tortilla and smothered in a red chile sauce
...revueltos	...scrambled
...tibios	...lightly boiled
Pan dulce	Pastries

Soups (sopas) and starters (entradas)

Botana	Any snack served with drinks; given free at traditional bars
Caldo	Broth (with bits in)
Ceviche	Raw fish pieces, marinated in lime juice and mixed with tomato and coriander
Entremeses	Hors d'oeuvres
Pozole	Stew of hominy (soft, hulled corn kernels) and pork
Sopa...	Soup...
...de frijoles	...creamy black-bean soup
...de verduras	...vegetable soup

Snacks (antojitos)

Chile relleno	Mild poblano green chile stuffed with meat or cheese and fried in batter
Enchilada	Rolled-up taco, covered in chile sauce and baked
Enchilada suiza	As above, with green chile and cheese
Flauta	Small rolled tortilla filled with red meat or chicken and then fried
Huarache	Chewy, thick oblong corn tortilla topped with assorted meats
Molletes	Split roll covered in beans and melted cheese, and often also with ham and avocado

Panucho	Like a *salbute*, but with black beans as well	**Taco al pastor**	Taco filled with spicy pork, often served with a slice of pineapple
Quesadilla	Toasted or fried tortilla topped with cheese	**Taco dorado**	Deep-fried meat taco
Queso fundido	Melted cheese, served with tortillas and salsa	**Tamal**	Corn-meal pudding, stuffed with meat and steamed or baked in banana leaves; plural *tamales*
Salbute	Crisp-fried tortilla topped with shredded turkey, lettuce, avocado and pickled onions	**Torta**	Bread roll filled with meat, lettuce and avocado
Taco	Soft corn tortilla with filling	**Tostadas**	Flat crisp tortillas piled with meat and salad

Fish and seafood (pescados y mariscos)

Calamares	Squid	**Corvina**	Sea bass
Camarón	Prawn	**Filete entero**	Whole, filleted fish
Cangrejo	Crab	**Huachinango**	Red snapper
Caracol	Conch	**Langosta**	Rock lobster
Cazón	Baby shark	**Merluza**	Hake
Coctel	Seafood served in a tall glass with spicy tomato sauce and avocado	**Ostión**	Oyster
		Pezespada	Swordfish
		Pulpo	Octopus
		Sábalo	Tarpon

Meat (carne) and poultry (aves)

Alambre	Kebab	**Filete**	Tenderloin or fillet
Albóndigas	Meatballs	**Guisado**	Stew
Arrachera	Skirt steak	**Hígado**	Liver
Barbacoa	Barbecued meat	**Lengua**	Tongue
Bistec	Steak (not always beef)	**Lomo**	Loin (of pork)
Cabeza	Head	**Milanesa**	Breaded escalope
Cabrito	Kid	**Pata**	Foot (usually pig's)
Carne…	Meat	**Pato**	Duck
…de res	Beef	**Pavo**	Turkey
…adobado	Barbecued or spicily stewed meat	**Pechuga**	Breast
		Pierna	Leg
Carnitas	Pork cooked with garlic until crispy	**Pollo**	Chicken
		Salchicha	Sausage or hot dog
Cerdo	Pork	**Salpicón**	Shredded beef and sliced radishes seasoned with vinegar
Chivo	Goat		
Chorizo	Spicy sausage		
Chuleta	Chop (usually pork)	**Ternera**	Veal
Codorniz	Quail	**Tripa**	Tripe
Conejo	Rabbit	**Venado**	Venison
Cordero	Lamb		
Costilla	Rib		

Vegetables (verduras)

Aguacate	Avocado
Arroz	Rice
Betabel	Beetroot (often as a juice)
Calabacita	Zucchini (courgette)
Calabaza	Squash
Cebolla	Onion
Champiñones/hongos	Mushrooms
Chícharos	Peas
Col	Cabbage
Elote	Corn on the cob
Espinacas	Spinach
Flor de calabaza	Squash blossoms
Frijoles	Beans
Huitlacoche	Corn fungus ("Mexican truffles")
Jitomate	Tomato
Lechuga	Lettuce
Lentejas	Lentils
Nopales	Cactus paddle, usually roasted or pickled
Papas	Potatoes
Rajas	Strips of mild green poblano pepper
Zanahoria	Carrot

Fruits (frutas) and juice (jugo)

Cherimoya	Custard apple (sweetsop)
China	Orange (only in Yucatán)
Ciruela	Plum
Coco	Coconut
Durazno	Peach
Frambuesa	Raspberry
Fresa	Strawberry
Guanábana	Soursop, like a large custard apple
Guayaba	Guava
Higo	Fig
Limón	Lime
Mamey	Like a large *zapote*, with sweet pink flesh reminiscent of sweet potato
Melón	Melon
Naranja	Orange
Papaya	Papaya
Piña	Pineapple
Pitahaya	Dragonfruit, a type of cactus fruit
Plátano	Banana/plantain
Sandía	Watermelon
Toronja	Grapefruit
Tuna	Prickly pear, a type of cactus fruit
Uva	Grape
Zapote	Sapodilla, fruit of the *chicle* tree

Drinks (bebidas)

Agua...	Water
...mineral/con gas	Sparkling water
...normal/sin gas	Still water
Café de la olla	Mexican-style coffee brewed in a clay pot
Cerveza	Beer
Jamaica	Cold drink of steeped hibiscus flowers
Licuado	Blended fruit drink
(Mi)chelada	Beer with (spicy) lime juice, ice and salt
Horchata	Creamy rice-milk drink, sometimes with coconut
Té	Tea
Vino	Wine

Sweets (dulces)

Cajeta...	Caramel confection, often served with...
...crepas	...pancakes
...churros	...cinnamon-covered fritters
Champola	Ice cream or sorbet in a tall glass filled with milk
Ensalada de frutas	Fruit salad
Flan	Crème caramel
Helado	Ice cream
Nieve	Sorbet
Paleta	Fruit popsicle
Raspada	Shaved ice with fruit syrup

Yucatecan specialities

Achiote	Spice paste made with orange annatto seeds, cloves, onion and garlic
Adobo	Chile-based spice paste similar to *achiote*
Brazo de reina	Large tamale filled with hard-cooked eggs and green pumpkin-seed paste
Cochinita pibil	Suckling pig seasoned with *achiote*, wrapped in banana leaves and slow-roasted in a pit
Habañero	Small, extremely hot chile pepper, made into red and green salsas
Mondongo kabic	Tripe stewed in *achiote* and bitter orange and green onions
Papadzules	Enchiladas filled with hard-cooked eggs, topped with green pumpkin-seed sauce
Poc-chuc	Pork marinated in citrus juice, then grilled
Pollo en relleno negro	Chicken in a black, slightly burnt chile sauce
Puchero	Meaty stew with sweet potato, seasoned with cinnamon and allspice
Queso relleno	Round of Dutch cheese hollowed out and filled with a spicy fruit-meat filling, topped with cream sauce
Sikil-p'aak	Spicy ground-pumpkin-seed dip
Sopa de lima	Broth with shredded chicken or turkey, tortilla strips and *lima*, an especially fragrant lime-like citrus
Tikin xic	Fish with *achiote* and spices wrapped in banana leaves and grilled
Xnipek	Raw *habañero* salsa; literally, "dog's nose" for the sweat it induces

Glossaries

Terms and acronyms

Ahorita diminutive of *ahora* (now) meaning "right now", but seldom applied as literally as a visitor might expect.

Auto-da-fé a public act of repentance, usually involving punishment or execution, and a product of the Inquisition; used most frequently in the Yucatán to refer to Fray Diego de Landa's burning of Maya texts in Maní in 1562.

Ayuntamiento city hall and/or city government.

Barrio area within a town or city; suburb.

Cambio foreign-currency exchange operation.

Camino blanco unpaved rural road, so called because it is paved with white limestone gravel.

Cantina bar, usually men-only.

Caseta telephone office.

Ceiba large tropical silk-cotton tree; also, the sacred tree of the Maya that represents the world.

Cenote natural sinkhole and underground water source, as found in the limestone of the Yucatán.

Chac Maya god of rain.

Chac-mool stone statue of a recumbent figure who may represent a sacrificial victim or a messenger to the gods.

Chultun underground cistern.

Colectivo shared van that provides service between towns.

Colonia neighbourhood or district (in the Yucatán, more commonly used than *barrio*).

Comal large, round, flat plate made of clay or metal and used for cooking tortillas.

Combi van that runs on fixed routes in cities, much like a bus.

Comedor cheap restaurant, literally "dining room"; also called a *cocina económica*.

Convento convent or monastery.

Cruzob Maya followers of the Talking Cross, a nativist political movement founded during the Caste Wars of the nineteenth century.

CTM central union organization.

Descompuesto out of order.

Don/Doña Sir/Madam (titles of courtesy used chiefly in letters, for professionals or when addressing the boss).

Ejido communally owned farmland or village property.

EPR Ejército Popular Revolucionario (the Popular Revolutionary Army), a guerrilla group not allied with the Zapatistas, whose first appearance was in Guerrero in 1996.

EZLN Ejército Zapatista de Liberación Nacional (the Zapatista Army of National Liberation), a guerrilla group in Chiapas.

Feria fair or market.

FONART government agency to promote crafts.

FONATUR government tourism agency.

Fray friar.

Gringo/a white man or woman, used chiefly of North Americans, though not necessarily intended as an insult; thought to originate with US troops, either because they wore green coats or because they sang "Green grow the rushes oh!".

Guayabera embroidered Cuban-style shirt, usually for men.

Güera/o blonde; also, a Westerner, a white man or woman; though often shouted after women in the street, not usually intended as an insult.

Hacienda plantation estate or the big house on it.

Hacendado plantation owner.

Henequen variety of agave cactus grown mainly in the Yucatán, the fibres of which are used to make rope.

Huipil Maya women's embroidered white smock dress or blouse, worn over a white petticoat, usually with a small checkered scarf.

IVA fifteen percent value-added tax (VAT).

Jarana popular dance blending Maya and Spanish styles, often performed at local *ferias*.

Kukulkán Maya name for Quetzalcoatl, the feathered-serpent god.

Ladino (of people) Spanish-influenced as opposed to Indian; now used chiefly with reference to clothing or culture rather than race.

Licensio common title, literally "graduate" or "licensed"; abbreviated Lic.

Malecón seafront promenade.

Mariachi quintessentially Mexican music, with lots of brass and sentimental lyrics; originated in northern Mexico, however, and is not particularly widespread in the Yucatán; see *trova*.

Maya people who inhabited Honduras, Guatemala, Belize and southeastern Mexico from around the second millennium BC, and still do.

Mestizaje the process that created mestizos: the birth of the first child to a Spaniard and a Maya, synonymous with the creation of modern Mexico.

Mestizo mixed race; of Indian and Spanish descent.

Metate flat stone for grinding corn; used with a *mano*, a grinding stone.

Milpa small subsistence farm plot, tended with slash-and-burn agricultural practices.

Mirador lookout point.

Muelle jetty or dock.

NAFTA North American Free Trade Agreement that includes Mexico, the US and Canada; see *TLC*.

Palacio mansion (not necessarily royal).

Palacio de Gobierno headquarters of the state or federal authorities.

Palacio Municipal headquarters of the local government.

Palapa palm thatch; also, any thatched-roof hut.

PAN Partido de Acción Nacional (National Action Party), a conservative party that took power when Vicente Fox became president in 2000.

Paseo broad avenue; also, a ritual evening walk around a plaza.

PEMEX Mexican national oil company.

Planta baja ground floor; abbreviated PB in lifts.

Porfiriato the three decades of Porfirio Díaz's dictatorship.

PRD Partido Revolucionario Democrático (Party of the Democratic Revolution), the left-wing opposition formed and led by Cuauhtémoc Cárdenas, which has the second largest number of seats in Congress.

PRI Partido Revolucionario Institucional (Party of the Institutional Revolution), the ruling party for eighty years until the PAN upset in the 1999 elections.

PT Partido del Trabajo (Workers' Party), a small party with opposition seats in Congress.

PVEM Partido Verde Ecologista de México (Green Party), a small opposition party.

Quetzalcoatl feathered-serpent god of the Toltec and Aztec civilizations, whose enigmatic image is widespread.

Sacbé ancient Maya road, paved with limestone; plural *sacbeob*.

Stele freestanding carved monument; plural *stelae*.

TLC Tratado de Libre Comercio, the Spanish name for NAFTA.

Toltec people who controlled central Mexico after the Teotihuacán and before the Aztecs.

Tope speed bump or other barrier for slowing traffic on rural roads.

Trova romantic Yucatecan song style popular in the early twentieth century and still played by *trovadores*.

Tula Toltec capital.

Tzompantli Aztec skull rack, or "wall of skulls".

Wetback derogatory term for a Mexican or other Hispanic (illegal) immigrant in the US; *mojado* ("wet") is the Spanish term, without the negative connotations.

Art and architectural terms

Alfiz decorative rectangular moulding over a doorway.

Arabesque elaborate geometric pattern of Islamic origin.

Artesonado intricate ceiling design, usually of jointed, inlaid wood.

Atlantean pre-Hispanic column in the form of a warrior, examples of which are found at Tula and Chichén Itzá.

Atrium enclosed forecourt of a churchyard or monastery; *atrio* in Spanish.

Azulejo decorative glazed tile, usually blue and white.

Camarín room in a church used for storing and dressing sacred statues.

Churrigueresque highly elaborate, decorative form of Baroque architecture (found chiefly in churches), named after the seventeenth-century Spanish architect José Churriguera.

Convento monastery residence that includes the cloister.

Corbel arch the distinctive Maya "false" arch, in which overlapping stones are stacked to meet at the top, forming a narrow, triangular shape; often extended into a vault in hallways.

Cornice decorative band around the top of a building.

Dado ornamental border on the lower part of an interior wall.

Escudo shield-shaped decoration.

Espadaña belfry, usually on top of the front wall of a church.

Fluting vertical grooves in a column.

Fresco technique of painting on wet or dry plaster.

Garita ornamental pinnacle or battlement which looks like a sentry box.

Grotesque ornamental style depicting fantastic birds, beasts and foliage.

Herrerian imperial style named after sixteenth-century Spanish architect Juan de Herrera.

Lintel piece of wood or stone framing the top of a doorway.

Lunette crescent-shaped space above a doorway or beneath a vault.

Mascarón mask.

Merlón decorative pyramidal battlement.

Mudéjar Spanish architectural style strongly influenced by Moorish forms.

Ogee curved, pointed arch.

Pila font or water basin; also commonly found in domestic buildings.

Pilaster flattened column that projects from a surface, used as decorative element.

Pinjante glove-shaped decorative pendant, popular in eighteenth-century architecture.

Plateresque elaborately of Spanish architecture) elaborately decorative Renaissance style.

Porfirian referring to the elaborate, eclectic architecture of the Porfirio Díaz period (also *porfiriano*).

Portal arcade; plural *portales*.

Portería entry portico to a monastery.

Predella base panel of an altarpiece.

Purista severe Renaissance architectural style, originating in sixteenth-century Spain.

Roofcomb decorative trim extending above the roof-line of a building that is particularly associated with ancient Maya architecture.

Zapata wooden roof beam, often decoratively carved.

Travel store

ROUGH GUIDES Complete Listing

UK & Ireland
Britain
Devon & Cornwall
Dublin **D**
Edinburgh **D**
England
Ireland
The Lake District
London
London **D**
London Mini Guide
Scotland
Scottish Highlands & Islands
Wales

Europe
Algarve **D**
Amsterdam
Amsterdam **D**
Andalucía
Athens **D**
Austria
Baltic States
Barcelona
Barcelona **D**
Belgium & Luxembourg
Berlin
Brittany & Normandy
Bruges **D**
Brussels
Budapest
Bulgaria
Copenhagen
Corsica
Crete
Croatia
Cyprus
Czech & Slovak Republics
Denmark
Dodecanese & East Aegean Islands
Dordogne & The Lot
Europe on a Budget
Florence & Siena
Florence **D**
France
Germany
Gran Canaria **D**
Greece
Greek Islands
Hungary
Ibiza & Formentera **D**
Iceland
Ionian Islands
Italy
The Italian Lakes
Languedoc & Roussillon
Lanzarote & Fuerteventura **D**
Lisbon **D**
The Loire Valley
Madeira **D**
Madrid **D**
Mallorca **D**
Mallorca & Menorca
Malta & Gozo **D**
Moscow
The Netherlands
Norway
Paris
Paris **D**
Paris Mini Guide
Poland
Portugal
Prague
Prague **D**
Provence & the Côte D'Azur
Pyrenees
Romania
Rome
Rome **D**
Sardinia
Scandinavia
Sicily
Slovenia
Spain
St Petersburg
Sweden
Switzerland
Tenerife & La Gomera **D**
Turkey
Tuscany & Umbria
Venice & The Veneto
Venice **D**
Vienna

Asia
Bali & Lombok
Bangkok
Beijing
Cambodia
China
Goa
Hong Kong & Macau
Hong Kong & Macau **D**
India
Indonesia
Japan
Kerala
Korea
Laos
Malaysia, Singapore & Brunei
Nepal
The Philippines
Rajasthan, Dehli & Agra
Shanghai
Singapore
Singapore **D**
South India
Southeast Asia on a Budget
Sri Lanka
Taiwan
Thailand
Thailand's Beaches & Islands
Tokyo
Vietnam

Australasia
Australia
East Coast Australia
Fiji
Melbourne
New Zealand
Sydney
Tasmania

North America
Alaska
Baja California
Boston
California
Canada
Chicago
Colorado
Florida
The Grand Canyon
Hawaii
Honolulu **D**
Las Vegas **D**
Los Angeles & Southern California
Maui **D**
Miami & South Florida
Montréal
New England
New York City
New York City **D**
New York City Mini
Orlando & Walt Disney World® **D**
Oregon & Washington
San Francisco
San Francisco **D**
Seattle
Southwest USA
Toronto
USA
Vancouver
Washington DC
Yellowstone & The Grand Tetons
Yosemite

Caribbean & Latin America
Antigua & Barbuda **D**
Argentina
Bahamas
Barbados **D**
Belize
Bolivia
Brazil
Buenos Aires
Cancùn & Cozumel **D**
Caribbean
Central America on a Budget
Chile
Costa Rica
Cuba
Dominican Republic
Ecuador
Guatemala
Jamaica
Mexico
Peru
Puerto Rico
St Lucia **D**
South America on a Budget
Trinidad & Tobago
Yucatán

D: Rough Guide **DIRECTIONS** for short breaks

Available from all good bookstores

Small print and

Index

A Rough Guide to Rough Guides

Published in 1982, the first Rough Guide – to Greece – was a student scheme that became a publishing phenomenon. Mark Ellingham, a recent graduate in English from Bristol University, had been travelling in Greece the previous summer and couldn't find the right guidebook. With a small group of friends he wrote his own guide, combining a highly contemporary, journalistic style with a thoroughly practical approach to travellers' needs.

The immediate success of the book spawned a series that rapidly covered dozens of destinations. And, in addition to impecunious backpackers, Rough Guides soon acquired a much broader and older readership that relished the guides' wit and inquisitiveness as much as their enthusiastic, critical approach and value-for-money ethos.

These days, Rough Guides include recommendations from shoestring to luxury and cover more than 200 destinations around the globe, including almost every country in the Americas and Europe, more than half of Africa and most of Asia and Australasia. Our ever-growing team of authors and photographers is spread all over the world, particularly in Europe, the USA and Australia.

In the early 1990s, Rough Guides branched out of travel, with the publication of Rough Guides to World Music, Classical Music and the Internet. All three have become benchmark titles in their fields, spearheading the publication of a wide range of books under the Rough Guide name.

Including the travel series, Rough Guides now number more than 350 titles, covering: phrasebooks, waterproof maps, music guides from Opera to Heavy Metal, reference works as diverse as Conspiracy Theories and Shakespeare, and popular culture books from iPods to Poker. Rough Guides also produce a series of more than 120 World Music CDs in partnership with World Music Network.

Visit www.roughguides.com to see our latest publications.

Rough Guide travel images are available for commercial licensing at www.roughguidespictures.com

Rough Guide credits

Text editor: Paula Neudorf
Layout: Umesh Aggarwal
Cartography: Swati Handoo
Picture editor: Sarah Cummins
Production: Rebecca Short
Proofreader: Jennifer Speake
Cover design: Chloë Roberts
Photographer: Dan Bannister and Sarah Cummins
Editorial: **London** Ruth Blackmore, Alison Murchie, Andy Turner, Keith Drew, Edward Aves, Alice Park, Lucy White, Jo Kirby, James Smart, Natasha Foges, Róisín Cameron, Emma Traynor, Emma Gibbs, James Rice, Kathryn Lane, Christina Valhouli, Monica Woods, Mani Ramaswamy, Joe Staines, Peter Buckley, Matthew Milton, Tracy Hopkins, Ruth Tidball; **New York** Andrew Rosenberg, Steven Horak, AnneLise Sorensen, April Isaacs, Ella Steim, Anna Owens, Sean Mahoney, Courtney Miller; **Delhi** Madhavi Singh, Karen D'Souza
Design & Pictures: **London** Scott Stickland, Dan May, Diana Jarvis, Mark Thomas, Chloë Roberts, Nicole Newman, Emily Taylor; **Delhi** Ajay Verma, Jessica Subramanian, Ankur Guha, Pradeep Thapliyal, Sachin Tanwar, Anita Singh, Nikhil Agarwal
Production: Vicky Baldwin
Cartography: **London** Maxine Repath, Ed Wright, Katie Lloyd-Jones; **Delhi** Jai Prakash Mishra, Rajesh Chhibber, Ashutosh Bharti, Rajesh Mishra, Animesh Pathak, Jasbir Sandhu, Karobi Gogoi, Alakananda Bhattacharya, Deshpal Dabas
Online: **London** George Atwell, Faye Hellon, Jeanette Angell, Fergus Day, Justine Bright, Clare Bryson, Aine Fearon, Adrian Low, Ezgi Celebi, Amber Bloomfield; **Delhi** Amit Verma, Rahul Kumar, Narender Kumar, Ravi Yadav, Debojit Borah, Rakesh Kumar, Ganesh Sharma
Marketing & Publicity: **London** Liz Statham, Niki Hanmer, Louise Maher, Jess Carter, Vanessa Godden, Vivienne Watton, Anna Paynton, Rachel Sprackett, Libby Jellie; **New York** Geoff Colquitt, Nancy Lambert, Katy Ball; **Delhi** Ragini Govind
Manager India: Punita Singh
Reference Director: Andrew Lockett
Operations Manager: Helen Phillips
PA to Publishing Director: Nicola Henderson
Publishing Director: Martin Dunford
Commercial Manager: Gino Magnotta
Managing Director: John Duhigg

ROUGH GUIDES

SMALL PRINT

Publishing information

This second edition published November 2008 by
Rough Guides Ltd,
80 Strand, London WC2R 0RL
345 Hudson St, 4th Floor,
New York, NY 10014, USA
14 Local Shopping Centre, Panchsheel Park,
New Delhi 110017, India
Distributed by the Penguin Group
Penguin Books Ltd,
80 Strand, London WC2R 0RL
Penguin Group (USA)
375 Hudson Street, NY 10014, USA
Penguin Group (Australia)
250 Camberwell Road, Camberwell,
Victoria 3124, Australia
Penguin Group (Canada)
195 Harry Walker Parkway N, Newmarket, ON,
L3Y 7B3 Canada
Penguin Group (NZ)
67 Apollo Drive, Mairangi Bay, Auckland 1310,
New Zealand

Cover concept by Peter Dyer.

Typeset in Bembo and Helvetica to an original design by Henry Iles.

Printed and bound in China

384pp includes index

A catalogue record for this book is available from the British Library

ISBN: 978-1-85828-805-5

1 3 5 7 9 8 6 4 2

Help us update

We've gone to a lot of effort to ensure that the second edition of **The Rough Guide to the Yucatán** is accurate and up to date. However, things change – places get "discovered", opening hours are notoriously fickle, restaurants and rooms raise prices or lower standards. If you feel we've got it wrong or left something out, we'd like to know, and if you can remember the address, the price, the hours, the phone number, so much the better.

Please send your comments with the subject line "**Rough Guide Yucatán Update**" to Ⓔmail@roughguides.com. We'll credit all contributions and send a copy of the next edition (or any other Rough Guide if you prefer) for the very best emails.

Have your questions answered and tell others about your trip at Ⓦcommunity.roughguides.com

Acknowledgements

Zora O'Neill would like to thank Lee Christie at Genesis, Sofi and Daniel at Marionetas, Jim and Ellen of YucatanLiving.com, Pedro and Eyal at Las Anclas, Sandra Dayton of Casa Cacahuate and Rob and Joanne Birce at Alma Libre Books, for keeping me in the loop and offering me hospitality; Matthew Robb, who clarified ancient Maya issues; *mi madre*, Beverly, for being a trooper; Paula Neudorf, for tireless editing; and all the readers who took the time to send in corrections, tips and criticism.

John Fisher: My thanks for their help in updating this edition go to Lupita Ayala and Luis Guillermo Rendon-Aguilar at the Mexican Tourist Board in London, Luciana Leguizamón, Leila Voight and Justa van Gorkum. A special mention to Paula Neudorf for an excellent, smooth edit, to my co-author Zora and as ever to A and the two Js.

The editor would like to thank Zora and John for their great work, patience and humo(u)r, as well as AnneLise Sorensen, Sarah Cummins, Umesh Aggarwal, Swati Handoo, Jennifer Speake and April Isaacs. Thanks are also and always due to Luca, Dave and Roxana, Eric Knuble and Britnei "The Britters" Merckle (project strength!).

Readers' letters

Thanks to all the readers who have taken the time to write in with comments and suggestions (and apologies if we've inadvertently omitted or misspelt anyone's name):

Lola Reid Allin, Elvira Anton Centenera, Heidi Cost, Jonny Hardaker, Nat Hill, Geoff Holden, Matthew Monahan, Allison Morris, Brian Mulligan, Ron Roskell, Rowena and Mike Sparling.

Photo credits

All photos © Rough Guides except the following:

Cover

Front picture: El Castillo from the Warriors Temple, Chichén Itzá © 4Corners/Borchi Massimo
Back picture: Spanish Colonial buildings, Campeche © Martin Norris/Alamy
Inside back picture: Gone to the Beach © Dan Bannister/Rough Guides

Introduction

French Angelfish, Cozumel © Dennis Sabo/iStock.com

Things not to miss

04 Sian Ka'an biosphere © Robert Fried/Alamy
05 Palenque © Andia.fr/Drr.net
12 Diver and sea turtle © Patrick Brown/Alamy
16 Whale shark © Reinhard Dirscherl/Alamy

Yucatán food colour section

Red chiles © Randy Faris/Photolibrary.com
Mayonnaise © Zora O'Neill
Making tortillas © Steve Burger/iStock.com

Maya culture colour section

Mayan seated king, from the Isle of Jaina © Boltin Picture Library/The Bridgeman Art Library
Loltun Caves © Alamy
Statue, Palenque museum © Zora O'Neill
Tzeltal Indian children outside church and school © Danita Delimont/Alamy
Maya woman with corn © Kenneth Garrett/Danita Delimont/Drr.net

Black and whites

p.95 Holbox tuktuk © Zora O'Neill
p.151 Spider monkey © Tony Rath/Drr.net
p.238 Flamingoes © iStock.com
p.292 Yaxchilan © Zora O'Neill
p.295 Wild Crocodile © Chris Haigh/Alamy
p.317 Tonina © Zora O'Neill
p.333 Henequen workers © Macduff Everton/Drr.net
p.344 Maya Calendar © iStock.com

Index

Map entries are in colour.

H

I

J

K

L

M

N

O

P

Q

R

S

T

Map symbols

maps are listed in the full index using coloured text

- International boundary
- Province boundary
- Chapter divisions boundary
- Motorway
- Major road
- Minor road
- Pedestrian road
- Unpaved road
- Steps
- Track
- Path
- River
- Ferry route
- Railway
- Wall
- Bridge
- One-way arrow
- Reef
- Waterfall
- Cenote
- Cave
- Ruins
- Maya site
- Hacienda
- Park entrance

- Gate
- Museum
- Point of interest
- Information office
- Telephone
- @ Internet access
- Transport stop
- Airport
- Petrol station
- Hospital
- Post office
- P Parking
- Golf course
- Monument
- Camping
- Lighthouse
- Baseball field
- Market
- Church
- Building
- Cemetery
- Park/reserve
- Beach
- Swamp

We're covered. Are you?